RBAN II EL CID OMAR KHAYYAM ST BERNARD OF CLAIRVAUX HILDEGAR
AI KHAN THOMAS AQUINAS ADAM DE LA HALLE ZHAO MENGFU MARC
NE GEOFFREY CHAUCER CHENG HO FILIPPO BRUNELLESCHI WAT TYLER DONATELL   RG HENRY THE
ICELLI JOHN & SEBASTIAN CABOT BARTOLOMEU DIAS HIERONYMUS BOSCH CH   ND & ISABELLA
GURU NANAK MOHAMMED TURRÉ ALBRECHT DURER NICOLAUS COPERNICUS   NEZ DE BALBOA
THER TITIAN HERNANDO CORTES SINAN HENRY VIII JACQUES CARTIER PARAC   HANS HOLBEIN
UEGEL GIOVANNI DA PALESTRINA PHILIP II IVAN THE TERRIBLE ELIZABETH I MARTIN FROBISHER HIERONI   RICIUS FRANCIS
ER GIOVANNI GABRIELI WALTER RALEIGH FRANCIS BACON JOHN DOWLAND CHRISTOPHER MARLOWE GALILEO GALILEI HENRY
GGIO PETER PAUL RUBENS WILLIAM HARVEY WILLEBRORD SNELL WILLIAM BAFFIN CARDINAL RICHELIEU JOHN WINTHROP THOMAS
EGO VELAZQUEZ CHARLES I PIERRE DE FERMAT ABEL JANSZOON TASMAN REMBRANDT VAN RIJN JOHN MILTON MOLIÈRE BLAISE
DE SPINOZA JEAN BAPTISTE LULLY JOHN LOCKE ANTONIE VAN LEEUWENHOEK SIR CHRISTOPHER WREN ROBERT HOOKE LOUIS XIV
NELL GWYN WILLIAM III DUKE OF MARLBOROUGH ARCHANGELO CORELLI K'ANG-HSI EDMOND HALLEY HENRY PURCELL DANIEL
G PHILIPP TELEMANN JEAN-PHILIPPE RAMEAU JOHANN SEBASTIAN BACH DOMENICO SCARLATTI GEORGE FRIDERIC HANDEL DANIEL
ANKLIN CAROLUS LINNAEUS LEONHARD EULER QIANLONG DAVID HUME JEAN JACQUES ROUSSEAU FREDERICK THE GREAT CAO
ANUEL KANT ROBERT CLIVE JAMES WOLFE THOMAS GAINSBOROUGH JAMES COOK CATHERINE THE GREAT LOUIS-ANTOINE DE
ESTLEY DANIEL BOONE JOHN ADAMS CHARLES COULOMB COUNT JOSEPH LOUIS LAGRANGE JAMES WATT LUIGI GALVANI THOMAS
SIR JOSEPH BANKS THOMAS JEFFERSON ALESSANDRO VOLTA TOUSSAINT L'OUVERTURE FRANCISCO DE GOYA EDWARD JENNER
LIAM BLAKE THOMAS TELFORD MAXIMILIEN DE ROBESPIERRE ADMIRAL HORATIO NELSON JAMES MONROE ROBERT BURNS MARY
ALTON ANDREW JACKSON TECUMSEH NAPOLEON GEORGES CUVIER DUKE OF WELLINGTON ALEXANDER VON HUMBOLDT LUDWIG
THOMAS YOUNG MERIWETHER LEWIS MATTHEW FLINDERS JANE AUSTEN ANDRE-MARIE AMPÈRE J. M. W. TURNER JOHN CONSTABLE
DE SAN MARTIN JOSEPH-LOUIS GAY-LUSSAC FABIAN VON BELLINGSHAUSEN ELIZABETH FRY RENÉ-THÉOPHILE-HYACINTHE LAËNNEC
ETT JOHN FRANKLIN BROTHERS GRIMM JOSEPH VON FRAUNHOFER SHAKA GEORG SIMON OHM LORD BYRON AUGUSTIN FRESNEL
BYSSHE SHELLEY NICKOLAI LOBACHEVSKI GIOACCHINO ROSSINI MATTHEW PERRY JOHN KEATS CHARLES STURT ROWLAND HILL
DIX ALEXANDER PUSHKIN RENE-AUGUSTE CAILLIC JOHN BROWN WILLIAM HENRY FOX TALBOT BRIGHAM YOUNG JAMES CHADWICK
ANS CHRISTIAN ANDERSEN MARY SEACOLE ISAMBARD KINGDOM BRUNEL BENITO JUAREZ JOHN STUART MILL GIUSEPPE GARIBALDI
DSTONE FRÉDÉRIC CHOPIN ROBERT SCHUMANN THEODOR SCHWANN P. T. BARNUM ELISHA GRAVES OTIS FRANZ LISZT HARRIET
OLE JOHN ALEXANDER MACDONALD OTTO VON BISMARCK THE BRONTËS HENRY DAVID THOREAU KARL MARX IVAN SERGEYEVICH
THONY FLORENCE NIGHTINGALE HARRIET TUBMAN ROBERT O'HARA BURKE FYODOR DOSTOEVSKY RICHARD BURTON HERMANN
GALTON GUSTAV KIRCHOFF ANTON BRUCKNER CHARLES BLONDIN WILLIAM KELVIN JOHANN STRAUSS II JOHN HANNING SPEKE
OTH EMILY DICKINSON JAMES CLERK MAXWELL ISABELLA BIRD EDOUARD MANET NIKOLAUS OTTO LEWIS CARROLL NILS ADOLF
WHISTLER DMITRI MENDELEYEV EDGAR DEGAS ERNST HAECKEL YUKICHI FUKUZAWA MARK TWAIN ADOLF VON BAEYER ANDREW
URY PYOTR IL'YICH TCHAIKOVSKY EMILE ZOLA CHIEF JOSEPH AUGUSTE RODIN JOHN DUNLOP CLAUDE MONET THOMAS HARDY
IEG ROBERT KOCH HENRY JAMES FRIEDRICH NIETZSCHE NICOLAY RIMSKY-KORSAKOV SARAH BERNHARDT THOMAS BARNARDO
ANNIE BESANT PAUL GAUGUIN W. G. GRACE FRIEDRICH LUDWIG GOTTLOB FREGE AUGUST STRINDBERG IVAN PAVLOV ROBERT
IL VON BEHRING LEOS JANÁCEK GEORGE EASTMAN NED KELLY KING CAMP GILLETTE RUDYARD KIPLING BOOKER T. WASHINGTON
RDINAND DE SAUSSURE EMMELINE PANKHURST EDWARD ELGAR ROBERT BADEN-POWELL RUDOLF DIESEL THEODORE ROOSEVELT
LE WILLIAM II ANTON CHEKHOV THEODOR HERZL GUSTAV MAHLER ANNIE OAKLEY JOSE RIZAL FRIDTJOF NANSEN DAME NELLIE
GEORGE HENRY FORD RICHARD STRAUSS WILLIAM BUTLER YEATS JEAN SIBELIUS ERIK SATIE BEATRIX POTTER WASSILY KANDINSKY
OTT JOPLIN NICHOLAS II CHARLES RENNIE MACKINTOSH FRITZ HABER VALDEMAR POULSEN MOHANDAS GANDHI HENRI MATISSE
MUNDSEN SERGEI DIAGHILEV LOUIS BLÉRIOT RALPH VAUGHAN WILLIAMS BERTRAND RUSSELL SERGEY RAKHMANINOV COLETTE
OBERT FROST WINSTON CHURCHILL MAURICE RAVEL D. W. GRIFFITH HIRAM BINGHAM CARL JUNG EGLANTINE JEBB MOHAMMED
IN ALBERT EINSTEIN SAMUEL GOLDWYN ALFRED WEGENER MARIE STOPES DOUGLAS MACARTHUR HELEN KELLER ANNA PAVLOVA
EIGER ROBERT GODDARD JACK HOBBS IGOR STRAVINSKY EAMON DE VALERA FRANZ KAFKA BENITO MUSSOLINI JOHN MAYNARD
BAN BERG NIELS BOHR AL JOLSON CLARENCE BIRDSEYE DIEGO RIVERA TY COBB MARX BROTHERS DAVID BEN-GURION MARCUS
NSTEIN GEORGIA O'KEEFFE KATHERINE MANSFIELD THOMAS EDWARD LAWRENCE JOHN LOGIE BAIRD EUGENE O'NEILL JIM THORPE
ORSKY CHARLIE CHAPLIN JOMO KENYATTA VLADIMIR ZWORYKIN MICHAEL COLLINS VASLAV NIJINSKY HO CHI MINH DWIGHT
ON-WATT FRANCISCO FRANCO HAILE SELASSIE JOSIP BROZ TITO WILFRED OWEN DOROTHY PARKER MAO ZEDONG MARY PICKFORD
NAGY BABE RUTH BUSTER KEATON JACK DEMPSEY F. SCOTT FITZGERALD AMELIA EARHART WILLIAM FAULKNER JOHN COCKCROFT
YSENKO GOLDA MEIR HENRY MOORE NINETTE DE VALOIS SUZANNE LENGLEN AL CAPONE HUMPHREY BOGART S. BANDARANAIKE
RÉDÉRIC & IRÈNE CURIE DENNIS GABOR CHARLES RICHTER AYATOLLAH KHOMEINI AARON COPLAND ENRICO FERMI CLARK GABLE
ED SUKARNO BOBBY JONES CHARLES LINDBERGH RICHARD RODGERS ANSEL ADAMS FERNAND BRAUDEL BARBARA MCCLINTOCK
MIR HOROWITZ KONRAD LORENZ TUNKU ABDUL RAHMAN RICHARD DREW ROBERT OPPENHEIMER PABLO NERUDA COUNT BASIE
RISTIAN DIOR JEAN-PAUL SARTRE GRETA GARBO MICHAEL TIPPETT PUYI DMITRI SHOSTAKOVICH JOHN HUSTON ALEC ISSIGONIS
AN FLEMING LYNDON B. JOHNSON SIMONE DE BEAUVOIR BETTE DAVIS HERBERT VON KARAJAN OLIVIER MESSIAEN DON BRADMAN
EAU MOTHER THERESA AKIRA KUROSAWA CHRISTOPHER COCKERELL ROBERT JOHNSON TENNESSEE WILLIAMS WILLIAM GOLDING
LY BENJAMIN BRITTEN JESSIE OWENS RICHARD NIXON MILDRED "BABE" DIDRIKSON JONAS SALK SCOBIE BREASLEY JOE DIMAGGIO
BANDARANAIKE FRANCIS CRICK YEHUDI MENUHIN JOHN F. KENNEDY INDIRA GANDHI ELLA FITZGERALD GAMAL ABDEL NASSER
FREDERICK SANGER JACKIE ROBINSON DAME MARGOT FONTEYN EDMUND HILLARY JAMES LOVELOCK CHARLIE PARKER ROSALIND
JAC YITZHAK RABIN CHRISTIAAN NEETHLING BARNARD JULIUS NYERERE JACQUES PICCARD IANNIS XENAKIS ROCKY MARCIANO
RE BOULEZ MARGARET THATCHER MARILYN MONROE JOHN COLTRANE MICHEL FOUCAULT MILES DAVIS CHUCK BERRY ELIZABETH
OAM CHOMSKY PAUL ELVSTRÖM GABRIEL GARCÍA MARQUEZ KARLHEINZ STOCKHAUSEN ANNE FRANK MARTIN LUTHER KING JR
LEY MILLER DEREK WALCOTT JAMES DEAN MIKHAIL GORBACHEV EDWARD HEATH TONI MORRISON ROGER PENROSE DESMOND
LE JANE GOODALL ALEKSEY LEONOV MARY QUANT NORMAN SCHWARZKOPF JOHN SURTEES ELVIS PRESLEY KING HUSSEIN WOODY
Y HOLLY F. W. DE KLERK ROBERT JARVIK VACLAV HAVEL ROLLING STONES STEVE REICH YVES SAINT LAURENT GARY SOBERS PHILIP
ARET ATWOOD GERMAINE GREER MAR   NICKLAUS PELÉ BRUCE LEE RICHARD DAWKINS
HEN HAWKING MARTIN SCORSESE AR   ATLÉS ROBERT DE NIRO BILLIE JEAN KING LECH
GEORGE LUCAS EDDY MERCKX STEVE   CRUYFF SALMAN RUSHDIE STEVEN SPIELBERG
GE VIV RICHARDS SEX PISTOLS FRANZ   IAN BOTHAM BILL GATES STEVEN JOBS GREG
EROS ERIC HEIDEN JEANNE LONGO MADONNA NICK FALDO MAGIC JOHNSON JOHN MCENROE AYRTON SENNA LINFORD CHRISTIE
ATARINA WITT BORIS BECKER PETE SAMPRAS MICHAEL SCHUMACHER TIGER WOODS VANESSA-MAE LOUISE BROWN...

1000
Makers of the
Millennium

DORLING KINDERSLEY
London • New York • Sydney • New Delhi
www.dk.com

A DORLING KINDERSLEY BOOK
www.dk.com

Senior Managing Editor Linda Martin
Senior Managing Art Editor Julia Harris
Senior Editor Fran Jones
Senior Art Editor Claire Legemah

Design/Editorial from Bookwork

DTP Designer Andrew O'Brien
Picture Research Maureen Cowdroy
Production Kate Oliver

Editorial Consultant James Harrison

Authors Simon Adams, Caroline Ashe,
Peter Chrisp, Emma Johnson,
Andrew Langley, Marcus Weeks

First published in Great Britain in 1999
by Dorling Kindersley Limited,
9 Henrietta Street, London WC2E 8PS

2 4 6 8 10 9 7 5 3 1

Colour Reproduction by Colourscan in Singapore
Printed and bound in Spain by Artes Gráficas Toledo, S.A.U.
D.L. TO: 1127 - 1999

Contents

Introduction

"*In the future everyone will be world famous for 15 minutes*" wrote the pioneer of Pop Art Andy Warhol in 1968. The artist's provocative comment gained him as much notoriety as his exhibitions of "re-packaged" soup cans and silk-screen representations of Marilyn Monroe and Elvis Presley. What's more, Warhol's view on fame neatly sums up the challenge for the compilers of *1000 Makers of the Millennium* – how to include everyone's favourite hero or heroine of the past 1000 years.

We hope we have risen to this challenge, and that our choice will satisfy readers looking for a quick source of reference on major figures of the past millennium. We are confident, at least, that the entries will invite comment and generate a lively debate about who should be in and who should be out. One thing is certain, our selection is as wide ranging as it is far reaching. Here is an incredible international collection of people who have made their mark by trying to improve the world, through words and deeds, as well as those who have proved themselves famous for their misdeeds. From painters to philosophers and military leaders to mayhem makers, you'll find every entry provides a fascinating insight into the lives of extraordinary people.

· THE SPIRIT OF THE AGE ·
From dramatically obvious entries, such as William Shakespeare, to less well-known inclusions such as John Napier or Mary Kingsley, this book presents a wide range of rulers and religious leaders, scientists, writers, composers, explorers, and stars of sport and film who all reflect the spirit of their age.

"*History is the essence*

The 20th century, for example, reflects the information revolution and the emphasis on entertainment (see pages on The Beatles, Marlon Brando, and Boris Becker). But as you'll discover on the pages in this book, entertainers have been performing since the start of the millennium. Read about the troubadour Blondel in the 12th century, or the tightrope acrobat Blondin later in the 19th century. And, of course, today people are famous just for being famous (or for being on TV or in magazines), so perhaps Andy Warhol's prediction has finally been realized.

Remember, names can have different spellings – even Sir Walter Raleigh can be spelled Ralegh – and many of them, especially Chinese and Japanese names, have three or four accepted ways of spelling (for example, Chiang Kai-shek is also known as Chiang Chieh-Shih, official name Chiang Chung-Cheng, and so on). Many people also achieved fame through a pseudonym rather than the name they were born with: so the founder of modern-day Yugoslavia is under "T" for Tito not "B" for (Josip) Broz, his real name.

You will also find several "composite" entries. For instance, although there is no individual entry for Jagger, Mick, he is listed with the 1960s band The Rolling Stones (and, of course, in the comprehensive index). You will also come across several "family" entries rather than "individual" treatments, such as the Cabots (15th/16th-century explorers), the Brontë sisters (19th-century authors), and the Marx Brothers (20th-century comedians). In these instances, the oldest person's birth date is the signpost for the chronological position in the book.

Cross-references within many of the entries then move you on to discover another person linked to your original line of enquiry. For example, reading about the 19th-century Scottish missionary and explorer David Livingstone will lead you on to Henry Morton Stanley, the journalist who tracked Livingstone down in the heart of Africa.

However, you can also simply dip in and out of the centuries on a random read, noticing as you do the "grouping" of particular skills, such as the number of explorers born in the 1450s, or composers in the 1680s, or computer wizards who arrived in the world in the 1950s.

1000 Makers of the Millennium takes you back through time, century by century. To complement the people, feature boxes outline key events such as the Crusades, the American Civil War, the French Revolution, and the Race for Space, while a year-by-year timeline highlights what was happening in the world when that person was born.

It's been our challenge to journey through the centuries and choose the makers of the millennium, now we'd like to know yours.

James Ham

Editorial Consultant

of innumerable biographies"

THOMAS CARLYLE, 1795–1881

• Each person is placed in chronological order by the date of their birth.
• The entries are listed by surname first, for example: Mandela, Nelson.

Full NAME
Birth and death dates
Nationality and achievement

Biography that describes life story and highlights key contributions.

11th CENTURY

At the dawn of the new millennium, Christians and Muslims began a "holy war" in Palestine, which was to last for nearly two hundred years. In Europe, a feudal system based on land ownership and military service governed everyday life, while on the other side of the world, the first Maoris settled in New Zealand after sailing from distant Polynesian islands.

Brian BORU
c.941–1014
Irish leader

Brian Boru was the first man to unite Ireland under one ruler. After the assassination of his brother in 976, he became king of Munster, in southwest Ireland. He eventually brought those responsible for his brother's death to justice and stamped out resistance. He then conquered each kingdom of Ireland in turn so that, by 1002, he was in control of almost the entire island. He governed his new kingdom wisely, in collaboration with the Catholic Church, but a revolt broke out in the east of the country in 1013. The two sides met at Clontarf in 1014 and although Brian won, he was killed in the battle. After his death, Ireland quickly fell apart, but for many generations to come, the Irish people have dreamt of uniting their country once again.

BASIL II
c.958–1025
Byzantine emperor

Basil was a fierce ruler who greatly extended Byzantine power across eastern Europe. He became emperor at the age of five, sharing the throne with army commanders. When he became sole ruler in 976, he defeated rebellions from the army and the aristocracy. He was helped by the support of Vladimir I of Russia, who had married Basil's sister Anna and converted to Christianity. Basil then began a campaign to destroy the growing power of the Bulgars in the north. He finally defeated them in 1014, taking their lands. He earned the nickname of *Bulgaroctonos*, or "Bulgar slayer", when he blinded thousands of Bulgarian prisoners from the battle, before sending them home.

ALHAZEN
c.965–c.1040
Iraqi mathematician

Born in Basra, Iraq, Alhazen wrote about optics – the study of vision. In 1270, his *Opticae Thesaurus* was translated from its original Arabic and published in Latin. This was the first study of refraction and reflection on curved surfaces and also one of the first detailed studies of the eyes. It is said that he spent a period feigning madness to escape a boast he had made that he could prevent the flooding of the Nile River.

Leif ERIKSSON
c.970–c.1025
Norse explorer

Known as Leif the Lucky, Leif Eriksson is reputed to have been the first European to visit North America. His father, Erik the Red, was a skilled explorer who gave Greenland its name and built the first Norse settlement there in 982–5. According to Icelandic sagas, Leif set off on his own voyage of exploration soon after the year 1000. He sailed west from Greenland to a rocky coast, which he named Helluland (Slabland). Sailing south, he found a forested country, Markland (Woodland), and a land with a mild climate where grapes grew. He named this place Vinland (Wineland), and spent the winter there, returning to Greenland in the spring. The exact location of Vinland is not known, but it is believed to have been somewhere on the North American mainland.

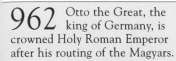

VIKING LONGSHIP
The Vikings used longships on raiding voyages and on long-distance journeys to discover new lands.

Murasaki SHIKIBU
c.978–1015
Japanese writer

Murasaki Shikibu was probably the author of the world's first full-length novel. Born in Kyoto, Japan, little is known about her other than that she began serving as a court lady in 1005, four years after her husband died. Shikibu's famous work, *The Tale of Genji*, was set in courtly society and is a romantic tale about the adventures of Prince Genji. The tone of the last 14 chapters is different from the rest of the book – either it was written by someone else, or the author was beginning to disapprove of her characters' vain and superficial lives.

AVICENNA
980–1037
Persian philosopher and physician

Born near Bokhara in Persia (modern Iran), Avicenna was famous for the vast extent of his learning. He wrote more than 200 works on science, religion, and philosophy, and was one of the main interpreters of the ancient Greek writer Aristotle for the Islamic world. He became physician to several sultans and his medical masterpiece, *Canon of Medicine*, became the standard reference book for generations of medical scholars.

---

962 Otto the Great, the king of Germany, is crowned Holy Roman Emperor after his routing of the Magyars. His victory ends the Magyar threat to Western Europe. Otto soon becomes king of Italy but Italian princes oppose his rule.

969 The Fatimids invade Egypt, building a new town, al-Qahirah, or Cairo, which becomes the capital of the Fatimid Empire. Cairo becomes a major centre for scientific studies, particularly astronomy. The empire declines after 1100.

Guido D'AREZZO
c.990–c.1050
Italian music theorist

Guido d'Arezzo was responsible for modern forms of musical notation. He was probably born in Arezzo, Italy, and taught singing at the cathedral before becoming a monk. In about 1026, he wrote a book explaining his new methods of teaching music,

Guido monachus   Theodal dususps

Micrologus de Musica. In this work, he described the use of lines and spaces to show the pitch of musical notes, and also introduced the syllables Ut, Re, Mi, Fa, Sol, La to name the notes of the musical scale.

CANUTE
c.995–1035
Scandinavian king

Canute was a king of such great power that some of his courtiers believed he could even control the tides. The younger son of King Sweyn I of Denmark, in 1013 Canute accompanied his father when he invaded England and forced the English king to flee. A year later King Sweyn died and the Danish settlers in England

chose Canute as king. In 1016, he defeated a rival English king and took control of the whole country. He became king of Denmark and southern Sweden in 1018, and king of Norway in 1028. He now ruled a vast empire around the North and Baltic seas and his reign was marked by great prosperity and generosity to the English Church. Legend tells that Canute had to sit by the sea and let the water wash over his feet to prove to his courtiers that there were limits to his powers after all.

GUIDO D'AREZZO
The Italian monk and musical theorist with his protector, Bishop Theodal (right).

William the CONQUEROR
c.1027–87
English king

William's conquest of England in 1066 was the last time the country was successfully invaded. He was born in Normandy, northern France, the illegitimate son of the Duke of Normandy. In 1051, he was promised the English throne by the childless English king, Edward the Confessor. Yet when Edward died in 1066, his brother-in-law, Harold, became king. William invaded England to claim his title, defeating Harold in battle at Hastings. As king of England, William was a strong ruler. He built a series of castles across the

country to assist in local government and, in 1086, ordered a survey of his entire kingdom, published as the Domesday Book.

URBAN II
1035–99
French pope who launched the Crusades

The crusades of Pope Urban II began centuries of warfare between Christians and Muslims. He was born Odo of Lagery, in France. After serving as a bishop and then a cardinal, he was elected Pope in 1088. In 1095, Urban called on the knights of western Europe to set off on a crusade, or holy war against the Muslim rulers of the Holy Land, to capture Jerusalem in Palestine. Perhaps

THE CRUSADES

In the late 11th century, the Muslim Seljuk Turks overran Palestine and began to attack Christian pilgrims to the Holy Land. The Byzantine emperor appealed for help to resist the Muslims. In response, the Pope, URBAN II, called in 1095 for a crusade, or holy war, against the Muslims. As a result, the Christian rulers of Europe launched a series of invasions of Palestine that lasted for over 200 years.

A EUROPEAN CRUSADE
People came from all over Europe to join the Crusades, some inspired by religious fervour, others by self-interest. Among the participants were RICHARD I of England (1157–99), nicknamed "the Lionheart" because of his bravery in battle; PHILIP II of France (1165–1223); and FREDERICK I, the Holy Roman Emperor (1123–90).

FAILURE
Despite the efforts of these and other leaders, the Crusades achieved little. Jerusalem was captured in 1099, but it was soon lost to SALADIN (p.11). The Crusaders were also less than Christian in their actions, massacring Jews and Muslims and looting what they could find. In 1204, Crusaders even sacked Constantinople, the capital of the

friendly Christian Byzantine Empire, and antagonized local Crusader kingdoms as well as the Muslims. By 1291, the Crusaders were thrown out of the Holy Land for good.

THE IMPACT
Although the Crusaders failed to hold Jerusalem, their actions did have a large impact throughout Europe. Great literature was written about the brave deeds of individual Crusaders and the code of chivalry among knights became very important. Although the hostility between Christianity and Islam grew even fiercer over the coming centuries, economic and cultural contacts formed between the two civilizations benefited Europe immensely.

1000
Viking Leif Eriksson and a crew of 35 men are probably the first Europeans to reach North America, five centuries before Christopher Columbus. They spend the winter there and name the new country Vinland.

1014
Rajendra I becomes king of the Cholas, a Hindu people who are very powerful in Southern India and Sri Lanka. He builds a huge temple in his capital city, Tanjore, to house hundreds, including 400 dancing girls.

CRUSADERS TAKE JERUSALEM
In July 1099, the Crusaders broke into Jerusalem after a five-week siege. They ransacked the city and killed all its Jewish and Muslim inhabitants.

as many as 130,000 people were inspired to leave their homes and set off on the first Crusade. In 1099, the Crusaders stormed Jerusalem, massacring every Muslim and Jew they could find.

El CID
c.1043–99
Spanish soldier

Legends about the life of El Cid have made him one of Spain's best-known national heroes. He was born Rodrigo Diaz de Vivar near Burgos. Very little is known for certain about his life, but he probably became a soldier in the army of King Sancho II of Castile. When Sancho was murdered in 1079, his brother Alfonso became king and sent Diaz into exile. Diaz, now El Cid (the Lord), assembled a small army and sold his services as a mercenary. He became a famous fighter, and conquered Valencia in 1094. His life was romanticized in the epic poem *The Song of the Cid* (c.1140).

Omar KHAYYAM
c.1048–c.1122
Persian poet, astronomer, and mathematician

Omar Khayyam was renowned in his own lifetime for his scientific knowledge, but nowadays he is better known for his poetry in *The Rubaiyat of Omar Khayyam* (first published in 1859). Born in Nishapuur, Persia, he was well educated and one of his first works was an influential piece on algebra. After a pilgrimage to Mecca, the religious capital of the Muslim world, Omar Khayyam became astronomer to the sultan, and revised the Muslim calendar.

Bernard of CLAIRVAUX
1090–1153
French reviver of the Cistercian Order of monks

Bernard of Clairvaux was one of the last founding fathers of the Catholic Church. He was born into a noble family, in a castle near Dijon in France. In 1112, he became a monk at a recently founded monastery at Citeaux. Bernard was a charismatic speaker and persuaded some 30 men to join him. The arrival of so many monks saved the failing monastery. Bernard went on to found a new monastery, called Clairvaux, which became the centre of a monastic revival. By 1152, his monks had founded 327 monasteries. They became known as the Cistercians, after Citeaux. In the 1120s, Bernard also helped to establish the Knights Templar, the crusading order of fighting monks. Bernard was later made a saint.

Hildegard of BINGEN
1098–1179
German abbess and composer

Hildegard is considered to be a saint in many parts of Germany. She was born into an aristocratic family and was educated at a convent. She stayed there as a nun, and became abbess (leading nun) of the convent in 1136. The convent moved to Bingen in about 1150. Hildegard had several mystical visions, which she described in her writings. She wrote an encyclopaedia of natural history, *Liber simplicis medicinae* (1150–60). She also wrote about the lives of the saints as well as poetry, some of which she set to her own music. She was probably one of the first composers in Europe, and certainly the first female composer.

HILDEGARD OF BINGEN
The German nun and mystic was one of the first composers in Europe.

1052 The Almoravids, a north African, Islamic dynasty, attack the wealthy kingdom of Ghana. Ghana had controlled trade on the Niger River and sold spices and gold. The Almoravids seize the capital, Kumbi, in 1076.

1080 Henry IV, the Holy Roman Emperor, is excommunicated and deposed by Pope Gregory VII. The argument concerns the question of whether bishops should be appointed by the Pope or by the emperor.

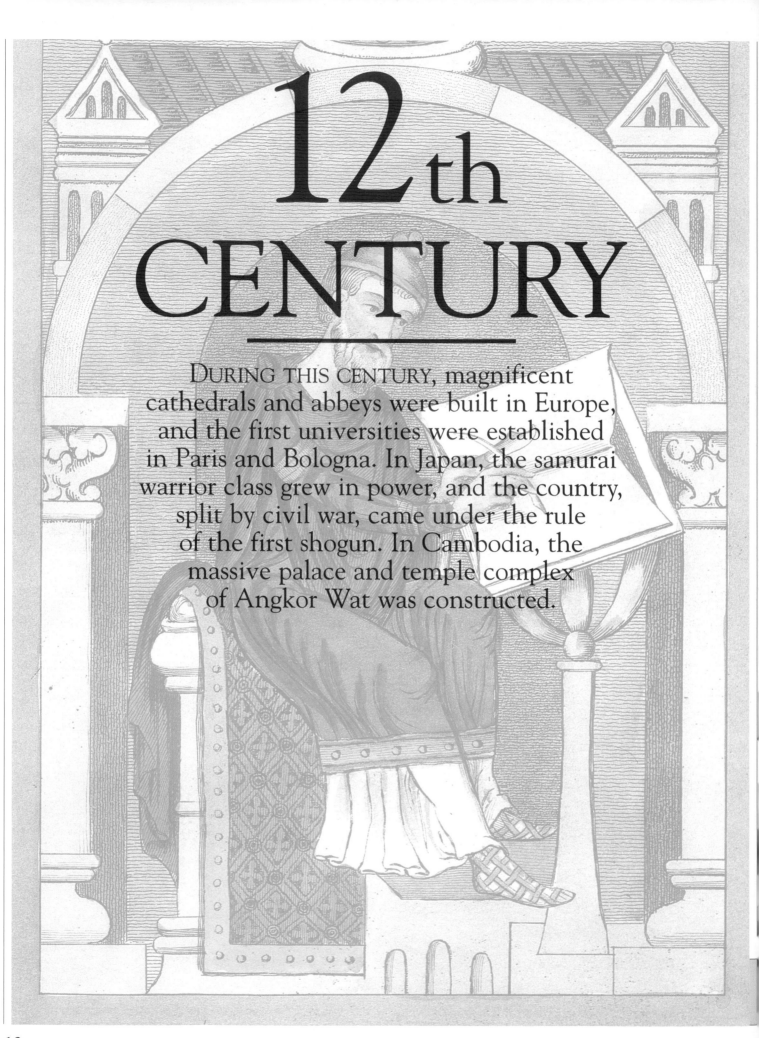

12th CENTURY

DURING THIS CENTURY, magnificent cathedrals and abbeys were built in Europe, and the first universities were established in Paris and Bologna. In Japan, the samurai warrior class grew in power, and the country, split by civil war, came under the rule of the first shogun. In Cambodia, the massive palace and temple complex of Angkor Wat was constructed.

Thomas BECKET
1118–70
English archbishop

Thomas Becket was murdered at Canterbury Cathedral after he argued with King Henry II. He had been promoted by the king, who made him chancellor in 1155 and then archbishop of Canterbury in 1162. But as archbishop, Becket put his religious duties first and resisted the king's attempts to control the Church. In 1170, frustrated and furious, Henry said: "Will no one rid me of this turbulent priest?" These words were answered by four knights, who murdered Becket. Within three years he had been proclaimed a saint, and his shrine at Canterbury became a site of pilgrimage.

Benjamin of TUDELA
c.1130–c.73
Jewish traveller

The rabbi (Jewish teacher) Benjamin of Tudela was the first great European traveller of the Middle Ages. Born in Tudela, Spain, between 1159 and 1173 he visited France, Germany, Italy, Greece, Syria, Arabia, Egypt, Assyria (Iraq), Persia (Iran), India, and the frontiers of China. Wherever he went he received hospitality from the small Jewish communities scattered across Europe, North Africa, and Asia. He wrote a book, *The Itinerary of Benjamin of Tudela*, which described the places he visited and the local Jewish communities. He was particularly interested in their customs, how they made their living, and how they were treated by their country's rulers.

HENRY II
1133–89
English king

Henry II was the first Plantagenet king of England. He was born in Le Mans, France, and inherited much of northern France from his father. He also acquired vast lands in southwest France when he married Eleanor of Aquitaine in 1152. In 1154, he became king of England. He now controlled a vast territory, known as the Angevin Empire, which stretched from the Scottish borders down to the Pyrenees mountains on the French-Spanish border. He extended this great empire by invading Ireland in 1171, beginning more than 800 years of English rule in Ireland. Henry was a strong and forceful leader, but he was also quarrelsome. In 1170, he famously fell out with his archbishop Thomas Becket, but later repented at Becket's tomb after his death. Henry introduced many sound legal reforms, laying the foundations of the English common law system. Remarkably, his empire remained intact until his death.

SALADIN
c.1138–93
Muslim leader

Saladin, or *Salah al-Din*, which means "the Welfare of the Faith", brought to an end Christian attempts to dominate Palestine. He was a brilliant military commander and administrator, and became grand vizier of Egypt in 1169. When the sultan died Saladin was pronounced successor and, in 1174, he became leader of Egypt. Having conquered Yemen and Syria, he came into conflict with the Crusaders, the Christian rulers of Palestine. In 1187, Saladin defeated Crusader armies at Hattin in Palestine and seized Acre and Jerusalem. In 1192, he made a peace with Richard I of England, guaranteeing Muslim control of the region.

Minamoto no YORITOMO
1147–99
Japanese shogun

Yoritomo established control over the whole of Japan after years of division. The country had been split between warring families, but Yoritomo gradually took over the eastern provinces of the country. By 1185, he was powerful enough to defeat the rival Taira family and set up a military government in the name of the emperor. In 1192, the emperor awarded him the title shogun, or "great general". The system of government he established lasted in Japan until 1868.

HENRY II
Effigies of Henry II and his wife Eleanor in the Abbaye de Fontevraud, France.

1126 In China, the Jin tribe attack the Song Empire, capturing the capital Kaifeng and much of northern China. One of the emperor's sons escapes and establishes a new southern Song Empire at Hangzou.

1139 Matilda, the widow of Henry V, makes a claim for the English throne which has been occupied by her cousin, Stephen of Blois, since 1135. She captures Stephen in 1141, but her reign is a disaster and he is reinstated in 1153.

Genghis KHAN
c.1162–1227
Mongol leader

Genghis Khan ruled over the biggest and most powerful empire in the world. Born Temujin, he succeeded his father, a Mongol chief, at the age of 13 and slowly built up Mongol power.

In 1206, a great assembly of all the Mongol tribes proclaimed him Genghis Khan, or "Lord Absolute Ruler". Over the next 15 years, his fearsome armies conquered northern China, Afghanistan, Central Asia, and much of Persia. He created an empire that stretched from the China Sea in the east to the Black Sea in the west. Genghis Khan also used his organizational skills to give the Mongols a code of law and an alphabet.

GENGHIS KHAN
in his tent or "yurt"

Leonardo FIBONACCI
c.1170–c.1250
Italian mathematician

Born in Pisa, Italy, Leonardo Fibonacci was responsible for spreading the use of Arabic numbers, which originated in India. His influential *Book of Calculation* (1202), demonstrated the efficiency of the new numerical system, showing how it could be used for complex calculations. His greatest work, *The Book of Square Numbers* (1225), contained highly advanced contributions to number theory. It was dedicated to his patron, the Holy Roman Emperor, Frederick II. He also discovered the Fibonacci sequence, in which each number is equal to the sum of the preceding two, for example, 1,1,2,3,5,8,13. He is thought to have been the most brilliant mathematician of the Middle Ages.

ST FRANCIS OF ASSISI
St Francis chose to lead a life of poverty. He founded an order of friars, called Franciscans, devoted to caring for the sick.

Llywelyn the GREAT
c.1170–1240
Welsh leader

Known as *Ap Iorwerth*, "the Great", Llywelyn was a Welsh noble who defended Wales against the English. By 1201, he had established control over northern Wales, and later extended his rule south and westwards. In 1211, King John of England threatened to invade Wales, but Llywelyn kept him out, building stone castles to defend his country. Through his good government he ensured semi-independence for the Wales, until its conquest in 1284.

Francis of ASSISI
c.1181–1226
Italian founder of the Franciscan Order

Francis of Assisi founded a new order of friars called the Franciscans. Francis, who came from a wealthy background, turned to religion after a long illness, and decided to follow Christ's example by living in poverty. He began to preach and care for the sick, begging for his daily food. As his reputation spread, he attracted followers who wanted to share his life. They settled near a leper colony at Assisi, Italy, where they lived in huts. In 1215, the Pope gave official approval to the group, who were known as the Friars Minor (Little Brothers). Their first general meeting, in 1219, was attended by 5,000 friars, and soon there were Franciscans in almost every large town in western Europe. Two years after his death, Francis was made a saint.

1170 The Normans, who already have a firm footing in England with Henry II on the throne, gain yet more power when Richard de Clare, known as Strongbow, invades Ireland. He is made king of Leinster the following year.

1174 Halfway through the building of a tower in Pisa, Italy, soil under the structure begins to subside, causing the tower to lean. Construction recommences in 1275 with a new design to compensate for the tilt.

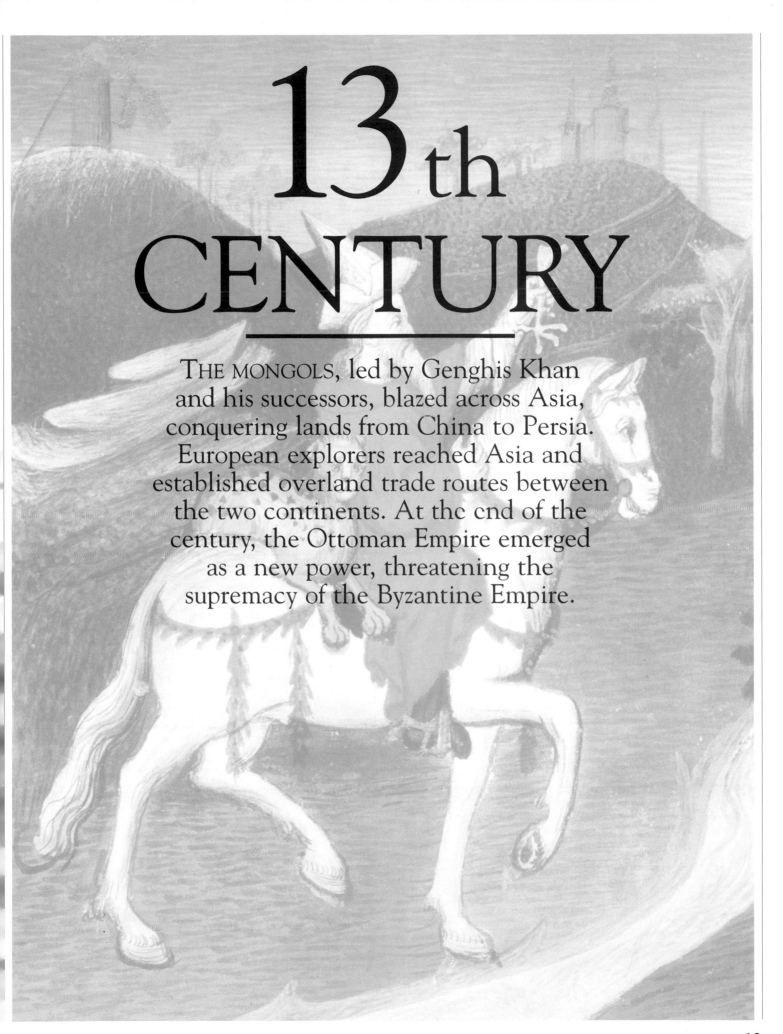

13th CENTURY

THE MONGOLS, led by Genghis Khan
and his successors, blazed across Asia,
conquering lands from China to Persia.
European explorers reached Asia and
established overland trade routes between
the two continents. At the end of the
century, the Ottoman Empire emerged
as a new power, threatening the
supremacy of the Byzantine Empire.

Kublai KHAN
c.1214–94
Chinese emperor

Kublai Khan was the leader of the most powerful empire in the world during the 13th century. He was the grandson of Genghis Khan (p.12), the first Mongol leader, and was elected Great Khan in 1260. Kublai Khan expanded the Mongol Empire so that by 1279, he had conquered all of China. As the first foreign-born ruler of China, he adopted many Chinese habits and practices. He was a harsh ruler, but did much to improve trade and commerce, particularly in the silk and porcelain industries. He also built new roads and canals and set up stores of food in case of famine. At his death, he ruled an empire stretching from China to the River Danube in Europe.

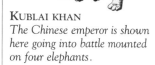

KUBLAI KHAN
The Chinese emperor is shown here going into battle mounted on four elephants.

Thomas AQUINAS
c.1225–74
Italian philosopher

Born near Naples in southern Italy, Thomas Aquinas was educated at the monastery of Monte Cassino. He entered the Dominican order of monks in 1244. The following year he moved to Paris, where he eventually became professor of theology. After 1259, he spent several years in Rome as adviser to the Pope before moving south to Naples, where he died. Aquinas was the greatest of all medieval thinkers, seeking to reconcile the teachings of the Catholic Church with the philosophy of the ancient Greeks, in particular Aristotle. He regarded society as a natural part of life and argued that people are not truly human if they are outside society. The basis of society is the family, and society provides a framework in which people can develop reason and moral sense and thus live well as Christians. This became known as Thomist doctrine and was popular with radical priests. In 1323, Aquinas was made a saint and in 1879, the ideas set out in his writings were recognized as the basis of modern Catholicism.

Adam de la HALLE
c.1240–c.86
French writer and composer

The composer Adam de la Halle who wrote the earliest French theatrical comedies and comic operas, was a *trouvère*, a northern French musician and poet. Born in Arras, France, he trained to be a priest, but spent much of his later life in Italy as a minstrel in the courts of Count Robert II of Artois and of Count Charles of Anjou. His work includes poems and plays such as *The Play of Robin and Marion* and *The Play of Adam*; and he composed courtly songs and choral pieces in all the popular styles. The songs of minstrels such as de la Halle had a far-reaching influence on the style and composition of late medieval music.

MARCO POLO'S TRAVELS
Marco Polo followed the Silk Road from Europe to Asia. The hazardous journey took him four years.

Zhao MENGFU
1254–1322
Chinese painter

Born in Wuxing, China, Zhao Mengfu was a descendant of an early Chinese emperor. He was educated in Chinese classics as well as artistic skills. At the same time he developed his skill in calligraphy (the art of beautiful handwriting), and was often called upon to inscribe celebratory texts. His paintings cover a huge range of subjects, including *Autumn Colours on the Mountains* (1296), *Red-robed Indian Monk* (1304), and *Watering Horses* in the *Autumn Fields* (1312). Zhao's dream-like landscapes, painted in pure ink on paper, are among the most famous expressions of medieval Chinese art.

Marco POLO
1254–1324
Venetian traveller

It was Marco Polo who first brought detailed news of Asia to the West. He was born in Venice, Italy, the son of a merchant. In 1260, his father and uncle travelled to the court of Kublai Khan, the Mongol ruler of China. On a second journey east, in 1271, they took Marco with them. According to his own account, Marco Polo became a valued member of Kublai Khan's court and travelled all over the Mongol Empire on the Khan's business. Marco Polo returned home in 1295, and joined the Venetian forces fighting Genoa. Taken captive, he spent two years in a Genoese prison, where he dictated his memoirs to a fellow prisoner. His *Descriptions of the World* (1298) introduced Europeans to the East. Many readers dismissed the work as fantasy. But others, including explorers Christopher Columbus (p.22) and John Cabot (p.22), were inspired to set out for Asia.

Dante ALIGHIERI
1265–1321
Italian poet

Dante Alighieri, usually known as Dante, wrote *The Divine Comedy* (1307–21), one of the most famous poems in literature. He became involved in politics at a young age which eventually led to his being exiled from his home in

---

1215 Forced by the barons, King John of England agrees to sign the Magna Carta, which secures their land-holding rights. John goes back on his agreement and dies shortly after. The barons have the charter made law in 1225.

1226 Frederick II, the Holy Roman Emperor, sends the Order of Teutonic Knights to convert Prussia (part of Germany) to Christianity. The Order succeeds in conquering large parts of the Baltic provinces and Russia.

Florence. Unusually, the long epic poem *The Divine Comedy* was written in Italian instead of the more conventional Latin, and helped to make Italian acceptable as a major literary language. The poem tells the story of a journey from hell, through purgatory, and into heaven, reflecting the medieval view of the afterlife, but it can also be seen as the story of Dante's life and exile. Virgil, the classical Roman poet, is Dante's guide through hell and purgatory, and his beloved Beatrice awaits him in Heaven. Dante's lifelong love for Beatrice, his ideal woman, is one of the most famous romances in literature.

Giotto di BONDONE
c.1267–1337
Italian painter

Giotto di Bondone's work changed the face of Western painting and had an enormous effect on a number of masters of the Italian Renaissance. Little is known about his early life, but he was born near Florence and was probably apprenticed to the painter Cimabue. His paintings broke away from the flat, formal Byzantine style which was then popular in Italy. His figures not only looked solid and natural, but conveyed emotion and drama in a new way. Giotto's greatest paintings are the frescoes in the Arena Chapel in Padua (c.1304–06). They include scenes of the Last Judgement and the Passion of Christ. In 1334, Giotto became architect of Florence Cathedral, where he designed the famous campanile, or bell tower.

THE CAMPANILE
Designed by Giotto in 1334, the Campanile in Florence is clad in white and pink Tuscan marble.

William WALLACE
c.1274–1305
Scottish military leader

In 1297, William Wallace sprang to fame. Little is known about his life prior to this. In 1296, King Edward I of England had conquered a large part of Scotland and expelled the Scottish king. Now Wallace gathered an army and led a rebellion against Edward. He defeated the English troops at the Battle of Stirling Bridge and moved south to attack the border counties. Scotland had won back her independence, but only briefly. In 1298, Edward's strengthened forces routed Wallace's army at Falkirk. He went into hiding and, in 1299 sailed to France to seek support for the Scottish cause. Wallace returned in 1303 and mounted a guerrilla war against the English. He was finally captured and hanged, drawn, and quartered in 1305.

Robert BRUCE
1274–1329
Scottish king

Robert Bruce freed Scotland from English rule. In 1297, he joined William Wallace's revolt against the English and after Wallace's death was crowned king of Scotland by the Scottish nobles in 1306. An English army quickly defeated him, but over the next eight years he organized a guerrilla campaign to expel the English from Scotland. Robert Bruce dismantled castles that had been seized from the English and avoided battles in order to build up his forces' strength. In 1314, he besieged Stirling Castle, defeating a huge English army under King Edward II at the Battle of Bannockburn. The fighting continued until Edward III recognized Scotland's independence by the Treaty of Northampton (1328).

Mansa MUSA
c.1280–1337
Mali emperor

Mansa Musa turned Mali into one of the most successful countries in 13th-century Africa. The ruler of Mali was traditionally a Muslim and when Mansa Musa became emperor in 1307, he vowed to go on a pilgrimage to Mecca, the sacred city of Islam. In 1324, he set out, causing a sensation in Cairo with his 500 slaves and 80 camels laden with gold. On his return, he brought back architects and scholars who turned his capital at Timbuktu into a centre of Islamic culture and learning. By the time he died, Mali was a rich, peaceful empire with a strong administration and trading links across the north and west of Africa.

1264 In China, the Mongol ruler Kublai Khan founds the Yuan Dynasty. The Mongol Empire now stretches from Germany to Korea. International trade along the Silk Route flourishes, increasing the empire's wealth.

1265 Having defeated and imprisoned English king Henry III a year earlier, nobleman Simon de Montfort invites leading citizens from major towns to take part in a parliament. It is the first time commoners have attended.

14th CENTURY

THE POPULATIONS OF EUROPE and Asia were decimated by the "Black Death". This deadly bubonic plague killed about one-third of the inhabitants of Europe – around 25 million people. In China, the Ming Dynasty was founded after the Mongols were driven out of the country, and, in West Africa, the state of Mali grew wealthy through trade across the Sahara Desert.

Guillaume de MACHAUT
c.1300–77
French composer

Born in Rheims, France, Guillaume de Machaut studied in Paris before becoming secretary to John of Luxembourg, king of Bohemia. He travelled with the king through Poland, Lithuania, and Italy. For his services he was made canon of Rheims Cathedral in 1337. This position allowed him to experiment with composing music. His most important composition is the *Messe de Nostre Dame* (Mass of Our Lady), which was in the new style known as *ars nova*, and is the earliest example of such a mass written by a single composer. His poetry, especially the long love poem *Voir-Dit* influenced Chaucer (p.18).

Ibn BATTUTA
c.1304–68
Moroccan traveller

In 1325, Ibn Battuta set off on a religious pilgrimage to Mecca, the centre of the Islamic faith, in Arabia. He enjoyed the journey so much that he decided to continue travelling, driven by a desire to see the whole world. Ibn Battuta spent the next 25 years on the move. He visited India, the Maldive Islands, Sumatra, China, Spain, Sardinia, West Africa, and East Africa. Back in Morocco in the 1350s, he dictated an account of his journeys, the *Rihlah* (Travels), which contains fascinating descriptions of the medieval Muslim world. Throughout his lifetime, it has been estimated that Ibn Battuta travelled an amazing 120,000 km (74,560 miles).

Francesco PETRARCH
1304–74
Italian scholar, poet, and humanist

Petrarch is best known for the series of love poems that he wrote for Laura, a woman he had admired from afar for many years. He perfected the Italian "Petrarchan" sonnet (a 14-line poem), breaking new ground by ignoring the ancient rules of poetry. Petrarch was also a humanist, which meant that he believed that man's reason and humanity were as important as the authority and rules of the Church.

IBN BATTUTA
with a native Egyptian

EDWARD III
1312–77
English king

Edward succeeded to the throne after his father, Edward II, was deposed by his mother, Matilda, and Roger Mortimer in 1327. Edward III wished to conquer France and to unite the nobility at home. In 1337, he announced his claim to the throne of France, thus starting the 100 Years' War, which was to last, with breaks, until 1453. He won many battles and gained large

EDWARD III
The warrior English king spent much of his reign fighting France.

tracts of land in northern and western France. At home, he promoted a class of nobility whose actions were motivated by chivalry. He reformed the laws and administration of the country, leaving behind a much stronger kingdom.

Kan'ami KIYOTSUGU
1333–84
Japanese playwright, actor, and musician

Japanese theatre pioneer Kan'ami Kiyotsugu directed a theatre group in Uamato. It was here that he formed the Yuzaki Theatrical Company, which became the Kanze school of Noh. Kan'ami is seen as the founder of Noh drama, where music (flutes, stringed insruments, drums, and song) helps to reveal traits about the characters. Kan'ami included aspects of other traditional Japanese theatres, adding popular song and dance, and elements from traditional harvest festivals.

1303 Guillaume de Nogaret, the emissary of Philip IV of France, captures and mistreats Pope Boniface VIII at Anagni in Italy. Local people rescue Boniface, but he dies soon after his ordeal.

1325 In Central America, the Aztecs found the city of Tenochtitlán. It is razed to the ground by Spanish soldier Hernando Cortés and his army in 1521, when he wipes out the Aztecs in pursuit of their gold. ay Mexico City stands there.

TAMERLANE
1336–1405
Mongol ruler

Also called Tamburlaine, and Timur, the mighty Mongol ruler Tamerlane was a descendant of Genghis Khan (p.12), and became ruler of the Mongol Empire in 1370. He began a series of wars in Persia, India, Syria, Turkey, and Central Asia. By 1402, Tamerlane had control of a vast empire. He was a military genius, with a reputation for cruelty: although he fought in the name of Islam, he plundered Muslim cities. However, he was a keen patron of the arts and sciences, and imported foreign craft workers to improve the Mongol capital at Samarkand.

Geoffrey CHAUCER
c.1340–1400
English poet

Geoffrey Chaucer was born in London, England. He began his career as a court page, then joined the army to fight the French during the 100 Years' War. He was taken prisoner and King Edward III (p.17) helped raise his ransom. Later, he travelled abroad on diplomatic missions for the king. Here, he was much influenced by Italian writers such as Dante (p.14) and Petrarch (p.17). *The Canterbury Tales*, written around 1387, is Chaucer's most famous work. It follows a group of pilgrims who are riding to Canterbury in Kent to visit the shrine of St Thomas Becket (p.11). The travellers, who include a knight, a miller, a monk, a nun, a cook, and the down-to-earth wife of Bath, pass the time by telling stories. The 24 tales, told in verse, portray a vivid, funny picture of medieval English life.

THE WIFE OF BATH
A character in Chaucer's Canterbury Tales, *the wife of Bath, showed that some women in the 14th century had a degree of independence.*

Cheng HO
1371–1435
Chinese admiral

In 1405, Chinese sailor and explorer Cheng Ho was ordered to lead a series of expeditions to the "Southern Ocean" south of China. Over a period of some 30 years, he made seven voyages, visiting Java, Sumatra, Malaya, Ceylon, India, Persia, Arabia, and East Africa. These were massive undertakings, with fleets of more than 60 ships, carrying thousands of men. Cheng Ho demanded tributes from the rulers of the lands he visited. He also traded with local merchants. His expeditions were the last of the Chinese voyages of exploration.

Filippo BRUNELLESCHI
1377–1446
Italian architect and sculptor

Filippo Brunelleschi transformed the architecture of Florence in Italy. He trained originally as a goldsmith, but gave it up when his designs for the baptistry doors of Florence cathedral were unsuccessful. He turned to architecture and studied the classical buildings in Rome. This was vital to his greatest triumph, the construction of the dome on top of Florence cathedral (1420–36). The dome, the largest in the world, was built without use of scaffolding. His work revived the architectural techniques of ancient Rome, making him the first important architect of the Renaissance.

Wat TYLER
died 1381
English rebel leader

In 1381, Wat Tyler led the Peasants' Revolt. His men marched on London from Kent to demand the abolition of the hated taxes and the end of serfdom, the system by which peasants were bound to the land. They stormed London and executed the king's ministers. Tyler was the chief spokesman, and put the demands of the peasants to King Richard II. He agreed to most of them, but Tyler was not satisfied with his response. During the confrontation that followed, Tyler was struck down and wounded. He was later beheaded.

1347
The Black Death, or bubonic plague, reaches Europe after devastating China and the Byzantine Empire. It kills around 25 million people in Europe – between one-third and one-quarter of the total population of the continent.

1358
In France, the Peasants' Revolt, known as the *Jacquerie*, is savagely suppressed. More than 20,000 lives are lost. The peasants and farmers were protesting against hordes of mercenary soldiers ravaging the countryside.

HENRY V
1387–1422
English king

Born in Monmouth Castle, Wales, Henry V became king of England in 1413. He had great ambitions for his country and immediately rekindled the 100 Years' War with France. In 1415, he defeated a far larger French army than his own at the Battle of Agincourt in northern France. After further victories, the French king Charles VI accepted Henry as his heir in 1420, giving him his daughter, Catherine, in marriage. Unfortunately, Henry died in 1422 before he could succeed to the French throne. He left his inheritance in the hands of his infant son, Henry, but within 30 years, England had lost all the territories Henry V had won. The 100 Years' War between the two countries ended in England's defeat.

THE 100 YEARS' WAR

In 1337, war broke out between England and France. The conflict lasted until 1453, but the armies did not fight every year, which is why it is known as the 100 Years' War. It began when EDWARD III OF ENGLAND (p.17) claimed the French throne through his mother, ISABELLA (1292–1358), daughter of the French king. From then on, every British king professed to be the king of France until GEORGE III (p.64) renounced his claim to the throne in 1801 during the French Revolution.

THE WAR
The first stage of the 100 Years' War lasted from 1337 to 1360 and was marked by decisive English victories at Crécy (1346) and Poitiers (1356). The English army was led by EDWARD THE BLACK PRINCE (1330–76), son of EDWARD III. His soldiers used the longbow, the arrows of which could pierce armour from a great distance, while the French used the slower, far more cumbersome crossbow. As a result, more than 10,000 French soldiers died at Crécy, compared with only 200 Englishmen. A peace treaty favouring the English was signed at Brétigny in 1360, but fighting continued sporadically.

THE FIGHTERS
In 1415, the war flared up again when HENRY V OF ENGLAND defeated the French army at Agincourt (1415). Henry became heir to the French throne but after his death in 1422, JOAN OF ARC (p.21) rallied the French armies to fight for their throne again. By 1453, the English had been thrown out of all of France except for the port of Calais, and the war was effectively over.

Donatello
DONATO
c.1386–1466
Italian sculptor

Donatello is considered one of the most important sculptors of the 15th century. He received his training in the workshop of sculptor Lorenzo Ghiberti in Florence, Italy. Here he developed a bold, highly original style of carving. His first great work was the marble statue of St George (1415–17). Though the figure appears relaxed, it also conveys strong emotion. Among Donatello's other notable pieces are his bronze David (c.1430–32), and the statue of the soldier on horseback, Gattamelata (1443–48). Later in life, he experimented with thinner, more distorted figures, such as the shocking carved relief of the Passion in the church of San Lorenzo in Florence.

Jan
VAN EYCK
c.1390–1441
Flemish painter

Very little is known about the early life of the painter Jan van Eyck except that he started his career as a manuscript illuminator. In 1425, he contributed to the great altarpiece depicting *The Adoration of the Lamb* (1432) in Ghent cathedral, Belgium. One of his most famous paintings is "*The Arnolfini Marriage*" (1434), now in the National Gallery, London, which shows his unusual style of capturing everyday detail. Van Eyck's pictures, filled with realistic detail, show his brilliant use of colour to convey the subtle differences of light and shade.

Henry the
NAVIGATOR
1394–1460
Portuguese prince

Born in Porto, Portugal, Prince Henry effectively launched the golden age of European exploration. He dreamt of leading a holy war against the Muslims of North Africa and wanted to learn if there were Christian rulers in Africa who could help him. To this end, he sent expeditions down the coast of Africa. His captains also sailed out into the Atlantic, discovering Madeira and the Azores. In 1446, they began to bring African slaves and gold back to Europe. Although Henry never went on a voyage himself, he certainly earned his nickname, "the Navigator".

Johannes
GUTENBERG
c.1398–c.1468
German inventor

Johannes Gutenberg was responsible for developing the printing press. A talented metalworker, from 1434 onwards, he worked tirelessly and secretly on his metal printing press. By 1455, he had produced his masterpiece – *The Gutenberg Bible* – the West's first printed book. His press was revolutionary because it had movable type – individual letters made from metal – which could be used over and over again. This method of printing meant that books were less expensive to produce and they became available to a wider audience.

THE GUTENBERG BIBLE
This gothic type used in Gutenberg's bible was modelled on German script.

1368 The Ming Dynasty is founded in China after almost a century of Mongol rule. Emperor Hung Wu rules as a dictator (someone who assumes leadership by force), but he restores order and prosperity to China.

1392 Having revolted against the Mongols and returned Korea to Chinese rule in 1354, Yi Song-gye seizes power himself in Korea and founds the Yi Dynasty. He sets up his capital in Kyon-Song, present-day Seoul.

15th CENTURY

DURING THE 15TH CENTURY, an international economy began to develop as trade routes brought continents and civilizations into closer contact with each other. In Europe, the Renaissance revitalized the role of art and learning in everyday life and ushered in a new cultural age. In the Americas, the powerful Aztec and Inca empires were at the height of their powers.

ANGELIC ART
This 15th-century triptych by Fra Angelico hangs in the Galleria Nazionale d'Arte Antica in Rome.

Fra ANGELICO
c.1400–55
Italian painter

The graceful style of Fra Angelico's frescoes (wall paintings) influenced many later Italian painters. He was born Guido di Pietro in Vicchio, Italy. At 19, he became a Dominican monk at Fiesole, near Florence, where he was known as Fra (Brother) Giovanni. It is thought that he began his artistic career by illustrating manuscripts, but the most famous of his works is the series of frescoes at San Marco Monastery in Florence, completed between 1438 and 1445. Fra Giovanni painted religious images of heavenly beauty, depicted in pastel shades and highlighted with gold leaf. Their beauty as well as their serene simplicity, inspired the nickname Fra Angelico (Angelic Brother). In 1445, he was summoned to work for the Pope in Rome, where he later died.

JOAN OF ARC
This bronze statue of Joan of Arc shows the French saint in a typically defiant pose. She led the French army to victory over the English in the 100 Years' War.

Joan of ARC
1412–31
French soldier and saint

A young French girl called Jeanne d'Arc, or Joan of Arc, was responsible for leading the French to victory in the 100 Years' War. Born the daughter of a farmer, at the age of 13 Joan began to hear "voices", which she claimed belonged to three saints. They told her to save France from the English. Joan travelled to the court of the *dauphin* (prince) at Chinon, and convinced him that the voices were genuine. In 1429, dressed in shining armour, she led the French to a series of victories at Orléans, resulting in the coronation of the *dauphin* as King Charles VII, at Rheims. In the spring of 1430, she was captured by the Duke of Burgundy, who handed her over to the English. Joan was tried and accused of witchcraft and heresy (false beliefs). On 30 May 1431, she was burned at the stake in Rouen. Joan of Arc was canonized as a saint in 1920.

PACHACUTI
c.1420–71
Inca leader

Pachacuti is credited with the vast expansion of the Inca Empire in South America. He was born Yupanqui, son of the Eighth Lord Inca, probably in their capital Cuzco, which is now in Peru. In 1438, Yupanqui overwhelmed the rival Chancas tribe and became Ninth Lord Inca with the name Pachacuti. He ran his empire with military efficiency, making Quechua the official language and setting up an efficient administration to govern every aspect of daily life. By the time of Pachacuti's death, the Inca Empire had expanded to cover modern-day Ecuador, Peru, Bolivia, and northern Chile.

William CAXTON
c.1422–91
English printer

England's first printing press was created by William Caxton. He began his career as an apprentice to a cloth merchant at the age of 15. In 1446, he went to Bruges in Belgium, where he prospered as a negotiator between English cloth merchants and the ruling dukes of Burgundy. From 1470 to 1472, he lived in Cologne, Germany, where he learnt about printing. Back in Bruges, Caxton set up a printing press and in 1475 printed the first English-language book, a translation of the French romance *Recuyell of the Historyes of Troye*. In 1476, back in England, he started a wooden press and, in 1480, used woodcuts as book illustrations. Among the 100 or so books that Caxton printed, the best known are Malory's *Morte D'Arthur* and Chaucer's *The Canterbury Tales* (p.18).

Sonni' ALI
c.1430–92
Songhai leader

Sonni' Ali led the large west African nation, Songhai, to independence. At the time of Sonni' Ali's birth, Songhai was part of the much larger Mali Empire to its west. In 1464, Ali ascended the Songhai throne and declared his nation independent. He captured the important trading cities of Timbuktu in 1469 and Jenné in 1473. Ali spent most of his reign in efficient but ruthless military campaigns. He also persecuted Islamic scholars, despite professing to be a Muslim himself. However, he encouraged commerce and trade, and on his death left behind a strong empire.

Josquin DESPREZ
c.1440–1521
French composer

The most influential composer of the High Renaissance period was Josquin Desprez. Little is known of his early life, except that he was born in the Picardy region of France and was a choral singer at Milan cathedral between 1459 and 1472. He remained in Italy, serving at various courts and singing in the papal choir until 1504, when an outbreak of the plague forced him back to France. He became a religious official at Condé, where he spent the rest of his life. Among his many religious works are 18 masses and more than 100 other choral works, but he also wrote many non-religious songs. Desprez gained admiration in Europe for his expressive style and sensitive setting of words to music. Luther (p.28) claimed Desprez was his favourite composer.

1405 Cheng Ho, a Chinese explorer, begins the first of seven expeditions to collect tributes for Ming emperors. The expeditions take him as far afield as Java, India, Persia, Arabia, and Africa. The final voyage ends in 1433.

1426 The Aztec Empire begins to grow when King Itzcoatl forms an alliance with Texcoco and Tlacopan, two adjacent states, and overthrows another neighbour, the Tapanecs. The Aztecs are both great traders and magnificent builders.

Sandro BOTTICELLI
1445–1510
Italian painter

Sandro Botticelli was one of the finest artists of the Renaissance period in Italy. Born in Florence, Botticelli trained first as a goldsmith, then as a painter under the artist Fra Filippo Lippi. He spent most of his life in Florence, working for wealthy patrons such as the Médici family and the Catholic Church. Many of his works depict mythical subjects, such as *Primavera* (1482) and *The Birth of Venus* (c.1485). Their delicate lines and poetic beauty brought him fame, and the Pope hired him to decorate the Sistine Chapel. Botticelli is also known for his images of beautiful Madonnas, and he later turned to exclusively religious themes. His style became unfashionable, however, and he died in poverty. Rediscovered in the 19th century, Botticelli has now become one of the best-loved of all Renaissance artists.

John & Sebastian CABOT
c.1450–98 & 1474–1557
Italian-English explorers

Born Giovanni Caboto in Genoa, Italy, John Cabot moved to Bristol, England, with his family. Like Columbus he believed Asia could be reached by sailing west across the Atlantic. Backed by Henry VII of England, he set off in the *Matthew* on 20 May 1497. On 24 June, Cabot reached Cape Breton Island, which he believed to be China. He explored the coast of Newfoundland before sailing home. In 1498, Cabot set off again with a fleet of five ships, hoping to trade with the Chinese. He was never heard from again, but his voyage led

the English to claim Canada. John Cabot's son, Sebastian, was a leading figure in 16th-century exploration. Between 1512 and 1547, he served the king of Spain as an explorer and cartographer. In 1547, back in England he helped set up the Company of Merchant Adventurers to find an eastern route to China. They were never to reach China, but they set up the first trade links between England and Russia.

Bartolomeu DIAS
c.1450–1500
Portuguese explorer

Bartolomeu Dias was the first explorer to round southern Africa's Cape of Good Hope. Nothing is known of his early life, until he was asked by the king of Portugal to find out if it was possible to sail around Africa to reach India. In 1487, Dias sailed south, following the African coastline until a storm blew his ships out of sight of land. After 13 days at sea, he sailed north and was amazed to see land to his left, rather than to his right. He had rounded Africa's southern cape (promontory), and the way to India now lay open. Dias sailed on two more voyages to the Indian Ocean, with Vasco da Gama (p.25) in 1497 and with Pedro Cabral in 1500. On this last voyage, he was lost at sea while rounding the cape he had discovered.

Hieronymus BOSCH
c.1450–1516
Dutch painter

The bizarre paintings of Hieronymus Bosch created a new art genre in the late 15th century and later inspired the Surrealists of the 20th century. Bosch took his name

from the town of his birth, s' Hertogenbosch in the Netherlands. Although his early paintings were conventional, he later developed the hellish images for which he is remembered. His largest work, *The Garden of Earthly Delights* (1505), is a triptych (three-panel painting) showing paradise, hell, and the seven deadly sins. Here, in a fantastic landscape, nightmarish figures demonstrate human foolishness and greed. In *The Temptation of St Anthony* (c.1505–10), the saint is surrounded by demons and other evils. Bosch's pictures gained fame because they reflected the fears of his time, such as plague, witchcraft, and what people believed the end of the world might be like.

Christopher COLUMBUS
1451–1506
Italian explorer

The most famous explorer of his time, Christopher Columbus discovered the "New World" of the Americas. Born in Genoa, Italy, Columbus believed that it was possible to reach Asia by sailing west from Europe across the Atlantic. After much persuasion, he won the backing of King Ferdinand and Queen Isabella of Spain (p.23). In 1492, he set sail across the Atlantic in his flagship the *Santa Maria*, accompanied by two smaller ships, the *Niña* and the *Pinta*. Columbus reached the islands of the Caribbean, still believing that China was only

1442
In western India, Ahmad Shah expands the kingdom of Gujarat and founds a new capital, Ahmadebad. In 1401, his grandfather, Zafar Khan, had proclaimed Gujurat's independence from the Tughluks.

1448
King Trailok, ruler of Siam (now southern Thailand) reforms land laws so that even the poor own land. Trailok expands his kingdom by warring with the northern states and moves his capital north to Phitsanulok.

a short distance away. On three further voyages he set up the first European settlement on the island of Hispaniola, and explored part of the mainland, but he never realized that he had not reached Asia. Columbus's discovery led to the European exploration and conquest of the Americas.

NEW WORLD EXPLORERS

At the end of the 15th century, Europeans believed that the Earth was very small and that Europe and Africa faced Asia across the Atlantic Ocean. Portuguese sailors were the first to open up sea routes to Asia by sailing east around Africa's Cape of Good Hope. CHRISTOPHER COLUMBUS then convinced the Spanish to sail west across the Atlantic in the hope of finding a new route to Asia and what they believed was its great wealth.

AN UNKNOWN CONTINENT
When CHRISTOPHER COLUMBUS landed in the Bahamas in 1492, he assumed the islands lay off the east coast of Asia. Other European sailors soon followed his route across the Atlantic. JOHN CABOT (p.22) discovered Newfoundland, and JACQUES CARTIER (p.29) sailed inland along the St Lawrence River into what is now eastern Canada. In 1513, VASCO NÚÑEZ DE BALBOA (p.26) became the first European to see the Pacific Ocean, confirming that this was indeed a separate continent, previously unknown to Europeans. By now, this new continent had a name, for in 1507, a German cartographer named it America after AMERIGO VESPUCCI (p.24), who claimed to have explored the South American coast between 1499 and 1502.

EUROPEAN DOMINATION
Within a century, most of North and South America was under European control. HERNANDO CORTÉS (p.29) conquered the Central American Aztec Empire (now much of modern-day Mexico) for Spain, while his compatriot, FRANCISCO PIZARRO (p.26), overran the Inca Empire in South America. The Portuguese gained control of Brazil, while Britain and France fought over control of Canada until the late 18th century.

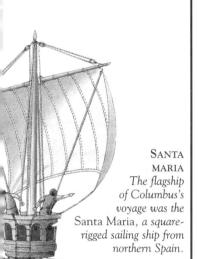

SANTA MARIA
The flagship of Columbus's voyage was the Santa Maria, a square-rigged sailing ship from northern Spain.

Ferdinand II of ARAGON & Isabella of CASTILE
1452–1516 & 1451–1504
Spanish rulers

When Ferdinand and Isabella unified Spain, they transformed it into one of the most powerful states in western Europe. In 1469, Ferdinand, heir of Aragon, married Isabella, heiress of Spain's largest kingdom, Castile, and together they ruled much of the country. In 1492, they conquered Granada, the kingdom of the Muslim Moors, and Spain was united. They built up Spanish power, using the Spanish Inquisition to enforce the power of the Catholic Church, and they supported Columbus's voyages of exploration. By 1516, Spain stretched from the Pyrenees to Gibraltar.

1450 High on a ridge in the Andes Mountains above the Urabamba River in Peru, the Incas build the city of Machu Picchu, including complex stone buildings and terraces for cultivating crops. Much of the city still survives.

1450 The settlement of Great Zimbabwe in south-central Africa is at its largest. Founded in the 10th or 11th century, Great Zimbabwe houses up to 3,000 people in thatched huts. The walls of the city are built of granite blocks.

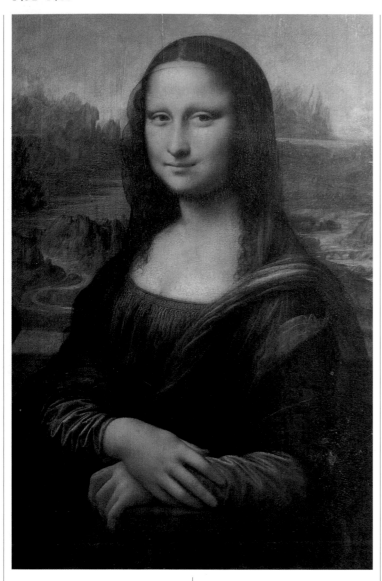

Amerigo VESPUCCI
1451–1512
Italian explorer

The explorer Amerigo Vespucci was the first person to use the phrase "New World" for the Americas, which were later named after him. Born in Italy, he went to Spain in 1492 and became a business partner of Christopher Columbus (p.22). In 1499, he crossed the Atlantic on an exploratory voyage, sailing down the coast of Brazil and seeing the mouth of the Amazon River. He made a second trip to Brazil in 1501. Vespucci published accounts of these voyages, implying that he had been the captain and that he had discovered the mainland, even though Columbus had done so in 1496. In 1507, a German cartographer suggested that the continent be named America in his honour.

Ludovico de VARTHEMA
c.1465–c.1510
Italian traveller

In 1508, Italian adventurer Ludovico de Varthema joined a group of pilgrims travelling to Mecca in Arabia. Posing as a Muslim, he became the first Christian to visit the holiest Muslim city and leave alive. He then joined another party of pilgrims on their way home to India, but was arrested in Aden as a Christian spy. He managed to win his release by feigning madness. Varthema's later travels took him to Persia and India, and his account of his amazing adventures, *Travels of Ludovico de Varthema* (1510), made him famous throughout Europe.

Desiderius ERASMUS
c.1466–1536
Dutch humanist

The theories of the Dutch scholar Erasmus helped pave the way for the Reformation of the Church. Born in Rotterdam in the Netherlands, he was trained as a Catholic priest, but his love of learning led him to study at the University of Paris. He taught throughout Europe and produced a stream of writings, including translations of the Greek New Testament (1516), classical texts, and satirical works such as *In Praise of Folly* (1509). Erasmus was a humanist, which meant that he valued human reason above the authority of the Church. He called for the reform of the Catholic Church and his ideas were to influence the Protestant Reformation. However, Erasmus remained true to his Catholic faith and criticized Protestant reformers such as Martin Luther (p.28) for what he saw as their narrow views.

Leonardo da VINCI
1452–1519
Italian artist, engineer, and writer

One of the most influential figures of his time, Leonardo da Vinci was not only a fine artist but also a ground-breaking mechanical engineer, typifying the ideal of the "Renaissance man". Born in Vinci, between Pisa and Florence, he was apprenticed to the Florentine artist Verrocchio. Leonardo soon outshone his master, producing remarkable works such as the *Baptism of Christ* and the *Adoration of the Magi*. In 1482, he went to Milan to work for Duke Ludovico Sforza, where he painted his masterpiece, *The Last Supper* (1495), and worked on numerous projects, from artillery design to diverting rivers. Leonardo worked for many patrons including Cesare Borgia, Louis XII, and Francis I of France (p.30). In about 1503, he finished his most celebrated painting, the *Mona Lisa*. Leonardo's thirst for knowledge inspired his vast range of interests. He produced pioneering anatomical drawings, plans for flying machines, and writings on mathematics. Much of his work was never finished, but he is still revered as a genius and a man ahead of his time.

AMERIGO VESPUCCI
The continent of America was named after this Italian navigator and business partner of Columbus.

| **1453** The Byzantine Empire comes to an end. Mohammed II bombards Constantinople with siege guns | for eight weeks and then sends 80,000 Ottoman troops into the city. Constantinople succumbs, despite fierce resistance. | **1456** Vlad Tepes rules Walachia, in present-day Romania, and has 50,000 of his 500,000 subjects put to death. | His favourite method is impaling people on stakes. Tepes's infamous cruelty is the origin of the legend of Dracula. |

Vasco da GAMA
c.1469–1525
Portuguese explorer

Vasco da Gama was the first person to open up the sea trading route between Europe and India. The son of a Portuguese nobleman, in 1497 he was chosen by his king to lead the first-ever sea expedition from Europe to India. He set off in July with a fleet of four ships. Instead of following the coast of Africa as previous explorers such as Dias (p.22) had done, da Gama sailed out into the Atlantic, then swung back eastward on the circular wind system. He reached India in May 1498, but the Indians were unimpressed with the Portuguese at first, because they had little of value to trade. Da Gama returned in 1502, this time with a fleet of 20 armed ships, and forced the local rulers to sign trade agreements with Portugal. These were to form the basis of Portugal's overseas empire.

Niccolò MACHIAVELLI
1469–1527
Italian political philosopher

Niccolò Machiavelli was born in Florence, Italy, and entered the civil service in 1498. He became Defence Secretary and conducted important diplomatic missions. When the Médici family returned to power in 1512, Machiavelli was sacked and he retired to the country to write and think. His fame rests on two books, *The Prince* (1513), modelled on ruthless general Cesare Borgia, and *The Discourses* (1513–18). In them he presents a tough and practical view of politics, in which the use of power to gain political ends is seen as more important than moral concerns. For Machiavelli, a good ruler was one who did what was necessary to achieve civic glory. Often accused of lacking principles, Machiavelli set out how to rule a country fairly and objectively.

GURU NANAK
The founder of Sikhism with the other nine gurus (shown with halos).

Guru NANAK
1469–1539
Indian religious leader

The founding father of the Sikh religion, Guru Nanak was born near Lahore, in what is now Pakistan. He was raised as a Hindu, the ancient Indian religion, but also studied Islam. One day he had a vision while bathing in a stream, and emerged saying: "There is no Hindu, there is no Muslim." He founded a new religion, combining the two older faiths. His followers were called Sikhs, meaning "disciples", and Nanak was their first guru (holy teacher). Today there are some 20 million Sikhs, most living in northwest India.

Mohammed TURRÉ
c.1470–1528
Songhai king

Mohammed Turré continued the work of Sonni' Ali (p.21) by leading the African kingdom of Songhai to further greatness. He was born in Gao, eastern Mali, and became a general in the Songhai army. After the death of Ali in 1492, he took over the throne. He created an efficient administration, introduced a system of taxation and standard weights and measures, and created a police force and an army. He also built a canal system on the River Niger to improve irrigation, and extended the empire northward to incorporate the rich salt mines of the Sahara Desert. Such was his wealth that on a pilgrimage to Mecca in 1495, he is said to have given away more than 250,000 gold coins. After his death the great Songhai Empire began to decline.

1462 Most of Russia is under Mongol (Tatar) control when Ivan III ascends the throne as the Grand Prince of Muscovy. The Tatars march on the Muscovite capital, Moscow, but fail to capture it. Ivan calls himself "Tsar of all the Russias".

1463 A 16-year war breaks out between Venice, the greatest trading power in the Mediterranean, and the Ottoman Turks. The Ottomans win and although Venice keeps some of its posts, it has to pay the Ottoman sultan.

Albrecht DURER
1471–1528
German painter and printmaker

Albrecht Dürer was the greatest artist of the Northern Renaissance. Born in Nuremberg in Germany, at 15 he was apprenticed to a local painter. He became expert in all areas of drawing, painting, and printing. He also studied the new Renaissance art styles and went to Italy to learn from artists there. Back in Nuremberg, he produced fine altarpieces, watercolour landscapes, and a series of self-portraits. His greatest achievement, however, was

LINE ENGRAVING
This engraving by Dürer is entitled, Knight, Death, and the Devil.

in printing. He developed the technique of line engraving on copperplate and wood blocks, producing works of great originality and technical mastery such as *The Knight, Death, and the Devil* (1513) and *St Jerome in his Study* (1514).

Nicolaus COPERNICUS
1473–1543
Polish astronomer

The great astronomer Nicolaus Copernicus was the first person to realize that the Earth revolves around the Sun. Born in Torun, Poland, Copernicus went to the university in Bologna, Italy, while waiting to take up a position as a priest. In Bologna, he studied the works of ancient Greek astronomers and soon became fascinated by the work of Ptolemy and his theory that the Sun revolves around the Earth. Many Greek astronomers disagreed with this theory, so when Copernicus returned home to be a priest, he pursued his interest, making detailed observations of the planets. He discovered that Ptolemy was wrong and that the Earth revolves around the Sun. Copernicus wrote about his findings but, against the advice of friends who recognized its importance, he refused to publish the work. At that time, the Church stated that the Earth was the centre of the universe and, as a priest, Copernicus felt he could not go against its teachings. It was only on his deathbed, in 1543, that Copernicus agreed to have his book, *On the Revolutions of the Celestial Spheres*, published. It was one of the most influential books ever written on astronomy, and had a deep impact on Western thought.

Francisco PIZARRO
1474–1541
Spanish conqueror

In conquering Peru for the Spanish, Francisco Pizarro brought about the fall of the Incas. In the 1520s, he made two voyages down the Pacific coast of South America in search of Peru's rich Inca Empire. He invaded with just 180 men and, in 1532, led his troops to Cajamarca, where the Inca ruler Atahualpa (p.32) was staying. Unafraid of so few men, Atahualpa agreed to meet Pizarro, but the Spanish attacked and took him prisoner. Pizarro promised Atahualpa his freedom for a roomful of gold, but after collecting the ransom, Pizarro killed the Inca ruler. Pizarro was later murdered by rivals in Lima, the new capital of Peru, which he had founded.

Vasco Núñez de BALBOA
1475–1519
Spanish explorer and conqueror

Vasco Núñez de Balboa was the first European to see the Pacific Ocean. Balboa sailed from his native Spain to the Caribbean in 1500, settling at first on Hispaniola and then joining an expedition to the American mainland as a stowaway. He convinced the other members of the expedition that they should found a settlement on the Gulf of Darien. In 1512, Balboa then led an expedition to the south and became the first European to discover the Andes mountains. The following year, he led a second expedition, this time towards the west. He crossed the Isthmus of Panama and, on 25 September 1513, he reached the Pacific, discovering the world's largest ocean. Wearing his armour and waving his sword, Balboa waded into the water, claiming the ocean and all its islands for Spain.

Michelangelo BUONARROTI
1475–1564
Italian artist

Usually known simply as Michelanglo, Michelangelo Buonarroti was the most revered Italian artist of the 16th century. At the age of 13, he became apprentice to the painter Domenico Ghirlandaio, but soon moved to a school supported by the wealthy Medici family. He was greatly influenced by the work of the earlier Italian masters Giotto di Bondone (p.15) and Tommaso de Giovanni di Masaccio. In 1496, Michelangelo moved to Rome, where he completed his major sculpture, the *Pietà* (1497).

1470 The Indian Chimu culture collapses in northern Peru. The Chimu are conquered and absorbed by the Incas, who began as a small tribe around 1300 and grew into a large and gold-rich empire over the next 200 years.

1471 Edward IV defeats Henry VI of England at Barnet during the Wars of the Roses. Henry is imprisoned in the Tower of London and later murdered. Edward IV succeeds as the new king of England.

THE RENAISSANCE

During the 1300s and 1400s, artists and writers became interested in the cultures of ancient Greece and Rome. These cultures had been largely forgotten in Europe since the end of the Roman Empire in the 5th century, but had been kept alive by the Arabs, who exported them back to Europe. The revival of ancient knowledge was known as the Renaissance, or rebirth.

THE ARTISTS
Before the Renaissance, artists only produced paintings to glorify God, but the new artists placed more emphasis on humanity, idealizing "Renaissance Man". GIOTTO (p.15), DONATELLO (p.19), BOTTICELLI (p.22), MICHELANGELO (p.26), RAPHAEL (p.28), TITIAN (p.28), and others painted the human body with realism, while writers such as DANTE (p.14), BOCCACCIO (1313–75), and PETRARCH (p.17) wrote about human nature in everyday Italian rather than Latin. The period also brought new ideas in science and technology. The architect of the *Duomo*, the cathedral in Florence, FILIPPO BRUNELLESCHI (p.18), was also an engineer, while painter LEONARDO DA VINCI (p.24) designed a helicopter, a water turbine, and also studied anatomy.

THE RENAISSANCE INFLUENCE
The first book on the Renaissance by painter GIORGIO VASARI (1511–74) became the definitive history of art.

Portrait of Lorenzo de' Medici, the wealthy patron of Renaissance artists.

With the invention of printing, the movement spread to western Europe, including the Dutch artist JAN VAN EYCK (p.19) and German engraver ALBRECHT DÜRER (p.26).

conquistador (conqueror) Hernando Cortés (p.29) led an army of some 500 men into the Aztec capital, Tenochtitlán (on the site of today's Mexico City). Aztec priests thought the arrival of this light-skinned man was the return of the legendary god, Quetzalcoatl, so the emperor made the invaders welcome. Cortés took Montezuma hostage and forced him to negotiate a truce. The Aztecs deserted him and revolted against the Spanish. In the chaos, Montezuma was killed. Cortés razed the great city of Tenochtitlán to the ground, bringing an end to the Aztec Empire and ushering in 300 years of Spanish rule in modern-day Mexico.

AZTEC *feather head dress*

Back in Florence, he produced the famous statue of David (1501–04) before returning to Rome to work for the Pope. Here he began his breathtaking decoration of the Sistine Chapel in the Vatican. Between 1508 and 1512, he painted the ceiling frescoes, which depict the Creation of Man, the Fall of Adam and Eve, and the great Flood from the Bible. In 1537, he returned to paint *The Last Judgement* on the altar wall. After completing the Sistine Chapel, Michelangelo concentrated on architecture, producing designs for the dome of St Peter's in Rome. His master-pieces convey a power and beauty which has inspired people for centuries.

Lucrezia BORGIA
1480–1519
Italian noblewoman

The illegitimate daughter of Pope Alexander VI, Lucrezia Borgia was born into one of the most powerful families in late-15th-century Italy. She earned a reputation, perhaps unfairly, for corruption and vice. She was married three times to further the ambitions of her father and brother, Cesare Borgia, first when she was only 12, to Giovanni Sforza, Lord of Pesaro, then, aged 13, to Alfonso of Aragon. After Alfonso was murdered by her brother in 1500, Lucrezia married the Duke of Ferrara. She used her position as Duchess to establish a brilliant court of artists and intellectuals and became a noted patron of the arts and education. Among the artists whose careers she furthered was Titian (p.28).

MONTEZUMA II
c.1480–1520
Last Aztec emperor

Montezuma II was the last emperor of the powerful Aztec Empire (in present-day Mexico). In 1502, he succeeded his father as ninth ruler of the Aztecs and proved a warlike and tyrannical leader. In 1519, the Spanish

Ferdinand MAGELLAN
c.1480–1521
Portuguese explorer

Ferdinand Magellan led the first round-the-world voyage. An experienced sailor, in 1519, the Spanish king asked him to find a western route to Asia. Magellan set off with five ships and sailed down the coast of South America until he found a passage to the Pacific (the Strait of Magellan). He thought Asia was close by, but it took him 90 days to reach the Philippines, where he was killed. Only one ship returned, completing the first-ever voyage around the world.

1479 The crowns of Aragon and Castile are united under Ferdinand and Isabella, forming the basis of modern Spain. They conquer Muslim-held Granada and suppress bandits with a new militia.

1480 The Spanish Inquisition begins. Jews and Muslims are accused of heresy and are forced to convert to Christianity. The Inquisitor, Torquemada, gives Jews three months to accept Christianity or be expelled from Spain.

frescoes Raphael painted for the Pope was his masterpiece, *The School of Athens* (1510–11), depicting a group of Greek philosophers. Raphael's graceful style and brilliant sense of composition influenced artists for generations.

most of northern India, from Afghanistan in the northwest to Bengal in the east. His land became known as the Mogul Empire because of his Mongol origins. Although a Muslim, Babur tolerated the Hindus in his new empire, and supported Indian arts and architecture. The empire survived until the British took over in 1858.

BABUR I
The Mogul emperor of India is depicted here invading Persia.

Erasmus (p.24), claimed that the Scriptures were the only source of truth. Luther used the new printing presses to publish his ideas, writing in German at a time when churchmen used only Latin. Many people in northern Europe agreed with Luther's ideas and broke with the Catholic Church to set up new Protestant churches.

TITIAN
c.1485–1576
Italian painter

Titian was the first painter of his time to use bold colours in religious images. Born Tiziano Vecellio, he trained as a painter at the studio of Giovanni Bellini in Venice, Italy. After Bellini's

TITIAN'S *statue in Pieve di Cadore, Italy*

RAPHAEL
1483–1520
Italian painter

The religious images painted by Raphael were among the most influential of the High Renaissance. Born Raffaello Sanzio, as a boy he helped his father with paintings for the Duke of Urbino. At 18 he travelled to Florence, where the influence of Michelangelo (p.26) can be seen in his paintings of the time, such as *The Entombment* (1507). In 1508, he was summoned to Rome to decorate the papal apartments. Among the series of lovely

BABUR I
1483–1530
Mogul emperor

Babur (the name means lion) was the first ruler of the Mogul Empire in northern India. He was born Zahiruddin Muhammad in Fergana (now Turkestan), a descendant of the Mongol leaders Genghis Khan (p.12) and Tamerlane (p.18). On inheriting the principality of Fergana, his first aim was to assert his authority over his uncle's territory of Samarkand. When that failed, he invaded Afghanistan, seizing control in 1504. In 1517, civil war broke out in India. Babur conquered

Martin LUTHER
1483–1546
German religious reformer

The founding father of the Christian Protestant faith was Martin Luther. Born in Eisleben, Germany, Luther became a monk and a university teacher. In 1517, he wrote 95 theses (arguments) in protest at the sale of indulgences (pardons for the sins of the dead). He stated that priests had no special powers and, influenced by

---

1483 The first major Ikko-ikki, or uprising of Ikko Buddhists, occurs in Japan. "The Age of Strife", which began in 1467, sees a disputed succession drag on until 1603 and heralds the establishment of the shogunate.

1485 Henry Tudor defeats Richard III at the Battle of Bosworth Field. Some of Richard's soldiers refuse to fight and others defect to Henry's side. Henry VII becomes the first Tudor king of England and Wales.

death in 1516, he became the city's official painter. A string of religious and mythological pictures followed, including the altarpiece *The Assumption of the Virgin* (1516–18) and *Bacchus and Ariadne* (1520–23). Titian's bold use of reds, golds, browns, and blues was startling and original. From 1530, he was commissioned to produce portraits of many leading statesmen, including two emperors, a pope, and the king of Spain. Later in life he returned to painting mythological scenes, such as *The Rape of Europa* (1562). His work influenced many later painters, including Rembrandt (p.45).

Hernando CORTES
1485–1547
Spanish conqueror

Cortés was the Spanish *conquistador* (conqueror) who destroyed the Aztec Empire. Born of a noble but poor Spanish family, he sailed to the Caribbean to make his fortune. In 1518, he led an expedition of 550 men to the coast of Mexico on the American mainland to look for gold. Here he learned of the wealthy Aztec Empire. Cortés marched inland to the capital, Tenochtitlán, forming alliances with enemies of the Aztecs on the way. He defeated the Aztec ruler, Montezuma (p.27) and captured Tenochtitlán. Cortés founded a new capital, Mexico City, on the same site, and in 1522 he was made governor of "New Spain". When he returned home to Spain in 1528, Cortés was received with honour by Charles V (p.32), but he later died in poverty.

MOSQUE INTERIOR
The Mosque of Suleiman the Magnificent in Istanbul is a fine example of the work of the great Ottoman architect Sinan.

SINAN
1489–1588
Turkish architect

The most prolific and influential architect of the Ottoman Empire, Sinan was born into a Christian family. He later joined the Muslim army of the Ottoman sultan and trained as a military engineer. In 1538, he was appointed chief architect to the great sultan Suleiman I (p.30). Over the next 50 years, Sinan designed a huge number of buildings, including more than 79 mosques, 55 schools, and 34 palaces, as well as hospitals, fortifications, and other public works. His finest buildings were religious, the greatest being the Mosque of Suleiman in Constantinople (1550–57) and the Selimye Mosque at Edirne, Turkey (1567–74). The Selimye Mosque, with its vast dome resting on eight pillars and surrounded by smaller domes, is one of the world's architectural masterpieces.

HENRY VIII
1491–1547
English king

Henry VIII was one of England's most powerful and influential rulers. Son of Henry VII, he ascended to the throne in 1509. For the first 20 years of his reign, he pursued a life of pleasure, leaving affairs of state to his advisers. But when the Pope failed to grant Henry a divorce from his first wife, Catherine of Aragon, Henry proclaimed himself head of the English Church. He broke links with the Pope and the Roman Catholic Church, dissolved (destroyed) the monasteries and seized their wealth, and divorced Catherine in favour of Anne Boleyn, mother of Elizabeth I (p.34). By the time of his death, Henry had married six times, beheaded two of his wives (Anne Boleyn and Catherine Howard), and killed 50,000 of his opponents. When he died, he left a bankrupt country to his only son, Edward.

Jacques CARTIER
1491–1557
French explorer

The explorations of Jacques Cartier in eastern Canada, formed the basis of the French claim to the region. Born in Brittany, France, in 1534 he sailed to North America in search of gold and a passage to the Pacific. He landed on a huge gulf, which he named the St Lawrence, and was welcomed by the local Huron people. He claimed the territory for France. On his second voyage in 1535, Cartier explored the St Lawrence River and heard stories of a wealthy kingdom to the west, called Saguenay. However, he found neither Saguenay nor gold. The French were so disappointed with the results of his voyages, that they did not return to North America for 50 years, but Cartier had given them grounds for their later claim to rule Canada.

1488 In China, the Ming emperors begin rebuilding the Great Wall of China. The wall had fallen into ruin since it was first built in 214 BC by the First Emperor. It is hoped the wall will defend China from invaders.

1489 James IV of Scotland marries Margaret, the daughter of King Henry VII of England. The union leads the way for a Scottish invasion of England in 1513, but the Scots are unsuccessful in taking over the throne.

PARACELSUS
1493–1541
German–Swiss physician

Paracelsus was one of the great pioneers of chemical medicine in the 16th century. Born Theophrastus Bombastus von Hohenheim, in Einsiedeln, Switzerland, he adopted the name Paracelsus after the great Roman physician Celsus. After studying alchemy and chemistry, he travelled throughout Europe, Russia, and the Middle East to learn about different medical practices. In 1526, he became town physician in Basle and lecturer at the university. But he upset the authorities and was forced to flee because he lectured in German rather than Latin, and publicly burnt the works of accepted scholars of medicine. Paracelsus revolutionized the practice of medicine by encouraging observation, experiment, and research. His study of miners' illnesses led to silicosis and tuberculosis being identified as occupational hazards. He also encouraged the careful preparation and measurement of medicines, and used laudanum – a derivative of opium – as a painkiller. Many of his ideas later became standard medical practice.

FRANCIS I
1494–1547
French king

During his reign, Francis I turned France into the artistic centre of the High Renaissance. Francis, Duke of Valois, became king of France in 1515. He was a typical Renaissance prince – rich, quick-witted, fond of the arts and learning, but also vice-ridden and cruel. He was a candidate for Holy Roman Emperor, but lost to Charles V (p.32), who became a lifelong enemy. For most of his life Francis conducted an unsuccessful campaign against Charles, who ruled Spain, most of Italy, Austria, and the Low Countries. Francis tried to enlist the support of Henry VIII of England (p.29) at the Field of the Cloth of Gold, but failed. By the time peace was declared with Charles in 1544, war had almost bankrupted France. However, Francis also turned the French court into an artistic centre, supporting the likes of Erasmus (p.24) and Leonardo da Vinci (p.24), and building the beautiful palace of Fontainebleau.

CHATEAU DE CHAMBORD
Francis I began work on the magnificent palace of Chambord in the Loire Valley.

SULEIMAN I
1494–1566
Ottoman emperor

Suleiman I was the most powerful and ambitious ruler of the Ottoman Empire. He succeeded his father, Selim, as emperor in 1520. During his reign, the empire expanded from the Atlantic Ocean to the Persian Gulf and from the border of Austria to the Sudan. Europeans called him "the Magnificent" for the brilliance of his court, but Ottomans knew him as *al-Qanuni*, (the Law-giver), because of his control of all aspects of daily life. After his death in 1566, the Ottoman Empire began a slow decline from which it was never to recover.

POETRY IN STEEL
Steel blades inlaid with lines of poetry were worn by Ottoman gentlemen at the court of Suleiman I.

Hans HOLBEIN
c.1497–1543
German painter

The brilliant portraits of Hans Holbein provide a unique record of England's Tudor court. Holbein the Younger was born in Augsburg, Germany, and trained in the studio of his father, also a successful painter. In about 1514, he moved to Basle in Switzerland, where he worked as a print designer and portrait painter, producing a best-selling series of woodcuts, *The Dance of Death* (1523–26). The turmoil of the Reformation forced him to look for work in England in 1526, and he settled there in 1532 as court painter to King Henry VIII (p.29). Among the masterpieces from this period are his double portrait *The Ambassadors* (1533) and a mural for Whitehall Palace (later demolished). Holbein's most famous achievement was the collection of lifelike portraits and drawings of the court of Henry VIII which survives to this day.

1494 Spain and Portugal agree to share the lands they discover in the Treaty of Tordesillas. It is agreed that Spain can claim the lands to the west and Portugal those to the east of an imaginary line of demarcation around the world.

1497 Vasco da Gama rounds the Cape of Good Hope and continues on to South Africa and India. He returns to India in 1499 and destroys Calicut in 1502 in revenge for the destruction of a Portuguese trading station.

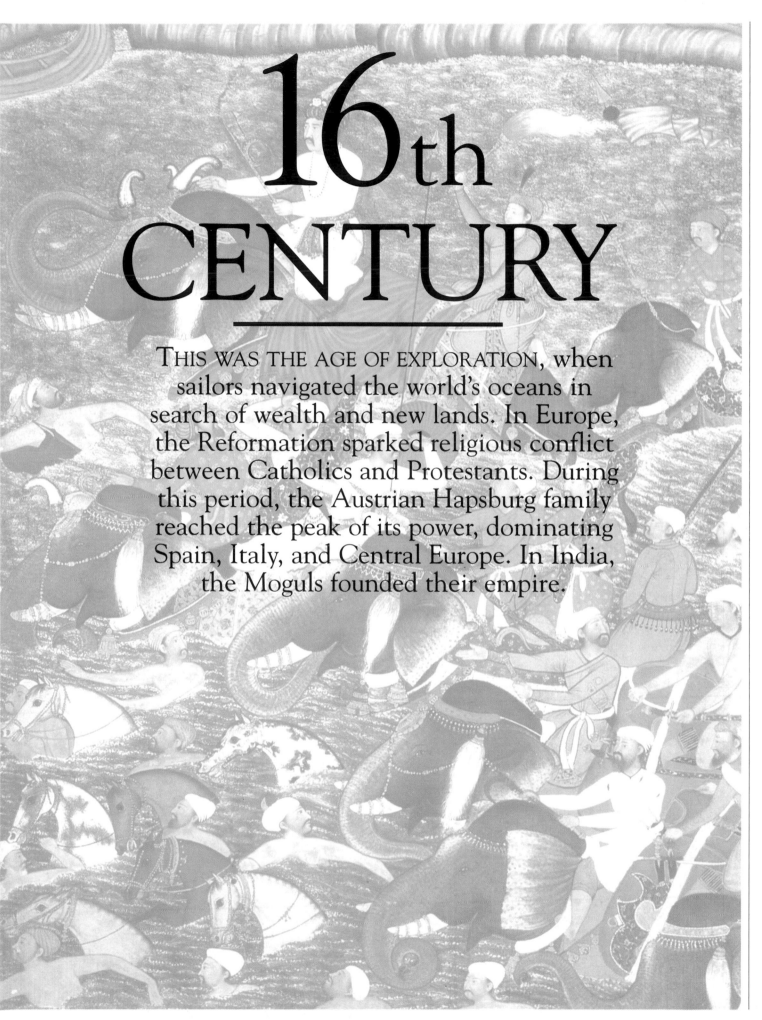

16th CENTURY

THIS WAS THE AGE OF EXPLORATION, when sailors navigated the world's oceans in search of wealth and new lands. In Europe, the Reformation sparked religious conflict between Catholics and Protestants. During this period, the Austrian Hapsburg family reached the peak of its power, dominating Spain, Italy, and Central Europe. In India, the Moguls founded their empire.

ATAHUALPA
c.1502–33
Last Inca emperor

As the last leader of the mighty Inca Empire in Peru, Atahualpa earned the respect of his people by defeating his brother, Huascar, in 1532, and extending his empire to southern Peru. Later that same year, Spanish troops led by Francisco Pizarro (p.26) arrived in Peru having heard of its great wealth. They captured Atahualpa and held him prisoner, demanding a huge ransom in gold from his people. The ransom was paid, but Pizarro executed Atahualpa nevertheless. Pizarro's troops went on to plunder the country of its riches, wiping out the entire Inca civilization.

CHARLES V
1500–58
Holy Roman Emperor

In the early 16th century, Charles V was the most powerful ruler in Europe. Born in Ghent, Belgium, Charles was the eldest son of Philip of Burgundy. In 1506, he inherited the Netherlands and Burgundy from his father, then in 1516, Spain,

Naples in southern Italy, and Spanish possessions in the Americas from his maternal grandfather. In 1519, his paternal grandfather left him the Hapsburg lands in Central Europe and Austria, as well as the title Holy Roman Emperor. Charles's control of much of western Europe led him into conflict with France and the Ottoman Empire. However, he made Spain the most powerful nation in Europe. In 1556, he abdicated and spent his last two years in a monastery.

CHARLES V'S
shield

VILLA ROTONDA
The elegant Villa Rotonda, near Vicenza, is the epitome of Palladio's architecture.

Andrea PALLADIO
1508–80
Italian architect

The most influential architect of his time, Andrea Palladio was noted for his use of symmetry and harmony. At 16, he was apprenticed to a stonemason in Vicenza, Italy, where he developed his talent for design and began to study architecture. His first work was the remodelled Basilica in Vicenza (1549). In following years he designed many palaces and villas for the wealthy families of Vicenza and Venice, including the famous Villa Rotonda (c.1552). Palladio based his buildings on classical Greek and Roman architecture. He wrote *Four Books of Architecture* in 1570. His buildings inspired other architects including Sir Christopher Wren (p.48).

John CALVIN
1509–64
French Protestant reformer

Born in France, John Calvin worked as a lawyer before turning his energies towards religion. Influenced by Martin Luther (p.28), the founder of the Christian Protestant faith, Calvin set out the first clear summary of Protestant ideas in his *Institutes of the Christian Religion* (1536). As governor of Geneva, Switzerland, Calvin put his strict Christian ideals into practice. Through his College of Pastors and Doctors and Consistorial Court of Discipline, he dominated every aspect of city life to create a "new Jerusalem". His successor, Theodore Beza, helped to spread Calvinism in Europe.

John KNOX
1513–72
Scottish Protestant reformer

John Knox was one of the founders of the Church of Scotland. Originally a Roman Catholic priest, John Knox converted to Protestantism under the influence of the religious reformer George Wishart. But when Wishart was killed for heresy (going against the beliefs of the Catholic Church), Knox went into hiding. In 1547, he was captured by French troops in Scotland and imprisoned in France. He was released two years later and went to England, but when Catholic Queen Mary I came to the throne in 1553 he fled to Europe. Knox returned to Scotland in 1559 to preach his Protestant doctrine. Then in 1560, he was instrumental in bringing about the Treaty of Leith which established the Church of Scotland.

1505 The Portuguese capture Sofala on the east coast of Africa. They colonize Mozambique and begin to do business on African trade routes. In 1513, they explore the Zambezi River, founding trade posts at Sena and Tete.

1515 The last Hindu empire of Java, Majapahit, collapses under pressure from the new Islamic states. Its rulers flee to the island of Bali, where they continue to practise their Hindu traditions.

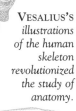

Andreas VESALIUS
1514–64
Flemish surgeon

The 16th-century surgeon Andreas Vesalius unravelled the mysteries of the human anatomy and paved the way for future medical advances. He came from a family of doctors, and attended the medical school at the University of Paris, France. It was here that he first learnt the skills of dissection that would make his name. While in Paris he dissected both dead animals and human corpses. At that time, the work of Galen, the ancient Greek physician, was considered the authority on anatomy. But in 1543, while at the University of Bologna in Italy, Vesalius challenged that authority. He concluded that Galen's theory of anatomy was based on the dissection of animals, since dissection of the human body was forbidden by the Catholic Church at that time. He shared these views in lectures at the university and wrote them down in his masterpiece, *De Humani Corporis Fabrica Libri Septem*, (*Seven Books on the Structure of the Human Body*) known as the *Fabrica*, which was printed in 1543. The book so impressed the Holy Roman Emperor Charles V that he employed Vesalius as his family physician. Thanks to Vesalius, anatomy became a recognized branch of science, and the study of medicine made a leap forward.

LI SHIH-CHEN
1518–93
Chinese biologist

Considered by many as the father of Chinese herbal medicine, Li Shih-chen was one of the most brilliant pharmacists of his day. In 1596, he published the *Great Pharmacopoeia*, which described in detail 1,000 plants, and included 11,000 prescriptions for herbal remedies. Li Shih-chen's remedies were highly advanced for the time. They included instructions for smallpox inoculation, as well as prescriptions for the use of iodine, mercury, and ephedrine.

Luis Vaz de CAMOENS
c.1524–80
Portuguese poet

Luis Vaz de Camoëns is Portugal's most revered poet. He was born in Lisbon and travelled extensively, particularly in India, returning to Portugal in 1570. Two years later he published his famous epic poem, *The Lusiads* (from the ancient Roman name for Portugal), which recounts the history of Portugal, including the dramatic story of Portuguese explorer Vasco da Gama (p.25), the first European to travel to India by sea. The poem is based on fact, but also features Roman gods who influence the fate of da Gama's expedition. *The Lusiads* was a landmark in Portuguese literature. Camoëns also wrote many beautiful lyrical poems, plays, and sonnets and he is now regarded as Portugal's national poet.

Pieter BRUEGEL THE ELDER
c.1525–69
Flemish painter

Pieter Bruegel the Elder was the first artist to capture Flemish peasant life on canvas. He was trained as an artist and, in 1551, joined the Antwerp painters' guild, although little

THE WEDDING FEAST
This painting by Bruegel is typical of his later works. He depicts the miserable lot of the peasants, taking part in a sorry celebration.

else is known of his early life. Bruegel's early works, such as the terrifying *Triumph of Death* (1562), were largely based on religious themes and influenced by the grotesque pictures of Hieronymus Bosch (p.22). It was while on a journey to Italy that he was inspired by the grandeur of the Alps, and many paintings after this depict panoramic landscapes filled with small peasant figures either at work or play. These include a series illustrating the seasons of the year, among them *Hunters in the Snow* (1565). Larger and far more detailed figures appear in his later scenes of rustic society such as *The Wedding Feast* (c.1567) and *The Peasant Dance* (c.1567). Bruegel brilliantly showed the toil and coarseness that existed beneath the quaint and idyllic image of country life that had been painted in the past.

1517 The Ottomans conquer Egypt, marking the end of the Mamluk Empire. Dominating the silk and spice routes of Egypt and Palestine had made the Mamluks rich, but corruption caused their empire to decline.

1521 The Spanish colonize Venezuela. In 1522, survivors of Magellan's 1521 expedition arrive back in Spain, having sailed around the world. Meanwhile, the Spanish are also exploring the Pacific coast of South America.

Giovanni da PALESTRINA
c.1525–94
Italian composer

Known for his smooth, flowing music, Giovanni da Palestrina was a prolific composer. He sang in the choir in Palestrina cathedral until the bishop of Palestrina (later Pope Julius III) took him with him when he moved to Rome. There, Palestrina worked as a singer and an organist at some of the greatest churches in the city. In 1551, he was appointed *maestro di cappella* (director of music) of the Julian choir at St Peter's, where he wrote the first of his Masses. He went on to direct many of Rome's choirs and composed 93 settings of the mass, nearly 400 choral compositions, and about 100 madrigals (songs for unaccompanied voices). Later composers who were influenced by Palestrina's style include Johann Sebastian Bach (p.54) and Wolfgang Amadeus Mozart (p.68).

PHILIP II
1527–98
Spanish king

Philip II of Spain inherited a great empire, but weakened it considerably through war. On the abdication of his father Charles V (p.32) in 1556, he became king of Spain, southern Italy, the Netherlands, and the Spanish possessions in the "New World" of the Americas. He was a conscientious ruler but as a devout Catholic he persecuted his Protestant subjects, causing the Dutch to rise in revolt in 1568. His Moorish subjects, the Moriscos, who had been forced to convert from Islam to Christianity, also revolted in 1569. Wars against the Ottomans, the French, and Elizabeth I of England – against whom he launched the ill-fated

SCENOGRAPHIA FABRICÆ ✝ S. LAVRENTII IN ESCVRIAL

Armada of 1588 – further damaged his empire and diminished Spanish power.

Ivan the TERRIBLE
1530–84
Russian tsar

Ivan became the first tsar (emperor) of Russia. Born in Muscovy, the area surrounding Moscow, Ivan became grand prince of Muscovy at the age of three on the death of his father. His mother and then a council of *boyars* (nobles) ruled on his behalf, but in 1547 Ivan took control himself. Until 1563, he pushed through a series of legal and administrative reforms, as well as conquering Kazan (1552), and Astrakhan (1556), and expanding Russian territory into Siberia. But in 1564, he began a reign of terror in an attempt to take control from the *boyars*, perhaps due to deteriorating mental health. Shortly before his death, he murdered his son and heir. Ivan had a violent nature, although his nickname, from the Russian *grozny*, is better translated as "awe-inspiring".

ELIZABETH I
1533–1603
English queen

Elizabeth I was one of the most effective and best-loved of all English monarchs. At the age of three, she was declared illegitimate by her father, Henry VIII (p.29) when he executed her mother Anne Boleyn for treason. Her older sister, the Catholic Queen Mary, later had Elizabeth imprisoned in the Tower of London because she feared her Protestant faith. Elizabeth survived these traumas and became queen at 25. She chose good advisers and proved an able ruler. Throughout her reign she faced many threats, not least from Spain, which sent an Armada to invade England in 1588, and from her Catholic cousin, Mary, Queen of Scots (p.36), who plotted against her. But under Elizabeth, England became increasingly prosperous and powerful, and experienced a flowering of the arts. Despite having many admirers, Elizabeth never married and became known as "the Virgin Queen". At her death, she was mourned by the entire nation.

The Escorial
Phillip II's imposing Escorial palace in Madrid is remarkable for the plain severity of its architecture.

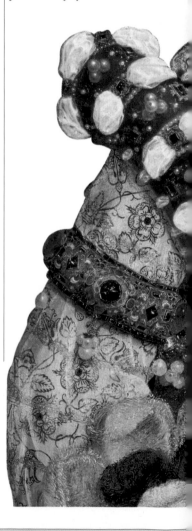

1526 In the Battle of the Mohács, the Turks defeat the Hungarians and Suleiman I declares Bratislava (then Pressburg) the capital of Hungary. The Turks remain in control until their defeat by the Hungarians in 1687.

1533 The Archbishop of Canterbury, Thomas Cranmer, dissolves the marriage of King Henry VIII to Catherine of Aragon and condones his marriage to Anne Boleyn. Henry is excommunicated from the Church by the Pope.

ELIZABETH I
Elizabeth was a strong ruler, who once famously inspired her troops by declaring that she had "the heart and stomach of a king".

Martin FROBISHER
c.1535–94
English explorer

Martin Frobisher explored much of what is now northern Canada. He made several trading voyages to North Africa in the 1550s and, in 1576, he sailed in search of a sea route to China, known as the Northwest Passage. North of the American mainland, he reached Baffin Island and found an inlet, now called Frobisher Bay. Here he became the first Englishman to meet the Native American Inuit (Eskimo) people, one of whom he captured to take back to England. He also found rocks which he believed to be gold. Frobisher made two more trips to Baffin Island, both gold-mining expeditions. After his third voyage, his rocks were identified as worthless. He spent the rest of his life raiding Spanish towns – an easier way to obtain gold.

Hieronymus FABRICIUS
1537–1619
Italian anatomist

Although he made many ground-breaking discoveries in anatomy, Hieronymus Fabricius is remembered for his studies of the development of human foetuses. Fabricus became Professor of Anatomy at Padua University, Italy, and students came from all over Europe to study under him – one of his pupils was the famous British anatomist William Harvey (p.41). Fabricius's most famous advances were in the field of embryology, but he also made studies of the larynx as a vocal cord, and was the first to show that the size of the eye's pupil alters in response to various emotions.

Francis DRAKE
1540–96
English sailor

Francis Drake was the first Englishman to sail around the world. He went to sea while still a boy, and in the 1570s, he became a privateer, or "official pirate", who attacked the enemies of his country. England's main enemy was Spain, and Drake spent most of his career raiding the rich Spanish settlements in the Americas. Between 1577 and 1580, he made a round-the-world voyage in his ship, the *Golden Hind*. On his return to England, he was knighted by Elizabeth I. His greatest success was the 1587 raid on Cadiz, Spain, where he burned a Spanish fleet preparing to invade England. He died aboard ship in the Caribbean.

William BYRD
1540–1623
English composer

Sometimes called the "father of British music", William Byrd was one of the greatest composers of the Elizabethan period. He studied under Thomas Tallis at the Chapel Royal in London. In 1563, he was appointed organist at Lincoln Cathedral, then became organist with Tallis at the Chapel Royal in 1572. Byrd was a Roman Catholic at a time when England was fiercely anti-Catholic, and he was often persecuted for his beliefs. He was, however, a favourite composer of Queen Elizabeth I, and was allowed to continue in his job and to print music. His religious music includes masses and choral pieces for both Catholic and Anglican services, but he also wrote songs, madrigals, and instrumental music.

1534 The Ottomans under Suleiman capture Mesopotamia and also Tunis in North Africa. The following year, Charles V, the Holy Roman Emperor, captures Tunis back for Europe, but the Ottoman Empire continues to grow.

1535 In England, the lord chancellor Thomas More disapproves of Henry VIII's marriage to Anne Boleyn. More refuses to recognize Henry VIII as the new head of the Church of England. He is imprisoned in the Tower of London, then executed.

El GRECO
1541–1614
Greek-Italian painter

The artist El Greco (the Greek) became known for his highly original style of painting, which often showed elongated and distorted figures lit by an eerie radiance. Born in Crete, his real name was Domenikos Theotokopoulos. Some time in the 1560s, he moved to Venice in Italy, where he trained as a painter of church icons (religious images). In 1577, he settled in Toledo, Spain, and produced his greatest series of portraits and religious paintings, including *The Burial of Count Orgaz* (1586) and the *Crucifixion* and *Resurrection* (1597–1604). El Greco wished to express the rapture of religious passion. His pictures, full of vibrant blues, yellows, and greens, are unlike those of any other artist.

Mary, QUEEN OF SCOTS
1542–87
Scottish queen

The last queen of Scotland, Mary is better remembered for her tragic personal life. She succeeded the Scottish throne one week after she was born, but her French mother sent her to France and, in 1558, she married Francis, heir to the French throne. She briefly became queen of France when he became king in 1559. After his death in 1560, Mary returned to Scotland, marrying her cousin, Lord Darnley. However, she fell in love with her secretary, David Rizzio, who was murdered by Darnley in 1566. Darnley was mysteriously murdered in 1567, and Mary then married the Earl of Bothwell. The unhappy Scottish lords forced Mary to give up the throne and flee to England. There, she was made a prisoner of her cousin, Elizabeth I (p.34), until she was named in a plot to overthrow Elizabeth and executed.

AKBAR
1542–1605
Mogul emperor

Akbar was the third Mogul emperor to rule India, taking the throne at the age of 13. Akbar's inheritance was fragile, but he soon consolidated his power and extended the empire across northern India to Bengal and south to Deccan.

AKBAR *organized tiger hunts to warn his enemies what to expect if they went to war with him.*

JAPANESE *fan depicting a party of noblemen*

A skilled administrator, he organized a strong civil service and reformed the tax system to help peasant farmers. Akbar was a Muslim, but he included Hindus in his government and married Hindu princesses. He supported artists and scholars, introducing many aspects of Persian culture to India. By the time of his death, he had firmly established Mogul rule over much of India and had done much to reconcile Muslims and Hindus in his empire.

Tokugawa IEYASU
1542–1616
Japanese shogun

Tokugawa Ieyasu was a powerful shogun (great general) of Japan who secured the rule of his family for centuries to come. In 1598, the Japanese dictator Hideyoshi died, and a fight to succeed him soon broke out. Ieyasu was the leading contender, but by 1600, Japan had lapsed into civil war. Ieyasu and his rival, Mitsunari, fought at Sekigahara, which ended in victory for Ieyasu. In 1603, he became shogun, restricting the powers of local governors and centralizing power in the capital, Edo. As a result of his success, his family ruled Japan until the abolition of the Tokugawa (or Edo) shogunate in 1867.

Tycho BRAHE
1546–1601
Danish astronomer

Tycho Brahe charted the position of the stars, producing an invaluable catalogue for later astronomers. In 1563, he found errors in existing astronomical tables and set about making new observations. He discovered a new star in Cassiopeia – the supernova now known as Tycho's Star – in 1572. In 1576, the Danish king helped him to build a new observatory called Uraniborg. He spent 20 years there and recorded the positions of 777 stars.

1545 The Catholic Reformation gathers steam after the Council of Trent. The Council suggests that priests should study in seminaries, bishops live in communities, and monks and nuns not accumulate wealth.

1546 Tabinshwehti takes the title of king of Burma, having conquered Pegu, the capital of the southern Mon kingdom. He makes it his capital and overruns Pagan in the north, later dying in a Mon rebellion.

1550

John NAPIER
1550–1617
Scottish mathematician

John Napier invented the calculation device of logarithms. He went to St Andrew's University, Scotland, at the age of only 13, but left before taking a degree. After travelling around Europe he devoted most of his leisure time to the study of mathematics. He first wrote about logarithms in his work of 1614, *Description of the Marvellous Canon of Logarithms*. He also invented a calculating machine, which used a set of rods called "Napier's Bones". Napier was a devout Protestant and his other published works centred on religious subjects.

Walter RALEIGH
c.1552–1618
English soldier and explorer

One of the most prominent figures of the English Renaissance, Walter Raleigh was born in Devon. He climbed the ranks of the navy and was knighted in 1584. Favoured by Queen Elizabeth I (p.34), Raleigh led several exploratory voyages to North and South America between 1584 and 1595. He is credited with introducing tobacco and the potato to England, which he brought back with him from the "New World". When James I acceded to the throne, Raleigh fell out of favour and was imprisoned for 13 years in the Tower of London. During that time he began to write

NAPIER'S BONES
This early method of calculation used sets of rods with numbers written at one end and along the sides. To find multiples of a particular number, the rods were laid side by side.

DON QUIXOTE
The most famous of Cervantes's characters, Don Quixote is depicted here setting out on an adventure with his servant, Sancho Panza.

Miguel de CERVANTES
1547–1616
Spanish writer

Miguel de Cervantes was the most popular writer of 16th century Spain. Born near Madrid, in 1571 Cervantes fought in the sea battle of Lepanto, where his hand was badly wounded. While returning home in 1575, his ship was captured by pirates, and Cervantes was sold as a slave in Algiers, North Africa. Eventually, in 1580, his family paid a ransom to free him. Back in Spain, Cervantes tried to earn his living as a playwright, but in 1594, he took a job as collector of revenues in Granada. In 1597, he was imprisoned briefly for financial irregularities, and it is believed that he began writing his great novel, *Don Quixote*, in prison. The publication of *Don Quixote* in 1605 finally brought Cervantes fame. One of the first novels, it tells the tale of Don Quixote, an elderly gentleman who tries to act out a life of heroism based on the romantic books he has read. He is accompanied on his adventures by his cunning servant, Sancho Panza, and his faithful old horse, Rozinante.

1549 A Spanish priest, Francis Xavier, is the first Christian missionary to go to Japan. He converts some Japanese people to Catholicism and more missionaries and traders follow from Spain and Portugal inspired by his success.

1550 Maoris in the North and South islands of New Zealand build *pa* (enclosures) to house their communities. Many of these are fortified, either with terraces or ditches, or by being built on a promontory or ridge.

The History of the World, which he never completed. Released in 1616, Raleigh led a final expedition to South America in search of gold, but was unsuccessful. On his return to England, he was tried and executed for treason. Renowned for his chivalry and learning, Raleigh was remembered as the ideal "Renaissance man".

Giovanni
GABRIELI
c.1555–1612
Italian composer

The music of Giovanni Gabrieli marked the turning point from the Renaissance to the Baroque style. Born in Venice, Italy, he studied music with his uncle, an organist at St Mark's Cathedral. On his uncle's death, Gabrieli took over his job and began composing choral and instrumental works for the cathedral, including ceremonial pieces such as the *Sacrae symphoniae* (1597, 1615). Much of his music is for choirs and instruments performing in different parts of the cathedral to give a "stereo" effect, using dramatic contrasts of volume.

Francis
BACON
1561–1626
English philosopher

Francis Bacon was the first philosopher to state that scientific theories must be based on realistic inquiries and research, rather than ideas. Bacon was educated at Cambridge University, and at Gray's Inn, London, where he qualified as a lawyer. He became a member of parliament in 1584, attorney general in 1613, and lord chancellor in 1618. In 1621, he was accused of taking bribes

FRANCIS BACON
The English philosopher hoped that new scientific discoveries could increase human well-being.

and was forced to retire. Unable to pursue his political career, he devoted the rest of his life to philosophy. Bacon argued that philosophy and theology should be two distinct disciplines, and that theories should be fully investigated, and discarded if they lacked sufficient proof of their worth. He believed that only through reason and scientific principles can people understand and control the laws of nature – that is, knowledge is power.

John
DOWLAND
1563–1626
English composer

Both a singer and lute-player, John Dowland is considered one of the finest songwriters of all time. While working for the English ambassador in France, Dowland became a Catholic, which made it difficult for him to find work in his native England. He studied at Oxford University, then travelled around Europe, singing and playing the lute in noble courts. After a period at the Danish court (1598–1605),

he returned to England, reverted to the Protestant faith, and became lutenist at the court of Queen Elizabeth I (p.34) in 1612. Dowland's four volumes of songs or "ayres", published between 1597 and 1612, were great successes, but he also wrote instrumental music, such as the *Lachrymae* collection (1605). This includes *Semper Dowland, semper dolens* (Always Dowland, always sad), which is typical of the melancholy mood of much of his music.

Christopher
MARLOWE
1564–93
English playwright and poet

Christopher "Kit" Marlowe was a successful playwright and a contemporary of Shakespeare (p.39). Born in Kent, England, Marlowe gained a scholarship to Cambridge University. While there, he went on secret missions abroad for Elizabeth I's (p.34) privy council. After university, he pursued a literary career in London, but continued to work for the government's secret service. His tragedy *Tamburlaine the Great* was performed around 1587. It was a huge success, and between 1588 and 1593, Marlowe followed it with four more plays: *The Jew of Malta* (c.1588), *The Tragical History of Dr. Faustus* (c.1588), *The Massacre at Paris* (c.1589), and *Edward II* (c.1590). He also wrote many poems, including the beautiful love poem *The Passionate Shepherd to his Love* (1599). Marlowe's death is still a mystery. He was killed in a fight in a tavern, two days after being arrested for supposedly writing blasphemous (anti-religious) pamphlets. Many historians believe that the secret service murdered him to keep him from revealing government secrets.

Galileo
GALILEI
1564–1642
Italian scientist

Galileo was one of the most influential scientists and inventors of his day. Born in Pisa, Italy, he studied at Pisa University and accepted the chair of mathematics. During this time he discovered the time-keeping properties of a swinging pendulum and developed a law of falling bodies. Shortly after the telescope was invented in 1609, Galileo built one of his own and it is said that he was the first to point it at the stars. Among many discoveries he made were Jupiter's four moons, the composition of the Milky Way, the phases of Venus, and the Sun's rotation. In 1613, his discoveries led Galileo to declare his support of the Copernican theory, which openly challenged the Church. Copernicus (p.26) stated that the Earth revolved around the Sun, whereas the Church taught that the Earth was the centre of the universe. Galileo received a warning from the Pope, yet in 1632, he angered the Church again with his book *Dialogue Concerning the Two Chief World Systems* (1632). Although it was judged a masterpiece by scientists, Church leaders were furious about its support of the Copernican view. In 1633, Galileo was put on trial in Rome. The charge was heresy – contradiction of the Church's doctrine. He was found guilty and condemned to spend the rest of his life imprisoned in his own home. However, he continued to work, producing perhaps his most important book, *Discourses on the Two New Sciences* (1638), on the science of mechanics.

GALILEO'S CLOCK
Galileo used the simple device of a swinging pendulum to measure time.

1558 Elizabeth I ascends the English throne. Elizabeth's reign is a golden age for England. The English defeat the Spanish Armada, send explorers around the world, and Shakespeare writes his most famous plays.

1562 African slaves are taken to the "New World" and sold as labourers by Sir John Hawkins, an English trader. This also marks the start of the slave trade to Europe, although Arabs already sell slaves to the Ottoman Empire.

William SHAKESPEARE
1564–1616
English playwright and poet

The greatest playwright in the English language, William Shakespeare was born in Stratford-upon-Avon, England. He attended the local grammar school and, in 1582 he married Anne Hathaway. Soon afterwards he went to London where he both wrote and acted in plays. Shakespeare wrote at least 37 plays, including tragedies such as *Romeo and Juliet* (1595), *Hamlet* (1599–1601), *Othello* (1602–04), *King Lear* (1604–05), and *Macbeth* (1606); comedies such as *The Taming of the Shrew* (c.1592), *Twelfth Night* (1601), and *A Midsummer Night's Dream* (1595–96); histories such as *Richard III* (1591–93) and *Henry V* (1599); and, later in life, some less easily classified plays such as *The Winter's Tale* (1610–11) and *The Tempest* (1611). He is also remembered for his 154 love poems written in the sonnet form. Quotations from Shakespeare's works, such as "To be or not to be; that is the question", "To thine own self be true" (*Hamlet*), and "Shall I compare thee to a summer's day?" (Sonnet 18), are so well known that they have become a part of the English language.

Henry HUDSON
1565–1611
English explorer

Henry Hudson explored the river that bears his name, a voyage that led to the Dutch settlement of New Amsterdam, now New York City. Between 1607 and 1610, Hudson made four voyages of exploration, three times for England, and once for the Dutch. He tried to find both a Northwest and a Northeast Passage to Asia. On his third voyage, he explored the Hudson River as far north as present-day Albany. On his final voyage, he reached the great Canadian bay also named for him, but his crew mutinied and cast Hudson adrift with his young son and seven sailors. They were never seen again.

THE GLOBE
Many of Shakespeare's plays were performed in this half-covered London theatre.

JAMES VI & I
1566–1625
Scottish and English king

James was the first king to unite England and Scotland under one throne. Born in Edinburgh, the son of Mary, Queen of Scots (p.36) and Lord Darnley, James VI became king of Scotland when he was a year old, after his mother was forced into exile. In 1603, he inherited the English throne from his childless cousin Elizabeth I (p.34), uniting the two countries under one crown as James I. James was a vain man who, although well educated, often used poor judgement – he became known as the "Wisest Fool in Christendom". His belief in the divine right of kings led him into conflict with parliament, and by the end of his reign he had squandered the legacy of strong government left to him by Elizabeth. He is also remembered for commissioning a new translation of the Bible, and publishing an attack on the recent fashion of smoking.

Samuel de CHAMPLAIN
1567–1635
French explorer

Samuel de Champlain founded the first French settlements in Canada and developed the fur trade there. As a young man, de Champlain served the Spanish by mapping the Caribbean. His map-making skills impressed the French king, who made him a royal geographer. In 1603, de Champlain sailed to Canada, and devoted the rest of his life to "New France". He explored widely, developed a prosperous trade in fur, and established the city of Quebec. In 1612, he was made Lieutenant of Canada. After 1615, he sent out explorers, and used the information they brought back to produce maps of Canada. His one major error was to make enemies of the powerful Iroquois people, who later helped the British to defeat the French in the battle for Canada in the 1700s. Lake Champlain on the Canada-US border is named after him.

1568 A minor lord, Oda Nobunaga, captures the Japanese capital, Kyoto. He deposes the last Ashikaga Shogun in 1573 and defeats other lords until his death in 1582. By 1591, his successor, Hideyoshi, is the unchallenged master of Japan.

1568 William, Prince of Orange, leads the Dutch in revolt against Spanish rule. In 1572, the Sea Beggars, a group of sailors, capture the Spanish-held port of Brill. The struggle goes on although William is assassinated.

Claudio MONTEVERDI
1567–1643
Italian composer

Claudio Monteverdi pioneered the genre of opera. He began his career in the choir at Cremona Cathedral, Italy, where he also learnt the violin and organ. He started composing at an early age, and some of his choral pieces were printed while he was still a teenager. Around 1591, he took a job with the Duke of Mantua as court musician, and worked there until 1612. His next post was as director of music at St Mark's Cathedral in Venice, where he stayed until his death in 1643. Monteverdi wrote mainly vocal music, including nine books of madrigals (songs for unaccompanied voices) and about 150 pieces of choral church music, the best known being the *Vespers* (1610). His greatest achievement, however, was in the field of opera. His work *Orfeo* (1607) is the earliest known opera and is still regularly performed today.

Guy FAWKES
1570–1606
English conspirator

The man linked with the Gunpowder Plot, Guy Fawkes aimed to blow up the Houses of Parliament and overthrow the Protestant king James I (p.39). In 1593, he joined the army of Catholic Spain, which was occupying the Netherlands, and in 1604, he joined other ardent Catholics in a plan to overthrow the English king.

THE GUNPOWDER PLOT
This famous engraving shows Guy Fawkes and his fellow conspirators plotting to kill King James I by blowing up the Houses of Parliament.

They intended to blow up Parliament and start a rebellion. The plotters rented a cellar beneath the House of Lords, and packed it with barrels of gunpowder. On 5 November 1605, when King James and his Parliament were sitting, Fawkes went to light the fuse. But he had been betrayed. He was arrested, tortured, and executed in 1606. Guy Fawkes Night is still remembered in England with bonfires and fireworks every year on 5 November.

Johannes KEPLER
1571–1630
German mathematician and astronomer

Kepler was the astronomer who discovered that the planets move in elliptical, rather than circular, orbits around the Sun. In 1594, he became professor of mathematics at Graz, Austria, where one of his tasks was to make logs of the weather by looking at the stars. This led him to focus on astronomy and while working as an astronomer, he wrote his first major work, *Mysterium Cosmographium* (1596). He sent copies to the major astronomers of the day, including Tycho Brahe (p.36), who invited Kepler to be his assistant in Prague. When Brahe died, he left Kepler his books of observations, and Kepler took over Brahe's position as imperial mathematician under the Hungarian king and Holy Roman Emperor Rudolf II. His study of Mars, and later the movement of the planets, were major breakthroughs in astronomy.

Michelangelo Merisi da CARAVAGGIO
1573–1610
Italian painter

Caravaggio was a ground-breaking artist who used light and shade to dramatic effect. At the age of 20, he gained the patronage of an influential cardinal in Rome, Italy, and his talent quickly matured. He painted many religious subjects using ordinary people as models for biblical characters. The sense of realism this produced proved highly controversial. His dramatic use of light and shadow influenced many later painters. Two of Caravaggio's most remarkable works are the *Conversion of St Paul* and the *Crucifixion of St Peter*. In 1606, Caravaggio fled Rome after killing a man who had beaten him at tennis.

1572 In France, Huguenots (French Protestants) gather on St Bartholemew's Day to celebrate the wedding of their leader, Henri of Navarre. King Charles IX is convinced they are about to revolt and massacres 80,000 of them.

1575 Stephen Batory is elected king of Poland. His rule starts well, with three successful battles against Ivan the Terrible, but he dies in 1586, before being able to implement campaigns against the Ottomans.

Peter Paul RUBENS
1577–1640
Flemish painter

The Flemish artist Peter Paul Rubens became one of the most influential artists of 16th-century northern Europe. He trained as a painter in Antwerp before moving to Italy in 1600. There, he was influenced by the Italian masters and Roman sculpture. In 1609, he became court painter to Archduke Albert in the Netherlands. He produced pictures on subjects ranging from state occasions to landscapes and portraits. His vigorous style made vibrant use of colour and often conveyed a joy in life. Some of his greatest works were on a grand scale, such as the 25 giant canvases glorifying Marie de' Medici of France. His painting *Descent from the Cross* (1611–14) in Antwerp Cathedral is considered his masterpiece.

Guy Fawkes

William HARVEY
1578–1657
British physician

The circulation of blood around the human body was first described with accuracy by William Harvey. He studied medicine at Cambridge University in England and then at Padua, Italy, under Hieronymus Fabricius (p.35). In 1607, he was appointed physician to St Bartholomew's Hospital in London and wrote his most famous work, *An Anatomical Exercise on the Motion of the Heart and the Blood in Animals* (1628). Harvey was the first doctor to realize that the heart is a muscle that pumps blood around the body via the arteries. His ideas contradicted those of the earlier, much respected expert Galen, and Harvey was ridiculed during his lifetime. It was not until Marcello Malpighi (p.47) demonstrated the truth of his theories with a microscope that Harvey's genius was finally acknowledged.

Willebrord SNELL
1580–1626
Dutch mathematician and astronomer

Willebrord Snell, also called Snellius, made the first accurate calculation of the Earth's radius, but he is better remembered for his studies of light refraction. Snell was born in Leiden, in the Netherlands, and became professor of mathematics at the university there. In 1621, he developed Snell's Law, which set out his scientific findings regarding refraction, and was published by the philosopher René Descartes (p.42) in 1637. His calculations revolutionized our understanding of the universe.

William BAFFIN
1584–1622
English explorer

William Baffin was the first navigator to measure longitude. Little is known of his early life, but he served as navigator on three voyages searching for the Northwest Passage – a sea route from Europe to Asia over the top of Canada. In 1612, 1615, and 1616, he explored the Greenland coast; Baffin Bay and Baffin Island are both named after him. He eventually decided that there was no Northwest Passage, (its entrance was blocked by ice in his time). Baffin was one of the best navigators of the 17th century and, in 1615, he was able to calculate his longitude (east-west position) by observing the Moon. Unfortunately, his method was too complicated to be widely used.

Cardinal RICHELIEU
1585–1642
French clergyman and statesman

Almost single-handedly, Cardinal Richelieu raised France to a dominant position in Europe. Armand-Jean Du Plessis, Duc de Richelieu, was made a bishop at 22 and, in 1614, became advisor to Marie de Medicis, who held the French throne on behalf of her son, Louis XIII. In 1622, he was made a cardinal and, in 1624, Richelieu became minister of state to Louis XIII. By 1629, Richelieu was ruler of France in all but name. He tried to reduce the influence in Europe of the Hapsburg family and, in 1635, he led France into the Thirty Years' War against Spain. His ruthlessness led to many French victories.

CARDINAL RICHELIEU
The influential French statesman sought to increase France's authority in Europe by weakening the power of the mighty Hapsburg family.

John WINTHROP
1588–1649
English first governor of Massachusetts

John Winthrop was a long-serving and influential governor of the Massachusetts Bay colony in North America. Winthrop was a Puritan, a Protestant who believed that the official English Church was not sufficiently reformed. In 1629, he joined the newly formed Massachusetts Bay Company, set up to establish an English colony in North America. Winthrop and other settlers founded Boston in 1630, which became the colony's capital. Winthrop dominated the colony, and was elected governor 12 times. He believed that God had chosen him to build a "godly commonwealth" – a perfect Christian society. Massachusetts was strictly governed, and those who disagreed with Winthrop's religious ideas were banished. But the colony was a lasting success. By 1640, some 20,000 settlers were living in Boston and many surrounding areas.

1584 Englishman Sir Walter Raleigh sends a party to explore Virginia in North America. Many of these early colonists die because of the cold winter, disease, and malnutrition. The colony eventually disappears.

1588 The English navy defeats the Spanish Armada. Stormy seas and more accurate cannons all contribute to their victory. Only 76 out of 130 Spanish vessels return to Spain. Philip II had believed his Armada could not be defeated.

Thomas HOBBES
1588–1679
English philosopher

The idea that an all-powerful state is required to control human nature was first developed by Thomas Hobbes. Educated at Oxford University, England, he became a tutor there. In 1640, he was forced to flee to France during the English Civil War because of his support for Charles I. Hobbes returned to England in 1651 and wrote many books, including his famous *Leviathan* (1651), which was much influenced by the political chaos of revolutionary England after the Civil War. It argues that people, if left to their own devices, are cruel and greedy, and live in continual danger and fear of violent death. In order to overcome these basic conditions of human nature, Hobbes argued the need for a strong state, with supreme power resting in the sovereign. He also believed rival sources of power must be removed. His theory of government has survived to the present day.

SHAH JAHAN
The Mogul court was at its most glittering under the rule of Shah Jahan. From his lavish palaces he encouraged painting, literature, and above all, architecture.

Shah JAHAN
1592–1666
Mogul emperor

Shah Jahan's reign marked the largest extent of Mogul rule in India, but he is probably best remembered for building the Taj Mahal. He inherited the Mogul throne in 1628 and conquered most of southern India, extending the empire to Persia, and strengthening the administration. A patron of art and architecture, he built a new capital at Delhi and ordered the building of the Taj Mahal at Agra to house the tomb of his wife. In 1657, he fell ill, and a war broke out between his sons. In 1658, he was deposed and imprisoned.

Artemisia GENTILESCHI
1593–c.1652
Italian painter

Artemisia Gentileschi was one of the few female artists of her time to earn an independent living. Born in Rome, she showed artistic talent at an early age and was encouraged by her father, Orazio. Influenced by Caravaggio (p.40), she began to paint in a forthright and realistic style, contrasting light and dark. In 1638, she visited England to help her father on a commission for King Charles I (p.45). Many of Gentileschi's pictures are of powerful women, often depicting the decapitation of men. The violence of such works as *Judith Slaying Holofernes* (c.1620) may have been a reaction to the treatment she suffered at the hands of men, including rape and torture.

Gustavus II ADOLPHUS
1594–1632
Swedish king

Gustavus II was a military commander of genius, organizing the most formidable standing army in Europe. Gustavus came to the Swedish throne in 1611. He quickly ended the wars he had inherited with Denmark (1613) and Russia (1617), gaining territory which cut Russia off from the Baltic Sea. By 1629, Sweden dominated the entire Baltic Sea. In 1630, Sweden entered the Thirty Years' War against the Hapsburgs. The Swedish army triumphed across Germany but, in 1632, Gustavus was killed during the Swedish victory at Lützen. During his reign, Gustavus also transformed the Swedish administration and developed industry.

René DESCARTES
1596–1650
French philosopher

René Descartes created a method of reasoning that could be used to test the logic of all scientific theories. He studied law in Poitiers, France, until 1618, when he went to the Netherlands to study mathematics. There he met physicist Isaac Beekman who encouraged him to study science. From 1619 to 1628, Descartes travelled around Europe gathering ideas. He rejected the belief that a probability was as acceptable as a certainty for proving a scientific theory. In his 1637 book *Discours de la méthode* (Discourse on Method), he stated that the existence of all things must be doubted until proven true. He did claim one certainty, however – *Cogito ergo sum* (I think, therefore I am).

1590 Shah Abbas I of Persia makes peace with Turkey. He introduces reforms and expands the kingdom, creating a magnificent court at Isfahan. Abbas blinds his children so they cannot overthrow him.

1592 Hideyoshi of Japan launches an invasion of Korea. The Korean king seeks aid from China and rallies his people to resist. Korean admiral Yi Sunsin commands the first armoured vessel, his "turtle ship", and defeats the Japanese.

Gianlorenzo BERNINI
1598–1680
Italian sculptor

Gianlorenzo Bernini was the finest sculptor of his day. He was trained in carving marble by his father, an eminent sculptor, who introduced him to many wealthy patrons such as the Borghese family. Bernini's early sculpted figures were so daring and original that, in 1629, he was appointed architect to St Peter's in Rome. He had already begun his first masterpiece, the huge bronze *baldacchino* (canopy) over the high altar (1624–33). Another of his great works is the marble sculpture *Ecstasy of St Teresa* in the Cornaro chapel in Rome (1645–52), showing the saint swooning, her face filled with bliss and agony. In 1656, he designed the piazza in front of St Peter's, with its spectacular double colonnades, completely changing the face of Rome.

BERNINI'S *angel in Sant' Andrea della Fratte, Rome*

Oliver CROMWELL
1599–1658
English parliamentarian

Oliver Cromwell was the first republican ruler of Britain. An East Anglian farmer, he entered Parliament as the representative for Huntingdon in 1628. He opposed the government of King Charles I and when civil war broke out in 1642, he joined the Parliamentary army. Cromwell developed an efficient military force which became known as the New Model Army. By 1645, he was the leading Parliamentary general and was instrumental in the defeat of the king. After the execution of Charles I (p.45) in 1649, Cromwell declared England a commonwealth and became Chairman of the Council of State. He defeated royalist armies in Ireland and Scotland, but failed to establish an effective system of government. In 1653, he abolished Parliament and became Lord Protector, ruling the country himself until 1656, when he was forced to recall Parliament. He named his son Richard Cromwell as his successor, but after Cromwell's death in 1658, Richard failed to maintain his father's iron grip. In 1660, the monarchy was restored and Charles II was invited to take the throne. Cromwell's body was later removed from the tomb of kings at Westminster Abbey and hung at Tyburn gallows.

Diego VELAZQUEZ
1599–1660
Spanish painter

Diego Velazquez's mastery of colour and light and ability to convey character made him one of the greatest of all Spanish painters. Velazquez became a master painter at only 18, painting mainly religious pictures, or portraits of everyday characters such as the *Waterseller of Seville* (c.1620). In 1623, he became court painter to King Philip IV and painted a series of grand royal portraits, pictures of court life, and fine historical paintings, such as *The Surrender of Breda* (1634–35).

1595 Alvaro de Mendana sails from Peru to the Marquesas Islands in eastern Polynesia for the second time. There are 380 potential settlers travelling with him, but most of them end up fighting with, and killing, many natives.

1598 The Edict of Nantes ensures tolerance of all religions in France. It is instituted by Henri IV, previously the Huguenot (Protestant) leader Henri of Navarre, who actually converted to Catholicism on taking the throne.

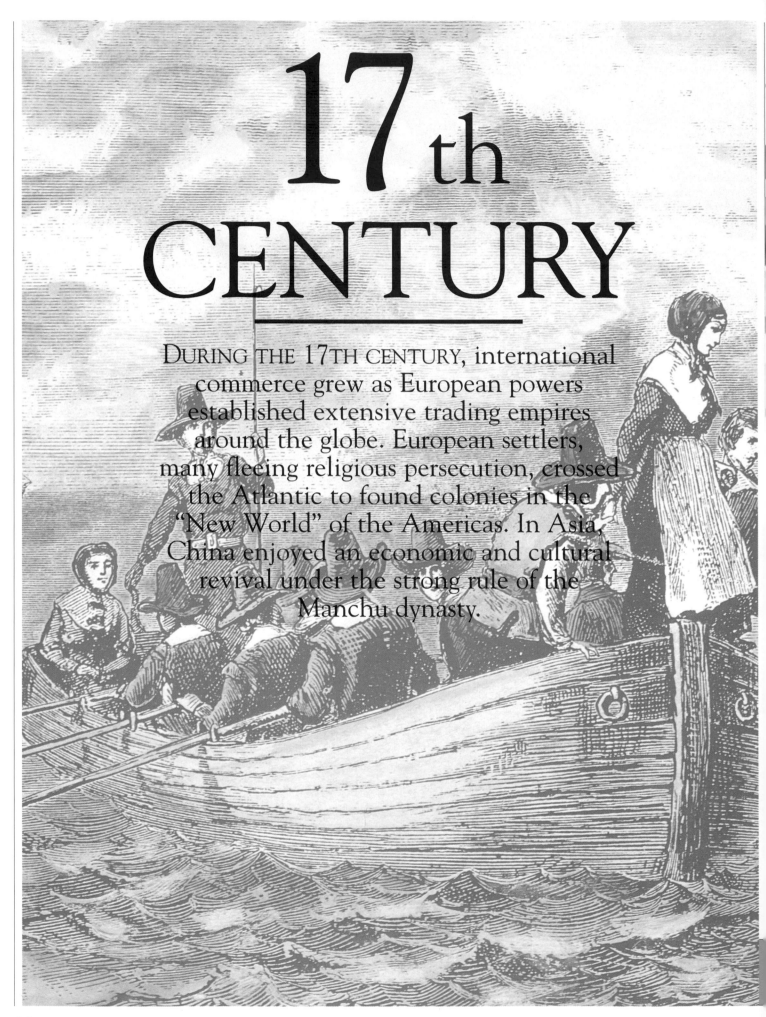

17th CENTURY

DURING THE 17TH CENTURY, international commerce grew as European powers established extensive trading empires around the globe. European settlers, many fleeing religious persecution, crossed the Atlantic to found colonies in the "New World" of the Americas. In Asia, China enjoyed an economic and cultural revival under the strong rule of the Manchu dynasty.

CHARLES I
1600–49
British king

Charles I was the only English king to be publicly executed. He believed in the divine right of kings and this idea that the king had absolute power brought him into immediate conflict with Parliament. In 1629, Charles dissolved Parliament and ruled without it until 1640, suppressing political and religious opposition to his rule through the royal courts. Short of money, Charles was forced to reinstate Parliament in 1640, but relations quickly deteriorated and, following rebellion in Scotland, civil war broke out in 1642. The king's royalist armies were no match for the Parliamentarian forces and, by 1649, Charles had been defeated. He was tried and, on 30 January 1649, beheaded for waging war against his country. Charles was a learned man who supported the arts, yet he was also stubborn and quarrelsome, which led to his untimely end.

Pierre de FERMAT
1601–65
French mathematician

Often described as the father of number theory, Pierre de Fermat was actually a lawyer by profession, and only practised mathematics as a hobby. De Fermat developed analytical geometry at around the same time as French mathematician René Descartes (p.42), and also made important advances in the field of probability. He is best remembered however, for "Fermat's Last Theorem", a mathematical problem that people tried to solve for 300 years. British mathematician Andrew Wiles finally cracked the puzzle in 1994.

REMBRANDT
Self-portrait of the artist in later life, painted only a few years before his death.

Abel Janszoon TASMAN
1603–59
Dutch explorer

In 1632, Abel Tasman joined the Dutch East India Company, a decision that would assure his future as an explorer. The company controlled Dutch trade in the Far East and was based on the Indonesian island of Java. In 1642, the governor of Batavia, Van Diemen, sent Tasman on a voyage of exploration. He sailed south of Australia and discovered an island which he called Van Dieman's Land after the governor. Sailing on, he became the first European to see New Zealand. Tasman's achievement is commemorated by the naming of the former Van Dieman's island as Tasmania, and in the Tasman Sea, which lies between Australia and New Zealand.

TASMAN *found exotic jewellery in Fiji, such as this necklace made from sperm whale teeth.*

Rembrandt van RIJN
1606–69
Dutch artist

Rembrandt van Rijn, commonly known as Rembrandt, is one of the most celebrated artists in the world. He studied painting under Pieter Lastman before becoming an independent master in 1625. He settled in Amsterdam and was soon successful. From mainly religious subjects, he moved on to portraits, notably the group portrait *The Anatomy Lesson of Dr Tulp* (1632). Rembrandt grew rich and fashionable, but in 1642, his painting *The Night Watch*, now celebrated as a masterpiece, was badly received, and his fortunes began to slide. He was declared bankrupt in 1656. Despite this misfortune, Rembrandt produced some of his finest works, including biblical scenes such as *St Matthew and the Angel* (1661) and *The Prodigal Son* (c.1669). Rembrandt's greatness lay in his use of light and shade, and in his genius for conveying character. This can be seen in his famous series of self-portraits.

John MILTON
1608–74
English poet

One of England's most respected poets, John Milton published his first important poem, the elegy *Lycidas*, in 1638. In 1665, he completed the famous 12-volume poem *Paradise Lost*, which is thought by many to be the greatest epic poem in the English language. It tells the story of the battle between the angels in Heaven and the Fall of Man, and was very much a work of political and religious allegory. Milton was politically active, supporting parliament in the English Civil War, and served as secretary to the new council of state after the execution of Charles I. The blindness of his later years did not prevent Milton from working. He continued to dictate his ideological essays and poetry to his daughters.

1600
In Japan, there is a struggle for the country's leadership following the death of the shogun, Hideyoshi. Tokegawa Ieyasu beats his rival Ishida Mitsunari at the Battle of Sekigahara. This is the beginning of the Edo period.

1608
In North America, the city of Québec is founded by 28 French settlers led by Samuel de Champlain. Having already explored Canada, de Champlain secures funding from French king Henri V to establish it as a colony.

MOLIERE
1622–73
French writer and actor

Jean-Baptiste Poquelin, or Molière as he is better known, was the most popular and famous French playwright of his day. After a good education at a Jesuit college, Molière joined a troupe of actors in order to master every aspect of the theatre. With money he inherited from his late mother, he founded the *Illustre Théâtre* in 1643, which was given official support by King Louis XIV (p.49). In 1664, Molière staged *Tartuffe*, one of his best-known comic plays, about a religious hypocrite. The play caused a huge scandal in Paris and afterwards, Molière was continually harassed by the authorities. Despite this, in 1666, *The Misanthrope* was acknowledged as a masterpiece. Among his most famous satires are *The School for Wives* (1662), *The Doctor in Spite of Himself* (1666), and *The Imaginary Invalid* (1673). Writer, actor, director, and manager, Molière devoted his entire life to entertainment, and died after collapsing on stage.

MOLIERE
This statue of Molière is in the Rue de Richelieu in Paris, close to where the famous playwright lived.

Blaise PASCAL
1623–62
French scientist and writer

At the age of only 16, the brilliant young Blaise Pascal published a theory on conics – the physics governing spherical shapes. The ideas he expressed were so advanced that the French philosopher René Descartes (p.42) refused to believe it could have been written by one so young. Pascal and his father carried out experiments using mercury to disprove the long-held theory that "nature abhors a vacuum".

This led to their joint scientific inventions of the barometer, the hydraulic press, and the syringe. Pascal contributed to the mathematical system of calculus as well as to the theory of probability. He also invented a calculating machine in 1647, but from 1654, he put aside scientific research and concentrated his energies on writing about religion. Between 1656 and 1657, he wrote 18 pamphlets entitled *Lettres Provinciales* (Provincial Letters). His famous notes on Christian truths were discovered after his death and published under the title *Pensées* (Thoughts).

George FOX
1624–91
English founder of the Society of Friends, or Quakers

The man who founded the Quakers, George Fox, had little formal education. He rebelled against the established Church, which was controlled by the state, and became a wandering preacher at the age of 18. He preached that all human beings have an "inward light", which comes from God. He thought people should be guided by this light, and not by rules laid down by any Church. He ridiculed the use of church buildings, which he called "steeple houses", and also refused to swear oaths, pay tithes (church taxes), or treat people in authority with special respect. Fox wrote a number of religious works and attracted many followers. He was sent to prison eight times for his beliefs. While on trial in Derby in 1650, he told the judge that he should "quake at the name of the Lord". The remark led to the nickname "Quakers" being given to Fox and his followers. Fox called them the "Friends of Truth".

Robert BOYLE
1627–91
Irish physicist and chemist

One of the most celebrated scientists of his day, Robert Boyle published Boyle's Law in 1662. It stated that "at a constant temperature, the pressure and volume of gas are inversely proportional". This means that if the pressure of a gas is doubled, then its volume halves, and vice versa. After completing his studies at Oxford University, Boyle conducted scientific experiments on air, combustion and vacuums with Robert Hooke (p.48) as his assistant. Boyle published his views in a book called *Sceptical Chymist* (1661), which emphasized the importance of chemical analysis. He researched the properties of metals, acids, alkalis, and crystals. Boyle also introduced the use of the plant extract litmus for identifying acids. He was a pioneer of scientific experiment and one of the founders of a group which, in 1645, became the Royal Society, devoted to the promotion of science. The Society influenced the rise in status of science as a discipline in the 17th century.

1618 The Thirty Years' War begins in Prague when Bohemians, claiming independence, throw two Catholic governors out of a window. European nations join in the fighting of Catholics against Protestants.

1620 The *Mayflower* sets sail from England with about 100 people bound for America. They settle in New England and set up a colony called the Plymouth Plantation, which flounders at first but eventually prospers.

John BUNYAN
1628–88
English writer and preacher

John Bunyan was the author of *The Pilgrim's Progress*. Following his wife's death in 1658, Bunyan devoted himself to religion. Joining the Baptist Church, he proved to be a gifted preacher. However, when Charles II was restored to the throne, Bunyan was imprisoned for refusing to give up his religion. He spent 12 years in Bedford County Gaol, England, then was released and imprisoned again. It is likely that he wrote his world-famous book, *The Pilgrim's Progress* (1678), while in prison. The book describes the adventures of a pilgrim called Christian. On his journey through life, he has to face many difficulties before finding salvation.

Marcello MALPIGHI
1628–94
Italian microbiologist

Marcello Malpighi studied philosophy and medicine at the University of Bologna, Italy and in 1691 became chief physician to Pope Innocent XII. Using the newly invented microscope, he made important discoveries about the structure of the liver, lungs, spleen, skin, glands, and brain. He discovered that capillaries transport blood – an idea that caused outrage at the time because it contradicted accepted medical opinion. He left an important legacy, making future scientists more aware of the possibilities of studying anatomy under the microscope. He was also the first to give a full anatomical account of an insect – the silkworm moth – which provided valuable insights into its respiratory processes.

Christiaan HUYGENS
1629–93
Dutch mathematician and physicist

While still at university, Christiaan Huygens acquired a reputation for brilliance following the publication of his mathematical book *Theoremata* (1651). In 1659, he discovered the true shape of the rings of Saturn using his new telescope lens. Huygens went on to invent the pendulum clock, based on the theories of Galileo (p.38). In his book *Treatise on Light*, published in 1690, he discussed reflection and refraction and developed his principle of light moving in waves.

Jan VERMEER
1632–75
Dutch painter

Little is known about the life of Jan Vermeer except that he trained as an artist and joined the Delft Guild of Painters as a master in 1653. He left very few pictures – between 35 and 40 are known. Many of these are calm interior scenes. His finest works include *The Milkmaid* (c.1660), *Lady Seated at a Virginal* (1674–75), and *The Artist's Studio* (c.1660), which showed him at work. From such simple scenes, Vermeer was able to conjure a magical sense of harmony and space, lit with a subtle radiance. He died a poor man and his work passed unnoticed for many years until a French critic rediscovered him in 1866 and initiated a revival of interest in Vermeer's work. Today, he is regarded as one of the greatest of Dutch painters.

Benedict de SPINOZA
1632–77
Dutch philosopher

Benedict de Spinoza was one of the great rationalist thinkers of the 17th century. He had a broad education and was familiar with medieval philosophy as well as the works of contemporary writers. His interest in astronomy and theology led to his expulsion from Amsterdam's Jewish community in 1656. He then became leader of a small philosophical circle which supported a strictly historical approach to the interpretation of biblical sources. His major work, *Ethics* (1677), published after his death, tried to deduce scientifically what was right and wrong for human beings.

Jean Baptiste LULLY
1632–87
Italian-French composer

Jean Baptiste Lully taught himself the violin and guitar and joined a band of minstrels. While in the service of Louis XIV, Lully became director of music at the royal court. Here he conducted the King's 24 Violins – one of the first real orchestras. His musical compositions include many of the first French operas, such as *Thésée* (1675) and *Acis et Galatée* (1686), in which ballet played a key role. He also collaborated with the popular French playwright Molière (p.46) on theatre pieces. In 1687, Lully injured his foot with his baton, and died of blood poisoning.

VERMEER
Head of a Girl with a Pearl Earring (c.1665).

1630 The Ottoman army takes Persia (then called Hamadan), which is ruled by Murad IV. In 1638, the Ottomans take Baghdad from the Persians and Mesopotamia becomes part of the mighty Turkish Empire.

1632 King Gustavus Adolphus of Sweden is killed at the Battle of Lützen when the Protestant Swedish forces defeat the Catholics during the Thirty Years' War. In his lifetime, he was known as "The Lion of the North".

John LOCKE
1632–1704
English philosopher

John Locke's *Essay Concerning Human Understanding* (1690) sets out his view that experience is the only source of knowledge (a theory known as empiricism). This idea provoked great debate among his contemporaries. Locke also helped to shape politics in Britain, the United States, and France, with *Two Treatises on Government* (1690). In them, Locke stated that government should be subject to tight control by its citizens. Such ideas formed the basis of liberal democracy and inspired a great many politicians.

Antonie van LEEUWENHOEK
1632–1723
Dutch scientist

Antonie van Leeuwenhoek brought the world into closer view by inventing the precision microscope in 1683. His observations extended the work of Marcello Malpighi (p.47) by accurately describing red blood corpuscles and capillaries. He discovered the existence of bacteria in the tartar of teeth in 1676.

Christopher WREN
1632–1723
English architect and scientist

Christopher Wren is best remembered as the architect who created many of London's most famous landmarks and effectively shaped the city's skyline. After gaining a degree from Oxford University in 1651, he became professor of astronomy there. However, he had a growing interest in architecture, which was helped by his knowledge of practical geometry. Wren designed or restored several major buildings in Cambridge and Oxford, including the Sheldonian Theatre in Oxford (1669). After much of London was destroyed by the Great Fire of 1666, Wren was appointed to the commission for planning the rebuilding. He redesigned some 50 churches, the most famous of which is the elegant St Paul's Cathedral (1675–1710), which has a refined, moderately Baroque style. Among his other masterpieces are Chelsea Hospital (1691) and Greenwich Hospital (1715).

St Paul's Cathedral *was designed by Wren after the Great Fire of London.*

Samuel PEPYS
1633–1703
English diarist

Samuel Pepys is famous for his detailed and fascinating diary, which he wrote from 1660 to 1669. In 1659, he travelled from France on the ship bringing the exiled Charles II back to London. He witnessed the Restoration of Charles II the next year, after which Pepys rose rapidly in the Admiralty, becoming secretary to the admiralty in 1672. During this period, Pepys also witnessed the Plague, and the Great Fire of London in 1666, writing his eyewitness accounts of these events in his diary as they unfolded. In 1679, he was imprisoned briefly for allegedly conspiring in a political plot, but was later reappointed to his job and made president of the Royal Society in 1684. Pepys's diary includes unique insights into life and society in England during the mid-17th century, particularly in the spheres of naval administration and the politics of the court. The lively and colourful style of his writing has made his diary a popular classic since 1825 when the manuscript, written in coded shorthand, was found, deciphered, and printed.

Robert HOOKE
1635–1703
English scientist

While at Oxford University, England Robert Hooke assisted Robert Boyle (p.46) on the construction of his air-pump. Five years later, he discovered the law of elasticity, now known as Hooke's Law, in which he states that the stretching of a solid body, such as metal, is proportionate to the force applied to it. The law was used by engineers to assess the effects of stress on a building. Hooke was also one of the first men to build a Gregorian reflecting telescope, which he used to discover the fifth star in the Orion group. He was also the first to suggest that the planet Jupiter rotates on its axis, a theory that was later proved to be true.

1632 In India, the Mogul emperor Shah Jahan orders work to begin on the Taj Mahal, an elaborate tomb for his beloved dead wife. It takes almost 20,000 people about 20 years to complete this beautiful memorial to love.

1633 William Laud is made archbishop of Canterbury by King Charles I. He introduces several controversial policies which are interpreted by some as Romanism, and fuel the build-up to the English Civil War.

North America, which he called Pennsylvania, in honour of his father. Penn described this new colony, which was to be a refuge for all separatists, as a "holy experiment". However, he found the colonists ungrateful and he died a disillusioned man.

Gottfried LEIBNIZ
1646–1716
German mathematician

Gottfried Leibniz was crucial to the development of mathematical theory, particularly with regard to statistics. In 1667, he obtained a position at the

court of the Elector of Mainz, where he studied the work of notable philosophers of the day. He also visited London and met important scientists. There, he was involved in a mathematical dispute with Isaac Newton – each believed he had discovered calculus first and the matter has never been conclusively settled. In 1700, Leibniz persuaded Frederick I of Prussia to found the Prussian Academy of Sciences of which Leibniz became the first president. His writings spanned the arts as well as mathematics.

GOTTFRIED LEIBNIZ
The German mathematician famously clashed with the English scientist Isaac Newton over who discovered calculus.

1650

Nell GWYN
1650–87
British actress

Although Nell Gwyn was an actress, it is as the mistress of King Charles II that she is best remembered. She began acting professionally while still in her teens, and quickly became famous. She had many admirers, including the poet John Dryden who wrote several parts especially for her. She became the mistress of Charles II in 1669, and had two sons by him. He remained devoted to her until his death.

WILLIAM III
1650–1702
English king

William's arrival in England to take the throne was the basis of the Glorious Revolution. He was a member of the House of Orange, the leading family in Holland, and in 1677, he married his cousin Mary, daughter of James II of England. In 1688, seven leading English Protestant noblemen asked William to rescue the nation from Catholicism by invading England and overthrowing the Catholic king, James II. William landed with a large army in Devon. James fled to France and William's army defeated all his followers. William's victory ensured that England remained Protestant. He defeated James at the Battle of the Boyne in Ireland in 1689. He governed England jointly with Mary until her death in 1694 and then by himself until 1702.

Duke of MARLBOROUGH
1650–1722
British general and statesman

John Churchill, Duke of Marlborough, was one of England's greatest generals. He served under James II and William III, but his military career reached its zenith during the reign of Queen Anne. In the War of Spanish Succession (1701–14), he commanded the British and Dutch forces, winning many victories against the French, most notably outside Vienna at the Battle of Blenheim (1704). His wife was one of Queen Anne's closest attendants, which helped Churchill to win royal favour – he was made a duke and earned Blenheim Palace as a reward for his victories.

1648 The Treaty of Westphalia takes power away from the Holy Roman Empire. Switzerland and the Netherlands become independent as do the German states of Saxony, Brandenberg, and Prussia.

1649 During the English Civil War, "Pride's Purge" expels all those from Parliament who are opposed to the army. The remainder, the "Rump Parliament", finds King Charles I guilty of treason and executes him on 30 January.

Archangelo CORELLI
1653–1713
Italian composer

The music of Archangelo Corelli had an enormous influence on composers such as Bach (p. 54) and Handel (p.55) in the 18th century. He was born in Fusignano, Italy, and studied music in nearby Bologna. He first made his name as a virtuoso violinist, playing in orchestras and small chamber groups. His compositions also became hugely popular, making him one of the most celebrated Italian musicians of his time. Unlike most other composers of the period, Corelli wrote nothing but instrumental music. Best known is the collection of 12 *Concerti Grossi* (concertos for orchestra), *Opus 6*, which includes the famous "Christmas Concerto". Although he wrote comparatively little, his music was highly original.

K'ANG-HSI
1654–1722
Chinese emperor

K'ang-hsi became the second Manchu emperor of China at the age of seven. He spent the early years of his reign crushing resistance from those loyal to the Ming dynasty, then turned to expanding the empire, incorporating Taiwan into China for the first time in 1683. K'ang-hsi was an open-minded leader, opening up ports to overseas traders, establishing diplomatic relations with Russia, permitting Catholic missionaries to convert the Chinese, and employing Jesuit priests to teach mathematics and to map his empire. During his reign, he toured China constantly to check up on the work of his government.

Edmond HALLEY
1656–1742
English astronomer and mathematician

Edmond Halley is famed for correctly predicting the arrival of a comet which now bears his name. In 1676, he travelled to the island of St Helena in the South Atlantic in order to make the first catalogue of the stars in the Southern Hemisphere. Later, his calculations concerning the orbits of 24 comets enabled him to predict with accuracy the return of a comet (Halley's Comet) in 1758 which had last been seen in 1583. He went on to make significant studies of Mercury and Venus. He also brought a great scientific masterpiece to the attention of the world when he persuaded his friend Isaac Newton (p.50) to print his *Principia Mathematica* (1687), even paying for the publication costs himself. In 1720, Halley was honoured for his work by being made Astronomer Royal of England.

COMET'S TAIL
Halley studied the comet's orbit, which can be seen here. As the comet gets closer to the Sun's heat, a huge tail of steamy gas is given off.

Henry PURCELL
1659–95
English composer

Henry Purcell is considered England's finest composer. He came from a musical family, and he and his brother served as choristers at the Chapel Royal, London. He later became composer for the king's violins. His duties at the royal court included providing music for state occasions, such as coronations and the funeral of Queen Mary. He also wrote about 65 anthems and six operas, including *Dido and Aeneas* (1689). Purcell's most popular work was the music he wrote for the theatre, particularly for the plays of John Dryden, William Congreve, and Aphra Behn (p.49).

Daniel DEFOE
1660–1731
English writer

Daniel Defoe has been called the father of modern journalism, though he is now more famous for his novels. After a spell in prison for writing a satire that mocked the Church, Defoe set up

---

1664 In North America, English warships sail into the harbour of New Amsterdam to intimidate the Dutch governor, Peter Stuyvesant. The English take control and rename the Dutch settlement New York.

1666 The Great Fire of London rages for four days, burning down 13,000 wooden houses. Much of the city is destroyed, but only six people die. An outbreak of bubonic plague in London the previous year claimed almost 70,000 lives.

The Review (1704–13), a commercial newspaper with columns on politics and scandal. It was the first of its kind. In 1719, Defoe published *The Life and Strange Adventures of Robinson Crusoe, of York, Mariner*, his famous tale of a desert-island castaway. Later, he wrote *Moll Flanders* (1722), one of the first novels to criticize a society that created and then punished criminals.

Thomas NEWCOMEN
1663–1729
English inventor

Thomas Newcomen was the inventor of an early atmospheric steam engine. He was a blacksmith by profession, but in 1698, he joined forces with Thomas Savery, who had patented plans for just such a steam engine. By 1712, Newcomen had produced an improved working machine. It became commonly used in mines for removing water, replacing the horses that had been used in the past.

BEAM ENGINE
Newcomen's engine had a huge beam at the top, which rocked back and forth.

Gobind SINGH
1666–1708
The last Sikh guru, or teacher

Gobind Rai was the son of Tegh Bahadur, the ninth Sikh guru. In 1675, his father was executed by the Muslim Moguls, who ruled much of northern India. Before he died, Tegh Bahadur named his son as 10th guru. In 1699, Gobind founded a military brotherhood called the Khalsa (Pure). All members of the brotherhood adopted a common surname – Singh (lion) for men and Kaur (lioness) for women. Gobind Singh was later driven into exile and assassinated. His four sons were also killed, ending the line of gurus, but the system Gobind Singh founded influences Sikhs to this day.

Jonathan SWIFT
1667–1745
Irish writer and clergyman

Jonathan Swift was the author of *Gulliver's Travels*. Born in Ireland, he moved to England in 1688 to become secretary to Sir William Temple. He became a clergyman in 1695, before writing *A Tale of a Tub* (1704), a criticism of religious corruption, published anonymously. After returning to Ireland, Swift published his best-known work, *Gulliver's Travels* (1726). It tells the story of an adventurer who travels through four strange countries, but it is actually a brutal satire of the politics, religion, and society of the day.

Peter the GREAT
1672–1725
Russian tsar

Peter the Great almost single-handedly dragged Russia into the modern world. In 1682, on the death of his brother, Feodor III, he became joint tsar, or ruler, with his mentally disabled half-brother, Ivan V. On Ivan's death in 1689, Peter became sole ruler. He was determined to modernize his country and travelled incognito throughout western Europe to learn about the latest ideas in everything from government to shipbuilding. He reformed Russia's institutions and built Russia's first navy, which he used to defeat Sweden in 1714 and thus gain Russia a "window on the West" on the Baltic Sea. Here he built his new capital of St Petersburg. By the time of his death in 1725, Peter had transformed Russia into a leading European nation.

Jethro TULL
1674–1741
English agriculturalist

Jethro Tull was responsible for revolutionizing British farming methods. He was educated at Oxford University and qualified as a lawyer but took up farming around 1700. In 1701, he invented the seed drill, which he used to plant seeds mechanically, evenly spacing them in rows. This was far more efficient than the haphazard scatter-throwing of seeds that people used up to that time. It made one job of the three tasks of drilling, sowing, and covering the seeds. He also designed a plough which is much the same as those used today. In 1733, he wrote his chief work, *The Horse-Hoeing Husbandry*.

1670 England has 12 colonies along the east coast of North America. The Hudson's Bay Company is founded to encourage English trade with Canada, and to discover a Northwest Passage to Asia.

1672 Turkey and Poland struggle over the Ukraine. In 1676, the Treaty of Zuravno grants Turkey the Polish Ukraine. The following year Turkey goes to war with Russia. It loses much of its share to Russia in 1681.

1675

Robert
WALPOLE
1676–1745
English politician

Robert Walpole was Britain's first effective prime minister. He was educated at Cambridge University, became a member of the Whig party, and entered the House of Commons in 1701. When George I took the throne in 1714, he appointed Walpole First Lord of the Treasury. Since George I could speak little English, Walpole had great freedom to make decisions. He took to meeting with a few ministers to decide policy, a system which evolved into today's British cabinet-style government. Walpole's residence at Number 10 Downing Street became the official London home of all future prime ministers.

Antonio
VIVALDI
1678–1741
Italian composer

The youngest son of a violinist at St Mark's church in Venice, Antonio Vivaldi became a priest in 1703. He left the priesthood to become violin teacher at a girls' orphanage, the *Ospedale della Pietà*. He maintained contact with the orphanage throughout his life and wrote much of his instrumental and sacred music for the conservatory there. He also frequently toured Europe with productions of his operas. His music includes more than 20 operas, and oratorios and other choral pieces, but he is best known for his instrumental music. He wrote about 550

LA PIETA
Vivaldi wrote music in this Venetian church.

concertos – more than half of them for solo violin and orchestra – including the collections *L'estro armonico*, Opus 3 (1711), *La stravaganza*, Opus 4 (c.1712), and *Il Cimento Dell' Armonia e Dell' inventione* (c.1725) which contains the "Four Seasons".

Georg Philipp
TELEMANN
1681–1767
German composer

Georg Philipp Telemann showed talent as a musician at a very young age. He became musical director of the Leipzig Opera in Germany and organist at the *Neue Kirche* (New Church) there. In 1721, he was appointed municipal musical director in Hamburg, where he stayed until his death. Telemann was the most popular German composer of his time, and one of the most

prolific ever. His output includes operas, oratorios, cantatas and other church music, and many concertos, overtures, and pieces for chamber groups and keyboard.

Jean-Philippe
RAMEAU
1683–1764
French composer

For much of his life, Rameau worked as an organist in several French cathedrals, and at first was more of a music theorist than a composer. In 1723, he moved to Paris, where he started to compose and teach music. Although his early compositions were for harpsichord, he soon began to compose operas. In 1733, his first opera *Hippolyte et Aricie* appeared, followed by operas that included *Castor et Pollux* (1737). Although "modern", his music soon became popular.

Johann Sebastian
BACH
1685–1750
German composer

Bach came from a musical family, and probably first learnt music from his father and his uncle. He became a choir singer and organist, and from 1708 to 1717, he was court organist at Weimar, Austria, where he composed mainly organ and church music. In 1723, the deeply religious Bach became musical director of St Thomas's Church in Leipzig, Germany, where he wrote many of his finest works, such as the *B Minor Mass* (1733), *The St Matthew Passion*, and brilliant keyboard studies such as *Art of the Fugue*. Bach married twice, and several of his 20 children also became composers. Although not as popular as some of his contemporaries, Bach is now considered one of the greatest ever composers.

Domenico
SCARLATTI
1685–1757
Italian composer

Domenico Scarlatti studied music with his father, Alessandro Scarlatti, who was director of music at the court of Naples, Italy, and a composer of operas and choral music. He became organist and composer under his father in Naples, and later in Rome, but left Italy in 1720 for the royal court in Lisbon, Portugal. When the king's daughter Maria Barbara married the crown prince of Spain in 1729, Scarlatti went with her to Seville, and settled in Madrid in 1733. He wrote mainly vocal music while he was in Italy, but is most famous for the keyboard music he composed in Portugal and Spain. He wrote more than 550 sonatas for harpsichord, organ, and

1678
Titus Oates fabricates the "Popish Plot", falsely claiming that Catholics are planning to murder Charles II so his brother James can become king. As a result, Parliament tries to prevent James from inheriting the throne.

1683
The forces of the Ottoman Empire are sent to beseige Vienna. The Austrians hold out for some time and then receive assistance from King John Sobieski of Poland to throw off their attackers.

possibly the newly invented pianoforte, all of which were very short pieces that used new techniques to dazzling effect.

George Frideric HANDEL
1685–1759
German/English composer

While studying law at Halle University in Germany, Handel became organist at the cathedral and switched his career to music. His opera *Rinaldo* was performed in 1711 in London, where he decided to settle. He enjoyed success in England as the composer of operas such as *Acis and Galatea* (1718), and also of orchestral pieces such as the *Water Music* (1717) and *Music for the Royal*

Fireworks (1749). Possibly his greatest work is the oratorio *Messiah* (1742), which includes the "Hallelujah Chorus".

Daniel FAHRENHEIT
1686–1736
German physicist

Instrument-maker Fahrenheit produced meteorological instruments for studying the weather. He also invented an alcohol thermometer in 1709, and a mercury thermometer in 1714. He was the first person to demonstrate that the boiling point of liquids varies at different atmospheric pressures, and used this as a principle for the construction of barometers. Fahrenheit also discovered that water can remain liquid below

its freezing point. His most famous invention remains the Fahrenheit scale for measuring temperature.

John HARRISON
1693–1776
English inventor

Long-distance sea navigation was revolutionized in 1735 when Harrison invented the first accurate chronometer for keeping time at sea. This was crucial for determining location and longitude when out of sight of land. Harrison developed his chronometer to win a £20,000 competition organized by the British government. After various trials, Harrison's chronometer was awarded first prize.

William HOGARTH
1697–1764
English painter and engraver

Hogarth painted comic scenes of everyday life that were teeming with satirical detail. Trained as an engraver, he became a professional portrait painter in about 1730. Soon afterwards, he developed the idea of a linked sequence of pictures, which he used to mock the manners of the day. The most famous is *A Rake's Progress* (1735), which shows a young man's fall from riches to imprisonment and madness, and *Marriage a la Mode* (1745), which charts the decline of a selfish married couple.

François VOLTAIRE
1694–1778
French writer and philosopher

French intellectual François Voltaire was a leading figure of the Enlightenment, the 18th-century movement that stressed the value of reason. His belief in religious, political, and social liberty often brought him into conflict with the French government, and he was twice imprisoned in the Bastille in Paris, and once banished to England, for his outspoken views. Despite such setbacks, Voltaire won the admiration of leading figures throughout Europe, notably Frederick the Great (p.58). Voltaire expressed his philosophy in various works, in particular *Letters Concerning the English Nation* (1733), which stated his support for Locke (p.48) and Newton (p.50); the *Philosophical Dictionary* (1764); and the satire *Candide* (1759), whose conclusion, "Let us cultivate our garden", encouraged common sense.

BAROQUE MUSIC

The revolution in music which lasted from 1600 to the death of Johann Sebastian Bach (p.54) marked one of the most important periods in the history of music. It is known as the "Baroque" period, which means something different or strange. Baroque music is characterized by the importance of the solo, whether vocal or instrumental, the separate qualities of the melody and the bass line, and an interest in expressive music.

VOCAL FORMS
The Baroque period had an important influence on all vocal forms of music, from opera to oratorio and cantata. The first major composer of opera was CLAUDIO MONTEVERDI (p.40) whose opera *Orpheus* (1607) represents the first flowering of his genius. Frenchman JEAN BAPTISTE LULLY (p.48) was also an important composer, as were ALESSANDRO SCARLATTI (1659–1725) and FRIDERIC HANDEL (p.55).

INSTRUMENTAL FORMS
The instrumental tradition began in Italy, again with the composer MONTEVERDI who, along with ARCHANGELO CORELLI (p.52) and ANTONIO VIVALDI (p.54), created and perfected the musical forms of sonata, concerto, and overture. Other important instrumental composers include GEORG TELEMANN (p.54) and most importantly JOHANN SEBASTIAN BACH (p.54), whose organ and church music remain the most powerful Baroque music.

The Music Party *by Philippe Mercier, c.1733*

1690 The Battle of the Boyne is fought in Ireland. William III of England defeats James II and takes control of Ireland. The Treaty of Limerick promises Catholics their lands and freedom of religion, but it is not honoured.

1692 The fortune-telling games of a group of young girls in the town of Salem, in North America, escalate into a wave of witchcraft accusations. The word of the girls is taken without any evidence, and 20 people are executed as a result.

55

18th CENTURY

THE 18TH CENTURY SAW A QUEST for knowledge, as new theories about government, personal liberty, religion, and science began to develop. Enlightenment ideas inspired the American and French revolutions, the effects of which were felt well into the next century. In 1788, the British established the first colony in Australia after landing in Botany Bay.

Daniel BERNOULLI
1700–82
Swiss mathematical physicist

After studying widely in Europe, Daniel Bernoulli joined the Academy of Sciences in St Petersburg, Russia, where he taught mathematics. Aged 32, Bernoulli went to Switzerland and worked as a professor first of anatomy, then botany, then physics. He is remembered for his work *Hydrodynamica* on the properties of flowing water, which was published in 1738.

Anders CELSIUS
1701–44
Swedish astronomer and inventor

Astronomer Anders Celsius published a book on the northern lights in 1733 and, in 1740, he built an observatory in his home town of Uppsala in Sweden. After many years' research in his observatory, Celsius discovered that the Earth is slightly flatter at the North and the South Poles. Celsius is most famous, though, for the method he developed of measuring temperature. In this system, 0 degrees is the temperature at which ice melts, and 100 degrees is the temperature at which water boils. He presented his idea to the Swedish Academy of Sciences in 1742, and within a few years of his death, other scientists were using his scale.

John WESLEY
1703–91
English founder of Methodism

While at Oxford University, England, John Wesley became disillusioned with the uninspiring spiritual leadership provided by the churches of the time. In 1729, he founded the Holy Club with his brother Charles. Its members were nicknamed "Methodists", because John Wesley had drawn up a methodical system for their spiritual improvement. Forbidden to preach in churches, Wesley decided to take Christianity to the people. For more than 50 years, he rode around the country on horseback and preached the Gospel in fields. He also travelled to North America, where his teachings created a wide following. In England, Wesley inspired a great religious revival and Methodism became hugely popular, particularly among the poor.

WESLEY'S CHAPEL
Wesley preached in this chapel in London until his death in 1791.

Benjamin FRANKLIN
1706–90
US statesman and scientist

Statesman, scientist, writer, and revolutionary, Benjamin Franklin became the most famous American of the 18th century. Born in Boston, he worked as a printer and, in 1732, he published the first edition of the bestselling *Poor Richard's Almanac*. He also founded the colonies' first lending library and fire insurance companies, and conducted groundbreaking experiments in electricity. Franklin spent 18 years in Britain and France as an agent for the Pennsylvania Colony, but returned to America in 1775 as conflict with Britain approached. He signed the Declaration of Independence before returning to Europe as the new nation's chief diplomat. In this role, he led the negotiations for a military alliance with France and the peace treaty with Britain. In his later years, Franklin founded an anti-slavery society and served as a delegate to the Constitutional Convention.

Carolus LINNAEUS
1707–78
Swedish botanist

Carolus Linnaeus's love of flowers began at an early age and he was nicknamed "the little botanist" when he was only eight years old. In 1735, he published his first major work, *Systema Naturae*, in which he set out a new system for the way plants were named and identified. The system of plant classification that he devised was binomial, that is, it had two parts. For example, the scientific name for the sunflower is *Helianthemum annuus*. The first part identifies the genus, or group of species, to which the sunflower belongs, and the second part identifies its particular species, or type. Linnaeus's method was much simpler than the scientific names of his day, which included as many as 10 words. At a time when explorers and botanists were continually discovering new plant species, this new classification system proved invaluable. It is still used by botanists today.

Leonhard EULER
1707–83
Swiss mathematician

In 1741, Frederick the Great (p.58) invited the brilliant mathematician Leonhard Euler to Germany to work as the director of mathematics and physics at the Berlin Academy. Euler published more than 800 books and papers on all aspects of mathematics, physics, and astronomy. Although he became completely blind, he continued to carry out research. In 1748, he published a definitive mathematical work on calculus and algebra. Euler's book remained a standard textbook for 100 years.

1701 Osei Tutu creates an army and defeats the West African state of Denkyira to whom his people pay taxes. The Asante Kingdom is born. It expands during and after Tutu's reign and takes over many neighbouring areas.

1703 Peter the Great founds the city of St Petersburg in Russia. He turns the country into a major power by reorganizing the army, church, and government according to successful European models he has observed.

QIANLONG
1710–99
Chinese emperor

In 1735, Qianlong, also called Hung-li, became emperor of China. Under his rule, the Chinese Manchu Empire reached its greatest extent, expanding northwards into Mongolia and westwards into Sinkiang and Tibet. He also established Chinese rule southwards over Nepal, Burma, and Annam (now part of Vietnam). So secure was his empire that, in 1757, Qianlong restricted all foreign traders to Canton. He refused to expand trade and would not establish diplomatic relations with the powerful British Empire. At home, he supported major agricultural and industrial developments which made China increasingly prosperous. The population grew quickly and millions moved from the country into the new towns, causing great social tension. His final years were marked by inefficient administration and widespread corruption. He abdicated in 1796, three years before his death. For most of his reign, though, Qianlong brought peace and prosperity to his vast empire.

David HUME
1711–76
Scottish philosopher

Philosopher David Hume was born and educated in Edinburgh, Scotland. During his lifetime, he was famous as a historian and author of the *History of England* (5 vols, 1754–62). He worked for the government as a military attaché, civil servant, and diplomat. While posted in Paris in 1763, Hume met and became friends with Swiss philosopher Jean-Jacques Rousseau. Hume's works form an important part of the British tradition of empiricism. The empiricists believed that experience rather than human reasoning was the basis of knowledge. Hume expressed his ideas in his ambitious first book, *A Treatise of Human Nature* (3 vols, 1739–40). Hume also attacked Rousseau's idea of the social contract. Hume argued that most people were constrained by culture, language, and habit to stay as they were, regardless of their government.

Jean-Jacques ROUSSEAU
1712–78
Swiss philosopher

In 1728, Jean-Jacques Rousseau left his home in Geneva, Switzerland, and travelled to Italy, where he converted to Catholicism. He then went to France, where he worked as a musician, as well as devoting himself to philosophy. In his most important book, *A Treatise on the Social Contract* (1762), Rousseau tries to imagine an ideal society where everyone has a responsibility to each other. He stated "Man is born free, and everywhere he is in chains", meaning that people are naturally good, but that they are exploited in most societies. Rousseau proposed that people should live by a "social contract" between all members of society for the common good. Thus, Rousseau rejected John Locke's (p.48) version of the social contract which was more concerned with the rights of the individual. Rousseau's ideas had a profound effect on the French Revolution.

FREDERICK THE GREAT *was an enlightened ruler, who turned Prussia into a powerful state.*

Frederick the GREAT
1712–86
Prussian king

Frederick II of Prussia turned his north German kingdom into one of the most powerful states in Europe. Throughout his reign he was often at war, exchanging enemies and allies in quick succession. However, he always managed to ensure that Prussia came out on top. By 1772, he had partitioned Poland with Russia and Austria, and extended Prussian power across northern Germany. At home, he exercised absolute power, but he also introduced many economic and social reforms, abolished torture, and freed the serfs (peasants who were forbidden to leave their landlord's property) on his own estates. Frederick, who became known as "the Great", was a highly cultured man who supported the arts and was a leading figure in the Enlightenment. His most influential legacy, though, was as a military commander who turned Prussia into the most important state in Germany.

1707 Following the death of Aurangzeb, the Mogul Dynasty – India's ruling group – starts to crumble after almost two centuries of power. Over the next 150 years, the Moguls lose their authority to the British.

1709 Mir Vais leads the Ghilzai people of Afghanistan against the Persian army. Following their decisive victory, the Ghilzai break away from the Persian Empire in order to establish their own state.

Cao CHAN
c.1715–63
Chinese writer

Little is known about Cao Chan's (also known as Ts'ao Hsueh-ch'in) early life, other than that he came from a wealthy family whose fortunes were in decline. In 1742, he was probably writing *The Dream of the Red Chamber*. When Chan died, he had completed 80 chapters. The book – totalling 120 chapters – and now regarded as China's greatest novel, was finished by another writer, Kao Eh. *The Dream of the Red Chamber*, published in 1791, tells of the Chia clan and its changing fortunes. It covers a series of events in the lives of 30 major, and 400 minor, characters and is partly based on Cao Chan's own life.

Lancelot "Capability" BROWN
1716–83
English landscape gardener

One of the greatest gardeners of his day, Lancelot Brown received his training at Stowe House in Buckinghamshire, England. He developed a new and more natural kind of garden design, which replaced the formal French style popular at the time. Brown wanted to create landscapes that looked natural, with rolling parkland, gentle hills, clumps of trees, lakes, and winding avenues. He gained his nickname because he claimed to see the "capability" of a landscape. He worked on at least 140 English estate gardens, including Blenheim Palace, Chatsworth House, and Harewood House. Brown's landscapes, which often involved massive labour, can still be seen today.

David GARRICK
1717–79
English actor-manager and playwright

After a slow and unpromising start to his acting career, David Garrick became an overnight success with his portrayal of Shakespeare's (p.39) Richard III in 1741. He became famous for playing tragic Shakesperian parts, particularly Hamlet, Macbeth, and King Lear, although he was also talented in comedy roles. Garrick's natural, unaffected style was considered highly original, as most acting then was artificial and melodramatic. He also worked as the manager of the Drury Lane Theatre in London, and was responsible for introducing new features in costume, stage lighting, and scenery. He dominated the English stage for more than 30 years.

Maria THERESA
1717–80
Austrian empress

Heir to the mighty Austrian Empire, Maria Theresa succeeded her father to the Hapsburg throne in 1740. Charles of Bavaria challenged her right to rule, and the War of the Austrian Succession broke out. When peace was restored in 1748, Maria Theresa retained all her lands apart from Silesia. Although military conflict was renewed in the Seven Years' War from 1756, Maria Theresa kept her country in one piece. A highly competent ruler, she introduced many far-reaching reforms. She won the admiration of her subjects and ensured the strength and independence of Austria throughout the next century.

Jean d'ALEMBERT
1717–83
French philospher and mathematician

While studying law, medicine, and mathematics in Paris, France, Jean d'Alembert proved a brilliant pupil. He developed many mathematical theories, including the principle named after him. He also worked with the philosopher Denis Diderot on Diderot's famous encyclopaedia, of which d'Alembert was the scientific editor. Later, he wrote his own examination of the philosophy of the French Enlightenment, called *Discours Préliminaire* (1751). He became famous all over Europe, but chose to stay and work in Paris, refusing invitations to the courts of Frederick the Great (p.58) and Catherine the Great (p.61).

Thomas CHIPPENDALE
1718–79
English furniture maker

Thomas Chippendale designed the most sought-after furniture in Europe during the mid-18th century. Born in Yorkshire, England, he trained as a carpenter before moving to London to open his own workshop. His firm was highly successful, producing furniture for notable architects such as Robert Adam. In 1754, Chippendale published *The Gentleman and Cabinet-maker's Director*, the first English book of household furniture designs. These were in the fashionable rococo style, which was elegant and playful, with curves and decorations. He worked mainly in mahogany, and his influence spread as far as the United States. Some of his pieces survive to this day.

CHIPPENDALE FURNITURE
This George III mahogany chair is designed in the style of the English furniture maker, Thomas Chippendale.

1715 In England, James Edward, the son of James II and his second wife, Mary of Modena, makes the first of two unsuccessful attempts to regain his place on the British throne. He becomes known as the "Old Pretender".

1716 Tokugawa Yoshimune becomes Shogun in Japan. He increases the amount of land used for rice crops to avoid suffering in case of a bad harvest. In 1720, he lifts a ban on contact with Europe and the study of European books.

Adam SMITH
1723–90
Scottish economist

From 1764 to 1766, Adam Smith travelled around Europe as a tutor, and began writing his most famous work, *Inquiry into the Nature and Causes of the Wealth of Nations* (1776). At that time, Britain was a wealthy country, but it was still dominated by old-fashioned aristocratic privileges and monopoly practices. Smith believed that these habits held back enterprise and economic progress. He proposed an open economy where the market itself dictated the value of both the price of goods and of labour and ensured a balance between the two. Smith's concept of the free market and arguments against government intervention in commerce had a profound effect on the science of economics.

Immanuel KANT
1724–1804
German philosopher

Immanuel Kant was one of Europe's most important philosophers. He wrote many books, notably *Critique of Pure Reason* (1781), which had a profound effect on the development of western thought. Kant was born in Königsberg, Prussia, where he lived all his life, becoming professor of logic and metaphysics at the university there. He became one of the deepest and most systematic thinkers of the Enlightenment (a movement that stressed the importance of reason and questioned existing ideas) and argued against the empiricism of David Hume (p.58) and the English philosophers. Kant believed that to understand the world, human beings have to use both their reason and their senses. Observations of the world take place in time and space, and Kant called our knowledge of these two forms "intuition". He stated that intuition is innate to all human beings and affects the way we experience things. Therefore, we can only ever know things as they appear to us and never have true knowledge of things "in themselves".

1725

Robert CLIVE
1725–74
Founder of the British Empire in India

Robert Clive is better known as "Clive of India" for his role in securing British colonial rule over the subcontinent. He rose to fame in 1751 when, with just a handful of soldiers, he held the town of Arcot against an assault by a large French-Indian army. In 1757, Clive was called upon to avenge the "Black Hole of Calcutta" incident. He recaptured Calcutta from the Nawab of Bengal, defeating 50,000 enemy troops with a mere 3,200 soldiers at Plassey. Clive went on to rule Bengal, India's richest province, on behalf of the British East India Company. In 1762, Clive was made Baron Clive of Plassey in recognition of his achievements, but in 1767, he was criticized in parliament for his handling of the East India Company's affairs. Although he was eventually cleared, Clive committed suicide in 1774.

CAPTAIN COOK'S SEXTANT
The English explorer used this navigational tool on his third Pacific voyage. It accurately measured the ship's latitude.

1720 The "South Sea Bubble" bursts, leaving many British speculators financially ruined. Investors risked fortunes on stock in overseas enterprises, which had been sold at inflated prices. Even the British government is affected.

1726 The tutor of young Louis XV, Cardinal Fleury, begins a 17-year period governing France following ten years of unstable regency rule. Louis takes over government from Fleury, who is in his 70s, as soon as he is of age.

James WOLFE
1727–59
English general

During the Seven Years' War (1756–63), James Wolfe commanded the British forces sent to Canada to defeat the French. Wolfe played a significant part in the siege of the French stronghold of Louisbourg in 1758. When Britain started to concentrate on removing the French from Canada, Wolfe conducted several attacks on the French general Montcalm in Québec. He found the French stronghold impenetrable until he led his army in a surprise attack on the Plains of Abraham above the city. After a short struggle, the French surrendered. Both Montcalm and Wolfe were killed, but Wolfe knew Québec had fallen – and Canada would now be a British, rather than a French, colony.

Thomas GAINSBOROUGH
1727–88
English painter

Thomas Gainsborough began his career as a portrait painter in Suffolk, England. His first masterpiece was *Mr and Mrs Andrews* (1749). In 1760, he moved to the fashionable city of Bath, where he quickly gained fame for his portraits of wealthy visitors. One of the best-known pictures from this period is *The Blue Boy* (1770). Gainsborough moved permanently to London in 1774. His success with portraits allowed him time for painting landscapes, which he preferred. He was one of the first British artists to paint realistic landscapes, rather than the ornate, imaginary ones of contemporary Italian art.

James COOK
1728–79
English explorer

Born in Yorkshire, England, James Cook joined the Royal Navy at 27. In 1768, aged 40, he was given command of the *Endeavour* and sent on a scientific mission to the South Pacific. He sailed to Tahiti and then to New Zealand, where he made the first map of New Zealand's coastline. The expedition continued to the east coast of Australia, which Cook claimed for Britain and named New South Wales. On his second voyage in 1772, Cook made the first crossing into the icy seas of Antarctica. Cook made a third Pacific voyage, in 1776, exploring the coasts of North America and Hawaii. He was killed in Hawaii by the islanders while trying to recover a stolen boat.

Catherine the GREAT
1729–96
Russian empress

In 1745, Catherine married the heir to the Russian throne. Her husband became Tsar Peter III in 1762, but within months, she overthrew her husband and was proclaimed tsarina (empress) in her own right. An energetic and resourceful leader, she extended Russian power south to the Black Sea and ended the independence of Poland to the west. At home, she developed industry and trade, reformed local government, and encouraged education, particularly among women. In continuing the work of Peter the Great (p.53), she did much to transform Russia into a powerful European country.

Louis-Antoine de BOUGAINVILLE
1729–1811
French explorer, soldier, and scientist

Antoine de Bougainville made the first French voyage around the world in 1766. He crossed the Pacific and became the second European explorer to visit Tahiti. Bougainville wrote a popular book about his journey, *Voyage around the World* (1771). His description of Tahiti led French missionaries and settlers to travel there in the 19th century, and France ruled the island from 1880. He gave his name to the plant genus, *Bougainvillea*, and to the island of Bougainville in the southwest Pacific.

Josiah WEDGWOOD
1730–95
English potter

Josiah Wedgwood was a key figure in the development of Britain's Industrial Revolution. He was born into a family of potters and after serving a long apprenticeship, he became a master potter in 1759. He founded his own business in Staffordshire, England, and ten years later, he opened the brand-new Etruria Works with his partner Thomas Bentley. Built in the countryside near Stoke-on-Trent, his new factory had a special village beside it to house the workforce. Wedgwood's organizational skills made it possible to mass-produce inexpensive earthenware pottery which most people could afford. He made his products tougher by using a newly discovered type of china clay from Cornwall. He also developed "Jasper Ware", a high-quality stoneware with classical designs in blue and green. Wedgwood china is now famous throughout the world.

WEDGWOOD CHINA
This cup is a fine example of the "Jasper Ware" range.

1727 The sugar industry in Brazil almost collapses when diamonds are discovered in central Brazil and people abandon the plantations in search of the precious stones. Native Americans and Africans labour as slaves in the mines.

1730 Danish explorer Vitus Bering is sent by Russian tsar Peter the Great to explore the entire Arctic coast of Siberia. He reaches the strait between Asia and North America, which is later named in his honour.

Henry CAVENDISH
1731–1810
English physicist and chemist

Born into an aristocratic English family in Nice, France, Henry Cavendish became one of the greatest scientists of his age. After university, he travelled in Europe before returning to London where he and his father devoted years to scientific research. In 1766, he discovered that air is made up of hydrogen and carbon dioxide and not a single element, as was commonly thought. He later demonstrated, in 1784, how hydrogen and oxygen combine to make water, and discovered nitric acid. In 1798, he performed the first "Cavendish experiment" which accurately measured the density of the Earth. He also carried out electrical experiments that anticipated many important discoveries. His work on electricity was not discovered and published until 1879.

Richard ARKWRIGHT
1732–92
English inventor

Richard Arkwright invented a mechanical spinning frame which played an important role in the early Industrial Revolution. Born in Lancashire, England, he began life as a barber, but his thirst for education led him into industry. In 1764, he began the construction of his first machine. The spinning frame was powered by water and produced a strong cotton yarn. Its success led Arkwright to open several factories using his new machinery which was very efficient. Some opposed this and, in 1779, one of his mills was destroyed by a mob of people who were fearful of losing their jobs.

ARKWRIGHT'S FLYER *worked by drawing out a thread, then twisting it as it was wound onto a spool or bobbin.*

George WASHINGTON
1732–99
1st US president

George Washington played an important part in the American War of Independence before becoming the nation's first president. Born in Virginia, which was then a British colony, he began to take an interest in politics at a time of growing unrest between Britain and its American colonies. At the outbreak of war with the British, he was chosen as commander-in-chief of the Continental Army. After hard-fought campaigns, and with the assistance of French allies, Washington forced the British army to surrender at the Battle of Yorktown in 1781. After a peace treaty was signed (1783), he retired to Mount Vernon, his Virginia plantation. In 1787, Washington presided over the Constitutional Convention, and two years later he was elected president of the United States. He was re-elected in 1793 and retired for good at the end of his second term. Washington's firm leadership, both military and political, was crucial to the establishment of the United States.

(Franz) Joseph HAYDN
1732–1809
Austrian composer

Born in Rohrau, Austria, Joseph Haydn was the first great Viennese classical composer. Educated at St Stephen's Cathedral Choir School in Vienna, Haydn worked as a freelance musician, teacher, and musical director. Then, in 1761, he went to work for Prince Esterházy, becoming musical director at the palace of Esterháza in 1766. He remained in the family's service for the rest of his life, composing and performing music for the palace. He wrote operas, church music, sonatas for piano, and chamber music, but is best known for his many string quartets and 104 symphonies – forms he helped to establish. Among Haydn's greatest works were the "London" Symphonies, *The Creation* (1798), and *The Seasons* (1801).

1733 The War of Polish Succession (1733–35) sees France and Sweden defeated by Russia and Austria. Europe soon suffers a second war of succession in 1740, when Frederick the Great of Prussia attacks Silesia.

1733 Georgia, the last of the 13 British colonies in North America, is founded. By the 1740s, the collective population of the colonies totals 1.5 million people, including 250,000 African-American slaves.

Joseph
PRIESTLEY
1733–1804
**English clergyman
and chemist**

Although he was a church minister, Joseph Priestley was a pioneer in the chemistry of gases. His family did not conform to the Church of England, and Priestley was sent to a Non-Conformist church academy, which offered a very broad education. In London, Priestley met Benjamin Franklin (p.57), who further aroused his interest in science. He worked on electrical experiments, but is best-known for identifying oxygen in 1774 and later isolating gaseous ammonia. He also invented soda water, using carbon dioxide. After accusations of atheism Priestley moved to America in 1794, where he lived until his death.

Daniel
BOONE
1735–1820
US pioneer

Daniel Boone was a hunter and trapper who opened Kentucky to settlement. In 1759, he was hired by the government to explore the land beyond the Appalachian Mountains, carve a route through the Cumberland Gap, and escort settlers to three settlements. Boone carried out his mission successfully, in spite of fierce opposition from the Native Americans in the area – he fended off repeated attacks and was captured twice, becoming a hero in the process. Boone founded Boonesborough on the Kentucky River and paved the way for the first westward migration of settlers from the east coast of what is now the United States.

John
ADAMS
1735–1826
2nd US president

Born in Massachusetts, John Adams graduated from Harvard College and was a rising young lawyer when he became involved in the Patriot cause. Conservative by nature, he nonetheless supported American independence, serving as a delegate to the Continental Congress and on the committee that drafted the Declaration of Independence. After a decade in Europe on diplomatic missions, he returned to the United States in 1788 to serve as George Washington's vice-president. In 1796, Adams was elected president, but his office saw domestic unrest, near-war with France, and bitter conflict with Thomas Jefferson (p.66), who succeeded him as president.

Charles
COULOMB
1736–1806
**French physicist
and engineer**

Born to wealthy parents in Angoulême, France, Charles Coulomb discovered many of the laws of magnetic attraction. After training as a military engineer and serving in the army, Coulomb devoted himself to the study of physics. During the French Revolution he fled Paris, but returned under Napoleon's (p.71) rule and was appointed Inspector-General of Public Instruction (1802–06). Coulomb is primarily remembered, though, for his work on the forces between positive and negative electric charges and magnetic poles. He devised sensitive instruments for measuring these forces, and the coulomb (symbol C), the unit of electric charge, was named in his honour.

AMERICAN WAR OF INDEPENDENCE

In 1783, a new nation – the United States of America – was born. After eight years of struggle, the 13 former British colonies became the first country in the world to break away from European colonial rule.

THE ROAD TO REVOLUTION
From the 1750s on, many colonial leaders felt it was unfair that the colonies had to pay taxes to Britain without any representation in parliament. After protesters dumped tea into Boston Harbour in 1773, troops occupied Boston and relations between Britain and the colonists grew strained. In April 1775, war broke out.

INDEPENDENCE
Delegates from the 13 colonies formed the Continental Congress and, in July 1776, adopted the Declaration of Independence drafted by THOMAS JEFFERSON (p.66). It took five years, many battles, and help from France and Spain before commander-in-chief GEORGE WASHINGTON decisively defeated the British army at Yorktown, Virginia.

American and British infantrymen.

Count Joseph Louis
LAGRANGE
1736–1813
French mathematician

The work of Joseph Lagrange was a major step in the early development of mathematical group theory. He was born in Turin, Italy of French parents and, as a young man, was much influenced by Edmond Halley (p.52), the English astronomer. Lagrange taught mathematics and published studies on astronomy and the nature of sound. Later, as director of the Academy of Berlin, he pursued his interest in number theory and the movements of the planets. Lagrange returned to Paris in 1787 and reformed the metric system. After the French Revolution, he was made Count of the Empire by Napoleon (p.71) in recognition of his work.

1736 The emperor Qianlong begins his reign over China. During his rule, Manchu China reaches the height of its power, destroying Mongol power, incorporating Turkestan, and forcing Nepal to accept Chinese rule.

1736 The great military leader Nadir Shah becomes shah of Persia and conquers Afghanistan. He also captures Kabul, Lahore, and Peshawar and finally sacks Delhi. Following his assassination in 1747, Persia loses Afghanistan.

James WATT
1736–1819
Scottish engineer/inventor

Scottish engineer James Watt made one of the major breakthroughs of the Industrial Revolution when he developed a new, and much improved steam engine. Watt began his working life as a mathematical instrument maker to the University of Glasgow in Scotland and opened a shop there in 1757. In 1764, while repairing a model of Newcomen's (p.53) steam engine, he discovered a way of making it three times more efficient by saving the water formed by condensation of the steam in a separate cylinder. He entered into partnership with Matthew Boulton in 1774 to produce the new engine. In 1781, Watt invented the sun-and-planet gear, a cog system that doubled the cycle of the engine. He went on to make many other improvements, obtained a patent for a smokeless furnace, and coined the term "horsepower". The modern unit of measure for power – the watt – is named after him.

Luigi GALVANI
1737–98
Italian scientist

Luigi Galvani was the first person to propose that animal tissues generate electricity. He was born in Bologna, Italy, and became a lecturer of anatomy in 1768, although he spent much of his career studying electricity. After observing dead frogs having convulsions while drying on an iron fence, Galvani surmised that animal muscles generate electrical charges. Alessandro Volta (p.66) later proved Galvani's ideas wrong, but Galvani's work stimulated research into electric currents. His name is remembered in many electrical terms, in particular the galvanometer, which is used to detect electric current, and the word "galvanized", which means to be spurred into action as if by an electric shock.

Thomas PAINE
1737–1809
English revolutionary

The radical Anglo-American political theorist Thomas Paine did much to advance the cause of liberty in both the United States and France. Paine was born in Norfolk, England, and became a customs officer. But in 1772, he was dismissed for agitating for higher salaries and emigrated to America. There he became involved in clashes between the colonists and the British government. In 1776, he published a pamphlet entitled *Common Sense*, which argued for the independence of the 13 colonies. From 1776 to 1783, he wrote a series of 18 pamphlets called *The Crisis*, which did much to encourage the colonists in their successful fight for independence. In 1787, he returned to England, and wrote his famous work *The Rights of Man* (1791–92) in defence of the French Revolution. *The Rights of Man*, which sold more than 250,000 copies in two years, argued that there are natural rights common to all people and that only democratic institutions can guarantee those rights. In 1792, Paine was prosecuted for treason. He fled first to France, where he became a member of the National Convention, and then to the United States, where he was shunned for his uncompromising atheism (disbelief in God).

GEORGE III
1738–1820
British king

The reign of George III witnessed a great expansion of the British Empire, the beginning of the Industrial Revolution, and the loss of the 13 British colonies in North America. He was born in London,

GEORGE III *ruled for 60 years, making him the second longest-reigning British monarch.*

1739 Encouraged by merchants and landowners, Britain goes to war with Spain. The War of Jenkins' Ear is fought over who controls the Caribbean and North America, where pirates often raid merchant ships.

1740 Central Africa is dominated by the Luba and Lunda peoples. The Lunda are particularly successful at sending out expeditions and setting up satellite, tribute-paying kingdoms.

and succeeded his grandfather George II as king of Great Britain and Ireland, and elector of Hanover, in Germany. As he was the first British monarch since 1714 to be born and raised in England, he wanted to be a good and fair ruler. He tried to rule by constitutional means, but his choice of prime ministers was sometimes ill-advised. His first minister, Lord Bute, had to be protected by bodyguards, while Lord North lost the American War of Independence. Yet George became a popular king, widely admired for his sense of duty and integrity. In 1788, he suffered an attack of porphyria, a disease which made him appear insane, and by 1811, he was incapable of ruling. Despite this misfortune, George created a role for the British monarchy which ensured that it survived the many changes of the times.

William & Caroline
HERSCHEL
William 1738–1822
Caroline 1750–1848
German-born British astronomers

William and Caroline Herschel were born in Hanover, Germany, but were members of a distinguished family of English astronomers. When William went to England in 1755 to pursue a musical career, Caroline accompanied him as his assistant. They settled in Bath in 1766, where their interests turned to astronomy. The high cost of telescopes led William to build his own. In 1781, William discovered the first planet to be found by telescope – Uranus – and in 1782, he was made private astronomer to George III. William's main studies were concerned with the stars and nebulae (clouds of

dust and gas in between stars). He spent the rest of his life examining the night sky using ever bigger telescopes. Caroline discovered, among other things, eight comets. After William's death she returned to Germany, and reorganized his catalogue of the nebulae.

Joseph & Jacques
MONTGOLFIER
Joseph Michel 1740–1810
Jacques Étienne 1745–99
French balloonists

Born near Lyons, France, Jacques and Joseph Montgolfier are famed for their invention of the first balloons capable of flight. They came from a family of 16 and their father ran a paper factory, in which both Joseph and Jacques worked. In June 1783, using heated air collected inside a large lightweight bag, the brothers oversaw the world's first manned balloon flight. They heated the air by burning straw, wool, and paper directly under the balloon, which rose 1000 metres (300 ft), sinking to the Earth after 10 minutes. By November, they had refined the experiment enough to carry two passengers 9 km (5.5 miles) over Paris. It was the first untethered balloon flight and made the brothers famous.

Karl Wilhelm
SCHEELE
1742–86
Swedish chemist

Karl Wilhelm Scheele was born in Stralsund (now in Germany). After settling in Köping, he started his own pharmacy. Scheele discovered oxygen, though his published

THE MONTGOLFIER BROTHERS *made aviation history in November 1783 when their hot-air balloon rose majestically into the skies above Paris with two passengers on board.*

account appeared after that of Joseph Priestley (p.63). Publication delays may have robbed Scheele of the glory of the discovery of oxygen, but he identified many other substances, including chlorine and hydrogen sulphide.

Antoine-Laurent
LAVOISIER
1743–94
French chemist

Antoine-Laurent Lavoisier has been called "the father of modern chemistry". He was born in Paris, France, and followed his father into the legal profession. But Lavoisier was fascinated by scientific problems and, while practising law, he worked on methods of providing light for towns. In 1768, he became a tax-collection official. This allowed him to indulge his interest in science, which Lavoisier hoped would improve French social and economic conditions. His achievements included improvements to gunpowder and agriculture. Lavoisier also proved that combustion needs only a part of the air, which he called oxygen. He wrote down his findings in his groundbreaking work *Treaty of Elementary Chemistry* (1789). As a tax collector, Lavoisier was later guillotined during the French Revolution.

1742 In the Kathmandu Valley, the Mallas, rulers of Nepal for 500 years, are overthrown by the Rajput leader King Prithvi Narayan Shah. The British East India Company refuses to help, and the king founds the nation of Nepal.

1742 Juan Santos takes the name Atahualpa II and leads the Native Americans of Peru in an unsuccessful revolt against the Spanish. The Peruvians revolt again in 1780, but independence is not won until 1821.

Joseph BANKS
1743–1820
English botanist

Born into a wealthy family in London, Joseph Banks gave Botany Bay in Australia its name. After receiving a large inheritance, he decided to travel and pursue his interest in botany. He went to Newfoundland and Labrador in 1766 and, two years later, he funded and accompanied Captain James Cook (p.61) on his voyage around the world. Banks developed many uses for plants and identified many diseases in crops. President of Britain's Royal Society for 41 years, he was much honoured in his lifetime.

Thomas JEFFERSON
1743–1826
3rd US president

The son of a Virginia planter, Thomas Jefferson studied law and went on to serve in Virginia's legislature. He became a delegate to the Continental Congress and was the principal author of the Declaration of Independence. Returning to Virginia as governor in 1779, he drafted a law establishing freedom of religion in the state. After serving as minister to France and as secretary of state in President George Washington's (p.62) cabinet, he became leader of the Democratic-Republicans, the faction that favoured states' rights over the authority of a strong federal government. Elected president in 1800, Jefferson made the Louisiana Purchase which doubled the size of the new nation. He was re-elected in 1804, but his second term was marred by tension with Britain and France. He retired to his estate, Monticello, in 1809.

Alessandro VOLTA
1745–1827
Italian physicist

Alessandro Volta developed the first electric battery. He became professor of physics at the Royal School in Como, Italy, in 1774, where his experiments led him to invent an "electrophorus" for generating static electricity. He went on to disprove Luigi Galvani's (p.64) ideas about animal electricity, finding that electricity is produced by the junction of two different metals rather than by animal muscle. He used this knowledge to produce the first electric battery, the voltaic pile, in 1800. The volt, a unit of electricity, is named after him.

Toussaint L'OUVERTURE
c.1746–1803
Haitian rebel slave

Pierre Toussaint's valiant life made him a symbol of the fight for liberty. He was born in Haiti in the Caribbean, then divided between France, Spain, and Britain. Though a slave, he educated himself by reading books on military history. With news of the French Revolution in 1791, the slaves rebelled and Toussaint became leader of the Haitian independence movement. Using his military knowledge, he gained his name *L'Ouverture* ("the Opening") for his skill in breaking through enemy lines. In 1793, France freed its slaves, but when that nation tried to restore rule over Haiti, Toussaint was put in prison, where he died.

THE FIRST BATTERY
Volta found that by making a "pile" of cells he increased the amount of electricity generated.

Francisco de GOYA
1746–1828
Spanish painter

Francisco de Goya was the most original painter of his age. He was born near Saragossa, Spain, and worked at the royal tapestry factory. He began painting portraits and religious subjects, and was made court painter in 1789. When he fell severely ill in 1792, Goya's work took on a more bitter, fantastical edge. His later portraits, such as the famous *Family of Charles IV* (1800), show the ugliness and vanity of the subjects. He also explored the themes of cruelty and terror, most horrifyingly in *The Disasters of War* (1810–14), a series inspired by the French invasion of Spain. After retiring in 1820, he decorated his home with even grimmer murals, now called "The Black Paintings" (1820–23).

Edward JENNER
1749–1823
English doctor

As a doctor in rural England, Edward Jenner noticed that milkmaids rarely contracted smallpox, a disease that killed and disfigured thousands, even though they often caught cowpox, a minor illness, from their cows. Jenner extracted fluid from the cowpox-infected hands of a milkmaid and injected it into the skin of eight-year-old James Phipps. The boy was later put into contact with children suffering from smallpox, but did not contract the disease. Jenner's new technique – vaccination – had made the boy immune to smallpox. It was a giant step forward in the fight against disease.

1745 Bonnie Prince Charlie, the Young Pretender, leads the second Jacobite uprising in Britain.

He fails to restore the Stuart dynasty to the British throne and is defeated at the Battle of Culloden Moor in April 1746.

1747 British forces capture the French fortress of Louisbourg in Canada as French and English rivalry

around the world escalates. . The French capture Madras in India from the British, but the British win it back in 1748.

Johann Wolfgang von GOETHE
1749–1832
German writer and statesman

Johann Wolfgang von Goethe was one of Germany's foremost writers. He was born in Frankfurt, Germany, and studied law in Leipzig, where he also began to write plays and poetry. In 1775, he went to work in the court of Charles Augustus, Duke of Saxe-Weimar, where he fell in love with Charlotte von Stein, the inspiration for much of his greatest romantic poetry. In 1808, Goethe published Part I of his masterpiece *Faust*, a dramatic poem about the legendary 16th-century scholar who sold his soul to the devil in return for knowledge and

GOETHE
Scenes from Faust *by Goethe, depicting the temptation of man.*

magical power. Goethe also developed a new German literary form, the *Bildungsroman*, or novel of character development, and wrote 14 volumes on science.

1750

James MADISON
1751–1836
4th US President

James Madison was responsible for drafting much of the Constitution of the United States (1787) and the Bill of Rights (1789), a role that earned him the name "Father of the Constitution". He succeeded Thomas Jefferson (p.66) as president in 1809 and was re-elected in 1812, but his second term was clouded by an unpopular war with Britain (1812–14). He retired to his farm in Virginia in 1817, where he spent his last years writing his *Advice to My Country*.

John NASH
1752–1835
English architect

John Nash's "Regency" style gave London some of its most dramatic architecture. He was born in London, and trained as an architect, setting up his first practice in Wales. For many years he designed country houses locally and in Ireland, often in partnership with the landscape gardener Humphrey Repton. His work impressed the prince regent (who later became King George IV). In 1811, the prince hired Nash to redesign London's West End. This huge scheme included Regent Street and Regent's Park (1811–30), which was bordered with sweeping terraces of houses built in brick faced with stucco (a kind of plaster). Nash also remodelled Buckingham Palace, Marble Arch, and later the Royal Pavilion in Brighton (1818–21).

MILESTONES IN MEDICINE

In the last 500 years, a number of important scientific discoveries revolutionized medicine. Before then, medicine was a mixture of folklore and superstition. Human dissections were not permitted until the 16th century, so little was known about the structure and workings of the body.

MEDICAL PIONEERS
In 1543, ANDREAS VESALIUS (p.33) published *On The Structure of the Human Body* based on actual dissections of human bodies. It was the first great anatomical work and paved the way for further medical advances. In 1628, English doctor WILLIAM HARVEY (p.41) also used experimentation to develop the first accurate theory of circulation. One of the greatest medical discoveries was made by EDWARD JENNER (p.66) in 1796 when he developed the technique of smallpox vaccination. Vaccines were subsequently produced for many life-threatening illnesses, including whooping-cough,

Jenner performs the first vaccination.

polio, and measles. Much later, in 1928, Scottish researcher ALEXANDER FLEMING (p.147) noticed that a fungus called *Penicillium* killed certain bacteria. His finding led to the development of antibiotic drugs, which cure infections by killing the bacteria that cause them. Large-scale production of penicillin since World War II has saved millions of lives.

LOUIS XVI
1754–93
French king

Louis XVI succeeded to the French throne in 1774, but he proved a weak king who failed to support those ministers who attempted to reform the crumbling French state. As France approached bankruptcy, Louis was forced to recall the *Estates-Général* in 1789 to raise taxes – the first time the French parliament had been called for 175 years. He refused to accept the many demands for reform, however, and was soon swept away by the tide of the French Revolution. The monarchy was abolished in 1792, and Louis was found guilty of conspiracy with foreign powers. As a result, he was beheaded on the guillotine as was his hated queen, Marie Antoinette.

1750 Sebastian de Carvalho (later Marquis of Pombal) is appointed to high office by Portugal's King Jose. In 1756, he is made prime minister and becomes perhaps the greatest statesman of modern Portuguese history.

1754 The colony of Virginia in North America feels threatened by a French fort on the Ohio River. Young George Washington leads a small force to capture the fort, but the following year the French take many British outposts.

MOZART
The Austrian composer was a brilliant pianist and violinist, and wrote many concertos in which he played the solo part himself.

Wolfgang Amadeus MOZART
1756–91
Austrian composer

A musical child prodigy, Wolfgang Amadeus Mozart went on to become the most popular composer of the 18th century. Born in Salzburg in Austria, Mozart was playing the harpsichord by the age of four, and he composed his first pieces at the age of five. His father recognized his musical genius and took the young Mozart on a tour of Europe to show off his talents. By the time he returned to Salzburg in 1773, Mozart had written 30 symphonies, four Masses, and two full-scale operas. He worked for the Archbishop of Salzburg (1774–81), then moved to Vienna, making his name with his piano concertos and operas. In the five years before his death Mozart produced the operas *Idomeneo* (1781), *The Abduction from the Seraglio* (1782), *The Marriage of Figaro* (1786), *Don Giovanni* (1787), *Così fan tutte* (1790), and *The Magic Flute* (1791), and symphonies 38–41. His final work, and one of his most ambitious, *Requiem* mass, was unfinished when he died.

John Loudon McADAM
1756–1836
Scottish roadmaker

John McAdam revolutionized road-making in Britain. At the age of 14, McAdam went to live with his merchant uncle in New York. Thirteen years later he returned a rich man and, at his own expense, set about improving the poor Scottish roads. McAdam tried many experiments in road-making, including raising the road to improve drainage, and building roads from layers of crushed, compacted rock. His methods were sanctioned by the government and, in 1815, he "macadamized" roads in Bristol, England. It was a great improvement and, by 1827 he was surveyor general of metropolitan roads in Great Britain. The word "tarmac" comes from the application of tar to a "macadamized" road.

William BLAKE
1757–1827
English poet, artist, and visionary

William Blake was an inspired poet and artist. He was born in London, and although he did not go to school, by the age of 10 he knew he wanted to be an artist. At 15, he was apprenticed to an engraver and later trained at the new Royal Academy of Arts in London. Blake composed deceptively simple poems which often had deeper meanings. Much of his work was illustrated with his own, highly original, hand-coloured engravings. Blake believed that imagination was one of the most important human qualities and also that God should be experienced personally, and not through the Church. He had powerful visions throughout his life, many of which inspired his art and poetry. Blake's best-known poems are *The Tyger* and *Jerusalem*, and his famous collections are *Songs of Innocence* (1789), *The Marriage of Heaven and Hell* (1793), and *Songs of Experience* (1794).

Thomas TELFORD
1757–1834
Scottish civil engineer

The bridges and canals of Thomas Telford changed the face of 18th-century Britain. Born in Scotland, Telford trained as a stonemason, but taught himself to be an architect. By 1786, he was surveyor of public works in Shropshire, working mainly on bridge construction. He built three bridges over the River Severn and two aqueducts which transported water and boats over the Ceiriog and Dee valleys in Wales. Telford went on to build over 1,450 km (900 miles) of roads, the Caledonian Canal, and two suspension bridges supported by cables over the River Conwy and the Menai Straits in Wales. He also built the Göta Canal in Sweden, the Harecastle Tunnel in Staffordshire, and St Katharine's Docks in London.

Maximilien de ROBESPIERRE
1758–94
French revolutionary leader

Maximilien de Robespierre led a movement that helped overthrow the French monarchy and form a republic. Born in the French town of Arras, Robespierre became a successful lawyer in Paris, and was elected to the *Estates-Général* (parliament) in 1789. Influenced by the writings of Rousseau (p.58), Robespierre demanded equality for all, and the right of people to govern themselves. He became a leader of the Jacobins, a political group influential in the French Revolution. After Louis XVI (p.67) was executed in 1793, Robespierre was elected to the Committee of Public Safety, which made him the most powerful man in

1756 Indian leader Suraj-ud-Daulah attacks a British trading station in Bengal. When 145 men surrender, they are imprisoned in a single tiny cell. By morning 123 are dead. The incident is known as the Black Hole of Calcutta.

1756 The Marquis of Pombal is made prime minister in Portugal a year after a massive earthquake devastates Lisbon. Pombal restructures Portugal and rebuilds the capital using wealth from the Portuguese colony of Brazil.

France. He was nicknamed "the Incorruptible", and his campaign against anyone who opposed the Revolution led to the Reign of Terror (1793–94), in which more than 17,000 people were put to death. This period of bloodshed turned many against him. In July 1794, Robespierre was guillotined. Though a cold and fanatical leader, he was also a dedicated French patriot.

Horatio NELSON
1758–1805
British admiral

Admiral Horatio Nelson led many successful naval campaigns for Britain and became a national hero. He joined the British navy in 1770, was on constant active service in the Mediterranean from 1793 to 1800, and lost an arm and the sight in one eye in battle. He was made a vice admiral in 1801 and sent to battle with the Danish. He was largely responsible for the British victory at Copenhagen and for negotiating peace with Denmark. In 1803, Nelson was made commander in the Mediterranean and for two years, he maintained a naval blockade of Toulon in southern France. In 1805, he defeated the combined French and Spanish fleets off Cape Trafalgar, making Britain safe from invasion. At the moment of victory, he was wounded by a bullet and died on board his ship, the *Victory*.

James MONROE
1758–1831
5th US president

With his famous Monroe Doctrine, President James Monroe ended European colonization of the Americas. He served in the American War of Independence and in 1790, became a US senator. Monroe was a US minister to France from 1794–96, and he later returned to France to help negotiate the Louisiana Purchase in 1803. The next four years were spent acting in diplomatic roles between the United States, Britain, and Spain. He was elected president in 1816 and his stable administration was known as "the era of good feeling". He signed the Missouri Compromise of 1820, and recognized the Spanish American republics in Central and South America. However, he is best remembered for proclaiming the Monroe Doctrine of 1823 which states: "the American Continents… are henceforth not to be considered as subjects for colonization by any European power."

Robert BURNS
1759–96
Scottish poet and songwriter

Robert Burns is Scotland's national poet. Born in Ayrshire, the son of a farmer, Burns' earliest influences were the countryside and its people. When his father died in 1784, he took over the family farm, but was an unsuccessful farmer. The following year he began writing poems, including *The Address to a Mouse*. In 1786, the publication of *Poems, chiefly in the Scottish Dialect* including *The Twa Dogs*, *To a Louse*, and *Address to a Haggis*, made Burns famous. He also wrote the narrative poem *Tam o' Shanter* and many songs, including *Auld Lang Syne*. In Scotland, his birth is celebrated every 25 January on Burns Night.

Mary WOLLSTONECRAFT
1759–97
English feminist and writer

Mary Wollstonecraft was an early campaigner for women's rights. Born in London, England, she spent her early working life as a teacher and French translator. She became involved with a political reform group called the English Jacobins, which included Thomas Paine (p.64), William Blake (p.68), and William Godwin. In 1792, she moved to Paris to see the French Revolution for herself. The same year she wrote *Vindication of the Rights of Women*, in which she called for equal opportunities for women in education and society. At the time, her ideas were shocking to many, but the book is now an early feminist classic. Wollstonecraft married William Godwin in 1797, but died after giving birth to her daughter, Mary (Shelley p.85).

THE FRENCH REVOLUTION

In 1789, revolution broke out in France. The government of Louis XVI (p.67) was swept away and a republic was established based on the ideals of "liberty, equality, and fraternity" of all citizens. The revolution transformed French society, and inspired both fear and admiration throughout the rest of Europe.

THE CAUSES
Three major wars since 1740 had left the French economy in ruins. King Louis XVI also ruled the country without a parliament, levying high taxes on the poor while the rich paid no taxes at all. Discontent erupted when Louis summoned the French parliament, the *Estates-Général*, for the first time in 175 years, to raise more money. On 14 July 1789, Parisians stormed the hated Bastille prison, triggering the revolution.

THE NEW GOVERNMENT
The *Estates-Général* then took control of France. It turned itself into a new form of government known as the National Assembly. It agreed a democratic constitution and drew up a Declaration of the Rights of Man, based on freedom and equality for all. In 1792, France became a republic and, in 1793, the former king and his extravagant and hated wife Marie Antoinette (1755–93) were executed. At first, leaders such as Georges Danton (1759–94) attempted a moderate course, but political extremists led by Maximilien Robespierre (p.68) took control in 1793. In what became known as the Reign of Terror, they executed all opponents by guillotine.

INTERNATIONAL IMPACT
The French Revolution drew on many of the ideals of the American War of Independence (1775–83) against Britain, and in turn inspired revolutionary movements throughout Europe. In France itself, however, the warring revolutionaries were unable to unite the country, and in 1799 Napoleon Bonaparte (p.71) seized power and ended the revolution.

1757 In India, Robert Clive defeats the Nawab of Bengal at the Battle of Plassey. This brings Bengal under the control of the British East India Company. Acting on their behalf, Clive takes over sole governorship of Bengal.

1757 Frederick II of Prussia defeats combined French and Austrian troops at Rossbach. After the war, Frederick decides to concentrate on domestic affairs. He grants people religious freedom and also abolishes torture.

William PITT THE YOUNGER
1759–1806
English prime minister

At the age of 24, William Pitt the Younger became Britain's youngest ever prime minister. After graduating from Cambridge University, Pitt entered parliament in 1781. By 23, he was already chancellor of the exchequer and, in 1783, with the help of the Tories, he became prime minister. His Act of Union in 1800 united Ireland with Britain, but in 1801, Pitt resigned when the king failed to grant Catholics political rights. The threat of invasion by Napoleon in 1803 persuaded him to return to office. He forged an alliance with Russia, Austria, and Sweden and, in 1805, the alliance defeated the French.

William WILBERFORCE
1759–1833
British politician and philanthropist

William Wilberforce was influential in ending slavery in Britain. The son of a wealthy merchant, at the age of 21, Wilberforce became an MP but, although a close friend of Pitt the Younger, he remained politically independent. In 1784, while touring Europe, Wilberforce became an Evangelical Christian. In 1788, he embarked on a 19-year struggle to abolish the slave trade. His determination to end this particular form of human suffering led to the abolition of slavery in the British West Indies in 1807. Wilberforce continued to fight for total abolition, but was forced to retire due to ill health in 1825. He died a month before his Abolition of Slavery bill was passed by parliament.

Alexander MACKENZIE
1764–1820
Scottish-Canadian explorer

Alexander Mackenzie was the first person recorded to have crossed the continent of America north of Mexico. Mackenzie emigrated with his father from Scotland to Canada and joined a fur trading company before setting off to look for a waterway to the Pacific. In 1789, he travelled to Canada's Great Slave Lake and found a river heading west. He followed its course, but was disappointed when he discovered that it flowed north into the Arctic ocean, rather than to the Pacific ocean. It is now called Mackenzie River, although the explorer named it the River of Disappointment. In 1793, he tried again by following several rivers and eventually reached the Pacific, travelling part of the way over the Rocky Mountains. His expeditions helped to open up the Pacific Northwest to European settlement.

Eli WHITNEY
1765–1825
US inventor

In 1794, Eli Whitney invented the cotton gin, a machine for separating cotton fibre from its seeds. One gin could produce 23 kg (50 lb) of cotton per day – around 50 times the amount produced by a manual worker. The design was so simple that in spite of Whitney's patent on it, people everywhere made their own versions. By greatly increasing the profitability of cotton plantations, Whitney's invention led to the rise of the "cotton kingdom" in the southern United States.

Thomas MALTHUS
1766–1834
English demographer

The studies of population growth carried out by Thomas Malthus were the first of their kind. A clergyman by profession, in 1798, Malthus published anonymously *An Essay on the Principle of Population . . .* It argued that humans would never achieve a perfect society, as suggested by Rousseau (p.58), because population growth would always exceed food supply. He accepted that war, famine, and disease regulated population numbers, and he encouraged taking positive action – such as late marriage and "moral restraint" – to slow down the birth-rate. This viewpoint raised the important question of human intervention to balance population and resources. Malthus's ideas had a profound impact on the social policies of the time. Some argued that to provide relief to the poor merely encouraged them to have more children, which worsened the problem of over-population. Although his conclusions were controversial, Malthus was the first person to address these serious concerns.

1762 In Russia, Catherine the Great starts a 34-year reign after deposing her husband. She promotes European culture and the arts, continuing the work of Peter the Great. However, she does not abolish the feudal system of serfdom.

1763 The Treaty of Paris ends the Anglo-French Seven Years' War. The English gain almost all French territory east of the Mississippi River in North America. Britain also becomes the dominant power in India.

John DALTON
1766–1844
English chemist and meteorologist

John Dalton's studies of atoms became the basis of modern chemistry. He began earning his living as a teacher from the age of 12, when he started instructing pupils at his local school. In 1793, he went to New College in Manchester, England, to teach science, and he later became a lecturer at the Royal Institute in London. His interest in meteorology inspired him to investigate the nature of air and other gaseous mixtures. This, in turn, led to his atomic theory of matter, in which he suggested that every chemical element consists of small particles called atoms. The idea of atoms was not new, but Dalton claimed that all atoms of an element are identical and unique to that element. He proposed that atoms of different elements could join up to form chemical compounds. Dalton's ideas changed the face of science.

ELEMENTS

	Wt.		Wt.
Hydrogen	1	Strontian	46
Azote	5	Barytes	68
Carbon	54	Iron	50
Oxygen	7	Zinc	56
Phosphorus	9	Copper	56
Sulphur	13	Lead	90
Magnesia	20	Silver	190
Lime	24	Gold	190
Soda	28	Platina	190
Potash	42	Mercury	167

DALTON'S ELEMENTS
Dalton's symbols for the atoms of the 36 elements he believed existed.

Andrew JACKSON
1767–1845
7th US President

Andrew Jackson was one of the most influential US presidents. Born on the South Carolina frontier, he fought in the American War of Independence as a boy before moving to Tennessee. There, despite his lack of formal education and a fondness for duelling, he practised law and entered politics. Jackson won fame as a general during the War of 1812, especially when he inflicted a humiliating defeat on the British at New Orleans. Narrowly defeated in the presidential election of 1824, Jackson was elected president in 1828. Throughout an often stormy, two-term administration, Jackson championed the rights of the "common people" over banks and corporations, and his coalition supporters formed the basis of the modern Democratic Party.

TECUMSEH
1768–1813
Shawnee leader

The great aim of Tecumseh was to unite the Native American Indians from Canada all the way down to Florida against new waves of white settlers. Because of his powerful public speaking, he became the spokesman for the Native American peoples. Tecumseh's plans suffered a setback when his brother Tenskwatawa, "the Prophet", was defeated at the Battle of Tippecanoe in 1811. The alliance of tribes built up by Tecumseh largely fell apart. He became a brigadier-general in the British army during the War of 1812, and died in battle in Canada.

SLAVE SHIP
used by Wilberforce in his campaign to abolish slavery.

TECUMSEH
The chief of the Shawnee tribe is seen here wearing a British medal. He became a British army officer in the Anglo-American War.

Napoleon BONAPARTE
1769–1821
French emperor

Napoleon was an awe-inspiring military leader who re-drew the map of Europe. Born on the French island of Corsica, he studied at military schools in France. During the revolutionary wars, he was promoted to brigadier-general. After successful campaigns in Italy (1796–97), and a less successful invasion of Egypt (1798–99), Napoleon seized power in 1799, and crowned himself emperor of France in 1804. Through a series of devastating military campaigns, he conquered vast areas of Europe, bringing an end to the Holy Roman Empire and crushing Prussia. Napoleon's invasion of Russia ended in disaster, however, and in 1814, he was overthrown by a coalition of European powers and exiled to the Mediterranean island of Elba. In 1815, he escaped to France in a bid to return to power, but

1767 Thailand is invaded by the army of the Burmese Kombaung Dynasty who destroy its capital, Ayuthaya.

The Thais submit, but the Burmese have to withdraw their overlordship when China invades shortly afterwards.

1768 European exploration of the African interior begins when James Bruce, a Scottish explorer, travels in Ethiopia. Mungo Park explores West Africa some years later under the directions of the African Association.

CUVIER'S TOUCAN
This tropical bird, with its long beak used for picking fruit, is named after the French zoologist Georges Cuvier.

he was decisively defeated by a German-British army at the battle of Waterloo (1815). He was banished to the South Atlantic island of St Helena, where he died six years later. Napoleon had a profound influence on the history of Europe and the modern legal code he developed remains the basis of French civil law and many other nations.

Georges CUVIER
1769–1832
French zoologist and anatomist

The science of palaeontology – the study of fossils – and the classification of fossil creatures was created by Georges Cuvier. Fascinated by natural history, Cuvier became an expert in animal anatomy and, from 1785, taught at the Museum of Natural History in Paris, France. Cuvier used his skill as an anatomist when examing fossils. By comparing the remains of fossil bones with the bones of living creatures, he was able to determine what an extinct animal had looked like. He also showed that rock layers of different ages contained different fossils. This became important when later biologists began to study the process of evolution.

Duke of WELLINGTON
1769–1852
British general and politician

Arthur Wellesley, Duke of Wellington, was a great military leader who led successful campaigns for the British. Born in Dublin, Ireland, he joined the army as an infantry officer. In 1797, his regiment was sent to India and he was later knighted for his work during the taking of Seringapatam. His campaigns against Holkar and Scindia resulted in the capture of Poona in 1803. In England, he was elected to parliament in 1806 and was appointed Irish Secretary in 1807. In 1808, he was sent to help the Portuguese and Spanish fight against Napoleon's armies in the Peninsular War, winning two major victories there. He secured ultimate victory against the French on the Spanish peninsula in the Battle of Salamanca (1812), and earned himself the title 1st Duke of Wellington. Together with the Prussian, General Blücher, Wellington finally defeated Napoleon's army at the battle of Waterloo in 1815. Although primarily remembered for his dazzling military exploits, the Duke of Wellington also had a significant career as a politician and served as prime minister for a short time from 1827.

Alexander von HUMBOLDT
1769–1859
German naturalist and explorer

Alexander von Humboldt broke new ground in the study of botany and helped popularize the science. Born in Prussia, Humboldt studied natural sciences at Göttingen University. He was interested in every aspect of nature, from botany and geology to meteorology. In 1799, he set off with famous French naturalist Aimé Bonpland on a five-year scientific expedition to South America. They travelled more than 9,700 km (6,000 miles), making maps and recording data. Humboldt and Bonpland collected 60,000 plant specimens, 6,300 of them previously unknown. In 1802, they climbed 5,800 m (19,280 ft) up Mount Chimborazo, the highest climb of their era. Humboldt spent 25 years publishing the results of his expedition in 34 volumes. The later naturalist Charles Darwin (p.93) described Humboldt as "the greatest scientific traveller who ever lived".

Ludwig van BEETHOVEN
1770–1827
German composer

The music of Ludwig van Beethoven broke away from the conventions of the Classical style and paved the way for composers of the Romantic period. Born in Bonn, Germany, Beethoven left home in 1787 to study with Wolfgang Amadeus Mozart (p.68) in Vienna, but soon returned to see his dying mother and help his alcoholic father look after the family. In 1792, he returned to Vienna, where he took lessons with Franz Joseph Haydn (p.62) and others, and started his career as a concert pianist and teacher. In 1800, Beethoven realized he was going deaf; within 20 years his deafness was total. Although his early compositions were in the style of Mozart and Haydn, from 1803 to 1812, he wrote his most original music, starting with the "Eroica" Symphony (No.3) in 1804, and including five more symphonies, piano sonatas, string quartets, and his only opera, *Fidelio* (1814). His most personal music, however, came in the last years of his life: the late string quartets and piano sonatas, and the magnificent "Choral" Symphony (No.9).

1769 English explorer James Cook sails around the coast of New Zealand and up the east coast of Australia past the Barrier Reef in his ship the *Endeavour*. He claims Australia as a British colony, naming it New South Wales.

1769 In northern India, the world's worst famine yet rapidly sweeps the region. More than 10 million Indian people in Bengal (present-day Bangladesh) die of starvation while rulers are helpless to intervene.

THE INDUSTRIAL REVOLUTION

In the late 18th century Britain experienced an industrial revolution that transformed the country. Within a century, Britain had become the world's first and richest industrialized nation, dominating the international economy and exporting goods all over the world. It wasn't long before other nations, such as Germany and the United States, also became industrialized.

MASS-PRODUCTION

The Industrial Revolution began when British inventors such as JAMES HARGREAVES (1720–88), RICHARD ARKWRIGHT (p.62), and SAMUEL CROMPTON (1753–1827) developed new machines to mass-produce textiles in place of manual spinning wheels and looms. JAMES WATT (p.64) and RICHARD TREVITHICK (p.73) built high-pressure steam engines to power these new machines, which were housed in large, purpose-built factories that employed many thousands of workers. Ironworks and coal mines also opened across Britain to produce the necessary raw materials, and in time other industries became mechanized as well.

THE IMPACT

The impact of the Industrial Revolution was immense. Canals and railways were built to transport goods to and from factories, while steamships carried them around the world. New towns and cities sprang up to house factory workers, and wealth based on land gave way to wealth based on industry and commerce. Not everyone accepted these changes: Luddites – named after NED LUDD, a Nottingham apprentice – claimed the new machines brought misery for workers, and many joined trade unions to protect their rights.

FULL STEAM AHEAD
Richard Trevithick built the first working steam locomotive in 1803.

continent largely unknown to Europeans. They chose Park to explore West Africa, and to trace the course of the River Niger. In 1795, Park travelled inland on horseback from the west coast. Among other hardships, he was robbed of his horse, fell ill, and was imprisoned for four months by an Arab chief. Yet he did locate the River Niger and traced its eastward course. Mungo Park returned to Africa in 1805, hoping to sail down the River Niger, but in April 1806, his boat was ambushed by local people. According to his African slave, Park drowned trying to escape.

Richard TREVITHICK
1771–1833
English mechanic and inventor

Richard Trevithick designed and built, among other things, the first steam railway locomotive. Born in a tin-mining district of Cornwall, England, Trevithick became a mining engineer and, despite his poor education, solved some of the major engineering problems of the day. Cornwall's lack of local coal meant that James Watt's (p.64) new steam engine had to be made more fuel-efficient. Trevithick built a high-pressure steam engine in 1797 by using the same amount of fuel in a smaller cylinder. By 1801, he had constructed a steam carriage that could travel uphill. In 1803, Trevithick's steam railway locomotive was used at an ironworks in Wales. He also used steam to drive the first steam iron-rolling mill, to propel a paddle barge, to work a farm threshing machine, and to power a dredger. He was no businessman, however, and after travelling in South America, where his engines were used in the silver mines, he died penniless in England.

Georg HEGEL
1770–1831
German philosopher

The ideas of Georg Hegel on the human condition were to be of great influence in the 20th century. Hegel studied theology, and in 1805, he became a professor at Jena University, Germany, later moving to Nuremberg, Heidelberg, and Berlin. As a philosopher, he set out to construct an explanation of all human existence and experience. His philosophy covers many areas, but he is remembered for two major ideas. The first is that human civilization is the story of moral and intellectual progress caused by the development of rational thought. The second is that human history is a series of conflicts in which the original state or idea – the "thesis" – contradicts the "antithesis" to produce a synthesis of the two. This idea of dialectic argument and of human progress influenced Karl Marx (p.96) and many other thinkers.

William WORDSWORTH
1770–1850
English poet

William Wordsworth was one of the most important English Romantic poets. In 1787, he went to Cambridge University. After spending a year in France, Wordsworth returned to England and moved to Dorset with his sister, Dorothy. His great friend, the poet Samuel Taylor Coleridge (p.74) lived nearby and together they published *Lyrical Ballads* (1798), containing Wordsworth's poem "Tintern Abbey". In 1802, Wordsworth married and moved to Grasmere in the Lake District with his wife and sister. During this period he toured Scotland and wrote some of his best poetry, such as the *Lucy* poems (1801), *The Solitary Reaper* (1803), and *Poems* (1807) which included "Intimations of Immortality" and "The Daffodils", one of the most famous English poems. In 1843, Wordsworth was made Poet Laureate. *The Prelude*, an autobiographical work, was published after his death.

Mungo PARK
1771–1806
Scottish explorer

Mungo Park explored much of West Africa. He first studied medicine and served as a ship's surgeon on a voyage to Asia. Then, in 1788, a group of British noblemen and scientists formed the African Association to explore Africa, then a

---

1769 In France, Nicolas Cugnot builds a three-wheeled steam carriage. The carriage crashes into a wall and overturns, but it is the first road vehicle to move under its own power. Motor cars are not perfected for another century.

1772 Following years of conflict between its neighbouring countries, Poland is divided up between the powerful nations of Prussia, Austria, and Russia. The partition is overseen by Russia's ruler, Catherine the Great.

Robert OWEN
1771–1858
Welsh social reformer

Robert Owen created several "ideal" communities in an effort to improve the lives of working people. Born in Newtown, Wales, Owen was a saddler's son who began work as an apprentice draper at the age of 10. By the time he was a young man, he was manager of a cotton mill. In 1800, he became part-owner of the New Lanark cotton mills in Strathclyde, Scotland. At the mill, Owen set up a welfare programme to improve housing and working conditions. The model worker's community included a school, day-care for children, evening classes for employees, and a village shop. Remaining true to his socialist beliefs, Owen went on to establish other communities, such as Orbiston near Glasgow in Scotland, and New Harmony colony in the United States, but these were unsuccessful. Later in life, Owen was active in the trade-union movement.

Samuel Taylor COLERIDGE
1772–1834
English poet

Samuel Taylor Coleridge was a major poet of the English Romantic movement. The son of a vicar, Coleridge was sent to Cambridge University to study for the Church, but in 1795 he married and moved to Dorset, where he met William Wordsworth (p.73). The two poets became friends and in 1798 they published *Lyrical Ballads*, which contained one of Coleridge's greatest poems, "The Rime of the Ancient Mariner". However, by 1800, Coleridge's marriage was failing and he had become addicted to opium; in 1802, he wrote "Ode to Dejection", which reflected his sense of failure. In 1810, he moved to London, where he wrote mostly essays and literary criticism, believing he had lost his poetic inspiration. He published a final collection of earlier poems in 1816, which included "Christabel" and "Kubla Khan", the poem that Coleridge claimed had come to him in a dream.

MERIWETHER LEWIS
Lewis and his friend Clark recorded details of mountains and rivers on their expedition into the American northwest.

Thomas YOUNG
1773–1829
English physicist

The work of Thomas Young in the field of physics uncovered some of the mysteries of light and colour. Young was a bright child – by the age of 16 he spoke nine languages, including Latin. He trained as a doctor, but after 1800, he devoted himself to scientific research. His work provided evidence that light travels as waves, and that colours are made up of light wavelengths. His theory was not immediately accepted, as many scientists believed light was made up of particles. (Today, scientists believe light consists of energy called photons, which behave as both waves and particles.) Young also proved that human eyes detect only red, green, and blue, and that all colours are a blend of these three.

Meriwether LEWIS
1774–1809
US explorer

Meriwether Lewis explored much of western North America and his notes provide a fascinating record of Native American life before the coming of white settlers. Born in Virginia, Lewis served in the army before becoming secretary and aide to President Thomas Jefferson (p.66). In 1803, the French sold their lands west of the Mississippi River to the United States, and Jefferson asked Lewis to explore the new territory. In May 1804, Lewis set off with his friend William Clark, an army officer and the expedition's co-commander. They travelled up the Missouri River to the lands of the Mandans, the first of several Native American peoples who welcomed them. They spent winter with the Mandans, and then found a Shoshone woman,

1773 Russian cossacks (free warrior-peasants) and peasants led by Emelian Pugachev revolt to protest at their poverty. Pugachev claims he is Peter III whom Catherine the Great had deposed.

1773 American colonists pay taxes to the British on various imported goods, yet have no parliamentary representation. In protest, some board ships in Boston and dump tea in the harbour.

Sacagawea, to guide them. Traversing the Rocky Mountains, they reached the Columbia River and in December 1805 arrived on the shores of the Pacific Ocean. The expedition returned overland after wintering in present-day Oregon.

Matthew FLINDERS
1774–1814
English explorer

Matthew Flinders charted large parts of the land he named Australia – from the Latin *australis* (southern). Flinders joined the British

navy at the age of 15 and became an expert navigator. In 1795, he sailed to Australia, mapping the southeast coast and making the first voyage around Tasmania. On a second voyage (1801–03), he sailed around Australia, mapping great stretches of the coastline. On his way home, he was captured by the French, who were at war with Britain. Flinders was only released after six years in captivity. He is remembered in the names of the Flinders River and Flinders Mountain Range in Western Australia, and Flinders Island, off the Australian coast.

AMPERE *was the first physicist to explain the connection between electricity and magnetism.*

1775

Jane AUSTEN
1775–1817
English novelist

The genre of "domestic" literature was created by Jane Austen, who wrote novels of keen wit with subtle observations of society. She was born in Hampshire, England, into the world of the country gentry in which her novels are set. She wrote from an early age and began publishing her work in 1811 with *Sense and Sensibility*, followed by *Pride and Prejudice* (1813), *Mansfield Park* (1814), and *Emma* (1816). *Northanger Abbey* and *Persuasion* were both published in 1818, after her death. Austen's work is often referred to as a "comedy of manners". Although on the surface, her novels deal with seemingly trivial matters of love and marriage, they also confront the deeper issues surrounding women's status in a male-dominated society.

André-Marie AMPERE
1775–1836
French physicist and mathematician

André-Marie Ampère discovered how to measure and monitor electrical flow through a circuit. Largely self-taught, Ampère became a lecturer in mathematics at the Ecole Polytechnique in Paris, then inspector-general at the Imperial University, and chair of experimental physics at the Collège de France. As a physicist, he discovered that two parallel wires carrying currents flowing in the same direction will attract, while currents flowing in opposite

directions will repel. He also invented the solenoid, a wire coil that behaves like a magnet when a current passes through it. The unit of electric current is now called the ampère.

J.M.W. TURNER
1775–1851
English painter

Joseph Mallord William Turner was one of the finest English landscape painters. He showed his talent for painting early, and entered the Royal Academy of Art in London at 14. A year later, he exhibited his first watercolour there. In 1802, he made his first visit to Europe, where the scenery of Switzerland and Italy inspired many later works. By 1810, Turner had developed a technique of swirling colours to depict natural elements in a new way, using either oils or watercolour. After 1830, he took his style to new levels, and later paintings, such as *Snow Storm* (1842) and *Rain, Steam and Speed* (1844) are almost abstract. The energy and originality of his work inspired the later Impressionists.

John CONSTABLE
1776–1837
English painter

The landscapes of John Constable beautifully captured ordinary country life in early 19th-century England. Born a farmer's son in Suffolk, Constable began sketching the countryside as a boy. In his twenties, he studied at the Royal Academy in London. He rejected the picturesque style of the late 18th century, stating his aim was to be a "natural painter". Pictures such as *The Vale of Dedham* (1814–15), *The Hay Wain* (1821), and *The Lock* (1824), reflect the true

1774 Warren Hastings becomes governor-general of British India. Hastings extends the power of the East India Company in India, improves justice, organizes the opium revenue, and wages a war with the Marathas.

1776 Spain creates the viceroyalty of La Plata in South America by attempting to merge Argentina, Bolivia, Paraguay, and Uraguay. The following year, the Treaty of San Idelfonso divides Brazil up between Spain and Portugal.

beauty of the Suffolk countryside with freshness and warmth. His sensitive portrayal of the fleeting effects of clouds and sunlight established him as one of the greatest English landscape painters.

OERSTED'S NEEDLE *showed that an electric current created a magnetic effect.*

Amedeo AVOGADRO
1776–1856
Italian physicist

Amedeo Avogadro is considered to be one of the founders of physical chemistry. Born in Turin, Italy, he served as professor of physics at Turin University for 25 years. In 1811, he set out his theory on gases, which stated that equal volumes of gases contain equal numbers of molecules (a term he introduced to describe combinations of atoms), when at the same volume and pressure. This is now known as Avogadro's Law.

Hans Christian OERSTED
1777–1851
Danish physicist

The discovery of electromagnetism is credited to Hans Christian Oersted. Born in Rudkøbing, Denmark, Oersted began assisting his father in the family pharmacy at the age of 11. He gained admission to Copenhagen University, where he studied physical science and pharmacy. He later became director of the Polytechnic Institute in Copenhagen. Oersted gave many public lectures on science, which

proved highly popular. During a lecture on electricity in 1820, he accidentally made the most significant discovery of his career. When he connected a wire to a battery's terminals, he noticed that the needle of a nearby compass was deflected, only swinging back to pointing north when the wire was disconnected. Oersted deduced that the electric current produced a magnetic field around the wire, and that this had disturbed the needle. His realization paved the way for the later discoveries of Ampère (p.75) and Faraday (p.83).

Karl GAUSS
1777–1855
German mathematician, astronomer, and physicist

Karl Gauss was the creator of the mathematical system of algebra. Born in Brunswick, Germany, to poor parents, his brilliance as a child brought him to the attention of the Duke of Brunswick, who paid for his entire education. In 1801, he published *Disquisitiones arithmeticae,*

which contained new findings in number theory. He also made a study of the Earth's magnetic field and developed new methods of calculating the orbits of planets. However, it was in mathematics that he made the greatest impact, when he established the fundamental theories of algebra, the branch of mathematics concerned with operations on sets of numbers that are often represented by symbols.

John ROSS
1777–1856
Scottish explorer

John Ross, together with his nephew James, discovered the North Magnetic Pole. Ross had joined the British navy at the age of nine, and he made his first voyage of exploration to the White Sea, north of Russia, in 1812. In 1829, a rich distiller, Sir Felix Booth, hired Ross to lead an expedition to find the Northwest Passage, the short route to Asia from the Atlantic to the Pacific along the coast of America. Ross sailed to the Canadian Arctic, where he discovered Boothia Peninsula and the Gulf of Boothia, which he named after his patron. In the course of the expedition, his nephew sledged to the North Magnetic Pole, the place to which compasses point. Ross's ship was trapped by ice for three winters before being crushed. The men were stranded until a whaling ship came to their rescue. Ross made a final Arctic voyage in 1850, searching without success for the lost explorer Sir John Franklin (p.80).

Humphry DAVY
1778–1829
English scientist

The Davy Lamp, also known as a miners' lamp, was invented by Sir Humphry Davy. Davy worked as a chemist and an apprentice surgeon, but in 1797, he began to concentrate entirely on science. Often risking his own safety and health, he made many discoveries, including the discovery of nitrous oxide ("laughing gas") and the fact that a diamond is a form of carbon. In 1815, the Society for Preventing Accidents in Coal Mines asked Davy to apply his mind to providing light underground without a naked flame, which ignites gas. The result, the miners' safety lamp, enclosed the flame in a double layer of wire gauze, which prevented the ignition of flammable gases. Davy was knighted in 1812 for his invention. In 1813, he employed the young Michael Faraday (p.83) as his assistant.

Joseph GRIMALDI
1778–1837
English clown and pantomimist

The archetypal image of a clown, with painted face and bright costume, was created by Joseph Grimaldi. Grimaldi came from a family of dancers and entertainers, and first performed in public when only two years old at Sadler's Wells theatre in London. He grew up to be an outstanding and versatile performer –

1776 The Continental Congress of American colonies passes the Declaration of Independence, signed by representatives from all 13 colonies. It states that the united colonies are, and should remain, free and independent.

1777 Moroccan ruler Sidi Mohammed abolishes Christian slavery. Britain outlawes the slave trade in 1807 and then abolishes slavery in the British Empire in 1833. Slaves are not freed in the United States until 1863.

he was a singer, acrobat, dancer, actor, and pantomimist. Grimaldi's greatest success was in 1806 at Covent Garden in London. In the pantomime *Mother Goose*, he created a new type of clown, combining innocent and

GRIMALDI
The English entertainer is credited with having created the modern clown.

roguish qualities in one character. It was a part he returned to frequently during his career, working tirelessly to perfect his clown character. The many new ideas he brought to the traditional role of the clown became part of the standard repertoire. To this day, clowns around the world are still called "Joey" after Joseph Grimaldi.

Bernardo O'HIGGINS
1778–1842
Chilean revolutionary and leader

Bernardo O'Higgins liberated the South American nation of Chile from Spanish rule. O'Higgins was the illegitimate son of Ambrosio O'Higgins, the Spanish governor of Chile. In 1812, he joined forces with the professional soldier José de San Martín in a revolution against Spain in Argentina. In 1817, San Martín and O'Higgins led a daring march into Chile across the Andes and defeated the Spanish at Chacabuco. They completed the liberation of Chile in 1818.

O'Higgins became head of the first permanent national government. However, he became increasingly dictatorial, and his policies eventually aroused so much opposition that he was overthrown in 1823.

José de SAN MARTIN
1778–1850
South American liberator

One of South America's greatest liberators, José de San Martín freed many nations from Spanish rule. Born near Paso de los Libres in Argentina, he grew up in Spain and served in the Spanish army until 1811, when he returned to Argentina. Spain had ruled much of South America for two centuries, but now Argentinians wanted their freedom. Under San Martín's leadership, Argentina declared its independence in 1816. This was just the beginning of his crusade. In 1817, he joined forces with Bernardo O'Higgins and the pair led their armies on an epic journey over the Andes into Chile. They defeated the surprised Spaniards and won Chilean freedom. In 1820, San Martín marched into Peru, declared it independent and made himself "protector". But after disagreements with fellow liberator, Simón Bolívar (p.80), San Martin retired to Europe.

Joseph-Louis GAY-LUSSAC
1778–1850
French chemist and physicist

Joseph-Louis Gay-Lussac led 19th-century research into the property of gases. Gay-Lussac studied engineering and then chemistry and, by 1801, was assistant to Claude-Louis Berthollet, a respected chemist. Gay-Lussac went up in hot-air balloons to observe the effects of changing temperature on gases, the Earth's magnetism, and atmospherics; in 1804, he rose to a height of 7,016 metres (23,018 ft), a new record. Next, he researched the proportions of hydrogen and oxygen in water (2:1), and the volume of other

1777 Christianity is introduced to Korea by Chinese Jesuits. The order, founded by St Ignatius of Loyola in the 16th century, has already undertaken considerable missionary work in Paraguay and Canada.

1778 Austria and Prussia fight the War of Bavarian Succession after Fredrick II of Prussia protests the transfer of Lower Bavaria to Austria. The war has no great battles. Austria eventually gives up most of Lower Bavaria.

reacting gases. His results were published in 1808, and became known as Gay-Lussac's Law. Many honours and professorships followed. Gay-Lussac later turned to pure chemistry, where his discoveries included the element boron.

Fabian von BELLINGSHAUSEN
1778–1852
Russian explorer

Fabian von Bellingshausen was the first explorer to see Antarctica, the last continent on Earth to be discovered. Bellingshausen was born in Osel, Estonia, then part of the Russian Empire. He joined the navy at the age of 10 and rose through the ranks. In 1819, the Russian ruler, Tsar Alexander, asked Bellingshausen to sail to the Antarctic, hoping to find land there. The English explorer James Cook (p.61) had made the first voyage around Antarctica from 1772 to 1775, but had seen only ice. In 1819, Bellingshausen set out with two ships on only the second voyage ever made to the Antarctic. He travelled farther south than Cook and, on 28 January 1820, made the first sighting of land. He also discovered Peter Island and Alexander Island, which he named after the Russian tsars.

Elizabeth FRY
1780–1845
English prison reformer

Shocked by the appalling conditions in which prison inmates were kept, Elizabeth Fry devoted her life to reforming prisons and asylums. Born into a Quaker family in Norwich, England, she married Joseph Fry, a Quaker merchant from London. In 1810, she

STETHOSCOPE
Laënnec's single-tube stethoscope was later developed into this 1855 version of the present-day design that has two earpieces.

became a preacher for the Society of Friends, the Quaker organization, and through the Society, came to visit Newgate Prison for women in 1813. This event was to change her life. Disgusted by the terrible conditions endured by the women and children there, she began a campaign for prison reform. In 1819, she produced a report on prison conditions with her brother, Joseph Gurney. Fry also founded one of the first hostels for the homeless in Britain and, although her husband became bankrupt in 1828, she continued to push for social reforms.

René-Théophile-Hyacinthe LAENNEC
1781–1826
French doctor

René-Théophile-Hyacinthe Laënnec invented the stethoscope, an instrument which enables doctors to listen to a patient's chest to detect disease. Formerly an army medical officer, Laënnec was appointed chief physician at the Hôpital Necker, Paris, in 1816. The same year he created the stethoscope, a wooden tube that magnified the noises of the lungs and the heart. In 1819, he published his research to demonstrate the importance of his invention. Ironically, Laënnec died of tuberculosis, a chest disease.

George STEPHENSON
1781–1848
English railway engineer

Modern rail travel owes its existence to the great engineer George Stephenson. While working as a mechanic in a coal mine, he educated himself at night school. By 1812, he was a chief mechanic and, in 1814, he built his first locomotive, the *Blucher*. This steam engine propelled itself forward at 6 km (4 miles) per hour and could pull eight wagons loaded with 30 tons of coal. Stephenson refined the steam engine until, in 1825, his *Active* (later the *Locomotion*) was able to pull the first passenger train. His next train, the *Rocket*, could travel at an amazing 58 km (36 miles) per hour. Having also been commissioned to build railways between Liverpool and Manchester, Stephenson also became a successful international railway consultant.

1779 British explorer James Cook is killed in Hawaii by local inhabitants while trying to recover a stolen boat. He was on his third expedition, an attempt to discover a northwest passage from Europe to Asia.

1780 A descendant and namesake of the 16th-century Inca Emperor Tupac Amaru leads a rebellion of native people in Peru against the Spanish colonialists. Tupac is killed in 1781, but it takes another year to crush the revolt.

Niccolò PAGANINI
1782–1840
Italian composer and violinist

Niccolò Paganini was one of the first of the virtuoso performer-composers of the 19th century. Born in Genoa, Paganini's father taught him the violin and guitar, and at the age of 11 he gave his first public performance. He toured Italy as a professional violinist in 1797, and became famous throughout Europe for his brilliant performances. However, he found that there was little music in the classical repertoire to show off his talents, and began to perform mainly his own compositions. Paganini's music is almost exclusively for solo violin or guitar and exploits the versatility of these instruments to the full. His work, which includes six violin concertos and 24 Caprices for solo violin, was admired by composers such as Franz Liszt (p.94) and Frédéric Chopin (p.93).

John C. CALHOUN
1782–1850
US political leader

Together with Henry Clay and Daniel Webster, John Caldwell Calhoun of South Carolina dominated the US Congress in the decades before the American Civil War (1861–65). Elected to the House of Representatives in 1810, he later served as secretary of war and as vice-president in two administrations. Calhoun is best remembered for his forceful arguments in support of slavery and against federal authority over individual states. From 1822 until his death, Calhoun was in the Senate, except for 1844 to 1845, when, as secretary of state, he negotiated the annexation of Texas to the United States.

Friedrich FROEBEL
1782–1852
German teacher and educational reformer

Friedrich Froebel reformed education in Germany by introducing learning through play. Froebel became a teacher in 1805, and in 1816 opened schools in Griesheim and Berne to train teachers in the importance of play in education. His philosophy was outlined in his work *Die Menschenerziehung* (*The Education of Man*) in 1826. In 1836, he opened the first kindergarten. For the rest of his life, Froebel organized schools and designed educational toys and games for young children.

ROCKET
This is a reproduction of the famous "Rocket" locomotive of 1929. Designed by George Stephenson, with assistance from his son Robert, the "Rocket" ushered in the age of the passenger steam train.

1780 Joseph II, co-ruler of Austria with Maria Theresa, becomes sole ruler on her death. He declares Austria independent of the Pope, publishes an Edict of Toleration for Protestants, and abolishes serfdom.

1781 The military phase of the American War of Independence comes to an end. British General Cornwallis is forced to retreat to Yorktown, Virginia. Reinforcements are slow in coming and Cornwallis surrenders.

Simón BOLIVAR
1783–1830
Venezuelan revolutionary leader

Simón Bolívar is still known throughout South America as "the Liberator". Born into a noble family in Caracas, Venezuela, he studied law at the University of Madrid in Spain. At that time, much of South America was under Spanish control. When Venezuela declared its independence from Spain in 1811, Bolívar left for Colombia, raised an army, then returned to Caracas to seize power. In 1814, he was driven out, but he made several further attempts to re-enter the country. It was not until 1824 that the last Spanish supporters were finally defeated. Bolívar became president of the new Republic of Colombia, which consisted of modern-day Venezuela, Colombia, and Ecuador. In 1824, he joined other rebels to drive the Spanish out of Peru and was the country's leader for a time. In recognition of Bolívar's role in freeing so much of the Americas from Spanish rule, Upper Peru was made a separate country and named Bolivia in his honour in 1825.

Carl Maria von WEBER
1786–1826
German composer

German opera owes its popularity to Carl Maria von Weber. Weber started composing at the age of 12. In 1804, he became director of Breslau Opera before directing operas at Prague (1813–16) and Dresden (1817). He was keen to promote German opera, rather than the fashionable Italian opera of the time. His first great success came with the opera *Der Freischütz* (1821), followed by *Euryanthe* (1823), and *Oberon* (1826). The most popular German opera composer of his time, his work paved the way for composers such as Richard Wagner (p.95).

Davy CROCKETT
1786–1836
US frontiersman and congressman

Davy Crockett is one of America's best-loved folk heroes. During Andrew Jackson's (p.71) presidency, Crockett made his name as a frontiersman fighting against the Native Americans. He won a place in the Tennessee government and later in Congress. As a congressman, Crockett opposed Jackson's harsh policy towards the Native Americans. He died fighting for Texas against Mexican troops at the Alamo in 1836. A series of books about his adventures helped turn Crockett into a legend.

John FRANKLIN
1786–1847
English explorer

Sir John Franklin was the leader of Britain's most disastrous Arctic expedition. His disappearance inspired a search that resulted in the complete exploration of the Canadian Arctic. In 1845, he set sail for the Arctic with 138 men in two ships in search of the Northwest Passage. He and his crew were never seen again. His disappearance was one of the great mysteries of the age and, by 1850, there were 14 ships looking for him. After an extensive search, a party found a tin cylinder buried in a pile of stones on King William Island. It contained a note

explaining how the ships had become stuck and crushed in the ice. After many months of hardship, the crew had perished.

Jacob & Wilhelm GRIMM
1785–1863, 1786–1859
German folklorists and writers

The Brothers Grimm were the collectors and publishers of the some of the world's most famous fairy tales. Their three-volume *Grimm's Fairy Tales* (1812–22) includes such favourite stories as *Hansel and Gretel*, *Rapunzel*, and *Snow White*. Both brothers studied law, but Wilhelm's health was bad, preventing employment. Jacob worked as librarian for

GRIMM'S FAIRY TALE
The Valiant Little Tailor sets off on a journey, meeting a giant on the way.

King Jérôme of the German state of Westphalia and also published a book on the similarities between languages. Although they are remembered for children's fairy tales, both were also respected academics.

Joseph von FRAUNHOFER
1787–1826
German physicist

Joseph von Fraunhofer invented the diffraction grating, which anticipated the spectroscope, an instrument that divides light into a spectrum of colours. He worked as a developer of scientific instruments before becoming

---

1783 In the first year of his reign, Rama I of Thailand continues the work of his predecessor P'ya Taksin. The previous year, the former general had seized power, put P'ya Taksin to death, and crowned himself Rama I, forming a new dynasty.

1783 The Treaty of Paris is signed, recognizing the independence of the 13 former British colonies in North America. In 1787, the Constitutional Convention establishes a new system of federal government.

director at the Bavarian Academy of Sciences. Fraunhofer first developed an instrument to see the dark lines in the spectrum of light from the Sun, now known as the Fraunhofer Lines, before inventing the diffraction grating in 1821.

SHAKA
c.1787–1828
Zulu leader

Shaka established the first Zulu Empire in southern Africa. The illegitimate son of a minor Zulu chieftain, Shaka suffered an unpopular and lonely childhood. He channelled his frustrations into fighting and acts of bravery, and soon emerged as a leader. When his father died in 1816, Shaka seized power by killing his brother and declaring himself king of the Zulus. He built up a fearsome army, training his warriors to be disciplined and skilful fighters. In battle, his men would advance behind two walls of shields, each flank, or "horn", spreading out on either side to engulf the enemy. With his relentless army, Shaka began to seize territory from his neighbours. Captured men and boys were absorbed into his forces as he conquered each new area. Within 12 years, Shaka had created a Zulu empire larger than Europe, and had plans to educate his people. However, in 1828, he was stabbed to death by jealous half-brothers.

SHAKA
The great Zulu warrior king was renowned for his military skill, but he was a ruthless man and became increasingly dictatorial and cruel.

Georg Simon OHM
1787–1854
German physicist

The relationship between voltage, current, and resistance within an electrical circuit was discovered by Georg Ohm, and it became known as Ohm's Law. Born in Bavaria, Germany, Ohm studied in Erlangen, then taught in Cologne as professor of mathematics at the Jesuit college. In 1827, he published his new and revolutionary theory, but it was not well received and he resigned. It was not until 1841 that his work was recognized by the Royal Society in London. The unit of electrical resistance – the ohm (Ω) – is named after him. The unit of conductance is known as mho – ohm spelled backwards.

Lord BYRON
1788–1824
English poet

The most glamorous poet of his time, George Gordon Byron inherited the family title at the age of 10. In 1812, after a tour of Europe, he published an epic poem, *Childe Harold's Pilgrimage*. It was instantly popular, and he followed it with *Giaour* (1813), *The Corsair* (1814), *Lara* (1814), and *The Siege of Corinth* (1816). London society was impressed by Byron's wild image, and the idea of the "Byronic hero" was born. After an affair with Lady Caroline Lamb, who described him as "mad, bad, and dangerous to know", he married heiress Annabella Milbanke, but she left him after a year. Byron moved to Venice, where he met Countess Teresa Guiccioli and began his most famous poem, *Don Juan* (1819–24). In 1823, he joined the Greek struggle against the Turks, but died of marsh fever.

Augustin FRESNEL
1788–1827
French physicist

The "Fresnel lens", which is still used in lighthouses, was invented by physicist Augustin Fresnel. Fresnel was an engineer, but from 1814, he began to concentrate on the study of light. The lens named after him uses multi-faceted mirrors to magnify and/or to concentrate the amount of light produced. Fresnel also developed devices to advance the theory, begun by Thomas Young, that light, like sound, can be measured in waves. His genius was not recognized in his lifetime.

1787 Lieutenant William Bligh sets sail for the Pacific on board the *Bounty*. In 1789, the crew, led by Fletcher Christian, mutinies and casts Bligh and others to sea without charts. They land in East Timor.

1788 A Fulani cleric from West Africa claims the king of Gobir, in Hausaland, northern Nigeria, is not governing according to Islamic law. This sows the seeds for a holy war against all Hausa kings, resulting in their defeat.

PIONEERS OF PHOTOGRAPHY

In the early 1800s, several inventors were trying to find a way to permanently record images using silver salts – chemicals that darken when exposed to light. The first practical method was LOUIS DAGUERRE's daguerrotype, a picture developed on a metal plate. But this method was expensive and could only be used to create an image once.

PHOTOGRAPHY FOR EVERYONE
The first breakthrough came in 1839, when WILLIAM HENRY FOX TALBOT (p.88) invented the first photographic negatives. These could be used to print multiple photographs on paper. Then, in 1888, GEORGE EASTMAN (1854–1932) introduced the Kodak box camera, which carried a roll of film. Relatively cheap and easy to use, the Kodak made photography available to everyone.

RECORDING EVENTS
Photography also proved a revolutionary way of documenting important events as well as unfamiliar places. In wartime, ROGER FENTON (1819–69) and MATHEW BRADY (1823–96) photographed what was happening in the army camps and battlefields in the Crimean War (1853–56) and the American Civil War (1861–65) respectively. Back in Britain, JOHN THOMSON (1837–1921) documented the lives of people living in the slums of London's East End.

In this Daguerrotype camera the shutter in front of the lens was moved aside to make the exposure.

Augustin Louis CAUCHY
1789–1857
French mathematician

The many theories developed by Augustin Cauchy greatly advanced the development of mathematics in the late 19th century. Trained as an engineer, Cauchy was forced to retire early due to ill health. He taught mathematics at the Paris Polytechnic, but left for Italy and Czechoslovakia after the 1830 revolution. He returned to Paris in 1838. Cauchy's most important mathematical work includes the wave theory of light, the theory of elasticity, and variable equations, but he is best remembered for the theory of functions of a complex variable.

William PARRY
1790–1855
English explorer

William Parry explored much of the previously unexplored Arctic region.

This Boat is left for Captain Parry and his party on their return from attempting to reach the North Pole. It is particularly requested that she may not be removed: as they will probably be much in want of her.

H.M. Ship Hecla. May 15th 1827.

CAPTAIN PARRY *left this message on a boat before setting out on his expedition to the North Pole.*

From the age of 13, Parry served in the British navy, eventually reaching the rank of admiral. He led three naval expeditions to the Canadian Arctic, in 1819, 1821, and

Robert PEEL
1788–1850
British prime minister

Robert Peel's political career was long and eventful. He entered parliament in 1809 as the Tory member for Cashel in Ireland. In 1812, he became Secretary of State for Ireland, where he earned the nickname "Orange Peel" because of his support for the Protestants (Orangemen) and his anti-Catholic views. In 1822, he became home secretary and set up London's Metropolitan Police Force – London policemen are still known as "Bobbies" in his honour. Peel stepped down in 1827 following the government's motion to allow Catholics the right to sit in parliament. He returned to politics in 1833 and was prime minister from 1834 to 1835 and 1841 to 1846. Unrest in Ireland returned to haunt him, and though he quelled it for a time, the Irish Potato Famine and repeal of the Corn Laws – a duty on grain – led to his downfall. He retired in 1846.

Louis DAGUERRE
1789–1851
French inventor

While working as a painter, Louis Daguerre noticed the effects of different lighting when exhibiting his art. He became interested in what was then called heliography, and later became known as photography. Nicéphore Niepce, another Frenchman, had already produced a photographic image in 1826. Daguerre went to work with Niepce and eventually developed his "daguerrotype" process, the first effective form of photography. The process involved exposing an iodized silver-coated plate to light for around 25 minutes and fixing the image with salt. His invention of the "daguerrotype" is dated as 1837.

1788 The first British convicts arrive in Botany Bay, Australia. When their sentences are finished, many convicts remain and obtain land. By 1868, 25,000 female and 137,000 male convicts have been sent to Australia.

1789 George Washington is elected the first president of the United States and serves two four-year terms.

Disputes begin between those who want a strong central government, and those who value individual states' rights.

1824, searching for the Northwest Passage. In 1827, Parry made the first ever attempt to reach the North Pole, dragging boats mounted on sledge-runners. He took boats because some experts believed that there was an open sea around the Pole. However, he found only ice and was forced to turn back, but not before discovering several islands there, including the Parry Islands which were named after him.

Michael FARADAY
1791–1867
English scientist

A pioneer in the study of electromagnetism and electrolysis, Faraday created the first generator and transformer. The son of an English blacksmith, Faraday started life as an apprentice bookbinder. He was inspired by the

science books he bound and frequently read, and attended the lectures of Humphry Davy (p.76) at the Royal Institute in London. He persuaded Davy to let him work as his assistant and toured Europe with him, meeting some of the top scientists of the day. When Davy retired, Faraday took over his position as professor of chemistry at the Royal Institute. He carried out research into many areas of

physics and chemistry, but he was particularly excited by a new field of study – electromagnetism. In 1831, Faraday built the first electric generator, or dynamo, after noticing that moving a magnet in and out of a wire coil made an electric current flow through the wire. He also invented the transformer, a device that alters the strength of an electricity supply, and pioneered electrolysis – the use of electricity to break down chemical compounds. Faraday's experiments and numerous discoveries became the basis for our understanding of electricity and magnetism.

VOLTAMETER
Michael Faraday used this voltameter to study how water is broken down by electricity. The two tubes were used for collecting oxygen and hydrogen.

Charles BABBAGE
1791–1871
English mathematician and inventor

The idea that mathematical tables could be calculated mechanically first occurred to Charles Babbage in 1812. He invented a small calculator that could carry out simple tasks such as addition and subtraction, up to a maximum solution of eight decimal numbers. Following on from this, in 1823, he obtained

a grant from the British government to design a machine with a 20-decimal capacity. During the 1830s, Babbage developed plans for a machine that was the forerunner of the modern digital computer; although the machine, called the analytical engine, was not completed during his lifetime. Babbage also helped establish the modern British postal system and invented a type of speedometer.

Samuel MORSE
1791–1872
US inventor

Morse Code, an electrically transmitted signal code, was named after its inventor, Samuel Morse. He developed the idea for an electric signalling system between 1832 and 1836 while professor of design at New York University. He eventually persuaded the United States' government to sponsor an experimental telegraph line between Washington and Baltimore. In 1844, he sent his first message, in the historic words "What hath God wrought!" The message was conveyed by his special code of dots and dashes. Morse's telegraph system and communications code was soon adopted around the world.

Percy Bysshe SHELLEY
1792–1822
English poet

Born into an aristocratic family, Percy Bysshe Shelley became one of the most revered but scandalous poets of his time. In 1811, he eloped with 16-year-old Harriet Westbrook, causing a rift with his family, who cut off his income. He published his first major poem, *Queen Mab*, in 1813. The following year he met 16-year-old Mary Godwin, daughter of Mary Wollstonecraft (p.69), whom he married in 1816, following Harriet's suicide. The Shelleys lived first in England, then Italy, where Shelley wrote his finest poetry, including *Prometheus Unbound*, the odes "To the West Wind" and "To a Skylark" (all 1819), and *Epipsychidion* (1821). Shelley drowned at sea when returning from a visit to Byron (p.81).

1789 The crippling cost of living for the peasantry, together with revolutionary ideas among the middle classes, create a mood of revolt in France. The storming of the Bastille prison in Paris sparks off the French Revolution.

1791 Louis XVI and Marie Antoinette try to escape from revolutionary France, but are stopped and brought back to Paris. Louis is guillotined in January 1793, and Marie Antoinette is executed the following October.

Nickolai LOBACHEVSKI
1792–1856
Russian mathematician

Nickolai Lobachevski developed one of the first geometrical theories in mathematics. He was born in Nizhni Novgorod, Russia. At 22, he became professor at Kazan University, where he stayed for the rest of his life. Ironically, theories similar to his were discovered at the same time by the Hungarian mathematician János Bolyai.

Gioacchino ROSSINI
1792–1868
Italian composer

The operas of Gioacchino Rossini, and in particular their exciting overtures, set the pace for Italian opera in the 19th century. Rossini was born on leap-year day in 1792 in Pesaro, Italy. His father was a horn player, his mother a singer, and Gioacchino studied the horn, singing, and composition in Bologna. His first opera was performed in Venice in 1810, and he was soon commissioned to write several more. He achieved international success in 1813 with *Tancredi* and *The Italian Girl of Algiers*, which were followed in the next 15 years by comic operas such as *The Barber of Seville* (1816), *Cinderella* (1817), and the more serious *Otello* (1816), *Semiramide* (1823), and *William Tell* (1829). Having made his fortune, Rossini retired at the height of his success. *William Tell* was his last opera and, after 1829 he wrote very little. However, his lively operas have remained immensely popular to this day.

ROSSINI
The Italian composer is famous for his often light-hearted operas.

Matthew PERRY
1794–1858
US explorer and naval officer

Commodore Matthew Perry is best remembered for opening up trade links with Japan after some 250 years of Japanese isolation. Perry lived a life of high adventure, fighting pirates in the West Indies and slave traders off the coast of Africa. In 1853, he sailed to Edo (now Tokyo) Bay with four ships and a letter from the US president requesting a treaty. At first the Japanese resisted, but Perry returned the following year with battle frigates and gained an audience with the aides of the emperor. The first trade treaty between Japan and the United States was signed in March 1854. The door was now open for other countries to form commercial links with Japan.

John KEATS
1795–1821
English poet

Together with Byron (p.81) and Shelley (p.83), John Keats was a leading poet of the Romantic movement. Not formally educated, Keats was apprenticed to a surgeon until 1817, when he devoted himself to writing poetry. His first two volumes – *Poems* (1817) and *Endymion* (1818) – were not well received at the time, but are now highly acclaimed. In 1818, he fell in love with Fanny Brawne, who was never to return his affections. The same year his brother Tom died of tuberculosis, and Keats learned that he was suffering from the same disease. Despite this, he wrote some of his best poems between 1819 and 1820: "La Belle Dame Sans Merci", "On the Eve of Saint Agnes", "Ode to a Nightingale", "Ode to a Grecian Urn", "Hyperion", and "Ode to Autumn". Keats's poetry is famous for its intense, romantic imagery. He died in Rome aged 26, searching for a cure for his tuberculosis.

Charles STURT
1795–1869
English explorer

Charles Sturt was the first European to cross the dry interior of Australia. Born in India, the son of an English judge, he joined the army and, in 1826, was sent to Australia. Europeans knew little about the Australian interior – an area known today as the Outback – but there were hopes that they might find an inland sea or river system which could be used to cross the continent. In 1828, Sturt made his first expedition into the interior, tracing the course of the Murray and Darling rivers. He made a second expedition in 1844. After crossing the Stony Desert, he made camp beside a creek. The dry season was beginning and Sturt could not risk moving away from this water. He spent seven months trapped there watching the creek's water level sink. When the rains finally came, he returned home with news that Australia had no inland sea.

1792 In France, the monarchy is abolished by the National Convention and a republic is established. The new order is based on "liberty, equality, and fraternity". Unlike England, the monarchy does not return.

1795 Caribbean slave leader Toussaint L'Ouverture negotiates with the French to win contol of most of Haiti. In 1801 he declares independence and abolishes slavery, but he is captured by French troops.

Rowland
HILL
1795–1879
English inventor

The idea of using postage stamps is attributed to Rowland Hill. In 1837, he wrote a book, *Post-office Reform*, in which he recommended that a uniform postage rate be paid for in the form of stamps. (Previously the addressee paid on receipt of a letter or parcel.) In 1840, a penny postage stamp was introduced in Britain. Hill became secretary to the postmaster general in 1846 and later to the Post Office.

Sadi
CARNOT
1796–1832
French scientist

Sadi Carnot advanced the study of steam engines to create thermo-dynamics. He developed a keen interest in science and technology at the Ecole Polytechnique in Paris. After graduating, he entered the army as a captain of engineers, a post he held until 1819, when he joined the general staff. From this point on, Carnot devoted his time to science and, especially, the design of steam engines. Steam power already existed but it was still inefficient, and Carnot was aware that France lagged behind other countries such as Britain. He prepared a scientific study of steam engines, which he published in 1824. It was largely ignored until 1834, when railway engineer Bénoit Clapeyron adopted Carnot's theories. They were used eventually to produce the first thermo-dynamic version of a steam engine, in which the heat produced by the steam was harnessed and turned into energy to power the engine.

FRANKENSTEIN
Frankenstein's monster, Mary Shelley's most famous creation, is seen here being played by Boris Karloff in the classic 1931 horror film.

Franz
SCHUBERT
1797–1828
Austrian composer

Born near Vienna, Austria, Franz Schubert became one of the most prolific composers of the early 19th century. He had already written a large amount of music by the time he became a teacher at his father's school in 1815. But his heart was not in teaching, and he continued composing songs, symphonies, and piano music, playing his music at private parties in Vienna known as "Schubertiads". In a tragically short life Schubert wrote more than 600 songs, including the collections *Die Schöne Müllerin* (1823), *Winterreise* (1827), and *Schwanengesang* (1828), as well as nine symphonies, and pieces for piano and chamber groups.

Mary
Wollstonecraft
SHELLEY
1797–1851
English writer

It is surprising to many that the genre of "horror fiction" was created by a 19th-century woman. Mary Godwin, the daughter of the philosopher William Godwin and feminist writer Mary Wollstonecraft (p.69), met Percy Bysshe Shelley (p.83) in 1814. They ran away together and married in 1816. While the couple were on holiday with the poet Lord Byron (p.81) in Switzerland that year, Byron suggested that they each write a ghost story. Mary wrote *Frankenstein* (1818), the story of a scientist who creates a living creature using electricity. She later wrote the novels *Valperga* (1823), *Perkin Warbeck* (1830), and *The Last Man* (1826), and published an edition of Shelley's poetry.

1796 Qianlong, Manchu emperor of China, abdicates after 60 years in power. His reign was good and prosperous until about 1770, when corruption set in and discontent broke out among the population.

1796 Catherine the Great, Empress of Russia since 1762, dies. She had vastly increased the size of her empire and was renowned throughout Europe for her intelligence and learning.

MOUNT FUJI
The famous Japanese mountain is visible in this painting by Hiroshige.

Hiroshige ANDO
1797–1858
Japanese painter

Hiroshige was one of the first Japanese painters to gain recognition in the western world. His early pictures, printed on woodblocks, were images of everyday Tokyo life, such as street scenes and bath houses. Hiroshige published his first collection of prints in 1818, but later concentrated on landscape paintings. His landscapes often showed vast panoramas with small human figures, skilfully executed in just a few brush strokes. His most famous series of pictures is *53 Stages on the Tokaido Road* (1833). Hiroshige's art was to have a huge influence on the French Impressionists.

Charles LYELL
1797–1875
Scottish geologist

Charles Lyell disputed many earlier theories of geology in an effort to explain the Earth's structure. He developed an interest in geology while at Oxford University and pursued this with the publication of *Principles of Geology* in 1830. The book raised new theories: instead of following the traditional line of thought that geological changes happen as a result of disasters, Lyell argued that many happen as a result of natural forces, a theory that was later proved true. Another work, *Geological Evidences of the Antiquity of Man*, provoked hostility from some people because of its support for Charles Darwin's (p.93) ideas on evolution, but Lyell was knighted for his work in 1848.

Sojourner TRUTH
c.1797–1883
US reformer

Born a slave in New York State, Sojourner Truth became one of the great campaigners for equal rights. Christened Isabella, she was sold to several different masters before gaining her freedom in 1827. Throughout her life she experienced visions and voices, and was convinced that she had been chosen by God to speak out for women and slaves. She changed her name to Sojourner Truth and travelled around the United States, denouncing slavery to huge crowds. During the American Civil War, Truth was active in getting supplies to African-American soldiers. After the war, she campaigned for equal rights for freed slaves and women.

Eugène DELACROIX
1798–1863
French painter

Eugène Delacroix was one of France's greatest Romantic painters. He trained in the studio of a Parisian artist, and learned from copying great paintings in the Louvre. He rejected the solemn Classical style of the time in order to paint dramatic subjects in vivid colours. Early works included *The Barque of Dante* (1822) and *The Massacre at Chios* (1824). The energy and richness of his style appeared most forcefully in his famous painting, *Liberty Leading the People* (1831), which he painted to celebrate the French Revolution. A visit to North Africa in 1832 inspired many of his later works, including *The Women of Algiers* (1834). Regarded as a rebel by many, Delacroix made a huge impact on the art world.

Alexander PUSHKIN
1799–1837
Russian poet, playwright, and writer

Alexander Pushkin was the first writer to use Russian as a literary language, and is still seen as Russia's greatest poet. Born in Moscow to an aristocratic family, Pushkin published the romantic poem *Ruslan and Lyudmila*, based on Russian folklore, in 1820. His writing reflected many of his childhood influences, such as his grandmother's stories about their ancestors, his nurse's Russian folktales, and the life led by the peasants on his parents' estate. After writing political verses, Pushkin was exiled from Moscow until 1826. He began his great novel in verse, *Eugene Onegin* (1833), while in exile. Pushkin eventually died in a duel, defending his wife's honour.

René-Auguste CAILLIE
1799–1838
French explorer

In the 1820s, the French Geographical Society offered a prize of 10,000 francs for the first European to report from Timbuktu, the fabled Muslim trading city on the edge of the Sahara desert in West Africa. René-Auguste Caillié was determined to win. The journey to Timbuktu was dangerous for non-Muslims – another explorer had already been murdered in 1826 – so Caillié spent a year in North Africa learning Arabic, allowing him to travel in disguise as a Muslim. He reached Timbuktu in 1828, but instead of a city of gold, he found "ill-looking houses, built of earth". On his return to France, he finally collected his prize.

1798 The Irish revolt against English rule. They are led by Wolfe Tone, a Protestant revolutionary, who is also supported by many Irish Catholics. The revolt fails and Tone is arrested, later cutting his own throat in prison.

1798 The strait between mainland Australia and Tasmania is navigated by George Bass and Matthew Flinders. They had earlier surveyed the coast of New South Wales. The strait is later named after Bass.

19th CENTURY

DURING THE 19TH CENTURY, an industrial revolution began in Britain and spread to cover much of Europe and the Americas. In their search for raw materials, the major European nations continued to establish colonies in Africa and Asia. In Europe, demands for democracy and national independence led to political unrest and the unification of Italy and Germany.

John BROWN
1800–59
US anti-slavery campaigner

As a boy in Connecticut, John Brown saw a white man beat a slave boy with a shovel. This kind of cruelty inspired him to devote his life to the abolition of slavery. He married twice and had 20 children, following five of his sons to the Kansas Territory in 1855. In 1856, Brown and four of his sons killed five pro-slavery settlers in revenge for their sacking the town of Lawrence. He went on to establish a refuge for runaway slaves, then planned an anti-slavery rebellion in the southern states. In 1859, Brown and his men raided the federal arsenal at Harper's Ferry, Virginia, for weapons. His small party captured the arsenal but was overpowered by a company of US marines and two of Brown's sons were killed. The wounded Brown was convicted of treason and hanged at Charleston, Virginia, but his name continued to inspire Union troops in the civil war that followed. "John Brown's Body" became their marching song.

William Henry FOX TALBOT
1800–77
English pioneer of photography

In 1839, William Henry Fox Talbot announced his invention of "photographic drawing", or photography – a method of producing photographic images on silver chloride paper. Fox Talbot was born in Dorset, England, into the landed gentry, and was educated at Cambridge University. In 1841, he patented the calotype, the first photographic negative

JOHN BROWN opposed the cruel practice of slavery, in which slaves had to wear collars, chains, and fetters.

from which prints could be made. He also invented the first flash photography in 1851. His book *Pencil of Nature*, published in 1844, was the first book to be illustrated by photographs. He also published influential works in the fields of astronomy and mathematics. In addition, Fox Talbot was a classical scholar and one of the first to transcribe cuneiform writing – an ancient pictogram script – at Ninevah, Assyria. He was also a member of Parliament from 1833.

Brigham YOUNG
1801–77
US Mormon leader

Brigham Young helped to shape the newly formed Church of Jesus Christ of the Latter-Day Saints, whose followers are known as Mormons. Young joined the Mormon Church in 1832 and three years later was appointed one of its 12 apostles. He embarked on a successful journey to Liverpool, England, to recruit more people to Mormonism, and on his return to the United States, Young was appointed head of the Mormon Church as successor to its murdered founder Joseph Smith. When the Mormons were driven from Nauvoo, Illinois, Young led the Mormon migration to the Great Salt Lake in Utah in 1847, founded Salt Lake City, and remained leader of the settlers until his death. Responsible for the city's infrastructure, Young encouraged industry and transportation, including the building of 100 miles of the Union Pacific Railroad. When he died, he left $2.5 million to his 17 surviving wives.

Victor Marie HUGO
1802–85
French poet, playwright, and novelist

Born in Besançon, France, Victor-Marie Hugo became one of France's leading literary figures. His father was one of Napoleon's (p.71) generals and the family travelled a great deal. When Napoleon's empire fell in 1815, Hugo finally settled down to study law, and began to write. The success of his five-act play *Hernani* (1830), and his most famous historical novel *Nôtre Dame of Paris* (1831) (later filmed several times as *The Hunchback of Nôtre Dame*) made him the leader of the French romantic school of writing. Hugo's work always showed his acute awareness of the sufferings of the common man. In 1851, his republican politics led to his exile from France until 1870. After the accidental death of his daughter and her husband in 1843, Hugo wrote a number of very moving poems, published as *Contemplations* (1856). But it is for his novels and their dramatizations, in particular *Les Misérables* (1862), that he is best remembered. On his death in 1885, Hugo was buried as a national hero in the Panthéon in Paris.

Christian Johann DOPPLER
1803–53
Austrian physicist

Christian Doppler explained a principle in the study of electromagnetic radiation that now bears his name. Born in Salzburg, Austria, Doppler showed an early talent for

PLACE DES VOSGES Victor Hugo lived in this beautiful square in the Marais district of Paris.

maths. After studying in Vienna, he became a professor of mathematics in Prague. Later he became a professor of physics at the Royal Imperial University of Vienna. He first published what he called "Doppler's Principle" in a paper in 1842. This explained why the frequency of waves seems to vary according to their distance from the observer; for example, why the sound of a vehicle seems to drop in pitch as it passes a listener. Doppler predicted that the same principle could be used to measure the speed of light. The Doppler effect can be applied to all forms of radiation and has been used in astronomy to calculate whether stars are approaching the Earth or receding from it – the latter is the phenomenon known as a red shift. Doppler thus helped provide important evidence about how our universe is constantly changing.

Hector BERLIOZ
1803–69
French composer

Hector Berlioz's ideas on orchestration had a great influence on many later composers. He was born in

1800 As the Industrial Revolution gets under way, factories are built throughout England. Machines invented in the 17th century are used in factories by businessmen who employ large workforces, transforming life in Britain.

1802 In Vietnam, the heir to Annam, Gia-Long, is finally crowned after 25 years in hiding. Conquering Tongking in the north, he becomes emperor of a newly united Vietnam, recognized by China.

88

La Côte St André, France. From an early age his father, a doctor, taught him the flute. However, Berlioz's father insisted that his son should study medicine. Hector was sent to medical school, but after a couple of years he left to study music. His first major composition was the *Symphonie Fantastique* (1830), inspired by his love for the actress Harriet Smithson, whom he later married. He was only moderately successful in his native France, so he toured Europe to get his music performed, and worked as a critic and writer to earn extra money. Berlioz was the most original French composer of his time, and used the orchestra to brilliant effect in concert overtures and symphonies such as the *Harold en Italie* (1834) and *Roméo et Juliette* (1839). Perhaps his greatest masterpieces, though, were the choral *Damnation de Faust* (1846), and his operas *Benvenuto Cellini* (1838), *Les Troyens* (1863), and *Béatrice et Bénédict* (1862). Despite these great works, Berlioz failed to win recognition in his native France, a source of lifelong disappointment to him.

Ralph Waldo EMERSON
1803–82
US philosopher, essayist, and poet

Ralph Waldo Emerson was at the centre of New England's literary and philosophical renaissance in the decades before the American Civil War. Born in Boston and educated at Harvard, Emerson served briefly as a Unitarian minister before travelling to Europe, where he met eminent writers and thinkers such as Samuel Taylor Coleridge (p.74) and Thomas Carlyle (1795–1881). Returning to Massachusetts, he developed the uniquely American philosophy later known as transcendentalism, which emphasized self-reliance, communion with nature, and the individual search for truth. Emerson outlined his philosophy in an 1837 lecture at Harvard, titled *The American Scholar*, which has been called "America's intellectual declaration of independence". Emerson wrote notable poems, but his main literary vehicle was the essay, many of which were published in the literary magazine *The Dial*.

Nathaniel HAWTHORNE
1804–64
US writer

Nathaniel Hawthorne used novels and short stories to explore the influence of Puritan ideals about sin, guilt, pride, and redemption on the American consciousness. Born in Salem, Massachusetts, he published his first novel, *Fanshawe*, anonymously in 1828. Hawthorne struggled for recognition until 1837, when *Twice-Told Tales*, a volume of short stories, won critical and popular success. He lived briefly at Brook Farm, a short-lived transcendentalist commune, before settling in Concord, Massachusetts, where he wrote another volume of short stories *Mosses from an Old Manse* (1846) and *The Scarlet Letter* (1850), the novel most critics consider his masterpiece. Appointed to a diplomatic post in Britain following his friend Franklin Pierce's election as US president, Hawthorne spent the years 1853 to 1860 in Europe.

George SAND
1804–76
French writer

George Sand (the pen name of Amandine Aurore Lucie Dupin) lived a highly unconventional life. An illegitimate child, Dupin was born in Paris, and was brought up by her grandmother. She married Baron Dudevant at the age of 18, but felt stifled by the marriage and left her husband, returning to Paris with her two children. Here she led what society saw as an outrageously independent life, including wearing trousers and smoking cigars. Dupin believed that women should have more freedom, and her first novel, *Indiana* (1832), which brought her immediate fame, was a passionate protest against an unhappy marriage. Between 1846 and 1849 she wrote her best-known novels, *The Haunted Marsh*, *Frances the Waif*, and *Little Fadette*, which are all concerned with life in the country. She did not marry again, but she was associated with several men, in particular the composer Frédéric Chopin (p.93).

Benjamin DISRAELI
1804–81
British politician and novelist

As prime minister, Benjamin Disraeli revitalized Britain's Tory (Conservative) party. Disraeli was born in London and first gained fame in 1826 with the publication of his novel *Vivian Grey*. He entered parliament as member for Maidstone in 1837, and helped bring down the Conservative prime minister Robert Peel (p.82) partly through disagreements on the Corn Laws. He had a brief spell as prime minister in 1868 and then returned in 1874. That year he annexed the Fiji Islands, and later the Transvaal (1877), and embarked on wars against the Afghans (1878–79) and the Zulus (1879). In 1876, Disraeli, a favourite of Queen Victoria (p.98), bestowed the new title of Empress of India on the queen, and he entered the House of Lords as Lord Beaconsfield. After the Russo-Turkish War, Russia threatened Constantinople, but thanks to Disraeli's negotiations in 1878, war was averted. The Tories fell from power in 1880, but Disraeli had reduced Russian power in the Balkans and upheld Britain's position as the world's leading imperial power.

1804 Meriwether Lewis and William Clark set out from St Louis, United States to explore the Louisiana Territory. The trek lasts 28 months and the knowledge they bring back proves invaluable to western expansion.

1804 Napoleon crowns himself emperor of France. He introduces the Napoleonic code – a legal system with many democratic elements. All people are equal before the law, but husbands have total authority over their wives.

Hans Christian ANDERSEN
1805–75
Danish writer of fairy tales

The fairy tales of Hans Christian Andersen have made him one of the world's greatest storytellers. Andersen was born in Odense, the son of a poor shoemaker and a washerwoman. He left his home town for Copenhagen at the age of 14 to try to find work in the theatre. He failed to find a job, but his talent for poetry earned him a place at an advanced school and eventually the support of

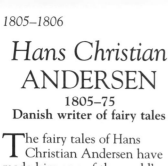

BRUNEL'S *Clifton suspension bridge spans the River Avon in Bristol, England.*

HANS CHRISTIAN ANDERSEN *This statue of the Danish writer in Central Park, New York is a landmark for children.*

King Frederick VI of Denmark. Andersen wrote adult novels and travel books, but it is for his children's stories that he is best remembered, notably *The Little Mermaid*, *The Emperor's New Clothes*, *The Ugly Duckling*, and *The Snow Queen*. These imaginative and touching stories, some of them based on folk tales, were originally produced as pamphlets. Since their publication, they have been translated into many languages, adapted into plays, musicals, and TV programmes, and recently into successful animated films.

Mary SEACOLE
1805–81
Jamaican nurse and war heroine

Born in Kingston, Jamaica, Mary Seacole gained fame for her work as a nurse in the Crimean War. After the death of her English husband, she returned to Jamaica from England, but when, in 1854, the Crimean War broke out in Europe, she went to England again to offer her services as a nurse. Turned down by the British Army because of her colour, Seacole went to the Crimea at her own expense. She set up a hostel for soldiers near Balaclava. From here, she was able to nurse the sick and wounded, becoming known as "Mother" Seacole in the process. At the end of the war she was bankrupt, but several British newspapers raised funds to get her out of debt.

Isambard Kingdom BRUNEL
1806–59
English engineer and inventor

Isambard Kingdom Brunel was one of the greatest engineers of the 19th century. He was born in Portsmouth, and studied at the Collège Henri Quatre in Paris. Brunel helped to plan the River Thames tunnel and drew up the plans (1829–31) for the Clifton suspension bridge over the River Avon in Bristol. The bridge was completed only after his death, but it remains a masterpiece of engineering that is still in use today. His shipbuilding designs included the *Great Western* (1837), the first steamship to cross the Atlantic Ocean regularly, and the *Great Britain* (1843), the first large iron ship powered by a screw propeller. The largest vessel ever built up to that time, the *Great Eastern* was also a Brunel design (1858). This ship later laid the first transatlantic telegraph cable. Brunel also worked on the Great Western Railway, and during the Crimean War (1854–56) he designed an innovative prefabricated hospital for the combat zone.

Benito JUAREZ
1806–72
Mexican president

Mexico's first Native American president was Benito Juárez. Juárez was born into a Zapotec Indian family in Oaxaca, Mexico. He qualified as a lawyer and was elected state governor in 1847, beginning a programme of electoral reform. This angered Mexico's dictator, Santa Anna, who sent him into exile in 1853. Juárez returned to Mexico in 1855, becoming the

1805 Mohammed Ali becomes the Ottoman viceroy of Egypt, despite opposition from Mahmud II, the Ottoman sultan of Turkey. Mohammed Ali has the Mamluk leaders murdered to free him to govern all of Egypt.

1805 At the Battle of Trafalgar, Horatio Nelson's British fleet captures the large Franco-Spanish fleet off Cape Trafalgar. Nelson is killed, but he ends Napoleon's hopes of challenging the British at sea for a long time.

country's president in 1861. He suspended payments of foreign debts, prompting an invasion by French forces to create an empire for Maximilian, brother of the Austrian emperor. After they withdrew, Maximilian was executed and Juárez became president once more.

John Stuart MILL
1806–73
English philosopher

John Stuart Mill was one of the most important liberal thinkers of the 19th century. He was born in England and educated privately by his father, the philosopher James Mill. He worked for the East India Company from 1822 until 1858, and for a brief time sat as a member of parliament. In writings such as *Utilitarianism* (1863), Mill suggested that actions are right if they bring about happiness and not right if they do not. In *On Liberty* (1859), Mill suggested that a mature society not only tolerates individual liberty but encourages it. In establishing these beliefs, Mill described the liberal democracy that would become a popular form of government in the 20th century.

Giuseppe GARIBALDI
1807–82
Italian patriot

Born in Nice, France, the son of an Italian sailor, Giuseppe Garibaldi was highly influential in the unification of Italy. He went to sea at 17, and joined the Italian nationalist movement, the *Risorgimento*. He was condemned to death for treason and forced to flee to South America. He returned to Italy in 1848 and fought for the Sardinian king against the

Austrians. Then he went to help Rome defend itself from the French. After another brief period of exile in the United States, he joined a crusade to unify Italy under Victor Emmanuel II of Sardinia. Gathering a volunteer army of 1,000 "Red-shirts", Garibaldi conquered Sicily and the kingdom of Naples in 1860. Italy (except for Rome and Venice) was now united under King Victor Emmanuel. But Garibaldi failed to take Rome and he finally retired to a farm.

NAPOLEON III
1808–73
French emperor

Louis Napoleon Bonaparte enjoyed great success as emperor of France, mainly as the result of his name, which evoked nostalgia for the glorious reign of his uncle, Napoleon I (p.71). Louis Napoleon spent his youth in exile. After two unsuccessful attempts to overthrow the French government (1836, 1840), he was imprisoned but escaped to England. After the French monarchy was overthrown in 1848, Louis was elected to the French assembly and was elected president of France the same year. In 1851, he seized power and became emperor as Napoleon III. He encouraged the industrialization of France and became a respected international leader. He pursued an aggressive foreign policy, uniting Nice and Savoy with France and winning colonies in Africa. However, in 1870 he unwisely declared war on Prussia. Captured, he was forced to abdicate.

NAPOLEON III
The French emperor was cruelly caricatured following France's defeat in the Franco-Prussian War.

Henry COLE
1808–82
English designer

The Great Exhibition of 1851, the showcase for the best in British industry, was designed by Henry Cole. Cole was born in Bath, and began his working life at the public records office, where he was responsible for preserving important fragile documents. Using an assumed name, Felix Summerly, Cole later set up his own firm to manufacture artistic objects such as a tea service. In 1856, he became the first Englishman to publish Christmas cards. He became director of the South Kensington Museum, which later became the Victoria and Albert Museum. His greatest achievement was to design the Great Exhibition of 1851, which was sponsored by Prince Albert.

Felix MENDELSSOHN
1809–47
German composer

Born in Hamburg, Felix Mendelssohn was a major figure in 19th-century music. A child prodigy, he played many instruments, and composed his first masterpiece, the *Octet for Strings*, at the age of 16. This was followed by the overture to *A Midsummer Night's Dream* the next year. After studying in Berlin, he travelled around Europe. During this time he wrote the *Hebrides Overture* (1830), and the *Italian Symphony* (1833). He became especially well known in England, which he visited ten times during his life. In 1835, he moved to Leipzig, where he conducted the Gewandhaus Orchestra and founded the Leipzig Conservatory. Characterized by delicacy and sensitivity, Mendelssohn's music combines romantic sensibility with classical forms. His 48 *Songs Without Words* are particularly well loved.

1807 Napoleon I's French army invades Portugal, and King John VI flees to Brazil. A year later, the Portuguese revolt and the French are driven out after the arrival of a British army commanded by the future Duke of Wellington.

1808 Britain's decision to prohibit slave trading has given rise to a new naval patrol. The squadron has about six small ships based at Freetown, Sierra Leone, to patrol the coastline and arrest the biggest maritime trade out of Africa.

EDGAR ALLAN POE
One of the great figures of American literature, Edgar Allan Poe showed a fascination for the mysterious and the horrific in much of his work.

in the Rue Morgue. In his stories and in poems such as *The Raven* Poe created a world both real and fantastic, beautiful and monstrous. A complex, tormented figure, Poe died of alcohol poisoning.

Edgar Allan POE
1809–49
US poet, writer, and editor

Edgar Allan Poe was one of the most original writers in American literature. Born in Massachusetts, Poe was orphaned at three, and was brought up by John Allan, a wealthy tobacco merchant. His early work was not a success, and Poe enlisted in the army. Allan's influence secured him a place at West Point, the US Military Academy, but he forced his own expulsion so he could write poetry. In 1837, Poe moved to Philadelphia where he worked for a magazine and wrote supernatural horror stories such as *The Fall of the House of Usher*. In 1841, he published the first modern detective story, *The Murders*

Louis BRAILLE
1809–52
French educationalist

The lives of countless visually impaired people have been improved by the work of Louis Braille. Born in Paris, France, Braille became blind at the age of three. When he was ten, he entered a school for the blind, where he finally became a teacher. In 1829, he developed a system of six raised dots, used in many different combinations to represent letters and words. This enabled the blind to read by moving their fingers over the script.

BRAILLE
By touching these raised patterns of dots, blind people are able to read.

Abraham LINCOLN
1809–65
16th US president

The US president most revered as a symbol of democracy and national unity was born in a Kentucky log cabin. Self-educated, Lincoln became a lawyer and then a politician, entering Congress in 1846. He was strongly opposed to the introduction of slavery into the United States's new territories. In 1860, Lincoln ran for president as the new anti-slavery Republican party's candidate. Lincoln's victory caused 11 Southern states to secede, or break away, from the Union to form the Confederate States of America. Lincoln declared that no state had the right to secede, and his refusal to agree to Confederate demands precipitated the outbreak of the American Civil War in April 1861. In his 1862 Emancipation Proclamation, Lincoln declared freedom for all slaves in areas of rebellion. In the Gettysburg Address of 1863, he declared his aim of preserving "government of the people, by the people, and for the people". Five days after Confederate forces surrendered, Lincoln was shot dead by a Confederate sympathizer, John Wilkes Booth.

AMERICAN CIVIL WAR

Lasting four years and leaving more than 600,000 dead, the Civil War pitted the Confederate States of America – the 11 southern states that seceded from the Union – against the states and territories that remained loyal to federal authority.

CAUSES OF THE WAR
While most people in the rapidly industrializing northern states did not oppose slavery in the South, many did oppose the spread of slavery to the West. However, southern politicians resisted any restrictions on African-American slavery. Political compromises kept the peace for a time, but southern states began leaving the Union after ABRAHAM LINCOLN'S election in 1860. In April 1861, the war began when Confederate forces shelled Fort Sumter in South Carolina.

NORTHERN VICTORY
The Union army halted Confederate invasions of the North in 1862 at Antietam, Maryland, and at Gettysburg, Pennsylvania in 1863. The Union's capture of Vicksburg, Mississippi split the Confederacy in two; in April 1865 General ROBERT E. LEE (1807–70) surrendered the main Confederate force to Union commander ULYSSES S. GRANT (p.101) at Appomattox Court House, Virginia.

Union soldier

Confederate soldier

1809 Spencer Perceval becomes Britain's prime minister. In 1812, he is shot dead by a man who had written to him with a complaint against the government. He is the only British prime minister ever to be assassinated.

1809 Rome is occupied by French troops and Napoleon declares the Papal States annexed to Rome. Pius VII excommunicates Napoleon but is taken prisoner in July, remaining in exile until the invasion of France in 1814.

92

Charles DARWIN
1809–82
English naturalist

Charles Darwin revolutionized biology by putting forward the theory of evolution. After graduating from Cambridge University, Darwin became a naturalist on HMS Beagle during its survey (1831–36) of South American waters. Here, in the Galapagos Islands off Ecuador, Darwin first formulated his concept of evolution. He believed that over time species adapt to their environment, or else they die out according to a process of

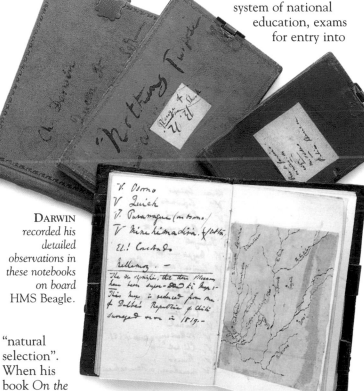

DARWIN recorded his detailed observations in these notebooks on board HMS Beagle.

"natural selection". When his book On the Origin of Species was published in 1859, public opinion was divided. Some considered Darwin's theory that man was descended from the ape was contrary to the creation story in the Book of Genesis in the Bible, and thus opposed to the teachings of the Church. Today, though, On the Origin of Species and Darwin's later book,

The Descent of Man (1871), are recognized as brilliant scientific achievements.

William GLADSTONE
1809–98
British prime minister

The dominant figure in Britain's Liberal Party from 1868 to 1894 was William Gladstone. He joined the Conservative government led by Robert Peel (p.82) in 1833. In 1859, however, Gladstone transferred his allegiance to the Whig Party, which later became the Liberal Party. He became prime minister in 1868. He achieved many reforms; the first system of national education, exams for entry into the civil service, vote by secret ballot, and parliamentary reform. His third ministry collapsed because of his support for Home Rule for Ireland. Gladstone's arch rival was Benjamin Disraeli (p.89), the other great figure in British politics during Victorian times.

1810

Frédéric CHOPIN
1810–49
Polish composer

Born in Zelazowa Wola, Poland, Frédéric Chopin brought romantic piano music to new heights of melodic expressiveness. Chopin grew up in Warsaw and made his first public performance at the age of eight. He studied music at the Warsaw Conservatory. Chopin became famous as a concert pianist and composer in Austria and Poland, but moved to Paris, France in 1831, where he gave private recitals and piano lessons, and frequented the fashionable artistic circles in the salons. The music composed for his concert performances before 1832 was designed to show off his fantastic technique, and includes two piano concertos. Later pieces, however, such as his nocturnes, waltzes, preludes, studies, and mazurkas, are more tuneful and less difficult to play. His eight-year affair with the novelist George Sand (p.89) shocked society at the time, but he was nevertheless universally admired as a composer and pianist. Chopin's health was never good, and he died of tuberculosis aged 39.

Robert SCHUMANN
1810–56
German composer

The music of Robert Schumann made him a leader of the Romantic movement. Born in Zwickau, Germany, Schumann originally trained as a lawyer, but gave up law to study music. Hand injuries prevented a concert career, but he continued composing and founded a music journal, the Neue Zeitschrift für Musik. In the 1830s, he wrote many pieces for piano, including two sonatas, and the collections Carnaval (1835), Fantasiestücke (1837), and Kinderszenen. His piano teacher refused permission for his daughter, Clara Wieck, to marry Schumann, and the late 1830s was an unhappy time for him. In 1840, the year he finally married Clara, he wrote more than 150 songs, including the collection Dichterliebe. He then turned to orchestral composition, including four symphonies and a piano concerto. In the 1850s, his health began to fail, and he was admitted to an asylum after a suicide attempt in 1852.

Theodor SCHWANN
1810–82
German physiologist

Some of the most important advances in cell biology were made by Theodor Schwann. Born in Neuss, Germany, he became a professor at Louvain, Belgium, in 1838, and in 1848, became professor at Liège. He discovered the enzyme pepsin – the chemical responsible for protein digestion – and investigated muscle contraction. He also brilliantly extended cell theory, showing that the cell is the basis of all animal and plant life. Part of his work included the study of digestion and cell tissues. He showed that the fermentation of sugar is a result of living yeast cells, and coined the term "metabolism" to describe the chemical processes that take place when food is broken down in the body.

1810 Miguel Hidalgo leads Indians and Mestizos in rebellion against the viceroy government in Mexico. After his defeat, Father Jose Maria Moreleos continues the revolt, and independence is eventually won in 1821.

1810 King Kamehameha the Great conquers islands not yet under his control to become king of all Hawaii using weaponry supplied to him by white traders. In 1848, Kamehameha III grants his subjects shares in the islands.

P.T. BARNUM
1810–91
US showman

The phrase "the greatest show on earth" can be attributed to Phineas Taylor Barnum, a flamboyant showman who began his career displaying curiosities to the public, many of which were fakes. Among his first exhibits was an elderly black woman, whom he alleged was the 160-year-old former nurse of George Washington. In 1841, Barnum opened the American Museum in New York City, filling it with real and fake attractions. They included the "Feejee" mermaid, "Siamese twins", and "General" Tom Thumb, a midget called Charles Stratton who was only 63 cm (25 in) tall. Barnum later formed a travelling circus and served as mayor of Bridgeport, Connecticut.

Elisha Graves OTIS
1811–61
US inventor

The lift, or elevator, was invented in the United States by Elisha Graves Otis. Otis was a master mechanic at a factory making bed frames when he was put in charge of building a new factory in New York City. The building had several floors connected by a lifting platform. Otis knew such platforms were dangerous, so he designed a spring-operated safety device which would hold the platform in place should the ropes holding it break. He patented his "elevator" in New York in 1854 and set up his own business to manufacture them. From the start, he received a flood of orders. His elevators were used in the first skyscrapers, making it possible for increasingly tall buildings to be built. Otis later went on to develop a steam-powered elevator in 1861.

Franz LISZT
1811–86
Hungarian pianist and composer

Franz Liszt was considered the greatest pianist of the 19th century. Born in Raiding, Hungary, he gave his first public concert aged nine. During his 'teens he toured France, England, and Switzerland as a concert pianist. In 1827, he settled in Paris, France, where he met Hector Berlioz (p.88) and Frédéric Chopin (p.93). He also met and fell in love with the Comtesse d'Agoult, with whom he had three children. Liszt continued to tour, becoming enormously popular and inspiring "Lisztomania" throughout Europe. In 1848, he went to Weimar, Germany, where he concentrated on composing, conducting, and teaching. Liszt's piano music includes his Sonata in B Minor (1853), *Transcendental Studies* (1851), and 20 Hungarian Rhapsodies. His orchestral music influenced many composers, including Richard Wagner (p.95), who married his daughter. Liszt's later compositions became more experimental.

Harriet Beecher STOWE
1811–96
US novelist

Harriet Beecher Stowe's novel *Uncle Tom's Cabin* (1852), about life on a Southern plantation, influenced many people to seek the abolition of slavery in the years before the American Civil War. A minister's daughter, Stowe had a strict religious upbringing which gave her a profound sense of right and wrong. Besides writing a second anti-slavery novel, *Dred*, in 1856, Stowe wrote many other books, the best loved of them about life in New England, such as *Old Town Folks* (1869).

Charles DICKENS
1812–70
British writer

Charles Dickens was one of the most popular British writers of the 19th century. He was born in Hampshire, England, and in 1822 his family moved to London. There, because of financial problems, the young Dickens was sent to work in a factory. He received only two years' schooling, and in 1831 he became a freelance reporter. Later, he began writing stories for magazines, and his *Pickwick Papers* (1836–37), published in serial form, was an immediate success. By the age of 25 Dickens was a famous writer. During his long career he wrote 14 novels, including *Oliver Twist* (1838), *A Christmas Carol* (1843), *David Copperfield* (1850), and *Great Expectations* (1861). His work combines comedy, tragedy, and social criticism, and his characters, such as Mr Pickwick, Oliver Twist, Scrooge, and Uriah Heep, remain some of the most memorable in literature.

1811 Textile workers in England smash the new weaving and spinning machines that have taken their jobs during the Industrial Revolution. The rioters become known as Luddites after their leader, Ned Ludd.

1812 President Madison of the United States declares war on Great Britain. The war goes badly for the Americans and, in 1814, the British invade and burn Washington, D.C. The Treaty of Ghent ends the war in 1814.

THE OWL AND THE PUSSYCAT
In this famous illustration by Edward Lear, the owl and the pussycat are asking the pig if he is willing to sell his ring.

Edward LEAR
1812–88
British poet and artist

Edward Lear was the creator of "nonsense verse". The youngest of 20 children, he was educated at home and showed a natural talent for drawing. In 1832, he was employed by the Earl of Derby to illustrate his menagerie (animal collection).

Lear became a successful artist, travelled widely, and even gave drawing lessons to Queen Victoria (p.98). Later, he began writing nonsense poems for Derby's grandchildren, illustrating them with his own sketches. In 1846, he published these anonymously as *A Book of Nonsense*. A further volume, *Nonsense Songs*, was published in 1870. His verses include *The Owl and the Pussy Cat*, *The Jumblies*, and numerous funny limericks.

on the Zambezi River in 1855. Livingstone wrote two books, *Missionary Travels* (1857) and *The Zambesi and its Tributaries* (1865). He exposed the horrors of the slave trade and suggested ways of establishing trade and Christian missions. In 1866, he set out to find the source of the Nile and disappeared into the interior. He was found in 1871 by Henry Morton Stanley (p.115) of the *New York Herald* who had been sent to look for him. Livingstone died in Africa.

Richard WAGNER
1813–83
German composer

Germany's most celebrated operatic composer, Richard Wagner changed the whole structure of opera. He had written his first opera by the age of 20 and continued with *Rienzi* and *The Flying Dutchman* (1843). His revolutionary politics forced him to flee to Switzerland, where he wrote the operas *Tannhäuser* (1845) and

Henry BESSEMER
1813–98
English engineer

Henry Bessemer revolutionized the steel industry. He learned metallurgy at his father's foundry. In 1855, he patented a new invention, the "Bessemer converter", which enabled him to change crude iron into steel without going through the costly wrought-iron stage. In 1859, Bessemer set up a steelworks in Sheffield, England, specializing in guns and steel rails, but his method of steelmaking had more success in the United States than in Britain.

Giuseppe VERDI
1813–1901
Italian composer

The beautiful melodies of Giuseppe Verdi's operas made him one of Italy's most popular composers. Born near Busseto, Italy, he learnt music

LIVINGSTONE *used this compass and magnifying glass on his journeys through Africa; the arrows were shot into his boat by hostile pygmies.*

David LIVINGSTONE
1813–73
Scottish explorer and missionary

By opening up Africa to Christianity and trade with the West, David Livingstone hoped to counteract the African slave trade. Born into a poor family, he became a doctor and a Christian minister. In 1841, the London Missionary Society sent him to South Africa, and he set off on a series of exploratory journeys, discovering the Victoria Falls

Lohengrin (1847). In 1864, King Ludwig of Bavaria invited him to Munich, where he wrote *Tristan and Isolde* (1865) and *The Mastersingers* (1868). He completed his famous series of operas called *The Ring* (*The Rhinegold*, *The Valkyrie*, *Siegfried*, and *Twilight of the Gods*) in 1874. Wagner wrote the words as well as the music for his operas, calling them "music dramas". He aimed to create a perfect fusion of words, music, and stagecraft, and he developed the *leitmotif*, a passage of music that reflects a character or episode. His ideas changed musical history.

from the local organist, and became assistant organist in 1829. Rejected by the Milan Conservatory, he studied with a composer from La Scala, Milan's great opera house. He returned to Busseto and married, but his wife and two children all died. He later remarried. His first opera, *Oberto*, was performed at La Scala in 1839, and he achieved his first international success with *Nabucco* in 1842. His best-known works are *Rigoletto* (1851), *La Traviata* (1853), *Don Carlos* (1867), *Aida* (1871), *Otello* (1887), *Falstaff* (1893), and a Requiem mass (1875).

1812 After years of bad relations between France and Russia, Napoleon Bonaparte decides to use armed force. However, the Battle of Borodino is one of the first major setbacks for Napoleon and the battle enters Russian folklore.

1813 After a revolution, Simón Bolívar becomes dictator of Venezuela. But divisions within Venezuelan society make the revolution difficult to sustain. The following year, Bolívar withdraws, not returning for two years.

George BOOLE
1815–64
English mathematician

George Boole was the first mathematician to express logic in algebraic form. Born in Lincoln, England, Boole's interest in mathematics started when he was young, and he was largely self-taught. Even though he had no university degree, he was made professor of mathematics at Cork University in Ireland in 1849. He did important work on differential equations, but his most famous works are *Mathematical Analysis of Logic*, published in 1847, and *Laws of Thought*, published in 1854. In these books he used various mathematical symbols to express logical equations. Boolean Logic is applied to two numbers – 0 and 1 – the binary numbers that are the basis for modern digital devices.

John Alexander MACDONALD
1815–91
Canadian statesman

John Alexander Macdonald led the campaign for Canada's independence and in turn became its first prime minister. Born in Scotland, he was taken to live in Ontario as a child. In 1857, he became prime minister of Upper Canada, before leading the movement for federation. He also expanded Canada's borders to include Rupert's land, Northwest Territory, and British Columbia.

JOHN ALEXANDER MACDONALD
led Canada through its period of early growth.

Otto von BISMARCK
1815–98
Prussian prime minister

Otto von Bismarck united the German states and became first chancellor of the new Germany. In 1862, he became prime minister of Prussia, the largest German state. His first act was to dissolve Prussia's parliament, with the agreement of King Wilhelm I, before beginning an aggressive policy to expand Prussian power. He provoked war – first with Denmark, then Austria, and finally France – securing Prussian victories in each campaign. Bismarck used his dominant position in Europe to reorganize the German states under Prussian rule. In 1871, he proclaimed a new German empire with Wilhelm I as kaiser (emperor) and himself as chancellor. Bismarck dominated German politics for the next 19 years, earning the nickname, "the Iron Chancellor". His rule ended when he clashed with the young kaiser Wilhelm II in 1890.

The BRONTES
Charlotte (1816–55), Emily (1818–48), and Anne (1820–49)
British novelists

The three Brontë sisters wrote some of the most remarkable fiction of the 19th century. In 1820, their father, Patrick Brontë, became rector of Haworth, a village on the moors of Yorkshire, England. Soon after, their mother and two other sisters died, leaving their father to bring up his daughters and their brother, Branwell. The children amused themselves by writing about two fantasy worlds, Gondal and Angria. In 1846, they published *Poems* under the

CHARLOTTE BRONTE
The English novelist based Jane Eyre *on her experience as a governess.*

male pseudonyms, Currer, Ellis, and Acton Bell. They followed this in 1837 with three novels: Anne's *Agnes Grey*, Emily's *Wuthering Heights*, and Charlotte's *Jane Eyre*. The intense passions of *Wuthering Heights* and *Jane Eyre* have made them classics of English literature. Sadly, all three sisters died young.

Henry David THOREAU
1817–62
US philosopher

A friend of Ralph Waldo Emerson (p.89), Thoreau put the transcendentalist ideal of a simple life lived close to nature into practice. His account of two years living in a log cabin, *Walden; or Life in the Woods* (1854), is a classic of US autobiography and philosophy. In 1846, Thoreau was jailed briefly for refusing to pay a tax to support the US war with Mexico. This led to an essay, *Civil Disobedience* (1849), in which Thoreau outlined a philosophy of nonviolent protest.

Karl MARX
1818–83
German philosopher and revolutionary

Karl Marx was the founder of communism. Born in Trier in Germany, he studied law at Bonn and Berlin before becoming a journalist. In 1843, he moved to Paris, where he participated in the 1848 Revolution. Exiled from Europe for his revolutionary activities, Marx moved to London and began working closely with the Manchester industrialist Friedrich Engels. Together they produced *The Communist Manifesto* (1848), which advocated a classless society in which private ownership had been abolished, and the means of production belonged to the workers. In 1864, Marx and Engels founded the International Workingmen's

1815 The Duke of Wellington enjoys his greatest victory at Waterloo. Napoleon attacks the allied Anglo-Dutch and Prussian armies in Belgium, but following the repulse of the imperial guard, the French are routed and surrender.

1816 The Congress of Tucumán declares independence of the United Provinces of South America. Under threat from the Spanish, they retreat to Buenos Aires, where they are overthrown by provincial opponents.

COMMUNISM

Beginning with the line, "The history of all hitherto existing society is the history of class struggles", *The Communist Manifesto* is one of the most influential books of the last 200 years. The manifesto was written in 1848 by KARL MARX and businessman FRIEDRICH ENGELS (1820–95); it urged workers to construct a new society based on communism.

THE THEORY

MARX and ENGELS believed that history is determined by economic factors. They predicted the class struggle between capitalists (property owners) and workers would end in victory for the working class when private property was abolished; everybody would be equal, and the state would wither away. In order to achieve this classless society, all governments would have to be overthrown.

WORLD COMMUNISM

These revolutionary ideas were largely ignored in the 19th century. But in 1917, the Bolsheviks under LENIN (p.137) and TROTSKY (p.145) seized power in Russia and set up the world's first communist state. By 1950, almost half the people of the world lived under communism, but with the break-up of the Soviet Union in 1991 and the introduction of reforms in China, very few countries now consider themselves communist.

Das Kapital was Marx's study of capitalism.

Association, but this fell apart in 1872. Marx's greatest work was *Das Kapital* (1867–94), a hugely influential analysis of economic and social history. Although his views had a limited impact in his lifetime, they exerted a strong influence in the 20th century.

Ivan TURGENEV
1818–83
Russian writer

The writings of Ivan Turgenev reflect a deep concern for the future of Russia. Born into a wealthy family, he grew up on a large country estate, where he observed the injustices suffered by the serfs (peasants forbidden to leave the land). After studying in Berlin, Germany, Turgenev came to believe that Russia needed westernization. In 1852 he published *A Sportsman's Sketches*, which contained sympathetic portrayals of the peasantry. His greatest novel, *Fathers and Sons* (1862), reflects the views of young Russian intellectuals, particularly their faith in science and dedication to their country's reform. However, it was criticized by both young radicals and conservatives. Turgenev reacted by leaving Russia and spending the rest of his life abroad.

James JOULE
1818–89
English physicist

James Joule discovered the relationship between heat and energy. Born in Manchester, he studied chemistry with the scientist John Dalton (p.71). In his experiments on heat, Joule calculated the amount of electrical energy that could be produced in relation to the amount of heat; this became known as Joule's Law. He also established the mechanical equivalent of heat, which became the basis of energy conservation. The joule, a unit of energy, is named after him.

Jean FOUCAULT
1819–68
French physicist

Born in Paris, Jean Foucault was the first scientist to calculate the velocity – rate of speed – of light, using mirrors. In 1850, he proved that light travels more slowly in water than in air, while in 1851, using a suspended pendulum, he proved that the Earth rotates. In 1852, he invented and constructed the gyroscope, and in 1857, the Foucault prism. He also improved the mirrors in reflecting telescopes. He became a physicist at the Paris Observatory in 1855 and invented high-quality regulators for driving machinery at constant speed. These were used in telescope motors and factory engines.

George ELIOT
1819–80
British writer

George Eliot was responsible for developing the psychological novel in which characterization plays an important role. Born Mary Anne Evans, early influences led to strong religious beliefs, but, aged 22, she met Charles Bray, a controversial free-thinker, who helped her break free of religious, political, and social traditions. She moved to London, working as a writer and meeting other radicals, including George Henry Lewes, with whom she was to live until his death 24 years later. Separated from his wife, their unconventional partnership isolated Evans from her family. She published her first novel, *Adam Bede*, in 1859 under the pen name George Eliot. This was followed by *The Mill on the Floss* (1860), *Silas Marner* (1861), and *Middlemarch*

1817 At a mass meeting in Manchester, England, the local magistrates take firm action to suppress a radical gathering. The troops ride through the crowd and 11 people are killed. The massacre becomes known as "Peterloo".

1819 After the British return the island of Java to the Dutch, the lieutenant governor of Java, Stamford Raffles, decides to try to establish a new port in the area. A Malay sultan agrees to cede Singapore to Britain.

(1871–72), which is considered her masterpiece. She depicts every level of Middlemarch society with detail and humour, and examines the thoughts, feelings, and motivations of her characters with great intelligence and compassion.

Herman MELVILLE
1819–91
US writer and poet

At the time of his death, Herman Melville was known only as a minor government official who had once published a few sea-stories. Today he is considered one of the US's greatest writers. Poverty forced the young Melville into a career at sea, and his experiences on a whaling voyage in the Pacific formed the basis of his first novels, *Typee* (1846) and *Omoo* (1847). He produced several more novels and short stories, none of which met with much popular success. In 1851 he published his masterpiece, *Moby Dick*, a novel in which a whaling captain's obsessive search for a white whale is a symbol of the human confrontation with evil. Melville's last great work, the novel *Billy Budd*, was published posthumously in 1924.

MOBY DICK
is Melville's most famous novel.

Walt WHITMAN
1819–92
US poet

Written in rhythmic free verse, sometimes expressing controversial ideas, and above all celebrating the ideals of freedom and democracy, the ground-breaking poetry of Walt Whitman is both highly personal and uniquely American. Born in Long Island, New York, the young Whitman worked as a printer and journalist. In 1855 he self-published *Leaves of Grass*, a collection of 12 powerful and innovative poems. The assassination of Abraham Lincoln affected Whitman profoundly, and his poems *O Captain! My Captain!* and

When Lilacs Last in the Dooryard Bloom'd memorialize the slain president. In 1873 a stroke left Whitman an invalid, and he spent his last years in retirement in Camden, New Jersey.

VICTORIA
1819–1901
British queen

Victoria was the longest-reigning British queen in history and did much to raise the profile of the monarchy. She ascended the throne in 1837 on the death of her uncle, William IV, and reigned until 1901. She was well advised, both by her prime ministers, notably William Gladstone (p.93) and Benjamin Disraeli (p.89), and by her husband Albert of Saxe-Coburg-Gotha, whom she had married in 1840. Victoria and Albert had nine children. When Albert died in 1861, the queen entered a long period of mourning, only returning to public life in the 1870s. During Victoria's reign, Britain reached the height of its powers, both at home and abroad; the domestic economy was transformed by industrialization, and the British Empire reached its greatest extent. She died a respected and popular monarch.

1820

Jenny LIND
1820–87
Swedish soprano

Jenny Lind was one of the first opera singers to achieve international fame. Born in Stockholm, Sweden, she studied singing and made her professional operatic debut in 1838. She then went to Paris, France, to study. She sang the title role in Bellini's *Norma*, with the Berlin Opera, to great acclaim, and embarked on a series of highly successful tours throughout Europe. She was particularly known for the purity of her voice, her wide range of notes (she could sing from B below middle C to high G), and her brilliant vocal control, all of which earned her the nickname the "Swedish Nightingale". In 1849, she withdrew from singing in opera, but continued to give concerts. She went to the United States where she toured with the great showman P. T. Barnum (p.94). Eventually, Lind retired from performing, although she continued to teach at the Royal College of Music in London, England.

1819 Florida moves from Spanish to American control after Andrew Jackson's capture of Pensacola in 1818. War with the Seminole Native Americans follows (1835–42) during which most are killed or removed to Indian Territory.

1820 After the Missouri Territory applies for statehood, a long debate in the US Congress ends in compromise: Missouri is admitted as a slave state balanced by the admission of Maine as a free state.

Susan B. ANTHONY
1820–1906
US reformer and advocate of women's rights

A leader of the US women's suffrage movement, Susan B. Anthony was, in many ways, a woman before her time. Born into a Quaker family in Massachusetts, Anthony became a teacher, then managed the family farm while working for the anti-slavery and temperance (anti-alcohol) movements. In 1848, she attended the first US women's rights convention at Seneca Falls, New York, and in 1852, helped form the Woman's State Temperance Society of New York. In the 1850s, she also campaigned on other women's issues, including equal voting rights, control of property, and guardianship of children after divorce. From 1868 to 1870, she co-edited the magazine *The Revolution* with her friend Elizabeth Cady Stanton. In 1869, the two formed the National Woman Suffrage Association but, in 1872, Anthony was arrested for violating voting laws. She was president of the Association from 1892 to 1900 and helped to compile the four-volume *History of Women's Suffrage* (1881–86).

FLORENCE NIGHTINGALE *organized the first modern wartime nursing service.*

Florence NIGHTINGALE
1820–1910
British nurse

Florence Nightingale single-handedly revolutionized nursing practices, sanitation in hospitals, and public health in the 19th century. Born in Florence, Italy, she trained as a nurse in Europe before taking a job in London

supervising a hospital for invalid women. When war broke out in the Crimea, Nightingale volunteered for duty, leaving for Scutari in 1854 with 38 nurses in her charge. She organized the barracks hospital after the Battle of Inkerman, and by introducing discipline and hygiene to hospitals she managed to reduce the death toll. When she returned to England in 1856, she was rewarded with a fund of £50,000 for training nurses at St Thomas's and Kings College hospitals in London. In 1859, she published her work *Notes on Nursing.*

Harriet TUBMAN
c.1820–1913
US abolitionist

Called "the Moses of her people", Harriet Tubman led more than 300 slaves to freedom in her fight to end slavery in the United States. An escaped slave herself, she devoted her life to smuggling other slaves to free territory by way of safe houses along the network known as the Underground Railroad. Rewards were offered for her capture, but she was never turned in. During the Civil War she enrolled as a nurse while acting as a spy for the North. Despite her courage, the US government refused her a pension until 30 years after the war had ended.

Robert O'Hara BURKE
1821–61
Irish explorer

The first man to cross Australia from south to north, Robert O'Hara Burke was born in Ireland, but emigrated to Australia in 1853. In 1860, the inexperienced Burke was chosen to lead a difficult expedition through the Outback. Leaving most of his men at a base camp, Cooper's Creek, he pressed on to the north coast with three companions. They struggled back, exhausted, to Cooper's Creek to discover that the others had left just hours before. Burke and his second-in-command, William Wills, both starved to death. A third man was looked after by aboriginals until rescuers arrived. Although the trip was a disaster, Burke had made the first crossing of Australia.

Fyodor DOSTOEVSKY
1821–81
Russian writer

Fyodor Dostoevsky was one of Russia's greatest novelists. Born in Moscow in 1849, he was exiled to Siberia for revolutionary activities. There he spent five years in prison, reading Dickens (p.94) and attending church. In 1861, he travelled in Europe, returning to Russia in 1871. Dostoevsky's novels include *Crime and Punishment* (1866), an intense portrayal of sin, remorse, and redemption; *The Idiot* (1868), the story of a doomed Christlike figure; and his masterpiece, *The Brothers Karamazov* (1880), which attempts to fathom the human soul. His work deals with dark themes, and was inspired by the widespread poverty and hardship he observed.

1821 The Battle of Carabobo, the final confrontation in Símón Bolívar's campaign to liberate Venezuela, takes place. Success allows the patriots to move south to engage the remaining Spanish forces in the Central Andes.

1821 Greece revolts against the Ottoman Turks. Egypt sends reinforcement troops to assist the Turks. Alarmed, Britain, Russia, and France destroy the Turkish-Egyptian fleet in 1827. In 1832, Greece wins independence.

Richard
BURTON
1821–90
English explorer
and writer

Richard Burton was
an intrepid man
who travelled to many
places previously
uncharted by
Europeans. Burton
was born in Devon,
England, and brought
up in France and Italy.
He was a brilliant
linguist, eventually
speaking more than
30 languages. After
serving with the
British army in India,
Burton became an
explorer. In 1853,
disguising himself
as a Muslim, he
travelled to Mecca
and Medina in
Arabia, and then
Harar, in East Africa
– all three Muslim
cities forbidden
entry to Christians.
In 1856, he went
to Africa with John
Hanning Speke
(p.103), to search for
the source of the River
Nile. They suffered
terribly from sickness;
Burton was paralyzed
and had to be carried,
while Speke went
temporarily blind. But together,
they reached Lake Tanganyika
while Speke, alone, found Lake
Victoria, the Nile's main
source. They were the first
Europeans to visit Africa's great
lakes. Burton published more
than 50 books during his life,
including a famous translation
of the stories known as the
Arabian Nights.

RICHARD BURTON
*The daring English explorer was
also a great scholar. As a British
army officer, he learnt Arabic and
more than 30 other languages.*

Hermann
HELMHOLTZ
1821–94
German physicist

Much of the knowledge we
have of the human eyes,
ears, and nervous system is a
result of the work of Hermann
Helmholtz. Born in Potsdam,
Prussia, Helmholtz became
professor of physiology at
Königsberg from 1849, Bonn
from 1855, and Heidelberg
from 1858. In 1871 he
became professor of
physics in Berlin. He
excelled in the fields of
physiology, physics, and
mathematics. He did
ground-breaking work
on vision, particularly
on the human
perception of colour;
he also invented the
opthalmoscope – an
instrument for the
close examination of
the inside of the eye.
Helmholtz was the first to
explain how the cochlea
in the inner ear works, and
the first to measure the
speed of nerve impulses.
He is also remembered
for his analysis of the
spectrum of light, as well
as the conservation of
energy in relation to
muscular action in the
body. He also researched
the development of electric
current in a galvanic battery.

Mary Baker
EDDY
1821–1910
US founder of
Christian Science

Mary Baker Eddy founded
the Christian Science
movement and advanced the
cause of faith healing. Born in
New Hampshire,
Eddy was
educated at
home by her
parents, spending much of
her time reading the Bible. In
1866, Eddy was badly injured
by a fall. She lay in bed,
reading accounts of Jesus's
miraculous cures. Suddenly, she
felt that she had been healed.
Eddy believed that sickness was
a matter of the mind, not the
body, and that it could be
cured by faith. She travelled
the country, lecturing on her
ideas and experiences. In 1875,
she explained her philosophy
in a book, *Science and Health
with Key to the Scriptures*. To
her followers, this is a holy
scripture second only to the
Bible. In 1879 Eddy founded
the first Church of Christ,
Scientist. Today, the church
has around 3,000 branches
in more than 50 countries.

Clara
BARTON
1821–1912
US founder of the
American Red Cross

After working for the
organization in Europe,
Clara Barton (full name
Clarissa Harlowe Barton)
founded the American branch
of the Red Cross. Born in
Massachusetts, Barton worked
as a schoolteacher from
1836–54, then in the Patent
Office in Washington D.C. But
when the American Civil War
broke out in 1861, Barton took
up nursing and also worked to
get badly needed medical
supplies to the battlefields.
After the war, while in Europe
recovering from an illness,
Barton joined the International
Red Cross and nursed the
wounded during the Franco-
Prussian War of 1870–71.
Back home she established an
American branch of the Red
Cross in 1881 and served as the
organization's first president
until 1904. Largely as a result
of her campaigning, the United
States signed the Geneva
Convention in 1882.

1822 Liberia is founded
in West Africa as
a home for freed US slaves. The
abolition of slavery in the British
Empire comes about in 1833.
The Thirteenth Amendment to
the Constitution outlaws slavery
in the United States in 1865.

1822 Brazil, which has
been agitating for
independence, is relieved when
King Joao VI leaves his son
Crown Prince Pedro in Brazil
and returns home. Pedro declares
Brazil independent and is made
emperor three years later.

Gregor Johann MENDEL
1822–84
Austrian botanist

Johann Mendel created the science of genetics. Born in Heinzendorf, Austria, Mendel became a monk, but he was also fascinated by science, and entered the University of Vienna in 1851 to study that subject. After graduating, he returned to his monastery, becoming an abbot in 1868. During this time, Mendel never ceased to be fascinated by how characteristics in humans, animals, and plants are passed down through generations. In the garden of his monastery, he began to carry out experiments with pea plants. By crossing certain varieties of pea, he realized that the passing on of characteristics such as height and flower colour depends on basic units in the makeup of living things – units we now call genes. These genes exist in either dominant or recessive forms, so that some characteristics, such as tallness, are dominant, and some, such as shortness, are recessive. Mendel's findings changed the way that scientists viewed nature's reproductive process, but fame came to him only after his death.

Ulysses S. GRANT
1822–85
18th US president

As a boy in Ohio and Illinois, Ulysses Grant had little interest in a military career. His father secured him an appointment to the US

MICROSCOPE
This microscope was presented to Louis Pasteur by Whitbreads in 1873.

Military Academy at West Point, New York, and Grant fought in the Mexican-American War (1846–48), but then resigned from the army. Returning to Illinois, he tried several business ventures, but all of them failed. At the outbreak of the Civil War he became a brigadier general and soon developed a reputation as one of the Union's best fighting commanders. Grant was given overall command of Union forces in 1864, and he finally took Lee's surrender in April 1865, ending the war. Grant was then the nation's greatest hero and in 1868 he was elected president on the Republican ticket. Although re-elected in 1872, Grant's presidency was marred by major scandals: many of his appointees and associates were corrupt. After leaving office he again went into business and again failed. Diagnosed with cancer, Grant managed to complete his memoirs – now considered a classic of military history – days before his death.

Louis PASTEUR
1822–95
French chemist and biologist

The process known as pasteurization, which keeps certain perishable products, such as milk, from turning sour, takes its name from its creator, Louis Pasteur. Pasteur studied physics and chemistry and became professor of chemistry at the University of Lille in 1854. Here he researched the process of fermentation and discovered that the presence of bacteria in alcohol turns wine sour. Pasteur soon discovered that the bacteria could be destroyed by heat to make the wine last longer. Wine could now be produced, preserved, and transported without turning "bad". The process, soon known as pasteurization, was then also applied to milk. Pasteur also proved that microorganisms cause disease, and was the first to develop vaccines for rabies, anthrax, and chicken cholera.

ETIENNE LENOIR
built the first car and an early internal-combustion gas engine.

Etienne LENOIR
1822–1900
French inventor

In 1859, Etienne Lenoir invented the first practical internal-combustion gas engine, fuelled by coal, gas, and air, which later revolutionized industry and transportation. In 1860, he built the first car, which was powered by his engine, and in 1886 he produced an engine-driven boat. However, the real value of his engine was for powering small machinery such as water pumps and printing presses – it was too big to be of long-lasting practical use in vehicles. Lenoir also invented an electric brake.

Francis GALTON
1822–1911
English scientist

Francis Galton was an enthusiastic, influential scientist who worked in several different fields. The cousin of Charles Darwin (p.93), Galton studied medicine at Birmingham Hospital and later at Kings College, London. From 1846, he travelled to Africa, exploring uncharted areas. In 1853, he published *Narrative of an Explorer in Tropical South Africa* and *Art of Travel*. His studies in meteorology, published as *Meteorographica* in 1863, laid the foundation for modern weather maps. He went on to study heredity, publishing *Hereditary Genius* in 1869, *English Men of Science: Their Nature and Nurture* (1874), and *Natural Inheritance* (1889). Galton was the first to suggest that mental and physical features are equally inherited. He also created the system of identifying people by their fingerprints, described in *Finger Prints* (1892).

Gustav KIRCHHOFF
1824–87
German physicist

Gustav Kirchhoff discovered the thermodynamics of radiation. Born in Königsberg, while still a student he devised Kirchhoff's Laws for electrical currents. He was professor at Heidelberg and Berlin universities, where he specialized in electricity and spectrum analysis. This led to the discovery of the elements caesium and rubidium. He also explained the Fraunhofer lines in the solar spectrum as the absorption of the spectral wavelengths in the Sun's atmosphere, devising Kirchhoff's law of radiation.

1823 President James Monroe proclaims the Monroe Doctrine, stating that the Western hemisphere is "off limits" for European colonization. The Doctrine is the work of Monroe's secretary of state, John Quincy Adams.

1823 The Irish Catholic Association is established by "the Liberator", Daniel O'Connell. He attracts so many Irish priests, lawyers, and professionals that the British government cannot suppress the organization.

Anton BRUCKNER
1824–96
Austrian composer

Anton Bruckner composed some of the finest symphonies of the 19th century. Born near Linz, Austria, he became a school teacher like his father, and was only a part-time musician until 1855, when he was appointed organist at Linz Cathedral. At this point he began to study music more seriously and, after hearing Wagner's (p.95) music in 1863, started composing his first major pieces. He became professor at the Vienna Conservatory in 1868. Bruckner wrote religious choral music such as the *Te Deum* (1884), but concentrated mainly on symphonies. He was not happy with his first attempt (he called it "Symphony No. 0"), but went on to write nine more, all masterpieces of the symphonic form.

Charles BLONDIN
1824–97
French acrobat

One of the world's most spectacular acrobats, Charles Blondin's claim to fame was walking the tightrope. Born Jean François Gravelet near Calais, France, he trained at the Ecole de Gymnase in Lyon from the age of five. Billed as "the Little Wonder", he made his first public appearance after only six months' training. In 1859, he crossed the Niagara Falls in Canada on a tightrope 49 metres (160 ft) above the

BLONDIN
This toy shows the amazing French acrobat riding a penny-farthing bicycle.

churning water. He performed this feat again on many occasions, with astonishing variations: blindfolded, pushing a wheelbarrow, walking on stilts, in a sack, with a man on his back – and once, he even stopped to cook and eat an omelette.

William KELVIN
1824–1907
British physicist

The absolute scale of temperature, now known as the kelvin, was just one of William Kelvin's discoveries. Kelvin was professor of physical sciences at Glasgow University, Scotland, where he created the first physics laboratory in a British university. In one of his early publications, he solved important problems of electrostatics. Kelvin was also chief consultant on the laying of the first

underwater Atlantic telegraph cable in 1857, but he finally made his fortune by inventing and patenting a device for speeding telegraphic transmission. He also improved the efficiency of ships' compasses and invented dozens of electrical instruments. Kelvin's house in Glasgow was the first to use electric, rather than gas, lights.

Johann STRAUSS II
1825–99
Austrian composer

Johann Strauss the Younger continued the work of his father in popularizing the Viennese waltz. Born in Vienna, Johann's father, Johann Strauss the Elder (1804–49), was a famous composer and conductor who had first made the waltz

---

1825 Having assisted Peru in expelling the Spanish, Simón Bolívar moves to Upper Peru, where he founds the republic later named Bolivia. Bolívar is also instrumental in winning independence for Colombia.

1827 Dom Miguel seizes the Portuguese throne despite the liberal constitiution sanctioned by his father Joao only a year earlier. Liberal exiles based in Britain invade northern Portugal sparking a two-year civil war.

popular throughout Europe. Young Johann was discouraged from becoming a musician by his father, but studied in secret, and started conducting his own orchestra in 1844. His brothers Josef and Eduard also became conductors. Johann Strauss the Younger composed more than 400 waltzes, including the famous *Blue Danube* (1867), *Tales from the Vienna Woods* (1868), and operettas such as *Die Fledermaus* (1874). After his father's death, he combined their two orchestras, which then performed in tours of Europe, Russia, and the United States. These tours made him even more famous than his father.

John Hanning
SPEKE
1827–64
English explorer

John Hanning Speke was the first person to discover the source of Africa's River Nile. In 1857, he went to Africa with Richard Burton (p.100) to search for the source of the Nile. When Burton was too sick to travel, Speke went on alone and discovered Africa's greatest lake, which he named Victoria, after his monarch (p.98). He later fell out with Burton, who refused to believe Speke's claim that the lake was the source of the Nile. In 1860–63, Speke returned to Lake Victoria and found further evidence that it was indeed the source. In 1864, he was due to debate his claims with Richard Burton in public. That day, Speke mysteriously shot himself while hunting. It was later proved beyond doubt that Speke had discovered the Nile's main source.

Joseph
LISTER
1827–1912
British surgeon

Joseph Lister pioneered the use of antiseptic in hospitals. He was educated at two Quaker institutions which emphasized natural history and science. Lister became professor of surgery first at Glasgow and Edinburgh universities in Scotland and later at Kings College, London. He transformed hospital practices when he introduced antiseptic surgery by using carbolic acid as a disinfectant. This dramatically reduced the risk of wounds becoming infected and therefore reduced death rates.

Josephine
BUTLER
1828–1906
English social reformer

A firm believer in women's education from an early age, Josephine Butler became a committed supporter of women's rights. Born in the north of England, she began a campaign against prostitution. She married George Butler, who was a church official in Winchester, a town where many soldiers were quartered. Butler strongly objected to the Contagious Diseases Acts, which made testing for sexually transmitted diseases compulsory for women living in seaports and military towns such as Winchester. She spent many years campaigning to bring an end to this practice. In 1896, she wrote an account of the campaign, *Personal Reminiscences of a Great Crusade*.

STEAM SPRAY
Joseph Lister invented the antiseptic carbolic steam spray in 1867. This version dates from around 1875.

Henrik
IBSEN
1828–1906
Norwegian playwright and poet

Born in Skien, Henrik Ibsen became Norway's finest playwright. He intended to study medicine, and at 15 apprenticed himself to a chemist. However, after writing his first play, *Catilina* (1850), he went into the theatre. In 1857, he became director of the Norwegian Theatre in Christiania (now Oslo), but it went bankrupt six years later, and Ibsen spent 26 years in Italy and Germany. No longer restrained by the theatrical fashions of Norway, he was free to use controversial subject matter, and refused to provide happy endings. In 1866, he published *Brand*, a long poem about a man who tries to overcome the small-mindedness of society, but who fatally ignores love. The hero of the play *Peer Gynt* (1867) is Brand's opposite; a lovable scoundrel. These two types feature frequently in Ibsen's work, which includes *A Doll's House* (1879) and *Hedda Gabler* (1890). Ibsen returned to Norway in 1891.

1828 The Test and Corporation Acts are repealed in Britain. They had laid down that office holders must take communion in the Church of England. The Repeal provides a precedent for the Catholic emancipation of 1829.

1828 In Africa, warrior-king Shaka, is murdered by his half-brothers. He had conquered neighbouring tribes to create a vast Zulu state. He left a professional army which successfully challenged European colonists.

Leo TOLSTOY
1828–1910
Russian writer

Tolstoy was a master of the psychological novel, in which characterization is all important. He was born Count Leo Nikolayevich Tolstoy on the family estate of Yasnaya Polyana in Russia. He studied law at Kazan University and, in 1851, he joined the army and later fought in the Crimean War. He moved back to his family estate to write his masterpiece, *War and Peace* (1863–69), an epic tale of two noble families during the Napoleonic wars. It contains vivid descriptions of military campaigns, portraying humans as mere victims of chance. His second great novel, *Anna Karenina* (1874–76), is the story of a married woman's love for an army officer and the tragic consequences of her passion. Tolstoy's religious writings brought him renown, but were so unorthodox that he was excommunicated by the Orthodox Church. As he grew older, he came to see truth only in simplicity, and renounced his earlier works as too stylized and sophisticated.

Joseph SWAN
1828–1914
English physicist and chemist

A pioneer of electric lighting and photography, Joseph Swan began work as a chemist, concentrating on manufacturing practices. He patented the carbon process for photographic printing in 1864 and invented bromide paper for producing colour photographs. He was also the first to produce artificial silk for practical use. Swan made one of the first miner's lamps and, in 1860, he invented an electrical lamp,

20 years before Edison (p.119). In 1897, when Edison had patented his own lamp, Swan invented an improved version. The two men joined forces to form the Edison and Swan United Electric Lighting Company in 1883. In all, Swan took out more than 70 patents for new inventions during his lifetime.

Friedrich KEKULE
1829–96
German chemist

Born in Darmstadt, Germany, Friedrich Kekule became an expert in organic chemistry. He set out to be an architect, but was persuaded to change course after hearing the lectures of well-known chemist Justus von Liebig. He studied chemistry at university and then worked in Liebig's laboratory for a year. In 1856, he took a teaching position in Heidelberg and built himself a private laboratory in his house in order to study structural organic chemistry. He published a multi-volume handbook on the subject between 1861–87.

GERONIMO
1829–1909
Native American warrior

Born in what is now New Mexico, Geronimo was an Apache who attempted to free his people from the US government's restrictions. In 1876, the US government planned to move the Chiricahua Apaches to a new reservation at San Carlos, Arizona Territory. Geronimo fled across the border into Mexico with other Chiricahuas. He was arrested and taken to

San Carlos in chains. Life there was harsh, with barren land, overcrowding, and little food. In 1882, Geronimo and others escaped to Mexico again, making raids across the border in an attempt to free their people. US troops attacked their stronghold in 1883 and Geronimo was forced to surrender and return to San Carlos. In 1885, he led 134 Chiricahuas on a final

break-out from Arizona, but in 1886 he had to surrender again. Confined to Fort Sill in Oklahoma, he became a tourist attraction in his last years.

GERONIMO *travels in a car with three other Native Americans. He was the most famous of all the Apache warriors who fought against the US government.*

1828 The Workingmen's Party, an early labour group, is founded by unemployed artisans in New York, USA. Its members seek electoral and banking reforms as a prelude to a radical programme of wealth redistribution.

1829 The first university boat race between Oxford and Cambridge universities is held on the River Thames in London. The first race, which is won by Oxford, was from Hambledon Lock to Henley Bridge.

104

William BOOTH
1829–1912
English founder of the Salvation Army

William Booth set up the Christian Mission in London, England, which later became the Salvation Army for the poor. Born into a poor family in Nottingham, William Booth converted to Methodism

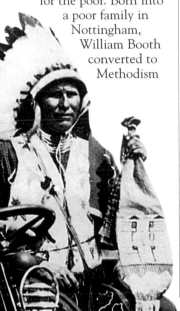

at the age of 15. Later, as a minister on Tyneside, he became frustrated at his inability to offer practical help to the poor and needy. In 1855, he married Catherine Mumford, a social worker, and together they set up the Christian Mission in London's poverty-stricken East End. They recruited men and women to provide shelter, food, and clothing for the homeless, and to help fight the evils of poverty, sweatshop labour, and child prostitution. Catherine believed that women had as much right to preach as men, and the couple were often imprisoned for preaching in public. Catherine died in 1890, but William carried on their work and the Army spread throughout the world. William Booth's book, *In Darkest England and the Way Out* (1890), outlines the beliefs and motives of the Salvation Army.

1830

Emily DICKINSON
1830–86
US poet

Emily Dickinson's poetry had a profound influence on later modern poets. Born in Amherst, Massachusetts, she led an uneventful and intensely private life. Her literary development was much influenced by her friends, with whom she corresponded regularly. She wrote 1,700 poems, but she was very secretive about her writing and published only seven of them during her lifetime. In her work, Dickinson experimented with different forms and combinations of rhyme and rhythm, and the expression of her thoughts on love, death, and religion were highly original.

After Emily's death, her sister published three volumes of her poetry in 1890, 1891, and 1896. Her vivid and unusual poems were recognized as works of genius.

James Clerk MAXWELL
1831–79
Scottish physicist

The work of James Clerk Maxwell paved the way for the great breakthroughs in physics of the 20th century. In 1856, he was appointed professor of natural philosophy at Aberdeen University, Scotland, and later at Kings College, London. In 1871, he was made professor of experimental physics at Cambridge University. He published papers on the kinetic theory of gases, established the nature of the planet Saturn's rings, and demonstrated the first colour photography with a picture of a tartan ribbon in 1861. His *Treatise on Electricity and Magnetism* (1873) provided the first evidence that light consists of electromagnetic waves. Maxwell was one of the greatest experimental physicists the world has ever known.

1830 Louise-Philippe, the son of the duc d'Orléans, is made king of France in a revolution. His extravagant lifestyle brings him criticism and he survives more assassination attempts than any other French leader.

1830 Belgium proclaims its independence from the Netherlands. The Belgians, who had resented the overbearing attitude of the Dutch, make the most of the revolution in Paris and rise up against the Dutch.

Edouard MANET
1832–83
French painter

The innovative work of Edouard Manet had a great influence on the Impressionist artists. Born in Paris, France, he was a pupil of the artist Couture from 1850, and was himself influenced by the earlier painters Goya (p.66) and Velazquez (p.43).

In 1863, Manet's painting *Déjeuner sur l'Herbe* shocked Paris by showing a nude woman picnicking with two clothed men on the grass. Another nude, his masterpiece *Olympia* (1865), caused even greater scandal, but Manet insisted that the visual effect of his pictures was more important than the subject matter. He worked with large, flat areas of colour, contrasting blocks of light and shade to convey a sense of immediacy, a style that inspired the Impressionists. Manet continued to paint a wide variety of subjects from modern life such as *The Execution of the Emperor Maximilian* (1867) and *A Bar at the Folies Bergère* (1882).

Nikolaus OTTO
1832–91
German engineer

Nikolaus Otto developed the four-stroke internal-combustion engine, which offered the first practical alternative to the steam engine. He built his first gasoline-powered engine in 1861. Three years later, he teamed up with a German industrialist and improved the engine. The pair won a gold medal for their invention at the Paris Exhibition of 1867. In 1876, Otto built an internal-combustion engine

Isabella BIRD
1831–1904
English traveller and writer

Born in Yorkshire, England, Isabella Bird was one of the first female travellers to detail her journeys around the world. In 1854, her parents sent her to Canada and the United States to recover from a spine operation. This journey led to her first travel book, *An Englishwoman in America* (1856). In 1873, Isabella travelled around the globe, visiting Australia, New Zealand, Hawaii, and the United States. She later published *A Lady's Life in the Rockies* (1879), an entertaining account of her adventures in the "Wild West" of America and her friendship with Rocky Mountain Jim, "a man whom any woman might love, but no sane woman would marry". In the 1880s, she trained as a nurse, and then spent several years travelling through Asia. She founded hospitals in India, China, and Korea, and an orphanage in Japan. She died in Edinburgh, aged 73, with her trunks packed for yet another journey.

EDOUARD MANET
The House at Rueil, 1882, oil on canvas, is in the National Gallery of Victoria, Melbourne, Australia.

1831 The *Risorgimento*, a resurgence of Italian nationalism, becomes a driving force for unification. The failure of revolts in Modena, Parma, and the Papal States, inspires Giuseppe Mazzini to found Young Italy.

1831 Pedro I, Emperor of Brazil since 1822, abdicates after an explosion of nationalist sentiment in Rio de Janeiro. On his return to Europe he leads a rebellion against his brother, Dom Miguel, but dies soon after its conclusion.

using the four-stroke cycle. It was patented by someone else, but is still generally known as the Otto Cycle. Otto's invention became most widely used in automobile engines.

ALICE AND THE DODO
Lewis Carroll's most famous creation was "Alice in Wonderland". This illustration of Alice and the dodo by the illustrator John Tenniel appeared in the book's first edition.

Lewis CARROLL
1832–98
English writer, mathematician, and photographer

The creator of "Alice in Wonderland" was born Charles Lutwidge Dodgson in Cheshire, England. He studied, and later taught, mathematics at Oxford University. There he befriended Alice Liddell, one of the daughters of the Dean of his college, for whom he wrote his famous stories. Under the pen name Lewis Carroll, he published *Alice's Adventures in Wonderland* in 1865. It was an immediate success, as was the sequel, *Alice Through the Looking-Glass* (1871). This was followed by *The Hunting of the Snark* (1876), a long narrative nonsense poem. Apart from the character of Alice, Carroll created such memorable characters as the Red Queen, the White Rabbit, the Mad Hatter, the Dormouse, and Tweedledum and Tweedledee. His quirky, imaginative stories are still popular with children all over the world.

THE EIFFEL TOWER
Many Parisians hated this huge structure when it was first built, but it soon became the symbol of the city.

Nils Adolf NORDENSKJOLD
1832–1901
Swedish explorer and scientist

Nils Adolf Nordenskjold was the first explorer to sail the Northeast Passage. Born in Helsinki, the son of a Swedish scientist, Nils Nordenskjold trained as a geologist and chemist. Between 1858 and 1876, he made seven scientific expeditions to the Arctic. He explored the Kara Sea, mapped the island of Spitsbergen, and tried twice, unsuccessfully, to reach the North Pole. This experience, however, convinced him that it was possible to reach the Pacific by sailing through Arctic waters, over the top of Russia. In July 1878, he set out from Norway on his ship, the *Vega*. He had almost reached his goal when his ship was trapped by ice. He had to wait ten months for the ice to melt before he was able to complete his journey, but he finally achieved one of the great goals of exploration.

Gustave EIFFEL
1832–1923
French engineer

The Eiffel Tower in Paris, France, is one of the most recognizable structures in the world, and was the work of Gustave Eiffel. After graduating from the College of Art in 1855, Eiffel began to specialize in metal construction, particularly bridges. He directed the building of an iron bridge in Bordeaux in 1858, followed by several other bridges, including one at Oporto, Portugal, and one in southern France which had a 162-metre (540-ft) arch spanning the Truyère River. He also designed the moveable dome over the Nice Observatory and the metal framework for the Statue of Liberty in New York in the United States. However, Eiffel made his name with the construction of the Eiffel Tower for the 1889 Paris Exhibition. At 320 metres (1,050 ft), it was the tallest building in the world until 1930. Eiffel designed it as a temporary structure, but it was so well built that it is still standing today.

Alfred NOBEL
1833–96
Swedish chemist

Alfred Nobel was the creator of dynamite, but is best known for giving his name to the Nobel Prize. In 1842, the Nobel family left Stockholm in Sweden and moved to St Petersburg in Russia. By the age of 16, Alfred was a competent chemist and fluent in five languages. He returned to Sweden and started to manufacture the explosive nitroglycerin. Soon afterwards, the factory blew up. Five people were killed, and Nobel was forbidden to re-open the factory. He experimented in secret and discovered that the explosive could be handled safely if mixed with a substance called kieselguhr. The resulting explosive was dynamite. He went on to perfect a more powerful substance, called gelignite. Nobel left the greater part of his fortune to establish the prestigious international award the Nobel Prize, awarded each year, unless there is a war, for achievements in science, literature, and world peace.

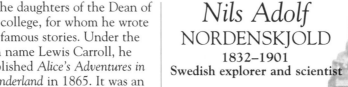

1833 Mohammed Ali is made ruler of Egypt. Administrative and economic innovations are established to support the army, which maintains his control. Scared of him, European powers force his withdrawal in 1841.

1833 A sermon by John Keble begins the Oxford Movement in Britain. The leaders of the movement reassert the authority of the Church of England as part of the Catholic Church, and its bishops as successors to the apostles.

Johannes BRAHMS
1833–97
German composer

The son of a double-bass player, Johannes Brahms was born in Hamburg and was a talented pianist as a child. He gave two concert performances in 1848–9, and his career took off with a concert tour in 1853, when he met Schumann (p.93) and Liszt (p.94). Schumann helped to publicize Brahms's music, and he became a close friend of the family, remaining devoted to Clara Schumann after Robert's death. He wrote his first piano concerto in 1859 while he was working as a conductor and teacher in Hamburg. He then moved to Vienna in 1862 to concentrate on composing. The success of his *German Requiem* in 1868 gave Brahms the confidence to complete his first symphony in 1876, and he went on to compose a further three symphonies, a second piano concerto, chamber music, and songs. Brahms's music was considered dry and academic in his own lifetime, but he is now recognized as one of the foremost composers of the 19th century.

Sitting BULL
c.1834–90
Native American leader

Sitting Bull was born into the Hunkpapa tribe of the Sioux, or Lakota, people. He won his name as a young man after showing bravery in a fight against another tribe. He became a medicine man (someone in close contact with the spirit world), and had a vision in which he saw the

SITTING BULL
In his native language, Sitting Bull was called Tatanke Iyotake.

Sioux defeating their enemies. In the 1870s, white miners poured into Sioux land in the Dakota territory. Sitting Bull, then leader of the Hunkpapa, told his people they must fight to save their homeland. At the Battle of Little Big Horn in 1876, Sioux and Cheyenne warriors wiped out US troops led by George Custer (p.112). The Sioux were forced to split up and Sitting Bull led his people to the safety of Canada. He returned to the USA in 1881 and lived on a reservation in Dakota. He was briefly a member of Buffalo Bill's Wild West Show. In 1890, fearful of an Indian uprising, police came to arrest Sitting Bull, but he was killed trying to escape.

William MORRIS
1834–96
English writer and designer

William Morris was born into a prosperous family near London. At Oxford University he became deeply interested in medieval art and went on to study architecture in 1856. He was close friends with the Pre-Raphaelite painters Rossetti (1828–82) and Burne-Jones (1833–98), but completed only one oil painting himself. In 1861 he formed (with others) a company to produce wallpaper, carpets, fabrics, and furniture. Morris hated Victorian mass-produced factory goods, and he ran the firm like a medieval guild, with craftworkers and designers producing their own work. He became active as a socialist, supporting the causes of workers and the unemployed. Morris was a prolific writer, producing mythical verse tales such as *The Story of Sigurd the Volsung and the Fall of the Niblungs* (1876), and idealistic fantasies such as *News From Nowhere* (1891). In 1890 he started a publishing company, the Kelmscott Press. Morris also designed typefaces, but it is his fabric and wallpaper for which he is best known today.

Gottlieb DAIMLER
1834–1900
German engineer

A major influence in the early development of the motor car, Daimler was born in Schorndorf and studied engineering in Stuttgart. In 1872 he worked with Nikolaus Otto (the man who invented the four-stroke internal-combustion engine) in Otto's factory, developing gas-powered engines. Wilhelm Maybach was the chief designer. Several

1833 In Spain, the first Carlist War is fought by followers of Don Carlos de Bourbon and his successors, who lay claim to the throne. They cannot challenge the loyalists and Carlism disappears as a force.

1833 Britain abolishes slavery in the British West Indies and 668,000 slaves are set free. Britain is the only country that enforces laws against the slave trade and has a permanent naval patrol in West African waters to prevent it.

IMRESSIONISM

During the 1860s, a group of French artists began to work together informally to develop a new style of painting. They tried to capture light and colour in their paintings and preferred working outside. In 1874 they organized their first exhibition, and critics gave them the derisory name of the Impressionists after a painting by Monet, *Impression – Sunrise*.

A FLEETING IMPRESSION

The Impressionists tried to achieve naturalism in their work. They ignored the strong outlines of an object in favour of capturing a fleeting impression of what they saw. At first they were scorned, but over the course of eight exhibitions held between 1874 and 1886 they began to prove themselves successful. Artists such as CAMILLE PISSARRO (1831–1903), EDGAR DEGAS, ALFRED SISLEY (1839–99), PAUL CEZANNE (p.112), CLAUDE MONET (p.114), BERTHE MORISOT (1841–95), and PIERRE AUGUSTE RENOIR (p.115) soon became famous. Many Impressionist paintings are of the countryside near Paris.

THEIR IMPACT

The Impressionists made an enormous impact on modern art, freeing painting from excessive realism and showing how it can capture feelings and impressions. Impressionist paintings are on display around the world, and exhibitions of their work draw huge crowds.

L'Absinthe (1875–76) by Edgar Degas

professor of chemistry at the University of St Petersburg. From 1868 to 1870 he wrote his book, *The Principles of Chemistry*, where he listed for the first time all the chemical elements known at that time, putting them in order of their atomic weight. He discovered that chemically similar elements tended to fall in the same columns he had arranged. This arrangement is called the periodic table. There were gaps in it but Mendeleyev predicted correctly that these would be filled later. The table became part of chemical theory and is now used worldwide. He was the first person to understand that all elements are related members of a single ordered system. Element number 101 is named mendelevium after him.

Edgar DEGAS
1834–1917
French painter and sculptor

Edgar Degas was born to a wealthy family in Paris. He trained first as a lawyer, but in 1855 he entered art school in Paris. He visited Italy to study the Old Masters and develop his drawing skills. Having a private income meant that Degas did not need to sell paintings to make a living. His plan was to paint historical subjects but he soon switched to scenes of modern life, especially ballet and the circus. His paintings of ballerinas, such as *The Rehearsal* (1873–74), *The Dancing Class* (1874), and *Awaiting the Cue* (1879) show the dancers in informal poses, practising, relaxing, or tying shoes. Degas did not try to make his sitters look beautiful – he wanted to show unusual body angles and a sense of movement. This can be seen in his nudes of women bathing. Degas was one of the greatest Impressionist painters.

years later he founded his own company to build engines in partnership with Maybach. In 1885, Daimler and Maybach patented one of the first high-speed internal-combustion engines and developed a carburettor that made possible the use of gasoline as a fuel. They first used a gasoline engine on a bicycle, then on a carriage, a boat, and finally a four-wheeled vehicle: this became the first commercially viable automobile in 1889. In 1890 he founded a company for the manufacture of automobiles and in 1899 the firm built the first Mercedes car. A Daimler-powered car won the first international car race from Paris to Rouen, France in 1894.

James McNeil WHISTLER
1834–1903
US painter

Whistler was born in Lowell, Massachusetts, but he spent most of his life outside the USA. He studied art in Paris, where his work was heavily influenced by that of French artist Gustave Courbet and Japanese artist Hokusai. Following a successful exhibition in Paris, he moved to London where he became well known for his portraits. In contrast to the sentimentality of British portraiture at that time, Whistler's subjects were often painted in stark colours with strident postures and confident rather than demure expressions. One of his most famous paintings is *Portrait of the Artist's Mother* (1871), which is now on exhibition at the Louvre in Paris. He drew many sketches and made beautiful etchings of scenes along the Thames.

Dmitri MENDELEYEV
1834–1907
Russian chemist

The youngest of 17 children, Mendeleyev was born in Tobolsk, Siberia. He studied science in St Petersburg, Russia, and Heidelberg, Germany, and later become

1834 The Whig Party is formed in the United States, in opposition to President Andrew Jackson.

Led by senator Henry Clay of Kentucky, the Whigs support trade restrictions to protect U.S. industry.

1834 Pressure on land in South Africa causes 15,000 Boers to set off on the Great Trek. They settle on land in the interior, outside the Cape Colony and British rule. The people who take part are known as "voortrekkers".

109

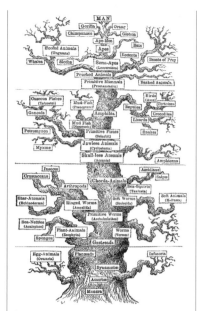

ERNST HAECKEL'S
Tree of Evolution

Ernst
HAECKEL
1834–1919
German zoologist

Ernst Haeckel was born in Potsdam, Prussia (now northeastern Germany). He studied at Würtzburg, Berlin, and Jena. He started to lecture at the University of Jena in 1861 and was professor of zoology there from 1862–1909. During his 47 years in the post, he went on many expeditions all over the world in search of zoological specimens. He became famous for his detailed zoological research and for his generalizations on biological themes. He had a fluent writing style and wrote many books on his discoveries while travelling. Haeckel was fascinated by evolutionary theories about how humans had been created and how they adapted to their environment. His outspoken views on this made him enemies, although they also brought him acclaim. Known as "the German Darwin", he was the first person to attempt to draw up a genealogical tree of all animals, showing the relationships between the various species.

Yukichi
FUKUZAWA
1835–1901
Japanese writer and educator

Son of a lower samurai, Yukichi Fukuzawa was born in Buzen, Japan. Fukuzawa trained in the new educational techniques, which included Western knowledge and science. In 1862 he wrote *Conditions in the West*, a simple explanation of the politics, economics, and culture of the West.

The book was instantly successful and hugely influential. In 1868 he was invited to enter the government but he refused, instead campaigning to introduce Western ideas to Japan, founding Japan's first independent university, and setting up a newspaper.

Mark
TWAIN
1835–1910
American writer

Born Samuel Langhorne Clemens in the Mississippi River town of Hannibal, Missouri, Mark Twain was a printer's apprentice, riverboat pilot, Confederate army deserter, prospector, and reporter before winning nationwide fame with the short story *The Celebrated Jumping Frog of Calaveras County* (1865). Adopting the pen name Mark Twain – a river pilot's term for "low water" – he went on to write novels which, although popular and funny, expressed some harsh truths about 19th-century American society, and about human nature in general. Twain's best-known works are *The Adventures of Tom Sawyer* (1876) and *The Adventures of Huckleberry Finn* (1884). Twain's keen wit – which he also exercised in lectures, journalism, and travel writing – made him a popular celebrity as well as a respected literary figure, but his last years were marred by personal tragedy and frequent depression.

Adolf von
BAEYER
1835–1917
German chemist

Adolf von Baeyer is best known for having synthesized the blueish-purple dye indigo in 1878. He was born in Berlin, Germany and studied at the University there, going on to become a lecturer in 1860. Later he was chemistry professor at the University of Munich, where he set up a laboratory in which many talented young chemists were trained. In 1863 he discovered barbituric acid, which was to become the main component of the hypnotic drugs known as barbiturates. In 1905 he was awarded the Nobel Prize for Chemistry.

HUCKLEBERRY FINN
Mark Twain's novel follows the adventures of the young boy Huck, and describes his friendship with the runaway slave Jim.

1834 Six farm workers from Dorset, England, are deported for trying to start a trade union. They become known as the Tolpuddle Martyrs. In 1836, they are pardoned and return home because of a public outcry.

1835 Juan de Rosas becomes dictator of Argentina, symbolizing the growing influence of the Creole landowners (those of Spanish ancestry). They have gained more land at the expense of the indigenous peoples.

Andrew CARNEGIE
1835–1919
Scottish-born US industrialist and philanthropist

The son of a weaver, Andrew Carnegie was born in Dunfermline, Scotland. At the age of 13 he and his family emigrated to the United States and settled in Pittsburgh. Then he worked at several different jobs, including factory hand and telegraph assistant. He joined the Pennsylvania Railroad, where he became a telegraph operator and rose to become superintendent of the railroad's Pittsburgh division. Carnegie invested his savings in the new oil industry. After the Civil War he put money into an iron-and-steel business which grew into the largest firm of its kind in the United States and made Carnegie a multi-millionaire. During the rest of his life he donated large amounts to worthy causes in Britain and America, including public libraries, universities, and institutions. In 1901 he retired from business and handed his vast empire over to the US Steel Corporation. He returned to his home country and lived for a while at Skibo, a castle in the far north. He later returned to the United States where he died.

ANDREW CARNEGIE
Carnegie believed that individual wealth, once acquired, should be used for the public's good. "The man who dies thus rich, dies disgraced", he wrote.

Isabella BEETON
1836–65
English writer

Isabella Mary Beeton (née Mayson) became famous for her *Book of Household Management*. The material for the book was first published as extracts in 1859 in a magazine on cooking and domestic science founded by her husband. The book was full of recipes and practical tips for running a household. "Mrs Beeton" could be found in most houses in Britain at a time when many middle-class people were starting to live without domestic servants for the first time. It was the first handbook on domestic science.

Elizabeth GARRETT ANDERSON
1836–1917
English physician

Elizabeth Garrett Anderson struggled to be recognized as a doctor in England at a time when women were discouraged from joining the medical profession. By her example, she championed the rights of other women to gain admission to professional education, particularly in medicine. Anderson was refused admission to medical school because she was female, so she studied privately with physicians in London hospitals and obtained her licence to practise in 1865 from the Society of Apothecaries. She was still not a full doctor but in 1866 she was appointed general medical attendant to St Mary's Dispensary, where she created a medical school for women. The Dispensary later became the New Hospital for Women. It was renamed the Elizabeth Garrett Anderson Hospital in 1918 in recognition of her work. She received a medical degree from the University of Paris and, in 1908, she was elected mayor of Aldeburgh, becoming the first woman mayor in Britain.

Georges BIZET
1838–75
French composer

Georges Bizet was taught music by his parents at an early age, and entered the Paris Conservatory before his tenth birthday. At 17, he wrote his Symphony in C Major. In 1857 he won the Prix de Rome, which led to his working for three years in Italy. Back in Paris in 1861, he concentrated on producing an opera for the Opéra Comique, and in 1863 *Les Pêcheurs des Perles* (The Pearl Fishers) was first performed. It was an immediate success. Apart from this opera and the music to the play *L'Arlésienne* (1872), Bizet's music was not popular during his lifetime. The premiere, in 1875, of his major opera, *Carmen*, was a failure. He was bitterly disappointed. Bizet died of a heart attack on the night of its 33rd performance.

Ernst MACH
1838–1916
Austrian philosopher and physicist

Ernst Mach studied at Vienna University and became professor of mathematics at Graz in 1864, of physics at Prague (now in the Czech Republic) in 1867,

1836 American settlers in the Mexican province of Texas declare their independence from the government in Mexico City. Despite initial setbacks, Texan forces defeat Mexican troops and establish an independent Texas.

1838 At the Battle of Blood River, a force of 470 voortrekkers, under Andries Pretorius, defeat some 3,000 Zulus under Dingane, the Zulu king. The battle leads to the establishment of the voortrekkers' republic of Natal.

and of physics at Vienna in 1895. During the 1860s he identified the phenomenon now known as Mach's bands – the tendency of the human eye to see bright or dark bands near the boundaries between areas of differing light strengths. In 1887 he established the principles of supersonics, and carried out many experiments on supersonic projectiles and on the flow of gases. His findings have proved very important for aircraft design. He also put forward the theory, now known as Mach's Principle, which states that inertia (the tendency of a body at rest to remain at rest, or of a body in motion to continue in motion in the same direction) results from the relationship of the body with all the matter in the universe.

GEORGE CUSTER
During the American Civil War, Custer became the Union's youngest brigadier-general at 23.

George CUSTER
1839–76
US soldier

George Armstrong Custer first came to prominence as a cavalry officer during the American Civil War (1861–1865). In 1866 he led the 7th Cavalry against the Native Americans of the Great Plains, and in 1874 he led an expedition that discovered gold in the Black Hills of the Dakota Territory and started a gold rush. The hills were sacred to the Cheyenne and the Sioux and relations between these peoples and the white invaders deteriorated. In 1876, Custer led the 7th Cavalry against an alliance of Cheyenne and Sioux warriors organized by Sitting Bull (p.108), Crazy Horse, and others. He went into battle against thousands of warriors in the valley of the Little Big Horn River. He and his main unit of 260 soldiers were all killed in what became known as "Custer's Last Stand".

Paul CEZANNE
1839–1906
French painter

Paul Cézanne was born in Aix-en-Provence and spent much of his life in the region. Against his father's wishes, he went to Paris to study art, although he was mostly self-taught. From 1863 he was greatly influenced by Impressionist painters such as Monet (p.114) and Pissarro. By the 1870s he was painting landscapes out of doors, concentrating on the basic structure of natural objects. He saw the hills and valleys of Provence in geometric shapes, and depicted them in blues, yellows, reds, and greens. His best-known work was produced after 1880, and includes many variations of *Mont Sainte-Victoire* (1885–1904), portraits of everyday figures such as *The Card Players* (1890–92), and the studies and paintings of *The Bathers* (1900–06). Little known in his own day, Cézanne is now viewed as a great and original artist.

George CADBURY
1839–1922
English social reformer

Son of Quaker businessman John Cadbury, George was born in Birmingham. In 1861, he and his brother Richard took over their father's small cocoa and chocolate company in the city. Together they transformed it into Cadbury Brothers, world-famous for its chocolate products. The brothers re-located the business in 1879 to a rural area that they called Bournville. George followed his Quaker beliefs in his business and introduced social welfare and improved living conditions for his factory workers. He became chairman of Cadbury Brothers in 1893 (Richard died in 1899) and the next year he started to establish a model village for his workers with pleasant small houses, gardens, and open spaces. Today, there is a museum at Bournville that highlights this successful experiment in modern social housing and tells the story of chocolate making.

1838 A People's Charter launches the Chartist Movement in Britain. The Charter's six points include vote by secret ballot and universal male suffrage. This mass movement for democratic rights flourishes until about 1850.

1839 The first Anglo-Chinese Opium War is fought when the Chinese government tries to suppress the traffic of opium and other foreign goods into China. The Chinese are forced to surrender and cede Hong Kong to the British.

1840

Pyotr Ilyich TCHAIKOVSKY
1840–93
Russian composer

A musically gifted child, Tchaikovsky studied music in 1862 at the St Petersburg Conservatory. He then taught harmony at the new Moscow Conservatory. In 1877, a disastrous marriage led to a nervous breakdown. Fortunately, he found an admirer of his music, Nadezhda von Meck, who financed his composing and encouraged him by letter, but never met him. Tchaikovsky threw himself into composing. He also toured Europe, and later the United States, as a conductor. Among his best-known works are the opera *Eugene Onegin* (1879); the ballets *Swan Lake* (1877), *The Sleeping Beauty* (1890), and *The Nutcracker* (1892); and the popular *Serenade for Strings in C Major* and the *1812 Overture* (both composed in 1880). He sank into depression after Nadezhda von Meck stopped his allowance, and died from cholera (possibly self-inflicted through intentionally drinking impure water) in 1893.

Emile ZOLA
1840–1902
French writer and political activist

E mile Zola was born in Paris but grew up in Aix-en-Provence, where he went to school with Paul Cézanne (p.112). When he returned to Paris, he was unemployed and knew real poverty, even having to trap sparrows for food. After two years, he found a job with the publisher Hachette and began to write articles. His first novel, published in 1865, established his belief that "The novelist should observe and record dispassionately, like the scientist." This became known as "naturalism" in literature. Zola's chief achievement was the 20-volume *The Rougon Family Fortune*, which he began in 1867. Each volume takes a different member of the family, in a different setting, and explores his or her personality against the family's common characteristics and background. Zola fought constantly against social injustice and was fearlessly outspoken. The Dreyfus Affair, in which the Jewish officer Alfred Dreyfus was wrongly convicted of spying by the French army, prompted Zola's famous open letter to a newspaper, accusing the judge of covering up for the army – "J'accuse" (I Accuse), it began. Zola died, probably accidentally, from carbon-monoxide poisoning when his chimney became blocked.

PYOTR TCHAIKOVSKY
The first Russian composer to gain recognition from Western audiences, Tchaikovsky loved his country and its folk songs, and his music reflects these influences.

Chief JOSEPH
c.1840–1904
Native American leader

J oseph was born into the Nez Percé people, whose homeland was in Oregon's Wallowa Valley. Joseph's father had converted to Christianity, and Joseph was taught at a mission school. He became leader of his tribe in 1871. White settlers had been encroaching on tribal lands in the Pacific Northwest since the 1850s. Pressed by the US government, Joseph reluctantly agreed to allow the Nez Percé to be resettled on a reservation in what is now Idaho. In 1877 the journey began. Fighting broke out between the soldiers and the Nez Percé, so Joseph led his people towards the safety of Canada. They walked more than 1,600 km (1,000 miles) through harsh country, pursued by soldiers. Joseph was forced to surrender – just 60 km (30 miles) short of Canada. He and most of his people were sent to a barren reservation in Native American territory (now Oklahoma), where many died. Joseph spent his last years in a reservation in Washington.

Auguste RODIN
1840–1917
French sculptor

A uguste Rodin was born in Paris. He began training as an artist at 14, but failed three times to get into art school, and first made his living as a stonemason. On a visit to Italy in 1875, he was inspired by the sculpture of Michelangelo. He began to model clay and wax shapes, which were then cast in bronze. In 1878, he completed his first major work, *The Age of Bronze*, and in 1880 was commissioned to create a door for a Paris museum. Rodin worked on this vast project – *The Gates of Hell* – for 20 years but never finished it. His other masterpieces include *The Kiss* (1898) and the famous *Thinker* (1902–04). Rodin's massive, passionate figures were so realistic that some thought he had cast them from human models. He was recognized as the greatest sculptor of his age and revived sculpture as an art form.

1840 In the United States, the Underground Railroad, a system of safe houses manned by people opposed to slavery, helps escaped slaves from the southern states flee to the northern states where slavery is outlawed.

1840 Russia, Britain, Prussia, and Austria form the Quadruple Alliance in support of Turkey. They offer Egypt and southern Syria to Mehemet Ali, provided he gives up Crete and northern Syria, which he refuses to do.

John DUNLOP
1840–1921
Scottish inventor

Scottish-born John Dunlop worked as a veterinary surgeon in Edinburgh and then Belfast in Northern Ireland. In 1887, while mending his child's tricycle wheels, he bound air-filled rubber hoses to the wheels instead of solid rubber tyres. The success of this idea led him to form a company in 1899 manufacturing pneumatic bicycle tyres. Dunlop also considered the possibility of using rubber tubes in car tyres. Dunlop's business became the Dunlop Rubber Company Ltd, and went on to produce the world's first pneumatic tyres for cars.

Claude MONET
1840–1926
French Impressionist painter

Claude Monet grew up in Le Havre and began his artistic career by drawing caricatures. He returned to Paris (his birthplace) in 1859 to study, and there he met Pierre Auguste Renoir (p.115), Camille Pissarro, and other Impressionist painters. After a period in England, where he was influenced by the work of J. M. W. Turner (p.75) and John Constable (p.75), Monet settled near Paris in 1871. He developed his Impressionist technique – painting outdoor scenes quickly to record the fleeting effects ("impressions") of light and weather conditions. This can be seen in early works such as

Impression – Sunrise (1872) and *La Gare St. Lazare* (1877). By the 1890s, he was taking this style even further, painting the same subject at different times of day to show the changing light. The best-known sequences are *Haystacks* (1890–91) and *Rouen Cathedral* (1891–95). In his last years, he produced a series of paintings inspired by his water-lily garden at Giverny, which was spanned by a Japanese bridge. The water-lily paintings established Monet as one of the greatest Impressionist painters.

MONET'S GARDENING BOOKS
These irises appear in a 26-volume set of books called The Flowers of the Gardens of Europe.

Thomas HARDY
1840–1928
English writer and poet

Thomas Hardy was born in Dorset, in the West Country of England, which was to be the setting for many of his later novels. His father was a stonemason, and after a rural childhood, the young Hardy spent five years working for a church architect in London. He returned home due to ill health. As well as poems, he began writing novels in 1862. It was not until his fourth novel, *Far from the Madding Crowd* (1874), that he felt confident enough to devote himself entirely to writing. Of the numerous novels that followed, Hardy is best remembered for *The Return of the Native* (1878), *Tess of the d'Urbervilles* (1891), and *Jude the Obscure* (1895). Later in life he again turned to poetry, producing volumes including *Wessex Words* (1898) and *Winter Words* published on his death).

Antonin DVORAK
1841–1904
Czech composer

Born in Nelahozeves, Bohemia, Antonin Dvorák studied at the Organ School in Prague. From 1863 he played viola in the Prague Provisional Theatre Orchestra, but left in 1873 to concentrate on composing. His Third Symphony (1874) won a prize in Austria, and brought him to the attention of Brahms, who helped to publicize his work. He gained international recognition with the *Slavonic Dances* (1878), and became especially popular in England, which he visited frequently. In 1891, he was made professor of composition at the Prague Conservatory, but the next year he left to become director of the National Conservatory in New York. Here he wrote his best-known works, the "New World" Symphony (1893), the "American" String

---

1840 British and Maori leaders sign the Treaty of Waitangi, which makes New Zealand a British Crown Colony and promises the Maoris British citizenship and land rights. The rights are not granted and war breaks out in 1843.

1841 The London Straits Convention is signed by all major European powers. It decrees that transit on the Bosphorus, the strait linking the Black Sea with the Mediterranean, will be restricted to the Turks in peacetime.

19TH CENTURY PARIS
The Dance at the Moulin de la Galette *(1876) by Renoir*

Quartet (1893), and the Cello Concerto (1895), before returning to Prague in 1895. His music, which includes elements of both Czech and American folk music, won many honours and awards.

Henry Morton STANLEY
1841–1904
Welsh-born US explorer and journalist

Henry Morton Stanley was born John Rowlands in Wales. While a teenager, he crossed the Atlantic as a cabin boy and was adopted by a merchant named Stanley. After serving with the Confederate army in the American Civil War, Stanley concentrated on journalism. In 1869, a newspaper sent him to Africa to contact the Scottish explorer David Livingstone (p.95). Stanley found him, greeting him with the famous words, "Dr Livingstone I presume." Stanley's account of his journey, *How I Found Livingstone* (1872), made him famous, and he decided to continue exploring. He traced the course of the Congo (Zaire) River in 1876–77, fighting African tribes along the way. He was a ruthless, but very effective, explorer.

Pierre Auguste RENOIR
1841–1919
French painter

Pierre Auguste Renoir was 13 when he began training as a painter of porcelain, and the delicacy of this work can be seen in his mature pictures. In 1862, he studied in Paris and met Claude Monet (p.114), Alfred Sisley, and others. With them he developed the ideas of Impressionist painting, working in the open air to record the changing effects of light and shade. Pretty women and children, jolly men, and beautiful landscapes were painted with feathery strokes. Renoir's early pictures, such as *Madame Charpentier and Her Children* (1878) and *The Luncheon of the Boating Party* (1881), brought him success, but after 1882 he reacted against Impressionism and worked in a more formal manner. Pictures like *The Umbrellas* (1881–86) and *Bathers* (1884–87) are full of lively, glowing colour, but their outlines are more solid. From the 1890s, Renoir suffered from rheumatism, but continued painting until his death.

Arthur SULLIVAN
1842–1900
English composer

Together with W. S. Gilbert, Arthur Sullivan developed the English form of operetta with a string of lighthearted and witty compositions. At 12, he joined the choir of the Chapel Royal in London and later studied at the Royal Academy of Music and at Leipzig. He worked as a conductor, teacher, and composer of serious music. His first comic opera was *Cox and Box* (1866), but he is best known for his collaborations with the poet W. S. Gilbert (1836–1911), writer of the popular *Bab Ballads*. Between 1875 and 1890, they wrote a series of comic operas for the Savoy Theatre in London. The "Savoy Operas", still the most popular comic operas in the English language, include *HMS Pinafore* (1878), *The Pirates of Penzance* (1880), *The Mikado* (1885), and *The Gondoliers* (1889). Sullivan's partnership with Gilbert broke down after an argument in 1890.

John William Strutt RAYLEIGH
1842–1919
English physicist

John Rayleigh graduated from Cambridge University in 1865. He was professor of experimental physics at Cambridge from 1879 to 1884, and of natural philosophy at the Royal Institution from 1888 to 1905. He conducted valuable studies in vibrations, the theory of sound, and the wave theory of light, earning the Nobel Prize for Physics in 1904. He was also responsible for calculating the three electrical units – the ohm, ampere, and volt – and for discovering argon gas.

THE MIKADO
This costume design is for Nanki-Poo, one of the characters in The Mikado *by Gilbert and Sullivan.*

1841 The American slave ship *Creole* is taken over by slaves, who murder the crew. They put into port in the British West Indies, where slavery is illegal. The British ignore American demands for the slaves to be returned.

1842 The *Nation* newspaper is founded by the Irish nationalist movement, Young Ireland. It publishes the work of a group of young intellectuals, advocating the study of Irish history and the revival of the Irish language.

ROBERT KOCH
This black-and-white pen cartoon jokes about Koch "culturing", that is teaching, bacteria.

Edvard GRIEG
1843–1907
Norwegian composer

Born in Bergen, Norway, Edvard Grieg was of Scottish descent. He studied music in Leipzig and was particularly influenced by the music of Schumann (p.93). While living in Copenhagen, Denmark, between 1863 and 1867, he met nationalist composers who used folk tunes in their music. This inspired him to write the Humoresker Op.6 (1865) for piano, and the acclaimed Piano Concerto (1868). In 1867 he married his cousin, Nina Hagerup, who was a talented singer, and he wrote many songs for her. Returning to Norway, he worked as a teacher and conductor in Christiania (now Oslo), and gained widespread popularity with his incidental music for the play *Peer Gynt* by Henrik Ibsen (p.103). He retired to Bergen in 1874.

Robert KOCH
1843–1910
German physician

Robert Koch developed techniques for isolating and testing bacteria and for cultivating and studying their growth. His systems became the basis of the modern study of bacteria (bacteriology). He isolated and identified the bacteria that cause anthrax, a disease that affects cattle and sheep. He also discovered the organism that causes cholera. In 1905 he was awarded the Nobel Prize for Medicine for his work on tuberculosis.

Henry JAMES
1843–1916
US writer

Brother of pioneering psychologist William James, Henry James was born in New York. The family moved frequently between the United States and Europe during James' boyhood, and as a young man he decided to settle in England and pursue a literary career. The theme of most of James's work is, in the words of one critic, "the drama, comic and tragic, of Americans in Europe and Europeans in America". Combining dense prose with sharp insights, James explored this theme in novels including *Daisy Miller* (1877), *The Portrait of a Lady* (1881), *The Bostonians* (1886), *The Wings of the Dove* (1902), *The Ambassadors* (1903), and *The Golden Bowl* (1904). James was a "writer's writer" rather than a popular success, and his work profoundly influenced later American novelists.

Friedrich NIETZSCHE
1844–1900
German philosopher

Friedrich Nietzsche's philosophical writings were highly original and ran against the progressive spirit of the age. He rejected religion and "conventional morality" in favour of a society where superior people would rise to greatness through "the will to power". (Nietzsche was not a racist nor an anti-Semite, as some critics later charged, but the Nazis and other fascist groups used distorted versions of his ideas to justify their cruelty.) Nietzsche was a powerful and persuasive writer, and his best books, including *Thus Spake Zarathustra* (1883) and *Beyond Good and Evil* (1886), are great literary as well as philosophical works. Nietzsche was plagued by mental illness, and following a breakdown in 1889 he was committed to an institution, where he died.

Nicolay Andreyevich RIMSKY-KORSAKOV
1844–1908
Russian composer

Rimsky-Korsakov came from a naval family near Novgorod. He was sent to naval training school in 1856, but was already interested in music. In 1861 he met the composers Balakirev, Borodin, Cui, and Mussorgsky, and started to compose in their nationalist style using Russian folk tunes. Together they became known as "The Mighty Handful", or simply "The Five". He became a professor at the St Petersburg Conservatory in 1871. As well as working on his own compositions, he revised the music of Borodin and Mussorgsky. The only professional composer of "The Five", Rimsky-Korsakov was famous for his colourful use of the orchestra in works such as the operas *Snow Maiden* (1882) and *The Golden Cockerel* (1907), and the orchestral fantasy *Scheherazade* (1888). His music was a great inspiration to his most famous pupil Igor Stravinsky (p.150).

Sarah BERNHARDT
1844–1923
French actress

Acclaimed in Europe and America, and one of the best-known actresses of her day, Sarah Bernhardt was barely noticed for many years. She entered acting school in Paris at age 16, encouraged by her mother's lover, the Duc de Morny. After many years "treading the boards" she eventually achieved theatrical success in 1868. The next year she performed in front of Napoleon III (p.91). In 1880, she formed her own travelling

---

1843 The South African state of Natal is proclaimed a British colony following the war between the Boers and the British. The region's economy is primarily agrarian, with the main exports being sugar and cotton.

1843 After his newspaper, *Rheinische Zeitung*, is banned in Germany, socialist thinker and writer Karl Marx moves to Paris. In the years that follow, he writes the works that become the cornerstones of communism.

SARAH BERNHARDT
This poster of Sarah Bernhardt shows the Art Nouveau style of Czech artist Alphonse Mucha.

Thomas BARNARDO
1845–1905
Irish philanthropist

Thomas Barnardo was born in Dublin, Ireland, the son of a furrier who had emigrated from Germany to Ireland. Barnardo left Ireland at 21 to study medicine in London in the hope of going to China as a missionary. He gave up this idea to teach and help poor families in London's East End instead. He raised money to provide homeless children with a place to sleep, and trained them to do jobs such as chopping wood, polishing boots, and making brushes. During his lifetime, more than 50,000 children were sheltered and trained in Dr Barnardo's Homes. Today, the charity finds foster homes for children, helps with adoption, and supports families of children with disabilities.

Wilhelm RÖNTGEN
1845–1923
German physicist

Wilhelm Röntgen, the man who discovered X-rays, studied at Zürich University, Switzerland, and was professor of physics at several German universities. In 1895, he discovered the electromagnetic rays that he called X-rays ("X" meaning unknown). Today, X-rays enable doctors and dentists to see inside the human body. He was awarded the Nobel Prize for Physics in 1901. He also did important work on the way crystals conduct heat, and on the specific heat of individual gases. Röntgen refused to accept any money for his discoveries because he believed that the results of scientific research should be made freely available to all.

company and became acclaimed internationally, touring extensively throughout Europe, America, and Australia. A legendary figure, she was generally thought to be the leading tragic actress of her day. She achieved her greatest fame as Cordelia in a French version of *King Lear* in 1872. Her other famous parts include the title role in Racine's *Phèdre*, and Marguerite in *La Dame aux Camélias*. She was extremely beautiful, had a mesmerizing presence on stage, and was renowned for the silvery quality of her voice. She injured her right knee when she jumped off the parapet in *La Tosca* by Sardou. Gangrene set in, and eventually she had to have the leg amputated. She continued to perform on stage with the aid of a wooden leg. She even visited troops during World War I, carried on a chair.

1844 *The Economist* weekly news magazine is founded in London to promote free trade. It develops into one of the world's foremost journals of news and opinion, giving high-quality coverage of general news.

1845 British engineer Isambard Kingdom Brunel's iron ship the *Great Britain* is the first propeller-driven liner to cross the Atlantic Ocean. Thereafter it makes frequent crossings between Britain and the United States.

Mary CASSAT
1845–1926
US painter

The Impressionist painter Mary Cassat studied in Spain, Italy, and Holland. In 1868, she settled in Paris, where she spent much of her life. She painted large, Impressionist-style studies, notably of women and children, and she popularized Impressionism in North America. One of her paintings, *Girl Sewing* (1880) typifies her style. Most of her work is in the Philadelphia Museum of Art.

WILLIAM CODY
Cody's battles with Native Americans were recounted in colourful detail in novels of the Wild West.

William "Buffalo Bill" CODY
1846–1917
US cowboy, scout, and showman

The nickname "Buffalo Bill" was given to Cody after he killed more than 4,000 buffalo to feed railroad workers on the Great Plains. He was an expert sharp-shooter and horseman who embodied the spirit of the American Wild West. He rode for the Pony Express and was a scout during the Sioux wars. In 1883, he began touring the United States with his Wild West Show. He took the show to Europe and performed for Queen Victoria (p.98). Sitting Bull (p.108) and Annie Oakley (p.129) were, for a while, members of his show.

Peter Carl FABERGE
1846–1920
Russian jeweller and goldsmith

Carl Fabergé was born in St Petersburg, Russia. His father was a jeweller who taught him his skills. Carl inherited the small family firm in 1880 and turned it into a thriving business empire with workshops all over Russia and offices in London and Paris. His craftsmen produced ingenious and beautiful objects in gold and silver, including miniature animals, pendants, cigarette cases, clocks, and brooches. In 1884, Fabergé was appointed jeweller to the Russian imperial family. He created his most famous pieces – a series of Easter eggs – for Tsar Alexander III. Inside each egg was a "surprise"– gold flowers, a jewelled cock that crowed, and even a clockwork train made of precious metals. The Russian Revolution of 1917 forced Fabergé into exile in Switzerland.

1846 Pope Pius IX is elected. He grants the Papal States a constitution, and is seen as a potential leader to unite Italy. Refusal to declare war on Austria costs him the support of the Liberals, and he is forced to flee Rome in 1848.

1847 Switzerland's Sonderbund War is fought between the cantons (small states), following the formation in 1845 of the Sonderbund – seven Catholic cantons opposed to anti-Catholic measures of Protestant cantons.

Jesse James

Jesse JAMES
1847–82
US outlaw

Sons of a Baptist minister, Jesse James and his brother Frank were raised on a Missouri farm. During the American Civil War (1861–65), they joined a Confederate guerrilla band and took part in looting and murdering. In the confusion after the war, they formed a gang and continued their robberies. They held up stagecoaches, trains, and banks, killing many innocent people. In 1871, a group of bankers hired detectives to catch Jesse. They threw a bomb into his house, killing his stepbrother. In 1881, a reward of $10,000 was offered for the brothers dead or alive. This led a gang member to shoot Jesse in the head, killing him. Frank gave himself up but was acquitted and returned home.

Alexander Graham BELL
1847–1922
Scottish–born US inventor

For two generations, the Bell family had been leading authorities on elocution and speech correction, and Alexander Graham continued the family tradition. In 1868, he became his father's assistant in London until the family moved to Canada in 1870. From 1871, Bell concentrated on teaching deaf people to speak and experimenting in sound. He began working with a mechanic to build an instrument for transmitting sound via electricity, and on 5 June 1875, he succeeded in transmitting an intelligible telegraphic message to his assistant. He patented the telephone in 1876 and formed the Bell Telephone Company in 1877. Bell defended his patent more than 500 times. Settling in Nova Scotia, he continued to work with the deaf for the rest of his life.

Thomas EDISON
1847–1931
US inventor

Thomas Alva Edison found it difficult to learn at school, and it was his mother who taught him and encouraged his interest in science. By the age of 10 he had made his own laboratory. In 1869, while working for the Western Union Telegraph Company, he devised a telegraph that could transfer messages to a printer. After this, he become a full-time inventor, and went on to take out patents for more than 1,000 inventions. Among these were the phonograph, an early form of record-player, and the motion-picture projector. His most famous invention was the light bulb, which he devised in 1879. In order to make it work better, he also built the world's first electricity plant. By the end of his life, Edison had proved himself one of the greatest inventors of all time.

Thomas Edison's early telephone

Annie BESANT
1847–1933
English socialist

Born in London of Anglo-Irish parents, Annie Wood married the Reverend Frank Besant in 1867 but separated from him in 1873. She became associated with the socialist Charles Bradlaugh with whom, in 1875, she published *The Fruits of Philosophy*, a paper in favour of birth control. Both were sentenced to six months in prison. The sentence was reversed on appeal, but Besant lost custody of her daughter. She became an advocate of theosophy (a mystic movement based on Hindu and Buddhist teachings) and went to India where she became involved in politics. She became president of the Indian National Congress and campaigned for Indian independence.

Paul GAUGUIN
1848–1903
French painter

Paul Gauguin was born in Paris, but spent his childhood in Peru. He joined the merchant navy at 17 and, in 1872, became a successful stockbroker. He began painting in his spare time and collected Impressionist pictures. In 1883 he took up painting full time. In 1888 he moved to Brittany and developed a personal style in such paintings as *The Yellow Christ* (1889), which used simple, well-defined shapes and intense colours. Gauguin's art was transformed by a journey to Tahiti in 1891, and he settled in the South Seas in 1895. Here he was inspired to paint a series of pictures of primitive life, notably *Where Do We Come From? What Are We?* and *Where Are We Going To?* (1897).

W.G. GRACE
1848–1915
English cricketer

Along with his two brothers, William Gilbert Grace was coached in cricket by his mother, and all three played county cricket for Gloucestershire, England. Although Grace qualified as a doctor and had a practice in Bristol, he devoted much of his spare time to playing cricket. He was the first great cricketer of the modern age. In 1871 he scored 2,739 runs in one season, becoming a national sporting hero. He was often depicted as a huge man with a thick beard, but he was athletic and a formidable cricketer. Grace captained England twice against Australia, in 1880 and 1882. During his career in first-class cricket (1865–1908) he scored 126 centuries, 54,896 runs, took 2,876 wickets, and held 899 catches. Grace played his last game of cricket in July 1914, aged 66.

Gottlob FREGE
1848–1925
German mathematician

Frege was educated at the University of Jena, Germany, and spent his whole working career there, becoming a professor in 1879. Although he is now regarded as the father of modern mathematical logic, little was known of his work during his own lifetime. His books on arithmetic were influential after his death, as were his philosophical essays in which he analyzed such concepts as meaning and sense. In 1902, he abandoned his attempt to derive all arithmetic from logic, after British philosopher Bertrand Russell published a theory that disproved his work.

1847
After conflict with non-Mormons, most of the Mormon community trek west from Nauvoo, Illinois, in search of a place in which they can live peacefully. Mormons found Salt Lake City in Utah in the United States.

1848
Inspired by the ideas of the French Revolution, in February a wave of nationalist feeling triggers revolutions in Austria, Hungary, Ireland, Switzerland, Denmark, and many German and Italian states. All uprisings are quashed.

August STRINDBERG
1849–1912
Swedish playwright and writer

August Strindberg was born in Stockholm. During his lifetime he had three failed marriages and several periods of mental instability, but he was determined to become a writer. His first major work, *Master Olof* (1872), is now recognized as the first modern Swedish play. In 1879 Strindberg wrote his satirical novel *The Red Room*, which made him nationally famous. His radical social criticisms led him to leave Sweden in 1883 and travel in Europe with his family for six years. Close to mental breakdown, and imagining persecution from every direction, he wrote about the sexes in conflict in *The Father* (1887), *Miss Julie* (1888), and *Creditors* (1888). He returned to Stockholm where he produced, among others, *A Dream Play* (1902). Strindberg was a major influence on modern theatre.

Ivan PAVLOV
1849–1936
Russian scientist

Pavlov was the son of a priest, but left his own studies for the priesthood to follow his interest in science and medicine. As director of the Institute of Experimental Medicine in St Petersburg, he researched digestion in dogs, the nervous control of saliva, and the role of enzymes. He trained a hungry dog to salivate at the sound of a bell, without even seeing or smelling food. He called this a "conditioned reflex". Pavlov's discoveries became the basis for studies of human psychological disorders. He received the Nobel Prize for Physiology in 1904.

1850

Robert Louis STEVENSON
1850–94
Scottish poet and novelist

Growing up in Edinburgh where he was born, Stevenson was a sickly child. He travelled abroad to escape the Scottish climate, and his first books describe his travels and his journey to California to marry Fanny Osbourne. He wrote the adventure novel *Treasure Island* in 1883, and it was an instant success. Stevenson's later novels include *Kidnapped* (1886), *The Strange Case of Dr Jekyll and Mr Hyde* (1886), and *The Master of Ballantrae* (1889). His novels embraced the themes of adventure, romance, and evil. In 1888, Stevenson settled in Samoa, hoping to find a cure for his tuberculosis, but he died six years later.

Antoine Henri BECQUEREL
1852–1908
French physicist

The young Antoine Becquerel grew up in a famous family of scientists and continued the work of his father and grandfather studying magnetism, energy, and optical phenomena. While researching fluorescent uranium salt, called pitchblende, he accidentally left some that had not been exposed to light on a photographic plate. He noticed that the plate had a faint image of the pitchblende on it. He came to the conclusion that these "Becquerel rays", as they became known, were a property of atoms – in other words he had discovered

LONG JOHN SILVER
This famous fictional pirate is one of the main characters in Stevenson's adventure story Treasure Island.

1850 After a revolution in Prussia, the king grants a new constitution. The new system is based on the British parliament. The king retains all executive power and the right to appoint and dismiss the government.

1851 By means of a coup d'état, Napoleon III restores the empire in France with the help of sections of the army. Despite the prosperity of his reign, republicans never forget the coup and overthrow Napoleon in 1870.

radioactivity. It is this work that led to the discovery of radium by Pierre and Marie Curie (pp.127/135). The three scientists shared the Nobel Prize for Physics in 1903.

MUTSUHITO
1852–1912
Japanese emperor

Mutsuhito was born in Kyoto and became emperor in 1867. He was given the reign-name Meiji, meaning "Enlightened Rule", after his death. In 1868, the shogunate – the military dictatorship that had ruled Japan since 1192 – was overthrown. The new government began to modernize and industrialize Japan, opening it up to foreign influences for the first time in centuries. In 1881, the emperor urged the introduction of a parliament, and in 1889 agreed a new constitution for the country. Meiji oversaw his country's transformation from an isolated, feudal society to a modern industrial and military power. Before he died, it had defeated Russia in 1904–05, acquired an empire in Taiwan and Korea, and become the most powerful nation in Asia.

Antoni
GAUDI
1852–1926
Spanish architect

Antoni Gaudí was born near Barcelona, where he trained as an architect and did most of his major work. His designs were influenced by the Moorish architecture of Spain, with its double arches, curved surfaces, and colourful tiling. He mingled this with the Gothic style and his own ideas. Many of his buildings have no straight walls or right-angles, and towers, roofs, and columns are twisted. Thin masonry walls are supported by diagonal

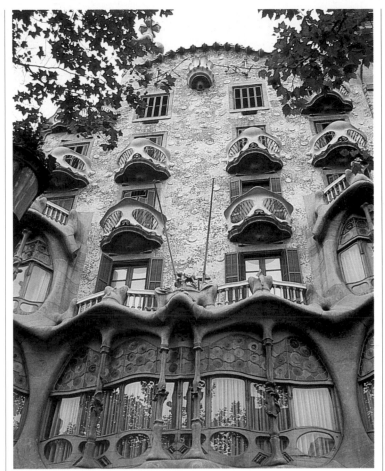

GAUDI'S STYLE
Gaudi designed two apartment buildings in Barcelona, the Casa Battló, above, and the Casa Milá.

buttresses and decorated with tiles or pieces of china. Gaudí's most famous buildings include the Casa Milá (1905–10) and the unfinished Church of the Sagrada Familia (1884–1926).

Vincent
VAN GOGH
1853–90
Dutch painter

The son of a pastor in the Brabant region of the Netherlands, Van Gogh failed at several jobs – art dealer, teacher, and preacher. In 1880 he became a full-time painter, depicting peasant subjects such as *The Potato Eaters* (1885). In 1886 he moved to Paris, where he was influenced by the Impressionists. He then moved to Arles in southern France,

where he produced a flood of pictures. He used intense primary colours and thick brush strokes to create masterpieces such as *Sunflowers* (1888) and *The Artist's Bedroom* (1889). However, Van Gogh suffered from mental illness, even cutting off his right ear lobe. Eventually he committed himself to an asylum, where he continued to paint. Van Gogh created more than 800 paintings, but sold only one in his lifetime. He committed suicide in 1890.

Cecil
RHODES
1853–1902
British-South African statesman

The son of a vicar, Rhodes went to southern Africa for health reasons. There he made a fortune in diamond mines –

by 1891 his company, De Beers, owned 90 per cent of world diamond production. Rhodes became prime minister of the British Cape Colony from 1890 to 1896. He wanted there to be a South African federation and a block of British territory from the Cape north to Cairo. Rhodes was responsible for the British annexing Bechuanaland (now Botswana) in 1885. He formed the British South Africa Company in 1889, which invaded Mashonaland and Matabeleland to form Rhodesia (now Zambia and Zimbabwe). He became prime minister of Rhodesia in 1890, but had to resign in 1896 due to his involvement in the disastrous Jameson Raid into Transvaal. In his will he left millions of pounds for overseas students to study at Oxford University – called Rhodes scholars today.

Oscar
WILDE
1854–1900
Irish poet and playwright

Oscar Wilde was born in Dublin. He went to Trinity College, Dublin and Oxford University. He became known for his affected artistic style and sharp wit. He wrote *The Happy Prince and other stories* (1888) for his two children. His only novel, *The Picture of Dorian Gray* (1891), was both praised and condemned (for immorality). *Lady Windermere's Fan* (1892) and *The Importance of Being Earnest* (1895) were among his successful plays. Wilde was a homosexual and had a relationship with Lord Alfred Douglas. Homosexuality was then illegal in Britian and Wilde was sent to prison for two years' hard labour. There he wrote *The Ballad of Reading Gaol* (1898). On his release, Wilde went to France, where he died friendless and broken.

1852 Following the lead of Mohammed Ali in Egypt, al-Hajj 'Umar launches a religious war to establish an Islamic state along the Senegal and upper Niger rivers. In 1863, he takes Timbuktu, but is killed a year later.

1853 Russia fights Turkey, France, Britain, and Sardinia in the Crimean War. The war is caused by arguments over access to the holy places in Palestine and a fear of Russian expansion in the Mediterranean and Middle East.

Paul EHRLICH
1854–1915
German bacteriologist

Paul Ehrlich trained in medicine at Leipzig and dreamed of finding a substance that would destroy germs in the body. He achieved this when he found a synthetic substance that would cure syphilis, and the science of chemotherapy (treating disease by chemical means) was born. He also made great advances in haematology (the study of diseases of the blood). In 1908, he won the Nobel Prize for Medicine.

VON BEHRING'S *vaccine*

Emil von BEHRING
1854–1917
German bacteriologist

Emil von Behring received his medical degree in 1878. While at the Institute of Hygiene in Berlin, he showed that it was possible to provide an animal with immunity to infection from tetanus by injecting it with the blood serum of another animal infected with the disease. He called this process antitoxic immunity, and used it to prevent diphtheria too. In 1901, Behring won the Nobel Prize for Medicine. In World War I, his tetanus vaccine saved so many lives that he became one of the few civilians ever to receive the Iron Cross.

Leos JANACEK
1854–1928
Czech composer

Born in Hukvaldy, Moravia (now part of the Czech Republic), Leos Janácek studied in Prague and Leipzig, Germany. At the age of 16 he became a choirmaster in Brno, where he spent the rest of his life. His early compositions, which include *Mass* (1908) and the opera *Jenufa* (1904), show the influence of Dvorák, but he developed his own style in the 1920s. Using Moravian folk melodies and a scientific study of speech patterns and rhythms, he developed a Czech style of composition, especially in the operas *Katya Kabanova* (1921), *The Cunning Little Vixen* (1924), and *From the House of the Dead* (1928), which established him as a great opera composer.

George EASTMAN
1854–1932
US inventor

Born in New York City and educated in Rochester, George Eastman gave up a career in banking for one in photography. In 1884, he produced a roll film for cameras. Then, in 1888, he invented the Kodak box camera, which started the spread of amateur photography. His work with Thomas Edison (p.119) made the moving-picture industry possible. In 1892 he formed the Eastman Kodak Company and produced the Brownie camera in 1900. In 1924, Eastman gave away half of his fortune – some $75 million – to charities and educational establishments, such as the Eastman School of Music at Rochester University and the Massachusetts Institute of Technology.

Ned KELLY
1855–80
Australian outlaw

Ned Kelly was born the son of a convict near Melbourne, Victoria. In tough surroundings, he grew up to be a fine horseman and excellent shot. At 15, he took part in an armed robbery, and in 1878 he and his brother were outlawed for shooting at a police officer. When the police pursued them, Kelly shot three of them dead and escaped into the bush. He and his brother formed a gang of bushrangers – outlaws ranging the country – making daring bank and police-station raids. They claimed to be fighting for poor workers, many of whom saw Kelly as a hero. A large band of troopers pursued the gang to a hotel in Glenrowan after a train ambush there. A gun battle ensued in which three of the gang were shot and killed. Kelly was the only survivor. He came out to fight wearing a home-made suit of armour, but he forgot to cover his legs and was shot down and captured. He was later hanged.

King Camp GILLETTE
1855–1932
US inventor

King Camp Gillette was born in Wisconsin and was educated in Chicago. He worked as a travelling hardware salesman. One day he placed a double-edged steel razor blade between two plates and used a "T" handle to hold the different pieces together:

NED KELLY
This famous Australian outlaw became a legend and was celebrated in books, films, and paintings.

1854 The Republican Party is founded in the United States. The party is formed in opposition to the Kansas-Nebraska Act and its doctrine of "popular sovereignty". This held that any territory could choose to have slavery or not.

1854 The Japanese make the Treaty of Kanagawa with the United States. It is Japan's first treaty with a Western nation. The treaty is signed following demands that Japan open its ports to US ships for supplies.

he had invented a safety razor and disposable blade. He started to market his Gillette razor in 1901 and found instant success. By the end of 1904, the Gillette Company had manufactured more than 12 million blades. Gillette was a committed socialist and contributed essays on the subject of social reform including *Gillette's Industrial Solution* (1900) and *The People's Corporation* (1924).

Booker T.
WASHINGTON
1856–1917
American educationist

Booker Taliaferro Washington was born into slavery in Virginia. Through discipline, study, and hard work – virtues he would later stress in his writings and speeches – he became an instructor at a Washington, D. C. school for freed slaves, before moving to Tuskegee, Alabama, in 1881. There he founded the Tuskegee Institute, which soon became a major centre of education and vocational training for young African-Americans. An 1895 speech at the Atlanta Exposition in Georgia and the 1900 publication of his best-selling autobiography, *Up From Slavery*, established Washington as the nation's foremost spokesperson for African-Americans. A moderate, Washington believed African-Americans should seek education and economic success, rather than demanding immediate civil and political rights, the strategy favoured by more radical African-American leaders such as W. E. B. DuBois.

Robert Edwin
PEARY
1856–1920
US explorer

Born in Pennsylvania, Robert Edwin Peary made the conquest of the North Pole a lifelong obsession. After joining the navy and doing survey work in Central America, Peary led

ROBERT PEARY
The Arctic explorer crossed the 2,000 km of Greenland on a sledge pulled by a team of huskies.

four expeditions to Greenland between 1886 and 1900. Two unsuccessful attempts on the pole followed. Peary set out again in 1908 aged 52. Travelling by dogsled from Ellesmere Island, Peary, his African-American assistant, Matthew Henson, and four Inuit (Eskimo) guides planted the US flag at the North Pole on 6 April, 1909. Peary returned to find that another explorer, Dr Frederick Cook, claimed to have reached the pole in 1908. Cook's claim was discredited, but it is uncertain whether Peary himself attained the pole, given the inaccurate navigational instruments then in use.

Woodrow
WILSON
1856–1924
US president

Born in Virginia, Woodrow Wilson was a well-known writer and educator before he entered politics as governor of New Jersey in 1909. Just three years later he became president as the Democratic party's candidate. Wilson urged strict US neutrality when World War I broke out in Europe in 1914, but after his reelection in 1916 the nation was drawn into the conflict. After fighting ended in 1918, Wilson personally represented the US at the peace conference in France. Wilson promoted US membership in the League of Nations, the proposed international peacekeeping body, but this was opposed by some Republicans in Congress. Wilson toured the US in support of the league, but he suffered a stroke and spent the remainder of his presidency as an invalid. Wilson was awarded the Nobel Prize for Peace in 1919.

1855 In Britain, *The Daily Telegraph* newspaper in founded in London. It becomes one of the best-known quality newspapers, reporting on world news as well as domestic affairs.

1855 A gold rush quadruples the population of Victoria, Australia in four years. The government tries to stem the rush by making people apply for licences. A riot breaks out at the Eureka mine, and the licence is later abolished.

Sigmund
FREUD
1856–1939
Austrian psychoanalyst

Sigmund Freud was born in Moravia (now part of the Czech Republic) and studied medicine at the University of Vienna. In the late 1880s, he began to use hypnosis to treat patients suffering from hysteria. Freud discovered that their symptoms were often the result of traumas experienced in early life. From this discovery he went on to develop an entirely new science concerned with the mind: psychoanalysis. The interpretation of dreams was an important part of Freudian psychoanalysis. Freud believed that the mind was divided by a conflict between the *id*, which is instinct, and the *superego*, which is social pressure to conform. Conflict between the two is regulated by the *ego*, which is concerned with reality. Freud popularized his theories in books starting with *The Interpretation of Dreams* (1900). Freud's ideas did not become widely known until after World War I, but psychoanalysis then became very popular, and Freudian concepts began to exert a profound effect on art, literature, and even daily life in Europe and North America. Freud remained in Vienna until 1938 when, following the Nazi occupation, he fled to England.

SIGMUND FREUD'S HOUSE
This waiting room of the house in Vienna where Freud lived from 1891 to 1938 has been lovingly restored.

J. J.
THOMSON
1856–1940
English mathematical physicist

Joseph John Thomson was born near Manchester, where he studied to become a railway engineer. In 1872, his father died, which meant that he could not afford to become an apprentice. However, he won a scholarship to Trinity College, Cambridge, and became physics professor there in 1884. In 1895, Thomson was investigating the rays produced when an electric current is passed through a vacuum in a glass tube. These rays, produced by the negative end of the tube (the cathode), were called cathode rays. Thomson showed that they consisted of negatively charged particles, which are found in every atom. These particles were named the electrons, and their discovery led to the beginning of the study of atomic structure. The machine he used in his experiments was the basis for the cathode-ray oscilloscope, which was used later in many experiments, as well as in televisions. Thomson won the Nobel Prize for Physics in 1906 and was knighted in 1908.

Nikola
TESLA
1856–1943
US physicist

Born in Croatia, Nikola Tesla emigrated to the USA in 1884. For a while he worked for American inventor Thomas Edison (p.119), but they argued, after which Tesla concentrated on his own inventions. He succeeded in improving dynamos – devices used for converting mechanical energy into electrical energy – as well as electric motors and a new type of transformer. He championed the idea of an electricity supply with an alternating current (AC) instead of the traditional direct current (DC), demonstrating the efficiency of lighting using an AC system in 1893. Tesla also predicted wireless communication two years before Guglielmo Marconi (p.141) developed it.

TESLA'S INDUCTION MOTOR
Tesla built his first induction motor in 1888. This was a major factor in the widespread adoption of AC supplies.

George Bernard
SHAW
1856–1950
Irish playwright

At the age of 20, George Bernard Shaw moved from his native Dublin to London to join his mother. She was a singing teacher and had left her husband some years earlier. Shaw wanted to be a writer. He was also attracted to socialism, and joined the Fabian Society. He was a successful journalist, and from 1898, the year of his marriage, onwards, Shaw wrote the plays that brought him fame, including *Arms and the Man* (1898), *Man and Superman* (1902), *Major Barbara* (1905), *Pygmalion* (1913) – the basis for the musical, *My Fair Lady* – and *St Joan* (1923). Much influenced by the playwright Henrik Ibsen, Shaw ignored theatrical traditions. His plays are superficially comic, but he challenged accepted social, economic, and political conventions. In 1925 Shaw was awarded the Nobel Prize for Literature.

Heinrich
HERTZ
1857–94
German physicist

The very first man to broadcast and receive radio waves was Hamburg-born Heinrich Hertz. In 1885 he was appointed professor of physics at Karlsruhe University, and in 1889 became professor at Bonn University. In 1887 he made his famous discovery of Hertzian waves, now better known as radio waves – building on the theories and predictions of earlier scientist James Clerk Maxwell (p.105). Hertz demonstrated that sound waves were prone to refraction and reflection, just as light and heat waves are. He went on to explore Clerk Maxwell's theories further and received several awards for his work on electric waves.

Ferdinand de
SAUSSURE
1857–1913
Swiss linguist

Ferdinand de Saussure was born in Geneva and studied languages at the universities of Leipzig and Berlin before lecturing, first in Paris and then, from 1891 until his death, at the University of Geneva. His theories were delivered to students in Geneva from 1907–11 and published as the *Course in General Linguistics*. Saussure

---

1856 The Peace of Paris ends the Crimean War after Napoleon III of France begins negotiations. The treaty ends the alliance system in which countries help each other, and starts an era of aggressive nationalist policies.

1856 Van Diemen's Land, an island state of Australia, is granted self-government and becomes known as Tasmania. Most Tasmanians support the federation of Australia, and Tasmania becomes an Australian state in 1901.

transformed linguistics by moving away from the study of how language evolved and concentrating instead on the structure of language as it is currently spoken. He believed that language is a system of signs that point to the meaning of what is being said, rather than a precise set of definitions. He also said that the study of language should not be divorced from the society and the environment in which the language is spoken. Such ideas revolutionized not just linguistics, but also all social sciences throughout the 20th century.

Emmeline PANKHURST
1857–1928
English suffragette

Born Emmeline Goulden in Manchester, she married Richard Marsden Pankhurst in 1879. Her husband was a radical lawyer who supported women's rights and introduced the first women's suffrage bill in Britain. Emmeline was soon

WOMEN'S RIGHTS

In most countries, women have at some time been denied equal rights with men. When the French Revolution proposed liberty, fraternity, and equality for all men, a women's movement slowly began to take shape to campaign for women to be guaranteed these rights, too.

THE FIRST CAMPAIGNS
In 1790, the French philosopher ANTOINE NICOLAS CONDORCET (1743–94) proposed that women gain full citizenship; in 1792, MARY WOLLSTONECRAFT (p.69) wrote *A Vindication of the Rights of Women*, in which she argued that the lack of education kept women in "ignorance and slavish dependence" on men. In 1848, women held the first-ever feminist convention, in Seneca Falls, New York.

GETTING THE VOTE
Many women saw that their situation would change only if they gained the right to vote. The US state of Wyoming was the first place to grant women's suffrage, in 1869. It was followed by New Zealand (1893), Finland (1906), and Norway (1913). In Britain, EMMELINE PANKHURST, and her daughter CHRISTABEL (1880–1958) waged an increasingly militant campaign with other suffragettes.

THE SUFFRAGETTE
This edition of a pamphlet published by the British suffragettes refers to a law passed in 1913 allowing the release of hunger strikers from prison, but only until they were well enough to return.

In 1918, women over 30 got the vote; all women got the vote in 1928. By then, the USA, USSR, Germany, and many other countries had granted women's suffrage. Full equality still had to be fought for.

caught up in the movement to obtain equal rights for women, and in 1889 she founded the Women's Franchise League. After her husband's death in 1898, she continued to campaign with her daughter Christabel, and together they established the Women's Social and Political Union in 1903. The struggle for women's

CHRISTABEL AND EMMELINE PANKHURST
In 1913, Emmeline was jailed and released 12 times under the "Cat and Mouse Act".

suffrage (the right to vote) became more radical and violent as women met with more resistance. On several occasions, both Emmeline and Christabel were arrested and sent to prison, where they went on hunger strike and were forcibly fed. During World War I, Pankhurst worked to bring about the mobilization of women in the workforce. The same year, her autobiography, *My Own Story*, was published. Equal voting rights for women was established in 1928, a few months before her death.

1856 Britain annexes Oudh, a historic region of Bengal in India. This increases the hostility to British rule. A year later, the revolt of Sepoys at Meerut begins an Indian mutiny against British rule, which is put down easily.

1857 The US Supreme Court's ruling on the Dred Scott case about a slave in a free state renders the Missouri Compromise unconstitutional. Northern fears of a "slave power" conspiracy to dominate government increase.

Edward ELGAR
1857–1934
English composer

Edward Elgar was born in Worcestershire and had an early interest in music. He worked for a while as an orchestral violinist and taught himself composition, which he took up full time in 1891. His first major success came with the *Enigma Variations* (1899), followed by the oratorio *The Dream of Gerontius* (1900). He was knighted in 1904 and appointed Master of the King's Music in 1924. Elgar's best-known music is the series of *Pomp and Circumstance* marches (1901–30), but his two symphonies and concertos for violin and cello are also acclaimed. He gave English classical music an international standing not reached since the days of Purcell (p.52).

Robert BADEN-POWELL
1857–1941
English founder of the Boy Scout movement

Baden-Powell was born in London. At the age of 19, he joined the British army and later served in South Africa. He became a hero when he led the 217-day defence of the town of Mafeking (1899–1900) during the Second Boer War. On his return to England, he discovered that his book *Aids to Scouting* was being used in schools, although he had written it for the army. He rewrote it for boys and founded the Boy Scouts in 1908. Two years later, he founded the Girl Guides and, in 1916, started the Wolf Cubs, a junior version of the scouts. Baden-Powell was World Chief Scout from 1920 until his death in Kenya.

Rudolf DIESEL
1858–1913
German engineer

Rudolf Diesel studied at the Munich Polytechnic. He trained as a refrigeration engineer and in 1885, began work on internal-combustion engines. He was commissioned to develop a "rational heat motor", which led to his demonstration of the first practical ignition engine in 1897. This diesel engine, as it became known, was about twice as efficient as an equivalent steam engine. Diesel established a factory at Augsburg, Germany, to make his engines. He died after falling overboard from a ship crossing the English Channel.

Theodore ROOSEVELT
1858–1919
US president

An advocate of the "strenuous life", Theodore Roosevelt was a rancher, explorer, hunter, writer, and soldier as well as a politician. He occupied several New York state and federal offices until war with Spain broke out in 1898. Roosevelt won fame fighting with the "Rough Riders" cavalry in Cuba, and he was elected governor of New York. In 1900, he became the Republican nominee for vice-president. In 1901, he succeeded to the presidency following President William McKinley's assassination, and was re-elected in 1904. He received the Nobel Peace Prize in 1905 for his role in negotiating an end to the Russo-Japanese War.

Giacomo PUCCINI
1858–1924
Italian composer

Born in Lucca, Tuscany, Puccini studied music with his uncle and became a church organist at the age of 14. His ambition was to write operas, and he won a scholarship to study at the Milan Conservatory in 1880. He wrote his first opera, *Le Villi*, in 1882, but his first real success came with *Manon Lescaut* in 1893. *La Bohème* followed three years later, but, to begin with, this opera was not popular with audiences. Puccini had a better reception for his next opera, *Tosca* (1900), which was in the new realistic "*verismo*" style. Puccini's tuneful music made him

1857 A mutiny disturbs British colonial rule in India. India is made a colony of the British Empire, to be ruled entirely from Britain. Indians are excluded from the upper ranks of the civil service and the army.

1858 The Irish Republican Brotherhood is founded in Dublin. An allied US movement gives the organization the name "Fenians". They aim to overthrow British rule in Ireland and create an Irish republic.

one of the most popular opera composers of all time, with works such as *Madama Butterfly* (1904) and *Turandot*, which he did not finish – he died of cancer with the incomplete score in his hands. The opera was completed in 1926 by Franco Alfano.

OPERA STYLE
This design is for a costume used in a production of the opera Turandot *by Puccini*

Ethel SMYTH
1858–1944
English composer

Ethel Smyth was born in London, and studied music in Leipzig, Germany, where she met Brahms (p.108), and began to compose. Her first operas, *Fantasio* (1898) and *Der Wald* (1902), were popular in Germany but she did not achieve international recognition until 1906, with the appearance of her greatest opera, *The Wreckers*. She was a fearless campaigner for women's rights, spent time in prison for her activities as a suffragette, and, in 1911, wrote the *March of the Women* as a campaign song for the Women's Social and Political Union. Later works include an opera, *The Boatswain's Mate* (1916), and orchestral works such as the choral symphony *The Prison* (1930). She was made a Dame of the British Empire in 1922.

Max PLANCK
1858–1947
German physicist

Max Planck studied at Munich and Berlin universities and went on to become a professor of physics at Berlin University. His work on the law of thermodynamics – the branch of physics concerned with the behaviour of energy in relation to pressure and temperature – led him to formulate his famous quantum theory in 1900. The quantum theory set out the way that, in thermodynamics, changes in energy take place in separate instalments, or quanta. This theory revolutionized scientists' understanding of atomic and sub-atomic physics. Max Planck was awarded the Nobel Prize for Physics in 1918.

Billy the KID
1859–81
US outlaw

His real name was Henry McCarty, but it is as Billy the Kid that this notorious gunfighter is remembered. In 1873, his family moved from New York to New Mexico, where he began a life of crime. He stole food and clothes, then horses and cattle. In 1877, he killed a man after an argument, ran away, and changed his name to William Bonney. He joined gunmen fighting a frontier feud in Lincoln County and killed at least four more men, including a sheriff. When the feud ended, each gunman was offered a pardon except for Billy the Kid, who continued rustling cattle. In 1880, local ranchers elected Pat Garrett sheriff and ordered him to hunt down Billy. By the time Garret trapped and shot him dead, in July 1881, Billy had killed at least 21 men.

PIERRE AND MARIE CURIE
In 1898, this husband-and-wife team of scientists discovered the radioactive elements polonium and radium.

Georges SEURAT
1859–91
French painter

Georges Seurat began studying at art school in Paris in 1878 and worked hard at drawing technique. He also examined theories of colour. Unlike the Impressionists, who recorded colours in dashing, instinctive brushstrokes, he worked out a more scientific method – covering the canvas with uniform dots of pure colour. When seen from a distance, these appear to merge, giving a radiant effect. Seurat's startling "pointillist" method was first shown successfully in *Une Baignade, Asnières* (1883–84) – although many people disapproved of it. He continued to work hard, producing intricately composed paintings such as *Sunday Afternoon on the Island of La Grande Jatte* (1884–86) and *Les Poseuses* (1887–88). He died of meningitis aged only 31. Other pointillists imitated his style, but none matched his skill.

Pierre CURIE
1859–1906
French physicist

Educated by his father in Paris, where he was born, Pierre Curie worked as laboratory assistant at the Sorbonne, where he was later appointed to the Chair of Physics. With his brother Jacques, he studied crystals and invented the electrometer that was later used by his wife, Marie, in her ground-breaking work on radioactivity. Pierre Curie proved that a ferromagnetic material loses its magnetic qualities at a certain point – now known as the "Curie point". From 1898 onwards, he worked with his wife on radioactivity and showed that the rays emitted by radium contained electrically positive, negative, and neutral particles. This discovery earned him the joint Nobel Prize for Physics in 1903, together with Marie Curie (p.135) and Antoine Henri Becquerel (p.120).

1858 Karageorge, the second son of the founder of the ruling Serbian dynasty, is deposed and forced to live in exile. Milosh Obrenovich, whose dynasty gave Serbia five rulers, is declared Serbian king after a struggle for supremacy.

1858 Brunel's ship *Great Eastern* is launched. This enormous vessel is considered to be the prototype of the modern ocean liner. This last ambitious effort strains Brunel's health and contributes to his early death.

Svante ARRHENIUS
1859–1927
Swedish chemist

Svante Arrhenius is said to have taught himself to read at the age of three. He went to school in Uppsala and studied chemistry and physics at the university. There, he put forward the idea that electrolytes – substances that dissolve in water to form a solution that conducts electricity – are separated into electrically charged particles, or ions, even when there is no current flowing through the solution. In 1891, he became a lecturer at Stockholm University and, in 1895, was made professor. He was awarded the Nobel Prize for Chemistry in 1903. In 1905, he became director of the Nobel Institute of Physical Chemistry in Stockholm. Arrhenius also made contributions to astronomy.

Arthur CONAN DOYLE
1859–1930
Scottish writer

Arthur Conan Doyle was born in Edinburgh, where he studied medicine. It was while practising as a doctor that Doyle began writing short stories about a private detective called Sherlock Holmes. Together with his friend Dr Watson and his arch enemy Professor Moriarty, Holmes appeared regularly in the *Strand Magazine* and in books such as *The Sign of Four* (1890). In 1893, Doyle killed off his hero in *The Final Problem*, but public opinion forced him to bring the detective back to life in *The Hound of the Baskervilles* (1902). Doyle was knighted for medical work in the Boer War in South Africa.

William II
1859–1941
Kaiser Wilhelm II
German emperor

William was born in Berlin, the eldest son of Frederick III. In 1888, he became king of Prussia and kaiser (emperor) of the newly united German empire. In 1890, he fired his great chancellor, Otto von Bismarck, and directed foreign policy himself. He wanted to make Germany a power in Europe. In 1914, he supported Austria-Hungary when it declared war on Serbia after a Serb assassinated the heir to the throne, Archduke Ferdinand. This led to World War I. In November 1918, when the defeat of Germany was imminent, William fled to the Netherlands, where he died.

SHERLOCK HOLMES
The fictional detective (right) worked on about 60 cases with the help of his friend Dr Watson.

1860

Anton CHEKHOV
1860–1904
Russian playwright and short-story writer

The son of a struggling grocer in Taganrog, Chekhov moved to Moscow with his family in 1879. While there he studied medicine at university and wrote comic sketches for various journals. In 1892, he bought a farm, but developed tuberculosis. In 1900, he moved to Yalta in the Crimea, and the following year he married Olga Knipper, who played most of the female roles in his plays. *The Seagull*, written in 1896, failed at first but was successfully re-staged in 1898. *Uncle Vanya* (1900), *The Three Sisters* (1901), and *The Cherry Orchard* (1904) are all internationally famous today. His technique has been called impressionistic, and his heroes are usually men who are downtrodden by the harsh material world and whose sensitivity leads to great suffering. Chekhov remains one of Russia's most popular international authors

Theodor HERZL
1860–1904
Hungarian Zionist leader

Theodor Herzl was the founder of modern Zionism – the movement to establish a Jewish homeland in Palestine. Born in Budapest, he studied law in Vienna, Austria. In 1894, he covered the Dreyfus trial for a Viennese newspaper (Dreyfus was a French Jewish officer falsely charged with giving documents to the Germans). Herzl was appalled by the anti-Jewish feeling the trial aroused, and he was convinced that the only solution to anti-Semitism was the creation of a Jewish state. He promoted this idea in an influential pamphlet, *The Jewish State* (1895). The pamphlet launched political Zionism. Herzl organized the first Zionist World Congress in Basle, Switzerland, in 1897, and founded the World Zionist Organization to promote the cause. Although he died more than 40 years before the establishment of the state of Israel, Herzl had paved the way and is now honoured as the "prophet of the Jewish state".

Gustav MAHLER
1860–1911
Austrian composer

Gustav Mahler was born in Kaliste, Bohemia (then part of the Austrian Empire, now in the Czech Republic). He was a very musical child and studied at the Vienna Conservatory from the age

1859 The US anti-slavery activist John Brown leads a raid on Harper's Ferry, the site of a federal arsenal in western Virginia, hoping to trigger a slave rebellion in the South. Brown is quickly captured and executed.

1859 The Pacific Northwest territory of Oregon becomes the 33rd state of the United States of America. Immigrants from the east develop logging and farming in Oregon's forested mountains and fertile valleys.

of 15. His first noted composition, the cantata *Das klagende Lied*, appeared in 1880. In his lifetime, he was better known as a conductor than as a composer. In 1897, he converted to Christianity, which also made it easier for him to be appointed as conductor of the Vienna Court Opera. After the death of his eldest daughter in 1907, his health began to fail and he spent winters in New York conducting and summers in Austria composing. His 10 symphonies and collections of songs, such as *Des Knaben Wunderhorn* (1892–98) and *Das Lied von der Erde* (1909), were largely ignored for 50 years after his death. They later came to influence many early-20th-century composers, including Dmitri Shostakovich (p.186) and Benjamin Britten (p.195).

Annie OAKLEY
1860–1926
US sharpshooter

Rodeo star and sharpshooter, Annie Oakley was often called "Little Sure Shot" – she was less than 1.5 metres (5ft) in height. She was a member of Buffalo Bill Cody's (p.118) Wild West Show, and her shooting skills were so good that, while performing in Berlin in Germany, Crown Prince William (later Kaiser William II) allowed her to shoot a cigarette out of his mouth. She was partially

ANNIE OAKLEY
Phoebe Anne Oakley could shoot the thin edge of a playing card from 30 paces.

paralyzed in a train crash in 1901, but went on entertaining audiences with her skill until her death. The legend of Annie Oakley grew even further when the US composer Irving Berlin wrote a fictionalized account of her life in the musical *Annie Get Your Gun*, in 1946.

José RIZAL
1861–96
Filipino patriot

José Rizal was born the son of a rich landowner in Calamba in the Philippines. At 17, he vowed to devote his life to reforming the way in which the Spanish ruled his country. He trained as a medical student and went to study in Europe in 1882. There he wrote two famous novels *Noli Me Tangere* (1886) and *The Reign of Greed* (1891), which exposed the harshness of Spanish rule in the Philippines. Rizal returned to his homeland in 1892 and started a movement for peaceful reform, calling for the legal equality of Filipinos with Spaniards and freedom of expression. In 1894, he was exiled to the Philippine island of Mindanao. In 1896, rebels launched an attack against the Spanish authorities. Although he had no part in it, Rizal was arrested, tried for treason, and shot. He is remembered both for his novels and for the inspiring example he set for Philippine nationalists.

Fridtjof NANSEN
1861–1930
Norwegian explorer and oceanographer

Fridtjof Nansen was born near Christiana (now Oslo). As a young man, he studied the Lapps, an Arctic people who live to the north of Norway, and the Inuit (Eskimos) of Greenland, to find out how best to live and travel in polar conditions. In 1888, he made the first crossing of Greenland on skis. Nansen then developed a theory that the Arctic, a mostly frozen ocean, has a strong current. To test his idea, he had a specially strengthened ship made – the *Fram*. In 1893, he deliberately allowed the *Fram* to become stuck in the Arctic ice and waited three years while the current carried it north. While his ship drifted, Nansen and a companion tried unsuccessfully to reach the North Pole using dog sleds and kayaks. Nansen later had a distinguished career as a diplomat and humanitarian. He became League of Nations High Commissioner for Refugees, and received the Nobel Prize for Peace in 1923.

1860 Victor Emmanuel of Sardinia drives the Austrians out of northern Italy. Other states unite with Sardinia and an Italian parliament is set up in Turin. Garibaldi's revolutionaries bring Sicily into the united Italy.

1861 The American Civil War begins between the northern and southern states over the spread of slavery. The North finally defeats the southern (Confederate) forces in 1865. More than 600,000 people die in the conflict.

Nellie MELBA
1861–1931
Australian opera singer

Christened Helen Mitchell, the young Melba grew up in Melbourne. (She later adapted the name of the city to create her stage name.) She gave her first public recital at the age of six, but did not begin to study singing until after her marriage to Charles Armstrong. She went to Paris to study, and her first operatic performance was as Gilda in Verdi's *Rigoletto*. She sang regularly in all the major opera houses in Europe and the USA,

DAME NELLIE MELBA
In 1887, Nellie Melba made her operatic debut in Brussels.

and was particularly associated with Covent Garden in London and the Metropolitan Opera in New York.

She was famed throughout the world for the purity of her soprano voice, which was particularly suited to roles such as Violetta in Verdi's *La Traviata* and Mimi in Puccini's *La Bohème*. Melba was extremely popular and was created a Dame in 1918. The great French chef Auguste Escoffier named his ice-cream and peach dish *pêche Melba* after her. Melba toast is also named after her.

Rabindranath TAGORE
1861–1941
Indian poet, playwright, and writer

Rabindranath Tagore was born to a wealthy family in Calcutta. After studying law in England he returned to India. He published his first book of poetry, *A Poet's Tale*, in 1878, followed by *Manasi* in 1890, which established his reputation as a poet. In 1901, Tagore started a school at Bolpur in his native province of Bengal, hoping to combine culture from both East and West; it later became Vishva-Bharati University. He wrote mainly in Bengali but his works, including *Binodini*, the first modern novel by an Indian writer, were translated into many languages. His other writings include the play *Chitra* (1892), the poetry collections *The Golden Boat* (1894), and *Gitanjali, Song Offerings* (1912), for which he received the Nobel Prize for Literature – the first Asian to win the award. He also composed more than 2,000 popular Bengali songs. Tagore was knighted by Britain's King George V in 1915, but resigned the knighthood after the Amritsar Massacre of 1919, in which British troops fired on unarmed Indian demonstrators.

Mary KINGSLEY
1862–1900
English explorer

The niece of Charles Kingsley, who wrote *The Water-Babies*, Mary Henrietta Kingsley lived a sheltered life in London for 30 years, educating herself and looking after her sick mother. Her father was a doctor who

1861 Italian unification is achieved at last, after a dual invasion by Garibaldi from the south, and by Victor Emmanuel from the north. The newly united state is dominated by the more-developed, prosperous, and populated north.

1861 Victor Emmanuel is proclaimed the first king of Italy. A brash monarch, he seeks to improve Italy's reputation through war and is often at odds with his ministers. After his death, in 1878, he is hailed as a great ruler.

travelled abroad and, as she read his letters from overseas, she was inspired to travel. When her parents died, she decided to become an explorer, – an amazing decision for a woman to make in Victorian times. In 1893, Kingsley set off for West Africa. She explored a previously unknown part of the Congo (now Gabon), collecting fish, insects, and plants. She climbed mountains, waded through swamps, and canoed down rapids. She wrote of her exploits in *Travels in West Africa* (1897). European explorers in Africa usually travelled in large well-armed parties, but Mary Kingsley had only a few hired helpers with her. She later died of fever in South Africa, nursing soldiers during the Second Boer War.

Claude
DEBUSSY
1862–1918
French composer

At the age of 10, the young Debussy went to study at the Paris Conservatory, where he won prizes for his composition. His early pieces were influenced by the music of German composer Richard Wagner (p.95), but he developed his own style in the 1890s, especially after hearing a Javanese gamelan orchestra in Paris. This new, atmospheric style was called "Impressionism", because of its similarities to the Impressionist paintings of the time. Such works as the *Prélude à l'après-midi d'un faune* (1894) were startling to listeners, and he gained international recognition with his opera *Pelléas et Mélisande* in 1902. This was followed by a large number of songs, pieces for piano, and orchestral works, including *La Mer* (1905). His totally new musical language was to have a huge influence on 20th-century composers.

Auguste & Louis
LUMIÈRE
1862–1954/1865–1948
French pioneers of the motion picture

The Lumière brothers were the sons of a photographer. At the age of 17, Louis invented a dry-plate process for printing photographs, which secured the family financially. By 1894 the Lumière business was producing 15 million plates a year. In the same year, after seeing a demonstration of the kinetoscope, which could record movement, the brothers were inspired to try to film moving pictures. Together, they invented the cinematograph – the first machine to project images on a screen. (The word "cinema" comes from this device.) On 28 December 1895, commercial cinema was born when their film *La Sortie des ouvriers de l'usine Lumière* was projected to a paying audience in Paris. The brothers spent the next years sending camera-operators and projectionists to destinations all over the world to shoot newsreels and to show films recording French life. Louis produced about 2,000 films. The brothers produced some of the earliest documentaries and comedy shorts.

Konstantin
STANISLAVSKI
1863–1938
Russian actor and theatre director

The son of a wealthy manufacturer, Stanislavski was born in Moscow and began acting in amateur performances while still in his teens. He became a professional actor and director, but rebelled against the stylized, artificial mode of acting that was then in fashion. He sought to develop a new, naturalistic style. He co-founded the Moscow Art Theatre, which opened in 1898, and one of his earliest productions was Chekhov's *The Seagull*, which demonstrated his innovative ideas and won critical acclaim. He went on to direct many plays by Chekhov (p.128) and other playwrights, and also opera, including Tchaikovsky's *Eugene Onegin* in 1922. Stanislavski's ideas had enormous influence on actors and directors in the West. Contemporary "method" acting – where actors look in detail at the personality and background of their character to give a more realistic performance – derives largely from his ideas.

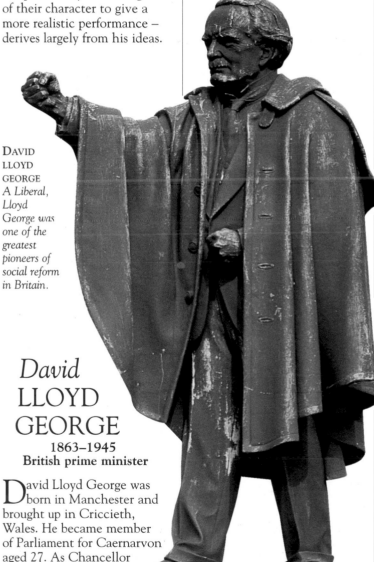

DAVID LLOYD GEORGE *A Liberal, Lloyd George was one of the greatest pioneers of social reform in Britain.*

David
LLOYD GEORGE
1863–1945
British prime minister

David Lloyd George was born in Manchester and brought up in Criccieth, Wales. He became member of Parliament for Caernarvon aged 27. As Chancellor of the Exchequer, he introduced old-age pensions in 1908 and National Insurance in 1911. His proposals in 1909–10 to tax the wealthy were rejected by the House of Lords, which led to the Act of 1911 which limited the Lords' powers. Lloyd George was Prime Minister from 1916 to 1922. During World War I, he waged war aggressively and was instrumental in negotiating the Peace of Versailles. He was a popular wartime leader but high postwar unemployment and the use of military police in Ireland (the Black and Tans) forced his resignation and left him on the sidelines of politics.

1862 In the United States, the Homestead Act promises farmers ownership of 65 hectares (160 acres) of land after they have cultivated it for five years. Thousands of settlers are lured to the lands west of the Mississippi.

1862 Bismarck becomes Prussian premier during a conflict between the government and the Liberal parliament. He wins the support of most Liberals through his foreign policy initiatives, such as wars with Denmark and Austria.

Henry FORD
1863–1947
US engineer

The "man who put America on wheels," Henry Ford grew up on a Michigan farm. His mechanical talent was apparent at an early age, and as a teenager he moved to Detroit, where he eventually became a chief engineer for the city's power-generating company. In the early 1890s Ford spent his spare time building a gasoline-powered automobile, which he successfully tested in 1895. After finding financial backers, he set up the Ford Motor Company in 1903 to build cars of his own design. Realizing that cars had to be affordable to the average worker if the automobile industry was to expand, Ford introduced the Model T in 1908. The boxy, no-frills car was cheap, reliable, and a phenomenal success. Ford refined the mass-production, assembly line system to manufacture the T in huge numbers, and he astounded the nation by offering workers the then-unheard-of wage of $5 per day. For all his success, Ford was a controversial figure. He published an anti-Semitic newspaper, led a much-mocked peace mission to Europe in 1916, and in the 1930s he bitterly opposed moves to unionize his factories. Nevertheless, Ford transformed American society by making cars accessible and affordable.

Richard STRAUSS
1864–1949
German composer

Son of the horn player in the Munich Court Orchestra, Richard Strauss began composing at the age of six. He studied at Munich and Berlin and began his career as a conductor in 1886. His first success as a composer came with the symphonic poem *Don Juan* (1889). In the 1890s, he wrote several more, including *Also sprach Zarathustra* (1896), *Don Quixote* (1897) and *Ein Heldenleben* (1898). From the 1900s, Strauss composed some impressive operas, including *Salome* (1905) and *Der Rosenkavalier* (1911). He composed little from 1920 until the 1940s, when, amongst other works, he wrote his last opera, *Capriccio* (1942).

Rudyard KIPLING
1865–1936
Indian-born English writer

Rudyard Kipling, famous chronicler of life in British-ruled India, wrote one of his first successful works *Plain Tales from the Hills* in 1888 while working as a journalist in Lahore. His tales for children, including his two *Jungle Books* (1894–95), *Kim* (1901), *Just So Stories* (1902), and *Puck of Pook's Hill* (1906), reveal his talent as an imaginative storyteller as well as his love of the exotic, as inspired by the wonders of India. Poems such as "If…" and "Gunga Din" also contributed to his popularity with readers all over the world. In 1907, he won the Nobel Prize for Literature – the first English writer to do so.

Drawing of W. B. Yeats by Kathleen Shackleton

William Butler YEATS
1865–1939
Irish poet

Considered one of the finest English-language poets of the 20th century, Yeats was born in Dublin and educated in England. Frequent visits to Sligo in western Ireland inspired Yeats with the beauty of the land and the rich folklore of its people, and his first volumes of poetry and verse-plays were both deeply mystical and rooted in Celtic mythology. An Irish nationalist, he helped establish Dublin's Abbey Theatre and later served in the senate of the Irish Free State. With *The Wild Swans at Coole* (1917), Yeats's poetry

MODEL T FORD
The first Model T went on sale in the USA on 12 August 1908 and cost $850. In all, 16,500 were made.

1863 The Polish uprising against Russia destroys the peaceful policy of the Russian tsar Alexander II.

The January Insurrection leads to defeat for the Poles in 1864. In the aftermath, Russia tries to destroy Polish national spirit.

1864 The Red Cross is formed to care for victims of battle during war, later aiding in the prevention and relief of human suffering generally. The Red Cross arose out of the work of Jean-Henri Dunant, a Swiss humanitarian.

grew increasingly philosophical, though highly lyrical and filled with stunning imagery. Yeats won the Nobel Prize for Literature in 1923 and produced some of his best work, including *The Tower* (1928) and *The Winding Stair* (1929), in old age. Among his best-known poems are "Easter 1916" and "The Lake Isle of Innisfree".

Jean SIBELIUS
1865–1957
Finnish composer

Jean Sibelius was born in Hämeenlinna. He learned piano and violin as a child, but went to Helsinki University to study law. He transferred to the Conservatory of Music and later studied music in Berlin and Vienna. Finland was part of the Russian

Empire until 1917, and Sibelius supported the Finnish nationalists – many of his compositions are based on Finnish legends. His first major work was the choral symphony *Kullervo* (1892), followed by the *Karelia Suite* (1893). In 1897, he received a grant from the government and spent his time composing. He wrote several symphonic poems including *The Swan of Tuonela* (1893) and *Finlandia* (1899). His seven symphonies made him one of the most significant symphonists of the 20th century.

Erik SATIE
1866–1925
French composer

Son of a ship's broker, Erik Satie was born in Honfleur. He went to the Paris Conservatory in 1879, but left after a year to make a living as a café pianist and songwriter. He started to compose pieces for piano in a light, simple style that was a reaction against the complex, heavy music of

contemporary composers like Wagner. He wrote three *Sarabandes* (1887), three *Gymnopédies* (1888), and three *Gnossiennes* (1890). Satie was eccentric and he gave his pieces titles such as *Three flabby pieces (for a dog)* (1913). His ballet *Parade* (1917) includes parts for typewriter, siren, and ship's whistle.

Beatrix POTTER
1866–1943
English writer and illustrator

Helen Beatrix Potter was brought up by nurses and governesses in London. As an adult, she wrote letters to her friends' children in which she illustrated stories about four rabbits called Flopsy, Mopsy, Cotton-tail, and Peter. Children loved them so she tried to get them published as *The Tale of Peter Rabbit*. Six publishers rejected it so she published it herself in 1900. In 1902, Frederick Warne & Co reprinted the book. This was followed by 22 more "little books for little hands", including *The Tale of Squirrel Nutkin* and *The Tailor of Gloucester*. Her engaging animal characters include Peter Rabbit, Jemima Puddle-Duck, Mrs Tiggy-Winkle, and Benjamin Bunny. In 1905, Potter became engaged to her publisher, Norman Warne, but he died before they were married. The same year she moved to Hilltop Farm in England's Lake District, bred sheep, and stopped writing. Her books are read and loved by children all over the world.

Wassily KANDINSKY
1866–1944
Russian painter

Wassily Kandinsky was born in Moscow. In 1896, he moved to Munich and studied painting. There he began creating what are thought to be the first abstract pictures. These spontaneous "improvisations" were painted in bright, pure colours. After a period back in Moscow, he returned to Germany in 1921 and taught at the Bauhaus School. He began to use geometric patterns and symbols in his paintings. Later works include *In the Blue* (1925), *Yellow-Red-Blue* (1925), and *Around the Circle* (1940). Kandinsky's paintings and books had a huge impact on 20th-century art.

H. G. WELLS
1866–1946
English writer and historian

Herbert George Wells was born in Bromley, Kent. At 18 he won a scholarship to study biology at what was to become the Royal College of Science. He became a teacher, and in 1891 married his cousin. Three years later, he ran away with a former pupil, whom he married in 1895, the year his first novel, *The Time Machine*, was published. This early science fiction was followed by many more short stories and novels, among them *The Invisible Man* (1897) and *The War of the Worlds* (1898). Wells's imagination produced many machines that scientists would later invent. He was committed to issues such as education, the League of Nations, and the rejection of Christian codes of behaviour, but it is as a science-fiction pioneer that he is remembered.

1866 War breaks out between Austria and Prussia because they cannot agree on the redistribution of power following their defeat of Denmark in 1864. The war lasts six weeks and ends with an Austrian defeat at Sadowa.

1866 While reading about one of Jesus's healings in the Bible, Mary Baker Eddy experiences a sudden recovery from an injury. She is prompted to found the Christian Science movement in the United States of America.

PIONEERS OF FLIGHT

The first powered flight by the WRIGHT BROTHERS in 1903 opened up a new form of travel. No longer were people restricted to land or sea. Now they could fly through the air.

FIRST FLIGHTS
In 1907, the first flight in Europe was made by the Anglo-Frenchman HENRI FARMAN (1874–1958). It lasted for just more than a minute. Two years later, LOUIS BLÉRIOT (p.139) flew his monoplane across the English Channel. By 1914, aircraft were regularly seen in the skies over Europe and North America.

WORLD WAR I AND AFTER. . .
The use of planes to fight, bomb, and observe the enemy led to big advances in aircraft technology during and after World War I (1914–18). In 1919, the British aviators

JOHN ALCOCK (1892–1919) and ARTHUR WHITTEN-BROWN (1886–1948) made the first transatlantic flight from Newfoundland to Ireland. The same year, daily passenger flights began between London and Paris, and the first regular international air service in the world was born. CHARLES LINDBERGH (p.178) flew across the Atlantic Ocean single-handed in 1927 and AMELIA EARHART (p.168) became the first woman to achieve the same feat in 1932. In 1930, AMY JOHNSON (p.180) flew solo from England to Australia in 19 days. The era of international flight was now well underway.

Wilbur & Orville WRIGHT
1867–1912 and 1871–1948
US inventors and aviation pioneers

The first to achieve powered flight, Wilbur and Orville Wright were born in Dayton, Ohio. They shared great mechanical talent, which they put to use in their bicycle-repair shop. They also built gliders – solving major aeronautical problems in the process – which they test-flew on annual visits to Kitty Hawk in North Carolina. In 1903, they fitted a 13-hp gasoline motor to their latest glider, and on 17 December, with Orville aboard, the first "Wright Flyer" made a 12-second flight. The

THE WRIGHT BROTHERS
Orville Wright was pilot for the first aircraft flight on 17 December, 1903.

Wrights refined their designs and travelled to Europe to promote their aircraft. Wilbur died three years later; Orville lived into the era of jet flight.

SUN YAT-SEN
1867–1925
Chinese revolutionary leader

Sun Yat-sen was the son of a Christian farmer. He went to Hong Kong to study medicine and became a doctor. Believing that China needed to join the modern world, Sun joined revolutionaries trying to overthrow the rule of the emperors of the Ching dynasty and establish a republic. He studied in Britain and the United States and organized

a revolutionary league in Japan. He returned to China for the 1911 revolution that overthrew the Chinese emperor and he became the provisional president of the republic. China then broke up into regions ruled by military warlords and Sun was forced to cede power to Yuan Shikai. Sun reorganized his revolutionary forces (the Kuomintang) and appointed Chiang Kai-Shek as head of a military academy. Sun died before he could defeat the warlords and unite China. Chiang Kai-Shek achieved this three years later by following Sun's political theories.

WOODEN SLEDGE
Early polar explorers, such as Robert Scott, used sledges to transport their heavy loads.

1867 Britain passes the North American Act. Under the Act, New Brunswick and Nova Scotia join Québec and Ontario to form Canada, which becomes a self-governing dominion within the British Empire.

1867 The Ausgleich Compromise is made between Francis Joseph I of Austria and the Hungarian leadership. It turns the Hapsburg Empire into Austria-Hungary and results in Hungarian control over Hapsburg affairs.

134

Marie CURIE
1867–1934
Polish-born French physicist

Marie Curie (maiden name Sklodowska) was born in Warsaw, daughter of a mathematics teacher. Her father lost his job, so Marie had to seek work as a teacher and later as a governess to earn money to study. At this time, women could not go to university in Poland, but she was able to pay for studies at the Sorbonne in Paris. Marie graduated first in her class in physical science and second in mathematics. In 1895, she married a successful chemist, Pierre Curie, and together they formed a working partnership studying magnetism and radioactivity and discovering the element radium, for which they jointly received (with Henri Becquerel) the Nobel Prize for Physics in 1903. Pierre died in 1906, and Marie took his place as the professor of physics at the Sorbonne – the first woman to teach there. In 1911, she won the Nobel Prize for Chemistry. During World War I, she continued her research into radioactivity but died of leukaemia, probably due to exposure to radiation.

Luigi PIRANDELLO
1867–1936
Italian playwright and writer

Luigi Pirandello was born in Sicily, and later went to universities in Rome and Bonn. He married in 1894 and his wife's money allowed him to write full-time. In 1904, his third novel, *The Late Mattia Pascal*, brought him success. After his wife went insane, Pirandello's growing interest in the human personality was reflected in his writing. He invented "theatre within a theatre" and his plays *Six Characters in Search of an Author* (1921) and *Henry IV* (1922) made him famous. In 1925, he established a theatre company and toured the world for two years. In 1934, he won the Nobel Prize for Literature.

Frank LLOYD WRIGHT
1867–1959
US architect

One of the most prolific and influential architects of the 20th century, Frank Lloyd Wright was born in Wisconsin.

He worked as a draughtsman in Chicago before setting up on his own in 1893. His early residential designs like Ward Willits House (1902) and Robie House (1909–10) helped define the "Prairie School" of architecture, with low horizontal forms echoing the midwestern landscape. Wright developed a philosophy of organic architecture, which emphasized the unity of building and site, expressed brilliantly in his best-known home, Fallingwater (1936–37), in Pennsylvania. A designer as well as an architect, Wright designed fittings, furniture, and decorations for his buildings in keeping with his organic approach. He taught architecture at two schools in Wisconsin and Arizona. Active into his 90s, his last great work was the Guggenheim Museum (1959) in New York City.

Robert Falcon SCOTT
1868–1912
English Antarctic explorer

Robert Falcon Scott was born in Devon. He joined the navy as a young man and in 1901, he was chosen to lead an expedition to the Antarctic. With two companions, he tried, unsuccessfully, to reach the South Pole. In 1910, Scott led another expedition. Rejecting the use of dogs as "unsporting", Scott and five companions man-hauled their heavy sledges. Scott's team reached the Pole on 17 January 1912, only to discover that the Norwegian explorer, Roald Amundsen (p.138), had arrived there a month earlier. Scott and his men died on the return journey, weakened by frostbite, scurvy, and exhaustion from hauling their sledges. Scott's diary, found near his frozen body 10 months later, was a stirring account of the suffering and bravery of his men.

Scott JOPLIN
1868–1917
US composer

The "King of Ragtime", Joplin was born to ex-slave parents near Texarkana, Texas. He studied piano as a child and spent years as a travelling musician. In 1899, Joplin composed the "Maple Leaf Rag", a piano tune written in the syncopated style that came to be known as "ragtime". The song became the first piece of music to sell more than a million copies in sheet-music form. Joplin's opera *Treemonisha* was staged in 1915, but ragtime's popularity was waning and Joplin was seriously ill. His music was revived in the 1970s and in 1976 he was awarded a Pulitzer Prize.

1867 The Second Reform Act in Britain is passed. It extends voting rights to homeowners if they have been resident in their homes for more than a year. Lodgers are also allowed to vote if their rent is at least £10 a year.

1867 The London Conference guarantees Luxembourg perpetual neutrality in European politics. The European powers make the duchy an independent state with its sovereignty invested in the royal House of Nassau.

NICHOLAS II
1868–1918
Last Russian emperor

Nicholas was born near St Petersburg and became tsar (emperor) of Russia in 1894, on the death of his father, Alexander III. He quickly announced that he intended to retain autocratic rule and began to suppress the opposition and persecute religious minorities. A heavy defeat by Japan in the war of 1904–05 led to a revolution, but Nicholas failed to give up power, and discontent grew. In 1914, Russia was drawn into World War I, in which Nicholas took personal command of the army. His incompetence led to a revolution against his rule in 1917, and he was overthrown. In 1918, he and the royal family were executed by the Bolsheviks to prevent them from falling into the hands of counter-revolutionaries.

Charles Rennie
MACKINTOSH
1868–1928
Scottish architect and designer

One of Glasgow's most famous inhabitants, Charles Rennie Mackintosh worked as an architect's apprentice and took night classes at the Glasgow School of Art. In 1900, he married Margaret Macdonald, a talented artist who would share the work on many of his future art projects with him. His architectural works, which include the

HIGH-BACKED CHAIR
Charles Mackintosh has only recently come to be regarded as a pioneer of modern design. This is one of his chairs, produced in 1900.

Glasgow School of Art, the Cranston Tearooms, and Hill House in Helensburgh, had a strong influence on European design, particularly in Austria. His interior designs, which combined strong lines and curved motifs, were influenced by the Art Nouveau movement, but as his style developed it became uniquely his own. He also turned his hand to furniture, glass, textiles, and metalwork. Towards the end of his life, Rennie Mackintosh concentrated on painting watercolours.

Fritz
HABER
1868–1934
German chemist

Fritz Haber taught physical chemistry at Jena, Karlsruhe, and Berlin. With his brother-in-law, Carl Bosch, he invented the process for creating ammonia from hydrogen, which was used in fertilizers, and also devised a process for producing nitric acid, which was used to make explosives during World War I. He was awarded the Nobel Prize for Chemistry in 1918. When Adolf Hitler rose to power in 1933, Haber went to Britain and worked at the Cavendish Laboratory in Cambridge.

Valdemar
POULSEN
1869–1942
Danish engineer

In 1900, while working for the Copenhagen Telephone Company, Valdemar Poulsen became the first person to demonstrate that sound could be recorded magnetically. A working model created for the Paris Exposition of 1900 generated great interest. Initially on a moving steel wire or tape, his device could record continuously for 30 minutes and was the forerunner of the tape recorder. Poulsen also worked on the development of what was to become long-wave radio broadcasting.

Mahatma
GANDHI
1869–1948
Indian leader

Mohandas Karamchand Gandhi was born in Porbandar. His mother was a devout Hindu and she passed on her peace-loving beliefs to her son. Gandhi studied law in London and later moved to South Africa to practice law. Gandhi remained in South Africa for more than 20 years, protesting about the discrimination against Asians. In 1914, he returned to India where he advocated non-violent civil disobedience against British rule. Imprisoned by the British authorities several times, he became the leader of the Indian Congress Movement for Indian freedom and campaigned for religious tolerance. Gandhi gave up the trappings of a Western lifestyle and associated himself with the poorest people in Hindu society, spinning cloth everyday and living a simple life. He taught that non-violent, passive resistance was the way to effect political

1868 In Japan, a treaty with the United States gives trade concessions to the West, which most Japanese people oppose, and a civil war is fought. Unity is restored under the young emperor, who takes the name Meiji – "enlightened ruler".

1869 The Suez Canal opens, linking the Mediterranean Sea to the Indian Ocean. The canal, cut with the permission of the ruler of Egypt, Sa'id Pasha, provides ships with a much shorter sea route to Asia.

change. His campaigns of 1919 to 1920 led to violence, notably in Amritsar, where hundreds of people were massacred by British troops. Gandhi's frequent arrests and hunger strikes made him an inspiration to fellow Indians and many joined his campaign. He negotiated with the British government until 1947, when India was finally granted independence. Gandhi was deeply saddened by the fighting between Muslims and Hindus that followed Indian independence. He was assassinated in 1948 by a Hindu fanatic.

Henri
MATISSE
1869–1954
French painter

Henri Matisse trained as a lawyer but gave this up in 1891 and moved to Paris to study art. His early paintings emphasized dark colours but Matisse was soon influenced by the Impressionists and used lighter, brighter colours. In 1905, Matisse and other painters shocked critics with an exhibition in Paris. Their primitive violent colours and style seemed to have no connection with what they were depicting, and they were dubbed the Fauves, meaning "Wild Beasts". Matisse produced the major Fauvist masterpieces, such as *The Joy of Life* (1906) and *The Red Room* (1908–09). After 1917, he worked mainly in the south of France, where he responded to the vivid sunlight by painting in even more vibrant tones and flowing forms. In his last years, he developed his own abstract style using cut-out shapes of brightly coloured paper to produce pictures like *The Snail* (1953). He was one of the most adventurous and influential artists of the 20th century.

1870

Vladimir Ilyich
LENIN
1870–1924
Russian revolutionary and founder of the USSR

Lenin was born into a middle-class family and trained as a lawyer. He turned to radical politics as a teenager after his brother was executed for his role in a plot to assassinate the tsar. Lenin became a Marxist and a revolutionary organizer and writer. Exiled to Siberia and then to western Europe, he became leader of the Bolshevik (minority) faction of Russia's Social Democratic Workers' Party. In 1917, he returned to Russia (with Germany's help) and led the Bolsheviks in their seizure of power during the October Revolution of 1917. Successfully withstanding challenges from political rivals and from the invading anti-Bolshevik armies of several nations, Lenin established the Soviet Union, or USSR, the world's first communist state. Ruthlessly crushing opposition and silencing dissent, Lenin ruled the new state as a virtual dictator. Several strokes in the early 1920s ruined Lenin's health, but he remained in power until his death in 1924.

VLADIMIR ILYICH LENIN
Lenin's real surname was Ulyanov. He was born in Simbirsk on the River Volga.

Jan Christian
SMUTS
1870–1950
South African prime minister

Smuts commanded the Boers (Dutch settlers) against the British during the Boer War (1899–1902). He later decided that co-operation was essential, and worked for peace between the warring sides. He was instrumental in the creation of the Union of South Africa in 1910 and was Minister of the Interior 1910–1912, and Defence Minister 1910–1920. During World War I, he commanded the South African forces in East Africa and was a member of the War Cabinet in London. He was Prime Minister of South Africa from 1919 to 1924. During World War II, he worked with the Allies to prevent Germany and Italy conquering North Africa.

Maria
MONTESSORI
1870–1952
Italian doctor and educational reformer

In 1894, Maria Montessori became the first woman in Italy to receive a medical degree. Her specialist fields were medical treatment of children and psychiatry. While working with mentally disabled children, she devised the "Montessori method", an education system for all children. Based on an informal approach, it allows children to develop at their own pace. The success of her methods, first used in a school she set up in Rome, and of her books – *The Montessori Method* (1912) and *The Secret of Childhood* (1936) – made her famous. Montessori schools have been set up throughout the world.

1870 The Prussian leader Bismarck provokes France into a war that he hopes will lead to a unified Germany under Prussian leadership. In the Treaty of Frankfurt, France gives up Alsace-Lorraine and pays heavy costs to Germany.

1870 John Rockefeller founds Standard Oil in the United States. He begins to control oil in other states and Standard Oil of New Jersey becomes one of the nation's most powerful "trusts".

Rosa LUXEMBURG
1871–1919
German revolutionary

Rosa Luxemburg was born in Zamosc, Poland, then part of the Russian Empire. As a teenager, she was inspired by the writings of Karl Marx (p.96). Faced with the prospect of prison for her communist activities, she emigrated to Zürich, Switzerland where she studied economics. In 1898, she moved to Germany where she joined the Social Democratic Party and became a leading revolutionary. She was imprisoned in 1915 for opposing World War I but was released in 1918. In 1919, she was arrested again, this time during disturbances in Berlin and was murdered on her way to jail.

Amundsen's boat the Gjoa

Marcel PROUST
1871–1922
French novelist

Growing up in Paris, Marcel Proust studied law and literature. He then mixed with the nobility in Paris, observing fashionable society. Ill-health and a growing dissatisfaction gradually made him more solitary. Disillusioned with the aristocrats, Proust threw his energies into writing. The vast work by which he is best known – *Remembrance of Things Past* – consists of seven books in 13 volumes. Within the novels, Proust explored the workings of memory and how taste and smell take one back to past times. The best-known volume of this autobiographical series is probably *Swann's Way* (1913), in which Proust remembers scenes from his childhood.

Ernest RUTHERFORD
1871–1937
New Zealand physicist

Ernest Rutherford was one of 11 children born and raised on a farm near Nelson, New Zealand. He did well at school and won a scholarship to Canterbury College, Christchurch, to study mathematics and physics. In 1895, he won a scholarship to Cambridge University in England, where he worked with J. J. Thomson (p.124) who had discovered the electron. Rutherford began work on X-rays. In 1898, he became a professor at McGill University, Montreal, Canada. His work there with Frederick Soddy (p.143) produced the idea that the atoms of some elements were not permanent but could disintegrate through radioactive decay (a discovery for which he was awarded the Nobel Prize for Chemistry in 1908). He returned to Britain in 1909 to work in Manchester. In 1911, Rutherford discovered the atomic nucleus and some of its properties. His work, for which he was knighted in 1914, was instrumental in the development of nuclear physics.

Roald AMUNDSEN
1872–1928
Norwegian explorer

Born in Borge, Norway, Amundsen made the first transit of the Northwest Passage, sailing a small sloop from the Atlantic to the Pacific through Arctic waters from 1903 to 1906. His hopes of being first at the North Pole were thwarted by Robert Peary's 1909 claim (p.123). Undaunted, Amundsen set out for the South Pole, and in 1911 he sailed to Antarctica. Amundsen and four companions reached the pole on 14 December, 1911, before his rival, Robert Scott (p. 135). He disappeared in the Arctic in 1926 while searching for the survivors of a downed airship.

Sergei DIAGHILEV
1872–1929
Russian ballet impresario

Diaghilev grew up with a passionate interest in the arts which was greatly encouraged by his stepmother. He moved to Paris in 1906 to pursue a musical career and began to arrange exhibitions and concerts of Russian art and music. In 1909, he founded his company, the *Ballets Russes*, which was to be a great influence on Western ballet. Diaghilev's brilliance lay in bringing together outstanding artists of the day – composers, artists, choreographers, and dancers. He worked with people of such international stature as Pablo Picasso (p.148), Igor Stravinsky (p.150), and Anna Pavlova (p.146). His most famous productions include Stravinsky's *The Firebird*, *Petrushka*, and *The Rite of Spring*. He was a temperamental but charming tyrant. The works he commissioned were genuinely innovative and full of vitality and imaginative fantasy.

LOUIS BLERIOT
The main frame of Blériot's monoplane was made of wood, with fabric stretched over it.

1871 The English Football Association Cup is established. The competition, now known as the FA Cup, is first won by Wanderers against the Royal Engineers. After 1923, the final is staged at Wembley Stadium.

1871 Germany is united under William I of Prussia. German chief minister Bismarck expands Germany by winning land from Denmark, Austria, and France. At home, he also courts north Germans with a liberal constitution.

Louis BLERIOT
1872–1936
French aviator

Louis Blériot was both an aircraft designer and a pilot in the early days of aviation. He pioneered the design of monoplanes – aircraft with one wing, instead of two. On 25 July 1909, just six years after the first-ever brief flight in a plane, Blériot flew a monoplane across the English Channel. He travelled from Baraques, France to Dover, England, covering a distance of 39.4 km (24.5 miles) in a mere 36.5 minutes. Blériot's monoplane design was widely copied, and his famous flight proved that aeroplanes were not just a novelty. They would be the transport of the future.

Ralph VAUGHAN WILLIAMS
1872–1958
English composer

Ralph Vaughan Williams studied at Trinity College, Cambridge University, the Royal College of Music in London, and in Berlin and Paris. He was particularly interested in English music of the Elizabethan period, as well as folksongs. These interests influenced his music and his work often shows a mixture of English folk styles and 20th-century techniques. His first major success was the *Sea Symphony* (1910), which was followed by a further eight symphonies, including the *London Symphony* (1914), *Pastoral Symphony* (1922), and *Sinfonia Antarctica* (1952). Other well-known pieces include *Fantasia on a Theme by Thomas Tallis* (1910) and *The Lark Ascending* (1914).

Bertrand RUSSELL
1872–1970
English mathematician and philosopher

Bertrand Arthur William Russell was the grandson of Liberal prime minister Lord John Russell. He gained first-class honours from Trinity College, Cambridge University, in mathematics and moral sciences (1893–94). After being elected a fellow of the college in 1895, Russell continued his work on the proofs of mathematics and logic, publishing *Principles of Mathematics* in 1903 and *Principia Mathematica* in 1910–13. Russell's controversial pacifism during World War I led to the loss of his Cambridge fellowship in 1916 and imprisonment in 1918. By World War II he was no longer a pacifist but, after a period of enthusiasm for atomic weapons, he became a supporter of nuclear disarmament from 1949 onwards. He continued his work for peace well into his 90s, opposing the Vietnam War. He won the Nobel Prize for Literature in 1950.

Sergey RACHMANINOFF
1873–1943
Russian composer

As a child, Sergey Rachmaninoff lived with his mother in St Petersburg and went to study at the Moscow Conservatory at the age of 12. He was a brilliant pianist and made his name both as a performer and for compositions such as the popular Prelude in C Sharp Minor, written when he was 19. The first performance of his Symphony No.1 (1897) was a disaster, however, because it

was poorly performed. Rachmaninoff became depressed and sought psychiatric help. In 1900, he resumed work as a pianist, conductor, and composer, and wrote the popular Piano Concerto No. 2. He toured the USA in 1909, premiering his Piano Concerto No. 3, and after the Russian Revolution made New York City his home. His romantically charged music includes three symphonies, choral music, and operas, but he is best-known for his dazzling and emotional pieces for piano and orchestra, notably the *Rhapsody on a Theme of Paganini* (1934).

1872 A Three-Emperors' League is formed between Germany, Russia, and Austria-Hungary. The agreement shows solidarity in the face of revolutionary movements and pledges support for Germany in a possible war with France.

1873 Isaac Butt's Home Government Association, founded in 1870, becomes the Home Rule League in Ireland. Its unexpected success in the 1874 general election leads to the formation of the Irish Parliamentary Party.

COLETTE
1873–1954
French writer

Sidonie-Gabrielle Colette was born and brought up in France. At 20, she married Henri Gauthier-Villars, who, in 1900, published her four *Claudine* books under his own pen name, Willy. They divorced in 1906, and Colette worked for a time as a music-hall performer, also writing *The Vagabond* and *The Hell of the Music Hall* (1913). She married again in 1912, and in 1920 she began to write the novels for which she is famous: *Chéri* (1920), *The Last of Chéri* (1926), and *The Wheat in the Grass* (1923). In 1935, she divorced again and married Maurice Goudeket. Her best-known work, *Gigi* (1944), was adapted as a play and a film.

COLETTE'S HOUSE
This house in the Burgundy area of France is where Colette was raised.

Ernest SHACKLETON
1874–1922
Irish explorer

Born in County Kildare, Ireland, Ernest Shackleton served in the British Merchant Navy before joining Robert Scott's first Antarctic expedition (1901–04). Shackleton returned to Antarctica in 1907–09 and made it to within 160 km (100 miles) of the South Pole. In 1914, Shackleton sailed south aboard the *Endurance*, hoping to make the first crossing of Antarctica. The ship was crushed by pack-ice, and after a gruelling journey the stranded crew made it to a small island. In an amazing display of courage and leadership, Shackleton and five others then sailed 1,287 km (800 miles) in an open boat to South Georgia Island to get help. After a dangerous crossing of the mountainous island, Shackleton reached safety and arranged the rescue of his men.

SHACKLETON'S HOOD
This windproof hood was worn by Shackleton in the Antarctic.

Harry HOUDINI
1874–1926
US escapologist

Houdini emigrated from Hungary to the United States with his family. He became a trapeze artist as a boy and established a reputation as an escapologist. He accepted seemingly impossible challenges, allowing himself to be tied up with ropes, handcuffs, chains, and strait jackets, and put in locked trunks. Houdini frequently added to the danger of his escapes by carrying them out underwater, or while hanging upside-down with his feet held by stocks. His tricks were based on skills and fitness. He claimed he could withstand any blow, but he died from peritonitis after a member of the public punched his stomach before he had had time to tense his muscles.

Lilian BAYLIS
1874–1937
English theatrical manager

The daughter of professional singers, Baylis began her career as a violinist, first in London, then in South Africa. She returned to London to help her aunt run the Royal Victoria Coffee Music Hall in the Old Vic theatre, where a variety of entertainments and lectures were put on for workers. After her aunt died, Baylis became the sole manager of the theatre. She introduced drama and opera into the repertoire and established the Old Vic's reputation for outstanding productions of Shakespeare. Baylis was a tireless promoter of the arts

HARRY HOUDINI
One of Houdini's escapes was carried out while he was suspended from the cornice of a skyscraper in New York.

1873 On his return from Europe, Rama V reforms Thailand, based on European models. He abolishes slavery and educates the children of the nobility. He reorganizes the government and taxation and opens a railway.

1873 A critic mocks the unfinished look of painter Claude Monet's *Impression – Sunrise*, but other artists seize on the name Impressionist and adopt it to describe an exhibition of their work.

and acquired another theatre, Sadler's Wells in Islington, which she rebuilt and opened in 1931. It became a venue for ballet and opera productions. Baylis founded the companies that were to become the Royal Ballet and the English National Opera.

Guglielmo MARCONI
1874–1937
Italian electrical engineer

After reading about the discovery of electromagnetic radio waves by Heinrich Hertz (p.124), Marconi built a device for converting them into electrical signals. He then tried to send and receive radio waves over increasing distances. In 1898, he transmitted signals across the English Channel and, in 1901, established communication in Morse Code between Newfoundland, and Cornwall in Britain. In 1909, Marconi received the Nobel Prize for Physics in recognition of his development of wireless telegraphy. In 1918, he sent the first radio message from England to Australia. Guglielmo Marconi also developed short-wave wireless communication.

W. Mackenzie KING
1874–1950
Canadian prime minister

William Mackenzie King was prime minister of Canada 1921–26, 1926–30, and 1935–48, holding the office longer than anyone else in Canada's history. A Liberal, he introduced Canada's first old-age pension and developed a foreign policy separate from Britain's. On the eve of World War II, King urged peace but, following Germany's attack on Poland, he declared war. He signed agreements on economic cooperation between US President Franklin Roosevelt and Canada at the founding conferences of the United Nations in 1945.

Arnold SCHOENBERG
1874–1951
Austro-Hungarian/ US composer

Viennese-born Arnold Schoenberg learned the violin as a child and began composing at an early age. He wrote his first important compositions, *Verklärte Nacht* (1899) and *Gurrelieder* (1900–11) in Berlin. Returning to Vienna in 1903, he worked as a teacher, with pupils including Berg and Webern. The three became known as the "Second Viennese School". His Chamber Symphony (1906) caused uproar because it abandoned traditional ideas of harmony and key. This new "atonal" style continued with works such as *Five Orchestral Pieces* (1909). In the 1920s, Schoenberg developed a system known as the 12-tone or serial method, first heard in the *Piano Suite* (1923). As a Jew, he was forced to leave Berlin in 1933 when the Nazis came to power and he settled in Los Angeles. His new methods of composition influenced many later 20th-century composers.

Charles IVES
1874–1954
US composer

Born in Connecticut, Charles Ives was first taught music by his father, a bandmaster. He later studied music at Yale University but chose a career in insurance, rather than becoming a professional musician or teacher. He composed an enormous amount of music in his spare time. His early works were rather conventional, but he later experimented with many different styles. Ives often mixed folk music, band tunes, and hymns in a single piece, with completely new techniques, such as using two or more keys simultaneously. Illness forced him to retire in the 1920s and most of his music was performed towards the end of his life. Ives was the first composer to develop a truly American style, best heard in his orchestral music, including *Unanswered Question* (pre-1908), the *Concord* piano sonata (1909–15), *Three Places in New England* (1908–14), and *114 Songs* (1919–24).

Robert FROST
1874–1963
US poet

One of America's best-loved poets, Robert Frost was born in San Francisco, California. In 1912, he travelled to Britain where, under the influence of such poets as Rupert Brooke, he published two volumes of poetry, *A Boy's Will* (1913) and *North of Boston* (1914), which made his name famous throughout the world. On his return to the United States in 1915, he was made Professor of English at Amherst College in Massachusetts. He continued to write poetry and was given the name "the voice of New England" because of the themes and speech patterns of his verse. Frost received the Pulitzer Prize for Poetry in 1924, 1931, and 1937. From 1939 to 1943, he was Professor of Poetry at Harvard. Two of his best-known poems are "The Road Less Travelled" and "Stopping by Woods on a Snowy Evening".

1873 The Ashanti War is fought between the Ashanti (Akan-speakers from the hinterland of present-day Ghana and the Ivory Coast in Africa) and the British. The Ashanti are defeated by a British expeditionary force in 1897.

1873 The 20-year period known as the Great Depression begins in Britain. It is a time of depression of prices, interest, and profits. It is as much a general feeling as an economic change, but there is a drop in Britain's international trade.

Winston CHURCHILL
1874–1965
British prime minister

Soldier, politician, statesman, writer, artist, and more, Winston Churchill led an amazing life, and his influence on 20th-century history was profound. Son of a wealthy American mother and an aristocratic English father, he first won fame as a young cavalry officer and war correspondent. Churchill was elected to Parliament in 1901 and remained there, almost without interruption, for more than 60 years, as both a Liberal and Conservative member, and in his career he held almost every major cabinet post. Churchill was a prominent and often controversial figure in British politics until the 1930s. In 1940, with Britain standing virtually alone against Nazi Germany, Churchill became prime minister. Rallying the British people with stirring speeches, convinced of ultimate victory, he proved a great war leader. In 1945, with victory over Germany won, however, he was defeated in his bid for reelection. Churchill again became prime minister in 1951, but ill health forced his retirement in 1955. Among his many honours was the Nobel Prize for Literature, which he was awarded in 1953.

Jin QIU
1875–1907
Chinese revolutionary

Jin Qiu, or Ch'iu Chin, was the youngest daughter of a government lawyer. When she was 18, a marriage was arranged for her and she moved to Peking. Following the failure of the Hundred Days Reform of 1898 and the Boxer Rebellion of 1900, she became involved in opposition to China's Manchu rulers. As a feminist, she spoke out against the ancient practice of foot-binding. Soon after this, she left her husband and two children to study in Tokyo where she joined a revolutionary group. She returned to China and became famous for her passionate public speeches. In 1906, she established a women's journal in Shanghai and became Principal of the Ta'Tung College of Physical Culture. She planned a rebellion with her cousin, Hsu, but before they could put their plans into action Hsu was arrested and executed. Qiu was imprisoned and tortured but would only repeat "The autumn rain and wind sadden us" – the seven Chinese characters. She was beheaded.

Maurice RAVEL
1875–1937
French composer

Maurice Ravel was born in Ciboure and brought up in Paris, where he studied at the Conservatory. He made his name as a composer with the *Pavane pour une Infante Défunte* (1899) for piano, which he arranged for orchestra in 1910. In the years before World War I, he wrote some of his finest music, including the *String Quartet* (1903) and the ballet *Daphnis et Chloé* (1912). During the war, he served in the ambulance corps and, in 1917, wrote *Le Tombeau de Couperin* in memory of friends killed in action. His later ballet, *Boléro* (1928), epitomized his intricate style. Forced to retire in 1928 because of a brain tumour, he had established himself as one of the masters of orchestral and piano composition.

Photo of Maurice Ravel, taken in 1902.

film. He is credited with developing many basic film-making techniques, including close-ups, long shots, fade-outs, and cross-cutting. In 1915, he directed *The Birth of a Nation*, set during and following the Civil War. It was hailed as a masterpiece but it was condemned for its racism. Griffith made *Intolerance* (1916) to answer his critics. It has been hailed as perhaps the finest silent film.

D. W. GRIFFITH
1875–1948
US film director

Born in Kentucky, David Wark Griffith was an actor and writer before becoming involved in the motion-picture industry. He developed techniques that turned film-making into an art form and revolutionized the language of

Hiram BINGHAM
1875–1956
US archaeologist and explorer

Hiram Bingham was born in Honolulu, Hawaii, son of a missionary who taught him mountaineering. Hiram was later educated at Harvard University and became an expert on the history of the Inca Empire in Peru. In 1911,

1875 An assembly of monarchists form the Third Republic in France, in the face of a resurgence of republicans and Bonarpartists. The Third Republic becomes the longest-lasting French regime since the Revolution of 1848.

1877 The Russo-Turkish War is fought as the former, mighty Ottoman Empire declines, and European powers vie for control of the Balkans. Russia has attempted to influence this area throughout the century.

he travelled into the mountains of Peru to search for Vilcabamba, the last stronghold of the Incas, which even the Spanish conquerors had failed to locate. With few clues, and the high Andes terrain to contend with, Bingham reached Vilcabamba in 1911. The abandoned mountain city, now known as Machu Picchu, contained wonderfully preserved stone buildings, walls, and plazas stretching over 40 hectares (100 acres). At 2,057m (6,750 feet) above sea level, Machu Picchu was one of the highest cities in the world. At the time Bingham did not realize he had located the lost city of the Incas, but he returned in 1912 to excavate it, and later wrote of his discoveries.

Carl JUNG
1875–1961
Swiss psychologist

For some time, Carl Jung collaborated with and supported Freud (p.124) in explorations of mental illness. Jung ultimately rejected Freud's focus on sexual problems as the basis of psychoanalysis, and instead developed what was to become analytical psychology. Jung lectured in psychiatry at the University of Zürich from 1905, but gave up his post in 1914 because he felt he could not continue to teach until he had worked out his own ideas more clearly. From then on, he developed analytical psychology. He defined people and behaviour by the attitude types extrovert (outward-looking) and introvert (inward-looking), and said that an imbalance of the types caused problems. Jung tried to correct this imbalance through mental and physical therapy, using the study of dreams and stressing the spiritual life of the person.

Eglantine JEBB
1876–1928
English philanthropist

Eglantine Jebb was born in Ellesmere, Shropshire. She was educated at home before going to Oxford University in 1895. Jebb became a teacher, but fell ill and went to live with her mother in Cambridge. For a time she threw herself into social work. Then, at the end of World War I, she went to Macedonia to organize relief for the victims of war, including millions of children. Save the Children, which grew out of her first Fight the Famine Council, was founded in 1919. At the Declaration of Geneva in 1924, Jebb persuaded the League of Nations to adopt her Children's Charter and, in 1925, joined the League of Nations Council for the Protection of Children. Save the Children International was established in Geneva, where Jebb stayed and continued to work for the organization.

Mohammed Ali JINNAH
1876–1948
Indian Muslim leader and founder of Pakistan

One of seven children of a prosperous merchant, Mohammed Ali Jinnah went to England as a young man to study law. At the age of 20 he set up a successful law practice in Bombay. India was still part of the British Empire, and Jinnah supported the National Congress Party in its efforts to achieve Hindu-Muslim

Jinnah is sworn in as Governor-General of Pakistan.

unity in India, but he later joined and became President of the Muslim League, which campaigned for a separate Muslim nation. Jinnah brought about the Lucknow Pact, which promoted peaceful co-existence with the Hindu-dominated Congress Party. During independence negotiations with Britain, he insisted on the creation of a homeland for Indian Muslims. He achieved his aim in 1947 and became the first Governor-General of the Dominion of Pakistan.

Frederick SODDY
1877–1956
English chemist

Born in Eastbourne, Frederick Soddy was educated in Wales and at Merton College, Oxford. He worked at McGill University, Montreal, Canada, with Ernest Rutherford (p.138). Together, they pioneered the theory of radioactivity and radioactive decay. On returning to England in 1903, Soddy continued this work and, in 1913, defined the alpha and beta particles emitted during radioactive decay. Soddy gave the name "isotopes" to atoms of the same atomic number but different atomic mass. For this work he was awarded the 1921 Nobel Prize for Chemistry. He predicted the use of isotopes in the ageing of rocks and foresaw atomic energy, but Soddy became concerned about its wider use.

1877 A rebellion of the samurai class is put down in Japan. Political, social, and economic reforms are brought in during the Meiji period. The capital moves to Edo, renamed Tokyo, and Japan starts to become a major power.

1878 The Congress of Berlin, a diplomatic gathering of European powers, takes place. The powers fear that Russia has gained too much by the Treaty of San Stefano, which was signed at the end of the Russo-Turkish War.

Isadora DUNCAN
**1878–1927
US dancer**

Daughter of a music teacher, Duncan was born in San Francisco. She was sent to ballet school and danced in an unconventional way, not liking the formalized movements she had to learn. She developed interpretative dance techniques, and was one of the first people to introduce the idea of natural movement as an expression of emotion. She danced barefoot in a loose, flowing tunic, using natural, instinctive movements, and frequently included running, skipping, and walking in her choreography. Her free style was not initially welcomed in the United States, but was admired in Europe and came to greatly influence the development of modern dance. Yet for many it is her bizarre death – her scarf became entangled in the wheel of a car in which she was travelling and strangled her – for which she is remembered.

Jack JOHNSON
**1878–1946
US boxer**

John Arthur Johnson, known as Jack, was born in Texas. He was the first black world heavyweight champion, defeating Tommy Burns, a Canadian, in Australia, in 1908. In spite of his obvious skills as a boxer, his victory provoked racial hatred and a "great white hope" was sought to defeat him. In 1910, the "hope" was found in James Jeffries, a former champion, but Johnson knocked Jeffries out in the 15th round. Johnson was married twice – to white women – and one of these relationships led to his conviction under the Mann Act for transporting a woman across state lines "for immoral purposes". Disguised as a baseball player, he fled to Canada and was a fugitive in Europe for seven years. He defended his championship in Paris three times but, in 1915, Johnson lost his title to Jess Willard in the 26th round of a fight in Cuba. He returned to the USA to serve his sentence and ended up working in carnival acts.

Lise MEITNER
**1878–1968
Austrian physicist**

After being awarded her doctorate in physics from the University of Vienna, Lise Meitner went on to Berlin, where she joined Otto Hahn to set up a nuclear physics laboratory. She spent some thirty years working with him on radioactivity, during which time they discovered the radioactive element proctactinium. In 1938, Meitner, a Jew, fled to Sweden to avoid persecution by the Nazis. When Hahn told Meitner about his discovery of radioactive barium, she and her nephew, Otto Frisch, worked with barium and described the way in which it produced nuclear fission. This later proved to be a breakthrough in nuclear physics.

Emiliano ZAPATA
**1879–1919
Mexican revolutionary**

Zapata was a Mexican rebel and folk hero who was born in the mountainous northwest of the country. Of Native American descent, he saw how wealthy farmers and miners seized land from his people. He was forced to serve in the Mexican army, but in 1910 he joined a revolt against the dictator Porfirio Diaz. Zapata built up his own guerrilla army and, by 1911, controlled his home state of Morelos, where he forced estate owners to give land back to the peasants. In 1914, Zapata and Francisco "Pancho" Villa rebelled against the government again and occupied Mexico City. A new president took power but would not agree to Zapata's demands for land reform. In 1919, Zapata was ambushed and killed.

EMILIANO ZAPATA
Under the slogan "Land and Liberty", Zapata fought to provide land for Mexico's impoverished rural people.

1878 Britain invades and gains control of Afghanistan to try to counter the increasing Russian influence. This is the second Afghan War; the first had ended with a British withdrawal in 1842, after a British force was annihilated.

1878 After the Turkish defeat in the Russo-Turkish War, European powers meet at the Congress of Berlin in order to determine restrictions on the extent of Russian power.

Leon TROTSKY
1879–1940
Russian revolutionary leader

Born in the Ukraine, Trotsky's real name was Lev Bronstein. He became a Marxist revolutionary and was exiled to Siberia in 1900 for his political activities. In 1902, he escaped to London, where he met Lenin (p.137) and other Russian socialists. He went back to Russia to take a leading part in the revolution of 1905, but was imprisoned and exiled to Siberia again. He escaped to Europe in 1907, but was expelled from France for his communist writings and settled in New York. Trotsky returned to Russia after the revolution of 1917 and, with Lenin, led the Bolshevik government. After Lenin's death in 1924, Stalin seized power and expelled Trotsky from Russia. He settled in Mexico, where he was murdered by a blow to the skull with an ice pick – on orders from Joseph Stalin.

Joseph STALIN
1879–1953
Soviet leader

Joseph Stalin was born Joseph Dzhugashvili in Georgia in the Caucasus Mountains. He studied for the priesthood, but was expelled from the seminary for his leftist politics. Taking the name "Stalin" – meaning "Man of Steel" – he became a radical activist. Stalin became an associate of Lenin (p.137) and after the Bolsheviks came to power in 1917 he served in several important party and government positions. Following Lenin's death, Stalin consolidated his own power and, from 1927 until his death, he ruled the Soviet Union with an iron fist. He succeeded in industrializing the nation and making it a world power, but at terrible cost: his official policies and personal paranoia caused the deaths of tens of millions of people, in addition to the 20–30 million Soviets who died in World War II.

Soviet dictator Joseph Stalin

Albert EINSTEIN
1879–1955
German-American physicist

Born in Germany, Einstein moved to Switzerland as a young man. He was working as a clerk in the Zurich patent office when, in 1905, he published his first major paper, now called the special theory of relativity, which held that mass and energy were equivalent. The general theory of relativity followed in 1912, and when a 1919 astronomical observation verified Einstein's theories, the shy academic found himself the most celebrated scientist in the world. The Nobel Prize for Physics came in 1921. He taught in Europe in the 1920s, but when the Nazis came to power in Germany, Einstein (a Jew) settled in the US. Much of his later life was spent in an unsuccessful effort to link all physics in a unified theory. His brilliant insights into the nature of matter helped make the atomic bomb a reality – something that Einstein, a pacifist, greatly regretted.

THE RUSSIAN REVOLUTION

In 1917, a revolution broke out in Russia that changed both that country and the rest of the world. The first stage of the revolution overthrew the tsar and his ministers and introduced a more liberal government; the second turned Russia into the world's first communist country.

THE REVOLUTION BEGINS
Under Tsar Nicholas II (p.136), Russia was badly governed and lagged far behind the rest of industrialized Europe. Wealth and power lay in the hands of a few nobles while the mass of people were poor. In 1905, a popular uprising led to some democratic reforms, but the tsar soon re-established his autocratic rule. In 1914, Russia entered World War I against Germany and Austria-Hungary. After initial successes, the Russian army suffered defeats, and morale collapsed. In 1917, protest marches by workers against bread shortages caused the tsar to abdicate. A provisional government attempted to introduce reforms, but kept Russia in the war.

THE COMMUNIST REVOLUTION
The Bolsheviks, led by Vladimir Lenin (p.137), opposed the war and gained strength as discontent rose across the country. In October 1917, they seized power, offering "peace, land, and bread". Power in the factories was given to the workers, private land was confiscated, and peace was made with Germany. Enemies of the revolution fought a civil war but, by 1920, Trotsky and the Red Army were in control, naming their country the Union of the Soviet Socialist Republics (USSR).

Leon Trotsky

1878 The Salvation Army, an international charitable movement operated on a small miltary scale, is founded by William Booth, a Methodist minister. It spreads across Britain and then overseas.

1878 The War of the Pacific, also known as the Nitrate War, between Chile, and both Peru and Bolivia is fought. Its origins lie in the growth of nitrate production in the disputed territory of the Atacama Desert.

145

1880

Alfred WEGENER
1880–1930
German meteorologist and geophysicist

Alfred Wegener originally studied astronomy and went on expeditions to Greenland as a meteorologist. In 1915, he published his theory of continental drift in *The Origin of Continents and Oceans*, causing great controversy. He stated that the continents had originally been part of one supercontinent, which he called Pangaea, and that this had broken up into several pieces in the Mesozoic era, about 200 million years ago. He claimed that the modern position of the continents was brought about by continental drift – continents moving into and away from each other over millions of years. His ideas were ahead of his time, and it was only in the 1960s that magnetic and oceanographic research confirmed that the Earth's plates have indeed moved over millions of years.

Marie STOPES
1880–1958
Scottish birth-control pioneer

Born in Edinburgh, Marie Stopes contributed greatly to a wider understanding of birth control and an acceptance of sexual education. She studied botany in England and Germany and became the first female science lecturer at Manchester University, where she was a specialist in fossil plants and coal-mining. When her first marriage broke down, she focused her attention on marital problems caused by ignorance of sex and birth control and she began to campaign for more information about contraception and family planning. Her most important book, *Married Love*, was published in 1918, but it was banned in the USA because of its frankness. Her other works include *Wise Parenthood* (1918) and *Contraception: Its Theory, History, and Practice* (1923). She opened the first birth-control clinic in London in 1918 with the support of her second husband, Humphrey Verdon Roe. After World War II, she promoted birth control in Asia.

Douglas MACARTHUR
1880–1964
US general

The son of a general, MacArthur graduated from West Point Military Academy in 1903. After service in the Philippines and Mexico he commanded the 42nd "Rainbow" Division in France in World War I. He retired in the mid-1930s to organize the military forces of the Philippines, but was recalled to duty as war with Japan loomed. After Pearl Harbour, MacArthur conducted a skilful but doomed defence of the Philippines before being ordered to safety. Made Commander-in-Chief, Southwest Pacific, he struck back against the Japanese in a series of "island-hopping" campaigns. In 1950, he commanded UN forces in the Korean War. A Chinese attack caught MacArthur by surprise, and when the general criticized President Harry Truman's (p.152) policies and urged a wider war against China, Truman fired him. The general retired amid public acclaim.

Helen KELLER
1880–1968
US writer and teacher

Helen Adams Keller was born in Alabama. After an illness at 19 months, she became blind, deaf, and mute. Given such disabilities, her later achievements as a scholar, writer, and lecturer are staggering. When she was six, Alexander Graham Bell (p.119), then a specialist in speech therapy, suggested that her parents employ Anne Mansfield Sullivan as a teacher. With Sullivan's help, Helen Keller learned to speak by feeling the vibrations in her throat, to read and write in Braille, and to "listen" to someone spelling words into her hands with a manual alphabet. Keller spent her life helping the deaf and the blind, speaking in public with a translator on overseas tours. She also wrote books, the best-known of which are *The Story of My Life* (1902) and *Helen Keller's Journal* (1938). In 1904, she graduated with honours from Radcliffe College, Massachusetts.

Anna PAVLOVA
1881–1931
Russian ballerina

The best-known ballerina in the world in her day, Anna Pavlova was born in St Petersburg and, despite a childhood dogged by poverty and sickness, she trained at the Imperial Ballet School to

Anna Pavlova

1880 In France, the scientist Charles Laveran demonstrates that a parasite in the blood causes the disease malaria. This dispels the popular myth that malaria is passed from person to person by breathing "bad air".

1881 Alexander III becomes tsar of Russia. He starts to persecute the Jews, blaming them for his father's murder. For 25 years, Pogroms (raids) take place in which Jewish homes are razed to the ground and people are killed.

become a prima (leading) ballerina. She left Russia and moved to Paris, where she worked with Sergei Diaghilev's (p.138) *Ballets Russes*, dancing opposite the brilliant Vaslav

Nijinsky. She formed her own company and toured extensively all over the world and to countries where ballet had hardly been seen before. Her performances contributed greatly towards popularizing classical Russian ballet in the West, and she opened up ballet to millions of people for the first time. One of her most famous roles, *The Dying Swan*, was created for her by choreographer Michel Fokine, and she choreographed several works herself, including *Snowflakes* (1915). From 1912, she was based in London and inspired many young dancers.

Mustafa Kemal ATATURK
1881–1938
President and founder of modern Turkey

Mustafa Kemal was born in the Turkish part of Salonika, Greece, and was determined to enter upon a military career, which he did in Istanbul, then capital of the Ottoman Empire. After military college, he joined other Turkish activists who wanted a modernized Turkey, free from the decay of the late Ottoman Empire. He led the Nationalist Congress after World War I and violently opposed the postwar division of Turkey under British and Greek rule. In 1919, he led the army that drove the Greeks out of Anatolia, and in 1921 set up a provisional government in Ankara. In 1922, the Ottoman

sultans were deposed and Turkey was declared a self-governing republic, with Kemal as president. He introduced many important social reforms in an effort to modernize Turkey, among them women's right to vote, in 1934, the introduction of the Latin alphabet to replace Arabic script, and better educational

Mustafa Kemal Atatürk

opportunities. He took the name of Atatürk, meaning "Father of the Turks", following the introduction of surnames to Turkey in 1935.

Béla BARTOK
1881–1945
Hungarian composer

As a child, Béla Bartók was taught music by his mother, and he gave his first piano concert at the age of ten. He studied music at Bratislava and Budapest and spent the years before World War I collecting folksongs around eastern Europe with the composer Zoltán Kodály.

During this period he composed his first important pieces, including the first String Quartet (1908) and his only opera, *Bluebeard's Castle* (1911). He was appointed professor at the Budapest Conservatory. After the war, he toured Europe performing his music. However, the rise of fascism in Central Europe eventually forced him to leave Hungary in 1939, and he settled in the USA. Bartók wrote his famous Concerto for Orchestra in 1943, a blend of modern classical and Hungarian folk styles.

Alexander FLEMING
1881–1955
Scottish bacteriologist

The man who discovered penicillin was born in Scotland, but moved to London with his family, where he was a brilliant medical student at St Mary's Hospital Medical School, Paddington. Fleming spent the rest of his career there. He was the first to use anti-typhoid vaccines on human beings and pioneered the use of salvarsan against syphilis. He was a medical officer in France during World War I, where he discovered the antiseptic powers of lysozyme, a substance present in tears and mucus. In 1928, quite by chance, Fleming noticed a curious mould, penicillin, which he found to have extraordinary powers of halting infections. He had to wait 11 years before his great discovery was revealed to the world, when Howard Florey and Ernst Chain (with whom he shared the 1945 Nobel Prize for Medicine) perfected a method of producing the drug.

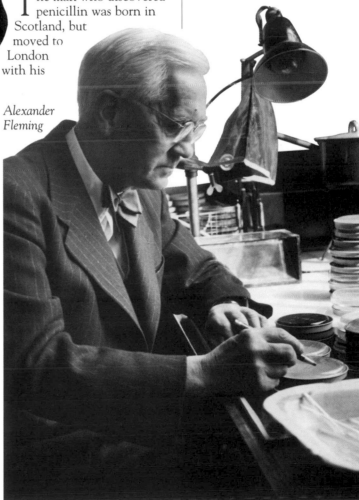

Alexander Fleming

1881 In Germany, the world's first public electric railway opens at Lichterfelde, just outside the city of Berlin. The new railway is 2.5 km (1.5 miles) long and represents the start of rail communications in Europe.

1881 The Boers defeat the British at Majuba Hill in the Transvaal, present-day South Africa, bringing the First Boer War to an end. Britain is forced to recognize the independence of the Transvaal.

Cecil B. DE MILLE
1881–1959
US film producer and director

Pioneer of the Hollywood film epic, De Mille came from a theatrical family and began his career as an actor. In 1913, he joined forces with Jesse Lasky and Samuel Goldwyn (p.150) to make the first US feature film, *The Squaw Man*. The film was to have an enormous impact on the film industry because, in order to provide facilities to make the film, De Mille converted a barn into a studio. The barn was in a little-known Los Angeles suburb called Hollywood. The film was a great success, and Hollywood established itself as the film capital of the world. De Mille is best-remembered for his epic biblical extravaganzas, featuring casts of thousands, among them *The Ten Commandments* (1923), *King of Kings* (1927), and *Samson and Delilah* (1949), and for being a co-founder of Paramount Films, one of the biggest Hollywood film studios.

CECIL B. DE MILLE
The film producer and director (left) was known for his famous biblical epics but he also made Westerns, comedies, and dramas.

Pablo PICASSO
1881–1973
Spanish painter

Even as a boy, Pablo Picasso was an exceptionally talented painter. By the age of 14, encouraged by his

YOUNG ACROBAT ON A BALL
This painting by Pablo Picasso is on display in the Pushkin Museum of Fine Art in Moscow.

father (also an artist), he had mastered drawing and oil painting and set up a studio in Paris. The early part of Picasso's long career can be roughly divided into periods. In the first, or Blue, period he painted poor and outcast people in gloomy shades of blue, such as *An Old Jew With a Boy* (1903). The Rose Period, from about 1905, saw him use warmer colours to depict livelier subjects including dancers and harlequins. His Negro Period, from 1906, was inspired by a study of African masks and sculpture, and produced one of his most important paintings, *Les Demoiselles d'Avignon* (1907). He continued to explore diverse forms, making use of classical, cubist, and surrealist ideas to express his feelings. His great painting *Guernica* (1937) was a testament of horror at the bombing of a Basque town in the Spanish Civil War. Besides being the most versatile and innovative painter of the 20th century, Picasso was also a pioneering sculptor, potter, theatre-set designer, and draughtsman. His work continues to influence our view of art today.

James JOYCE
1882–1941
Irish novelist

One of the most innovative novelists of the 20th century, James Augustine Aloysius Joyce was born in Dublin – the setting for much of his writing. His most famous novel, *Ulysses* (1922), broke traditional rules of writing with its disregard for grammar, and for the way in which ideas were set down in a seemingly unstructured "stream of consciousness". It was first published in Paris, where Joyce lived after World War I, but was banned at first in Britain and the USA for obscenity. A record of events that take place on one day in Dublin, *Ulysses* became the epitome of the modern novel, and the literary movement Modernism grew up around it. His earlier work *Dubliners* (1914), a collection of short stories, was more traditional and naturalistic in style, as was *A Portrait of the Artist as a Young Man* (1916), much of which is autobiographical. Joyce became disillusioned with what he saw as the narrow-mindedness of traditional Irish life. He spent most of his life in France, Italy, and Switzerland, often in poverty. His last novel, *Finnegan's Wake*, was published in full in 1939, having appeared in parts in 1927.

1881 The infamous outlaw and murderer Billy the Kid is shot dead in New Mexico, while trying to evade capture, at the age of 21. He becomes an American folk hero celebrated in songs and stories.

1882 In Germany, engineers Wilhelm Maybach and Gottlieb Daimler begin working to develop a high-speed gasoline engine. The results of their work alter the course of the motor industry for ever.

Hans GEIGER
1882–1945
German physicist

Hans Geiger gave us the geiger counter, the first successful detector of individual alpha particles, or radioactivity. He studied for his PhD in Erlangen, Germany, before travelling to Manchester, England where he worked with Ernest Rutherford (p.138). In 1908, the two men designed an instrument that could detect and count alpha particles – particles emitted by radioactive decay. Geiger returned to Germany in 1912 and became head of the Radioactivity Laboratories in Berlin. In 1928, he worked with Walther Müller to produce a more sensitive version of his counter. The final model, called the Geiger-Müller counter, also detects electrons and radiation.

Robert GODDARD
1882–1945
US rocket pioneer

Robert Goddard's pioneering rocket experiments greatly influenced both military rocketry and space exploration. While a professor at Clark University in Worcester, Massachusetts, Goddard theorized that liquid-fuel rocket engines were more efficient than the solid-fuel engines, and that rockets could provide thrust in a vacuum – concepts crucial to the development of rocket propulsion. Goddard began building and launching rockets in 1926. By the mid-1930s, his rockets had broken the speed of sound. Goddard's last years were spent as a war consultant to the United States' military.

F. D. ROOSEVELT
1882–1945
32nd US president

The only four-term US president, Franklin Delano Roosevelt was born into a wealthy New York family. Educated at Harvard and Columbia, he was a rapidly rising politician when, aged 40, he was partly paralyzed by polio. Refusing to let disability halt his career, "FDR" was elected governor of New York and then, in 1932, won the presidency as the Democratic candidate. Taking office in the Great Depression, he reassured Americans through his radio "fireside chats", and helped ease the ravages of poverty and unemployment through his administration's innovative New Deal programmes. Re-elected in 1936 and 1940, FDR led the nation through the worst years of World War II and was again victorious in the election of 1944, but died of a stroke in 1945.

Jack HOBBS
1882–1963
English cricketer

John Berry Hobbs was one of the greatest batsmen of his time. He began his career in 1904, playing county cricket for Cambridgeshire. A year later, he joined Surrey, where he played for almost 30 years. Between 1907 and 1930, Hobbs played in 61 Test matches and made 5,410 runs. In 1926, he captained England against Australia, making 316 runs, the then highest score at Lords. At the Oval in the same series, he scored 100, helping England to win the Ashes. In his career in first-class cricket, Hobbs scored 61,237 runs. He was the first English cricketer to be knighted.

VIRGINIA WOOLF
This portrait of Virginia Woolf was painted by her sister, Vanessa Bell.

Virginia WOOLF
1882–1941
English writer and critic

Virginia Adeline Stephen was born in London. In 1904, she moved to Bloomsbury, an area of London now firmly associated with the literary world and with the group of artists and writers called the Bloomsbury Group. She married Leonard Woolf in 1912 and published her first novel, *The Voyage Out*, in 1915. Three years later, the Woolfs founded The Hogarth Press, publishing work by themselves and others such as T. S. Eliot and E. M. Forster. Virginia Woolf's best-known works include *To the Lighthouse* (1927), *A Room of One's Own* (1929), and *The Waves* (1931). Overcome by wartime worries and her mental instability, she committed suicide, leaving her last novel, *Between the Acts*, unfinished. Her influence on novel writing continues to this day.

1882 The St Gotthard railway tunnel through the Alps is completed, connecting Göschenen in Switzerland with Airolo in Italy. It is 15 km (9 miles) long and improves commerce between the two countries.

1882 Prussian leader Otto von Bismarck establishes the formation of the Triple Alliance between Germany, Austria, and Italy to protect their territories from their powerful and aggressive neighbours, Russia and France.

Igor STRAVINSKY
1882–1971
Russian-born composer

Born near St Petersburg, Igor Stravinsky originally studied law, but later studied composition with Rimsky-Korsakov (p.116) and started to write in the Russian nationalist style. When Sergei Diaghilev (p.138) invited Stravinsky to compose for the *Ballets Russes*, this led to his first great successes: *The Firebird* (1910), *Petrushka* (1911), and *The Rite of Spring* (1913). The last of these literally caused a riot with its ultra-modern sound and became a turning point in 20th-century music. Stravinsky settled in Switzerland in 1914, where he switched to a more "neoclassical" style with the ballet *Pulcinella* (1920), inspired by 18th-century music. He became a French citizen in 1934 but moved to California, in 1940, where he spent the rest of his life.

Samuel GOLDWYN
1882–1974
US film producer

The man who was known for such "Goldwynisms" as "Anyone who goes to a psychiatrist needs to have his head examined," was born Samuel Goldfish in Warsaw, Poland. He moved to the USA and became involved in the newly emerging film industry, eventually becoming one of the most influential producers in Hollywood. He founded the Metro-Goldwyn-Mayer Company (MGM). He was a shrewd businessman who brought together outstanding talents and produced a huge number of films, including *Wuthering Heights* (1939) and *Porgy and Bess* (1959).

Eamon DE VALERA
1882–1975
Irish prime minister

Born in New York but brought up in Ireland, Eamon De Valera started his career as a maths teacher but joined the Irish Volunteers who opposed British rule in Ireland. He was sentenced to death in 1916 for his part in the Easter Rising, but was reprieved due to his US citizenship. He joined the Sinn Féin Party, which was committed to home rule for Ireland, and was elected MP for East Clare. In 1918, he went to the USA to raise funds for the nationalist movement. The trip raised vast sums and De Valera returned to lead Sinn Féin against the British. He worked alongside Michael Collins, but the two men fell out. De Valera then started the Fianna Fáil party, which won the election of 1932, and was prime minister until 1948. Ireland became an independent republic in 1955 and De Valera became, in turn, taoiseach (prime minister) and president of the Irish Republic until 1973.

Franz KAFKA
1883–1924
Czech-born German writer

Franz Kafka was born in Prague, now the capital of the Czech Republic, the son of middle-class German-Jewish parents. Kafka always felt separated from other people, isolated by his inability to communicate properly. Most of Kafka's characters are full of fear, despair, and confusion, living in isolated nightmare worlds. Kafka moved to Berlin in 1923, but the tuberculosis that was to kill him forced him to return to Prague. Kafka did not publish much in his lifetime, *Metamorphosis* (1916) being one of a few long stories. The unfinished novels, *The Trial* (1925) and *The Castle* (1926) were published after his death and against his wishes.

Benito MUSSOLINI
1883–1945
Italian dictator

A blacksmith's son, Mussolini became a radical journalist whose philosophy – extreme nationalism acting through an all-powerful state – became known as fascism. Mussolini rose to national influence in Italy following World War I, and in 1922 he seized power with the help of his supporters, the "blackshirts". Proclaiming himself *il Duce* ("the leader"), Mussolini promised to restore Italy to the days of the Roman Empire through public works and foreign conquests. In the 1930s, Italian forces conquered Ethiopia and Albania and helped Franco's forces in the Spanish Civil War. He also joined forces with Adolf Hitler. This "Rome-Berlin Axis" proved Mussolini's undoing during World War II. Italian forces were defeated in Africa and, by 1943, Italy had been invaded by the Allies. Mussolini was arrested, rescued by German troops but then killed by resistance fighters.

Benito Mussolini

1883 The Orient Express rail service makes its first journey, carrying passengers between Paris, France, and Constantinople in present-day Turkey. It was intended as a luxurious form of transport and it still runs today.

1883 The world's first skyscraper is built in Chicago. It is 10 storeys tall – a staggering height for its day. With the commercial manufacture of lifts, it soon becomes possible to build ever taller skyscrapers.

150

John Maynard KEYNES
1883–1946
English economist

The creator of "macroeconomics", influential economist John Maynard Keynes was educated at Cambridge University. He then pursued a dual career as an academic and as an adviser to the British treasury. His first international fame came in 1919, when he published *The Economic Consequences of the Peace*, which criticized the financial aspects of the peace treaty forced on Germany at the Versailles Conference. Keynes's best-known work was *The General Theory of Employment, Interest and Money* (1935), which held that government intervention in the economy could smooth out the cycle of "boom and bust" that had affected Western nations since the Industrial Revolution. By the 1970s, most Western nations had incorporated at least some Keynesian ideas into their economic policies.

Clement ATTLEE
1883–1967
British prime minister

Clement Attlee was born in London and educated at Oxford University. While a teacher at the London School of Economics, he came into contact with London's slums, which made him aware of social problems. He joined the Independent Labour Party in 1910. In 1919, he became the first Labour mayor of Stepney, in London, and in 1922, he became a member of parliament. He was appointed parliamentary secretary to the Labour leader Ramsay MacDonald, and served as deputy leader under George Lansbury. By 1935, Attlee had become leader of the Labour Party and, when war broke out in 1939, he was made deputy prime minister in Churchill's cabinet. At the end of the war, Labour won the general election and Attlee became Labour's first prime minister (1945–51). He started the welfare state, introducing the National Health Service, building new council houses to replace slums, and setting up a national insurance scheme. Attlee's government also granted independence to India and Burma. Attlee was a respected leader and accepted an earldom on retiring from politics in 1955.

Walter GROPIUS
1883–1969
German architect

Walter Gropius trained as an architect in Munich and Berlin and, in 1908, became assistant to the designer Peter Behrens. Gropius believed in using only modern materials such as sheet glass, steel, and concrete. He put his revolutionary ideas into practice in his designs for the Fagus shoe factory at Alfeld (1911). The façade is almost all glass, in steel frames that mask the supporting wall. In 1919, Gropius founded the Bauhaus School in Weimar, later designing new buildings for it at Dessau (1925). Here, students were trained by teachers who included painters such as Klee and Kandinsky (p.133). When the Nazis took power in 1934, Gropius moved to England, finally settling in the United States in 1937.

Coco CHANEL
1883–1971
French dress designer

Gabrielle Chanel, known as "Coco", dominated Parisian *haute couture* (high fashion) for nearly 60 years. She was born near Saumur and was an orphan by the age of six, but little else is known about her childhood or early adulthood. She opened a small dressmaking and millinery shop in the fashionable French resort of Deauville in 1913. Soon her casual styles of skirts and sweaters became popular and, in 1924, she opened a fashion house in Paris. Here she introduced comfortable and easy-to-wear suits and dresses in jersey material or soft tweeds, with chunky costume jewellery as decoration. Her designs were deceptively simple and included several classics, including bell-bottom trousers, trenchcoats, and the "little black dress". Her perfumes, notably Chanel No. 5, were also phenomenally successful.

Eleanor ROOSEVELT
1884–1962
US humanitarian

One of America's greatest first ladies and a major figure in her own right, Anna Eleanor Roosevelt had a privileged but unhappy childhood. After completing her education in England, she married her distant cousin,

COCO CHANEL *revolutionized women's fashions in the 1920s.*

1883 In Indonesia, the volcanic island of Krakatowa erupts; 36,000 people are killed by the explosion. The eruption can be heard 4,800 km (3,000 miles) away and is the loudest sound ever heard by human beings.

1884 The War of the Pacific, fought between the South American countries of Peru, Bolivia, and Chile, ends with a Chilean victory. bolivia and Peru have to yield valuable land to Chile in the peace settlement.

Eleanor and Franklin Roosevelt

Franklin Delano Roosevelt (p.149) in 1905. In 1921, FDR contracted polio. Although he regained some mobility, his convalescence in the 1920s allowed Eleanor to develop an independent career, including journalism and social work. She became her disabled husband's "eyes and ears" and continued this role during FDR's presidency. Following his death, Eleanor Roosevelt remained involved in humanitarian causes, including helping to draft the United Nations' Universal Declaration of Human Rights (1948). At the end of her life she was hailed as "first lady to the world".

Harry TRUMAN
1884–1972
33rd US president

Born in Lamar, Missouri, Harry S. Truman was a farmer and businessman before entering politics in the late 1920s. A Democrat, he served as a judge and in local posts before his election to the Senate in 1934. When World War II broke out he served on an important military committee, winning a reputation for honesty and plain-speaking. Nominated for vice-president in 1944, he became president in April 1945 upon Franklin Roosevelt's (p.149) death. He made the decision to drop the atomic bomb on Japan, ending World War II, and took a firm stand against the expansion of communism in the early years of the cold war, including sending troops to South Korea after its invasion by North Korea in 1950. Narrowly re-elected in 1948, he left office in 1953.

D. H. LAWRENCE
1885–1930
English writer, poet, and painter

David Herbert Lawrence wrote powerful prose, dealing with intimate personal, marital, and sexual feelings. Many people at the time considered this shocking and wanted the works banned. Lawrence was born in Nottinghamshire to a mining father and a dominant school-teacher mother. He left home at 22 and went to teach in Surrey. He had already been writing poetry for some years when, in 1911, *The White Peacock*, a novel he had begun in about 1906, was published. He gave up his job to write another novel and some poetry. In 1912, he ran away to Europe with Frieda Weekley, the wife of his former teacher. Here, he finished *Sons and Lovers* (1913), probably his most popular novel. A sensational scandal and court case surrounding publication of *Lady Chatterley's Lover* greatly affected his reputation. Its alleged "obscene" contents meant that it was not published in England until 1961, although it was published overseas in 1928. Other works by Lawrence include *The Rainbow* (1915) and *Women in Love* (1920), as well as many short stories.

Alban BERG
1885–1935
Austrian composer

A composer of atonal music, Alban Berg was self-taught until he took composition lessons with Schoenberg in 1904–10. Berg then moved away from the 19th-century style of his early compositions, such as the *Piano Sonata* (1908), and adopted the atonal and serial methods of his teacher. He developed his own tuneful style, first heard in the *String Quartet* (1910). Works for which he is best known include the operas *Wozzeck* (1925) and *Lulu* (1935, unfinished), and the Lyric Suite (1925). Berg died of blood poisoning as the result of an insect bite.

Niels BOHR
1885–1962
Danish physicist

Born in Copenhagen, Niels Bohr moved to Britain where he later worked with J. J. Thomson (p.124) and then Ernest Rutherford (p.138). He returned to Denmark in 1916 and won the 1922 Nobel Prize for Physics for research into the atom. Bohr worked with other physicists on quantum theory and later on atomic fission. In 1943, he left German-occupied Denmark, escaping to the USA where he joined the atom bomb programme. After the war, he helped to set up CERN, the European Nuclear Research Centre, and organized the first Atoms for Peace Conference in 1955.

1885 A Muslim Sudanese leader called the Mahdi (messiah) rebels against the Egyptian occupation of the Sudan. The British general Gordon tries to rescue Egyptian forces in Khartoum, but the city is besieged and Gordon is killed.

1885 The Indian National Congress is founded to convince the British to trust more Indians with civil service and senior army positions. Many Muslims break away from it, suspicious of its Hindu leadership.

THE ARRIVAL OF THE TALKIES

By the 1920s, cinema had become the most popular form of mass entertainment with leading stars such as CHARLIE CHAPLIN (p.160) AND RUDOLPH VALENTINO (p.166) drawing audiences in their millions. The silent age ended in 1927, when the first full-length sound picture *The Jazz Singer* was released. Audiences were amazed when they saw and heard AL JOLSON singing his hits and exlaiming "You ain't heard nothin' yet!"

HOLLYWOOD

The centre of the film industry was Hollywood in Californa, USA. A big Hollywood studio was like a factory, turning out up to 50 films a year. Each studio had its own distinctive style. MGM made lavish production with Hollywood's biggest stars, such as GRETA GARBO (1905–1990) and CLARK GABLE (p.176). Warner Brothers specialized in gangster films, featuring HUMPHREY BOGART (p.171) and JAMES CAGNEY (1889–1986), while RKO's most popular films were musicals, starring the great song and dance team of FRED ASTAIRE (1899–1987) and GINGER ROGERS (1911–1995).

WORLD CINEMA

Although the industries of other countries could not match the output of Hollywood, they produced some of the greatest directors. INGMAR BERGMAN (1918–), FREDERICO FELLINI (1920–93) and JEAN RENOIR (1894–1979) showed that cinema was a true art form.

Poster of Al Jolson in The Jazz Singer

Al JOLSON
1886–1950
US singer and actor

Born in Lithuania as Asa Yoelson, Jolson emigrated to the USA with his family in 1894. He took to show business at an early age, and by 1909 he was a featured singer on the vaudeville circuit. Jolson sang the sentimental popular songs of the day in an enthusiastic, expressive style that owed debts both to African-American music and the Jewish cantor tradition. By the 1920s, Jolson's records and stage appearances won him the accolade "World's Greatest Entertainer". In 1927, he made history by starring in *The Jazz Singer*, the first-full length sound movie. Changing musical tastes slowed his career, but he continued entertaining until his death.

AL JOLSON
Two films were made about Jolson's life –The Jolson Story and Jolson Sings Again.

Clarence BIRDSEYE
1886–1956
US inventor

While working as a fur trader in Labrador, Canada, Clarence Birdseye was struck by the ease with which food could be frozen to preserve it in an Arctic climate. When he returned to the USA, he discovered that the same effect could be obtained by freezing prepared food rapidly between two refrigerated metal plates. To market his frozen products, he set up the General Sea Foods Company in 1924 and later developed the quick-frozen foods that we know today. Among his other inventions were the recoilless harpoon gun, and a method of removing water from food in order to preserve it.

Diego RIVERA
1886–1957
Mexican painter

Best-known for his huge, colourful murals, Diego Rivera was one of Mexico's most famous painters. He was born in Guanajuato and trained as a muralist in the Mexican folk tradition. In 1907, he travelled to Europe, where he was greatly influenced by the work of Gauguin, the cubists, and Picasso, whom he met in Paris. On his return to Mexico in 1921, Rivera was commissioned to produce a series of murals celebrating the Mexican people and their long struggle against oppression. Using dramatic colours and often portraying scenes of ancient Aztec life, Rivera painted the walls of many public buildings in Mexico City. His large-scale murals depicted Mexican history in a brash, energetic style, attacking capitalism and the Church and praising ordinary workers. From 1930, he also painted murals in the USA including one for the Rockefeller Center in New York, which was removed because it was claimed to include a likeness of the communist leader Lenin.

1885 In Britain, Francis Galton proves that no two people's fingerprints are identical and that prints stay the same throughout a person's life. His discovery proves invaluable in police work.

1885 The French fear Samori Ture, the creator of a Mande Empire in the upper Niger regions. Ture's plans for an Islamic state are unpopular with his subjects. French troops force Samori eastwards. He is captured and exiled in 1898.

Ty COBB
1886–1961
US baseball player

Tyrus Raymond Cobb was nicknamed the "Georgia Peach" (he was born in Narrows, Georgia). From 1905–26 he played for the Detroit Tigers, moving to the Philadelphia Athletics team and playing for them until 1928. In a 23-year career with these two teams, he scored more than 4,000 base hits in major-league baseball. Cobb was one of the great offensive players in the game. He was a brilliant base runner and batter, who had a hit more than once every three times – an all-time record. He entered the Baseball Hall of Fame in 1936. Both on and off the field, Cobb was notorious for his hot temper and eccentric personality. In 1994, Cobb was immortalized in a film about his life (*Cobb*) starring Tommy Lee Jones.

MARX BROTHERS
Chico 1886–1961, Harpo 1888–1964, Groucho 1890–1977, Zeppo 1901–77
US film comedians

The Marx Brothers formed the most successful comedy quartet of the 1930s. They started as "The Six Musical Mascots" in about 1904 with another brother, Gummo, and their mother, Minnie, and were a top-billing vaudeville stage act. Gummo left the act and the four Marx Brothers took to screen comedies in the 1920s. They became famous for their slapstick and quick-witted humour. They had nicknames: Chico, because he "chased chicks", Harpo, who never spoke but played a harp, Groucho, the bad-tempered wise-cracker who "duck-walked" with an oversized moustache and cigar, and Zeppo, born at the time of the first zeppelins. Actress Margaret Dumont was often the unruffled butt of their antics. Their films include *Animal Crackers* (1932), *Duck Soup* (1933), and *A Night at the Opera* (1935). They disbanded in 1949. Groucho continued as a solo performer, hosting television and radio shows during the 1950s and 1960s.

David BEN-GURION
1886–1973
Israel's first prime minister

Known as "Father of the Nation", Ben-Gurion was born David Gruen in Plonsk, Poland. He attended local Jewish schools before emigrating with his father to Palestine (then part of the Turkish Ottoman Empire) in 1906. He became a Zionist – a campaigner for an official Jewish state in Palestine. He studied law in Constantinople, then went on to fight with the British against the Turks during World War I. After the war, Ben-Gurion became leader of the Jewish political group in Palestine (at that time under British rule). In 1935, he was appointed chairman of the Jewish Agency, part of the World Zionist Organization. He campaigned tirelessly to create a Jewish state in Palestine and on 14 May 1948, delivered Israel's declaration of Independence. He became Israel's first prime minister until 1953, leading resistance to Arab attacks and overseeing the entry of more than one million Jews into Israel.

THE MARX BROTHERS
A scene from Duck Soup with (l to r) Groucho, Zeppo, Chico, and Harpo.

1886 In North America, the Canadian Pacific Railway transcontinental route is completed. It is 4,635 km (2,880 miles) long in total. This leads to more railways across the country, which improve communications dramatically.

1886 The first efficient tandem bicycles are manufactured in Britain. They have a saddle, handlebars, and pedals for two riders, and immediately become a big hit with people in countries all over the world.

Marcus GARVEY
1887–1940
Jamaican-US activist

Marcus Garvey was born in Jamaica, West Indies. Forced to find work in South America, he was appalled by the discrimination against West Indians he found there. Later, in England, he learned about African history and met African leaders. Garvey founded the Universal Negro Improvement Association (UNIA) to promote pride among black people and a "back to Africa" movement to create a new black-governed state in Africa. In the 1920s, Garvey became the most influential black leader in the US, famous for his brilliant speeches, but his belief in racial purity and separatism put him in conflict with other black leaders. In 1925, he was accused of fraud and deported to Jamaica. In 1935, he moved to London, where he died in obscurity.

Erwin SCHRODINGER
1887–1961
Austrian physicist

Born and educated in Vienna, Schrödinger was the son of a manufacturer. In 1926, he published the papers that began the branch of physics known as wave mechanics. He then moved to Berlin to take over from Max Planck (p.127) as professor of theoretical physics, but left when the Nazis came to power in 1933. Schrödinger shared the 1933 Nobel Prize for Physics with Paul Dirac for their work on atomic particles. In 1938 Schrödinger became a professor at the Institute for Advanced Studies in Dublin. He returned to Vienna in 1956.

Le CORBUSIER
1887–1965
French architect

The influential architect and town planner Le Corbusier was born Charles Edouard Jeanneret in La Chaux-de-Fonds, Switzerland. He studied at the local art school and, in 1908, moved to Paris, where he worked as a painter. From 1916, he developed the "International Style" of architecture. This aimed to create brighter, "freer" buildings by using modern techniques and materials. Le Corbusier's designs include columns to raise the building off the ground, flat roofs with gardens, and continuous windows. Among his major works was the *Unité d'Habitation* in Marseille (1947–52), which is a complete community of apartments, shops, and leisure facilities. He also planned much of Chandigarh in India (1950–51). He died suddenly while swimming and was mourned in a national funeral.

Marcel DUCHAMP
1887–1968
French artist

Marcel Duchamp's innovative art was full of irony stemming from his belief that life was essentially absurd. Duchamp was born near Rouen and moved to Paris, where he met many young modernist artists. He quickly developed ideas that challenged traditional theories about art. His painting *Nude Descending a Staircase, No. 2* (1912) made him famous when it shocked critics at a New York exhibition. After this, Duchamp spent eight years creating *The Large Glass* (1915–23), made of paint and metal between large sheets of glass. He presented everyday objects as art, calling them "ready-mades". They included a bicycle wheel on a stool, a hat-rack, and a porcelain urinal entitled *Fountain* (1917). He stated that an artist did not have to make a work of art, but simply choose it.

Boris KARLOFF
1887–1969
English actor

The man who is known for his film portrayal of Frankenstein's monster was born William Henry Pratt. He emigrated to Canada, where he began acting, then moved to Hollywood and was cast as the monster in the early horror film *Frankenstein* (1935). His role brought him overnight success and he became "the king of horror", typecast as the villain in films and Broadway plays. He starred in Frankenstein sequels and other films including *The Mask of Fu Manchu* (1932). He appeared on Broadway in *Arsenic and Old Lace* in 1941, and was widely acclaimed as Captain Hook in *Peter Pan* in 1950.

CHIANG KAI-SHEK
A supporter of Sun Yat-sen (p.134) Chiang Kai-shek fought in the Chinese revolution of 1911.

Chiang KAI-SHEK
1887–1975
Chinese general and politician

Chiang Kai-shek (or Jiang Jieshi) was born in Fenghwa, China. He received his military training in Tokyo. In 1926, Chiang Kai-shek commanded the Kuomintang army and attempted to unify China by force. He achieved this in 1928, and became the first president of the Republic of China. His rule was threatened by corruption within his party and by the communists under Mao Zedong (p.164). War with Japan also weakened his power because it increased poverty and hardship in the country and made people eager to believe in Mao and his promise of a better life. In 1948, the Kuomintang collapsed and Chiang Kai-shek was forced to flee to Taiwan, where he became president.

1886 The Statue of Liberty is unveiled in New York Harbour. It is a gift from the French government. It rapidly becomes a symbol of the promise of the freedom and opportunity the United States offers to immigrants.

1887 The Ottomans renege on the Treaty of San Stefano, in which they had agreed to return land to Bulgaria. North and South Bulgaria are reunited under King Ferdinand, and Bulgaria becomes the leading Balkan state.

Bernard
MONTGOMERY (OF ALAMEIN)
1887–1976
British field marshal

The most famous British commander since the Duke of Wellington (p.72), Bernard Montgomery was born in London and trained at the Royal Military College, Sandhurst. In World War II, Montgomery commanded the British Eighth Army in North Africa, driving German general Erwin Rommel's Afrika Korps from the region after the Battle of El Alamein in 1942. After leading Allied forces in Sicily and Italy, he served as Allied ground commander for the invasion of Normandy in 1944. "Monty" occasionally clashed with his fellow Allied generals, but he was a master of the set-piece battle, and his concern for his soldiers' well-being was legendary.

Artur
RUBINSTEIN
1887–1982
Polish-US pianist

Rubinstein was a child piano-playing prodigy. He began to study music when he was only three years old and began playing the piano in public at six. He made his European debut in Berlin when he was 13 years old and went on to perform all over the world. Rubinstein redefined the classical piano repertoire, but he is especially remembered for his playing of Chopin. Several composers wrote works especially for him, among them Manuel de Falla. He gave his final London concert in 1976 at the age of 88. By then he was widely regarded as one of the virtuoso pianists of the 20th century. He was also a man of charm and wit, who spoke eight languages.

Georgia
O'KEEFE
1887–1986
US painter

An important pioneer of modernist painting in the USA, Georgia O'Keefe was born in Wisconsin and studied art in Chicago, and Columbia University in New York City. She became an art teacher in Texas, and it was the desert landscape of the southwestern USA that had a huge influence on her work. In the 1930s, she began visiting New Mexico and settled there in 1946. She painted simple desert shapes and natural forms on a large scale, such as rocks, animal skulls, and desert flowers. Her clear and elegant style can be seen in *Black Iris* (1926) and *Summer Days* (1936). She also produced precise and eerie views of New York, such as *Radiator Building* (1927), as well as abstract designs.

Katherine
MANSFIELD
1888–1923
New Zealand
short-story writer

Many of Katherine Mansfield's short stories evoked her early life and memories of New Zealand, but she wrote most of them in England, where she settled at the age of 19. Personal misfortunes – early in life she had a miscarriage, and she left her first husband within hours of the marriage – contributed to her subtle themes of internal struggles and disillusionment that made her short stories internationally famous. In 1911, she met the British writer and critic John Middleton Murry, marrying

LAWRENCE OF ARABIA
This poster for the film Lawrence of Arabia *shows the actor Peter O'Toole in the part of T. E. Lawrence.*

1887 The English writer Arthur Conan Doyle invents the fictional detective Sherlock Holmes when he writes *A Study in Scarlet*. Holmes and his friend Dr Watson soon become two of the world's best-loved characters.

1887 Tragedy hits China when the Huang He River bursts its banks and floods huge areas of land nearby. Nearly one million people later die of starvation because of the crop damage caused by this natural disaster.

him after her divorce in 1918. *Prelude* (1918) and *Bliss and other stories* (1920) were followed by *The Garden Party* (1922), her best-known collection of stories. Katherine Mansfield died of tuberculosis and much of her work was published after her death.

T. E. LAWRENCE
1888–1935
British soldier and writer

The man who became famous as "Lawrence of Arabia" was born in North Wales and educated at Oxford University. In 1911, Lawrence joined an archaeological team in Carchemish on the Euphrates River, where he first met the nomadic Bedouin Arabs. Lawrence got to know both the land and the people well – he became an expert camel rider and wore Arab dress. When World War I broke out, he was enlisted to help with intelligence work in Cairo because of his knowledge of Arab affairs. In 1916, he became convinced that Britain should support the Arab rebellion led by King Faisal I against the Turks, who were Germany's allies. With British approval, he became involved in the Arab rising and quickly became its military brains. Lawrence and Faisal led a successful guerrilla campaign against the Turks and, in 1917, joined forces with British commander General Allenby. Together they captured Jerusalem, followed by Damascus in 1918. By this time, Lawrence was exhausted and disillusioned by the Arabs' inability to stop

fighting among themselves; he returned home just before the end of the war. His brilliant account of the Arab revolt, *Seven Pillars of Wisdom*, was published in 1926. Lawrence was killed in a motorbike accident aged 46.

THE TELEVISOR
Baird's early television had a tiny screen and could not broadcast sound and pictures together.

John Logie BAIRD
1888–1946
Scottish electrical engineer

The "father", if not the inventor, of television, John Logie Baird gave the first public demonstration of televised moving objects to a gathering at the Royal Institution in London in January 1926. He had been working on television as early as 1912 and had transmitted outline objects in 1924 and recognizable human faces in 1925. His demonstration in 1926 opened up the possibilities of television that we know today. Baird researched radar and infrared television, and also developed video recording on both wax records and magnetic steel discs. He demonstrated colour television in 1928 and, in 1929, the newly formed BBC (British Broadcasting

Corporation) made its first broadcast using Baird's equipment. Later, the BBC adopted the Marconi EMI rival system for its broadcasts, but before that, Baird had been responsible for the first "location" broadcast – the 1931 Derby horse race.

JIM THORPE *won a Gold Medal in the Stockholm Olympics.*

Eugene O'NEILL
1888–1953
US playwright

Son of a popular touring actor, Eugene O'Neill was born in New York City and spent his childhood "on the road". In 1912, O'Neill developed tuberculosis and spent six months in bed. It was then that he discovered his writing talents: he spent the rest of his life writing for the theatre. O'Neill's best-known plays include *The Iceman Cometh* (1946), *A Moon for the Misbegotten* (1947), and *Long Day's Journey into Night* (first performed in 1956 after O'Neill's death). His portrayals of human suffering are very perceptive, and his own life was full of sadness: one son committed suicide and another was mentally unstable. In 1936, he was awarded the Nobel Prize for Literature.

Jim THORPE
1888–1953
US athlete

Born in Oklahoma, of Native American descent, Jim Thorpe was an all-round athlete of exceptional ability. His first sports were American football and baseball. In the 1912 Olympic Games in Stockholm, he won the gold medal in the pentathlon and the decathlon. He was later disqualified on the grounds that he was not an amateur because he had once played semi-professional baseball. After his death, the American Athletics Union reinstated him as an amateur athlete for the years 1909–12 and his Olympic titles and medals were posthumously restored. From 1913–19, Thorpe played professional baseball for the New York Giants, the Cincinnati Reds, and the Boston Braves. Then, from 1919–26, he played professional football. Later, he became the first president of the National Football League. In 1950, American sports writers voted him the greatest American athlete and best football player of the first half of the 20th century.

1888 In Britain, John Dunlop makes an air-filled pneumatic tyre for his son's bicycle. He develops the idea further and eventually creates the modern tyre, and founds his own company for their manufacture.

1888 In Germany, Kaiser (emperor) William II begins his reign, which lasts for 30 years. His support of Austria against Serbia in 1914 is one of the major contributing factors to the outbreak of World War I that year.

T. S. ELIOT
1888–1965
US-born English poet

Thomas Stearns Eliot was born in St Louis, Missouri, USA, and studied at Harvard and in Paris. In 1914, he met the poet Ezra Pound and settled in England working for the publisher of poets such as Stephen Spender and W. H. Auden. One of Eliot's most famous poems, "The Love Song of Alfred J Prufrock", was published in 1917 in his first volume of poetry, *Prufrock and Other Observations*. *The Waste Land* (1922) and *The Hollow Men* (1925) brought Eliot international fame. *Old Possum's Book of Practical Cats* (1939), a book of children's verse, inspired the popular musical, *Cats* (1981). Eliot's last major poem was possibly his greatest: *The Four Quartets* (1944). His plays include *Murder in the Cathedral* (1935). In 1948, Eliot was awarded the Nobel Prize for Literature.

Chandrasekhara Venkata RAMAN
1888–1970
Indian physicist

A major force in the study of physics in India, Raman was born in Trichinopoly and studied at Madras University. At that time, there were few opportunities for scientific research in India, so Raman worked in the Indian Civil Service. During his time there, he conducted research on sound and diffraction in his spare time. In 1917, he was appointed professor of physics at Calcutta University, a post he held until 1933. His discovery that light scattered by molecules shows shifts in frequency is known as the Raman effect. It provided confirmation of quantum theory and led to a method of finding out about the motion and shape of molecules, known as Raman spectroscopy. Raman was knighted in 1929 and, in 1930, became the first Asian to win the Nobel Prize for Physics.

THE RISE OF FASCISM

In 1922, a new political movement took power in Italy. It was known as fascism, from the bundles of rods or fasces bound with thongs that were the symbol of political power in the Roman Empire. Fascism soon came to be the dominant movement in European politics.

FASCISM
The Italian Fascist party, the *Fascio di Combattimento*, was formed by BENITO MUSSOLINI (p.150) in 1919. Fascists believed in a strong state led by a dictatorial leader who personified the nation. Individual human rights were reduced, democratic institutions abolished, and military discipline used to build up the power and authority of the state. Fascism was violently opposed to communism, although it adopted similar styles of propaganda and organization.

THE INSPIRATION
The success of Mussolini's Italy led to the spread of fascism throughout Europe. In 1933, ADOLF HITLER came to power in Germany as leader of the Nazi Party. ANTONIO SALAZAR (1889–1970) introduced fascist rule in Portugal after 1933, and GENERAL FRANCO (p.162) established a fascist government in Spain in 1939. In Britain, the National Union of Fascists was formed under SIR OSWALD MOSLEY (1896–1980) and the Blue Shirts were established in Ireland under EOIN O'DUFFY (1892–1944). With the defeat of Germany and Italy in World War II fascism was discredited all over the world.

Bust of Adolf Hitler

Adolf HITLER
1889–1945
German dictator

Adolf Hitler is one of the most infamous figures in 20th-century history. He was born in Austria and took up painting at 16. During World War I, he served in the Bavarian army and won an Iron Cross for bravery. He blamed Germany's defeat in the war primarily on the Jews. In 1920, Hitler helped to found the Nazi party. In 1923, the Nazis attempted to overthrow the Bavarian government in the "beer hall putsch". The attempt failed and Hitler went to prison, where he wrote *Mein Kampf* in 1925. The book was full of hatred for the Jews and his plans for world domination. As Germany plunged into depression, many people began to support the Nazis, attracted by Hitler's powerful oratory. His anti-communism helped him to win the support of Germany's financiers. In 1933, President Hindenburg of Germany appointed Hitler chancellor in an effort to control him. In the election of 1934, 88 per cent of the German people voted for him to become chancellor and Hitler took on dictatorial

1889 A new Meiji constitution is introduced in Japan, which takes a more liberal approach to democracy. The first general election to be held under the terms of this constitution takes place in 1890.

1889 Malietoa Laupepa is finally recognized as King of Samoa by Britain, Germany, and the United States. He had been ruling there for some time with the three European countries as joint supervisors.

powers, using his secret police, the Gestapo, to crush opposition. He established forced-labour "concentration" camps in which to put the groups of people he hated, including communists, Jews, homosexuals, and gypsies. More than six million Jews were murdered. Hitler began to absorb neighbouring states into the "Third Reich". In 1939, he invaded Poland, starting World War II. By 1940, his armies had occupied most of Europe. By 1944, the Allied powers had beaten Germany back and Hitler narrowly escaped assassination. He finally shot himself rather than face capture by Soviet troops.

Ludwig
WITTGENSTEIN
1889–1951
Austrian philosopher

The philosopher whom some people believe brought philosophy to an end was born in Vienna. After studying aeronautics at Manchester University, Wittgenstein went to Cambridge University to study philosophy. During World War I, he fought in the Austrian army, then taught at an elementary school in Austria and practised architecture in Vienna before returning to England in 1929 to lecture at Cambridge. He wrote two major works, *Tractatus Logico-Philosophicus* (1921) and *Philosophical Investigations* (1953), which transformed philosophy completely. In the *Tractatus* he argued that philosophical problems are not real problems, but are arrived at in an attempt to push philosophy beyond the limits imposed on it by language. In the *Investigations*, he changed his views somewhat and argued that philosophy must be chiefly concerned with the analysis and proper use of language.

Edwin
HUBBLE
1889–1953
US astonomer

Through his research, Edwin Hubble was able to provide the first evidence that the universe is expanding – when it was long thought to be static. This was a fundamental shift in our understanding of the cosmos. Born in Marshfield, Missouri, Edwin Powell Hubble embarked on a legal career, but soon gave it up in order to study astronomy. After World War I, he joined the Mount Wilson Observatory and in the 1920s, he studied hundreds of galaxies. By measuring the movement of some galaxies away from each other he was able to calculate that the universe was expanding. Hubble's name is remembered through the system of classification that he proposed for the shapes of galaxies (spiral, elliptical, and regular) and in the Hubble Space Telescope, launched from the space shuttle *Discovery* in 1990. This telescope allows people to view space without the distortion produced by the Earth's atmosphere.

Jawaharlal
NEHRU
1889–1964
Indian prime minister

When India gained independence from Britain in 1947, Nehru became its first prime minister. Nehru was educated by English governesses and then sent to boarding school in England at the age of 16. He studied law and then returned home to serve in the High Court of Allahabad. He became a member of the pro-independence group, the Indian National Congress, and, in 1928, he became its president. He was imprisoned by the British for his political activities and spent a total of ten years in jail (1921–45). After that, he led negotiations for independence from Britain. As prime minister of an independent India, he put his country on the international map as an important supporter of the British Commonwealth and the United Nations. Nehru promoted the industrialization of India and parliamentary democracy.

Igor
SIKORSKY
1889–1972
Russian-born US aircraft and helicopter engineer

Sikorsky conducted his first experiments with building helicopters in 1909–10. He then turned to aircraft design, building and flying the first four-engined aeroplane, *Le Grand*, in 1913: among its innovative features were a completely enclosed cabin for pilots and passengers. This plane became the basis of the four-engined bombers that Russia used during World War I. After the Russian Revolution, he emigrated first to France, then to the US, where he founded the Sikorsky Aero Engineering Company in 1923. He built several flying boats, including the *American Clipper*, but in the late 1930s, he returned to helicopter design and achieved his major breakthrough with the VS-300 – the world's first successful helicopter. He test-flew it (he insisted on trial-flying all of his designs) on 14 September 1939.

SIKORSKY HELICOPTER
This R-4 helicopter, designed by Igor Sikorsky, is one of more than 400 built for the US army during World War II.

KK995

1889 In Brazil, the emperor Pedro II is deposed from his throne and is forced to leave the country following a powerful army revolt. As a result, Brazil is proclaimed a democratically run republic with a president.

1889 The first Pan-American Conference is held in Washington D.C. Its aim is to promote peace between the different states of the Americas and development within the region as a whole. The conferences still take place.

Charlie CHAPLIN
1889–1977
English film actor and director

Chaplin's silent movie character – the seedy but soft-hearted tramp with baggy trousers, a moustache, bowler hat, and walking stick – made him one of the world's first and most popular box-office stars. Charlie Chaplin was born in London. His father was an alcoholic and died when Chaplin was a young boy, and his mother was mentally unstable. He was brought up in orphanages and boarding schools and became a child actor. While on tour in the USA, he was signed up for films by the Keystone Company and began to act in films in 1914. *The Tramp* (1915) established Chaplin as a great comic actor and gifted mime artist. In 1919, he co-founded United Artists with Mary Pickford, Douglas Fairbanks, and D.W. Griffith, and from then on produced his own films, including *The Gold Rush* (1924), *City Lights* (1931), and *Modern Times* (1936). He returned to the US in 1972 – having spent the previous 20 years in self-imposed exile in Switzerland – to receive a special Oscar. He was knighted in 1975.

Jomo KENYATTA
1889–1978
Kenya's first president

Kamau Ngengi was born into the Kikuyu tribe in the East African highlands and educated there by Scottish missionaries. In 1922, he joined the Kikuyu Central Association. Its main aim was to reclaim tribal lands that were lost when Kenya became a British colony in 1920. He often went to Britain to lobby Parliament and studied for a year at London University. He changed his name to Jomo, meaning "Burning Spear", Kenyatta and became president of the Pan-African Federation. In 1946, he returned to Kenya, where he was elected president of the Kenyan African National Union (KANU) – an organization committed to Kenya's independence. In 1953, following the Mau Mau uprising by Kikuyus against European settlers, he was sentenced to seven years' hard labour for allegedly directing the rebellion. In his absence, he was chosen as president of the KANU Party. Following Kenya's independence in 1963, he became president of the Republic of Kenya in 1964. In his 15-year term he turned Kenya into a stable country with a prosperous economy.

Vladimir ZWORYKIN
1889–1982
Russian-born US inventor

Vladimir Zworykin developed the first entirely electrical television system. In 1923, he used a cathode-ray tube, which he called the kinescope, to produce television images. By 1938, he had produced the first practical television camera, which he patented as the iconoscope. He also developed colour television.

CHARLIE CHAPLIN
This scene is from Chaplin's 1936 film Modern Times.

1890

Michael COLLINS
1890–1922
Irish nationalist

Michael Collins was born in County Cork. At 15, he went to work as a clerk in London. There he joined the Irish Republican Brotherhood, a group dedicated to fighting for Irish independence from Great Britain. In 1916, he returned to Ireland and took part in the unsuccessful Easter Rising in Dublin, after which he was jailed. On release in 1918, he became a Sinn Féin ("Ourselves Alone") Member of Parliament in the Irish Assembly. Most Sinn Féin members were still in prison and Collins arranged for their leader, Eamon De Valera (p.150), to escape. He became an Irish Republican Army (IRA) commander, directing guerrilla warfare against British troops. Following a truce in 1921, Collins helped frame the treaty that created the Irish Free State, a British dominion with allegiance to the Crown. De Valera and others wanted complete independence and civil war broke out in 1922. Collins led the Free State army against the IRA but was ambushed and murdered by the IRA in west Cork.

1889 A new speed record for trains is set when a steam locomotive reaches a remarkable 143 km/h (89 mph).

This exciting feat is achieved in France on the track between the capital city Paris and Dijon in the east of the country.

1889 Following a serious rail crash, automatic brakes are made compulsory on all British trains.

This is done to minimize the chance of trains colliding with each other. Other countries soon follow suit with similar laws.

VASLAV NIJINSKY in the ballet L'après-midi d'un Faune

Vaslav NIJINSKY
1890–1950
Russian ballet dancer

In a 10-year period, from 1909–19, Nijinsky established himself as the greatest male ballet dancer of his day. He was born in Kiev, into a family of celebrated dancers, and learned to dance as a very young child. His remarkable talent was quickly recognized and he was called the "eighth wonder of the world". He was acclaimed for his technique, sensitive interpretation, and dramatic ability. When dancing, he seemed to defy the laws of gravity with his spectacular leaps and *entrechats* (crossing and uncrossing the legs in mid air). In 1909, he left Russia and moved to Paris, where he joined Diaghilev's *Ballets Russes* and became an overnight sensation. At 29, he had to retire because of his mental instability. He was later diagnosed as schizophrenic.

Dwight EISENHOWER
1890–1969
US general and 34th US president

Nicknamed "Ike", Eisenhower was born in Texas and graduated from West Point Military Academy in 1915. He served as a staff officer in World War I, and by 1939 had risen to chief military assistant to General MacArthur (p.146) in the Philippines. Although he had never been in action, he was now a brigadier general. In 1942, he took command of the Allied forces in North Africa, and in 1944 was made supreme commander of the cross-channel invasion of mainland Europe. In 1950, he was chief of staff of the US army. He was invited to be supreme commander of NATO forces in Europe but, in 1952, he was swept to victory in the "I like Ike" presidential campaign. He was re-elected in 1956. Despite his lack of political training, Eisenhower was a natural diplomat. His terms in office saw Alaska and Hawaii join the union, and the start of the US space programme.

Ho Chi MINH
1890–1969
Vietnamese leader and statesman

Born in Vietnam when it was part of the French colony of Indochina, Ho Chi Minh helped to establish a united Vietnam. He became leader of the Viet Minh movement fighting for liberation. At the Battle of Dien Bien Phu in 1954, the Viet Minh were successful against French colonial forces. The Geneva Conference that followed divided Vietnam. Ho Chi Minh became president of North Vietnam, which was communist, while South Vietnam remained capitalist. From 1960, Ho Chi Minh was a forceful leader in a civil war against South Vietnam. This developed into the Vietnam War when US troops came to support the South. Ho Chi Minh did not live to see his army reunite North and South in 1975.

Charles de GAULLE
1890–1970
French general and president

The man who would lead France through the postwar years was born in Lille. He was wounded and captured in World War I and when World War II broke out in 1939, he commanded a tank division. During the German occupation of France, de Gaulle escaped to England, where he became leader of the French resistance movement. He led the Free French forces into Paris on its liberation in 1944. He was elected president in 1945 but resigned after only ten weeks due to differences within his party. De Gaulle formed a new party called Rally of the French People in 1947, which he led until 1953. He became president again in 1958. In 1959, he resolved a long-running political problem by giving all the French African colonies the right to govern themselves. He was re-elected in 1965 and again in 1968. He resigned in 1969.

Sergey PROKOFIEV
1891–1953
Russian composer

The composer who wrote the children's music classic *Peter and the Wolf* (1936) was encouraged by his piano-playing mother to study music. Prokofiev was composing at five years of age and had written two operas by the age of 12. He studied at the St Petersburg Conservatory (1904–14) and made his name as a pianist and composer with his first two Piano Concertos (1912 and 1913). He moved to London, where he composed works including "Classical" Symphony No. 1 (1917), and then to the US, where he wrote the opera *The Love for Three Oranges* (1919). From 1920, he lived in Paris, working on another opera, *The Fiery Angel* (1923), and his second and third symphonies. He was homesick, though, and returned to Russia in 1933. He composed music for films such as *Lieutenant Kijé* (1933) and *Alexander Nevsky* (1938)

1889 In Paris, France, the Eiffel Tower is completed. It is the tallest building in the world at the time, but with an increasing number of skyscrapers being built around the world, it does not hold this record for long.

1890 The last major conflict between Native Americans and the US Army takes place at Wounded Knee Creek in South Dakota, USA. The army attack Sioux people in a reservation and about 350 Sioux are killed.

James CHADWICK
1891–1973
English physicist

James Chadwick studied at Manchester, Berlin (under the German physicist Hans Geiger, p.149), and Cambridge, and went on to work with Ernest Rutherford (p.138). In 1934, Chadwick was able to confirm the existence of the neutron (a neutral particle with no electrical charge) in the atom. This discovery was of great significance in the understanding of atoms and earned him the Nobel Prize for Physics in 1935. The same year, he built Britain's first cyclotron (an apparatus used for accelerating charged atomic particles) in Liverpool. During World War II, Chadwick went to the USA to lead the UK's work on the atomic bomb. He was knighted in 1945.

Arthur COMPTON
1892–1962
US physicist

Arthur Compton studied the effects of X-rays on electrons and revealed the transfer of energy from photon to electron – the Compton effect. He was educated at Princeton and Cambridge, England, and took up teaching posts in St Louis and Chicago. In 1927, he won the Nobel Prize for Physics (with Charles Wilson), for work on the wavelength of scattered photons. Compton became a leading authority on nuclear energy, X-rays, and plutonium production and, in 1941, was asked to help to produce plutonium for the atomic bomb. He became a major contributor to the Manhattan Project (the atomic bomb) in Chicago. In 1942, he built the first nuclear reactor with the nuclear physicist Enrico Fermi (p.176). His book *Atomic Quest*, published in 1958, describes the project and his work in it.

J. B. S. HALDANE
1892–1964
Scottish scientist

John Haldane started studying science when assisting his father, a well-known physiologist. In 1924, Haldane produced the first proof that enzymes obey the laws of thermodynamics. He was convinced that natural selection was the true process of evolution. In 1932, he estimated for the first time the rate of mutation, or change, of a gene. In 1936, he showed the genetic link between the blood disorder haemophilia and colour blindness. In 1957, he went to India in protest at the Anglo-French invasion of Suez. He was made professor of genetics in Orissa and took Indian citizenship in 1961.

J. R. R. TOLKIEN
1892–1973
English writer

Author of the epic trilogy *Lord of the Rings*, John Ronald Reuel Tolkien was born in Bloemfontein, South Africa and came to England aged four. He went to Oxford University where he then taught until 1959, specializing in Anglo-Saxon and other Old English languages. This interest is clearly reflected in *The Hobbit* (1937), which is set in a mythical world called Middle Earth. Tolkien returned to the same world many years later in *The Lord of the Rings* (1954–55), which is made up of three volumes: *The Fellowship of the Ring, The Two Towers,* and *The Return of the King.* The adventures of his hobbits and elves were originally intended to amuse himself and his children but today, many of his characters, such as Bilbo Baggins, Gandalf, Gollum, Tom Bombadil, and Smaug the dragon, have achieved cult status with young people and adults.

General Franco

Robert WATSON-WATT
1892–1973
Scottish physicist

The man who first gave practical application to radar was a descendant of James Watt (p.64), who developed the steam engine. Robert Watson-Watt attended university in Dundee and St Andrews, Scotland. His first job was in the meteorological office and, in 1940, he became scientific adviser to the air ministry. Watson-Watt played a major role in the development and introduction of radar, which helped ground defences pinpoint in-coming enemy aircraft by day or by night. He was knighted for his discovery in 1942. Before the US joined the war, Watson-Watt was sent there to advise on radar.

Francisco FRANCO
1892–1975
Spanish general and dictator

Francisco Franco ruled as dictator of Spain for 36 years. He was born in Galicia and graduated from Toledo military academy in 1910. He gained rapid promotion through the ranks to become

---

1891 The German government introduces the first compulsory senior citizens' pension plan in the world. Germans can draw a pension from the age of 70. The programme is a huge success and other countries follow suit.

1891 Two Frenchmen – Emile Levassor and Rene Panhard – design the first car with an engine at the front instead of the back. The design is immediately popular. It takes off and alters the design of cars for ever.

Europe's youngest general in 1926. In 1931, the Spanish king left the country and Spain became a republic. In 1936, Franco joined the conspiracy to overthrow the republican government, leading to the Spanish Civil War. Franco's close ties with rebel forces led to his appointment as "generalissimo" of the rebels and chief of the Nationalists. With support from Hitler and Mussolini, he overturned the republicans in 1939 and became *caudillo* (general dictator) of Spain, with no opposition until his death in 1975. During the 1950s he regained the confidence of Western powers by his anti-communist stand. Ironically, it was the economic reforms that he introduced to Spain that undid his regime and led to the return of democracy. In 1969, he announced that on his death, the monarchy would be reinstated and Juan Carlos, grandson of Spain's last ruling king, would take the throne.

Haile SELASSIE
1892–1975
Ethiopian emperor

The Ethiopian leader, whom the Rastafarian religious and political movement regards today as divine, was born into Ethiopian nobility. Ras (prince) Tafari Makonnen became regent and heir to the throne in 1917. He sought to modernize his country's institutions and succeeded in gaining Ethiopia's admission into the League of Nations in 1923. He was also the first Ethiopian ruler ever to travel abroad. He was crowned king in 1928 and then emperor, as Haile Selassie, in 1930. He lost power when Italy invaded his country in 1935–36, but regained control with British help in 1941. He became the father-figure of African liberation as the only leader of an independent Black African state. In 1963, he helped to found the Organization of African Unity, whose headquarters were established in Addis Ababa. He slowly lost touch with the rising social discontent in the country and was deposed in 1974.

TITO
1892–1980
Yugoslav leader

The ruler of Yugoslavia from 1945 to 1980, Josip Broz was born in Croatia. During World War I, he was taken prisoner by the Russians, under whose influence he became a communist,

HAILE SELASSIE
An important leader of his day, he was a symbol of the aspiration of Black Africa.

serving in Lenin's Red Army during the Russian Civil War. Returning to the new Yugoslavia, he became active in the communist movement, which led to his imprisonment for five years. He then did much undercover work for the communists, adopting the name Tito. During World War II, Tito led the partisan movement against the German occupation. At the end of the war, he forced the abdication of King Peter II and ruled the new Federal Republic of Yugoslavia from 1945. His reforms were disapproved of by his former ally Stalin and he broke his ties with the Soviet Union in 1948. He pursued a neutral policy, neither aligned with the USSR nor the USA. He made Yugoslavia the most liberal communist nation in Europe, providing some 30 years of stability – which only shattered as Yugoslavia fragmented in the 1990s.

Louis-Victor Duc de BROGLIE
1892–1987
French physicist

Louis-Victor was part of a high-ranking family in northern France. He studied history, but his work at the Eiffel Tower radio station in Paris during World War I sparked an interest in science. In 1924, he gained a science doctorate at the Sorbonne in Paris. He set out to prove the reverse of Einstein's theory that waves can behave as particles (in other words that particles can behave as waves). This idea was of great importance in the development of quantum mechanics. In 1929, de Broglie won the Nobel Prize for Physics for his pioneering work on electron waves, which are called either de Broglie or matter waves.

1891 German inventor and flight enthusiast Otto Lilienthal makes the first of a series of glider flights in Germany, launching himself into the wind from high places. He dies in 1896 when one of his gliders crashes.

1892 Following the increase of high-rise public buildings in many cities within the USA, the moving escalator is invented by Jesse Reno. It saves people from having to climb up and down huge numbers of steps.

Wilfred OWEN
1893–1918
English poet

One of England's great World War I poets, Wilfred Owen was born in Shropshire. When he was 20, he went to France as a tutor. He fought in World War I and, in 1917, he was invalided home where he met the poet Siegfried Sassoon in hospital. The resulting friendship greatly influenced Owen's work. His poetry expresses horror and anger at the pointlessness and brutality of war. In August 1918, he returned to France where he was awarded the Military Cross, the highest award for bravery in battle. On 4 November, a week before the war ended, Wilfred Owen was killed in action, aged only 25. The terrible honesty of his beautifully crafted poems is evident in "Strange Meeting", "Dulce et decorum est", "Futility", "Exposure", and "Anthem for Doomed Youth".

Dorothy PARKER
1893–1967
US poet and writer

Poet Dorothy Parker was famous for her "one-liners": her comment on being told of the death of the somewhat reserved President Coolidge was "How can they tell?" She was born Dorothy Rothschild in New Jersey. After a privileged but short education, she began her literary career when, in 1916, the magazine *Vogue* accepted some poems for publication. She married Edwin Pond Parker II in 1917. Later, as drama critic for *Vanity Fair*, and reviewer and writer for the *New Yorker*, she achieved a reputation for a sharp wit and, in 1926, her first book of poems, *Enough Rope*,

was instantly popular. She followed it with *Sunset Guns* (1928, the year of her divorce) and *Death and Taxes* (1931). Two collections of her short stories, *Laments for the Living* (1930) and *After Such Pleasures* (1933) were equally successful.

Mao ZEDONG
1893–1976
Chinese Communist leader

One of the founders of the People's Republic of China, Mao Zedong (or Mao Tse-tung) was one of the founders of the Chinese Communist Party. He broke

away from the ruling regime of Chiang Kai-shek (p.155) and in 1934–35 led his army on a 10,000-km (6,000-mile) strategic retreat known as the Long March. In 1937, the Japanese invaded China and Mao fought an underground war against them, gaining popularity when Japan left. By 1949, Mao had taken power from Chiang Kai-shek to become the first chairman of the People's Republic of China. In 1958, he organized the Great Leap Forward, a programme of planned industrial growth. This failed, and Mao lost his chairmanship but remained Communist Party leader. He directed the Cultural Revolution, in

which thousands of political opponents and intellectuals were persecuted. In the 1970s, Mao's health deteriorated, but he stayed in power until his death. His *Little Red Book* became one of the most printed books in the world.

Mary PICKFORD
1893–1979
US film star

Pickford captivated audiences all over the world with her girlish charm and long blond curls. Born Gladys Mary Smith in Toronto, Canada, she began acting as a child and made her

THE CULTURAL REVOLUTION

During the 1960s, China was gripped by a revolutionary uprising. The Cultural Revolution, as it was called, began in 1965 as a move to return to the basic principles of the Communist Party. By the time it finished in 1968, the country was in turmoil and its economy was seriously weakened as schools and colleges closed and industry shut down.

RED GUARDS
After the communists took power in 1949, China was run by Chairman MAO ZEDONG, who stamped his mark on every aspect of society. During his semi-retirement in the early 1960s, more liberal, "reformist" ideas from Russia were encouraged by President LIU SHAOQI (1898–1974). In October 1965, the Minister of Defence, LIN BIAO (1908–71), urged college pupils to uphold Mao's ideals and return to basic communist principles. Supporters of Mao, known as the Red Guards, held parades and put up wall posters criticizing writers, intellectuals, and all supporters of the president. This encouraged a personality cult of Mao and a purge of the Communist Party.

THE INSPIRATION
By 1966, the Cultural Revolution was out of control and the economy was seriously weakened. The veteran leader ZHOU ENLAI (p.170) urged restraint and, in October 1968, President LIU SHAOQI was dismissed and order restored.

Mao Zedong addressing his supporters

1892 Rudolf Diesel takes out a patent for a new internal combustion engine in Germany. These diesel engines become used in most heavy road vehicles and mean that freight can now be transported successfully by road.

1893 In Hawaii, Queen Liliuokalani is overthrown by a revolt led by the island's sugar planters. The previously independent kingdom is made a republic in 1894. It is annexed to the USA in 1898, becoming a territory in 1900.

MARY PICKFORD
Known as "Baby Gladys" when acting as a child, Mary Pickford later became known as "America's sweetheart" because of her qualities of sweetness and innocence.

first film when she was 16. Her best-known silent films include *Rebecca of Sunnybrook Farm* (1917) and *Pollyanna* (1920). Her role in her first "talkie" *Coquette* (1929) earned her an Academy Award. She had an astute business mind and co-founded the film studio United Artists with D. W. Griffith (p.142), Charlie Chaplin (p.160), and Douglas Fairbanks (whom she married). Pickford retired in 1933 and then became a virtual recluse.

Nikita KHRUSHCHEV
1894–1971
Soviet leader

Khrushchev was born into a peasant family. He joined the Communist Party and, in 1938, was made a full member of the Politburo – the Soviet government. In 1940, after Soviet forces had invaded Poland, the then leader, Joseph Stalin (p.145), placed Khrushchev in charge of integrating Poland into the Soviet Union. In 1953, on the death of Stalin, Khrushchev became leader and distanced himself from Stalin's brutality. He allowed the publication of a Solzhenitsyn book which denounced Stalin's repression, and let Soviet tourists travel overseas for the first time. However, he was swift to crush an Hungarian uprising. He also attempted to place nuclear missiles on Cuba in 1962, which brought the world to the brink of nuclear war. Generally, Krushchev tried to improve relations with the West. He promoted the Soviet space programme, which earned the Soviets great international acclaim when they launched the first man into space in 1961.

Shoji HAMADA
1894–1978
Japanese potter

Hamada ranks as one of the most important potters of the 20th century. He was born near Tokyo and studied ceramics at the Technical College there. In 1916, he joined the Institute of Ceramics in Kyoto working mainly in stoneware. He met the English potter Bernard Leach and went with him to England in 1920. The pair set up a studio in Cornwall, where they produced strong, simple pottery decorated with rich and subtle glazes. Hamada returned to Japan in 1924, where he developed traditional techniques and launched a Japanese folk crafts movement. He continued to create bold, uncomplicated designs, using age-old tools such as brushes made of dog's hair or dry grass, and local clays and glazes. He was awarded the Order of Cultural Merit in 1968.

Robert MENZIES
1894–1978
Australian prime minister

Robert Menzies was prime minister of Australia for 16 consecutive years. He encouraged European immigration and industrial growth and strengthened ties with the USA. In 1934, he became member of parliament for Kooyang. He was Commonwealth Attorney General from 1935 to 1939 and prime minister from 1939 to 1941 and again from 1949 until 1966. He secured his position by exploiting the rifts within the opposition Labor Party and fostering economic growth. His last years in office were overshadowed by Australia's role in the Vietnam War.

1893 Leading the way in social reforms, New Zealand is the first country to grant women the right to vote. In 1897, the government introduces an eight-hour working day and, in 1889, old-age pensions are instituted.

1894 Indian-born British author Rudyard Kipling writes *The Jungle Book* about Mowgli, a boy who is brought up by wolves. This becomes one of his best-loved children's stories and it is later made into a Disney cartoon.

Konosuke MATSUSHITA
1894–1989
Japanese industrialist

The man who would own one of the world's largest electrical companies started work as an errand boy. By the time he was 16, Matsushita was working for the Osaka Electric Light Company. When he was 23 he left to set up his own company selling electric plugs that he had designed himself. His company was called Matsushita Electric Industrial Company Limited, and, by the 1950s, it was Japan's leading manufacturer of washing machines, refrigerators, and televisions. Under brand names such as Panasonic, National, JVC, and Technics, he exported electrical equipment, computer chips, and video recorders. Matsushita concentrated on the mass-production of consumer goods at the lowest cost possible. This had a huge influence on Japanese industry in the second half of the 20th century.

RUDOLPH VALENTINO *The "Great Lover" Valentino is seen here in a scene from the 1926 United Artists film* Son of the Sheik.

Martha GRAHAM
1894–1991
US dancer and choreographer

Martha Graham was born in Pennsylvania and trained as a dancer in Los Angeles. She rejected classical ballet with its stylized movements, wanting to use her entire body in dance movements. Eventually she set up her own dance company. Her ideas were highly influential, and she evolved a new language of dance, using flexible movements as a way of expressing complex but universally shared emotions. In later years she concentrated on making dance reveal the "inner man", and her ballets became ever more psychological in content. The movements were often angular and jagged, rather than smooth and graceful as they are in traditional ballet. She wove her ballets around social, psychological, and literary themes, and drew inspiration from Greek tragedy. Her ballets include *Primitive Mysteries* (1931), *Appalachian Spring* (music by Aaron Copland, 1944), and *Legend of Judith* (1960).

Rudolph VALENTINO
1895–1926
US film actor

The Italian-born Rodolfo Guglielmi was to become Hollywood's silent movie "Great Lover" of the 1920s. Rudolph Valentino moved to the USA while in his teens and lived in Hollywood where he played small parts in a number of films. His first starring role was as Julio in *The Four Horsemen of the Apocalypse*, which led to him becoming a star overnight. He played the romantic hero, and his smouldering good looks made him the subject of unsurpassed female adulation. Subsequent performances in films such as *The Sheikh* (1921) established his status as a matinée idol of the 1920s. He became a legend of the silent screen, but died at the age of 31 from a ruptured ulcer. There were reports of hysteria and suicides at his death, and his funeral was a national event.

László MOHOLY-NAGY
1895–1946
Hungarian artist

Amazingly versatile in painting, photography, cinematography, and industrial design, László Moholy-Nagy was a challenging and inspiring artist. He was born in southern Hungary, studied law at Budapest University, and served as a soldier in World War I before becoming a full-time artist. In 1921, he moved to Berlin, where he began to experiment with many different art forms besides oil painting. These included collage (building images by pasting cuttings, pictures, and texts to a flat surface) and photography, from which Moholy-Nagy created abstract "photograms" by using a camera without a lens. From 1923–28 he taught at the famous Bauhaus School of applied arts in Weimar. Here he branched out still further, working in film, theatre design, and sculpture. In 1935, he moved to London, where he designed furniture and film sets

1895 The world's first official road race for cars takes place through the streets of northern France. For the race, the cars have to follow a route from Paris to Bordeaux, in the southwest of France, and back.

1895 Pretending to assist foreign workers in the Transvaal goldmines, but actually out for his own gain, Leander Jameson leads an anti-government rebellion. He and his secret supporter, Cecil Rhodes, are caught.

LASZLO MOHOLY-NAGY
This self-portrait is in the Magyar Nemzeti Gallery in Budapest.

– notably for *Things to Come* (1936). Finally, he settled in the US, where he became director of the Chicago Institute of Design.

Babe RUTH
1895–1948
US baseball player

Babe Ruth was one of the most popular baseball players in the history of the game, and the man against whom most baseball batting feats are judged. He was born George Herman Ruth in Baltimore, Maryland. He joined the Boston Red Sox in 1914, playing as a left-handed pitcher, and soon became a great all-rounder. He was

Buster KEATON
1895–1966
US comedian, actor, and director

One of the greatest comic stars of the silent film era, Joseph Francis Keaton began acting in his parents' miming and acrobatic vaudeville act.

His name, Buster, came after he fell down some stairs but did not break any bones. On screen, he was renowned for his deadpan expression; his films include *The Navigator* (1924), *The General* (1926), and *The Cameraman* (1928). The arrival of talking pictures ended his career, although he made a few short films and had a small role in Charlie Chaplin's film *Limelight* (1952). In 1959, he was presented with a special Academy Award for his contribution to cinema.

Jack DEMPSEY
1895–1983
US boxer

The heavyweight boxer called the "Manassa Mauler" was born William Harrison Dempsey in Colorado. As known by the nicknames "Babe" and "Bambino" as well as "the Sultan of Swat". He played mainly for the Red Sox and the New York Yankees and by 1925 he was earning more than the president. In 1935, he moved to the Boston Braves and, in 1938, became coach for the Brooklyn Dodgers. During his career, he played in ten World Series, and held the record of 714 regular season home runs until 1974.

BABE RUTH
Seen here playing for the New York Yankees, Babe Ruth became the greatest all-rounder in the history of baseball.

a young man, he worked in the copper mines before taking to the boxing ring as "Kid Blackie" at the age of 19. Dempsey showed great ability as a heavyweight boxer and, in 1919, he won the world heavyweight title, defeating Jess Willard. In 1926, he lost the title to Gene Tunney. In a rematch, he lost again, but only on points and after Tunney suffered a knock-down. Dempsey continued to box for several more years, appearing in fighting exhibitions, but he never won the heavyweight title again. In 1940, he retired from the ring and opened a restaurant called Dempsey's on Broadway in New York City.

F. Scott FITZGERALD
1896–1940
US writer

Francis Scott Key Fitzgerald's novels and short stories famously depicted the Jazz Age in the USA of the 1920s. He was born in Minnesota. After university he joined the army and, in 1920, published his first novel, *This Side of Paradise*, which made him famous. He followed it with *The Beautiful and the Damned* (1922) and *The Great Gatsby* (1925), his best-known novel. He and his wife, Zelda, lived on the French Riviera, and became celebrities as part of a group of flashy US expatriates. Fitzgerald began to drink too much while his wife's mental health deteriorated. Her breakdown led to the moving novel *Tender is the Night* (1934). Now regarded as a major US writer, Fitzgerald fell into debt and alcoholism. He died from a heart attack at the age of 44.

1896 In Athens, Greece, 13 countries take part in the first of the modern Olympic Games. The idea of Frenchman Baron Pierre de Coubertin, the modern Olympic Games are based on the ancient Greek games held at Olympia.

1896 Italy recognizes the independence of Ethiopia at the Treaty of Addis Ababa. By 1914, Ethiopia and Liberia were the only countries on the whole of the African continent not to be under some form of European "protection".

Amelia
EARHART
1897–1937
US aviator

A daring pilot, Amelia Earhart was the first woman to fly across the Atlantic Ocean. She paid for flying lessons with money she earned from her early jobs, and in 1928 she became the first woman to fly the Atlantic – as a passenger. In 1932, she flew the Atlantic again, in just more than 15 hours, achieving the first solo crossing by a woman. Three years later, she set another record, flying solo from Hawaii to California. In 1937, she took off on a round-the-world trip with a navigator, Frederick Noonan. Earhart managed to travel more than two-thirds of the distance but, after taking off from New Guinea, her plane disappeared over the Pacific Ocean. Despite a massive search, no trace of her was found. In her last letter to her husband, Earhart wrote: "Women must try to do things as men have tried. When they fail, their failure must be but a challenge to others."

William
FAULKNER
1897–1962
US writer

William Faulkner created some memorable American fiction and experimented with the form of the novel. He was born in Mississippi and in World War I joined up as a trainee pilot in Canada. The war ended before he even learned to fly, and he went home. After various university courses and temporary jobs, *Soldier's Pay* (1926) launched Faulkner as a novelist. Of the titles that followed, he is best-known for *As I Lay Dying* (1930), *Sanctuary* (1931), *Absalom, Absalom!* (1936), and *The Reivers* (1962), a nostalgic comedy that appeared a month before his death. Many of his novels are set in the fictional Yoknapatawpha County, a microcosm of the South, which allowed him to address the basic questions of humanity n a controlled situation. He received the Nobel Prize for Literature in 1949.

AMELIA EARHART
Clues found on a Pacific Island suggest that Earhart and her co-pilot may have survived a crash, only to die of thirst.

John
COCKCROFT
1897–1967
English nuclear physicist

John Douglas Cockcroft's work with protons helped the development of the H-bomb and nuclear fusion. Born in Yorkshire, he studied at Manchester and Cambridge universities, then became professor of natural philosophy at Cambridge. He was in charge of constructing a nuclear power station in Canada during World War II, then returned to England and became director of the Atomic Energy Research Establishment at Harwell. Working under Ernest Rutherford (p.138) at the Cavendish Laboratory in Cambridge, he built (with Ernest Walton) an apparatus to accelerate particles. The device was essential for understanding nuclear structures. In 1932, they used it in the first successful experiment to split an atom. The two men won the 1951 Nobel Prize for Physics. Cockcroft was knighted in 1948.

1897 A new era in sailing begins when Charles Parsons's ship *Turbinia* reaches the astonishing speed of 34.5 knots (64 km/h [40 mph]). The *Turbinia* uses a turbine engine rather than the less efficient reciprocating model.

1898 In China, the unpopularity of foreigners leads to violent attacks on them, often ending in murder. This period becomes known as the Boxer Rebellion after one of the leading groups, whose name means "righteous harmony fists".

Enid BLYTON
1897–1968
English children's writer

The colourful children's characters Noddy and Big Ears were created by Enid Mary Blyton. Born in London, Blyton trained as a nursery school teacher then turned to education journalism. She started writing for children and published a collection of poems in 1922, *Child Whispers*. In 1930 she began her output of fiction for children that was to tally more than 600 books, and be translated into many different languages. Best known for very young children are the *Noddy* books. For older children she wrote adventure tales in the *Secret Seven* and the *Famous Five* series. Until the 1970s, her stories were considered good reading material for children, but teachers and librarians came to think that her attitudes towards the sexes and class were politically incorrect. In the late 1990s Noddy won over a new generation of fans in Britain and the USA when his Toytown antics were made into an animated TV series.

ENID BLYTON
This illustration from The Enchanted Wood, *written by Enid Blyton in 1939, shows a scene from* The Land of Birthdays.

George GERSHWIN
1898–1937
US composer

Born Jacob Gershvin in Brooklyn, New York, Gershwin was the son of Russian Jewish immigrants. He learned the piano and taught himself composition as a child, and started to write popular songs in his teens. His first success came with *Swanee* in 1920, followed by hit musicals (usually with lyrics by his brother Ira) such as *Lady Be Good!* (1924) and *Girl Crazy*

(1930). In 1924, he wrote *Rhapsody in Blue* for the Paul Whiteman band, the first of his more "serious" pieces, which also included a Piano Concerto (1925) and the orchestral *An American in Paris* (1928). He was cleverly able to bridge the gap between popular and classical music, which he did most effectively in his "American folk opera" *Porgy and Bess* (1935).

Sergei EISENSTEIN
1898–1948
Russian film director

An innovative director of silent films, Eisenstein served with the Red Army, then became a theatrical scene designer. He was appointed by the Soviet government to make propaganda films on the history of the Russian revolution. He developed a new technique of film editing, called montage, where images run into each other at breakneck speed. His views were not always in line with those of the government and he fell in and out of favour. His films *Battleship Potemkin* (1915), *October* (1928), *Alexander Nevsky* (1938), and the epic *Ivan The Terrible* (1942–46) influenced many directors.

Bertolt BRECHT
1898–1956
German playwright and poet

Brecht was born in Bavaria in southern Germany and studied philosophy and medicine at university. His dislike of middle-class values developed into Marxism and, in 1933, he fled from Hitler's Nazi regime. He settled in the USA in 1941 but was forced to leave after being suspected of "Un-American Activities"; he returned to East Germany. Among Brecht's works are *The Threepenny Opera* (1928), *Mother Courage and her Children* (1941), *The Caucasian Chalk Circle* (1949), and *The Resistible Rise of Arturo Ui* (1958).

C. S. LEWIS
1898–1963
English scholar and writer

An important writer on Christianity, Clive Staples Lewis is best remembered as the author of the *Chronicles of Narnia*. He was born in Belfast and, after being wounded in World War I, went to Oxford University. He stayed there – as scholar, fellow, and tutor – until 1954, when he became a professor at Cambridge University. Lewis excelled in every area in which he wrote. The *Screwtape Letters* (1942), instructions from a senior devil to a junior devil on temptation techniques, was a best-seller. The brilliant *Cosmic Trilogy*, three science-fiction novels, was finished in 1945. He continued his Christian themes in the seven books set in the magical land of Narnia, beginning with *The Lion, the Witch and the Wardrobe* (1950) and finishing with the ultimate fight between good and evil, *The Last Battle* (1956).

Howard FLOREY
1898–1968
Australian scientist

In 1945, Florey – together with Ernst Chain and Alexander Fleming (p.147) – was awarded the Nobel Prize for Medicine for making pencillin available for use as an antibiotic. Born in Adelaide, Florey attended Oxford University. He was professor of pathology at Sheffield University and later at Oxford. Together with Ernst Chain, he experimented with penicillin, first discovered by Fleming in 1928, and made the breakthrough in 1935. The antibiotic was widely used in Europe during World War II and helped to save countless lives.

1898 Following the success of London's underground system, Paris decides to follow suit. Work begins on the Metro, which is due to open a year later, although the underground building work takes longer than anticipated.

1898 In the Sudan, Africa, British and French forces face each other at the Nile fort of Fashoda. Both Britain and France are seeking to expand their African empires. The French eventually retreat, averting an Anglo-French war.

Zhou ENLAI
1898–1975
Chinese statesman

The first prime minister of the People's Republic of China, from 1949 to his death, Zhou Enlai was educated in Japan and Paris. While in Paris, he became a founding member of the overseas Chinese Communist Party (CCP). He strongly believed in a city-based communist revolution in China along the lines of the Russian Revolution and organized a revolution that failed in Nanchang in 1927. In 1935, he supported the election of Mao Zedong (p.164) as leader of the CCP and remained a loyal supporter of him for the next 40 years. From 1937 to 1946, he acted as a liaison officer between the CCP and the Nationalist government led by Chiang Kai-shek (p.155). In 1949, he became prime minister. Throughout his career, he acted as a peacemaker, representing China in a diplomatic role abroad. He was a key influence in working towards a relaxation of relations between China and the US in the early 1970s. He always took a moderate line and was a stabilizing influence during the more extreme episodes of Mao's regime, such as the Cultural Revolution.

Paul ROBESON
1898–1976
US singer, actor, and black activist

Paul Robeson was a talented athlete and American football player while at college, but decided against becoming a professional sportsman and studied law instead. However, legal career opportunities for blacks in the USA at that time were few, and, in 1923, Robeson drifted into acting and singing African-American folk songs. Within a year, his reputation was established when he appeared in the title role

of *The Emperor Jones* by Eugene O'Neill (p.157). He also appeared in the film version of the play and in other later films. He became famous for singing "Ol' Man River" in the musical *Showboat* and was widely acclaimed for his portrayal of *Othello* in London and on Broadway. His outspoken left-wing politics led the US State Department to withdraw his passport in 1950 after he went on a highly public visit to Russia. His career was seriously affected. He finally returned to the US in 1963, but died a virtual recluse.

Trofim LYSENKO
1898–1976
Russian biologist

As leader of Soviet scientists under Stalin (p.145), Trofim Lysenko was so powerful he could officially dismiss Gregor Mendel's (p.101) theory of inherited characteristics. Instead, he put forward his own theory that changes were acquired during an individual's lifetime. His theories were later proved wrong, but he had some success in other areas of genetics. By supporting vernalization – a method of making plant seeds germinate quickly in the spring – he achieved large increases in the amount of crops grown. However, Lysenko's position gave him dictatorial powers, which he used to silence any scientists who opposed him. Lysenko thus did much to impede the progress of Russian science, until Nikita Khrushchev (p.165) came to power and dismissed him in 1965.

PAUL ROBESON
The African-American activist was famous for his singing of spirituals as well as folk songs.

Golda MEIR
1898–1978
Israeli prime minister

Golda Meir was a founder and fourth prime minister of the state of Israel. She was born into a Jewish family in Kiev, Ukraine, and when she was eight years old her family emigrated to the USA. She was married in 1917 and moved to Palestine, then controlled by the British, where she lived on a kibbutz (communal farm) and became active in the Labour movement. After World War II, Meir signed Israel's independence declaration in 1948. She worked as Israeli ambassador to the Soviet Union from 1948 to 1949 before taking up posts as minister of labour and then foreign minister in the Israeli government. In 1969 Meir was elected prime minister. She worked hard to achieve peace in the Middle East between the warring Arabs and Israelis, but her efforts were ignored and, in 1973, the fourth Arab-Israeli war broke out. In 1974, she resigned and, upon her death in 1978, it was revealed that she had been suffering from leukaemia for 12 years.

Henry MOORE
1898–1986
English sculptor

Monumental, primitive, and often displayed outdoors, Henry Moore's sculptures set him apart from other English artists of the 20th century. He was born into a Yorkshire coal-mining family. After serving as a soldier in World War I, he studied at Leeds School of Art and the Royal College of Art in London. He became an art teacher in 1925, living first in North London and then in

1898 When a US battleship is sunk by an explosion in the harbour at Havana, Cuba, the USA declares war against Spain. (Cuba was under Spanish control.) After months of fighting, the USA wins and Cuba becomes independent.

1898 In the United States, Henry Ford forms his Detroit Automobile Company (later the Ford Motor Company). He vows that his factory will ensure that "horseless carriages" or automobiles, will become as common as bicycles within a few years.

Hertfordshire. His early wood carvings were influenced by sculptures from Mexico, Africa, and Polynesia, which helped him to create simplified, flowing human forms such as *Reclining Figure* (1935). Moore strove to relate his sculptures to their natural surroundings and several of them were intended for outdoor settings, such as *King and Queen* (1953) and the bronze *Three Piece Reclining Figure* (1961–62). Many of his works in wood, stone, or bronze were pierced with openings to increase the surface area of their curves.

Dame Ninette de VALOIS
1898–
Irish ballerina

Founder of the Royal Ballet, Ninette de Valois grew up in Ireland as Edris Stannus. She trained as a ballet dancer, performing in a variety of shows from pantomimes to revues and opera. In 1923, she joined Diaghilev's (p.138) *Ballets Russes* as a soloist and went on to found her own ballet school in London. The London venue Sadler's Wells was opened by Lilian Baylis in 1931 and Valois became a founding member of the Vic-Wells Ballet (later to become the Sadler's Wells Ballet and The Royal Ballet). Valois was highly involved with the Royal Ballet and remained artistic director until 1963. Widely regarded as a pioneer of British ballet, she helped create a distinctive style of ballet, inspired by literature, music, and paintings. Her choreographed works include *The Rake's Progress* (1935) and *Don Quixote* (1950). She was created a Dame of the British Empire in 1951.

Suzanne LENGLEN
1899–1938
French tennis player

Born in Compiègne, Suzanne Lenglen dominated amateur tennis from 1919–26. A brilliant tennis player from an early age, she was trained by her father and, in 1914, won the women's world hard-court singles championship in Paris. Lenglen was the French women's champion from 1920–23 and from 1925–26. She won both the singles and doubles tournaments at Wimbledon in 1919–23 and 1925, and the mixed doubles in 1920, 1922, and 1925. She won Olympic gold medals in the singles and mixed doubles in 1920. Lenglen turned professional in 1926 and toured the US. When she retired a year later, she founded the Lenglen School of Tennis in Paris. She was perhaps the greatest female tennis player in the history of the game. After her death, she was awarded the French Legion of Honour.

Al CAPONE
1899–1947
US gangster

Alphonse Capone was born in Brooklyn, New York. He worked for the gang leader Johnny Torrio, following him to Chicago in 1919. He earned his living collecting "protection" money and earned the nickname "Scarface" after being cut in a knife fight. With Torrio, he controlled prostitution and gambling dens and traded in illegal alcohol during the Prohibition era (1919–33). His wealth was estimated to be $100 million. By 1925, Capone was in control of much of Chicago's crime. In 1929, his gang gunned down seven men in what became known as the St Valentine's Day Massacre. Capone made sure he was on holiday at the time. He was eventually arrested and jailed for tax evasion in 1931. When he emerged ten years later his influence had disappeared.

HUMPHREY BOGART
Although famous for playing tough-guy roles, Bogart won an Academy Award for his portrayal of a drunken, ageing boatman in The African Queen.

THOMPSON *Sub-machine gun favoured by gangsters*

Humphrey BOGART
1899–1957
US film star

The classic Hollywood "tough guy" screen actor was born the son of a doctor in New York City. Humphrey Bogart began his career as the manager of a touring theatrical company. He soon started acting in films and he made his name with a series of gangster movies. He played characters who were tough, cynical, and world-weary, but faithful to their own moral code. He was also capable of more sympathetic roles. His films include *The Maltese Falcon* (1942), *The Big Sleep* (1946), where he played opposite Lauren Bacall (who became his fourth wife), *The African Queen* (1951) co-starring Katharine Hepburn, and *Casablanca* (1942), with Ingrid Bergman. It was in this film that he is supposed to have said to the piano player in his café, "Play it again, Sam". In fact, what he says is "Play it, Sam". His films have become perennial favourites.

1899 Famous outlaw Butch Cassidy, together with his gang, the Wild Bunch, and his partner Harry Longabaugh, better known as the "Sundance Kid", hold up a Union Pacific train at gunpoint and get away having robbed it of $60,000.

1899 The British Empire is at its largest. Territories include India, Canada, Australia, New Zealand, parts of the Middle East and Africa, as well as the key islands of Hong Kong, Singapore, Jamaica, and Ceylon (Sri Lanka).

Solomon BANDARANAIKE
1899–1959
Sri Lankan statesman

Bandaranaike changed the course of history in his native Ceylon (now Sri Lanka). He studied law at Oxford University and qualified as a lawyer in 1925. On his return to Ceylon, he entered politics, became a leading member of the United National Party and, in 1948, was elected to the House of Representatives when Ceylon became free of British rule. He resigned from government in 1952 to form the Sri Lanka Freedom Party. In 1956, he formed an alliance of opposition parties, which won an election that year and Bandaranaike became prime minister. Turmoil between the country's two ethnic groups – the majority Sinhala, which Bandaranaike supported, and the Tamil minority – led to violence. Bandaranaike was assassinated in 1959 by a Buddhist monk.

Ernest HEMINGWAY
1899–1961
US writer

Hemingway's short, simple sentences and vigorous prose stemmed from his training as a journalist and a "macho" lifestyle, and influenced writers all over the world. He was born in Illinois. His father was a doctor, and Hemingway trained as a reporter. In World War I, despite a bad eye, Hemingway joined the Red Cross as an ambulance driver. He was badly injured in Italy and sent home. He married in 1921 and travelled abroad as a roving reporter. In 1928, he moved to Florida and began his famous drunken, wild, and adventurous lifestyle in earnest: skiing, sailing, fishing, and hunting (when he was not writing). The works that made him famous include *The Sun Also Rises* (1926), *A Farewell to Arms* (1929), *For Whom the Bell Tolls* (1940), and *The Old Man and the Sea* (1952). In 1954 he received the Nobel Prize for Literature. He suffered later from extreme depression and shot himself.

ERNEST HEMINGWAY *worked for the loyalists during the Spanish Civil War.*

Francis POULENC
1899–1963
French composer

Paris-born Francis Poulenc wrote several pieces as a teenager, but first became well known in 1919 with the songs in *Cocardes*, written in collaboration with the poet Jean Cocteau. Poulenc and five other young French composers became known as "*Les Six*", and they set out to create a new French style of composition distinct from Claude Debussy's (p.131) impressionism. Influenced by the music of Stravinsky and Satie, Poulenc wrote many songs in a light and witty style in the 1920s, including *Poèmes de Ronsard* (1924), some piano pieces, and the ballet *Les Biches* (1924). However, from about 1935, he concentrated on more serious songs and religious pieces. His *Dialogues des Carmélites* (1953–56) is thought one of the finest 20th-century operas.

Duke ELLINGTON
1899–1974
US jazz composer, pianist, and band leader

A major force in jazz music, Edward Kennedy Ellington grew up in Washington D.C. His elegant appearance and manners earned him his nickname, Duke. He moved to New York City and made his name playing in venues such as the Cotton Club in Harlem. He formed his own band, employing top-class musicians, many of whom stayed with him for years, and toured all over the world throughout his life, composing wherever he went. He was among the most influential arrangers in jazz, and one of his many talents was the way in which he brought together instruments from different sections of the band, forming unusual sounds. He also wrote fully orchestrated works, and Stravinsky (p.150) cited him as an influence. He was also the first African-

1899 The Second Boer War begins between the British and the Boers of the African Transvaal and the Orange Free State in southern Africa. Although the British win, the war eventually leads to the creation of the modern state of South Africa.

1899 Tsar Nicholas II of Russia suggests setting up a court in The Hague in the Netherlands to decide disputes between different nations. The US Senate ratifies the decree a year later and the International Court of Arbitration is set up.

American composer to be commissioned to write film soundtracks. His best-known works include *Mood Indigo*, *In a Sentimental Mood*, and *Do Nothin' Til You Hear from Me*.

Jorge Luis BORGES
1899–1986
Argentine writer and poet

Jorge Luis Borges helped popularize South American fiction worldwide. He was born in Buenos Aires, son of a literary father. His first language was English, but he learned French and German in Geneva then joined the ultraist writing group in Spain. This was an extremely modern movement that rebelled against all traditional forms of poetry. Borges is credited with introducing ultraism to South America, but he later denied this. He returned to Buenos Aires in 1921 and wrote a series of poems celebrating the beauty and history of the city: *Fervour of Buenos Aires, Poems* (1923). After a severe illness, Borges's creativity accelerated and he began to write his famous fantasy-led short stories, collected in, among others, *Fictions* (1944 and 1946), *The Aleph* (1949), and *Death and the Compass* (1951). By 1955, Borges was too blind to write and instead dictated his work to friends and family.

Alfred HITCHCOCK
1899–1989
British film director

Generally acknowledged as the "master of suspense", Hitchcock was one of a few film directors whose name on a film could attract audiences as much as a movie star's. He started his career as a commercial artist but became a film director, making his name with films such as *The Thirty-nine Steps* (1935) and *The Lady Vanishes* (1938). He moved to Hollywood in 1940 and won an Academy Award for his first American film, *Rebecca* (1940). Hitchcock was renowned for his ability to build and maintain suspense using innovative camera work and editing techniques. He made such brilliant thrillers as *Dial M for Murder* (1954), *Rear Window* (1954), *Vertigo* (1958), *Psycho* (1960), and *The Birds* (1963). He always gave himself a small role in any film he made and his cameo appearances became a trademark.

HITCHCOCK FILM
Robert Donat and Madeleine Carroll starred in Alfred Hitchcock's film The Thirty-nine Steps.

Friedrich von HAYEK
1899–1992
Austrian economist

Friedrich von Hayek was born and educated in Vienna. He lectured at the London School of Economics before moving to Chicago during the 1950s. In his first and most famous book, *The Road to Serfdom* (1944), he attacked proposals for economic planning after World War II as being close to totalitarian government. He proposed that only the market-place could set prices and production levels effectively. Government intervention, he said, should be restricted to setting the supply of money so that inflation was stopped. These free-market, monetarist ideas were scorned at first, but found favour later with the US and British governments. He won the Nobel Prize for Economics in 1974.

1899 The French pronounce the country of Laos in Southeast Asia a French protectorate. They gained control of much of Laos following a successful blockade of Bangkok in 1893 and finally gain control of all of Laos in 1904.

1899 The Anglo-French Convention ends the tension surrounding the Fashoda incident in Sudan, Africa. Britain and France agree to limit expansion of their African empires, and in 1904, they sign the Entente Cordiale.

20th CENTURY

ALTHOUGH THE 20TH CENTURY was shaken by two world wars, as well as revolutions in Russia and China, it also saw the establishment of the United Nations and, in many societies, the guarantee of rights to oppressed groups. The exploration of space began, and astronauts landed on the Moon. There was also an increased interest in sports and entertainment, which were made more accessible by the advent of film, television, and, towards the end of the century, the computer revolution.

Kurt WEILL
1900–50
German composer

Kurt Weill's music covers orchestral and chamber pieces, including two symphonies, but he is best known for his stage operas with their social and comedic satire. He was born in Dessau and studied music in Berlin. In the 1920s, he was influenced by jazz and incorporated elements of popular and ragtime music in his own work. His collaboration with the playwright Bertolt Brecht (p.169) led to his first and most famous success, *The Threepenny Opera* (1928), and *The Rise and Fall of the City of Mahagonny* (1927–30), with its strong political message. In 1926, he married the singer Lotte Lenya. Because Weill was both a socialist and a Jew, his music was banned by the Nazis. He fled to Paris in 1933, where he composed *The Seven Deadly Sins* with Brecht, before settling in the USA as a composer of popular songs. His "Mack the Knife" has been covered by many popular artists, including Louis Armstrong and Ella Fitzgerald.

Frédéric & Irène JOLIOT-CURIE
1900–58, 1897–1956
Husband and wife French physicists

Frédéric Joliot was born in Paris and studied at the Ecole Supérieure de Physique et de Chimie Industrielle. He joined the Radium Institute in 1925 and became professor of nuclear physics at the Collège de France in 1937. Irène Curie was the daughter of Pierre (p.127) and Marie Curie (p.135) and was born and educated in Paris. She began work in her mother's Radium Institute in 1921 and, in 1926, married Joliot, one of her mother's pupils. She became a professor at the Sorbonne in 1937 and director of the Radium Institute in 1946. The couple worked closely together on radioactivity and the transmutation of elements, discovering, in 1934, that when they bombarded certain elements with alpha particles, radiation continued after the bombardment stopped. The alpha particles were producing a radioactive isotope of phosphorus not found in nature. For this discovery of artificial radioactivity, they were jointly awarded the Nobel Prize for Chemistry in 1935. Irène died of leukaemia caused by over-exposure to radioactivity, as her mother had done.

Dennis GABOR
1900–79
Hungarian-born British physicist

Gabor conceived of the idea of holography and invented a way of demonstrating it. He was born in Budapest and studied at the Budapest Technical University and then at Berlin, where he worked until he fled to Britain in 1933 to escape the Nazis. He was professor of applied electron physics at Imperial College, London. In 1947, Gabor invented the holographic method of three-dimensional photography and, in 1971, was awarded the Nobel Prize for Physics.

AYATOLLAH KHOMEINI
The name "ayatollah" means religious leader.

Charles RICHTER
1900–85
US seismologist

Charles Richter was educated at the University of Southern California. He became professor of seismology – the study of an earthquake's strength – at the California Institute of Technology in 1952. He introduced the Richter scale in 1935, originally to measure just local California earthquakes: the weakest ones were given a value of 0, and the scale went up in units that equalled a tenfold increase in the earthquake's magnitude. No earthquake has yet exceeded 9.

Ayatollah KHOMEINI
1900–89
Iranian leader

In 1979, Ayatollah Khomeini (originally Ruhollah Musawi) returned from exile to seize power in Iran after the pro-Western regime collapsed. He instigated the stormy "Islamic Revolution", which had a huge impact on everyday life in Iran. His fundamentalist rule unsettled Middle East politics as he "sponsored" Islamic terrorism, including the seizing of the US embassy and Western hostages. Khomeini soon became the *rahbar*, the absolute political and spiritual ruler of Iran. In 1980, he plunged the country into an eight-year war against its neighbour Iraq, which left up to a million dead. He provoked further Western unease in 1989 by declaring a *fatwa*, a death sentence (since revoked) on British author Salman Rushdie for his allegedly blasphemous book *The Satanic Verses*. Khomeini's death later that year sparked an outpouring of mass public grief.

1900 Psychologist Sigmund Freud publishes *The Interpretation of Dreams*. His theories about the unconscious lay the foundations for the modern science of psychoanalysis. His ideas have a profound impact on the understanding of the human mind.

1900 German inventor Ferdinand von Zeppelin builds the first airship named after him. Zeppelins are used as luxury passenger ships and as military craft. They are used by the German Army for reconnaissance work during World War I.

Aaron COPLAND
1900–90
US composer

Probably the best-known American composer of the 20th century, Copland was born in Brooklyn, New York. He was taught piano by his older sister and later studied music theory in New York. Like many composers of his generation, he then went to France to study with Nadia Boulanger, where he was influenced by the music of Stravinsky (p.150). When he returned to the USA, he worked as a teacher and composed music in the neo-classical style, with some elements of jazz, but developed his own style in pieces such as *Statements for Orchestra* (1935). In the 1940s, he adopted a more popular style using American folk tunes and produced the ballets *Billy the Kid* (1940), *Rodeo* (1942), and *Appalachian Spring* (1944), which established him as a distinctively American classical composer.

Enrico FERMI
1901–54
Italian-born US physicist

Enrico Fermi's experiments produced nuclear fission and opened up the possibilities of the atomic bomb and nuclear power. A child prodigy, Fermi attended the University of Pisa and was awarded his doctorate for a thesis on radioactivity. Between 1927 and 1933, he and his colleagues worked in atomic physics, which led them to split apart a uranium atom by bombarding it with neutrons. He was awarded the 1938 Nobel Prize for Physics and immediately left Italy for the USA. In 1942, he constructed the first US nuclear reactor in a basement squash court at the University of Chicago and produced the first controlled nuclear chain reaction there.

Clark GABLE
1901–60
US film star

A romantic leading film star, Clark Gable began his career in the movies with bit parts. While trying to break into acting, Gable worked in factories and oil fields. Eventually he was given starring roles and for many years he was the most popular leading man in cinema. He was known as the "King of Hollywood" and, for many people, epitomized American manhood and masculinity. He immortalized himself as Rhett Butler in one of Hollywood's most successful box-office hits, *Gone With the Wind* (1939), with the words, "Frankly my dear, I don't give a damn." While best remembered for his role in *Gone With the Wind*, he also starred

CLARK GABLE
In the film Gone with the Wind, Gable starred opposite Vivien Leigh, who played Scarlett O'Hara.

in *Mutiny on the Bounty* (1935), *San Francisco* (1936), *The Misfits* (1961), in which he played opposite Marilyn Monroe, and *It Happened One Night* (1934), for which he won an Academy Award.

Walt DISNEY
1901–66
US film animator and producer

The creator of Mickey Mouse, Donald Duck, and Disneyland was born in Chicago and began his career as a commercial artist. He set up his own studio and made his first Mickey Mouse film in 1928. He provided his own voice for Mickey. The film was a great success, and he went on to create other cartoon characters, among them Minnie Mouse, Donald Duck, Pluto, and Goofy. He had an instinctive awareness

1900 The King of Italy, Umberto I, called "Umberto the Good" by some people, is assassinated by an anarchist at Monza. It appears that the murder is in revenge for Umberto's instructions to crush a workers' rebellion in 1898.

1900 The World Exhibition, the biggest of its kind, opens in Paris in April. In the next few months, the second modern Olympic Games are also held in Paris. The new Métro underground system opens.

ALADDIN
The Disney company continued to produce animated films after Walt Disney's death, including Aladdin (1994), shown here.

LOUIS ARMSTRONG
The trumpet player was often seen with a handkerchief in one hand, ready to mop his sweating brow.

of popular taste, and provided entertainment for "children of all ages" throughout the world. His animated feature films include *Snow White and the Seven Dwarfs* (1937), *Fantasia* (1940), *Bambi* (1942), *Dumbo* (1940), and *Mary Poppins* (1964). In 1955, he realized a long-cherished ambition and built the theme park Disneyland in Anaheim, California.

Alberto GIACOMETTI
1901–66
Swiss sculptor

From 1935, Alberto Giacometti developed his own unmistakable sculpting style, refining the human form until he was left with thin and elongated figures. He achieved this by constructing a metal framework and adding clay to it before casting the whole in bronze: in contrast, most sculptors started with a mass of material and chiselled to find a form underneath. He was born in Stampa, the son of an Impressionist painter. After studying at art schools in Geneva and Italy, he settled in Paris in 1922 and trained as a sculptor. His early work was surrealist in tone, the best-known being *The Palace at 4 a.m.* (1935). Giacometti spent World War II in Geneva and returned to Paris in 1945. His finest work comes from this time, including the single figures *Man Pointing* (1947) and *Walking Man* (1960). With their blank faces and pitted surfaces, these stick-like humans convey a powerful sense of loneliness.

Achmed SUKARNO
1901–70
Indonesia's first president

Born in eastern Java, Sukarno became a political activist working for the independence of Indonesia from the Netherlands. He formed the Partai National Indonesia in 1927. During World War II, Sukarno co-operated with a local government set up by the Japanese to replace Dutch rule. After the war, in 1945, he became president of the new Indonesian Republic, becoming president for life in 1966. His power and popularity diminished at home and abroad as Indonesia became poor and chaotic, and Sukarno pursued a strongly anti-Western foreign policy. After surviving a communist coup in 1965, Sukarno was ousted from office by his former Chief of Staff, Suharto, in 1967.

Louis ARMSTRONG
1901–71
US jazz trumpeter and singer

Born in New Orleans – the breeding ground for early jazz – Armstrong watched brass bands as a child and was a professional trumpet player in his teens. He soon formed his own bands and began to make recordings. His unique talents turned him into the first individual star of popular music. He led numerous big bands during the 1930s and '40s and his instinctive understanding of harmony and phrasing made him one of the outstanding influences in popular music. He established his own style of playing in such numbers as *Potato Head Blues* (1927) and *West End Blues* (1928). He was known not only as an instrumentalist, but also as a singer. His most popular hits were *What a Wonderful World* and *Hello Dolly*. He appeared in many films, notably *High Society* (1956). He was often known by his nickname "Satchmo" – Satchel Mouth shortened.

Joe DAVIS
1901–78
English snooker player

Joseph Davis made snooker a popular sport in the 1920s. He was born in Derbyshire and, as a child, watched the clients at his father's hotel playing billiards. He went on to become a billiards and snooker champion, winning every title including the first world snooker championship in 1927 and the billiards championship the following year. Davis was unbeaten at snooker until he retired from world championship play in 1946. He continued to play both snooker and billiards and, in 1955, made the first snooker maximum break of 147. Considered by many to be the "Father of the game", Joe Davis was awarded an OBE in 1963. Joe and his brother Fred are the only players to have won both billiards and snooker world championships.

1901 The first Nobel Prizes are awarded. Established by the industrialist and inventor Alfred Nobel, they are intended for "Those who, during the preceding year, shall have conferred the greatest benefit on mankind".

1901 On 1 January, the Commonwealth of Australia is formed to unify the different states and give them one voice in social, economic, and defence affairs. Australia is now self-governing although it is still part of the British Empire.

Margaret MEAD
1901–78
US anthropologist

Margaret Mead challenged the conventions of Western society with her book *Coming of Age in Samoa* (1928). It was a study of the differences in temperament between Western and Samoan people. She argued that personality characteristics, especially as they differ between men and women, are shaped by cultural conditioning rather than heredity. She expanded on this subject in later works, making her valuable studies accessible to a wide audience. She had a strong personality and was outspoken on issues ranging from pollution to world hunger and drug abuse. A year after her death, she was awarded the Presidential Medal of Freedom.

Lee STRASBERG
1901–82
US theatre director and teacher

Strasberg taught many of Hollywood's top box-office stars from the late 1950s with his "method acting" technique – getting them to get "under the collar" of a character and to "live" the role. The result was a new realism not seen before on screen. He was born in Austria but emigrated to the USA as a child. He became an actor and stage manager with the Theatre Guild. In 1931, he helped to form the Group Theatre in New York, where he became involved in developing method acting. It deals with the psychology of interpretation in acting. Although he continued to direct and act throughout his life, Strasberg devoted a great deal of his time to training actors in the technique. Among the stars that he taught were Marlon Brando, James Dean, Paul Newman, Anne Bancroft, and Robert de Niro.

HIROHITO
1901–89
Japanese emperor

Hirohito was born in Japan and became regent in 1921, before succeeding to the imperial throne in 1926. The early years of his reign were marked by an aggressive military policy that led to the invasion of Manchuria in 1931, the invasion of China in 1937, and to war against the USA and Britain in 1941, following the bombing of Pearl Harbor. In 1945 Hirohito intervened for the first time in the conduct of the war to force the armed services to accept unconditional surrender: for

HIROHITO *This photo shows the emperor in the uniform of a lieutenant colonel.*

many Japanese this was the first time they had heard their emperor speak. In 1946, he renounced his divinity and accepted his new role as hereditary head of state in the newly democratic Japan. As such, Hirohito played an important part in transforming Japan from a military to an economic power in the period following World War II.

Linus PAULING
1901–94
US chemist

Pauling was the first man to win two unshared Nobel Prizes: one for chemistry in 1954, and one for peace in 1962. Pauling's work provided the first clear insight into the structure of all carbon compounds. His book *The Nature of the Chemical Bond* (1939) was highly influential in the study of chemistry. His investigations on immunology and sickle-cell anaemia were later confirmed. His work was also influential in the search for DNA. Pauling's criticism of nuclear arms policy made him unpopular for a time, particularly when he published *No More War!* in 1958. Pauling presented a petition to the UN signed by 11,021 scientists from 49 countries urging an end to the testing of nuclear weapons.

Bobby JONES
1902–71
US golfer

The son of an Atlanta attorney, Robert Tyre Jones was a sickly child and played golf to help him recover from illness. He later studied law, which he began practising in 1928. Always an enthusiastic amateur golfer – throughout his playing career he never turned professional and earned his living from his legal practice – Jones became one of the greatest players in the history of the game. He won the US Open Championship four times (1923, 1926, 1929, 1930) and the British Open three times (1926, 1927, 1930). In 1930, he won both the British and US Open and Amateur Championships in one year. At the age of 28, Jones retired from competitive golf and, in 1934, built his dream course in Georgia. It became the venue for the US Masters tournament. Following a spinal injury in 1948, he was confined to a wheelchair, but he continued designing golf courses.

Charles LINDBERGH
1902–74
US aviator

In 1927, Charles Augustus Lindbergh achieved world fame when he made the first-ever solo transatlantic flight from New York to Paris – in a Ryan monoplane, *The Spirit of St Louis*, in 33 hours 30 minutes. He was born in Detroit and worked as an air-mail pilot between St Louis and Chicago. After his daring non-stop crossing he was awarded the Congressional

1901 Booker T. Washington, a teacher and founder of the Tuskegee Institute, an educational centre for African Americans, becomes the first black man to dine at the White House.

1901 Queen Victoria dies aged 81 after a 63-year reign. Her own position and the alliances of her nine children relate her to the monarchs of six other European countries. Not only the "mother of Empire", she is the "grandmother of Europe".

Medal of Honour. Lindbergh later pioneered many of the first commercial airline routes. When World War II broke out in Europe he urged the USA to remain neutral. He was awarded a 1954 Pulitzer Prize for his autobiography, *The Spirit of St Louis*.

Richard RODGERS
1902–79
US composer

Rodgers' stage and film musicals remain a mainstay of popular entertainment around the world in the late 1990s. Richard Rodgers formed a working partnership with Lorenz Hart while still a university student, and they began to write musical shows together. He composed the music and Hart wrote the words. They moved away from traditional song and dance routines and were among the first to create musical dramas. Their greatest successes were *Babes in Arms* (1937), which includes the songs *The Lady is a Tramp* and *My Funny Valentine*, covered by many popular singers, and *Pal Joey* (1940), which includes *Bewitched, Bothered and Bewildered*. When Hart died in 1943, Rodgers started to collaborate with Oscar Hammerstein II and together they created a string of successful stage musicals such as *Oklahoma!* (1943), *South Pacific* (1949), *The King and I* (1951), and *The Sound of Music* (1959), all of which were turned into successful Hollywood films.

Ansel ADAMS
1902–84
US photographer

Ansel Adams first earned his living as a piano teacher, but in 1930, he became a full-time photographer and established his name with dramatic pictures of the American wilderness. Born in San Francisco, Adam was given his first camera at the age of 14 and began working part-time in a photographic shop. From 1920, he led expeditions in Yosemite National Park, California, and took many pictures there. Among these was *Monolith, the Face of Half Dome* (1927), which became one of his most famous photographs. He produced images of dramatic landscapes using "straight" techniques with large cameras and small apertures. Adams exhibited in New York in 1933 and wrote the manual *Making a Photograph* in 1935. In 1940, he helped to found the Department of Photography at New York's Museum of Modern Art and, in 1941, began a series of vast photo-murals including *Moonrise, Hernandez,* and *New Mexico* (1941). Adams helped photography to be accepted as an art form.

ANSEL ADAMS
A love of nature influenced Adams's photographs and spilled over into his work as a conservationist.

Fernand BRAUDEL
1902–85
French historian

Fernand Braudel transformed the study and writing of history in the 20th century. He was born in a small village in eastern France and educated at the Sorbonne in Paris. He then taught in Algeria, France, and Brazil before starting at the Ecole des Hautes Etudes in Paris in 1937. As a prisoner of war in Germany during World War II, Braudel wrote his famous history study – *The Mediterranean and Mediterranean World in the Age of Philip II* – entirely from memory in a prison camp. In 1948, he returned to the Ecole where he worked until his retirement in 1968. As an historian, Braudel rejected the traditional narrative history of events in favour of the *longue durée*, a global approach to history concerned with examining subjects from many different angles rather than just one. He thus considered geography, economics, population changes, technology, and many other subjects in order to get to grips with his theme. Braudel also wrote the three-volume *Capitalism and Material Life 1400–1800* (1967–80).

1902 In Egypt, the massive Aswan dam is completed after four years of work by 11,000 labourers. Its purpose is to hold the annual flood waters of the Nile and release them gradually for irrigation during the dry season.

1902 The UK and Japan make an alliance intended to preserve both nations' interests in China and Korea. Russia and China agree that Manchuria (a region of northeast China) be returned to Chinese control.

Barbara McCLINTOCK
1902–92
US geneticist

Barbara McClintock's research on the genetics of corn led her to the idea that some genes can control others and can move within the chromosome from generation to generation. This helped to explain how identical cells take on different functions as skin, muscle, bone, and nerve. It also explained how new species could evolve. She studied at Cornell University and conducted her research at the Carnegie Institution laboratory in New York. Her findings were ignored for many years, but in 1983 she received the Nobel Prize for Physiology and her research is now recognized as providing a breakthrough in the study of genetics.

Lou GEHRIG
1903–41
US baseball player

Lou Gehrig was one of the first American baseball players to achieve national hero status. A native New Yorker, Gehrig began his career with the New York Yankees in 1925. He was often overshadowed by his team-mate Babe Ruth (p.167), whom he followed in the Yankees' batting order. During the next 14 years he broke all baseball records, achieving a batting average of .340 and playing 2,130 consecutive league games. He took early retirement in 1939, when he began to feel that his physical strength was deteriorating. That same year he was diagnosed with a rare and fatal disease of the nervous system, which was officially named Lou Gehrig's Disease after his death in 1941.

Amy JOHNSON
1903–41
English aviator

Amy Johnson was a pioneer long-distance pilot of the 1930s. Born in Hull, she became the first woman to pass the test for the British Ground Engineer's Licence and, in 1930, became the first woman to fly solo from England to Australia. She married Jim Mollison – another aviator whose Australian record she had been trying to beat. The following year, she flew across Siberia to Japan and back. In 1932, and again in 1936, she flew from England to South Africa, on each occasion breaking records for the flight time. When World War II broke out, Amy joined the Women's Auxiliary Air Force, ferrying fighter planes from the factories to the aerodromes. She was killed when her plane went down over the Thames in bad weather.

George ORWELL
1903–50
English writer

George Orwell was born Eric Arthur Blair in Bengal, India. His father was a minor British official in the Indian Civil Service with little income. George won a scholarship to Eton, one of England's leading schools, where he was taught by Aldous Huxley. He refused to go to university, joining the Indian Civil Police in Burma instead. In 1927, ashamed of the British and their colonialism, he returned to Europe and began writing full-time. *Down and Out in Paris and London* (1933) was written after Orwell spent time in the slums and with the homeless, trying to atone for the racism that he had experienced in Burma. In 1945, Orwell wrote *Animal Farm*. The story of the pigs' ambitions, a clear and horrifying allegory of Stalin's (p.145) communist purges, made him world famous. *1984*, his last book, was published in 1949. It condemns dictatorships and describes a world where "Big Brother" is always watching you.

John von NEUMANN
1903–57
Hungarian-born US computer scientist

John (or Johann) von Neumann was a mathematician who developed computer theory, such as the notions of memory and random access, long before personal computers were invented. He was born in Budapest, and emigrated to the USA in 1930. In 1933 he became a member of the new Institute for Advanced Study at Princeton. In 1943 he was a consultant for the Manhattan Project, a programme for the construction of the nuclear bomb, and in 1954 a member of the Atomic Energy Commission. His most important mathematical work was on the theory of linear operators. During World War II, he studied computers and designed some of the earliest models. In his book *The Theory of Games and Economic Behaviour* (1944), he set out a theory that could be applied to games of chance and games of skill, such as chess.

Mark ROTHKO
1903–70
US painter

Rothko's development of "colour field" painting – expanses of intense colour on immense canvases – made him a major figure in 20th-century art. He was born in Latvia but his family settled in Oregon, USA, in 1913. His early subjects included animals, plants, and street scenes. In the late 1940s, he produced huge canvases covered with rectangular "fields" of colour. Rothko gave these colours simplified shapes and blurred edges and applied them in many thin layers, producing a soft, luminous effect that he hoped would convey basic human emotions. His works are often titled according to their colours, such as *Green on Blue* (1956), *Light Red over Black* (1957), and *Black on Maroon* (1958–59). He also created a group of murals for the chapel named after him in Houston, Texas (1967–69).

JOHNNY WEISSMULLER *was as famous for his portrayal of Tarzan in films as he was for his feats in the swimming pool.*

1902 The Prussian government in Germany forbids women from forming political associations.

Some months earlier, Norway had given women the right to vote, although this was still only in local elections.

1902 An exhibition of modern art, or "Art Nouveau", opens in Paris at the Société Nationale des Beaux-Arts. This new decorative style is characterized by curling patterns. It is used in architecture, interior design, and the applied arts.

LEAKEY FAMILY

**Louis 1903–72,
Mary 1913–96,
Richard 1944–
English palaeo-anthropologists**

The field work of this amazing family revealed that humans are far older than previously believed and their origins centred in Africa rather than Asia. Louis Leakey's parents were missionaries in Kenya, Africa. He took part in several archaeological expeditions in East Africa, where he made a study of the Kikuyu people and wrote a great deal on African anthropology – the study of people. In 1959, together with his wife, Mary, he discovered early pre-human fossils in East Africa. They unearthed the skull of *Zinjanthropus*, thought to be 1.7 million years old. In 1964, he found the remains of *Homo habilis*, an earlier form of being than our ancestor *Homo sapiens*, thought to be 2 million years old. He also unearthed evidence of human habitation in California that was more than 50,000 years old. Mary Leakey's fossil findings in East Africa also revolutionized ideas about human origins. Richard Leakey, their second son, was born un Africa and found his first fossil bone at the age of six. He became a distinguished palaeo-anthropologist, studying the origins of the human species. He also discovered the remains of *Homo erectus* on the eastern shores of Lake Turkana, Africa. He later worked in wildlife conservation and ran Kenya's game reserves.

Johnny WEISSMULLER

**1903–84
US swimmer and actor**

From swimming champion to screen idol, Peter John Weissmuller was born in Freidorf, Romania, the son of Austrian parents. When he was four years old, the family emigrated to the USA. He had an athletic build and soon became a strong swimmer. In 1922, Weissmuller made history when he became the first man to swim 100 metres in under a minute and later 400 metres in under five minutes. He won five gold medals in the 1924 and 1928 Olympics and in 1932 became a professional swimmer. His athleticism led to his being cast as Tarzan in a Hollywood film about the "King of the Jungle". Eighteen Tarzan films later, Weissmuller had established himself as one of the most popular film stars.

Barbara HEPWORTH

**1903–75
English sculptor**

Hepworth's work was influenced by the rolling hills of her home county of Yorkshire. She saw the shaping of wood and stone as echoing the natural forces which shaped the landscape. Her sculptures were mostly abstract. *Hollow Form with White Interior* (1963) is smoothly polished on the outside but roughly chiselled inside. Some works are strung with cord or wire, such as *Pelagos* (1946).

Konrad LORENZ

**1903–89
Austrian zoologist**

The study of animals was Lorenz's life's work. Whenever possible, he studied animals in their natural environment, while most of his contemporaries studied them in laboratories. He had some eccentric working practices – such as talking to goose eggs so that when they hatched, the goslings would respond to his voice – but he got results. He did a lot of work on the influence of external stimulants on animals and, in 1935, he published his studies on the behaviour of young birds. He noted how they learn to respond to parents at a very early stage. In 1973, he won the Nobel Prize for Physiology.

1903 In Bulgaria (part of the Ottoman Empire at the time), 50,000 people are massacred when Turkey sends 240,000 troops to stop an uprising in Macedonia. The area was later divided between Greece and Serbia.

1903 Police turn a blind eye while Russian peasants in Kishinev attack the homes and businesses of the 50,000 Jews that make up half the city's population. The pogrom is sparked off by the alleged murder of a Christian boy.

Tunku ABDUL RAHMAN
1903–90
Malaysian prime minister

Independent Malaya's and later Malaysia's first prime minister, Abdul Rahman was born in Kedah when Malaya was still part of the British Empire. He studied law at Cambridge University and entered the civil service in Kedah in 1931. In 1945, he founded the United Malay's National Organization and in 1952 he was elected to the executive and legislative councils of the Federation of Malaya. He became chief minister in 1955 and prime minister when the country became independent in 1957 (not to be confused with Tuanku or "Paramount Ruler" Abdul Rahman who became head of state). Rahman negotiated the formation of the Federation of Malaysia, including Singapore, Sarawak, and Shaib and remained prime minister of the largest nation when it was established in 1963. After the outbreak of violent riots between Chinese and Malays in Kuala Lumpur, Rahman retired from his post.

Charles Richard DREW
1904–50
US surgeon

Drew was a black US surgeon whose most important discovery was that blood plasma has a longer life than whole blood and therefore is the best part to use for transfusion. He was born in Washington D.C. and studied medicine. He became a professor of medicine at Howard University Medical School in 1942. In 1939, he set up a blood bank for use in transfusions and during World War II he was in charge of collecting blood for British Army casualties. In 1941, he was put in charge of the American Red Cross blood bank in New York, which collected blood for the US army. He resigned when the Red Cross decided to segregate blood according to the race of the donor.

ROBERT OPPENHEIMER *was awarded the Enrico Fermi award in 1963.*

(Julius) Robert OPPENHEIMER
1904–67
US nuclear physicist

J. Robert Oppenheimer was was born in New York and studied in the USA, England, Germany, and Switzerland. He became assistant professor at the California Institute of Technology in 1929 and, in 1942, was made director of the Los Alamos laboratory in New Mexico, which was working on the construction of the atomic bomb. He resigned from this post in 1945 after achieving the first successful nuclear explosion. He went on to become chairman of the advisory committee to the US Atomic Energy Commission. When he realized the dangers of radioactivity, Oppenheimer campaigned for international control of atomic energy. He strongly objected to the further development of the hydrogen bomb on moral grounds. In 1953, he was accused of being a security risk and was suspended by the Atomic Energy Commission. His case became an international *cause célèbre.*

Pablo NERUDA
1904–73
Chilean poet

Known as the People's Poet, Neruda was born Neftalí Ricardo Reyes Basoalto in Parral, Chile. He began to write poetry at age ten and took the pen name of Pablo Neruda to disguise authorship. In 1923, he published his first collection of poems, *Crepusculario.* His next book, *Twenty Love Poems and a Song of Despair* (1924), was a huge success. He became a militant communist, was exiled from Chile, and visited Russia, where he was given the Stalin Prize. Neruda returned to Chile in 1952 and, in 1971, was awarded the Nobel Prize for Literature. His love poems remain passionate, but other poems recall his isolation.

Count BASIE
1904–84
US jazz musician and band leader

William Basie led a jazz big-band called the Count Basie Orchestra from the late 1930s. It became internationally famous for its

1903 Army officers burst into the royal palace and assassinate the king and queen of Serbia. King Alexander had repealed the liberal constitution and replaced it with a more reactionary one.

1903 In Britain, Emmeline Pankhurst sets up the Women's Social and Political Union to fight for women's right to vote. Women attend demonstrations and some go on hunger strike in support.

easy swing style, and jazz and blues rhythms and tones. Basie was born in New Jersey and began his career playing the piano in Harlem dance halls. He acquired his nickname when he was doing a radio broadcast with a group called the Barons of Rhythm and the DJ called him "count". Basie became leader of his own band with which he performed for nearly 20 years. The band recorded with Ella Fitzgerald and Frank Sinatra. Basie was also a composer. His most popular pieces are "One O'Clock Jump" and "Jumpin' at the Woodside".

Ding
LING
1904–86
Chinese writer

Ding Ling (or Ting Ling), one of China's most popular contemporary authors, was born Jiang Bingzhi in the Hunan province of China. In 1921, she went to Shanghai, developing strong opinions on women's rights. Moving to Beijing, she fell in love and then lived with a struggling poet, Hu Yeh-p'in, who, as a communist, was arrested by Nationalists and executed in 1931. Ding Ling also joined the Communist Party and began writing for left-wing literary magazines. In 1931, she published a novel, *Shui (Flood)*, which was much acclaimed. Despite this, Ding Ling was imprisoned in 1933, but she escaped in 1936 and joined the communists under Mao Zedong (p.164). In 1948, she wrote her best-known book, *The Sun Shines over the Sanggan River*, which won the Soviet Union's Stalin Prize. In 1970, during China's Cultural Revolution (Mao's purge of old-guard communists), Ding Ling was again imprisoned, this time for five years. It was not until 1979 that she regained popularity.

Frederick
ASHTON
1904–88
English ballet dancer and choreographer

Frederick Ashton became interested in ballet after seeing Anna Pavlova dance in Peru, where he was brought up. (He was born in Ecuador.) He moved to London and studied under Marie Rambert, and became resident choreographer and principal dancer of the Vic-Wells company (later the Sadler's Wells Ballet and then the Royal Ballet). He eventually succeeded Ninette de Valois as director of the Royal Ballet company. Ashton created a great many ballets, both traditional and abstract, and was widely considered to be the leading British choreographer of his day. His best known works include *Cinderella* (1948), *La Fille Mal Gardée* (1960), *The Dream* (1964), and *Rhapsody* (1980), and he choreographed and acted in the film *The Tales of Beatrix Potter* (1971). Although Ashton created new ballets for young dancers, for many years Margot Fonteyn was his favourite dancer and in 1963 he created Marguerite and Armand especially for Fonteyn and Rudolf Nureyev. He was knighted in 1962.

FREDERICK ASHTON *with Claire Luce in the ballet* The First Shoot

Isamu
NOGUCHI
1904–88
US sculptor

The son of a Japanese poet, Noguchi was born in Los Angeles, brought up in Japan, and attended school back in the USA. He began training in sculpture in 1922, moving to Paris in 1927. By 1928, he was constructing works from sheet metal, stone, and wood. Noguchi visited China and Japan from 1931–32, where he was influenced by local pottery and garden design. Back in the USA, he broadened his range of work, creating ballet and theatre sets, playgrounds, public sculptures, and murals. Among the finest of his works are the sculptures *Endless Coupling* (1957) and *Red Cube* (1968), concrete bridges for the Hiroshima Peace Park (1951), and *Monument to Ben Franklin* (1984).

Vladimir
HOROWITZ
1904–89
Russian pianist

Horowitz was famous for his virtuoso piano playing. He played a wide range of music, from Liszt to Prokofiev and Rachmaninoff. He was born in Kiev in the Ukraine and studied at the conservatory there. He began giving concerts while in his early 20s and astounded audiences with the flawless quality of his playing. In 1930, he gave a performance of a Rachmaninoff concerto in London with the London Symphony Orchestra that has become legendary. While touring in the USA, he decided to settle there and became a US citizen in 1944. He largely retired, but played in concerts on occasion and performed in Russia in 1986.

1904 In an attempt to prevent an alliance with Russia, British troops enter Lhasa in Tibet and force the Dalai Lama to make an exclusive treaty with them. They kill many unarmed Tibetans.

1904 The African Herero people kill 123 German colonists in protest at losing grazing lands and water sources to German settlers. Then, 14,000 troops crush the rebellion and drive the Herero people into the desert.

Salvador DALI
1904–89
Spanish artist

The painter who created dream-like worlds where clocks melted like cheese and a sleeping face balanced on crutches, was Salvador Dali. Many of his later paintings reflect the barren landscape of Catalonia. After 1929, he became one of the leading painters in the Surrealist style, which placed familiar images in unfamiliar situations. Dali's *Accommodation of Desire* (1929), *The Persistence of Memory* (1931), and *Sleep* (1937) are among the best-known Surrealist works. He also co-created, with director Luis Buñuel, the Surrealist film, *Un Chien Andalou* (1929).

SALVADOR DALI
Dali's nightmarish paintings and eccentric lifestyle made him famous throughout the world.

SURREALISM

Surrealism was a new movement in art and literature that emerged after World War I. The term "surrealism" was first used by the French poet ANDRÉ BRETON (1896–1966) in 1924, with the publication of *The Surrealist Manifesto*. The word "surreal" means "super real", and describes a way of looking at the world that is above or beyond reality.

THE MOVEMENT
The Surrealists claimed to create art through imaginative impulse or even by accident. Familiar objects and figures were painted in great detail and placed in unlikely settings.

THE INSPIRATION
The style emerged from the "anti-art" Dada movement. The Surrealists saw the subconscious as the source of imagination and much of their art tried to recreate the world of dreams. The movement was also inspired by the psychoanalyst SIGMUND FREUD (p.116), whose work on the analysis of dreams had a profound influence on Surrealist artists. Salvador Dali once described his paintings as "hand-painted dream photographs".

THE ARTISTS
Famous Surrealist painters include MAX ERNST (1891–1976), JOAN MIRÓ (1893–1983), and RENÉ MAGRITTE (1898–1967). Their work proved highly influential in the world of modern art.

Sleep (1937) by Salvador Dali

In 1937, he was expelled from the Surrealists, partly because of his support for Franco during the Spanish Civil War. He lived in the USA until 1955.

B. F. SKINNER
1904–90
US psychologist and writer

Burrhus Frederic Skinner invented the "Skinner box", an enclosed box in which the process of learned behaviour can be observed. In the box, a rat presses a lever and learns to repeat the behaviour because it is rewarded with food. Skinner also designed a "baby box", a controlled soundproof environment in which young children can be observed. His own daughter was partly raised in such a box until the age of two. He argued that an ideal society can be achieved only if human behaviour is modified using conditioning – learning certain patterns of behaviour. Skinner wrote a popular novel, *Walden II*, to support his ideas.

Graham GREENE
1904–91
English novelist

Graham Greene was one of the great voices of 20th-century literature. He was born in Berkhamsted and went to the school there where his father was headmaster. He later began work as a journalist for *The Times* newspaper in 1926 and converted to Catholicism the same year. His religion was to have a major influence on his work, which often dealt with the conflict between good and evil – *The Power and the Glory* (1940), *The Heart of the Matter* (1948), and *The Quiet American* (1955) all explore this theme. Although many critics consider his novels to contain an underlying sadness, Greene himself described many of his books, such as *The Man Within* (1929) and *The Honorary Consul* (1973) as "entertainments". One of Greene's most famous characters is Pinkie, the amoral gang-leader from the novel *Brighton Rock* (1938).

1904
Japan mounts a surprise attack on the Russian fleet off the coast of Korea. The Japanese follow up the attack by declaring war on Russia and sending forces into Korea. They march unopposed towards the capital, Seoul.

1905
The Sinn Fein party is founded in Ireland. Its name means "Ourselves Alone". The aim of members of the party is to secure full independence for Ireland from Britain and create an Irish republic.

Deng
XIAOPING
1904–97
Chinese political leader

Deng Xiaoping (Teng Hsiao-p'ing) was born in Sichuan province. While a student in Paris, he met Zhou Enlai and joined the Chinese Communist Party (CCP). In 1934, Deng Xiaoping took part in the Long March, led by Mao Zedong (p.164). In the 1960s, he entered the CCP Politburo, or government, under President Liu Shaoqi. In the Cultural Revolution, Deng was branded a state enemy and sent to work in a factory. He was rescued by Zhou Enlai, who was prime minister, and took over from him after Zhou Enlai's heart attack. He became deeply unpopular when he allowed the Chinese army to massacre more than 2,000 demonstrators in Tiananmen Square, Beijing, in 1989. He officially retired from politics shortly afterwards, but maintained an advisory role.

John
GIELGUD
1904–
English actor

Gielgud is one of the finest Shakespearean actors of the 20th century. He was born in London, studied drama at the Royal Academy of Dramatic Art (RADA), and made his debut at the Old Vic theatre when he was 17 years old. His performance of Hamlet in 1929 established his reputation as an actor. He performed all over the world with his one-man show, *The Ages of Man*, and has performed in and produced a variety of plays and appeared in many film and television dramas. He received a knighthood in 1953, and won an Academy Award for his comedy role in *Arthur* (1980).

1905

Christian
DIOR
1905–57
French fashion designer

Christian Dior made Parisian fashions the most popular and profitable in the world in the post-war years. His outfits needed so much material that women could not adapt their wartime clothes to match and the fashion conscious had to buy a new wardrobe. Dior was born in Granville. He trained as a diplomat, but by the 1930s, was working as a fashion artist for the weekly magazine *Figaro Illustré*. He became a designer for Parisian fashion houses in 1938 and, after World War II, set up his own company, financed by a textiles manufacturer. His first collection of "New Look" clothing in 1947 made him instantly successful. After the austerity of wartime, women were eager to wear clothes that were elegant and feminine.

Jean-Paul
SARTRE
1905–80
French writer, playwright, and philosopher

A major philosopher of the 20th century, Jean-Paul Sartre was born and brought up in Paris. He studied at the Sorbonne before teaching in France and Berlin. He formed a lifelong relationship with Simone de Beauvoir (p.189) although neither believed in marriage. In Paris, Sartre published the novel *Nausea* (1938) in which the main character becomes increasingly revolted by all material things, including his own body. After the war, Sartre became more concerned with social responsibility, writing novels such as *The Age of Reason* (1945). He also wrote plays, including *The Flies* (1943). Sartre supported the student rebellion in Paris in the 1960s and campaigned against the war in Vietnam. In 1964, following publication of his autobiography, *The Words* (1963), Sartre won the Nobel Prize for Literature, but he refused it.

DIOR MODEL
As shown by this outfit, Christian Dior designed for small waists, full bosoms, and sloping shoulders.

Greta
GARBO
1905–90
Swedish film star

Greta Gustafsson began her career in Sweden. She moved to Hollywood in 1925 and became one of the most popular silent-movie stars. When talkies were introduced, audiences adored her husky voice and accent. Garbo retired from films in 1941 after *Two-Faced Woman* was given bad reviews. For the next 40 years she lived a private life and became a legendary recluse. Her famous remark, "I want to be alone", was actually said by her character in *Grand Hotel* (1932). Her best-known films include *Anna Karenina* (1935), *Queen Christina* (1933), and *Camille* (1936).

1905 Mutiny erupts on board the Russian battleship *Potemkin* when the first lieutenant shoots a sailor who complains about the food. Workers in Odessa, where the ship is docked go on an all-out strike.

1905 Japan beats Russia in war to gain control of Manchuria, an area rich in resources, formerly ruled by the Chinese Manchu dynasty. Japan also annexes the independent state of Korea.

Michael TIPPETT
1905–97
English composer

A London-born composer of international repute, Michael Tippett studied at the Royal College of Music and worked as a teacher and conductor but composed little until in his thirties. His first major success was the oratorio *A Child of our Time* (1941), a moving depiction of Jewish oppression in Nazi Germany. A life-long pacifist, Tippett was imprisoned as a conscientious objector in World War II. After the war, he became internationally known for his chamber music, especially the six string quartets and orchestral pieces, which include four symphonies, and the oratorio *The Mask of Time* (1982). He also wrote a number of operas including *The Midsummer Marriage* (1955) and *The Knot Garden* (1970). He was knighted in 1966 and awarded the Order of Merit in 1983.

Puyi
1906–67
Last Chinese emperor

Puyi (P'u-i) was born in China and became emperor as Xuan Tong (Hsuan T'ung) in 1908 at the age of two. Overthrown by the Chinese Revolution in 1911, Puyi was given a pension and continued to live in the imperial palace in Beijing with extensive privileges. However, his presence served as a focus for pro-monarchist forces, who restored him to the throne for 12 days in 1917. In 1924, he was forced to flee and seek Japanese protection. In 1932

he became the nominal ruler of Manchuria, the puppet state set up by the Japanese in northern China. Deposed and captured by Russian forces in 1945, he was tried in China as a war criminal in 1950, pardoned in 1959, and became a private citizen. His death marked the end of the 2,000-year-old imperial era of China.

THE CHILD EMPEROR
Puyi's life was chronicled in the film The Last Emperor *(1987).*

Dmitri SHOSTAKOVICH
1906–75
Russian composer

Dmitri Shostakovich earned an international reputation as a composer with his *Symphony No.1* (1926), written while still a student. Born in St Petersburg he was taught first by his mother and then studied at the Conservatory. Despite his early success, he was soon in trouble with the authorities over his operas *The Nose* (1930) and *A Lady Macbeth of Mtensk* (1934), which Stalin found "anti-Soviet". Shostakovich wrote his *Symphony No.5* (1937) in a more acceptable style as "a reply to just criticism". During World War II he was in Leningrad at the time of the siege, which inspired his *Symphony No.7*. Still occasionally clashing with the authorities, he became the leading Soviet composer, writing 15 string quartets, several concertos (two each for piano, violin, and cello), and some film music; but he is best-known for his symphonies, some of the finest of the 20th century.

John HUSTON
1906–87
US film director

Huston's father was a celebrated actor and John spent his early life touring with his parents. He worked in a variety of jobs, including a spell as a professional boxer and a competitive horseman in Mexico. Eventually he took up writing, beginning as a journalist but later turning to screenplays. In 1941, he directed his first film, the detective thriller *The Maltese Falcon*, starring Humphrey Bogart (p.171), which made his

(and Bogart's) name. He went on to act in and direct many films including classics such as *The Treasure of the Sierra Madre* (1948) – which won several Academy Awards – *The African Queen* (1952), *The Misfits* (1961), and *Prizzi's Honour* (1985). His daughter Angelica Huston continues the acting dynasty.

Alec ISSIGONIS
1906–88
British automotive designer and engineer

Sir Alec Issigonis changed the face of motoring when he designed the Morris Minor car in 1948 and the Mini Minor in 1959. Previously, motor cars had been large and unaffordable to most British people. His Morris Minor became the first British car to sell a million. Issigonis had Turkish parents but his mother brought him to England after World War I, where he went to technical college and later worked for Morris Motors. Issigonis wanted to create a vehicle that was a convenient size and affordable to everyone. The Mini was launched in 1959 with major design innovations, including rubber suspension and gears located in the oil pan. It is still one of the most popular small cars.

Grace HOPPER
1906–92
US computer scientist

Grace Hopper made a major impact on computers' coming of age. She was educated at Vasser and Yale, and during World War II, she volunteered for duty with the Naval Office Computation Project. In 1945, she was sent to Harvard University to assist

---

1905 At least 5,000 people are killed or injured when Tsar Nicholas II orders his troops to open fire on workers in St Petersburg. The workers had been petitioning for an improvement in their working conditions.

1905 A group of young artists led by Henri Matisse hold an exhibition in Paris. Their use of bold, bright colours leads to the name by which the group came to be called – Les Fauves, meaning "wild beasts".

MINI
This small car was an icon of the 1960s and remains a design classic.

Howard Aiken in the building of a computer. She created the first computer language and the compiler necessary to translate it into a form that the computer could work with. In 1959, she was invited to join a Pentagon team attempting to create a single, simple computer language for commercial use. This led to the invention of COBOL, still one of the most widely used computer languages.

Rachel CARSON
1907–64
US biologist

Rachel Carson was a key figure in making people aware of the effects of pollution on the environment in the latter half of the 20th century. Her first book, *The Sea Around Us* (1951), was a bestseller and won several literary awards. It was followed by *The Edge of the Sea* (1955) – an ecological study of the seashore. Her most famous book, *Silent Spring*, published in 1962, attacked the indiscriminate use of pesticides. It inspired a raised awareness in the public and the first environmental movements were established.

W. H. AUDEN
1907–73
Anglo-US poet

Wystan Hugh Auden was born in Yorkshire, and his first poem was published when he was 17 and at Oxford University he belonged to a group of revolutionary intellectuals where he made his name as a witty social commentator. *Poems* was published in 1930, followed by *Look Stranger!* (1936). Whilst earning his living as a teacher, Auden continued to write and publish verse, often in partnership with his friends, in particular Christopher Isherwood and Louis MacNeice. In 1939, he settled in the USA and was naturalized in 1946. Auden's output was immense and his poems include the popular "Funeral Blues", "Tell Me the Truth About Love", "As I Walked out one Evening", and "In Memory of W.B. Yeats". Auden's poetry received a boost and new audience when it was recited in the film *Four Weddings and a Funeral* (1994).

John WAYNE
1907–79
US film star

The man who was born Marion Morrison in Iowa came to epitomise on screen the tough guy, the gritty cowboy, the patriotic US soldier. He had a summer job at the Fox Film Corporation and struck up a friendship with the director John Ford. He assumed the name Wayne in 1930 and was given bit parts in several films. He became a star after John Ford cast him as the lead in *Stagecoach* (1939), in which he played the familiar tough, fearless, but warm-hearted character for which he became famous. Other notable Westerns include *Red River* (1948), *The Searchers* (1956), *True Grit* (1969), for which he won an Oscar, and his last film *The Shootist* (1976). "The Duke" or "Big John", as he was known, appeared in more than 150 feature films, and was loved by cinema audiences the world over. When he died, the US Congress authorized a special gold medal to be struck in his honour.

Georges HERGÉ
1907–83
Belgian cartoonist

The cartoon-strip boy detective Tin-Tin and his faithful dog Snowy came from the pen of Hergé – the pen name of Georges Rémi, who was born near Brussels. His first cartoon strip was *Totor*, in 1926, for a boy scouts' weekly publication. Tin-Tin, the boy-hero with whom Hergé is forever linked, first appeared in the children's supplement to *Le Vingtième Siècle* and was published as a book in 1930: *Tin-Tin in the Land of the Soviets*. Twenty-two books followed, selling more than 25,000,000 copies. The name Hergé was derived from his initials, RG.

TIN-TIN
The popular hero is shown setting out on an adventure with his dog, Snowy.

1906 French army captain Alfred Dreyfus, a Jew convicted of treason as a result of anti-Semitism, is re-tried and cleared of all charges. He returns to the French army after spending 11 years in prison.

1906 In the USA, a violent earthquake hits the city of San Francisco in northern California. A fire started by the quake sweeps the city, razing it to the ground. At least 1,000 people die in the disaster.

Nikolaas TINBERGEN
1907–88
Dutch-born British zoologist

Along with Konrad Lorenz (p.181), Tinbergen pioneered the study of animals' behaviour in relation to their environment. He specialized in the study of instinctive behaviour. In *The Study of Instinct* (1951), Tinbergen showed that the aggressive behaviour of the male three-spined stickleback is stimulated by the red colour on the underside of other males during the mating season. He also demonstrated that the courtship dance of the male is stimulated by the sight of the swollen stomach of the female when it is ready to lay eggs. In *The Herring Gull's World* (1953), he describes the social behaviour of gulls, highlighting the importance of stimulus response in territorial behaviour. In 1973, he shared the Nobel Prize for Medicine with Konrad Lorenz and Karl von Frisch.

Laurence OLIVIER
1907–89
English actor and director

Olivier was one of the most outstanding stage and film actors of his generation. He was born in Surrey and studied at the Central School of Dramatic Art. After touring with a repertory company, he joined the Old Vic theatre company and performed in Shakespeare's *Hamlet*. Olivier went to the USA and became famous with his roles in *Wuthering Heights* (1939) and *Rebecca* (1939). In 1944, he produced, directed, and starred in *Henry V*. He continued to develop Shakespearean theatre and also directed and starred in non-Shakespearean productions such as *The Prince and the Showgirl* (1957). In 1962, he became the first director of the National Theatre in London. He was the first actor to receive a knighthood (1947) and life peerage (1970). In the 1980s, his television performances in *Voyage Round My Father* and *Brideshead Revisited* attracted new audiences.

Frank WHITTLE
1907–96
English engineer

Frank Whittle produced the first British jet engine. In place of an engine with a propeller, his engine was a rocket, or gas turbine, that had already been in development for some 20 years. He was born in Coventry and joined the British Royal Air Force (RAF) as a trainee. He tried to persuade the RAF that gas-turbine jet propulsion was the future for aviation and, in 1930, patented the basic design for the turbo-jet engine; but the RAF was not interested at that time. Whittle continued his work on jet propulsion and, in May 1941, the *Gloster E 28/39* first flew with the Whittle jet engine. With the outbreak of World War II, the RAF backed Whittle's work and, by 1944, jets were in RAF service. His jet engine went on to power many modern aeroplanes.

Frank Whittle with a Proteus turbo-jet engine

Ian FLEMING
1908–64
English writer

The creator of the British Secret Service Agent 007, James Bond, was born in London. After attending military college at Sandhurst, Ian Lancaster Fleming studied languages overseas, then worked as a journalist in Moscow. He then became a banker and stockbroker and, during World War II, he was a high-ranking naval intelligence officer. After the war, Fleming published his first James Bond novel, *Casino Royale* (1953). This was followed by 11 more 007 novels, which together sold more than 18 million copies around the world, among them *From Russia with Love* (1957), *Dr No* (1958), and *Goldfinger* (1959). The Bond films, based loosely on Fleming's dashing British spy and his glamorous adventures, were equally successful. Fleming also wrote *Chitty Chitty Bang Bang* (1964), which became a classic children's film when Roald Dahl wrote the screenplay.

JAMES BOND
The first and most famous film version of 007 was Sean Connery.

Lyndon Baines JOHNSON
1908–73
36th US president

LBJ was born in Texas into a Baptist family. He qualified as a teacher then worked as a congressman's secretary before being elected as a Democrat candidate in 1937. He was elected senator in 1948 and became vice president in 1960.

1907 In South Africa, Indian-born lawyer Mohandas Gandhi begins a campaign of civil disobedience against a law that requires Indian residents to carry passes. He is arrested and jailed many times.

1907 The islands of New Zealand become an independent dominion within the British Empire. Although a British colony since 1840, New Zealand has been largely self-governing since 1856.

Having been sworn in as president after John F. Kennedy's assassination, Johnson became president in his own right with a landslide victory in the election of 1964. During his administration, the Civil Rights Act introduced by Kennedy was passed in 1964 as well as the Voting Rights Act, both of which made improvements to the lives of African-Americans. Under the slogan "The Great Society", he introduced a series of economic and social reforms, including the Medicare programme for the aged and measures to improve education. From 1965 on, his presidency was clouded by the war in Vietnam, which led to a decline in his popularity. In 1968, he retired from politics.

Simone
DE BEAUVOIR
1908–86
French writer, socialist, and feminist

Simone de Beauvoir is principally remembered for her two-volume *The Second Sex* (1949): a classic feminist work demanding equality of the sexes. She was born in Paris and educated at the Sorbonne, where she met Jean-Paul Sartre (p.185), the famous philosopher and writer with whom she had a life-long relationship. De Beauvoir taught for 12 years before writing full-time. Her scholarly *The Second Sex* was a social and historic study of the role of women and the need to banish certain myths of femininity. Described by early feminists as "the mother of us all", de Beauvoir's courage and intelligence is remarkable: her life reflected her works and beliefs in every way. Many of her novels are auto-biographical, among them *Memories of a Dutiful Daughter* (1959) and *Adieux: A Farewell to Sartre* (1981).

Bette
DAVIS
1908–89
US film star

Best-known for playing very intense and often unlikeable celluloid characters and for her clipped way of talking, Bette Davis relied on her forceful character rather than beautiful looks to establish her film reputation. Born Ruth Elizabeth Davis in Massachusetts, she changed her name to Bette as a young girl. She began by acting in small repertory companies and eventually made her way to Hollywood. Her film debut was in *The Bad Sister* (1931), in which she co-starred with Humphrey Bogart (p.171). But it was her role as Mildred in *Of Human Bondage* (1934) that made her a star. She won Academy Awards for *Dangerous* (1935) and *Jezebel* (1938) and critical acclaim for *All About Eve* (1950) and finally *Whatever Happened to Baby Jane?* (1962), in which she terrorized her crippled sister, who was played by Joan Crawford.

Bette Davis was first hired by Universal Studios in 1931.

Herbert
VON KARAJAN
1908–89
Austrian conductor

A child prodigy on the piano, Herbert von Karajan was born, grew up, and studied in Salzburg. He began his conducting career in Ulm and Aachen in Germany, then made his name conducting the Berlin State Opera. He joined the Nazi party in 1933 and was not permitted to work after World War II until 1947. He survived his association with the Nazis and was made principal conductor of the Berlin Philharmonic Orchestra in the mid-1950s. He was artistic director at the Salzburg Festival and often conducted at the Vienna State Opera and other major opera houses and orchestras all over the world.

Olivier
MESSIAEN
1908–92
French composer

Olivier Messiaen was born in Avignon and studied at the Paris Conservatory. He was organist of La Trinité in Paris and wrote many pieces for the organ. His fascination with birdsong and eastern rhythms is reflected in the *Quartet for the End of Time* (1941), which he wrote while he was a prisoner of war in Germany. The quartet was first performed at the prison camp. On his release, he became a professor at the Paris Conservatory and married one of his students, Yvonne Loriod. His interest in birdsong can be heard in the *Catalogue des Oiseaux* (1958) for piano and the orchestral piece *Oiseaux exotiques* (1956). It is combined with his profound Catholicism in the opera *St François d'Assise* (1983).

1908 Austria annexes Bosnia and Herzegovina with Russian approval. The Serbs demand the return of these territories, which they had controlled for about 600 years. Austria arms itself in readiness for war.

1908 France and Spain recognize Moulay Hafid as the new Sultan of Morocco in northwest Africa. Hafid promises to control tribal uprisings and to cooperate with the international powers.

Stéphane
GRAPPELLI
1908–98
French jazz violinist

With his group called the Quintette du Hot Club de Paris, co-led by the Belgian gypsy virtuoso guitarist Django Reinhardt, violinist Stéphane Grappelli brought a European influence into jazz music. He was born in Paris and trained as a classical musician but turned to jazz in his twenties. Reinhardt and Grappelli made many recordings and performed all over the world. Their recordings are jazz standards with their bright, swing-based style and lyrical, sweet tone. Grappelli also made some recordings with the great violinist Yehudi Menuhin (p.198). His urbane and sociable manner made him a popular guest on television chat shows.

Don
BRADMAN
1908–
Australian cricketer

Donald Bradman, an Australian stockbroker from Cootamundra, New South Wales, is considered to be one of the greatest batsman in the history of the game. As a boy, he practised playing cricket on his own, hitting a soft ball against a corrugated water tank. His well-trained eye took him on to score 28,067 runs. From 1928–48 Bradman played cricket for Australia and captained the team from 1936–48. During his career, he played in 52 Test matches and had an astonishing average in Test matches of 99.94 runs per

innings, itself a record. (His average would have been over 100 had he not been bowled for 0 in his last Test innings as captain of Australia in 1948.) He made 117 centuries and his score of 452 not out against Queensland in 1929–30 was a record for nearly 30 years. In 1949, Bradman was knighted for his contribution to cricket. In retirement, he acted as chairman of the Australian Cricket Board from 1960–63 and 1969–72.

Henri
CARTIER-BRESSON
1908–
French photographer

Henri Cartier-Bresson is recognized as the greatest of 20th-century photographers. He was born near Paris and from 19 he studied painting but later turned to photography. In 1931, he travelled in West Africa, taking pictures with a small camera. This proved easy to use and allowed him to remain an unobtrusive observer, which he continued to do as a full-time photographer, travelling widely for newspapers and magazines. His careful compositions brought great personality to ordinary street scenes, in such photographs as *Hyeres: France* (1930) and *Madrid* (1933). In 1940 he was imprisoned by the Germans, but escaped and worked with the French Resistance. His photographs of this period, such as *Exposing a Gestapo Informer* (1945), have become classic images. In 1947, he helped to found the Magnum photographic agency.

Kwame
NKRUMAH
1909–72
Ghanaian president

Kwame (the name means Saturday, the day of his birth) Nkrumah was born in Nkroful, on Africa's Gold Coast. He went to the US to go to university and, in 1945, visited Britain. On his travels, he met people working for black equal rights. After his return to Africa, he formed the Convention People's Party in 1949 to overthrow British rule. They campaigned strongly for self-government. Nkrumah was imprisoned for his political campaigns in 1950, but was elected to Ghana's parliament while still in jail. On his release, in 1951, he served as the country's acting leader, becoming prime minister in 1957 when Ghana was granted independence. In 1960, Ghana became a republic and Nkrumah became president. He tried to improve relations between African countries through the 1961 Charter of African States, and pursued a policy of "African socialism" pursuing links with communist countries. His rule became increasingly dictatorial and, while he was visiting communist China in 1966, his regime in Ghana was overthrown by a military coup. He sought refuge in Guinea, where he remained in exile.

THE EUROPEANS
This photograph of a man ploughing was taken by Cartier-Bresson in Calvados, France, in 1960.

1908 The British parliament passes an act entitling retired people to claim a pension. In 1909, Prime Minister Lloyd George introduces a radical budget to finance the claims, but the House of Lords rejects it.

1908 In China, the infant Hsuan T'ung, or Puyi, becomes emperor on the death of Emperor Kuang-Hsu. Puyi's father, Prince Chun, will rule the nation as regent until Puyi comes of age.

190

AFRICAN INDEPENDENCE

On 6 February 1957, the British flag came down for the last time over the British colony of the Gold Coast in West Africa. In its place flew the new flag of Ghana, the first African country to win independence from its colonial rulers. A new dawn was breaking over Africa.

COLONIAL RULE

The first European colonies in Africa were established by the Portuguese during the 15th century, but despite increasing European influence, most of Africa remained independent for the next 400 years. During the 1880s, this changed as European powers scrambled to set up colonial empires. Within a decade, the whole of Africa had been carved up, apart from Ethiopia in the east and the free slave state of Liberia in the west.

AFRICAN RULE

Inspired by the successful independence movement in India, and by a desire for self-rule, African leaders campaigned for independence. KWAME NKRUMAH in Ghana, JOMO KENYATTA (p.160) in Kenya, JULIUS NYERERE (1922–) in Tanzania, KENNETH KAUNDA (1924–) in Zambia, PATRICE LUMUMBA (1925–61) in the Congo, and many others led their countries to independence. The French and the Belgian colonies gained independence by 1962, the Spanish and Portuguese colonies by 1975, and the final British colony, Zimbabwe, in 1980. The transition from colony to country was not always smooth and vicious civil wars and military coups often disfigured the continent.

Kwame Nkrumah in 1961

1910

William SHOCKLEY
1910–89
US physicist

William Shockley was one of the scientists who made the era of micro-electronics possible. He was born in England but educated at the California Institute of Technology and Harvard, before taking up a job at the Bell Telephone Laboratories in 1936. During World War II, he directed anti-submarine warfare research. On his return to Bell Telephones, he worked with John Bardeen and Walter Brattain on the invention of the transistor, which largely replaced the bulkier vacuum tube and led to the miniaturization of circuits in televisions and radios. They were jointly awarded the Nobel Prize for Physics in 1956.

Dorothy HODGKIN
1910–94
British chemist

Dorothy Hodgkin was only the third woman to win the Nobel Prize for Chemistry. Born in Cairo, Egypt, she studied and taught at Oxford and Cambridge universities. She later married Thomas Hodgkin. She carried out the first analysis of a complex organic molecule to be done entirely by the use of X-ray crystallography. She used the same method to determine the structure of penicillin, insulin, and vitamin B12. She was the first to use a computer to analyze the molecular structure of complex chemicals and this enabled her to produce three-dimensional models. Hodgkin was one of only two women to be awarded the British Order of Merit (Florence Nightingale was the other recipient).

Jacques COUSTEAU
1910–97
French underwater explorer and inventor

Cousteau was famous for his television series *The Undersea World of Jacques Cousteau* (1968–76), in which he revealed life beneath the waves. He joined the navy and worked for naval intelligence during the Nazi occupation of France in World War II. From 1936, he tried different diving techniques and, in 1943, invented the aqualung for safe deep-sea diving and a process for filming underwater for television. In 1951, he began the first of many televised expeditions on the ship *Calypso*.

CORAL WORLD
Fire coral in the Red Sea, southern Egypt.

Elia KAZAN
1909–
US film and theatre director

The person who directed Marlon Brando in *On the Waterfront* and James Dean in *East of Eden* was born Elia Kazanjoglous in Istanbul, Turkey. His Greek parents took him to to the USA aged four. He began his career with Lee Strasberg (p.178) at the Group Theatre, the home of "method acting", and became involved in radical theatre. He made a name for himself directing Broadway productions, especially those written by Arthur Miller and Tennessee Williams, such as *A Streetcar Named Desire* (1947) and *Cat on a Hot Tin Roof* (1955). Kazan began to direct films in 1944 and in them he expressed his social and political beliefs. *Gentleman's Agreement* (1947) and *On The Waterfront* (1954) both won him an Academy Award for best director.

1909 The Cape of Good Hope, Natal, Transvaal and Orange River agree a draft constitution that will result in a unified South Africa. They insist that "Coloureds" and "Natives" cannot vote.

1910 The ocean passenger liner *Mauretania* leaves Liverpool in Britain and crosses the Atlantic to New York City in the United States in less than five days, setting a new speed record for the route.

Mother TERESA
1910–97
Albanian humanitarian

Mother Teresa personified faith and charity to people the world over for her work as a missionary in India. Born Agnes Bojaxhiu in Yugoslavia, of Albanian parents, she grew up in Skopje, Macedonia, and joined a convent at the age of 12. In 1928, she entered a convent school in Calcutta, India, as a teacher. She wanted to help the poorest people on the streets and asked to leave the convent which she was allowed to do. In 1950, she moved to the slums and founded the Order of the Missionaries of Charity – her Indian nuns donned saris rather than traditional nun's habits. Mother Teresa was devoted to helping the city's abandoned and dying and her work brought the plight of India's poor, orphans, and lepers to international attention. She was awarded the Nobel Peace Prize in 1979 for her unstinting humanitarian work. Mother Teresa retired in 1990, but her work continues in more than 200 centres in Africa, America, Europe, Australia, and Asia.

MOTHER TERESA
In 1971, Mother Teresa was awarded the first Pope John XXIII Peace Prize.

Akira KUROSAWA
1910–98
Japanese film director

Kurosawa's most famous film, *The Seven Samurai* (1954), was turned into the Hollywood top box-office Western *The Magnificent Seven* (1960) with Steve McQueen, perhaps proving that imitation is the sincerest form of flattery. Kurosawa was born in Tokyo and worked for several years as a film editor and screenwriter, making his debut as a director with *Judo Saga* (1943). He came to international attention with *Rashomon* (1951), a film set in medieval Japan that tells the same story from different characters' perspectives. It was the first Japanese film to achieve success in the West. Kurosawa often took violent dramatic stories from Japanese history, giving some of his films an "eastern Western" quality. He became one of the most well-known Japanese film-makers. His other international successes include *Kagemusha* (1980) and *Ran* (1985), which is generally considered to be his masterpiece.

Christopher COCKERELL
1910–99
English engineer

The father of the hovercraft – the air-cushioned vehicle that can travel over land and water – was Christopher Cockerell. He was born and educated in Cambridge. He worked for the Marconi Company, where he made a valuable contribution to aircraft radio navigation and communications. In the 1950s, he began working on an air cushion that could support a ship – something that other scientists had tried to produce but failed, their main problem being how to keep the cushion full of air. Cockerell experimented with a cat-food tin inside an inverted coffee tin with air blowing down through the space between. The success of this simple research led to his forming a company Hovercraft Ltd and testing the first hovercraft in 1959 along the English south coast. The vessel travelled at 30 knots (55 km/h) and climbed effortlessly onto the beach. The hovercraft made its first Channel crossing from Calais in France to Dover in England later that year.

COCKERELL'S HOVERCRAFT
One of the first hovercraft, the Princess Margaret, on the Thames in London.

1910 Civil war breaks out in Mexico when Liberal landowner Francisco Madero and charismatic peasant leader Emiliano Zapata revolt against Porfirio Diaz's autocratic rule. Madero is murdered three years later.

1910 Twenty-year-old King Manuel II of Portugal is deposed and the country declared a republic. The revolution comes after ten years of discontent about royal extravagance in the face of widespread poverty.

Robert
JOHNSON
1911–38
US blues singer, songwriter, and guitarist

In the 1930s, blues singers used the guitar with equal intensity as the voice, and Robert Johnson was unmatched in this. He was born in Hazlehurst, Mississippi, and was a self-taught guitarist.

Robert Johnson

His life has not been well documented, but he is part of blues folklore. He recorded only 29 songs, but his falsetto voice and resonating slide guitar had a great impact on blues and rock musicians including Muddy Waters, Eric Clapton, The Rolling Stones, and Ry Cooder. His recordings include "Love In Vain", "Crossroads", "Hellhound on My Trail", and "Me and the Devil Blues". He was, allegedly, stabbed or poisoned by a jealous husband or woman.

Tennessee
WILLIAMS
1911–83
US playwright

The dramatist whose tales of romantic Southern gentility underlaid a world of simmering sex and violence was born Thomas Lanier "Tennessee" Williams in Mississippi. He was not formally educated and wrote short stories while working in a shoe factory. In 1938 he completed a university degree, and wrote his first play, *Battle of Angels*. It was not a success, but *The Glass Menagerie* (1945) earned him real recognition as a playwright. *A Streetcar Named Desire* (1947) and *Cat on a Hot Tin Roof* (1955) cemented his reputation and he won the Pulitzer Prize for both. Usually set in the southern United States, Williams's plots centre around the downfall of women who are not in tune with the world in which they find themselves. In 1969, Williams had a severe breakdown and his later plays were not successful.

William
GOLDING
1911–93
English writer

In 1953, *Lord of the Flies* was published to immediate acclaim. Golding's story of a group of schoolboys shipwrecked on an island and their rapid decline into savagery both shocked and intrigued readers. William Golding was born in Cornwall and went to school at Marlborough, where his father taught. After graduating from Oxford University, Golding became a teacher in 1939. A year later, he joined the navy. After the war, he returned to his teaching. In his writings, Golding maintained that, "Man produces evil as a bee produces honey." Among Golding's many other novels, *The Inheritors* (1955) and *Rites of Passage* (1980) are particularly praised. Golding won the Nobel Prize for Literature in 1983 and was knighted five years later.

Juan Manuel
FANGIO
1911–95
Argentine racing driver

Fangio dominated Formula 1 motor racing in the 1950s. He was born in Balcarce, Argentina, of Italian parents. His first job was as a car mechanic and, after building his own car, he entered several South American racing events. In 1949, he entered Formula 1 racing, eventually winning 24 Grand Prix events for Alfa Romeo, Mercedes-Benz, and Maserati. By 1957, Fangio had won the world championship five times – in 1951 and 1954–57 – a record bettered only by Jim Clark in the 1960s. After his retirement from motor racing in 1958, Fangio worked for Mercedes-Benz back home in Argentina.

Jackson
POLLOCK
1912–56
US painter

Jackson Pollock pioneered the art of "action painting", which involved dripping and throwing paint, often over massive canvases. Born in Cody, Wyoming, he studied art in New York and developed his own brand of abstract expressionism with his first drip painting in 1947. In works such as *Number 1A* (1948) and *Blue Poles* (1952) he daubed, smeared, and even flung paint in sweeping gestures using sticks and knives. He produced dynamic patterns and lines as he tried to express feeling in a vital, abstract way. He said his painting was influenced by Surrealism and Native American and Chinese art. He was killed in a car crash.

Woody
GUTHRIE
1912–67
US folk singer and chronicler of the Great Depression

Woody Guthrie grew up in Oklahoma, but left home with his harmonica and guitar at 15 to travel as a hobo (itinerant) on freight trains – along with many other poor Americans during the Great Depression of the 1930s. He was moved by the plight of hobos and out-of-work farm and factory workers during these years of economic hardship. He began writing about them in songs, including his "dust bowl ballads" – populist protest songs publicizing the plight of the poor and the social injustices they faced. "This Land is Your Land" is the most famous of his 1,000 songs and is considered by many to be a kind of alternative national anthem. His career was cut short in the 1950s by Huntington's chorea, a disease of the nervous system. A young Bob Dylan (p.228), among others, paid homage to him in his hospital bed. Woody's son, Arlo, became a well-known protest folk singer of the late 1960s, performing at the Woodstock Festival and recording "Alice's Restaurant".

1911
Swedish explorer Roald Amundsen reaches the South Pole with good weather contributing to his success. A month later, his rival Robert Scott arrives after battling against the worst storm recorded in the region.

1911
The National People's Party leads a revolution to rid China of interference by other countries and to grant everyone democratic rights and a guaranteed income. China becomes a republic.

Wernher von BRAUN
1912–77
German-born US rocket scientist

Wernher von Braun was a gifted physicist and from an early age was passionate about rocket technology. He worked on Germany's rocket programme during World War II. His most famous invention was the V2 rocket. At the end of the war, he went to the USA, full of admiration for the work there of rocket pioneer Robert Goddard (p.149). Braun became a US citizen in 1955 and was instrumental in setting up the US space programme, working in the newly formed NASA to develop the large space launch Saturn vehicles that later powered the US *Apollo* missions to the Moon.

Patrick WHITE
1912–90
Australian writer

Many of White's books are set in the Australian outback and he cleverly created a sense of isolation and savagery, reflecting the country's terrain. White was born in London and grew up in Australia. He went to Cambridge University and his first novel, *Happy Valley*, was published in 1939. After the war, he settled in Australia and established his reputation as a writer with *The Tree of Man* (1954). He also published short stories and plays and won the Nobel Prize for Literature in 1973. He used the prize money to establish the Patrick White Literary Award, an annual grant for writers who have not achieved critical or financial recognition. Among White's most famous novels are *Voss* (1957), *Riders in the Chariot* (1961), and *The Twyborn Affair* (1979).

John CAGE
1912–92
US composer

John Cage's work calls into debate the meaning of the word "music" and has had an enormous influence on composers since World War II. He was born in Los Angeles and became interested in experimental music from an early age. He became a pioneer of avant-garde techniques of composition and wrote pieces for percussion ensembles and the "prepared piano" – his own invention, which modified the strings of a piano with things such as screws and bits of rubber. Cage's interest in Eastern philosophy, especially Zen Buddhism, led him to introduce chance procedures into his music, such as the tossing of coins or dice, and eventually to the infamous 4'33" (1952), which contains 4 minutes 33 seconds of silence. He was also a pioneer of electronic music.

Gene KELLY
1912–96
US dancer and film star

Famous for his athletic, acrobatic, but always graceful dancing performances, Gene Kelly was one of the first people to integrate dance

with drama in films successfully. He was born Eugene Curran Kelly in Pittsburgh and graduated from college with an economics degree. He tried a variety of jobs, including that of dance instructor, and became a dancer himself. In 1951, Kelly received a special Academy Award for his "brilliant achievements in the art of choreography on film". Among his best-known films are *On the Town* (1949), *An American in Paris* (1950), where he danced with Jerry the animated mouse, and *Singin' in the Rain* (1951), in which he did his famous dance with an umbrella. He directed a number f films including *Hello Dolly!* (1969).

GENE KELLY
Kelly choreographed his dance routine to the title song of the film Singin' in the Rain.

1912 On her first voyage, the British liner *Titanic* hits an iceberg and sinks. More than 1,500 people drown.

The ship was thought to be unsinkable and was not carrying enough lifeboats for all its passengers and crew.

1913 King George I of Greece is assassinated in Salonika, where he has been staying since his

troops captured the town from the Turks some months earlier. He is succeeded by his son Crown Prince Constantine.

Benjamin BRITTEN
1913–76
English composer

Born and raised in Lowestoft, Suffolk, Benjamin Britten studied music and wrote his own compositions. He became the foremost British opera composer since Purcell in the 1600s. Britten produced his first major works while still at the Royal College of Music. After a spell in the USA, he concentrated on opera, achieving success with *Peter Grimes* (1945), *Billy Budd* (1951), *The Turn of the Screw* (1954), and *A Midsummer Night's Dream* (1960). Much of his music is vocal, with parts for his lifelong companion, the tenor Peter Pears. Works include *War Requiem* (1961) and the songs *Winter Words* (1953). His instrumental music includes *The Young Person's Guide to the Orchestra* (1946). Britten founded the annual Aldeburgh Festival in 1948, where his music is regularly featured. He was made Baron Britten of Aldeburgh in 1976 – the first composer ever to be knighted.

Jesse OWENS
1913–80
US athlete

In 1935, James Cleveland Owens competed for the Ohio State University athletics team and, in the space of an hour, set three world athletics records and equalled another. Owens became one of seven African-American athletes to take medals the next year at the 1936 Berlin Olympics. Hitler (p.158) had staged the event to showcase Aryan (white) supremacy. However, Owens took four gold medals – the 100 metres, 200 metres, long jump, and the 4 x 100-metres team relay – and his athletic prowess infuriated Hitler, who left the stadium rather than congratulate a black athlete. Sadly, Owens's achievement was not acknowledged at home either. On his return, he was forced to run races against animals to earn a living. His recognition as the greatest sprinter of his generation came 20 years later. He was elected to the Illinois Athletics Commission and in 1956 went to the Olympics as President Eisenhower's personal representative. At the age of 63, Owens was awarded the Presidential Medal of Freedom.

Richard NIXON
1913–94
37th US president

Richard Milhous Nixon, the only US president to resign from office, was born in California into a Quaker family. He ran for Congress for the Republicans in California in 1946. His outspokenness and shrewd tactics meant that he rose swiftly through the political ranks. In 1952, he became vice-president under Dwight Eisenhower (p.161). He lost the presidential election in 1960 to John F. Kennedy by a tiny margin. He won in 1968 and was re-elected in 1972. During his administration, the Vietnam War attracted increasing public protest, particularly following the invasion of Cambodia in 1970 and the heavy bombing of North Vietnam, which resulted in a cease-fire in 1973. Nixon's staff were implicated during an official investigation into a break-in at the Democratic National Committee's headquarters in the Watergate building in Washington. Nixon attempted a "cover up" by preventing White House staff from being questioned and refusing to hand over tapes of relevant conversations. In 1974, after several leading members of his government had been found guilty of involvement in the Watergate scandal, Nixon was found to have been responsible for organizing the cover-up and he resigned from office to avoid certain impeachment. He was later given a full pardon by President Gerald Ford.

"Babe" Didrikson ZAHARIAS
1914–56
US golfer and athlete

Mildred Ella Didrikson was born in Port Arthur, Texas. As a young woman, she was a great all-round athlete, excelling in many sports, including tennis, swimming, golf, and rifle-shooting. From 1930–32, Didrikson was in the women's All-American basketball team before changing to athletics and winning two gold medals – javelin and 80-metres hurdles – in the 1932 Olympics. She also competed in the high jump and would have broken the world record if she hadn't been disqualified for using the new Western roll technique. Later, she turned to golf and won the US National Women's Amateur Championship in 1946, followed by 17 other championships, including the British Ladies Amateur Championship in 1947. She became a professional golfer in 1948, winning the US Women's Open three times, in 1948, 1950, and 1954. Didrikson married the wrestler George Zaharias.

BABE DIDRIKSON *was one of the USA's most versatile female athletes.*

Jonas SALK
1914–95
US physician

Salk's medical research led to the first safe vaccine for polio. He was born and raised in New York City, where he also studied medicine. In 1942, he joined Thomas Francis at the University of Michigan School of Public Health to develop an immunization against influenza. In 1947, he moved to the Pittsburgh School of Medicine, where he began research into the various strains of virus that cause polio. Salk identified three separate strains. He then demonstrated that vaccines containing killed virus of each of these could cause the formation of protective antibodies in monkeys. The vaccines were then given to children and were found to reduce the incidence of polio.

1914 The Panama Canal opens in Central America, linking the Pacific and Atlantic Oceans and the Caribbean Sea. The United States controls land on both banks, ensuring free passage for US ships.

1914 Archduke Franz Ferdinand, the heir to the Austrian throne, and his wife are assassinated in the Bosnian capital, Sarajevo. The killer is Gavrilo Princip, a young Serbian nationalist. The action provokes the start of World War I.

Joe DIMAGGIO
1914–99
US baseball player

The superb baseball hitter Joe DiMaggio was known by the nicknames "Joltin' Joe" (featured in Simon and Garfunkel's hit "Mrs Robinson") and "The Yankee Clipper", because of his powerful hitting. He was born Joseph Paul DiMaggio in Martinez, California, and played for the New York Yankees throughout his career (1936–51). DiMaggio was voted Most Valuable Player three times and won the batting championship twice, in 1939 and 1940. He was also an outstanding fielder and he holds the record for scoring a hit in 56 consecutive games, in 1941. In 1954, he married his second wife, the film star Marilyn Monroe (p.209) and, although the marriage lasted only a short time, the two stars remained friends throughout her life.

Scobie BREASLEY
1914–
Australian jockey

Arthur Edward Breasley, popularly known as "Scobie", was a successful jockey in Australia for 20 years. He then went to Britain in 1950 and won his first classic race in 1951 – the 2,000 Guineas, on Ki Ming. The jockey from Wagga Wagga, New South Wales, went on to win the 1,000 Guineas classic on Festoon in 1954. He then joined the stable of the great trainer Sir Gordon Richards in 1956 and became champion jockey four times, in 1957, 1961, 1962, and 1963. His astonishing record included winning two English Derbies when he was in his 50s – on Santa Claus (1964) and Charlottown (1966). After one of the longest careers as a flat-racing jockey, he finally retired from riding in 1968 and became a trainer of racehorses, winning the Irish Derby with Steel Pulse in 1972.

Thor HEYERDAHL
1914–
Norwegian adventurer

Thor Heyerdahl put his firmly held theories of how early civilizations might have spread in ancient times into practice with two famous ocean expeditions. He believed that the ancient Peruvians and Egyptians were both able to cross oceans and therefore cross-fertilize ideas and discoveries with other civilizations. In 1947, he decided to prove that the Peruvians could have reached the islands of the Pacific. Heyerdahl built a balsa wood raft, the *Kon-Tiki*, based on ancient Peruvian boats. He then sailed 6,900 km (4,290 miles), from Callao in Peru to the Tuamotu islands in the Pacific. His raft was wrecked there, but he had established the proof he wanted. In 1948, he published a book, *Kon-Tiki Expedition*, in which he described the progress of the expedition in detail. In 1969, Heyerdahl made a second voyage, in order to show that the Ancient Egyptians could have reached Central America. He attempted to cross the Atlantic in a replica of an ancient Egyptian reed boat that he called the *Ra*. Heyerdahl was forced to abandon ship half way across. He tried again in 1970 and reached Barbados. These journeys were described in the book *Ra Expeditions* (1971). Despite his many exploratory voyages, few experts believe that the ancient Peruvians and Egyptians did cross oceans.

1915

Billie HOLIDAY
1915–59
US jazz singer

Despite having had no formal training, Billie Holiday is generally considered to be one of the greatest jazz and blues singers of all time. She was born Eleanora Fagan in Baltimore, Maryland, the daughter of a jazz guitarist, and began singing in nightclubs in Harlem, where she was discovered by the record producer John Hammond. He introduced her to Benny Goodman, with whose band she made her first recordings. She had a distinctive style, singing slightly behind the beat, which gave her songs a wistful air. She toured throughout the 1940s and 50s, but encountered racial prejudice and humiliating obstacles in the southern US states. She also suffered private problems, especially with drugs, which brought about her early death. Her story was made into the film *Lady Sings the Blues* (1973), starring Diana Ross.

BILLIE HOLIDAY
Billie Holiday made many jazz recordings and appeared with Louis Armstrong in the film New Orleans (1947).

1914 World War I breaks out in Europe. Austria and Germany eventually surrender to the Allies – Britain, France, Russia, Italy, and the United States – in 1918. Ten million soldiers die and twice that many are wounded.

1914 With the paramilitary Ulster Volunteer Force reputedly 100,000 strong, Ireland appears to be moving towards civil war. A crisis meeting with King George V over the issue of Home Rule resolves nothing.

Ingrid
BERGMAN
1915–82
Swedish film star

At the height of her fame, Ingrid Bergman was one of the most popular actresses of her generation, symbolizing freshness, vitality, and naturalness. She was born in Stockholm and was a well-known actress in Sweden before she moved to Hollywood. Among Bergman's best-known films are the classic *Casablanca* (1943), where she played opposite Humphrey Bogart, *For Whom the Bell Tolls* (1943), *Gaslight* (1944), for which she won an Academy Award, *Spellbound* (1945), and *Notorious* (1946), both directed by Alfred Hitchcock. She also starred in *Stromboli* (1950), which was directed by Roberto Rossellini, who became her husband. She won a third Academy Award for *Murder on the Orient Express* (1974).

Orson
WELLES
1915–85
US film director, producer, writer, and actor

Orson Welles was born in Wisconsin. He travelled widely as a child and became an actor in Ireland and then Chicago, mainly in Shakespearean roles. He directed an all-black cast for *Macbeth* in 1934 and set up his own theatre company. In 1938, he produced a radio broadcast of H. G. Wells's *War of the Worlds*, in which invaders from Mars attack New Jersey. The production was so realistic that people thought it was a real invasion and Welles had to apologize. When he was only 26, he co-wrote, produced, directed, and starred in *Citizen Kane* (1941), one of the most influential films ever made. He made other films, including *The Lady of Shanghai* (1948), but none equalled his earlier work. Welles was also a successful actor and one of his most famous roles was as Harry Lime in Carol Reed's film *The Third Man* (1949).

Frank
SINATRA
1915–98
US singer and film star

Known as "The Voice", Sinatra was one of the first "pop stars". Born Francis Albert Sinatra in New Jersey, he started his singing career on the radio with bands such as the Tommy Dorsey Orchestra. He made many recordings, including a string of hit albums and singles for Capital Records, such as *Songs For Swingin' Lovers*. He turned to acting and won an Oscar for his role in *From Here to Eternity* (1953). Other films include *Guys and Dolls* (1955), *The Manchurian Candidate* (1962), and *High Society* (1956). He was one of the original "Rat Pack", which included Dean Martin, Sammy Davis Jr, and Peter Lawford and socialized with John F. Kennedy and Marilyn Monroe. He performed live well into his 70s, including many stints at Las Vegas where alleged Mafia connections had threatened to upset his career.

FRANK SINATRA
Sinatra's four wives included Ava Gardner and Mia Farrow.

Stanley
MATTHEWS
1915–
English footballer

Known as "the wizard of dribble", Matthews won 54 international caps. He was born in Hanley, Staffordshire, the son of a boxer. Stanley began his sporting career as a sprinter but soon took up football and joined Stoke City in 1931. He transferred to Blackpool in 1947 and, at the age of 20, he was picked for the England squad. He was 38 before he won a medal – in the FA Cup Final in 1953. In 1961, he returned to play for Stoke City and continued to play first division football into his 50s. He was twice voted Footballer of the Year (1948 and 1963) and was the first European Footballer of the Year in 1956. Matthews went on to manage Port Vale and his autobiography, *The Stanley Matthews Story*, was published in 1960. In 1965, he was knighted for his contribution to the game – the first British footballer to achieve this honour.

1915 Czech nationalist leader Thomas Masaryk publishes a manifesto calling for the establishment of a Czech National Council and urging that Czech forces join the Allies against the Austro-Hungarian Empire.

1915 Leading his armies in the field, the South African prime minister Louis Botha captures German South West Africa, an area of 777,000 sq km (300,000 sq miles). 3,500 prisoners are taken and 1,769 soldiers die in the war.

Arthur MILLER
1915–
US playwright

Arthur Miller was born in New York City and grew up much affected by the economic depression of the 1930s. Miller had to work to earn enough money to go to college in Michigan, where he began to write plays. *All My Sons* (1947) was his first success, but it was *Death of a Salesman* (1949), the tragic story of a small man destroyed by society, that established his reputation. Miller married Marilyn Monroe (p.209) and wrote the script for her last film, *The Misfits*, in 1961, the year of their divorce. His plays concentrate on society's imperfections and on the inner life of his characters. His play *The Crucible* (1953) was based on witchcraft trials in Massachusetts in 1692, which Miller considered to be relevant to the McCarthy anti-communist trials to which he was subjected in the 1950s.

YEHUDI MENUHIN
The celebrated violinist spent much of his time teaching young musicians, including the British violinist Nigel Kennedy.

Yehudi MENUHIN
1916–99
US-born English violinist

Menuhin was one of the greatest violin virtuosos and teachers and played all over the world to great acclaim. He was born in New York City and studied the violin from the age of four. He was a child prodigy and played with the San Francisco Symphony Orchestra when he was only seven years old. While still in his teens, he completed a world tour and was admired for his technical ability and sensitive interpretation. He gained attention for introducing little-known and new compositions into his concert repertoire, in particular music from India. After World War II, Menuhin moved to England and broadened his range of musical

activities. He started to conduct, became a director of music festivals, and founded the Yehudi Menuhin School for musically talented children.

Sirimavo BANDARANAIKE
1916–
Sri Lankan prime minister

Sirimavo Bandaranaike became the world's first woman prime minister when her party won the 1960 Ceylon (Sri Lanka) general election. She was born in Ratnapura and later married the prime minister Solomon Bandaranaike (p.172). He was assassinated in 1959 but Sirimavo followed in his footsteps and became leader of the Sri Lanka Freedom Party. She was prime minister 1960–1965 and 1970–1977. Her second term was difficult, with a rebellion in 1971 by the People's Liberation Front as well as the establishment of a new republican constitution in 1972, and a spell of economic instability. The United National Party government deprived her of her civil rights in 1980, forcing her to give up the leadership in favour of her son. In 1994, she was re-elected prime minister.

Francis CRICK
1916–
English molecular biologist

Francis Crick was one of a trio of men who were awarded the Nobel Prize in 1962 for their work on DNA – the building-blocks of life. After World War II, he worked at Cambridge University researching the structure of molecules within living organisms. In 1951, US biologist James Watson joined him. Watson convinced him that it was worth studying the nucleic acid DNA, which plays a central role in the hereditary characteristics of cells. The two men published their findings in 1953. Using theories already written by Maurice Wilkins, they identified the structure of DNA strands and the pattern that governs the reproduction of cells, which explained how genes are copied.

Edward HEATH
1916–
British politician

Prime minister, sailor, conductor, and elder statesman of British politics in the 1990s, Edward Heath was responsible for gaining British entry into the European Economic Community (EEC). Born in Kent and educated

1916 With the war still raging in Europe, US President Woodrow Wilson proposes a "league of nations" for the future that can decide international disputes, guarantee the freedom of the sea, protect small countries, and prevent war.

1916 At Easter, Irish Nationalists seize public buildings in Dublin to protest against the British failure to grant them Home Rule. The uprising is severely crushed, but the southern part of Ireland gains self-government in 1923.

at Oxford University, he served in the army in World War II. In 1950, he became a Conservative MP. After the Conservatives' defeat in the 1964 election and Douglas-Home's resignation as leader of the party, Heath took over as leader in July 1965. In the election of 1970, he swept to victory and became prime minister. Troubles in Ireland and a dispute with the miners' union meant that he lost the election in 1974. The next year he was replaced as leader of the Conservatives by Margaret Thatcher (p.208) whose policies he criticized. He retained his seat in the 1997 election.

John F.
KENNEDY
"JFK"
1917–63
35th US president

When a sniper killed President John Kennedy on 22 November 1963, in Dallas, the world mourned. Kennedy was born in Massachusetts and graduated from Harvard in 1940. He was elected to the House of Representatives as a Democrat in 1946 and won a seat in the Senate in 1952. In 1953, he married Jacqueline Lee Bouvier. Kennedy won the presidential election for the Democrats in 1960, becoming the youngest-ever president. His early legislation addressed civil rights, education, medical care, and improvements to the space programme. The reforms to make the "Great Society" that his successor, Lyndon Johnson, drove through were Kennedy's legacy. He was immensely popular at home in spite of foreign policy crises, such as a stand-off with the Soviet Union about stationing Soviet missiles in Cuba, which brought the world to the brink of nuclear war in 1962.

Indira
GANDHI
1917–84
Indian politician

Indira Gandhi was the daughter of Jawaharlal Nehru (p.159), the first prime minister of independent India. She served as her father's assistant and rose through the Congress Party, becoming a member of the Central Committee on Indian Congress in 1950, president of the Indian Congress Party in 1959, and prime minister of India in 1966. In 1975, following her conviction for vote rigging, she declared a state of emergency in India, imprisoning opponents and passing laws to limit personal freedom. In the national elections of 1977, she and her party were defeated. Gandhi resigned from Congress in 1978 but returned to power in 1980. She was assassinated in 1984 by members of her bodyguard.

Ella
FITZGERALD
1917–96
US jazz singer

Ella used her voice as an instrument and was well-known for her unique style of "scat-singing", improvising as a saxophone or trumpet as in her famous songs "Lady be Good" and her version of "Mack the Knife". Ella Fitzgerald was born in Virginia and grew up in New York City. When she was 14, her mother died and Ella made a living on the streets, singing and dancing for money. She entered a talent contest in Harlem, was spotted by the drummer Chick Webb, and then sang with his band for several years. At the end of the era of the big band, she began to develop her career as a solo singer, giving audiences her high-speed jazz improvization, touring the world with such legends as Count Basie (p.182) and Duke Ellington (p.172).

Gamal Abdel
NASSER
1918–70
Egyptian statesman

Nasser was one of the most important Arab leaders of the 20th century. He founded the military group that brought down the corrupt Farouk regime in 1952 and helped General Mohammed Neguib rise to power. When the two began to disagree, Nasser assumed the presidency and deposed Neguib. He was officially elected president in 1956. His nationalization of the Suez Canal that year led to the Israeli invasion of Sinai. When Anglo-French forces became involved, the affair turned into an international crisis, but the outcome was to Nasser's political advantage because it gave him pre-eminence within the Arab world. He created a union with Syria and Yemen to form the United Arab Republic. He suffered a setback when Syria pulled out of the union, followed by Yemen in 1961, but Syria later re-joined. Following heavy losses during the six-day Arab-Israeli War, in 1967, Nasser resigned. He died a year later, back in office.

GAMAL ABDUL NASSER
President Nasser aimed to build an Arab empire across North Africa.

1917 The Russian Revolution begins when troops are ordered to fire on striking factory workers in St Petersburg but instead join the revolt themselves. The tsar abdicates and the Soviet Union is established.

1918 The Arab revolt to dismantle the Ottoman Empire continues. Emir Faisal and T. E. Lawrence take Damascus in October. This follows their success in leading troops all the way from Arabia against the Turks.

199

Richard
FEYNMAN
1918–88
US physicist

The brilliant mind of Richard Feynman laid the foundations of quantum electrodynamics – the theory explaining the interactions between electromagnetic radiation (protons) and charged subatomic particles (electrons). Feynman graduated from Massachusetts Institute of Technology. After working on the Manhattan Project to develop the atomic bomb, he left to teach and study theoretical physics at Cornell University and then at the California Institute of Technology. He developed a system – known as Feynman Diagrams – to represent interactions between particles and how they move from one space-time frame to another. This visual approach simplified some of the complicated mathematical calculations used to observe and predict such interactions. *The Feynman Lectures on Physics* (1963) became a standard work. Feynman shared the Nobel Prize for Physics in 1965.

Leonard
BERNSTEIN
1918–90
US composer and conductor

Leonard Bernstein was among the first composers of the 20th century to combine modern themes and classical music. Born in Massachusetts, Bernstein studied music at Harvard University and the Curtis Institute before becoming musical director of the New York Philharmonic from 1958–59. He wrote symphonies such as *The Age of Anxiety* (1949), ballets such as *Fancy Free* (1944), and stage musicals such as *Wonderful Town* (1953) and *Candide* (1956). His work with lyricist Stephen Sondheim produced *West Side Story* (1957), a musical adaptation of Shakespeare's *Romeo and Juliet*, set on the gang-ridden streets of New York City's Lower East Side. It has remained one of the most popular musical works of the 20th century. Bernstein was a highly respected conductor but a flamboyant and volatile personality – his temper flaring famously with opera singers José Carreras and Dame Kiri Te Kanawa (p.232) in a documentary about a new recording of *West Side Story*.

Denis
COMPTON
1918–97
English cricketer and soccer player

Rare in British sports, Denis Charles Scott Compton had a successful career as both an international cricketer and soccer player. He was born in London and, at the age of 18, he scored more than 1,000 runs playing for Middlesex county. He went on to play for England in 78 Test matches and, in his first-class career, scored more than 38,000 runs, including 123 centuries. In the 1947 season, he scored a record 18 centuries. Compton was also a talented soccer player. He won an England Cap in 1943 and played as outside-left for Arsenal. In 1950, he was a member, with his brother Leslie, of the Arsenal team that won the FA Cup. In 1955, after being injured playing soccer, his kneecap was removed, which curtailed both his cricket and soccer careers. Such was his status in cricket, however, that the kneecap is now kept in a biscuit tin in the MCC archive at Lords cricket ground, London. From 1957 he became a well-known journalist and broadcaster.

Ingmar
BERGMAN
1918–
Swedish film director

The son of a Lutheran pastor, Bergman was born in Uppsala. While at university, he became involved in writing and acting in plays.

WEST SIDE STORY
In this Bernstein musical, rival gangs called the Jets and the Sharks fight on the streets of New York City. Shown here is a scene from the film, which won ten Academy Awards.

(p.232)

1918 President Wilson of the United States puts forward 14 points for a post-war peace plan. They include freedom of navigation on the seas, removal of trade barriers, and a reduction in arms to the lowest possible level.

1918 Nicholas II, tsar of Russia before the communist revolution of 1917, is murdered by Bolshevik soldiers together with the rest of the Romanov family. It is not known for certain whether Lenin issued orders for the assassinations.

He first made his mark as a theatre director before he turned his attention to films. He came to international attention with his film *The Seventh Seal* (1956), a medieval moral tale, and most of his films quickly became art-house favourites. Bergman worked closely with cinematographer Sven Nykvist to create extremely intense pictures dealing with personal issues such as guilt, emotional repression, and death. His films are often extremely pessimistic. He is well-known for his sensitive portrayals of women and for the photographic artistry present in his films. Other notable films include *Wild Strawberries* (1957), *Cries and Whispers* (1972), and *Fanny and Alexander* (1982). Many people consider Bergman one of the greatest directors of modern film.

Fanny BLANKERS-KOEN
1918–
Dutch athlete

Affectionately nicknamed "the flying Dutch housewife", Francina Blankers-Koen captured the imagination of the public after winning four gold medals in a single Olympics – the first woman ever to do so. She was born in Amsterdam and quickly proved herself a fine all-round athlete. She was 18 when she competed in the high jump at the 1936 Olympics, but she achieved her greatest success relatively late, at the age of 30, at the 1948 Olympic Games in London: she dominated the women's track and field events and won gold medals in the 100 metres, 200 metres, 80 metres hurdles, and 4 x 100 metres relay. She also achieved world records in seven track-and-field events including high jump, long jump, hurdles, and pentathlon between 1938 and 1951.

Billy GRAHAM
1918–
US evangelist

To many, Billy Graham is the embodiment of Christian evangelism (preaching and spreading the gospel). Born William Franklin Graham in North Carolina, he found his calling as an evangelist at the age of 17 when he attended a revival meeting. Gaining a reputation as a street preacher, Graham began, in 1954, to hold evangelistic campaigns around the world and he formed the Billy Graham Evangelistic Association. His energetic mass rallies are seen as "crusades" to convert thousands of spectators around the world to Christianity. With their rise in

BILLY GRAHAM
A Protestant evangelist, Graham is known for his dramatic preaching.

popularity, he used radio, television, and film to reach even greater numbers with his religious message. He was friendly with a succession of presidents including Truman, Eisenhower, Johnson, Nixon, and Reagan. In 1992, Graham announced that he was suffering from Parkinson's disease and handed most of his work to his eldest son.

Nelson MANDELA
1918–
South African leader

Nelson Mandela was born in the Transkei, son of a tribal chief, and given the middle name Rolihlahla, meaning "stirring up trouble": the name proved to be highly prophetic. He qualified as a lawyer and established the first black legal practice in South Africa. As an active member of the African National Congress (ANC), Mandela was involved in the movement to overthrow the apartheid policy that segregated blacks and whites and made blacks second-class citizens with no vote. In 1960, the government banned the ANC after the Sharpeville massacre, in which 69 protesters were shot down by police. This led Mandela away from peaceful protest to more

aggressive opposition. In 1964, he was found guilty of carrying out acts of sabotage and treason and sentenced to life imprisonment. During his many years in prison on Robben Island, off Cape Town, Mandela became a symbol of the struggle against apartheid. As worldwide pressure built up, Mandela was finally released in 1990 by President F. W. de Klerk (p.223) who, one week earlier, had lifted the ban on the ANC and had also begun to dismantle apartheid. In 1993, Mandela was awarded the Nobel Prize for Peace jointly with de Klerk. The following year the first all-race elections were held in South Africa. The ANC won and Mandela became South Africa's first black president. He retired from politics in 1999 after one term in office, aged 81.

Frederick SANGER
1918–
English biochemist

The first scientist to earn two Nobel prizes in the same field (for chemistry in 1958 and 1980), Sanger was born in Gloucestershire and studied biochemistry at Cambridge University before taking a post at the Medical Research Council (1951–83). Sanger defined the structure of the insulin molecule crucial to the health of millions of people suffering from diabetes. For this he received his first Nobel Prize. Twenty-two years later, he was again awarded the Nobel Prize for Chemistry for his work on DNA (the molecular structure that reveals genetic codes, thus giving us information on inherited characteristics). With two other scientists, he established methods of determining the sequence of nucleotides strung together along strands of DNA.

1918 On 11 November, after more than four years of bitter conflict, the German leaders finally admit defeat and sign an armistice with the Allies ending World War I. The historic event takes place in northern France.

1918 Led by Prince Faisal and advised by British officer T. E. Lawrence, Arab forces celebrate the capture of the ancient city of Damascus in Syria. Arab armies have been in open revolt against Turkish rule since 1916.

Jackie ROBINSON
1919–72
US baseball player

The first African-American player in major league baseball, Jack Roosevelt Robinson attended the University of California, where he excelled at baseball, football, and basketball. He became a star infielder and outfielder for the Brooklyn Dodgers, from 1947–56. He led the Dodgers to six National League pennants and one World Series in 1955. Robinson retired in 1956 and, in 1962, was elected to the Baseball Hall of Fame.

Margot FONTEYN
1919–91
English ballet dancer

Margot Fonteyn was an outstanding ballerina who helped popularize dance in Britain and whose world tours established her as an international star. She was born Margaret Hookham in Surrey, but first studied dancing while living in Hong Kong with her parents. On returning home, she joined the Vic-Wells Ballet, which later became the Royal Ballet Company, and stayed with the company throughout her career. Her exceptional talent was quickly recognized by Ninette de Valois (p.171).

She was given leading roles and became a prima ballerina. She excelled in the great classical ballets such as *Swan Lake* and *The Sleeping Beauty* and was made a dame in 1956. The choreographer Sir Frederick Ashton (p.183) created several ballets with parts for her and, in 1963, she began her famous partnership with the Russian dancer Rudolf Nureyev (p.226). She was one of the finest dancers of the 20th century, renowned for her technical skill and her characterizations.

MARGOT FONTEYN *dances the role of the White Swan, Odette, in Tchaikovsky's Swan Lake.*

James LOVELOCK
1919–
English chemist

Dr James Lovelock is probably best known for his Gaia hypothesis (1972) that describes planet Earth and its air, oceans, and land surface as a single, constantly renewing organism. The idea, named after the ancient Greek goddess of the Earth, stressed the importance of climate control and how the ecosystem responds to it. Lovelock was educated at the University of London and Manchester University and holds a Ph.D in medicine. In the 1960s, he invented the electron capture detector – a device for measuring minute traces of atmospheric gases called chloro-fluoro-carbons (CFCs) in the atmosphere. Although he did not describe the damage they had done to the ozone layer at that time, CFCs are now recognized as highly harmful and emissions, such as those from refrigerators, are now regulated. Lovelock was elected a Fellow of the Royal Society, London in 1974, and was awarded the first Amsterdam Prize for the Environment by the Royal Netherlands Academy of Arts and Sciences in 1990.

EDMUND HILLARY *After their successful ascent of Everest, Hillary and Tensing sit together drinking tea.*

1919 In Amritsar, India, British soldiers fire into a crowd of civilians protesting against the new security laws. Gandhi predicts that continued British rule in India will result in a "sea of blood".

1919 After six months of negotiations, German delegates sign a peace treaty at Versailles in France officially ending World War I. The terms are so harsh that the German chancellor first resigned before finally agreeing to sign.

Edmund HILLARY
1919–
New Zealand mountaineer and explorer

Former beekeeper Edmund Hillary was the first person to reach the summit of the world's highest mountain, Everest, together with Tensing Norgay. Hillary was born in Auckland and became an expert mountaineer, climbing in the New Zealand Alps and in the Himalayas of Asia. In 1953, he joined the British Everest expedition, led by Colonel John Hunt, to climb the summit between Nepal and Tibet. Hillary was chosen to make the final ascent, along with the Nepalese climber and guide Tensing Norgay. On 29 May, 1953, Hillary and Tensing reached the peak. Hillary was knighted later that year and Tensing received the George Medal. Hillary went on to become an explorer, travelling to the South Pole by tractor and exploring the highlands of Alaska and Nepal. In 1977, he led the first jet-boat expedition up the Ganges River in India, climbing to its source in the Himalayas. Since the 1980s, he has campaigned against the destruction of Nepal's forests. Despite all these achievements, he will always be remembered for conquering Everest.

1920

Charlie PARKER
1920–55
US jazz musician

Charles Christopher Parker was one of the most important jazz musicians of his generation. Known as "Bird", short for "Yardbird", Parker was born and grew up in Kansas City. His mother gave him a saxophone when he was 11 and when he left school he played in local jazz venues. To begin with, he played in big bands, alongside the trumpeter Dizzy Gillespie, but then moved to New York City and worked as a freelance musician, leading small groups playing the "bebop" style of jazz. By the time he was 25 years old, Parker's skill and fluency as an improviser were legendary. His compositions include "Ornithology" and "Now's the Time". He suffered from mental instability, and also alcohol and drug addiction – the latter finally killed him.

Rosalind FRANKLIN
1920–58
English scientist

Rosalind Franklin studied physical chemistry at Cambridge University. From 1947, she worked at the State Chemical Laboratory in Paris, France, studying X-ray techniques. In 1951, she went to London to work on DNA. Using her research here, she published X-rays of DNA and determined its molecular structure. She died of cancer a few years before Watson and Crick shared their Nobel Prize for Physiology in 1962.

Kath WALKER
1920–93
Australian writer and poet

Oodgeroo Noonuccal (she reverted to her Aboriginal name in 1988) was born in Brisbane, Queensland, and grew up on Stradbroke Island. She left school at 13 and, when World War II started, she joined the Australian Women's Army Service. After the war, she campaigned for Aboriginal rights and was involved in the campaign that resulted in Aboriginals being given constitutional recognition in 1967. In 1964, she published *We Are Going*, the first book of poetry to be published by an Aboriginal writer. She followed this with other works, including *The Dawn Is at Hand* (1966) and *The Rainbow Serpent* (1988).

JOHN PAUL II
1920–
Polish pope

Karol Wojtyla took the name John Paul II in 1978, when he became the first non-Italian pope for more than 450 years. Wojtyla was born in Wadowice, the son of an army officer. He was a keen athlete, but became a priest in 1946. He taught at the University of Lublin and then rose through the ranks of the Catholic Church in Poland, being made bishop (1958), archbishop (1964), and cardinal (1967). As pope, he has campaigned for peace and justice and attacked oppressive regimes, but he is strongly conservative in his opposition to women priests and birth control. In 1981, he was wounded in an assassination attempt in Rome. He has travelled more than any other pope and has visited more than 60 countries, preaching to many millions of people.

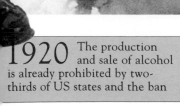

1920 The production and sale of alcohol is already prohibited by two-thirds of US states and the ban is now made nationwide. New York's mayor predicts that 250,000 police will be needed to enforce the city's law.

1920 In Ireland, 14 British officers are killed by the Irish Republican Army. British forces retaliate by firing into a crowd of people. Twelve people are killed and 60 injured on what becomes known as "Bloody Sunday".

Isaac ASIMOV
1920–92
US science fiction writer

Isaac Asimov is considered one of the greatest science-fiction writers of all time. During his career he wrote some 200 books including *I, Robot* (1950) and the *Foundation Trilogy* (1951–53), which recounted an empire's collapse in a future universe. He also wrote many books on science, helping to popularize the subject, and, in 1980, he completed his autobiography.

Andrei SAKHAROV
1921–89
Russian physicist

Andrei Sakharov attended the Soviet Academy of Sciences and worked out the theoretical basis for controlled thermonuclear fusion. With his knowledge of nuclear physics, he then began to argue for a worldwide reduction in nuclear arms and increased cooperation

THE WIZARD OF OZ
As Dorothy, Judy Garland goes to find the Wizard with the Scarecrow and the Tin Man.

between the nuclear powers. In 1970, he founded the Soviet Human Rights Committee, arguing for civil liberties in the USSR. As a leading dissident, he was often harassed by the Soviet authorities, especially after he was awarded the 1975 Nobel Prize for Peace.

Alexander DUBCEK
1921–92
Czech statesman

Dubcek joined the ruling Communist Party in Czechoslovakia, becoming First Secretary in 1968. He was a major reformer, instituting policies such as the abolition of censorship. The USSR became concerned and their tanks rolled in to Czechoslovakia in August 1968. Under pressure from the USSR, the Czech Communist Party replaced Dubcek in 1969. He was arrested by Soviet troops and expelled from the party in 1970. He spent the next 18 years working as a clerk in a lumber yard.

John GLENN
1921–
US astronaut and senator

John Herschel Glenn Jr was the first astronaut to orbit Earth. Glenn was selected by NASA in 1959 for the *Mercury* manned spacecraft programme. In February 1962, he flew around Earth in the spacecraft *Friendship 7*. The flight lasted 4 hours and 55 minutes. Glenn retired from space travel in 1964 and became senator for Ohio from 1974. In 1998, Glenn, aged 77, returned to space aboard the space shuttle *Discovery* as part of a NASA study on the effects of space on elderly people.

Judy GARLAND
1922–69
US film star and singer

Born Frances Gumm in Michigan, Judy Garland first appeared on stage when she was

three years old, touring with her siblings as "The Gumm Sisters". She was signed up by the MGM studio aged 13, changed her name, and made her movie debut when she was 14. For her role as Dorothy in *The Wizard of Oz* (1939), she won a special Academy Award. She starred in many other films, including *Meet Me in St Louis* (1944) and *A Star is Born* (1954). Despite problems with alcohol and drugs, she was a superstar in films and concerts.

Jack KEROUAC
1922–69
US writer and poet

Jean-Louis Kerouac was born in Massachusetts. He turned to writing after attending Columbia University and serving in the merchant marines. His first novel, *The Town and the City* (1950), was not successful, but *On the Road* (1957) was both a bestseller and very influential novel. A fictionalized account of Kerouac's cross-country travels with friends and lovers, the book appealed to young people dissatisfied with 1950s American society – the so-called "Beat Generation". The book and follow-ups like *Big Sur* (1960) made Kerouac a celebrity, but his last years were spent struggling with alcohol and depression.

Yitzhak RABIN
1922–95
Israeli soldier and prime minister

Yitzhak Rabin was born in Jerusalem. At the outbreak of World War II, he joined the army and rose to be chief of staff in 1964. After heading the armed forces during the six-day Arab-Israeli War of 1967, he

1921 One-quarter of Berlin's children are malnourished or diseased. Germany looks set to continue suffering from its defeat in World War I, with reparations of £10 million due to the Allies over the next 40 years.

1921 Russia is in the grip of a major famine that has claimed the lives of about 18 million people. There are reports of peasants eating clay and twigs and instances of cannibalism. The civil war and drought are blamed.

THE TRIESTE
The bathyscape was designed by Auguste Piccard to allow scientists to research deep under the sea.

became ambassador to the USA. He became leader of the Labour Party in 1974 and was prime minister (1974–77 and 1992 95). In 1985, Rabin withdrew troops from Lebanon, but treated Palestinian rebels in other occupied territories severely. In 1993, he signed an agreement with the Palestinian Liberation Organization (PLO), granting self rule to the Palestinians in Jericho and Gaza and promising to withdraw Israeli troops. He won the Nobel Peace Prize in 1994, but his concessions were opposed by some people in Israel. He was assassinated at a peace rally in Tel Aviv.

Christiaan
BARNARD
1922–
South African surgeon

In 1967, Christiaan Neethling Barnard led a team of 20 surgeons to perform the first human heart transplant.

Barnard was born in Beaufort West and studied medicine in Cape Town and the USA. He returned to Cape Town to work at Groote Schuur Hospital, where he experimented on heart transplants in dogs. The first human transplant took place on a terminally ill patient, Louis Washkansky. He died 18 days later from pneumonia, but a second patient, in 1968, survived for nearly two years. When Barnard retired in 1983, some of his patients had survived for several years.

Julius
NYERERE
1922–
Tanzanian politician

Son of a village chieftain, Julius Nyerere was born near Lake Victoria. He went to Edinburgh University to study

history and economics and returned home to Tanganyika (now Tanzania) in 1954. He reorganized the Nationalist Party to form the Tanganyika African National Union, of which he became president, entering the Legislative Council in 1958. In 1960, he became chief minister and then prime minister when Tanganyika was granted self-government from Britain in 1961. He retired for a short time, but was elected president when Tanganyika became a republic. In 1962, Nyerere organized the union of Tanganyika and Zanzibar into Tanzania. He resigned in 1985.

Jacques
PICCARD
1922–
Swiss underwater explorer

In 1960, Jacques Piccard took his bathyscape (deep-sea diving vessel) the *Trieste* down 10,912 m (35,800 ft) to the bottom of the Marianas Trench in the Pacific Ocean – a world record. He was born in Brussels, the son of Auguste Piccard, who had designed a cabined balloon and ascended to double the height of Mount Everest. In 1948, Auguste had also designed the first deep-sea vessel able to operate without the support of a ship on the surface. In 1953, Jacques helped his father test the bathyscape the *Trieste*, diving to 3,150 m (10,330 ft) in the Mediterranean Sea. Jacques then moved to the USA to continue further undersea exploration in bathyscapes and was employed by the US Navy during his world record dive.

1921 In India, riots break out in Bombay when Mohandas Gandhi, leader of the Indian Congress Party, burns a pile of clothes in protest against the import of foreign cloth during a visit by the Prince of Wales.

1921 Struggling with unemployment and inflation following World War I, Italy elects Benito Mussolini prime minister. He promises to fight communism and make Italy strong again, but he soon becomes a dictator.

Iannis XENAKIS
1922–
Romanian-born French composer

Iannis Xenakis's scientific approach to composition – he originated music using computers and mathematical probability – has made him one of the most influential composers of the late 20th century. He was born in Braïla, Romania, to Greek parents. The family returned to Greece in 1932 and Iannis studied engineering in Athens. He was injured fighting for the Resistance during World War II. In 1947, he moved to Paris, where he worked with the architect Le Corbusier (p.155), and started to compose. His first piece, *Metastasis* (1954), for orchestra was composed using formulas from the world of architecture and engineering. In later works, such as *Atrées* (1962), he developed a complex mathematical method of composition called "stochastic music". Most of his music is instrumental and often very difficult to play.

Rocky MARCIANO
1923–69
US boxer

Born Rocco Francis Marchegiano in Brockton, Massachusetts, Marciano took up boxing while serving in the forces during World War II. Rocky soon earned his nickname "the Brockton Blockbuster". He was a powerful hitter and in his career as a heavyweight boxer won 43 of his 49 bouts by knockouts. He turned professional in 1947 and made his name in 1951 when he defeated Joe Louis, the former world champion. The following year he took the world title from Jersey Joe Walcott. When Rocky Marciano retired in 1956 at the age of 33, he became the only undefeated world heavyweight champion, with an incredible record of 49 victories out of 49 fights. All attempts to persuade him to make a comeback from retirement failed. Marciano died in a plane crash in Newton, Iowa, the day before his birthday.

ROCKY MARCIANO
The fight for the 1953 heavyweight title took place in New York City. Marciano (left) beat Roland la Starza to retain the title.

Maria CALLAS
1923–77
US opera singer

Known for performing roles that were highly demanding, soprano Maria Callas became famous internationally for her passionate, dramatic style, that was both intense and exciting to watch. Born Maria Cecilia Sophia Anna Kalogeropoulos to parents of Greek descent in New York City, she studied singing at the Athens Conservatory. Her first major performance was at Verona in 1947, and she won international acclaim with her performance in Bellini's *Norma* at Covent Garden in London and the Metropolitan Opera in New York City. For the next two decades she was the best-known opera singer in the world, appearing at major opera houses in Europe and the USA. Her private life and relationship with wealthy Greek businessman Aristotle Onassis was of great public interest. Two of her most famous roles were in Cherubini's *Medea* and Puccini's *Tosca* – the latter was her final performance in 1965.

Nadine GORDIMER
1923–
South African writer

Gordimer's writing depicts the narrow, restricted lives of white South Africans especially during the years when official racial segregation – apartheid – was in force in the country. Born near Johannesburg, Nadine Gordimer had a religious education. As a voracious reader, she came to learn about

1922
The tomb of the young pharaoh Tutankhamun is discovered at Luxor in Egypt by a team led by British archaeologist Howard Carter. The following year, the sarcophagus is opened, revealing a priceless gold effigy of the king.

1923
About 2.5 million Japanese people become homeless in Tokyo and Yokohoma and more than 300,000 people die, when a huge earthquake razes the cities to the ground and rivers burst their banks.

and loathe apartheid. Her first book, *The Soft Voice of the Serpent* (1952), a collection of short stories, looked at the terrible effects state-sponsored racism had on ordinary South Africans. Gordimer's recurring theme was continued in *The Lying Days* (1953), a novel about a girl's fight against her parents' racism. Her best-known book is probably *The Conservationist* (1974). She continued to write and receive critical acclaim well into the 1990s. In 1991, she received the Nobel Prize for Literature.

Jack
KILBY
1923–
US electrical engineer

Jack Kilby, together with Alfred Noyce, another engineer working in what became Silicon Valley, California, is credited with co-inventing the integrated-circuit microchip, or silicon chip, in 1975. Kilby was born in Montana and studied electrical engineering at universities in the Midwest. After working for Centrelab, a company making radio and television parts, he moved to Texas Instruments in Dallas in 1959. The chip that Kilby and Noyce invented opened up the future for personal and home computers. Kilby continued to work on integrated chips, registering patents for many of his discoveries.

Marcel
MARCEAU
1923–
French mime artist

The best-known modern performer of mime, Marcel Marceau was born in Strasbourg and studied at the School of Dramatic Art at the Sarah Bernhardt Theatre,

MARCEL MARCEAU
Tours around the world brought Marceau international recognition and he influenced many other artists, including the English pop star David Bowie.

Paris. He became famous internationally as the white-faced clown character "Bip", based on the traditional French clown Pierrot and Charlie Chaplin's (p.160) tramp. His mimes include *Le Manteau* (1951), *Un Jardin Public* (1955), and *Paris qui Rit, Paris qui Pleure* (1959), all of which have been filmed.

Marlon
BRANDO
1924–
US film actor

Brando has frequently portrayed macho rebels and is famed for his moody on-screen persona and blurred way of speaking. Born in Omaha, Nebraska, he started acting in New York City and became a leading exponent of "Method" acting taught by Lee Strasberg (p.178). He first came to public notice with brilliant reviews for his theatrical performance as Stanley Kowalsky in Tennessee Williams's (p.193) *A Streetcar Named Desire*. He also appeared in the film version in 1951. Other well-known films include *On the Waterfront* (1954), for which he won an Academy Award, and *The Godfather* (1972), for which he was given his second Academy Award. He refused this in protest against the film industry's treatment of Native Americans. In 1978, he again gained notoriety by being paid more than $18 million for a nine-minute appearance as Superman's father in *Superman*. His acting reputation was restored with the Vietnam War allegory *Apocalypse Now* (1979). He now spends much of his time on his private Polynesian island.

Robert
MUGABE
1924–
Zimbabwean statesman

Robert Mugabe was prime minister in the first government of independent Zimbabwe and later he became the country's first elected president. He was born in Kutama, southern Rhodesia, and became a teacher in various African countries before returning home in 1960. In 1961, he became deputy secretary general to the Zimbabwe African People's Union (ZAPU), which opposed British sovereignty over Rhodesia. He was imprisoned, but escaped to found the Zimbabwe African National Union (ZANU) in 1963. He went on to become its president and to qualify as a lawyer. Mugabe went to Mozambique to oversee the guerrilla war against the white regime. Back home, he joined with Joshua Nkomo, president of ZAPU, to press for black majority rule and led their combined party to victory in the elections of 1980. When Joshua Nkomo agreed to merge his ZAPU with Mugabe's ZANU, Mugabe took over as leader of the new one-party state. He was re-elected as president in 1996.

1923 General Mustapha Kemal declares Turkey a republic with himself as the new president. He is moving the captital from Constantinople to Ankara and intends to turn the new Republic of Turkey into a modern state.

1924 Soviet leader Vladimir Ilyich Lenin dies at the age of 54. The death of the "Father of the Russian Revolution" leaves a serious power vacuum in Russia. His possible successors include Leon Trotsky and Joseph Stalin.

1925
MALCOLM X
1925–65
US political activist

Malcolm Little was born in Nebraska and raised in Lansing, Michigan, where he saw his family home burned by the Ku Klux Klan. In his teens he moved to Boston, and later New York, and became a petty criminal. In 1946, while serving a sentence for burglary, Little joined the Nation of Islam. Taking the name Malcolm X after his release, he followed the Nation of Islam's strict code of behaviour and tirelessly promoted its goals of African-American

separatism and racial pride. A powerful speaker, Malcolm soon had a nationwide reputation, but he was controversial: he defended violence as a means of African-American self-defence, denounced white people, and rejected the more moderate approach of civil rights leaders like Martin Luther King, Jr (p.213). In 1964, Malcolm X left the Nation of Islam and set up a rival organization. On becoming an orthodox Muslim, he renamed himself El-Hajj Malik el-Shabazz after making the Haj (pilgrimage) to Mecca. He also began to moderate his anti-white, pro-separatist views. In 1965, Malcolm X was assassinated at a rally in Harlem.

MALCOLM X
The X of his name represented the African surname his ancestors lost when they were sold into slavery.

Yukio MISHIMA
1925–70
Japanese writer

Yukio Mishima was the pen-name of Hiraoka Kimitake. Born in Tokyo, he failed his physical for the military and worked in a factory during World War II. He then studied law. His first novel, *Confessions of a Mask* (1949), was semi-autobiographical and won him instant acclaim. In Mishima's novels, his characters usually fail to live up to impossible ideals. The best-known of these is *The Temple of the Golden Pavilion* (1956). Despite the intensely Japanese settings, the solid plots and studies of humanity gave Mishima's novels a worldwide readership. Mishima was obsessed with the traditions and ideals of Imperial Japan – martial arts, quests for beauty, and heroic death. He formed a society dedicated to the Samurai code of honour. When his attempts to convert the nation to his ideals failed, Mishima committed suicide by disemboweling himself.

Pierre BOULEZ
1925–
French composer and conductor

Pierre Boulez was born in Montbrison. He took lessons in composition at the Paris Conservatory with Messiaen (p.189). His early music concentrated on the avant-garde. By the 1960s, he had become known internationally as a conductor with the BBC Symphony, New York Philharmonic, Chicago Symphony, and Cleveland Symphony orchestras. Among Boulez's innovative pieces are such works as *Sonatine* (1949), *Structures Book 1* (1952), and *Pli selon pli* (1960).

Margaret THATCHER
1925–
British prime minister

In 1979, Margaret Thatcher became Britain's first woman prime minister. Born in Leicestershire, she studied chemistry at Oxford University. In 1959, she became a Conservative member of parliament. She was made secretary of state for education in 1970, leader of the Conservative Party in 1975, and prime minster from 1979 to 1990. Her rigid approach to policy making and her dominance of her all-male cabinet earned her the name "the Iron Lady". Her leadership during the Falklands War against Argentina, her firm stand against terrorism, and her famous phrase "This lady's not for turning" helped to make the name stick. She resigned in 1990 after the Conservative Party lost faith in her leadership. She remained in the House of Commons until 1992 and was made Baroness Thatcher of Kesteven in 1992.

1925 In a joint initiative, Britain and Australia announce plans to encourage up to 450,000 Britons to emigrate to Australia in the coming decade. Immigrants are to be given money and training to establish new farms.

1925 In the United States, the state of Tennessee makes it illegal for Darwin's theory of evolution to be taught in schools because it contradicts the Bible. School teacher John Scopes of Dayton is prosecuted under the new ruling.

Marilyn
MONROE
1926–62
US film star

The life and death of Marilyn Monroe has come to symbolize the glamour and tragedy of 20th-century stardom. She was born Norma Jean Baker in Los Angeles and spent an unhappy childhood in orphanages and a series of foster homes. She started out as a photographers' model and, after several small film parts, she became famous internationally as a "sex symbol", but also an actress, showing her comedic talents in such films as *Gentlemen Prefer Blondes* (1953) and *Some Like it Hot* (1959). She also demonstrated a serious side to her acting in *The Misfits* (1961), her last film, written for her by her third husband Arthur Miller (p.198). She was also married to baseball star Joe DiMaggio (p.196). In 1961, Monroe sang "Happy Birthday Mr President" to John F. Kennedy (they were rumoured to be having a relationship). She died when she was 36 from an overdose of sleeping pills.

John
COLTRANE
1926–67
US jazz musician

Renowned for his fluid improvisation, John Coltrane became the most influential jazz musician of the the 1960s and 70s. He played in a navy band before joining a rhythm-and-blues group. Once he was established as a musician, he began playing tenor and alto saxophone with Dizzy Gillespie and, in the mid

MARILYN MONROE
Marilyn took up this famous pose in the Billy Wilder-directed film The Seven-Year Itch *(1955).*

1950s, with trumpeter Miles Davis, where he developed his "sheets of sound" technique, most notably on Davis's *Kind of Blue* (1959). In 1960, he formed his own quartet and recorded the powerful and uptempo "Giant Steps". Coltrane was a highly popular jazz artist: his *My Favourite Things* sold 50,000 copies at a time when jazz albums might muster 5,000. Coltrane popularized the saxophone as an instrument and was also interested in and influenced by music from India and Africa.

Michel
FOUCAULT
1926–84
French philosopher
and historian

From his writings on the way society defines itself, Foucault led social scientists to reconsider social institutions and relationships. He was born in Poitiers and studied at the Ecole Normale Supérieure in Paris. He held academic posts in France and Sweden before becoming a professor at the Collège de France in 1970. In his books, Foucault argues that knowledge and power are inseparable. He showed that power can be both a positive and a negative force. Much of Foucault's work is easy to read but difficult to understand.

Miles
DAVIS
1926–91
US jazz musician

Miles Dewey Davis III was given a trumpet at the age of 13 by his father. He studied at the Juilliard School in New York City, but left to play bebop in bands with Charlie Parker (p.203), Dizzy Gillespie, and others. Davis was the pioneer of "cool" jazz in the 1950s, when improvization became totally free. In 1970, he led the way with another new movement in jazz when he incorporated popular music into his work, successfully fusing jazz and rock together. His bands from this period featured electronic instruments and synthesizers. Davis was probably the most popular jazz musician of the post-war era. Among his prolific recorded works are the notable *Round Midnight* (1956), *Kind of Blue* (1959), *Bitches Brew* (1969), and *Tutu* (1986).

1925 Adolf Hitler writes his manifesto, *Mein Kampf (My Struggle)*, while in jail for attempting to overthrow the government in Bavaria two years earlier. His vision of a German empire is rooted in his deep hatred of Jews.

1926 In a public demonstration in London, Scottish inventor John Logie Baird reveals an innovative system for transmitting moving images via airwaves. The flickering images appear on a device called a televisor.

Chuck BERRY
1926–
US rock'n'roll musician

The guitar riffs and chords that Chuck Berry introduced in the 1950s became the staples of rock'n' roll music. He was born Charles Edward Berry in St Louis, Missouri, and learned to play guitar as a teenager. He led a blues trio in the South, then moved to Chicago. He quickly gained popularity among young, white US teenagers with a series of simple songs with humorous lyrics, such as "Maybellene" (1955), "Roll Over Beethoven" (1956), and "Johnny B Goode" (1958). His success helped to bring about the rise of rock music and influenced many later musicians such as The Beatles and The Rolling Stones. In 1972, he topped both the US and UK charts with his jokey "My Ding-A-Ling".

ELIZABETH II
1926–
British queen

When she was just ten years old, Elizabeth became heir to the British throne, when her father, George VI, became king. In 1947, she married Philip Mountbatten, who was then created Duke of Edinburgh. In 1952, she succeeded her father and became queen. An astute ruler, she has overseen the transformation of the British Empire into a commonwealth of independent states and has presided over massive social and economic change at home. Her famous "walkabouts" when meeting the public, her annual televised Christmas message, and her natural dignity have endeared her to the nation, but the failed marriages of three of her four children have attracted unprecedented media coverage and considerable controversy during the 1990s.

QUEEN ELIZABETH II
In spite of the gradual modernization of the royal family, the queen still appears in official dress at many state occasions.

It may be due to the Queen's personal standing and her efforts to modernize the role of the royal family that the British monarchy remains intact to face the challenges of the next millennium.

Joan SUTHERLAND
1926–
Australian opera singer

The most famous Australian operatic soprano, Dame Joan Sutherland was born in Sydney and grew up studying piano and singing with her mother. She made her singing debut as Dido in Purcell's *Dido and Aeneas* in 1947, then came to London to study at the Royal College of Music. She joined the Royal Opera, Covent Garden, and gained recognition for her roles in Donizetti's *Lucia di Lammermoor* and Handel's *Samson*. She sang in major opera houses all over the world and was widely acclaimed for the beauty of her voice and her impeccable technique, which developed under the guidance of her husband, the Australian conductor Richard Bonynge. She retired in 1990.

Bob FOSSE
1927–87
US choreographer

Robert Louis Fosse was born in Chicago, went to a school that taught dance, and first performed professionally at the age of 13. As a young man, he danced in the chorus in Broadway musicals and his work on *The Pajama Game* (1954) established him as a choreographer. Fosse was known for his angular groupings of dancers and exaggerated, stylish staging. He choreographed 11 Broadway shows, including *Damn Yankees* (1955), *Redhead* (1959), and *Dancin'* (1978). He moved into films and was both director and choreographer of *Cabaret* (1972), for which he won an Academy Award, and *All That Jazz* (1979).

Fidel CASTRO
1927–
Cuban revolutionary

Cuban leader Fidel Castro made his country the first communist state in the western hemisphere. His father was a wealthy sugarcane farmer and Castro attended Catholic boarding schools and later studied law in Havana. As a lawyer, he fought cases for the poor and for victims of the corrupt Cuban government. In 1953, he led an unsuccessful uprising against Cuba's dictator, Fulgencio Batista, and was imprisoned. After a year, he fled to the USA and Mexico and continued to work to overthrow the Cuban government. In 1956, he landed in Cuba with a band of 80 rebels, including Che Guevara (p.211), but was ambushed and forced to hide in the mountains. From here, he organized guerrilla attacks against the army. As conditions in Cuba worsened, more people joined Castro and, in 1958, he had enough support to force Batista out. Castro became prime minister in 1959. He managed to weaken US control over the country's economic trade and, in 1961, defeated its attempt to end his regime in the Bay of Pigs invasion. The USSR became Cuba's main ally. When it installed its nuclear weapons on Cuba, in 1962, the USA became wary. It agreed to leave Castro alone if the weapons were withdrawn. The collapse of the USSR in 1991 forced Castro to relax his trade and tourism laws.

1926 In Japan, 25-year-old Hirohito becomes emperor when his father Yoshihito dies. He will be crowned in a few years, taking his place on the "August Heavenly Throne" and becoming a living god.

1926 Britain sees its first-ever general strike when the Trades Union Congress votes to support coal miners against mine owners. White-collar workers step into the breach to keep trains running and to provide other services.

Theodore MAIMAN
1927–
US physicist

In 1960, at the Hughes Research Laboratories in Miami, Theodore Maiman constructed the first working laser. He was born in Los Angeles. After military service in the Navy, Maiman received his PhD from Stanford University in 1955, then joined a research laboratory in Florida. He developed the first laser from the "maser" (micro-wave amplification by stimulated emission of radiation), using beams of light instead of micro-waves. The wavelengths of light from a laser are all the same length and travel in a straight line. The laser has many uses today, including micro-surgery and compact disc players. In 1962, Maiman set up the Korad Corporation, which manufactures high-powered lasers.

SHIRLEY TEMPLE
Shirley's blonde curls and cheery personality captured the world's heart.

Shirley TEMPLE
1927–
US actress

The most successful child star of all time, Shirley Temple began making films at the age of two. Simplistic musicals such as *Bright Eyes* (1934), in which she sang one of her most popular songs, "On the Good Ship Lollipop", *Curly Top* (1935), and *Dimples* (1936) became consistent successes at the box office. Temple's childhood image was so popular – there were Shirley Temple dolls, comics, dresses, and colouring books – that she was unable to make the transition to adult roles and retired from the cinema in her 20s.

Later, as Shirley Temple Black, she began a political and diplomatic career, first as US Representative to the United Nations (1969–70), then as US Ambassador to Ghana (1974–76) and Czechoslovakia (1989–92).

Che GUEVARA
1928–67
Argentine revolutionary

With his beret and beard, Ernesto "Che" Guevara became a revolutionary icon at a time when many young people were politically active against oppressive regimes. He was born in Rosario, Argentina, into a middle-class family. He studied medicine in Buenos Aires, where he became a revolutionary, convinced that society could be improved only by forcibly overthrowing unjust rulers. In Mexico, he met the Cuban rebel leader Fidel Castro and joined his invasion of Cuba in 1956. By 1959, the rebels had taken control of the island and Guevara was Castro's chief aide. He was put in charge of the National Bank and organized land reforms. His real interest, however, was in revolutionary struggle. In 1965, he left Cuba and eventually travelled to Bolivia, where he led a guerrilla band against the government there. He was killed by Bolivian soldiers.

Andy WARHOL
1928–87
US painter

The man who claimed that everyone would be famous for 15 minutes, Andy Warhol was a leader of the Pop Art movement. He became famous in the 1960s with his pictures of household products such as soup cans, drinks bottles, and soap-pad boxes. He was born Andrew Warhola in Pennsylvania and studied art in Pittsburgh before moving to New York City in 1949. Here, he worked as a commercial artist, designing and illustrating advertising material. Following his successful "soup can" exhibition in 1962, Warhol worked on photographic silk-screen images of celebrities, which he repeated many times in garish colours. Warhol mass-produced his art in his New York studio, which he called The Factory. He later turned to cinema, directing experimental films such as *Sleep* (1965), which shows a man sleeping for six hours, and produced the influential 1960s rock band The Velvet Underground. Critics argue over whether Warhol was a remarkable artist or a brilliant self-promoter.

CHE GUEVARA
In the 1960s, Che's face was a popular image on student posters and T-shirts.

Maya ANGELOU
1928–
US writer

One of America's leading writers and poets, Maya Angelou was asked to write and read a poem for the inauguration of President Clinton in 1993. She was born Marguerite Johnson in Missouri. She had a traumatic childhood that left her mute for five years and she became pregnant at 16, giving birth to a son – experiences she wrote about in her autobiography *I Know Why the Caged Bird Sings*. Angelou embarked on a career of singing, acting, dancing, waitressing, and cooking. In 1950, she moved to New York City and began to write. In the 1960s, Angelou campaigned for black civil rights, later spending some years in Ghana and Egypt. In 1970 she published the first volume of her autobiography, which became a bestseller, followed by four more volumes. She has written several volumes of poetry, of which *And Still I Rise* (1987) is possibly her best known.

1927 US pilot Charles Lindbergh becomes the first person to fly non-stop across the Atlantic in his single-engine monoplane, *The Spirit of St Louis*. The 5,793 km (3,600 mile) journey took Lindbergh 33.5 hours.

1927 The capital of Australia is moved north from Melbourne in Victoria to the new city of Canberra in the Australian Capital Territory. The first meeting of the Australian parliament takes place there.

Noam CHOMSKY
1928–
US linguist

Chomsky has transformed linguistics (the study of language), arguing that language reveals the way in which knowledge is acquired and stored. He studied mathematics and philosophy at the University of Pennsylvania. He also studied at Harvard University before teaching at the Massachusetts Institute of Technology. In such works as *Syntactic Structures* (1957), Chomsky theorized that linguistics was not a single subject, but a major branch of psychology. He argued that children are born with an inbuilt knowledge of the basic principles of language. Chomsky also became one of the foremost critics of the US government's foreign policy in Vietnam and the Middle East.

Paul ELVSTROM
1928–
Danish yachtsman

The only yachtsman to win Olympic gold medals in four events, Paul Elvström was born in Copenhagen and grew up to be a fine dinghy sailor. He won in the Firefly class and Finn class at four consecutive Olympics, in 1948, 1952, 1956, and 1960. At the 1984 Olympics, Elvström came fourth in the Tornado class with his daughter Trine.

Gabriel García MARQUEZ
1928–
Colombian writer

Famous for his "magic realism" stories, Márquez describes ordinary events as

CIVIL RIGHTS

After the abolition of slavery in 1865, African-Americans became US citizens and could vote for the first time. Many southern states continued to discriminate against them, however, placing legal obstacles in their way to prevent them from voting and segregating education, transportation, and public places. During the 1950s, African-Americans demanded equality.

WE PROTEST!
In 1954 the US Supreme Court ruled that racial segregation was unconstitutional. Armed with this verdict, African-Americans began a series of protests to end segregation. In Montgomery, Alabama, ROSA PARKS (1913–) was arrested for sitting in the white section of a bus, leading to a year-long boycott of the bus system led by MARTIN LUTHER KING, JR. Other non-violent protests included sit-ins, boycotts, voter registration drives, and other forms of direct action.

LEGAL VICTORY
In 1963, more than 200,000 people marched on Washington to demand civil rights. President LYNDON JOHNSON (p.188) later signed the Civil Rights Act of 1964 and the Voting Rights Act of 1965, outlawing racial discrimination in employment, voting, education, and public housing. As racial tension increased in the USA during the 1960s, and economic conditions worsened for non-whites, the civil rights movement split between those who supported King's non-violent campaign to achieve equality, and those, led by MALCOLM X (p.208) and the Black Panthers, who favoured "any means necessary" to secure African-American liberation.

Martin Luther King in Washington DC, 1963.

extraordinary and impossible and represents fantastical things as quite ordinary. Gabriel García Márquez was born in Aracataca, Colombia. Despite the poverty of his family, he studied law and journalism at university in Bogota. Márquez started writing in 1944 and, from 1948, he worked as a journalist in Italy, France, USA, Mexico, and Spain. In *The Leafstorm and Other Stories* (1955), he introduced Macondo, the fictional village where much of his later work was to take place. From 1965, he devoted himself to writing and, in 1967, wrote *One Hundred Years of Solitude*, his best-known novel, which follows the history of a family and their house and town, Macondo, from the beginning to the end of time. It was for this novel, one of the great books of the 20th century, that Márquez was awarded the Nobel Prize for Literature in 1982. It sold more copies than any other fictional work set in Latin America. His other novels include *Love in the Time of Cholera* (1985) and *The General in his Labyrinth* (1991).

Karlheinz STOCKHAUSEN
1928–
German composer

A leading exponent of electronic experimental and serial music, and a major influence on avant-garde musicians, Karlheinz Stockhausen was born in Mödrath. He studied at nearby Cologne and in Paris with Messiaen (p.189), where he learned the techniques of electronic music. Early pieces, such as *Kontrapunkte* (1952), show the influence of Webern and Messiaen, but Stockhausen took the principles of serial composition even further in his eleven *Klavierstücke* (1953–56) and *Gruppen* (1957) for three orchestras. After visiting the USA in 1958, he was influenced by John Cage's (p.194) use of chance procedures and applied these to his own music. His later compositions, such as *Licht* (1970) are more conventional.

1928 In China, Nationalist forces led by Chiang Kai-shek enter the capital, Peking, bringing an end to the civil war. Now that he has successfully taken control of the capital, Chiang may be regarded as effective ruler of China.

1928 Revolution erupts in Afghanistan when King Amanullah attempts drastic modernization including the abolition of the veil for women. The proposed new regime is said to be influenced by the king's Russian and Turkish advisors.

Anne FRANK
1929–45
German-Jewish diarist

The diary of an unknown teenage Jewish girl, who was forced to spend her youth in hiding from Nazi persecution during World War II, has become world-famous. The diary was published in 1947 and has been translated into more than 50 languages. It was written – with no sense of despair – in the form of letters to an imaginary friend called Kitty. Annelies Marie Frank was born in Frankfurt. She was the second of two daughters and, in 1933, her father took his family to Amsterdam, Holland, when the Nazis took power in Germany. In 1941, the Germans invaded Holland and the family went into hiding in secret rooms above the office of the Frank firm. They lived there from July 1942 to August 1944. This was the period in which Anne kept her diary. Friends, in particular

ANNE FRANK'S DIARY
As well as being published as a book, Anne's story has been brought to the world's attention in plays and a film.

Miep Gies, helped the family survive by smuggling food to them. On 4 August, 1944, the Germans discovered the hide-out; they had been betrayed. The family was sent to the Auschwitz concentration camp, where Anne's mother died. Anne and her sister were sent on to Bergen-Belsen (another camp), where they died of typhus. Her father, Otto, survived and spent the rest of his life promoting Anne's diary.

Martin Luther KING, JR
1929–68
US civil rights leader

Son of a Baptist preacher, Martin Luther King, Jr was born in Atlanta, Georgia. When he was 15, he went to college on a scholarship and, in 1948, he gained his degree in divinity and became a Baptist minister. In the 1950s, African-Americans in the southern states were still segregated from whites in public places such as buses and schools. When King moved to Alabama, he soon became a leading figure in the civil-rights movement and a

founder and leader of the Southern Christian Leadership. He was influenced by the philosophy of the Indian leader Gandhi (p.119) and pushed for non-violent resistance to segregation laws and discrimination. He made brilliant speeches, including his rallying cry, "I have a dream…" spoken in 1963, when he organized a peaceful march on Washington DC. The next year, the Civil Rights Act became law and King was awarded the Nobel Peace Prize for his work and commitment to a peaceful struggle. On 4 April, 1968, King was assassinated by a sniper in Memphis, Tennessee. In his last speech before he died, he said, "I may not get to the promised land with you, but I want you to know tonight that we as a people will."

Yasser ARAFAT
1929–
Palestinian leader

In 1993, Arafat and the prime minister of Israel, Yitzhak Rabin (p.204), signed a peace agreement in which Israel

Yasser Arafat

agreed to withdraw from Jericho and the Gaza Strip and the areas were transferred to Palestinian control. Both men received the Nobel Peace Prize for this in 1994. Born in Jerusalem, Yasser Arafat attended Cairo University, where he became leader of the Palestinian Students' Union. In 1956, while in Beirut, he co-founded Al Fatah, which was to become the leading military wing of the Palestinian Liberation Organization (PLO), formed in 1964. By 1969, the PLO was controlled by Arafat's Al Fatah group. As leader of the PLO, Arafat campaigned tirelessly for an independent Palestinian state, free from Israeli influence. He managed to keep control of the many opposing splinter groups of the organization and gradually gained world recognition for the PLO and its aims. He came to favour a policy of political persuasion rather than terrorism. In the 1980s, the PLO splintered into several factions and Arafat was forced to leave Lebanon but he remained leader of the majority PLO. In 1985, he made an agreement with King Hussein of Jordan (p.220) to recognize the state of Israel provided that, at the same time, some Israeli territory was restored to the Palestinians. This pact failed, but it was nevertheless the start of many important peace initiatives.

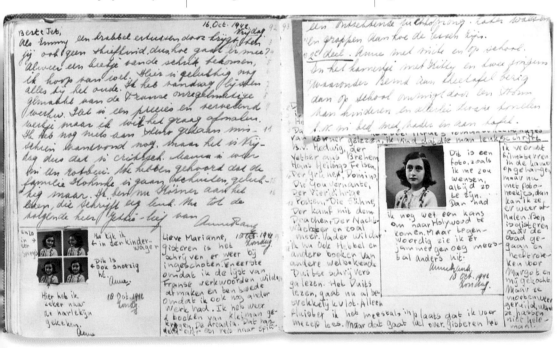

1929 The US movie industry holds its first award ceremony in Hollywood, California. The Academy of Motion Picture Arts and Sciences votes William Wellman's film *Wings* best picture of 1927–28.

1929 Wall Street slumps after the New York Stock Exchange crashes, marking the start of the Great Depression in the USA. Banks and companies collapse and many people in both the USA and Europe lose all their savings.

Roger BANNISTER
1929–
English athlete and neurologist

Shortly after completing his medical training at St Mary's Hospital, London, in 1954, Roger Bannister became the first person to run a mile (1.609 km) in less than four minutes (3 minutes, 59.4 seconds). Later in the same year, he broke his own record against John Landy of Australia at the Empire Games, by running the mile in 3 minutes 58.8 seconds. Roger Gilbert Bannister was born in Harrow, Middlesex, and read medicine at Oxford. At the height of his amateur athletics career (1947–54), he won the mile event in the Oxford versus Cambridge match four times and was a finalist in the 1,500 metres at the 1952 Olympic Games in Helsinki. He was knighted in 1975 for his services to sport as chairman of the Sports Council. In 1985, he was appointed Master of Pembroke College, Oxford, following a distinguished career as a neurologist.

Arnold PALMER
1929–
US golfer

One of the post-war golfing greats, Arnold Palmer attracted a huge number of fans, known as "Arnie's Army", on both sides of the Atlantic. He is credited with turning golf from an elitist sport into a popular pastime. He was born in Latrobe, Pennsylvania. In 1954, he was US amateur champion and a year later, as a professional, he won the Canadian Open Championship. In 1960, Palmer won the US Open and, in 1961 and 1962, he won the Open championship. Twice captain of the US Ryder Cup team, he won the US Masters in 1958, 1960, 1962, and 1964, supported by his fans. In 1968, Palmer became the first golfer to earn $1 million playing golf.

Edward O. WILSON
1929 –
US biologist

Recognized as the world's leading authority on ants, Edward Wilson extended his insect research into studying the social behaviour of humans and this is whatmade him famous. He was born in Alabama and became interested in animals and insects as a child. From his early studies on ants in the 1950s, he discovered pheromones, the chemicals with which ants communicate with each other. He developed the study of sociobiology and in his *Sociobiology: the New Synthesis* (1975) asserted that our behaviour is a result not only of our cultural upbringing, but also of our genes. In *The Diversity of Life* (1992), he warned of the danger of losing species through extinction. In 1995, he received the Audubon Medal for his contribution to conservation and to environmental protection.

1930

Ted HUGHES
1930–98
English poet

One of Britain's foremost poets, Hughes was appointed Britain's Poet Laureate in 1984. Edward J. Hughes was born in Mytholmroyd, Yorkshire. He won a scholarship to Cambridge University. Having begun a degree in English literature, he changed to

THE RACE FOR SPACE

In 1957, the USSR sent the artificial satellite *Sputnik 1* into orbit around Earth, starting a space race between the USSR and the USA. Both countries wanted to boost their national pride and feared the other might exploit space for military use.

TO THE MOON
At first, the USSR led the race for space. In 1961, YURI GAGARIN (p.218) became the first person in space and, in 1965, his compatriot ALEKSEY LEONOV (p.219) became the first person to walk in space. Soviet successes prompted the USA to begin the Apollo programme that aimed to land a man on the Moon by 1970. In 1966, the USSR landed the unmanned *Luna IX* on the Moon, but the USA won the race in July 1969 when NEIL ARMSTRONG and EDWIN "BUZZ" ALDRIN (1930–) stepped out of *Apollo 11*.

INTO SPACE
After the Moon landings, both countries concentrated on exploring the rest of the solar system, sending out unmanned flights as far as Neptune and Pluto. Space travel proved expensive, so the countries started to work together. Soviet and US craft first linked up in 1975 and, by the late 1990s, the two nations were building an orbiting space station together. The space race had ended in a peaceful draw.

Edwin "Buzz" Aldrin walks on the Moon.

1929 Seven gangsters are gunned down in Chicago, USA, in "the St Valentine's Day massacre". The killers are believed to have been acting for gangster Al Capone in a fight for control of the illegal alcohol trade during Prohibition.

1929 Factional squabbling between people in the kingdom of the Serbs, Croats, and Slovenes gives King Alexander no choice but to dissolve Parliament and set up a dictatorship. The country is renamed Yugoslavia.

archaeology and anthropology. Nature in its primitive, cruel, and beautiful forms mesmerized Hughes. He married the American poet Sylvia Plath in 1956 and published his first volume of verse, *The Hawk in the Rain*, a year later. Plath and Hughes lived in the USA for some years before moving to London and Devon, England. They separated in 1962 and the following year Plath committed suicide, an action that profoundly affected Hughes. It was three years before he began the explosion of verse that continued until his death in 1998. *Crow* (1970) and the children's story *The Iron Man* (1968) are among his best-known works. *The Birthday Letters*, a collection of poems published only months before his death, tells, for the first time, his version of his relationship with Plath.

NEIL ARMSTRONG
This photo shows Armstrong inside the lunar module of Apollo 11.

Neil
ARMSTRONG
1930–
US astronaut

On 20 July, 1969, the words "That's one small step for [a] man, one giant leap for mankind" were the first spoken by a human being standing on the surface of another world. It was astronaut Neil Armstrong who uttered this sentence as he stepped from the Apollo landing craft to become the first person to walk on the Moon. He was born in Ohio and was always looking to the sky – he had a pilot's licence before he learned to drive a car. After serving as a fighter pilot in the Korean War, he became a test pilot. In 1962, Armstrong was selected to take part in the US space programme. He made his first space flight in 1966, aboard the *Gemini 8*. The mission ended after less than 11 hours due to engine failure. Three years later, he commanded the *Apollo 11*, the first human expedition to the Moon. Watched by millions on live television, Armstrong took his leaps on the Moon with Buzz Aldrin and the goal of the US space programme had been achieved.

Jean-Luc
GODARD
1930–
French film director

Godard remains one of the most influential and controversial of contemporary film makers. He was born in Paris. After college he became a film critic, writing for the influential film magazine *Cahiers du Cinéma*. He teamed up with another famous director-to-be, François Truffaut, to make his first feature film, *A Bout de Souffle* (*Breathless*) (1959). Godard uses improvised dialogue, disjointed storylines, and unconventional techniques in cutting and shooting in the film. These methods were developed further in later films, such as *Alphaville* (1965), and established him as the leader of the French "New Wave" movement. Throughout his career, Godard made few concessions to popular taste, but his work has been absorbed by more commercial directors.

STANLEY MILLER
The biochemist became professor of chemistry at the University of California in San Diego.

Stanley
MILLER
1930–
US biochemist

Stanley Miller greatly increased our understanding of how life might have begun on this planet. After university, Miller went to Chicago, where, together with Harold Urey, he tried to recreate the formation of life on Earth. He added an electrical discharge to water under a gas mixture of methane, ammonia, and hydrogen. After a week, he found that amino acids, the ingredients of protein – an essential constituent of all living organisms – had been formed. Since 1960, he has taught at the University of California.

1930 Spanish dictator General Primo de Rivera resigns and General Damasco Berenguer is appointed prime minister. Madrid is the scene of clashes between police and students. After 15 months, the country becomes a republic.

1930 Emperor Haile Selassie of Ethiopia is crowned in a ceremony attended by foreign dignitaries and conducted by the Archbishop of the Coptic Church. Liberia is the only other African country with a black African ruler.

Derek
WALCOTT
1930–
Caribbean poet and
playwright

It is for his poems that Derek Walcott is most famous. His early poetry is lyrical, and celebrates the natural beauties of the Caribbean, but his later work develops into a tighter style as he examines his increasing isolation from his homeland. Born in St Lucia, Derek Alton Walcott was educated at the University of the West Indies and, by the age of 20, his plays were being produced in Trinidad. In 1958, with a Rockefeller Foundation grant, he went to New York City to study theatre, thereafter teaching part-time at Boston University. In 1962, he published *In a Green Night: Poems 1948–60*. He published several more volumes before his *Collected Poems* in 1986 and *Odyssey* in 1993. In 1992, Walcott was awarded the Nobel Prize for Literature.

JAMES DEAN was the first actor to receive a posthumous nomination for an Academy Award for his role in East of Eden.

James
DEAN
1931–55
US actor

A symbol of youthful rebellion, James Dean became a worldwide cult figure with young people – although he made only three films. He was born James Bryon in Indiana. His mother died when he was only five and he grew up on his uncle's farm. He began acting and attended the Actors' Studio in New York. He appeared on stage and television before landing the starring role in *East of Eden* (1955). This was followed by *Rebel Without a Cause* (1955), in which his performance as a sensitive, troubled youth earned him nationwide fame. He was killed in a car crash, age 24, before the release of his last film *Giant* (1956).

Mikhail
GORBACHEV
1931–
Soviet statesman

Born and raised on a farm, his mother a farm hand and his father a tractor driver and Communist Party official, Mikhail Gorbachev joined the Communist Party in 1952. He became a member of the Politburo, the Soviet governing body, in 1980 and became Premier Chernenko's right-hand man during the administration of 1984 to 1985. On Chernenko's death, he became party general secretary. Gorbachev set about the most significant reform of the USSR since the Russian Revolution under the twin banners of *glasnost*, meaning "openness" and *perestroika*, "restructuring". He met US President Ronald Reagan in a series of summits (1985–88) in order to improve relations between the Soviet Union and the West. To this end he was frequently seen in the West with his wife, Raisa (up to then, Soviet officials did not travel much). Gorbachev went on to sign agreements to reduce nuclear forces and pulled Soviet forces out of Afghanistan. During this time, the more radical Boris Yeltsin grew increasingly powerful and, in 1991, Gorbachev resigned when the Communist Party was abolished and the Soviet Union dissolved.

Toni
MORRISON
1931–
African-US writer

In her novels, Morrison deals with the African-American story with courage and in a style that is poetic yet brutally cold-blooded. Born in Ohio, Chloe Anthony Wofford (Toni Morrison is her pen name)

1932
A "peaceful revolution" in Thailand, during which only the palace chief of staff is killed, removes King Prajadhipok from office. The military intends to make Thailand a constitutional rather than absolute monarchy.

1932
The capture of Shanghai by Japanese forces confirms the belief that the Manchurian Incident (which began with a surprise attack on Mukden) was planned as a preliminary skirmish before a full-scale invasion of China.

grew up in the Midwest, attending college in both Washington, D.C., and New York City. She taught writing at Howard University in Washington then, in 1965, moved to New York. She edited fiction for a publishing house before writing her first novel, *The Bluest Eye* (1970). *Song of Solomon* (1977) and *Tar Baby* (1981) shot Morrison to fame and, in 1988, *Beloved* won the Pulitzer Prize for fiction. In 1993, she was awarded the Nobel Prize for Literature.

Roger
PENROSE
1931–
English astrophysicist

Born in Colchester, Roger Penrose studied at University College, London, and at Cambridge University. He was professor of mathematics at Birkbeck College, London, then moved to Oxford University. With Stephen Hawking (p.230), he developed some of the theorems that describe black holes, notably the singularity theorems, which state that once the gravitational collapse of a star has reached a certain point, singularities, which form the centre of a black hole, are inevitable. He proposed the idea of cosmic censorship, in which some events are hidden to observers outside a black hole, and has devised a new model of the universe with basic building blocks that he calls twistors.

Desmond
TUTU
1931–
South African archbishop and anti-apartheid campaigner

An exuberant clergyman, Desmond Tutu did much to draw world attention to the inequalities of South African society and to support Nelson Mandela (p.201). Tutu was born in Transvaal. After working as a teacher, he trained for the Anglican priesthood and was ordained in 1960. He became the first black person to become Dean of Johannesburg (1975), Bishop of Johannesburg (1985), and Archbishop of Cape Town (1986). As archbishop, he was head of South Africa's Anglican church. Tutu was a leading spokesman in the struggle against apartheid, which denied equal rights to South Africa's non-white population. In 1984, he won the Nobel Peace Prize for his dedication to non-violent campaign methods. Apartheid was finally abolished in 1993. Since 1995, Tutu has headed the Truth and Reconciliation Commission, which has aimed to heal the bitter divisions of his country.

Louis
MALLE
1932–95
French film director

Born into a wealthy French sugar-producing family, Malle began his career as assistant to the explorer Jacques Cousteau (p.191) on the underwater film *Le Monde du Silence* (*The Silent World*) (1956), for which they shared an Academy Award. He made his directorial debut with *Ascenseur pour l'échaffaud* (*Frantic*) (1957) and was associated with the "New Wave" movement. His second film, *Les Amants* (*The Lovers*) (1958) was a critical and commercial success and established Malle's reputation as a director and Jeanne Moreau's (1928–) as an actress. Later films include *Lacombe Lucien* (1974), *Atlantic City* (1980), and *My Dinner with André* (1981).

CORY AQUINO
When she became president of the Philippines, Cory Aquino became a symbol of opposition to an oppressive regime.

Cory
AQUINO
1933–
Filipino politician

After a long campaign against the dictator Ferdinand Marcos, Cory Aquino was proclaimed Philippine president in 1986. She was born Maria Corazon Cojuangco to a wealthy family north of Manila. She gained a degree in mathematics in the USA. In 1956, she married Benigno Aquino. He was imprisoned for life by Marcos for political opposition in 1972, but was released because of a heart condition and the couple lived in exile in the USA. In 1983, on his return to the Philippines, Benigno was assassinated by a military guard at Manila airport. Cory Aquino decided to continue her husband's work and ran in the 1986 presidential elections. She was officially declared the loser but, when it was proved that the ballot had been rigged, she took power and Marcos fled the country. Military opposition marred her presidency and, on the sixth attempt at a coup to overthrow her, the US Army had to intervene. In 1992, she chose not to run for president again.

1932 Bolivia and Paraguay go to war over the Chaco region, a wilderness area supposedly rich in oil deposits. After three years of fighting, with heavy losses and no winner, the Chaco is divided, with Paraguay receiving the lion's share.

1933 Adolf Hitler becomes chancellor of Germany, beginning the period of the Third Reich. Trade unions are banned and the organized persecution of Jews and other minorities begins with the setting up of concentration camps.

James BROWN
1933–
US soul singer

With more than 30 years of hit records and touring, James Brown earned the nickname "The Godfather of Soul". He also pioneered the punchy rhythmic guitar-and-horns style that became known as funk. Brown had a troubled childhood and was arrested for armed robbery at age 16. He began his professional career backed by a former gospel group, The Famous Flames and later mixed gospel and blues music in his own unique style. By the early 1960s, he had become America's leading rhythm-and-blues star. His first international success was "Out of Sight" (1964) and other best-selling hits include "Papa's Got a Brand New Bag" (1965), "Sex Machine" (1970), and "Living in America" (1986). Brown was back in prison in 1989 on drug charges but was released in 1990 and continued to tour well into 1999.

Richard ROGERS
1933–
English architect

Richard Rogers was one of the new wave of post-war architects. At first, he had

MILLENNIUM CELEBRATION
The Dome building in Greenwich, London, was designed by Richard Rogers to celebrate the year 2000.

more recognition overseas than in Britain, but his buildings are now acclaimed worldwide. He studied architecture in London and at Yale, where he was influenced by the work of Frank Lloyd Wright (p.135). His early designs include the Renault Factory in Swindon (1967), which was pre-fabricated in steel. He pioneered the "high-tech" style with a house for his parents made of steel and plastic. With Renzo Piano, he designed the Pompidou Centre in Paris (1971–77), which has coloured service ducts and escalators on the outside and a visible steel skeleton. Rogers used similar ideas for the Lloyd's Building in London (1979–87), which is clad in stainless steel.

Yuri GAGARIN
1934–68
Soviet cosmonaut

The first man to travel in space was born near Gzhatsk in the USSR. In 1957, he joined the Soviet air force, flying fighter planes in the Arctic. Excited by the launch of the first space satellites, he applied to join the Soviet space programme and was chosen to make the first ever manned space flight. On 12 April, 1961, he took off in *Vostok 1*, orbiting Earth once and then returning safely. He was later killed in a plane crash. His home town was renamed Gagarin in his honour.

Brigitte BARDOT
1934–
French film actress

A famous film star of the 1960s, Brigitte Bardot later became a recluse devoted to campaigning for animal rights. She was born Camille Javal in Paris, to wealthy parents. She studied dancing and, at 13, went to the Paris Conservatory. She worked as a model in her mother's dress shop and, when she was 15, posed for the cover of *Elle* magazine, as Brigitte Bardot. After playing bit parts in films, she came to the attention of film director, Roger Vadim, who made her an international star in *Et Dieu créa la femme (And God Created Woman)* (1956).

Hank AARON
1934–
US baseball player

The baseball player nicknamed "Hammerin' Hank" was born Henry Louis Aaron in Alabama. Aaron set almost every batting record in his 23-season career. He scored 2,297 lifetime runs, 1,477 extra-base hits, and 755 career home runs, breaking Babe Ruth's (p.167) long-standing record. Aaron played for the Milwaukee Braves, the Atlanta Braves, and the Milwaukee Brewers. A fine all-round player, Aaron's skill was never fully appreciated and he was named Most Valuable Player only once. When he retired, he became a spokesman for minority groups in baseball. In 1982, he was elected to baseball's Hall of Fame. His autobiography, *I Had a Hammer*, was published in 1990.

BRIGITTE BARDOT
Famous for her stunning looks and blonde hair, "BB", or "Bébé", became a movie sex symbol.

Harrison BIRTWISTLE
1934–
English composer

Birtwistle studied at the Royal Manchester College of Music and the Royal Academy of Music. He worked as a clarinetist and teacher before taking up composition full time. He came to public attention with *Tragoedia* (1965) and the opera *Punch and Judy* (1968), works which showed his interest in medieval music as well as the influence of Stravinsky (p.150) and Varèse. In the 1970s, he developed a slow, ritual style and included some electronic instruments in his music. While he was associate director of the National Theatre in London (1975–88), he wrote another opera, *The Mask of Orpheus* (1986), followed by *Gawain* (1990) and *The Second Mrs Kong* (1994). He was knighted in 1988 and made a professor at King's College, London, in 1993.

1933 In the United States, President Franklin Roosevelt announces his strategy for dealing with the economic depression. His "New Deal" sets aside $3 billion for public works and increases government regulation of industry.

1934 In Nicaragua, members of the National Guard kill General Sandino, who has just dined with the president. They are enraged by his criticism of their leader, General Somoza, who now seems likely to launch a coup.

Jane GOODALL
1934–
English naturalist

Jane Goodall's studies into chimpanzee behaviour were conducted first-hand in Africa. They revealed, among other things, that these primates use tools, when it was thought only humans did so. Goodall was born in London and, as a child, was passionate about animals. She worked to save money for a passage to Africa and, in Kenya, she worked for Louis Leakey (p.181), the famous fossil-hunter. In 1960, Goodall set up an observation camp in the Gombe Stream Game Reserve to research chimpanzee behaviour. Her studies revealed the astonishing complexities in the social lives of chimpanzees, including their practice of hunting other animals for food. Goodall stayed in Kenya until 1975. Thanks to her research, Goodall worked out the best way to protect chimps. The Jane Goodall Institute focuses attention on their plight. Today, Goodall works in conservation and writes about her experiences and research.

JANE GOODALL
A wild chimpanzee exhibits sufficient trust to accept bananas directly from animal behaviour specialist Jane Goodall.

Aleksey LEONOV
1934–
Soviet cosmonaut

Leonov was born near Kemerovo, USSR, and was a fighter pilot in the Soviet air force from 1957 to 1959, when he was selected to be a cosmonaut. On 18 March 1965, he took off in *Voskhod 2* with Pavel Belyayev. After orbiting Earth twice, Leonov put on a spacesuit and stepped out through an airlock to make the first-ever spacewalk. He floated for 10 minutes, looking down at Earth. He said it was like "swimming over a vast, colourful map". Ten years later, he made a second space flight, commanding *Soyuz 19* in the first Soviet–US mission. On 17 July, 1975, two craft docked in space and Leonov shook hands with US astronaut Tom Stafford.

Mary QUANT
1934–
English fashion designer

Mary Quant's fashion designs include some of the most recognizable symbols of the 1960s. Quant studied at Goldsmiths College, London. In 1955, she opened a boutique and pioneered a revolution in women's clothing – her mini-skirt design, worn several centimetres above the knee, was controversial but popular and remains a major fashion creation of the 20th century. Her geometric designs in bright colours or black and white were sold at affordable prices, marking the start of "high-street fashion". She expanded into cosmetics and textile design and was awarded the British Council's Hall of Fame Award in 1990.

Norman SCHWARZKOPF
1934–
US army general

Popularly known as "Stormin' Norman", General H. Norman Schwarzkopf served as commander-in-chief of the Allied forces during the Gulf War with Iraq in 1990. He was born in Trenton, New Jersey. He graduated from the US military academy at West Point in 1956. During the Vietnam War, he was awarded a Silver Star for bravery and led the US ground forces during the Grenada invasion of 1983. When Saddam Hussein invaded Kuwait, Schwarzkopf led troops in Operation Desert Shield, the allied build-up in Saudi Arabia. This was followed by Operation Desert Storm – a six-week aerial attack designed to destroy Iraq's communications, followed by a brief ground war. Schwarzkopf retired from the army in 1992 and became a public speaker and consultant. In 1992, he published his autobiography, *It Doesn't Take A Hero.*

John SURTEES
1934–
English motorcyclist and racing driver

John Surtees is the only man to win world titles on two and four wheels. He was born in Westerham, Kent. Before turning to car racing, he won seven world motorbike championships, including the 350 cc motor-cycling world title (1958–60) and the 500 cc title (1956 and 1958–60) on an MV Agusta motorbike. In 1964, Surtees won the world motor-racing title in a Ferrari. On his retirement from motor sports he became a manufacturer of racing cars.

1934 In Russia, the assassination of Sergei Kirov, a Communist Party leader, leads to the summary trials and executions of at least 100 people. Stalin claims the purges are intended to eliminate enemies of the working class.

1934 Mao Zedong leads Chinese communists on the "Long March" to escape the Chinese Nationalist Army. Only 10,000 of the original 100,000 make it to Shaanxi Province, having crossed 24 rivers and 18 mountain ranges.

1935

Elvis PRESLEY
1935–77
US rock 'n' roll singer

Known as the "King of rock 'n' roll", Elvis Aaron Presley was the biggest popular music star in the world until the rise of The Beatles in the mid-1960s. He began singing country-and-western songs in Memphis, Tennessee. His style combined white country music with African-American rhythm-and-blues. In 1953, Elvis paid to make a record for his mother's birthday at Sun Records Studio in Memphis. The owner, Sam Phillips, offered him a recording contract. The result was "rock 'n' roll", as Presley instantly caught the imagination of record-buying teenagers with songs like "Heartbreak Hotel" (1956), "Blue Suede Shoes" (1956), and "Hound Dog" (1956). Presley became a sensation with his concerts and television appearances. He later concentrated on film roles, among them *Love Me Tender* (1956) and *Jailhouse Rock* (1958), but his records continued to outsell any other performer – he recorded 97 gold singles. As The Beatles and The Rolling Stones came to dominate pop music, Elvis began to stay more at his home, Graceland, in Memphis. He died from heart failure.

ELVIS PRESLEY
An electrifying stage performer, Elvis served in the army from 1958 to 1960. On his return to music, he never quite regained his former success.

Jiving was a typical rock 'n' roll dance style

THE ROCK 'N' ROLL YEARS

In July 1954, ELVIS PRESLEY walked into Sun Records in Memphis, Tennessee, and recorded a blues song, "That's All Right". It transformed the history of modern entertainment because what Elvis had done was to invent a new form of music – a form that was later to become known as rock 'n' roll, or rock.

ROCK ORIGINS
Elvis's music led to the explosion of popular music. African-American musicians, such as CHUCK BERRY (1926–) and LITTLE RICHARD (1932–), popularized a hard-driving sound with its roots in rhythm-and-blues, while white musicians, such as BUDDY HOLLY (p.222), produced softer pop songs.

ROCK WORLDWIDE
In the 1960s, rock music became an international phenomenon, with groups such as the BEATLES (p.227) and the US Beach Boys. BOB DYLAN (p.228) married rock music with folk, while the ROLLING STONES (p.223) and JIMI HENDRIX (p.229) updated blues music, and ARETHA FRANKLIN (p.230) mixed gospel music with the blues to produce soul.

King HUSSEIN
1935–99
Jordanian ruler

King Hussein was educated in England at Harrow School and Sandhurst military college. He ascended the throne of Jordan in 1953 at the age of 17. Within days, he announced a series of reforms, including the right to freedom of speech. By 1960, his country had begun to see dramatic economic growth. In 1967, Hussein lost all areas of his kingdom west of the Jordan River during the Arab-Israeli wars. He finally renounced Jordan's claim to the West Bank in 1988 and signed a peace treaty with Israel in 1994. Hussein was regularly

1935 In Germany, the Nuremberg Laws deprive Jews of citizenship, bar them from working in education and the media, and restrict them from working in law and medicine. Marriage between Jews and non-Jews is forbidden.

1935 Ethiopia appeals to the League of Nations to prevent an Italian invasion but, in a speech broadcast throughout Italy, the country's dictator, Mussolini, boasts that he will not be bowed by the league.

employed as a mediator in the Middle East, particularly between the Israelis and the Palestinians. He attempted to prevent the outbreak of the Gulf War in 1990 and, after the war, reluctantly supported Saddam Hussein. He died of cancer, and was succeeded by his eldest son, Abdullah, from his second marriage, to English-born Antoinette Gardiner (Princess Muna).

Woody ALLEN
1935–
US film director and actor

Actor-writer-director Woody Allen was born Allen Konigsberg in Brooklyn, New York. He dropped out of college to become a comedy sketch writer for television. In the early 1960s he was a stand-up comic, which helped him to develop his on-stage personality of a neurotic, wisecracking, intellectual misfit in a complex and hostile world. His films are highly personal and made outside the Hollywood system. They are often set in a contemporary urban situation, and range from bittersweet comedies to serious dramas. His films include *Play It Again, Sam* (1972), *Love and Death* (1975), *Annie Hall* (1977), *Hannah and Her Sisters* (1986) – the latter two winning Academy Awards – and *Bullets Over Broadway* (1994). His most recent film is *Celebrity* (1999).

Giorgio ARMANI
1935–
Italian clothes designer

The name "Armani" on clothes became a byword for understated chic during the 1980s and 1990s. The man who gave his name to these

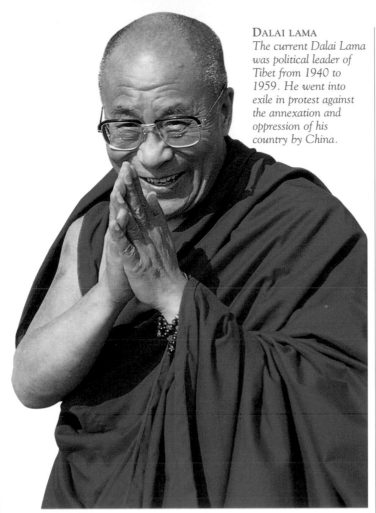

DALAI LAMA
The current Dalai Lama was political leader of Tibet from 1940 to 1959. He went into exile in protest against the annexation and oppression of his country by China.

fashionable items was born Giorgio Armani in Piacenza. After studying medicine at Milan University and doing military service for a while, he became a window dresser in a department store. In 1961, he joined the men's clothing company Cerruti as a designer. He established his own fashion consultancy in 1975 and quickly gained success as a producer of clothes for both men and women. His relaxed style is based on elegant textures and simple outlines.

Dalai LAMA
1935–
Tibetan Buddhist leader

The Dalai Lama is the spiritual and political leader of the Tibetan people. They believe he is the living Compassionate Buddha, who has been reborn in a series of incarnations (bodies). When he dies, buddhist monks search for his new incarnation among recently born boys. The present Dalai Lama is the 14th incarnation. He was born Tenzin Gyatso into a peasant family in Amdo Province, Tibet. At the age of two, he was selected as Dalai Lama and taken away from his parents to be brought up by monks. He has spent his life campaigning for independence from the Chinese, who took over Tibet in 1950 (when he was 16) with violence and the destruction of monasteries. For the next nine years, he sought peaceful co-existence but, in 1959, he was forced to flee in disguise over the border to India, where he set up a government in exile. In 1989, he was awarded the Nobel Peace Prize for his non-violent opposition to China.

CHRISTO
1935–
Bulgarian-born US artist

Christo Javacheff was born in Bulgaria. He studied art in Sofia, Prague, and Vienna before moving to Paris in 1958. He began to create "packaged", or "wrapped" art. He started with small household objects such as bottles, cans, and furniture and moved on to cars and trees, wrapping them in plastic or canvas sheeting tied with ropes. Christo believed that by hiding an object, he emphasized its basic form. Since 1961, he has worked in partnership with his wife, Jeanne-Claude, and the pair settled in New York in 1964. Since then, they have "packaged" large buildings and pieces of landscape, including part of the coastline near Sydney, Australia (1969), the Pont Neuf, Paris (1975–85), and the Reichstag, Berlin (1995). These later wrappings were, of course, only temporary.

Sylvia EARLE
1935–
US marine biologist and undersea explorer

Sylvia Earle became famous in 1970 when, with four other women, she lived for two weeks in a specially constructed shelter on the sea-bed. She was born in New Jersey, and, when she was 13 her family moved to Florida. Sylvia studied botany at university and learned to scuba dive so that she could study the plant life of the ocean at first-hand. From the late 1960s, she began to make record-breaking dives. In her 1995 book, *Sea Change*, she describes the threat to the oceans caused by human pollution: "If the sea is sick we feel it. If it dies, we die. Our future and the future of the oceans are one."

1935 Japanese forces march into Beijing, China, to set up a new state. The Autonomous Federation for Joint Defence against communism recognizes Chinese sovereignty but plans to work with Japan to rescue China from communism.

1935 Despite an anti-monarchist revolt led by the former prime minister Eleutherios Venizelos in March, a referendum by the people in November restores the monarchy to Greece. King George II returns after a 12-year exile.

Issey MIYAKE
1935–
Japanese clothes designer

Although famous for some startling items, Issey Miyake has always aimed to create enduring designs rather than passing fashions. He was born in Hiroshima and educated at Tama University. He moved to Paris in 1965 to study fashion design. There he worked in the fashion houses of Laroche and Givenchy before settling in New York City in 1969, where he founded his own business in 1971. Miyake revealed a bold individual style in his first two shows, in 1971 and 1973, which blended ideas from the West and Japan. His clothes had flowing, sculpted lines that wrapped the body in several loose layers. During the 1980s, he created sensational items using geometric shapes, such as stiff bodices, which curved up around the shoulders, and moulded silicone bustiers.

Luciano PAVAROTTI
1935–
Italian opera singer

Pavarotti has sung in opera houses, concert halls, parks, and outdoor arenas, and on television and on CDs, reaching a wider audience than any other opera singer. He was born in Modena and quickly rose to international stardom. He first sang at La Scala, Milan, in 1965 in Verdi's *Rigoletto*. He then toured with Joan Sutherland (p.210) in Australia. Pavarotti is a lyric tenor, noted for the purity of his voice and his ability to reach the highest notes in a tenor's range. He is one of the most successful opera singers in the world. In 1990, he sang with Placido Domingo and José Carreras as "The Three Tenors" at a televised concert in Rome, marking the soccer World Cup, and his recording of Puccini's aria *Nessun Dorma* ("Nobody is sleeping") topped pop charts around the world.

Lester PIGGOTT
1935–
English flat-racing jockey

A naturally fearless rider, Lester Piggott rode his first winner at the age of just 12. He was born in Wantage, Berkshire, into a horse-racing family and, by the time he was 15, he had been placed 11th in the list of top British jockeys. At 19, he rode his first Derby winner, Never Say Die. Piggott was taller than most jockeys and gained the nickname "The Long Fellow".

During his career, he rode 4,349 winners in Britain, a record of 29 Classic winners, and nine Derby winners. Piggott was so successful that he was considered a safe bet, becoming a favourite with the punters. After retiring from riding, Piggott became a trainer of racehorses. He was given a three-year prison sentence for tax offences in 1987, but was released on parole after a year. He returned to racing in 1990, and in 1992 won his 30th Classic race, the 2,000 Guineas at Newmarket.

LESTER PIGGOTT
In 1954, Piggott won the English Derby at Epsom on Never Say Die, the first of nine wins in the race.

Gary PLAYER
1935–
South African golfer

Gary Player helped to lay the foundations of modern golf. Born in Johannesburg, he was a natural athlete and his commitment to muscle-building exercises, diet, and continuous practice made him a great competitor. In his highly successful career, lasting for more than 40 years, Player won the British Open three times (1959, 1968, 1974), the US Masters three times (1961, 1974, 1978), the US Open once (1965), and the US Professional Golf Association title twice (1962, 1972). He also won 13 South African Open titles and six Australian Opens. When Player gave up competitive golf, he became a member of the US Seniors Tour. He returned to live in South Africa, where he breeds horses.

Buddy HOLLY
1936–59
US rock'n'roll singer

Buddy Holly was one of the most influential of the early rock 'n' roll singers. With self-

---

1935 Europe is arming itself. Germany introduces conscription and creates an air force. France doubles the period of national service for soldiers, and Britain announces plans to expand all its defence forces.

1936 On the orders of Adolf Hitler, German troops march into the Rhineland, a region lost by Germany to France at the end of World War I. French politicians want to take military action, but the British urge restraint.

penned songs such as "That'll be the Day" (1957), "Rave On" (1958), and "It Doesn't Matter Any More" (1959), he became the first rock 'n' roll artist to regularly write his own hits. He was also the first rock 'n' roll artist to record with a string orchestra. He was born Charles Hardin Holley in Texas and his early musical interests included country-and-western, Mexican, and African-American music. He formed a group called The Crickets, with which he toured, although he split from them shortly before his death. The Crickets were the first group to use two guitars, bass, and drums, in what was to become the classic musical combination for a rock band. He was killed in a plane crash while flying between concerts, aged only 22. His popularity increased after his death and he became a cult pop figure.

BUDDY HOLLY
Holly (left) and members of his band, The Crickets, recorded many hits that have since become classics.

F. W. DE KLERK
1936–
South African politician

In 1990, South African president F.W. de Klerk lifted the 30-year-old ban on the opposition movement, the African National Congress (ANC) and released its leader, Nelson Mandela (p.201), from prison. The two were jointly awarded the Nobel Peace Prize in 1993. Born in Johannesburg, de Klerk had a legal practice in Vereeniging and became a popular member of the National Party. He served in the cabinet of P.W. Botha from 1978 and, when Botha fell ill in 1989, de Klerk took over as leader of the National Party and acting state president. By 1994, he had abolished the apartheid system and South Africa had its first all-race national election. Mandela became president and de Klerk was vice-president.

Vaclav HAVEL
1936–
Czech writer and statesman

Born in Prague, Havel later became resident writer there. His most famous early plays are *The Garden Party* (1963) and *The Memorandum* (1965). He became a prominent figure in the Czechoslovakian "Prague Spring" reforms of 1968 under Alexander Dubcek (p.204). After the Soviet clampdown on the country, his plays were banned and his passport was seized. During the 1970s and 1980s, he was arrested several times and spent four years in prison for his attempts to improve human rights in Czechoslovakia. He was a co-founder of Charter 77 – a group dedicated to freedom of expression – and circulated the work of banned writers. He continued to lead underground anti-communist groups until 1989, when the Communist Party collapsed. In 1992, Havel oversaw the peaceful separation of Czechoslovakia into the Czech Republic and Slovakia and was elected president of the Czech Republic in 1993.

THE ROLLING STONES
Bill Wyman 1936–
Charlie Watts 1941–
Mick Jagger 1943–
Keith Richard 1943–
Brian Jones 1942–69
Jones drowned and was replaced by guitarist Mick Taylor (1948–), then Ron Wood (1947–)

Self-styled as the "the world's greatest rock 'n' roll band", The Rolling Stones formed in 1962 and soon acquired a reputation as the rebellious, dishevelled "bad boys" of rock 'n' roll. They recorded such classic 1960s singles as "(I Can't Get No) Satisfaction", "Jumping Jack Flash", and "Honky Tonk Woman" and their best-known albums include *Let It Bleed* (1969), *Sticky Fingers* (1971), and *Exile on Main Street* (1972). During the 1970s and '80s, band members pursued solo careers. Watts went into big band jazz, and Wyman left the group, but the Stones went on performing sell-out concerts, such as the 1999 Bridges to Babylon tour.

1936 In Britain, police surround Cable Street in London's East End to prevent a march by 7,000 supporters of British fascist leader Sir Oswald Mosley. Riots follow and about 80 people are arrested in the Battle of Cable Street.

1936 Civil war erupts in Spain when General Franco leads an army rebellion against the republican government. Franco warns the government that "The Spanish Restoration Movement will triumph very shortly".

Steve REICH
1936–
US composer

Inspired by African percussion music and the Balinese gamelan, Steve Reich became one of the foremost composers (along with Philip Glass) in a style of composition – using repeated patterns that gradually change shape – called "minimalist". He was born in New York City, and trained as a drummer before studying philosophy at Cornell University, and later music at the Juilliard School and Mills College. In 1966, he formed a group of musicians, mainly percussionists, to perform his music. His first success came with *Drumming* (1971), in which purely rhythmic patterns slowly get out of phase, but went on to apply the same minimalist techniques to melody and harmony in *Music for 18 Musicians* (1975) and *Tehillim* (1981). Later pieces, such as *Desert Music* (1984) for orchestra and *Different Trains* (1988) for voices and string quartet, moved away from strict minimalism. By the 1990s his records were bestsellers, and he has become internationally popular. He has worked with contemporary classical and jazz artists such as the Kronos Quartet and Pat Metheny.

Yves Saint LAURENT
1936–
French clothes designer

One of the most important post-war fashion designers, Yves Saint Laurent was born in Oran, Algeria, to French parents. When he was a 17-year-old student in Paris, he entered a competition to design a wool cocktail dress – and won first prize. This led to a job with the fashion designer Christian Dior. On Dior's death in 1957, Saint Laurent took over the firm, presenting his first collection at the age of 21. After a year's military service overseas, he returned to Paris to open his own fashion house in 1962. Over the next decade he launched many influential designs for women, including pea jackets, smocks, thigh-length boots, knickerbockers, safari jackets, and trouser suits. In 1966 he opened the first boutique in the Rive Gauche chain (there were eventually 160 of them around the world). Stylish yet casual, Saint Laurent's clothes were perfectly suited to the relaxed atmosphere of the 1960s.

Gary SOBERS
1936–
West-Indian cricketer

Arguably the finest all-round cricket player, Garfield St Auburn Sobers captained the West Indies as one of the strongest and most entertaining teams in world cricket. He was born in Bridgetown, Barbados. Not only was he a first-rate fast, medium, and slow-spin bowler, but also a brilliant batsman. Until Brian Lara hit 375 in 1994, Sobers held the world record for the highest Test innings (365 not out against Pakistan at Kingston, Jamaica in 1958). He scored just over 8,000 runs in Test cricket, including 26 centuries. Sobers is also one of a select number of players to have scored 36 runs in one over (six "sixes" off six balls). His 20-year career was rewarded with a knighthood in 1975, the year after he retired from cricket.

HAUTE COUTURE *Yves Saint Laurent's beautiful clothing designs continue to influence the fashion world.*

Philip GLASS
1937–
US composer

In the 1960s, along with other experimental composers such as Steve Reich, Philip Glass developed a system of composition using repeated patterns known as "minimalism". Glass studied music at the Juilliard School in New York City and with Nadia Boulanger in Paris. He became influenced by African and Indian music and elements of jazz and rock. His early compositions are mainly for small ensembles, but in the 1970s he became famous through the production of his first opera, *Einstein on the Beach* (1976). Since then he has concentrated on works for the stage, from *Satyagraha* (1980), to *The Making of the Representative for Planet 8* (1988), and *The Voyage* (1992), which have been performed all over the world. *Songs From Liquid Days* (1986) featured popular singer-songwriter Paul Simon (p.229).

1936 In the Spanish Civil War, Italy and Germany send military aid to General Franco's Nationalists, while Russia and the volunteer International Brigade help the Republicans. In 1939, Franco wins, becoming dictator of Spain.

1936 Edward VIII, king of England, abdicates in order to marry the twice-divorced American Mrs Wallis Simpson. He announces his decision on a radio broadcast that stuns the whole nation. He is succeeded by his brother.

Dawn FRASER
1937–
Australian swimmer

Dawn Fraser was chosen as Australia's greatest female athlete in 1988 for her outstanding Olympic and world swimming records. She was born in Sydney, and as a schoolgirl swam at the local harbourside pool in Balmain, which now bears her name. Her swimming talent was soon discovered and she went on to win 29 Australian Championships. Fraser qualified for the Olympics and won gold medals in the 100 metres freestyle at three successive Olympic Games (in Melbourne in 1956, Rome in 1960, and Tokyo in 1964), each time setting a new Olympic record. She was the first woman swimmer to achieve this feat. She also took six Commonwealth Games Gold Medals and broke 27 world records in her career. In 1964 she became the first woman to break the "magic minute" for the 100 metres freestyle, with a time of 59.5 seconds. She was awarded the MBE in 1967.

DAWN FRASER *became a national heroine after winning two gold medals in the 1956 Olympics, aged only 19.*

David HOCKNEY
1937–
English painter

One of the most important and versatile of post-war British artists, David Hockney was born in Yorkshire. He studied at Bradford College of Art and at London's Royal College of Art, and showed himself to be a brilliant draughtsman. After two years of national service, he became a full-time painter, moving away from his early abstract style to become a leader of the 1960s Pop Art movement in Britain. In 1967, inspired by a visit to California, he began a series of "swimming pool" paintings in bright acrylic colours. These included his most famous image, *A Bigger Splash*. Hockney later settled in California, where he featured in a film about himself, also called *A Bigger Splash* (1974). He has also worked extensively for the stage, designing the costumes and sets for productions of the operas *The Rake's Progress* (1975) and *The Magic Flute* (1978). During the 1980s he turned to photography, using multiple images to create photographic collages.

Marcian "Ted" HOFF
1937–
US inventor and electronic engineer

Ted Hoff was the first person to recognize that a computer could be powered by a tiny microchip. Hoff was born in Rochester, New York, and he gained a degree and a doctorate in electrical engineering before joining the Intel electronics company in 1962. By 1980 Intel was one of the largest computer companies in the world, and Hoff was named first Intel Fellow. He helped develop the single-chip microprocessor, delivered in 1971. Now standard in high-performance computers, such microprocessor chips are also used in household appliances such as fridges, air-conditioning units, and video recorders.

Renzo PIANO
1937–
Italian architect

Renzo Piano was greatly influenced by the work of R. Buckminster Fuller, who believed that technology should be used to solve social problems. Born in Genoa into a family of builders, he studied architecture in Milan. In 1970, Piano and Richard Rogers (p.218) won the commission to design the Pompidou Centre in Paris. Their solution was an uncluttered space inside, with elevators and brightly coloured pipes and ducts on the outside. Piano's notable later works include the Kansai Airport buildings, Japan (1988) and a multiple-use tower complex in Sydney, Australia (1996).

RUSSIA'S *Valentina Tereshkova was the first woman in space.*

Valentina TERESHKOVA
1937–
Soviet cosmonaut

The first woman to travel in space, Valentina Tereshkova was born in Maslennikovo, USSR. In 1961, inspired by cosmonaut Yuri Gagarin's (p.218) prediction that "there's no doubt a woman will fly in space", she wrote to Moscow asking to join the space programme. Although not a pilot, Tereshkova was accepted for training because she was a skilled parachutist. On 16 June 1963, Tereshkova took off alone in the *Vostok 6* spacecraft, orbiting the Earth 48 times in 70 hours and 50 minutes – and providing the USSR with another triumph in the US–USSR "space race".

1936 The Olympic Games are held in Berlin, Germany. Hitler transforms the event into a propaganda exercise for the Nazi regime and is furious when the African-American athlete Jesse Owens becomes the star of the Games.

1937 The first ever feature-length animated film, *Snow White and the Seven Dwarfs*, premieres. It cost Walt Disney a staggering $1.5 million to produce and took a team of artists and animators over four years to complete.

Rudolf NUREYEV
1938–93
Russian ballet dancer

Acclaimed as the greatest male ballet dancer since Nijinsky (p.161), Rudolf Nureyev danced all over the world in classical and contemporary works. He was born in Siberia and trained at the Kirov School in St Petersburg, where he became a principal dancer for the Kirov Ballet. In 1961 he defected from the Soviet Union and sought political asylum in Paris. He began a partnership with the British ballerina Margot Fonteyn (p.202), dancing the principal roles in ballets such as *Swan Lake* and *Giselle*, and together they helped to popularize ballet. Nureyev is credited with re-establishing the importance of the role of the male dancer in ballet. From 1983 to 1989 he was artistic director of the Paris Opéra Ballet.

Rod LAVER
1938–
Australian tennis player

In 1969 Rodney George Laver became the first tennis player to repeat the "grand slam" of four major tournaments (Australia, France, Britain, and the USA) in one year. He had achieved this first in 1962. Born in Rockhampton, Queensland, Laver acquired his nickname, "the Rockhampton Rocket", from his powerful left-handed play. He won the Wimbledon singles title as an amateur in 1961, and again in 1962. As a professional player, Laver won the world singles title five times between 1964 and 1970; and, in 1968, when the Wimbledon tournament allowed professionals to take part, he won the singles title, repeating his success the following year during another grand slam. Until 1978, Laver won more money playing professional tennis than any other player.

RUDOLF NUREYEV
The Russian ballet star was well known for his versatile and acrobatic dancing.

Margaret ATWOOD
1939–
Canadian writer and poet

Margaret Atwood began writing at the age of five. She was born in Ottawa, but spent much of her early life in the northern bush country of Canada. After graduating from Toronto University she taught English literature. Her first collection of poems, *The Circle Game*, was published in 1966. In 1969 a novel, *The Edible Woman* (1969), was published to great critical acclaim. *The Handmaid's Tale* (1985), *Cat's Eye* (1989), and *Alias Grace* (1996) were all nominated for the Booker Prize. Atwood's work often focuses on women and their role in the world.

She is one of Canada's most accomplished writers, who has also written children's books such as *Princess Prunella and the Purple Peanut* (1996).

Germaine GREER
1939–
Australian feminist

Author of *The Female Eunuch* – a detailed examination of women's liberation – Germaine Greer championed women's sexual freedom in the early 1970s, and her book was a bestseller around the world. She was born in Melbourne and educated at convent schools and at the universities of Melbourne and Sydney.

In 1964 she moved to England to study at Newnham College, Cambridge. From 1967–73 she taught drama at the University of Warwick. While in Britain, she became involved in alternative and radical politics. In her ground-breaking book *The Female Eunuch* (1970) she argued that society symbolically castrates women, keeping them as inferior beings and thus enslaving both men and women. She examined how society oppresses women through such institutions as marriage and the family. Greer's views on feminism have continued to be enormously influential. Her books include *The Obstacle Race: The Fortunes of Women Painters and Their Work* (1979), *Sex and Destiny: The Politics of Human Fertility* (1984), and *The Whole Woman* (1999).

THE BEATLES
Album cover of "Sgt Pepper's Lonely Hearts Club Band", designed by artist Peter Blake.

1938 Adolf Hitler makes Austria into a province of Germany. The dictator drives through the streets of the capital, Vienna, in a spectacular procession led by tanks and field guns. He is greeted by cheering crowds.

1938 Orson Welles throws the population of the USA into hysteria with his radio broadcast of H.G. Wells' novel, *The War of the Worlds*. The broadcast simulates a Martian invasion and one million listeners believe it is real.

1940

THE BEATLES
**John Lennon 1940–80
Ringo Starr
(Richard Starkey) 1940–
Paul McCartney 1942–
George Harrison 1943–**

The Beatles became the most famous rock group of the 1960s and revolutionized all the pop music that followed. The group was formed in 1959 as the Silver Beatles, and played rock 'n' roll and rhythm and blues by American artists, as well as their own Lennon-McCartney penned numbers, at the Cavern Club in Liverpool. In 1962 they recorded "Love Me Do", which became a minor hit. It was followed by "Please Please Me" (1963), which began a string of 20 Top Ten hit singles. Soon, they were the best-known group in Britain, and "Beatlemania" spread around the world after

they toured the USA in 1964. The group made several hit movies, including *A Hard Day's Night* (1964), *Help!* (1965), and the animated full-length feature *Yellow Submarine* (1968). The Beatles gave up performing live after 1966, and Lennon and McCartney concentrated on experimentation in their music. The result was the ground-breaking album *Sgt Pepper's Lonely Hearts Club Band* (1967). More influential albums followed, continuing their domination of popular music, but the band were already disintegrating and The Beatles broke up in 1970. John Lennon was murdered on the steps of his New York home.

Mario ANDRETTI
**1940–
Italian-born US racing driver**

For longevity and diversity Mario Andretti ranks among the greatest drivers in motor racing history. Born in Montona, Italy, during World War II, he grew up in refugee camps before his family moved to the USA when he was 15 years old. Living in Nazareth, Pennsylvania, Mario and his twin brother Aldo began racing on the local dirt tracks in 1958. He started his career in midget and sprint car racing, going on to become three-times champion in the US Automobile Club Circuit (1965, 1966, 1969). In 1967 he switched to stock car racing and won the Daytona 500. He went to Formula One the next year, but also won the Indianapolis 500 race in 1969. In Formula One he won 16

Grand Prix and in 1978 Andretti won the Racing Drivers World Championship. His son, Michael, joined him with the Newman/Haas Indy Car racing team and somewhat overshadowed him from 1989–92. In 1993 Mario achieved his 52nd Indy Car racing victory, giving him a total of over 100 motor racing victories in five decades.

Bernardo BERTOLUCCI
**1940–
Italian film director**

One of the Italian "New Wave" directors, Bertolucci's interest in cinema came from his father, who was a film critic. As a child in Parma, Bertolucci attended many screenings with his

father. He left college to work as an assistant director, and his directorial debut was with *La Commare Secca* (*The Grim Reaper*, 1962). His early films studied the impact of fascism on Italian life. Working with his cinematographer Vittorio Storraro, Bertolucci developed a highly personal visual style, using atmospheric colours and extravagant camera movements. His films have been controversial, and *Last Tango in Paris* (1972), starring Marlon Brando, caused an international scandal because of its explicit sexual content. Other films include *Novecento*

(1900) (1976) and *La Luna* (1979), but his greatest success came with *The Last Emperor* (1988), which won nine Academy Awards, including best director.

Jack NICKLAUS
**1940–
US golfer**

The "Golden Bear", as he is known because of his size and blond hair, has won more major golf tournaments than any other player in the world. Born in Columbus, Ohio, Jack Nicklaus won two US Amateur Golf championships while still a student at Ohio State University. In 1960, as an amateur player, he was runner-up to the great Arnold Palmer in the US Open. He played in the prestigious Walker Cup twice before turning

MARIO ANDRETTI
The famous racing driver is seen here in a 1994 Indy Car race.

professional in 1962, and won the US Open that year. In a remarkable career, he dominated world golf from the 1960s to the 1980s, winning four US Opens (1962, 1964, 1972, 1980), three British Opens (1966, 1970, 1978), five Professional Golf Association championships (1963, 1971, 1973, 1975, 1980), and a record six US Masters (1963, 1965, 1966, 1972, 1975, 1986). Nicklaus is the first player to become a multi-millionaire through earnings from golf.

1939 Adolf Hitler invades Poland. After he fails to respond to an ultimatum from British prime minister Neville Chamberlain, World War II begins. By 1941, Germany occupies much of western Europe, and has Italy on its side.

1940 France surrenders to Germany and signs an armistice in the same railway carriage in which the Germans surrendered in November 1918. French resistance quickly collapses and, in June, German troops march into Paris.

PELE
1940–
Brazilian soccer player

In 1969 Pelé scored his 1,000th goal in senior soccer, bringing accolades from around the world and confirming his standing as one of the greatest ever soccer players. Edson Arantes do Nascimento, who was born in Tres Coraçoes, Brazil, has been known simply as Pelé throughout his career as a soccer player. He got this nickname at an early age from his skill at *pedala*, a simple version of soccer. Pelé made his international debut in 1956, aged 16. In 1958 he won his first World Cup medal and scored two goals in the final against Sweden. He won two more winner's medals in 1962 and 1970. For most of his first-class soccer career (1955–71) he played for the Brazilian club Santos. In 1975, he signed a multi-million dollar contract with the New York Cosmos and led the team to the 1977 North American Soccer League Championship.

Bruce
LEE
1941–73
US actor and
martial arts expert

Bruce Lee shot to international stardom in the film *Fists of Fury* (1971), in which he became recognized as a martial-arts sensation. Born in San Francisco to Chinese parents, Lee became a child actor, appearing in over 20 Hong Kong film productions. He became well known in both Hong Kong and the USA as a martial arts expert, and he started to teach actors while developing his own unique style of martial arts called Jeet Kune Do. He played Kato in the US television series *The Green Hornet* (1966–67). Lee made his first film in English, *Enter the Dragon*, in 1973, but tragically died before its release.

Richard
DAWKINS
1941–
British zoologist

Dawkins has succeeded in making his ideas on sociobiology – the social behaviour of humans and animals in the context of evolution – accessible to ordinary readers. He was born in Nairobi, Kenya, and educated at Oxford University, where he has taught since 1975. In *The Selfish Gene* (1976), he argued that genes are the driving force of evolution. He went on to explore the transmission of cultural values in human societies. *The Blind Watchmaker* (1986) summed up his theories of evolution.

BRUCE LEE *in the film* Enter the Dragon.

BOB DYLAN *wrote anti-war "protest" songs such as Blowin' in the Wind.*

Bob
DYLAN
1941–
US singer-songwriter

One of the most influential folk and rock musicians from the 1960s through to the 1990s, Dylan was born Robert Zimmerman into a middle-class family in Duluth, Minnesota. He later moved with his family to the iron-mining town of Hibbing, where his father had an appliance store. Influenced by folk singer Woody Guthrie (p.193), he started singing in Greenwich Village coffee bars in New York City in the 1960s, having taken the name Dylan from the Welsh poet Dylan Thomas. He released "The Times They are a-Changing" (1962) and "Blowin' in the Wind" (1963), which were quickly adopted and championed by the civil rights movement. His early songs were laden with social, political, and anti-war messages, in tune with the youth culture of the 1960s. However, in the mid-1960s he upset many of his folk fans by taking up the electric guitar to perform songs such as "Like a Rolling Stone" and "Subterranean Homesick Blues" (1965). Of his prolific album output, both legal and bootleg, his *Highway 61 Revisited* (1965) and *Blonde on Blonde* (1966) were highly influential, as was the simpler, country-tinged *Nashville Skyline* (1969). *Blood on the Tracks* (1975) is often considered his finest album. Dylan continued to be an influential figure in popular music in the late 1990s, recording the award-winning *Time Out of Mind* in 1997.

Jesse
JACKSON
1941–
US political activist

One of the major voices for African-American civil rights in the USA from the 1970s onwards, Jesse Jackson started his political life supporting Martin Luther King, Jr (p.213) in the 1960s. Jackson began work as a Baptist preacher, a career that led to his reputation as a fine public speaker. In 1983 he was influential in getting Chicago's first African-American mayor elected, and he founded the National Rainbow Coalition, intended to represent a spectrum of ethnic interests.

Edward
ROBERTS
1941–
US electrical engineer

The man who invented the world's first personal computer, Edward Roberts eventually retired to a farm in Georgia, where he now practises as a doctor. Roberts

1941 Japan makes an unprovoked attack on a US naval fleet at Pearl Harbor in Hawaii. The USA declares war on Japan and Germany, thereby entering the war. Japan captures around 138,000 Allied troops.

1941 The German advance on the Soviet Union begins to slow down. After many easy victories, the Germans are halted on their march to Moscow by the savage Russian winter, which causes their tanks and trucks to freeze up.

obtained his university degree in electrical engineering in the US Air Force. He invented a hand-held electronic calculator and began a company called MITS (Micro Instrumentation and Telemetry Systems). In 1974, he invented the first personal computer (PC), the Altair 8800. It was a huge success, despite the fact that it was sold as a self-assembly kit. Two students, Paul Allen and Bill Gates (p.238) developed a version of the BASIC programming software to run on the Altair. MITS sold 50,000 PCs before Roberts sold his company to the Pertec Corporation in 1977.

Paul SIMON
1941–
US singer-songwriter

Paul Simon was half of one of the most successful pop partnerships of all times; the folk-rock duo Simon and Garfunkel. He is also a noted lyricist and performer in his own right. Born in Newark, New Jersey, he began playing guitar with singer Art Garfunkel in the 1950s. Their songs, such as "Mrs Robinson" (1968, from the film *The Graduate*), captured the spirit of youth rebellion of 1960s America. Their album *Bridge over Troubled Water* (1970) remains one of the most successful recordings in pop history. Simon went solo at the height of their fame and produced a string of finely crafted albums including *Still Crazy After All These Years* (1975), which used the cream of New York's jazz session musicians. In 1986 he had a worldwide hit with *Graceland*, the result of a collaboration with many South African, Cajun, and other ethnic artists.

Jimi HENDRIX
1942–70
US rock guitarist

One of the most innovative electric guitarists, a rock superstar of the 1960s, and a legend because of his untimely death, James Marshall Hendrix continues to influence popular music. He was born into a poor neighbourhood in Seattle.

MUHAMMAD ALI
The US boxer was a great showman, both inside and outside the boxing ring.

Hendrix was a self-taught musician, and although left-handed, he played with a right-handed guitar. He started out as a backing guitarist, and was then spotted by British rock musician Chas Chandler, who persuaded him to come to London. There, he formed the trio the Jimi Hendrix Experience, whose best known songs include "Hey Joe" (1967) and "Purple Haze" (1967). Hendrix played at all the big outdoor festivals in the 1960s, including Woodstock (1969) and the Isle of Wight (1970). In his hands the guitar became an independent object, and his stage act was spectacular – he would play the guitar with his teeth, behind his head, and sometimes set fire to it. He died from an overdose of drugs.

Muhammad ALI
1942–
US boxer

Self-proclaimed "The Greatest", Ali was certainly the dominant heavyweight champion boxer of the late 1960s and 1970s. He was born Cassius Clay in Louisville, Kentucky, but changed his name to Muhammad Ali after joining the Nation of Islam in his mid-twenties. At the age of 18 he won an Olympic gold medal and the amateur light-heavyweight title. Ali turned professional and won the world heavyweight title in 1964, but was stripped of his title in 1967 after refusing to serve in the US Army on religious grounds. He became heavyweight champion again in 1974 after beating George Foreman in Zaire (documented in the Academy Award-winning film *When We Were Kings*, 1997). Ali was known for immodest references to himself, including his claim to "float like a butterfly, sting like a bee". He was the first heavyweight to win the world championship three times, regaining the title twice – in 1974 and 1978. He retired from boxing in 1981, and remains one of the all-time most popular sports heroes.

1941 In Germany, all Jews over the age of six are required to wear the Star of David in public as a "mark of shame". Within a year the Nazis open a death camp at Treblinka for the mass murder of the Jewish people.

1942 In the Pacific, the US Navy secures its first major victory against the Japanese in the Battle of Midway, sinking four Japanese aircraft carriers. The Americans used a special code-breaking machine to uncover Japanese plans.

Daniel
BARENBOIM
1942–
Israeli pianist and conductor

A child prodigy on the piano, Barenboim was born in Argentina, and grew up and studied music in Salzburg, Austria. Both his parents were pianists, and he made his performance debut at the age of seven. The family moved to Israel in 1952 and Barenboim went on to give concerts throughout Europe and the USA in the late 1950s. He turned to conducting in 1962, and toured all over the world, often with the English Chamber Orchestra. In 1967 he married the brilliant cellist Jacqueline du Pré (p.233). Barenboim was musical director of the Orchestre de Paris for over a decade, but was dismissed in 1989 amid controversy. He became conductor of the Chicago Symphony Orchestra in 1991.

Aretha
FRANKLIN
1942–
US soul singer

The "Queen of Soul", Aretha Franklin was one of the first soul singers to be regarded as a star by white audiences, and many of her singles and albums have sold more than a million copies. She was born in Memphis, Tennessee, but grew up in Detroit, where her father was a well-known preacher. Visitors to their home included leading singers and musicians like Mahalia Jackson, B. B. King, and Dinah Washington. Franklin began by singing gospel music, but gradually expanded her repertoire, gaining widespread popularity in 1967 with hits such as "Baby I Love You". One of her songs, "Respect", became a signature

tune of the civil-rights movement. Her popularity continued throughout the 1970s. In the 1980s, her duet with George Michael, "I Knew You Were Waiting (For Me)", topped the US and UK charts.

Stephen
HAWKING
1942–
English physicist

A uthor of *A Brief History of Time* (1988) – one of the best-selling science books ever – Stephen Hawking has helped to popularize the study of black holes and the big bang theory of the origins of the universe. He studied mathematical physics at Oxford University and went on to do his PhD at Cambridge, where he was made a research fellow. Shortly afterwards, he contracted an incurable neuro-muscular disease which made him dependent on a wheelchair and a computer-enhanced voice-box. In spite of this, he continued to make amazing progress in the field of physics. His special area of research and interest is the theory of relativity and black holes, where space-time is curved due to the gravitational collapse of a star. He has predicted that when a black hole disappears, it is possible for mass to escape from its gravitational pull. This is known as the Hawking process.

Martin
SCORSESE
1942–
US film director

O ne of the "movie brats" who came out of film school and gave US cinema a "second golden age" in the 1970s, Martin Scorsese was born and grew up in New York City. He tried, without success, to become a Roman Catholic priest. He loved films as a

child, and studied film at New York University. He began directing in the 1960s, and made his name with *Mean Streets* (1973) which, like many of his subsequent films, dealt with the sordid and violent aspects of New York street life, and the conflict and inequality between men and women. The film also starred Robert de Niro, who has appeared in many of Scorsese's films, among them *Taxi Driver* (1976), *Raging Bull* (1980), *Goodfellas* (1990), and *Casino* (1995). Scorsese's work can be highly controversial – in *The Last Temptation of Christ* (1988), Christ is portrayed as a flawed character. Scorsese has also made costume dramas and black comedies, notably *The King of Comedy* (1983).

MARTIN SCORSESE
The influential film director is seen here directing Robert de Niro in his 1980 film Raging Bull.

1942 The British Eighth Army, led by General Montgomery, succeeds in halting the German Afrika Corps at El Alamein outside Cairo in Egypt. Commander Rommel returned from sick leave to find his forces being defeated.

1943 As Allied leaders meet for a conference in the North African city of Casablanca, film-goers flock to see the new film, *Casablanca*, a war drama starring Humphrey Bogart and Ingrid Bergman.

Arthur ASHE
1943–93
US tennis player

The first African-American winner of a major men's tennis single championship (the US Open), Arthur Ashe was also the first to head the US tennis players' ranking. He was one of the great "touch" players of the game whose pace and accuracy defeated many volley-and-serve players. Ashe started playing tennis at seven, and won a tennis scholarship to the University of California. His breakthrough came in 1968 when he won the US national singles and the US Open championships. He turned professional in 1969 and toured the world with the Davis Cup team. In 1975, Ashe won the men's singles at Wimbledon in a thrilling final against the reigning champion, Jimmy Connors (p.236). He was now ranked first in the world – the first African-American player to achieve this. He retired from tennis in 1980.

Jocelyn Bell BURNELL
1943–
English astronomer

In the late summer of 1967, while working as a graduate assistant to Antony Hewish, Jocelyn Bell Burnell became the first person to detect pulsating radio stars (pulsars). Pulsars are the remains of dead stars, and they send out radio waves at even intervals of time. Educated at Glasgow and Cambridge universities, Burnell received the Royal Astronomical Society's Herschel Medal in 1989 and, in 1991, became professor of physics at the Open University.

Robert DE NIRO
1943–
US film star

De Niro's dedication to acting is legendary. He grew up in New York City, and decided to become an actor in his teens. He studied at the Actors' Studio and has retained a life-long commitment to the method acting inspired by Lee Strasberg (p.178). De Niro is noted for the versatility of his acting, and his devotion to authenticity in his characters. He has had a long-standing professional collaboration with the director Martin Scorsese, starring in such films as *Raging Bull* (1980) – for which De Niro put on 27 kilograms (60 pounds) and learnt how to box – earning an Academy Award for the role. His other starring roles include *The Godfather Part II* (1974) (also an Academy Award-winning role) and *The Deer Hunter* (1978). He directed his first film, *A Bronx Tale*, in 1994.

Billie Jean KING
1943–
US tennis player

One of the dominant figures in women's tennis in the 1960s and 1970s, King won a record 20 Wimbledon titles, including the singles title six times (1966–68, 1972–73, 1975). Born in Long Beach, California, Billie Jean Moffitt became a natural athlete and dedicated tennis player at an early age. At her first attempt, in 1961, she won the Wimbledon women's doubles with Karen Susman. Aside from the British titles, King went on to win 13 US titles (four singles), four French titles, and two Australian. In 1973 King played Bobby Riggs in the "Battle of Sexes" and won. A year later she became the first president of the Women's Tennis Association. King has written several instructional books. Towards the end of her career as a player she was a leading voice for better playing conditions and prize money for women.

BILLIE JEAN KING
The record-breaking tennis player in action on the Centre Court at Wimbledon in 1983.

Lech WALESA
1943–
Polish president

Lech Walesa led millions of Polish workers in the country's first independent trade union and went on to become president of Poland. He was born in Popowo and received only a very basic education before beginning work as an electrician at the Lenin Shipyard in Gdansk. He founded *Solidarnoshc*, meaning "solidarity", an independent trade union. This organization initiated several strikes under Walesa's leadership. He drew a great deal of public support, and forced the Polish government to make some important

1943 Weakened by the harsh Russian winter, the German Sixth Army suffers a heavy defeat by the Soviet Red Army at Stalingrad. Five months later, the Soviets smash the German forces' finest divisions in a great tank battle at Kursk.

1943 In one of the most daring air-raids of the War, a small number of British Lancaster bombers blast three dams and cause floodwaters to destroy much of the Ruhr, Germany's industrial heartland. They use new "bouncing" bombs.

political and economic changes between 1980 and 1981. However, *Solidarnoshc* was outlawed and Walesa imprisoned. He was released in 1983 and awarded the Nobel Peace Prize. After leading another series of major strikes in 1988, *Solidarnoshc* was legalized again and a new socialist democracy established. Following democratic elections, he was Polish president from 1990 to 1995.

KIRI TE KANAWA *at the Glyndebourne Festival Opera in England in 1998.*

Kiri Te KANAWA
1944–
New Zealand opera singer

Of Maori descent, Kiri Te Kanawa is a gifted soprano singer, who won many awards in New Zealand and Australia before leaving for England in 1965. She joined the Royal Opera Company and, in 1970, appeared in her first major role in Mozart's *The Marriage of Figaro*. In 1981 she sang at the wedding of the Prince and Princess of Wales. In 1982 she was created a Dame – Commander of the British Empire. Eager to cross the borders of classical and popular music, she recorded the role of Maria in Leonard Bernstein's *West Side Story* in 1985.

Reinhold MESSNER
1944–
Austrian mountaineer

In 1986, Reinhold Messner became the first person to climb all 14 of the world's mountains higher than 26,250 ft (8,000 metres). He was born in the mountainous Tyrol region of Austria, and by the age of 13 was making difficult ascents in the Alps. In 1970, he climbed Nanga Parbati in Pakistan, one of the world's highest mountains. Reinhold made a point of climbing without oxygen cylinders, a method calling for almost superhuman fitness. In 1978, with Peter Habelar, he made the first ascent of Everest without oxygen. Two years later, he repeated the climb alone. He also made the first crossing of Antarctica on foot.

Peter WEIR
1944–
Australian film director

A dream-like film, based on the true story of the disappearance of some schoolgirls in the Australian outback, *Picnic At Hanging Rock* (1975) established Peter Weir as one of the most influential directors in Australia's "New Wave" of the 1970s. He was born in Sydney, and educated at the university there. He started working at a television station and began directing short films. His first feature was *The Cars That Ate Paris* (1974). His films explore the relationships of ordinary people in unfamiliar environments, or people who are overtaken by extraordinary events. Among them are *The Year of Living Dangerously* (1982), *Witness* (1985), *Dead Poets Society* (1989), and *Green Card* (1991).

George LUCAS
1944–
US film producer and director

George Lucas is the creator of the hugely successful *Star Wars* films. He was born in Modesto, California, and studied at the film department of the University of Southern California before working for the Warner Brothers studio. His first major film, *American Graffiti* (1973), won considerable critical acclaim and received five Academy Award nominations, but it was the *Star Wars* trilogy that established him as a major filmmaker. *Star Wars* (1977), an intergalactic adventure boasting breathtaking special effects, was an extraordinary box office success, becoming the largest selling motion picture in history. It was followed by two further episodes in the saga, *The Empire Strikes Back* (1980) and *Return of the Jedi* (1983). Lucas returned to the Star Wars universe in 1999 with the release of *Star Wars: Episode I – The Phantom Menace*, the first of three prequel films in the series. Lucas's clarity of vision as a storyteller and zeal for developing innovative special effects technology has revolutionized the art of motion pictures. In 1978 he set up his own production company, Lucasfilm Ltd, which contains the special-effects division Industrial Light and Magic.

STAR WARS *The droids C3-PO and R2-D2 are characters in George Lucas' Star Wars films.*

1944 In an operation codenamed "Overlord", two Allied armies, with over 100,000 US, British, and Canadian troops, land on the Normandy coast in northern France. 3,000 Allied casualties are sustained on "Omaha" beach.

1944 After four years of Nazi occupation, Paris is liberated by Allied forces on 25 August. The French Fourth Armoured Division, led by General Jacques Leclerc, are the first troops to greet the jubilant Parisian crowds.

1945

Bob MARLEY
1945–81
Jamaican reggae musician

The first reggae (Jamaican roots music) group to become internationally famous was led by Robert Nesta Marley. He was brought up in Trenchtown, Kingston. In 1963 Marley co-formed the group The Wailers with Peter Tosh and Bunny Livingstone, and became the group's lead singer and chief songwriter. His songs, which preached Rastafarianism and anti-establishment politics, succeeded in reaching a world-wide audience, but they also made him a controversial figure: in 1975 he survived an assassination attempt. Among his hit songs are "No Woman, No Cry", "I Shot the Sheriff", and "Get Up, Stand Up". Influential albums include *Exodus* (1977) and *Uprising* (1980). Marley is regarded as a national hero in Jamaica.

Jacqueline DU PRE
1945–87
English cellist

An internationally acclaimed cellist, Jacqueline du Pré was a gifted artist who died tragically young. She was born in Oxford and studied at London's Guildhall School of Music, winning numerous prizes as a student. She began her professional career at the age of 16 and went on to play cello all over the world. In 1967 she married the pianist and conductor Daniel Barenboim (p.230), and they often performed and recorded together. Du Pré became renowned for her playing of Elgar's Cello Concerto. Her instinctive feeling for music, and the wide range of her style, made her an exceptional soloist. Unfortunately, multiple sclerosis eventually confined her to a wheelchair and stopped her from performing.

Franz BECKENBAUER
1945–
German soccer player

One of the great heroes of German soccer, Franz Beckenbauer was born in Munich. Throughout the 1970s he was a powerful player for Bayern Munich and for Germany, playing in both the 1966 and 1970 world championships. As a player, coach, manager, and administrator he earnt the nickname "Kaiser". In 1972 he was the captain of the West German national side when they won the European Nations Cup, and he was named European soccer player of the year. Beckenbauer captained West Germany again in 1974 to win the World Cup. In 1986 he became manager of the West German team.

Aung San SUU KYI
1945–
Myanmar (Burmese) political leader

The daughter of General Aung San, who led the Burmese independence movement against British rule, Suu Kyi was born in Burma (now Myanmar), and educated there, in India, and in Oxford, England. In 1972 she married academic Michael Aris and settled in Oxford. However, in 1988, she returned to Burma and found the country in turmoil from military rule. She became a focus of political opposition and was placed under house arrest for the next six years. This did not stop her from fighting for political freedom and becoming leader of the National League for Democracy (1989–91), as well as the organization's General Secretary from 1995. In 1991 Suu Kyi won the European Parliament's Human Rights Prize and the Nobel Peace Prize. The following year she won the Simón Bolivar Prize. Her husband died of cancer in 1999.

Eddy MERCKX
1945–
Belgian racing cyclist

The most successful rider in the history of his sport up to the mid-1970s, Eddy Merckx (known as "the Cannibal") won over 445 cycling races in his career – more than any other rider. He was born in Woluwe St Pierre, near Brussels. He enjoyed soccer and basketball at school, but from the age of 14 concentrated his efforts on cycling. Merckx became the World Amateur Road Race champion at the age of 18, later winning the professional title three times. Between 1966 and 1978 he won the Giro d'Italia (Tour of Italy) five times, and in 1969 he won his first Tour de France, dominating the sprint, time-trial, and endurance "king of the mountain" sections. He went on to win four more Tour de France races in 1970–72 and 1974. He won the Milan-San Remo race seven times in all. Merckx retired from the sport in 1978 to run his own bicycle manufacturing company.

1945 On 8 May, peace is declared in Europe after German forces surrender unconditionally to the Allies in Reims, France. The day is known as VE (Victory in Europe) Day and is celebrated in London, Paris, and Rome.

1945 On 6 August, US bomber plane *Enola Gay* drops a single atom bomb on the Japanese city of Hiroshima killing around 80,000 people. On 15 August, the Japanese surrender, sparking celebrations in the USA and Australia.

Steve BIKO
1946–77
South African political activist

Born in King Williams Town, South Africa, Stephen Biko was involved in politics from an early age. He began studying medicine, but gave it up to follow his political activities. He became involved in the black activist movement against apartheid (the segregation of blacks and whites), and helped to establish the Black People's Convention. In 1973 the South African government served a banning order on him, which severely restricted his movements and right to speak publicly. He was arrested on several occasions and, in 1977, he died in brutal circumstances while in police custody. When it was examined, his body showed signs of severe beating. At a time when Nelson Mandela (p.201) was still in prison and apartheid dominant, Biko's murder made him a symbol of the oppression of blacks by the South African government.

Robert JARVIK
1946–
US medical pioneer

On 2nd December, 1982, the Jarvik-7, designed by Robert K. Jarvik, was surgically implanted into a patient by William C. DeVries. The first permanent artificial heart to be placed in a patient replaced the two lower chambers of the natural heart. No oxygenation was required, because with an artificial heart the patient's lungs were not bypassed. This first patient survived 112 days and died as a result of various physical complications caused by the implant. Several

ARTIFICIAL HEART
The plastic and metal Jarvik-7

subsequent patients who received artificial hearts fared little better. The consensus was that the existing technology could not yet produce a permanent artificial heart that functioned as well as a natural one. Doctors decided that artificial hearts should be used only as temporary replacements in needy patients until suitable natural hearts could be obtained for transplantation.

George BEST
1946–
Irish soccer player

Born in Belfast, Northern Ireland, George Best showed early promise as a soccer player and at the age of 15, was signed up to play for England's Manchester United. He became homesick, however, and returned to Northern Ireland. He was persuaded to rejoin Manchester United when he was 17 and became their top goal scorer. In the 1967–68 season, he scored the highest number of goals in the soccer league's first division. In 1968 he also won a European Cup medal and was voted European player of the year. Best's good looks and top-class skills inspired a huge following, and fan clubs sprang up all over Europe. However, his unstable private life and drinking problems brought an early end to his career, which was effectively over by his late twenties. He attempted several come-backs with smaller soccer clubs, but these proved unsuccessful and he never returned to his earlier form. Best is still remembered as a great soccer talent, though, and one of the first superstars of the game.

GEORGE BEST *in action for his team Manchester United.*

John ADAMS
1947–
US composer

An important composer at the forefront of modern classical music, John Adams learnt the clarinet as a child and studied music at Harvard. He wrote some early electronic pieces, but developed his own tuneful minimalist style. His first important piece was *Shaker Loops* (1978) for solo strings and later a string orchestra, which was followed by *Harmonium* (1981) for choir and orchestra, and the enormously popular *Grand Pianola Music* (1982). Other key works include the opera, *Nixon in China* (1987), and the fanfare *Short Ride in a Fast Machine* (1986) – one of the most popular pieces of classical music to have been written by a living composer.

Johann CRUYFF
1947–
Dutch soccer player

One of the most exciting and talented centre-forwards in European soccer, Johann Cruyff joined the football club Ajax Amsterdam at the age of ten. Noted as a gifted player in his early years, he made his debut in Dutch league soccer at 19. As a powerful forward, Cruyff won 11 Dutch League and Cup medals and helped Ajax to win three European Cups in succession (1971–73). In 1973, Cruyff joined Barcelona, winning Spanish League and Cup medals with the club. He captained the Dutch team in the 1974 World Cup, when they reached the final. In 1983, he went back to Holland to play for Feyenoord and then in 1988 he returned to Spain as manager of Barcelona, guiding the team to win the European Cup for the first time in 1992.

JURASSIC PARK *Stephen Spielberg scored another major box-office success with his 1993 film about dinosaurs.*

1947 India gains its independence after 163 years of British rule. It is feared there will be conflict between Hindus and Muslims, and there are plans to partition India, creating a separate Muslim state, Pakistan.

1948 Jewish leaders Chaim Weizmann and David Ben-Gurion declare the independence of the new Jewish state of Israel. The announcement seems certain to commit the new state to war with neighbouring Arab states.

Salman RUSHDIE
1947–
British writer

As famous for being the recipient of an Islamic *fatwa* (death sentence) as that of numerous literary awards, Ahmed Salman Rushdie was born in Bombay, India. He emigrated to Britain in 1965 and published his first novel, *Grimus*, in 1975. It was *Midnight's Children*, in 1981, which won him international fame and the Booker Prize. However, in 1988 he wrote *The Satanic Verses*, which upset many Muslims around the world for what was considered to be blasphemy against Islam and Mohammed. The *fatwa* issued against him by Ayatollah Khomeini, with a bounty of $6 million on his head, forced Rushdie into hiding. In 1998 the *fatwa* was withdrawn, and Rushdie published *The Ground Beneath Her Feet* (1998).

Steven SPIELBERG
1947–
US film director and producer

Spielberg is the most commercially successful director in cinema history. He studied film at California State College. He began directing features in his twenties, and showed his directorial style for building up tension and drama with *Duel* (1972). International success came with *Jaws* (1975), which broke all previous box-office records. His films – admired for their storytelling, technical brilliance, special effects, and high standards of production – include *Close Encounters of the Third Kind* (1977), *Raiders of the Lost Ark* (1981), *E.T.* (1982), and *Indiana Jones and the Temple of Doom* (1984), as well as the war-time dramas *Schindler's List* (1993) and *Saving Private Ryan* (1998), which both won Academy Awards.

Andrew LLOYD WEBBER
1948–
English composer

Andrew Lloyd Webber's varied rock-based musicals revitalized a declining art form. With lyricist Tim Rice, he wrote his hits *Joseph and the Amazing Technicolour Dreamcoat* (1968) and the "rock opera" *Jesus Christ Superstar* (1970). In 1978, their musical *Evita* was another hit. Lloyd Webber parted company with Rice to work on *Cats* (1981), using T. S. Eliot's *Old Possum's Book of Practical Cats* as his lyrics. In 1991, he made history by being the first person to have six shows running consecutively in London's West End. Webber's blend of strong melodies and flashy stage shows continued with later successes such as *Starlight Express* (1984), *The Phantom of the Opera* (1986), and *Sunset Boulevard* (1993).

1950

Mark SPITZ
1950–
US swimmer

The first athlete to win seven gold medals at one Olympic Games, Mark Spitz was hailed as the greatest swimmer in the history of the games. He started swimming from the age of two. At the age of 18 he won two gold medals in team events at the Mexico City Olympics. Spitz was 22 when he achieved his seven-gold-medal success at the 1972 Munich Olympics – he also broke the world record with each victory. A dashing and athletic figure, in 1968 and 1972 he had earned a total of 18 medals – nine gold, five silver, and four bronze. Spitz turned professional in 1972.

Stevie WONDER
1950–
US singer-songwriter

Steveland Judkins Morris was blind from birth, but despite this, proved to be talented on the piano, harmonica, and drums. Signed to Detroit's Motown Records at the age of ten, he first recorded as Little Stevie Wonder. After a string of hit singles in Europe and the USA in the 1960s and 1970s, Wonder went on to produce a series of accomplished albums – notably *Talking Book, Songs in the Key of Life*, and *Innervisions* – in which he played all the instruments and pioneered the use of synthesizers in songs such as "Superstition" (1972). He received an Academy Award for "I Just Called to Say I Love You" (1983).

1949 Western European countries and the United States agree to form a new military alliance to deter Soviet attack. The alliance of 12 countries is to be called the North Atlantic Treaty Organization, or NATO.

1949 In Beijing, China, communist leader Mao Zedong proclaims the birth of a new People's Republic. Mao has declared himself chairman and promises freedom of speech and religion and equal rights for all Chinese citizens.

SEX PISTOLS

**Paul Cook 1950–
Johnny Rotten
(John Lydon) 1956–
Sid Vicious
(John Ritchie) 1957–79
Steve Jones 1957–**

The Sex Pistols exploded on the London music scene with their loud, abusive punk sound. Their appearance – safety pins, spiked hair, and ripped T-shirts – mocked all that had gone before them. Under their manager Malcolm McLaren, the group attracted media attention with songs such as "Anarchy in the UK" (1976) and their irreverent "God Save the Queen" (1977), which was banned from public broadcast in the UK. Their only studio album, *Never Mind the Bollocks, Here's the Sex Pistols* went to Number One in 1977's UK charts. Bass player Sid Vicious' rendition of the Frank Sinatra classic "My Way" seemed to epitomize the group's wild ways. Vicious died of a heroin overdose in 1979 after he was accused of murdering his girlfriend. Lead singer Johnny Rotten continued to perform with Public Image Limited, using his real name John Lydon.

Stephen WOZNIAK

**1950–
US computer engineer**

Wozniak's technical wizardry created the first Apple computer, which changed the face of technology and created a path for the information age. While working for Hewlett-Packard, Wozniak formed a business partnership with Steven Jobs (p.238), another computer enthusiast. Jobs recognized Wozniak's engineering skill, and together they began to design personal computers. Wozniak and Jobs founded the Apple Computer Company in a garage and, in 1977, introduced the Apple II computer – one of the first pre-assembled computers with application software. In 1984, Apple revolutionized the personal-computer industry with the Macintosh, which featured a graphical, mouse-driven operating system and built-in sound and graphics capabilities. Apple's success made both men multi-millionaires but, disillusioned with big business, Wozniak left the company in 1985. He continues to work on small-scale electronic designs.

Sally RIDE

**1951–
US astronaut**

Sally Kristen Ride was the first American woman to journey into space. Born in Los Angeles, California, Ride achieved national ranking as a student tennis player. After studying for a PhD in astrophysics she was accepted by NASA (as one of only six women) for the Space Shuttle flight crews. In 1983, she went into space on a *Challenger* mission, and was preparing for her third space flight when the *Challenger* exploded in 1986. In 1987 she retired from NASA, and from 1989 was professor of physics at the University of California.

Nickolay ANDRIANOV

**1952–
Russian gymnast**

Between 1972 and 1980 Andrianov won 15 Olympic medals, achieving a record for male gymnasts. Born in Vladimir, Russia, Andrianov started gymnastics at the age of 12 – late for this sport – and was selected for the 1972 Munich Olympics where he won three Olympic medals. At Montreal he excelled with seven medals, including gold for rings, floor, vault, and combined exercises. In 1980, at Moscow, he won a further five medals. He also won 12 world championship medals, including the overall individual title in 1978.

Jimmy CONNORS

**1952–
US tennis player**

A jester on the court, a superb athlete, and a devastating double backhander, James Scott Connors was a dominant tennis player in the 1970s and early 80s. He was born in Belleville, Illinois, where his mother taught him tennis at an early age – at eight he competed in the US boys' championship. The left-handed Connors was one of the first players to use the two-handed backhand, making it one of his characteristic winning shots. In 1974, he became Wimbledon champion at the age of 21.

Connors also won the US and Australian Open in that year. He went on to win the US Open in 1976, 1978, and in 1982–83. In 1982 he won the Wimbledon men's final again, this time beating John McEnroe. In 1984 Connors became the first player to win 100 singles titles, and went on to an all-time record of 109 titles.

JIMMY CONNORS *was affectionately known on and off the courts as "Jimbo".*

Chen KAIGE

**1952–
Chinese film director**

Together with Zhang Yimou, Chen Kaige spearheaded a dramatic revival in Chinese cinema in the 1980s. Kaige was born in Beijing, where his

---

1950 In Korea, the communist People's Republic of North Korea invades the Republic of South Korea with the intention of unifying the peninsula. The United States and Soviet Union soon become involved in the war.

1951 In Africa, the Convention People's Party led by Kwame Nkrumah wins the first election in Ghana after Britain allows the country limited home rule. Full independence is granted to Ghana in 1957.

mother was a teacher and his father a filmmaker. When he was 15 years old, he was sent to work on a rubber plantation in rural China, where he was extremely moved by the poverty and hardship he saw around him. He studied film at the Beijing Film Academy and, after graduating, became a leading member of the "fifth generation" of Chinese filmmakers (which included Zhang Yimou, who directed *Raise the Red Lantern* in 1991). Experimenting with colour, natural landscapes, and sweeping camera movements, Kaige's films sensitively portray the lives of Chinese people in the past. His first film, *Yellow Earth* (1984), was well received, and his fifth film, *Farewell, My Concubine* (1993), was joint winner of the Palme d'Or at Cannes and brought him international acclaim.

Viv RICHARDS
1952–
West Indies cricketer

A formidable batsman who often wore a peaked cap rather than a safety helmet, Viv Richards captained the West Indies from 1985–91. In 121 Test matches he scored 8,540

runs, including 24 centuries. Born Isaac Vivian Alexander Richards, in St Johns, Antigua, the promising young cricketer left the West Indies to play for the English county of Somerset and later for Glamorgan. In 1976 he scored a record 1,710 Test runs in one calendar year. Wherever he played his style of attack, together with his powerful right-handed batting, was feared by bowlers. His incredible timing

VIV RICHARDS *during the West Indies tour of England in 1991.*

and power enabled him to score the fastest Test century (off 56 balls) in cricket history against England in 1986.

Franz KLAMMER
1953–
Austrian skier

Born in the Alps, in Mooswald, Austria, Franz Klammer was a brilliant snow skier from an early age. At the height of his skiing career, from 1974 to 1984, he won a record 25 World Cup downhill races – winning eight out of nine races in this event in 1975. The next year at the Winter Olympics

in Innsbruck, Austria, he thrilled the crowd with his display of courage, control, and speed as he took the gold medal from the defending champion Bernhard Russi, beating him by just one-third of a second.

Bob GELDOF
1954–
Irish musician and charity worker

Pop singer Bob Geldof succeeded in putting famine relief at the forefront of international concerns through his charity-based, fund-raising activities. As lead singer with the rock band The Boomtown Rats (1975–86), Geldof had several chart successes including "I Don't Like Mondays" (1979). In 1984, moved by a television documentary about the famine in Ethiopia, and angered by the lack of any government intervention, Geldof, (with fellow musician Midge Ure) formed Band Aid, a group of international rock stars. Their record, "Do They Know It's Christmas?" sold three million copies – then the biggest-selling single ever in the UK – raising millions of pounds for famine victims. On 13th July 1985 he staged Live Aid, two charity rock concerts, which were broadcast globally via satellite. The event raised some £70 million. In 1986 Geldof received an honorary knighthood. The concept of celebrity-led charity fund-raising was now firmly established.

BOB GELDOF *visiting Ethiopia to find out how best to use the money raised by Band Aid.*

1953 In the Himalayas, two climbers from a British party – Edmund Hillary of New Zealand and Tensing Norgay of Nepal – are the first to reach the summit of Mount Everest, the world's highest mountain.

1953 Queen Elizabeth II of Great Britain is crowned in Westminster Abbey, London. She succeeds her father, George VI. The coronation of the 27-year-old queen is watched by millions of television viewers across the world.

Tim
BERNERS-LEE
1955–
English Internet pioneer

Tim Berners-Lee is the creator of the World Wide Web, the leading information retrieval service of the Internet which is accessed by personal computer. Lee studied physics at Oxford University, during which time he built his own personal computer. In 1978 he began designing computer software, but it was while working in Switzerland for an international scientific organization called CERN that Berners-Lee designed his own private programme for storing information called Enquire. This programme formed the basis of the first World Wide Web, which Lee placed on the market in 1991. The web allowed people from around the world to work together and access information via computers, and it has changed the face of international communications forever. Lee continued to work on refining the web until 1994, when he joined MIT (Massachussets Institute of Technology) as a director of development of the World Wide Web.

Ian
BOTHAM
1955–
English cricketer

One of the best all-rounders in cricket, Ian Terence Botham was born in Heswall in Cheshire. He joined Somerset in 1974 and played with the county until he moved to Worcestershire. Botham has played in 102 Test matches for England, 65 of these consecutively, and in 12 as captain of the England team. He held a record number of test wickets (383 at an average of 28.40 runs) until overtaken

THE COMPUTER AGE

The second half of the 20th century has seen faster change than any other period in history. Just one invention has facilitated many of these changes in our society: the computer.

A powerful information tool, the computer works at high speed with detailed instructions in the form of electronic signals representing the 1s and 0s of the binary code.

EARLY COMPUTERS
The first programmable computer was conceived in the 1830s by British mathematician CHARLES BABBAGE (p.83). Then, in 1890, US statistician HERMAN HOLLERITH (1860–1929) automated the US census counts by programming a machine to read perforated cards. But it was not until 1946 that the first programmable computer was built in the US. Called ENIAC (Electronic Numerical Integrator and Calculator), it was so big that it filled a large room.

SMALLER AND SMALLER
In the last 50 years, computers have evolved extremely rapidly, becoming progressively smaller and more powerful. Early computers such as ENIAC were powered by unwieldy vacuum tubes, but by 1959 these had been replaced by smaller, more reliable transistors. In 1971 US engineer TED HOFF (p.225) invented the tiny single-chip microprocessor, enabling computers to become smaller and even more efficient.

TECHNOLOGY TODAY
The computer's vast electronic memory has proved useful in lots of applications, from reliable medical technology to efficient washing machines. But, as BILL GATES predicted, it is the personal home computer – bringing faster, cheaper, global communication via e-mail, and access to the Internet, the "information superhighway" – that has had the most impact on people's lives.

by the New Zealander Richard Hadlee, another brilliant all-rounder. In Botham's Test career he scored 5,200 runs, including 14 centuries and has a fine record of 10 wickets in a match on four separate occasions. Botham moved to play for Durham county in 1992 and a year later retired from first-class cricket.

Bill
GATES
1955–
US computer engineer and businessman

The richest man in the world at the end of the millennium, William Henry Gates made his fortune though computer software. Born in Seattle, Washington, Gates created his first computer programme while still at high school, and adapted the computer language BASIC for use in the fledgling personal computer industry while still an undergraduate at Harvard University. Gates became convinced that personal computers would eventually be used by every office and home in the developed world. In 1975, aged 19, he dropped out of Harvard to set up the Microsoft computer company with Paul Allen. His foresight paid off. In 1980, Microsoft licensed the computer operating system MS-DOS to IBM – then the biggest computer company in the world. This, and the success of later products such as Windows 95, made Microsoft the largest producer of computer software in the world – Microsoft operating systems now run more than 90 per cent of the world's personal computers.

Steven
JOBS
1955–
US computer designer

A computer hobbyist, Jobs designed one of the world's first personal computers with his friend Stephen Wozniak (p.236). Born in California, Jobs formed a partnership with Wozniak while they were both working for Hewlett-Packard. They combined Wozniak's technical skill with Jobs' marketing talents to form the Apple Computer company. In 1975 they developed the first pre-assembled personal computer, the Apple II, which helped create the personal-computer market. Ousted in 1985 from the company he helped create, Jobs returned 12 years later to rescue Apple from the brink of almost certain bankruptcy.

1955
Twenty-seven-year-old US actor James Dean dies in a car crash outside Los Angeles. Dean's performance in *East of Eden* was highly acclaimed. His other two movies, *Rebel Without a Cause* and *Giant*, are yet to be released.

1955
Walt Disney fulfils his dream of creating a "Never-Never Land" for children when he opens his amusement park, Disneyland, near Los Angeles in California, USA. Over five million visitors are expected each year.

GREG NORMAN
*in action at the British
Open at Royal
Lytham and
St Anne's
in 1996.*

Greg NORMAN
1955–
Australian golfer

The "Great White Shark" (as Norman is called on the golf circuit) is almost as famous for being the golfer who never quite won the US Masters as he is for winning virtually everything else in professional golf. Gregory John Norman was born in Mount Isa, Queensland, and has been a professional golfer since 1976. As an assistant pro, earning £14 per week, he gambled on golf to earn his fare to Europe. His straight, long-playing shots became legendary. In 1986 he was rated the world's number one player, and won the Australian Open in 1980, 1985, and 1987, the British Open in 1986 and 1993, and the World Match Play Championship in 1980, 1983, and 1986. A favourite with golf crowds all round the world, Norman has come tantalizingly close to winning the US Masters only to see a six-stroke lead destroyed by Nick Faldo in 1996, and Larry Mize chip an unlikely play-off winner in 1987. He now owns a company that builds golf courses in Asia.

Alain PROST
1955–
French racing driver

In 1987 Formula One racing driver Alain Prost bettered Jackie Stewart's record of 27 Grand Prix wins, becoming the most successful driver in the history of racing. As a young man, Prost was sufficiently skilled at soccer to consider becoming a professional player, but he opted for racing instead. During his Formula One career Prost won 51 races from 199 starts. In 1981 he won his first Grand Prix, and in 1983–84, and 1988, he was runner-up in the World Championships, becoming World Champion in 1985–86, driving for McLaren-Porsche. He won the World Championship again for McLaren in 1989, and a fourth time for Williams in 1993, when he retired. His 798.5 championship points set a world record unbeaten today. Since 1996 he has managed the Prost Formula One racing team.

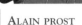

ALAIN PROST
The French racing driver ranks alongside Juan Manuel Fangio as the most successful Formula One driver ever. He is seen here during Formula One testing at Estoril in 1993.

Bjorn BORG
1956–
Swedish tennis player

One of the most consistent tennis players ever, Bjorn Rune Borg combined stamina and athleticism with a deft touch. He was born in Södertälje and was a talented all-round athlete in his youth. At the age of 14 he left school to concentrate on his tennis game. Only the next year he was selected for the Swedish Davis Cup team and, at the age of 16, he became Wimbledon junior champion. In the 1970s – the highpoint of his tennis career – he won the Wimbledon singles title five times in succession (1976–80, a record beaten only by Pete Sampras), including 41 consecutive matches undefeated until John McEnroe finally beat him. Borg's incredibly steady baseline play, his powerful double backhand, and deft ground strokes wore down his opponents. He won the Italian championship twice and the French Open six times between 1974–81. Borg always played with conventional wooden rackets, even when the first synthetic rackets arrived. Later in his career he failed to stage a comeback using this "old technology". He retired from tennis at the age of 26, having made a considerable fortune and inspired a generation of young players in Sweden and elsewhere. He ventured into designer clothing in the 1990s.

1956 In Alabama, USA, an African-American woman, Rosa Parks, is arrested for sitting at the front of a bus in a section set aside for whites. Protesters organize a bus boycott and 115 are jailed. The fight for civil rights continues.

1956 Hungary tries to break away from Soviet rule. Rebels destroy the huge bronze statue of Stalin in Budapest and thousands die fighting with the Soviet forces stationed in Hungary. The Soviet Union sends in troops.

Olga KORBUT
1956–
Russian gymnast

Olga Valentinovna Korbut captivated the world at the 1972 Munich Olympics with her near-perfect displays on the beam and bars, and her acrobatic grace in the floor exercises. She was born in Grodno, Belarus, and took up gymnastics at the age of ten. She showed great promise in competitions and was selected for the Soviet Olympic team. At the 1972 Olympic Games, only a slip on the asymmetric bars prevented her from winning a medal in the overall competition. However, she did win gold medals in the beam and floor exercises, and a silver for her daring performance on the parallel bars. As a member of the winning Russian team, she won another gold medal. At the 1976 Olympics, she once again won a silver medal for her exercises on the beam. In 1977 Korbut retired and married rock musician Leonid Bortkevich. She taught gymnastics in the USSR before emigrating to the USA in 1991 to teach in Atlanta, Georgia.

OLGA KORBUT
The 17-year-old Russian gymnast hit the headlines by winning three gold medals at the 1972 Olympics.

Spike LEE
1956–
US film director and actor

Lee was born in Georgia and grew up in New York. His father is a jazz musician who often writes the music scores for Lee's films. Lee studied film at New York University Film School, where he was an outstanding student, winning prizes with his student film *Joe's Bed-Stuy Barbershop: We Cut Heads* (1982). His first feature *She's Gotta Have It* (1986) was made on a shoestring budget, but it succeeded in establishing him internationally as a brilliant new talent. His follow-up, *Do The Right Thing* (1989), was an explosive story about inner-city racial rivalry from an African-American viewpoint – until then still a rare subject in Hollywood. Lee became the most influential African-American filmmaker of his generation. His work continues to be controversial and highly political in content, dealing with issues such as ethnic stereotypes and racism. His other films include *Jungle Fever* (1991) and *Malcolm X* (1992), a biopic about the political activist.

Sugar Ray LEONARD
1956–
US boxer

Sugar Ray Leonard was born in South Carolina. After winning an Olympic gold medal in Montreal in 1976, he embarked on a professional boxing career, during which he fought 12 world title fights and won titles in each of the various weights. Between 1977 and 1987 he was beaten only once in 35 fights – by Roberto Duran, who took the welterweight title on points in 1980. In 1981 Leonard became the undisputed welterweight champion. In 1991 he finally retired from boxing after sustaining a detached retina.

Joe MONTANA
1956–
US football player

One of the American football greats, Joseph Montana Jr was born in Monongahela, Pennsylvania. A talented passer and quarterback for Notre Dame, he went on to lead the San Francisco 49ers to victories in four Super Bowls in 1982, 1985, 1989, and 1990. A well-liked and inspirational team leader, Montana was named the National Football League's Most Valuable Player in 1989, when he led the NFL in passing the ball. He played with the Kansas City Chiefs from 1993–95.

Martina NAVRATILOVA
1956–
Czechoslovakian-born US tennis player

The first woman tennis player to earn more than $1 million in a season, from an early age Martina Navratilova showed great promise as a tennis player in her native country. Born in Prague, she played for Czechoslovakia in the Federation Cup for three years before defecting to the USA in 1975. She came to the attention of US tennis superstar Billie Jean King (p.231), who encouraged her to train hard to increase her stamina. Navratilova's new life in the USA marked the start of a brilliant career in tennis, during which she won 54 Grand Slam events. She still holds the record for the greatest number of Wimbledon singles titles, winning nine times between 1978 and 1990, six times in a row from 1982–87. Her finals were often thrilling duels against Chris Evert. Wimbledon has always been Navratilova's favourite Grand Slam venue, and she received a standing ovation from the crowd there when she played in the singles finals for the last time in 1994. Today, she often works as a tennis commentator, and her autobiography, *Being Myself*, was published in 1985.

Seve BALLESTEROS
1957–
Spanish golfer

The most exciting golfing talent to emerge in the mid-1970s, and the first Spanish golfing superstar, Severiano Ballesteros was born in Pedrena, northern Spain. The youngest of four brothers who all became professionals, he started as a youngster by sneaking out onto courses he was not allowed to play on and practising into the evenings. At 17 he turned professional and, in just five years, became one of the world's leading golfers, with a reputation for

1956 President Nasser of Egypt seizes control of the Suez Canal, the long waterway used for carrying oil from the Arab nations to Europe. England and France invade Egypt, but are forced to withdraw by the United Nations.

1957 *West Side Story*, a new musical by US composer Leonard Bernstein and lyricist Stephen Sondheim, opens on Broadway in New York. Based on Shakespeare's *Romeo and Juliet*, it is a moving love story set in New York's gangland.

adventurous play and an ability to recover from difficult positions with amazing winning shots. At the age of 22, Ballesteros was the youngest player to win the British Open in the 20th century – and the first continental European to win it for 72 years. A year later, in 1980, he became the youngest player ever to win the US Masters tournament and only the second European to wear the green jacket (he won it again in 1983). He again won the British Open in 1984 and in 1988. He was a key member of Europe's Ryder Cup team victories over the USA in 1985 and 1987. He continued to play into the late 1990s, but could not recapture the glory days of the 1980s.

Eric
HEIDEN
1958–
US speed skater and cyclist

A versatile athlete who had success in both speed skating and cycling, Eric Heiden was born in Madison, Wisconsin. As a medical student, he was only able to train as a skater for short periods of time. He performed well at his first Winter Olympic Games in 1976, coming seventh in the 1,000 metres race. The following year he became the world speed skating champion and in 1977, 1978, and 1979 the senior world all-round champion. At the 1980 Winter Olympics he won five gold speed skating medals in the 500 metres, 1,000 metres, 1,500 metres, and 10,000 metres. In 1981 he became a professional cycle racer, winning the US Professional Cycling Championship in 1985.

MADONNA
Madonna has been highly successful in adapting her image and musical style to keep up with current trends.

Jeanne
LONGO
1958–
French cyclist

B orn in Annecy, on the French-Swiss border, Jeanne Longo is considered to be the best female road cyclist of all time. Although she never won an Olympic gold medal, she had other numerous and prestigious wins, including the Women's Tour de France three times, the Colorado equivalent four times, and the world title a record eight times. She came out of retirement for the Barcelona Olympics in 1992 and won a silver in the road race that year.

MADONNA
1958–
US singer and actress

M adonna Louise Ciccione has emerged as the most successful female popular music artist of the late 20th century. She was born

in Rochester, Michigan, and trained as a dancer. She started with a string of disco-tinged hit singles, such as "Like a Virgin" (1984) and "Material Girl" (1985). Her album *True Blue* (1986) was Number One in 28 countries. She became a symbol of success and sexual liberation, attracting young female fans nicknamed "wannabes" for aspiring to be like their idol. Known as much for her continually changing image as for her music, each new look is keenly observed by both fans and fashion designers. Madonna has pursued a less successful film career but, in 1996, played Eva Perón to critical acclaim in the film *Evita*. Madonna changed her image yet again with the Grammy award-winning *Ray of Light* (1999), which reflected the latest dance-music styles.

1958 The Brazilian soccer team wins the sixth World Cup, beating the host nation Sweden 5–2 in the final. Seventeen-year-old Brazilian Pelé scores two of the final goals and emerges as a dazzling new soccer star.

1958 In France, wartime leader General de Gaulle is elected president. It is hoped that de Gaulle, who is intent upon a compromise with rebellious Algerian nationalists, will steer the country through a difficult time.

Nick FALDO
1959–
English golfer

Twice winner of the US Masters and three times British Open Champion, Nick Faldo was the foremost British golfer of the 1980s and early 1990s. He was born in Welwyn Garden City, Hertfordshire, and was good at all sports as a boy. However, when he picked up a golf club at the age of 14, he knew that he had found his game. Faldo's early successes included winning the Professional Golf Association Championships three times, in 1978 and 1980–81. A determined player and a perfectionist, he practised unceasingly, and changed his golf swing under David Leadbetter's instruction. The hard work resulted in his winning the British Open at Muirfield for the first time in 1987. In 1989 he won the US Masters, retaining it in 1990 and winning it for a third time in 1996. He won the British Open again in 1990 and 1992.

MAGIC JOHNSON
The US star (pictured here in the middle) used his commanding physique and height (6 ft 9 in) to great advantage on the basketball court.

John McENROE
1959–
US tennis player

The first "tennis brat" of the game, John Patrick McEnroe made his mark on the game as much by his tantrums and haranguing of umpires over dubious line calls as by his superb agility, speed, and poise. He was born in Wiesbaden, Germany. A promising young tennis player, he was sent to the USA to train at Port Washington Tennis Academy in New York State. At the age of 18, McEnroe was the youngest man to reach the Wimbledon finals and, in 1981, he won the men's singles title for the first time. From the late 1970s onwards he won numerous tournaments, including the US Open singles titles four times (1979–81 and 1984), Wimbledon on two more occasions (1983–4), and the Grand Prix three times (1979 and 1984–5). He was also the World Championship Tennis winner in 1979, 1981, and 1983–4. In 1986 McEnroe married Tatum O'Neal, the film actress, but the couple separated in 1993. McEnroe withdrew from top-class tennis before he was 30, and became a tennis commentator and art gallery owner.

Magic JOHNSON
1959–
US basketball player

Born Earvin Johnson in Lansing, Michigan, "Magic" Johnson is one of the greats of basketball. From 1979 he played basketball with the Los Angeles Lakers, and he was a member of the National Basketball Association (NBA) championship teams in 1980, 1982, 1985, 1987, and 1988. His autobiography, *Magic*, was published in 1983 when he was just 24 years old. In 1992 he was part of the US "dream team" that dominated the basketball event at the Olympics, winning the Gold Medal, but later that year he retired from the game after revealing that he had been diagnosed as HIV positive. In 1992 he published his second book, *What You Can Do To Avoid AIDs*. Johnson made a brief, but disappointing, comeback in 1993, and then coached the LA Lakers for a short time. In 1996 he played again for the team.

1960

Ayrton SENNA
1960–94
Brazilian racing driver

Ayrton da Silva Senna began racing go-karts when he was four years old in Sao Paulo where he was born. As a young man, he moved to Formula Three racing in Britain and, in 1981, joined a Formula One team. Senna made his Grand Prix debut in 1984 with the Toleman team and, a year later, he was driving for Lotus (1985–87) and, after that, for McLaren (1988–93) and Williams (1994). He was Formula One world champion in 1988, 1990, and 1991, but lost his title to Nigel Mansell in 1992. His success in motor racing led to success in another area – a major business marketing Senna products, which he built up in Sao Paulo. His career in motor racing was marked by his rivalry with Alain Prost, who was the only driver to better Senna's 41 Grand Prix wins. In 1994 Senna died after crashing in the San Marino Grand Prix.

Linford CHRISTIE
1960–
English sprinter

In 1993 Christie held the World, Olympic, Commonwealth, and European titles for the 100 metres, marking him as a supreme athlete of his generation. Born in St Andrews, Jamaica, Christie was brought up by his grandmother until the age of seven, when he joined his parents in England. At school he was encouraged to join the

1959 Following a coup on the Caribbean island of Cuba, President Batista flees to the Dominican Republic. The former guerrilla leader, Fidel Castro, rides triumphantly into the capital, Havana, and becomes Cuba's premier.

1959 The Dalai Lama, Tibet's Buddhist spiritual leader, is smuggled out of the capital, Lhasa, and flees to India to avoid arrest by the Chinese. He is met by 7,000 Tibetans at the West Bengali town of Siliguri.

athletics team. After leaving school he worked as an accountant, pursuing his career as a budding runner in his spare time. He made his international debut for Britain in 1980 and, in 1986, established himself as the fastest male sprinter outside the USA when he won the 100 metres in the European Championships. In 1980 he won a silver medal at the Seoul Olympics, repeating his success in 1990, when he also won a gold medal at the Commonwealth Games. At the age of 32, competing at the 1992 Olympics in Barcelona, Linford Christie won the 100 metres gold medal – the oldest man to do so. Christie retired in 1997 – having made over 50 appearances for Britain.

Diego
MARADONA
1960–
Argentinian soccer player

Soccer superstar Diego Maradona is probably best remembered for apparently scoring his first goal against England during a 1986 World Cup match with his fist and later attributing it to "the hand of God". Born in Lanus, Maradona played for his home country club, Boca Juniors, as a teenager. At the age of 17 he became Argentina's youngest international player and, five years later, in 1982, played in the World Cup in Spain. He was sent off in the match against Brazil, but afterwards the Spanish club Barcelona paid a record £5 million for him, making him the most expensive player in the world. A strong, speedy player with good balance and great flair, Maradona was not at his best in his first two seasons with Barcelona. Illness and injury seemed to plague him and consequently he played very little top-class soccer. In 1984

he moved from Barcelona to the Italian club Napoli, this time for a record £6.9 million. His health restored, he captained the Argentinian team to victory in the World Cup in Mexico, in 1986. In 1987 Maradona helped Napoli to win their first Italian championship. He led Argentina to another World Cup final in 1990 but they lost 1–0 to West Germany and his career started to founder amid accusations of drug use. Nevertheless, he is still considered to be one of the most gifted natural players of his generation.

Diana
PRINCESS
OF WALES
1961–1997
British princess
and humanitarian

Diana Spencer was born in Sandringham, Norfolk, youngest daughter of the 8th Earl Spencer. She came to the public's attention in 1981 when she was engaged to marry Charles, the Prince of Wales. Their spectacular royal wedding later that year was watched on television by millions of people around the world. She endeared herself to the British people with her genuine sense of caring in her charity work for those not so well off, and for the glamour and fashion she added to royal tours and functions. She and Prince Charles had two children, William (1982–) and Henry (1984–), but the marriage came under strain and they separated in 1992. Diana continued to work strenuously with

a number of charities, most notably on behalf of children and AIDS sufferers, and she led an anti-landmine campaign. She was killed in a car crash in Paris, on 31 August 1997. Her tragic death resulted in a spontaneous outpouring of grief all over the world.

FASHION ICON
Diana, Princess of Wales, brought glamour to the British Royal Family with her natural style and elegance.

1960 In the township of Sharpville, in South Africa, 69 black demonstrators are killed by white police officers. The demonstrators were protesting against the apartheid system and new laws restricting their freedom.

1960 Mrs Sirimavo Bandaranaike of the Freedom Party is elected in Sri Lanka, becoming the world's first female prime minister. She entered politics a year earlier when her husband, the prime minister, was assassinated.

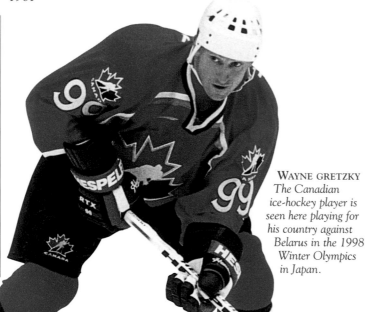

WAYNE GRETZKY
The Canadian ice-hockey player is seen here playing for his country against Belarus in the 1998 Winter Olympics in Japan.

Nadia COMANECI
1961–
Romanian gymnast

At just 13, Nadia Comaneci was already a gymnastic sensation. She won four of the five gold medals at the European Championships of 1975, and the following year she represented Romania at the Montreal Olympics, winning gold medals in the beam, floor, and vault exercises. Born in Onesti, Moldavia, she was educated at the College of Physical Education and Sports in Bucharest. Always a graceful gymnast with superb concentration, Comaneci scored a perfect score of ten on the asymmetric bars – the first athlete to achieve this, and at the age of only 14. She again took gold medals for beam and floor exercises in the 1980 Moscow Olympics when she was 18. Comaneci retired in 1984 and became a judge of gymnastics and junior team coach for five years. In 1989 she caused a stir by defecting to the USA, where she was granted refugee status. She later became a dancer and gymnastics entertainer.

Wayne GRETZKY
1961–
Canadian ice-hockey player

Known as "The Great One" during his career in ice-hockey, Wayne Gretzky was born in Brantford, Ontario. In 1979 he joined the Edmonton Oilers ice-hockey team and was voted the Most Valuable Player in the National Hockey League (NHL) on nine occasions (1980–89). As well as being the National Hockey League's leading scorer ten times, Gretzky holds 61 records in the sport, and scored more goals in one season than any other player (92 in 1981–82). In 1988 he transferred to the Los Angeles Kings for $15 million – another record – and in 1996 moved to St Louis and then to the New York Rangers, retiring in 1999.

Carl LEWIS
1961–
US athlete

Frederick Carlton Lewis, born in Birmingham, Alabama, was a brilliant all-round athlete. He won the world long jump gold medal at the 1981 World Cup, and three gold medals in the World Championships in 1983. At the Los Angeles Olympics in 1984, Lewis won four gold medals for track and field events – the 100 metres, 200 metres, 4 x 100 metres relay, and long jump – repeating the success of Jesse Owens (p.195) in 1936. More gold medals followed: at the 1988 Seoul Olympics for the 100 metres and long jump, and the 1992 Barcelona Olympics for the long jump. For many years Lewis held the world record in the 100 metres.

Wynton MARSALIS
1961–
US musician and trumpeter

Born into a musical family (his father and brothers were all jazz musicians), the young Wynton Marsalis was given his first trumpet at the age of six. He studied music throughout his childhood, and at the Juilliard School of Music in New York. Marsalis studied both jazz and classical music and showed virtuosity in both genres. As a young man he played with many jazz greats, including Art Blakey and Herbie Hancock, as well as recording an album with his father and brother Branford, called *Fathers and Sons* (1982). In 1983 he released the albums *Think of One* (jazz) and *Trumpet Concertos* (classical).

WYNTON MARSALIS
The US trumpeter is a talented classical and jazz musician.

1961 The Berlin Wall is erected, separating East and West Berlin. The heavily guarded wall and electric fences will prevent Germans from escaping the hardships of the communist regime in East Germany.

1963 US President John F. Kennedy is shot in the head as he is driven in an open-topped car through Dallas, Texas. The police arrest a lone gunman, Lee Harvey Oswald, for the assassination. Oswald himself is later shot by Jack Ruby.

He won Grammy awards for each as best soloist in 1984 – the first musician to win Grammy awards in both classical and jazz categories – and the next year repeated the rare double.

Michael
JORDAN
1963–
US basketball player

With the highest-scoring career average in US professional basketball, Michael Jordan was probably the finest all-rounder the game produced in the 20th century. Born in Brooklyn, New York, he acquired his reputation as a talented basketball player at college. After helping the University of North Carolina to the national championship and the US team to the 1984 Olympic gold medal, Jordan joined the Chicago Bulls as a professional player. He carried the team to victory in six National Basketball Association championships – in 1991, 1992, 1993, 1996, 1997, and 1998. He earned his nickname "Air Jordan" through his athleticism and ability to jump high. He was a member of the US Olympic gold-medal winning basketball team in 1984 and 1992 and was the first basketball player to be named Most Valuable Player five times by the NBA. One of the highest scorers in the game, Jordan made more than 50 points

on 36 different occasions and holds the record for the most points (63) in a NBA play-off, against Boston, in 1986. Jordan retired in 1993 to play baseball, but rejoined the Bulls in 1995 and led them to three NBA Championships in 1996–98, after which he finally retired.

Katarina
WITT
1965–
German figure skater

A stunning figure skater, Katarina Witt dominated the sport in the 1980s. She was born in Karl-Marx-Stadt, East Germany. In 1982 she was the East German champion figure skater and, in 1983, won the first of six successive European titles. She was the World Champion in 1984–85 and 1987–88, and Olympic Champion in 1984 and 1988. After the reunification of Germany in 1989 Witt immediately took advantage of greater freedom and decided to perform professionally in ice shows in Europe and the USA. She bought an apartment in New York and, in 1991, won an Emmy Award for her performance in *Carmen on Ice*. In 1996 Witt was first in the Legends Championship.

Boris
BECKER
1967–
German tennis player

In 1985 Becker became the youngest-ever winner of the men's singles at Wimbledon, as well as the first unseeded player to win the title. Born in Leimen, he was a successful product of the German tennis leagues. He was first noticed in 1984, when he finished runner-up in the US Open tournament. Becker went on to win Wimbledon for the first time in 1985, and for seven years (1985–91) was in the finals six times, winning again in 1986 and 1989. He also had victories in the US Open in 1989 and 1994 and the Australian Open in 1991 and 1996, as well as a gold medal for Germany in the doubles at the Barcelona Olympics in 1992. His form deserted him in the mid-1990s and in 1998 he failed to play at Wimbledon for the first time in 13 years. He returned in 1999 in a bid to secure one more win, but did not make it to the semi-finals.

BORIS BECKER
The German tennis player's power and accuracy of play on court earned him the nickname "Boom Boom" Becker.

1964 In the United States, President Lyndon Johnson signs the Civil Rights Act outlawing racial discrimination.

President Johnson publicly shakes hands with civil rights leader Martin Luther King after the signing.

1969 US astronaut Neil Armstrong becomes the first person to walk on the Moon. With the famous words

"That's one small step for man, one giant leap for mankind", he steps out of his lunar module and into the history books.

Michael SCHUMACHER
1969–
German racing driver

Born in Hürth-Hermuhlheim, Michael Schumacher began racing at the age of five. In his early twenties he became the German and European Senior Kart Champion, moving on to Formula Ford in 1988 and Formula Three in 1989. He made a remarkable Formula One debut in the 1991 Belgium Grand Prix, when he qualified in seventh place. Two weeks later he joined the Benetton team and became world champion in 1994 and 1995. A year after his second world championship victory, Schumacher signed a $26 million contract with Ferrari. Schumacher is widely regarded as the most technically proficient driver on the Formula One circuit.

1970

Pete SAMPRAS
1971–
US tennis player

One of the greatest tennis players ever, Pete Sampras completely dominated the game and the record books at the end of the 20th century. By the time he was 27 years old, he had won 12 Grand Slam Championships (US Open, Wimbledon, and the Australian Open). Born in Washington DC, he proved a formidable opponent on the US college circuit, and soon established a name for his powerful serve-and-volley game. Sampras went on to win the US Open tournament four times – in 1990, 1993 and 1995, 1996 – and Wimbledon

six times (1993, 1994, 1995, 1997, 1998, and 1999 – finally surpassing Bjorn Borg's tied record of five Wimbledon wins.

Tiger WOODS
1975–
US golfer

Already an unbeatable amateur player, "Tiger" Woods shot to fame as a world-class professional golfer after winning the US Masters at Augusta, Georgia, in devastating style in 1997. The son of an African-American father and Thai mother, Tiger Woods was born Eldrick Woods in Cypress, California. His nickname "Tiger" is a tribute to a friend with whom his father served in Vietnam. Tiger studied at Stanford University in California and won junior and amateur US golf titles – he retained the amateur title for a record three consecutive years – before turning professional in 1996. At the age of 21 he became the youngest as well as the first black winner of the US Masters tournament and was immediately hailed as a budding golf superstar. He continues to attract the largest crowds and is hailed as the saviour of the game for the new millennium.

Vanessa-MAE
1978–
Singaporean musician

Vanessa-Mae Vanakorn Nicholson was born in Singapore but moved to Britain with her family when she was four. A musical child prodigy, she began piano lessons at the age of three, violin lessons at five, and studied at both the Central Conservatory in

Beijing, China, and the Royal College of Music in London before making her concert debut in 1989, aged 11. After recording three highly successful classical records (1990–92), she broadened her outlook and recorded *The Violin Player* (1995), a "techno-acoustic fusion recording" that mixed classical and rock music and sold more than one million copies. Vanessa-Mae's extraordinary violin technique, combined with a strong stage personality, makes her a much sought-after public performer. Through her many records and concert performances, she has attracted listeners who might normally avoid classical music, and has done much to popularize violin music.

Louise BROWN
1978–
English "test tube" baby

In July 1978, Louise Brown was born as the first person to be conceived outside the womb. Louise's mother, Lesley Brown, could not conceive a child because she was sterile. One of her eggs was removed and fertilized by her husband's sperm in a test-tube before it was re-implanted in her womb to grow naturally through to birth. The revolutionary technique was developed by Patrick Steptoe (1913–88), a gynaecologist at Oldham General Hospital, where Louise was born, and Robert Edwards (1925–), a physiologist at Cambridge University. The process is called *in vitro* fertilization.

VANESSA-MAE *gives a typical shimmering performance at a concert at London's Royal Albert Hall.*

1979 In the Middle East, President Sadat of Egypt and Prime Minister Begin of Israel sign a peace treaty at the White House in Washington, DC. However, problems such as the future of the Israeli-occupied West Bank are not resolved.

1999 One of mankind's greatest joint ventures is the International Space Station. The station is being built 402 km (250 miles) above the Earth's surface, and 16 countries are involved in putting the pieces together.

FACT FINDER

THROUGHOUT THE MILLENNIUM, Britain has produced many people of international importance, who feature in the main part of this book. But for every famous monarch or political leader, poet or astronomer, there are many more, who, in their own way, made their mark on British society. They are listed here, alongside Nobel Prize and Academy Award winners, as well as US presidents.

KINGS & QUEENS

For more than 1,000 years, an unbroken thread has run through British history. With one brief exception in the 17th century, Britain has been ruled by hereditary monarchs, with the throne passing down within royal houses (families) from father to son, or sometimes daughter, despite wars, revolutions, and the occasional beheading. In the year 1000, England, Scotland, Ireland, and Wales were separate kingdoms. In 1171, England began the invasion of Ireland, and in 1284 ended the independence of Wales. For centuries, Scotland fought to remain independent but the two thrones merged in 1603. By 1801 the country as we know it today was united.

SAXON & VIKINGS

The years after 1000 were marked by Viking domination of England; under Canute, England became part of a Scandinavian empire which included Denmark, Norway, and part of Sweden. In 1042 the Saxon Edward the Confessor became king, although he was heavily influenced by his Norman advisers and even promised the throne to William of Normandy – William the Conqueror – who invaded England in 1066 to claim his title.

978–1013	Ethelred the Unready
1013–1014	Swein Forkbeard
1014–1016	Ethelred the Unready (restored)
1016	Edmund II Ironside
1016–1037	Canute
1037–1049	Harold I Harefoot
1040–1042	Harthacnut
1042–1066	Edward the Confessor
1066	Harold II

THE NORMANS 1066~1154

The Normans were originally Vikings who had settled in northern France in the early 10th century and built up a powerful state. In 1066 William, Duke of Normandy, invaded England and seized the throne at the Battle of Hastings, ending 400 years of Saxon rule. The Normans introduced strong central government, squashed all dissent against their rule, and began to build magnificent stone castles and cathedrals. Both William I and Henry I were capable and effective kings, although William II quarrelled with the Church and his leading supporters and anarchy ruled during the reign of King Stephen.

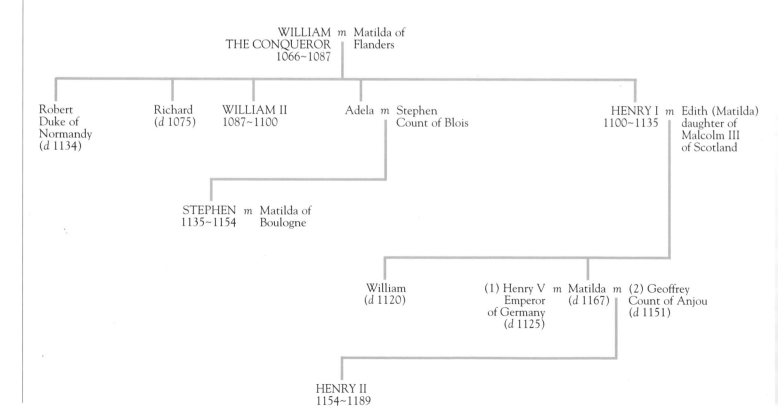

THE PLANTAGENETS 1154~1399

The Plantagenets took their name from the sprig of flowering broom (*Planta genista*) Geoffrey of Anjou – father of Henry II – wore as a badge. With few exceptions, the Plantagenets were energetic, warlike kings who extended English rule west into Wales and Ireland, attempted to conquer Scotland, and carved out a vast empire in France which stretched down to the Pyrenees mountains. That empire was lost during the reign of John, but in 1337 Edward III renewed the English claim to the French throne and attempted once again to conquer France. Under the Plantagenets, England prospered.

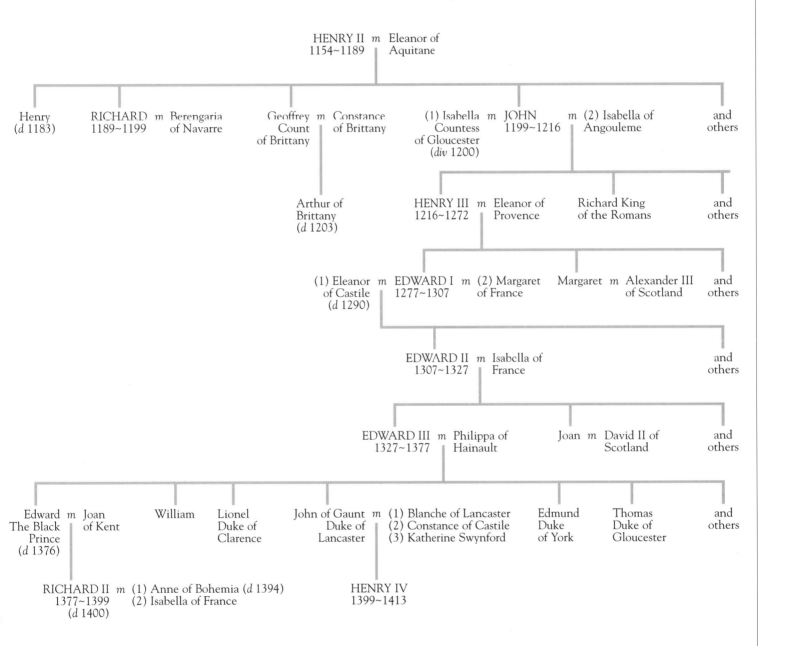

HENRY II 1154–1189
When he became king at the age of 21, Henry inherited an empire that stretched from the Scottish borders down to Spain. Intellectually and physically strong, Henry regulated the powers of the Church, laid the foundations of common law, and established the jury system.

RICHARD I 1189–1199
Richard was an absentee king, spending all but seven months out of England on crusades in the Holy Land. His courage in battle earned him the name *Coeur de Lion* (Lionheart).

EDWARD I 1272–1307
A renowned warrior, Edward invaded Wales and also attempted to conquer Scotland, earning himself the name "Hammer of the Scots". His son, Edward II (1307–1327) was weak and ineffectual; he was deposed and murdered on his wife's orders.

EDWARD III 1327–1377
In 1337 Edward laid claim to the French throne and declared war. The 100 Years' War was not continual, but the conflict brought considerable wealth to England at the expense of the French.

THE HOUSE OF LANCASTER 1399~1461

Abranch of the Plantagenet family, the three Lancastrian kings were descendants of John of Gaunt, Duke of Lancaster and the fourth son of Edward III. In 1399 Henry Bolingbroke, Duke of Lancaster, seized the throne from his cousin Richard II, who was deposed and died in prison the following year. The Lancastrian period was marked by almost continual warfare, with a revolt in Wales, uprisings by discontented barons, renewed fighting in France, and then civil war as the Yorkists, descendants of the third and fifth sons of Edward III, claimed and seized the throne in the Wars of the Roses.

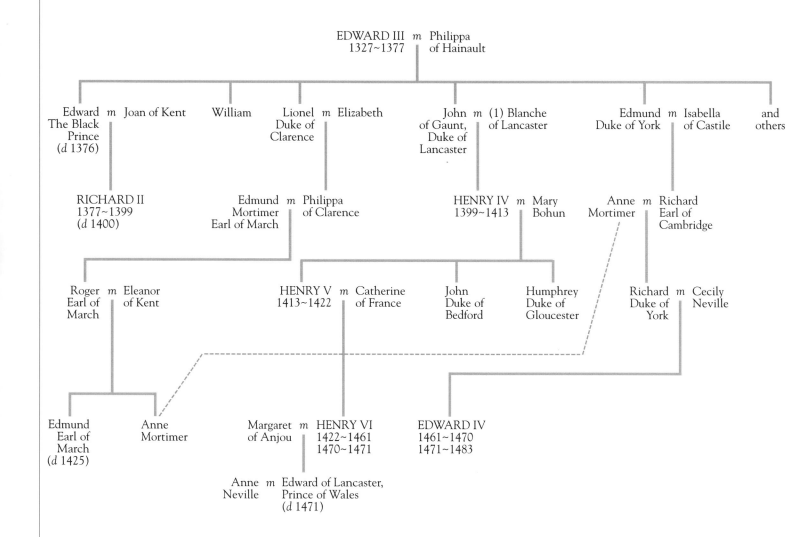

HENRY IV 1399–1413
A strong and able ruler, Henry spent his reign overcoming revolts in Wales, led by Owain Glyndwr, and by powerful barons, led by the Percy family of Northumberland. Even his own son, Henry of Monmouth (later Henry V), challenged him by setting up his own royal court.

HENRY V 1413–1422
Within months of his succession, Henry reopened the 100 Years' War, which had ended in 1374 with the loss of almost all English possessions in France. Henry invaded in 1415 and defeated the French at Agincourt. In 1420 he married the daughter of Charles VI of France and became heir to the French throne, but died before he could become king.

HENRY VI 1422–1461, 1470–1471
Henry VI became King of England when he was nine months old; two months later he became King of France after the death of Charles VI. His rule in France was soon ended by the campaigns of Joan of Arc, and by 1453 the English were driven out of France, with the exception of Calais. Throughout his reign, Henry suffered from mental illness; his cousin, Richard of York, became Protector in 1454 and in 1455 rose in revolt, starting the Wars of the Roses between Lancastrians and Yorkists. Henry was deposed in 1461, and although he briefly regained the throne in 1470, he was again deposed and murdered in the Tower of London in 1471. Henry was a devoutly religious man with a great enthusiasm for education. He sponsored King's College at Cambridge University and built its famous chapel.

THE HOUSE OF YORK 1461~1485

Another branch of the Plantagenet family, the Yorkists had a better claim to the throne than the Lancastrians. Led by Richard, Duke of York, and then by his son, Edward, the Yorkists rose in revolt in 1455, seizing the throne in 1461 when Edward became king as Edward IV. Although the Yorkist family ruled for only a short period, the country was well-governed and enjoyed considerable commercial prosperity. Music, literature, and architecture flourished, and in 1476 William Caxton set up England's first printing press.

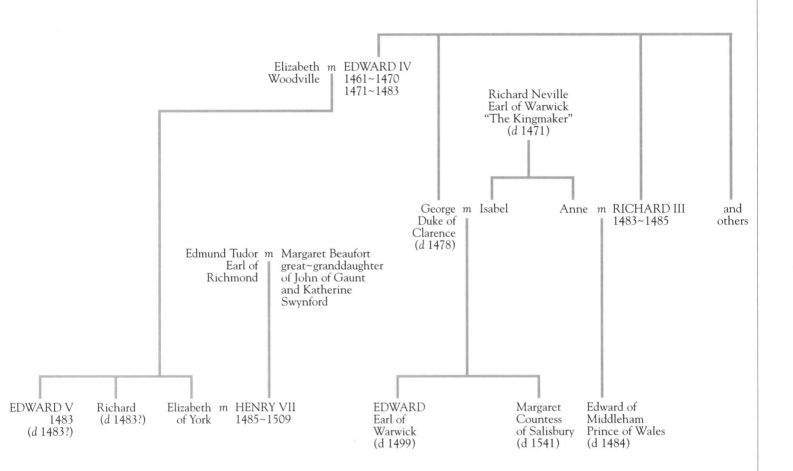

EDWARD IV 1461–1470, 1471–1483
Only 18 when he came to the throne, Edward set out to restore good government and improve the royal finances. He achieved both these ends by reforming the legal system, encouraging the wool trade, allowing German merchants to trade in England, and keeping the country out of foreign conflicts. During his reign, England enjoyed a period of well-deserved peace and prosperity.

EDWARD V 1483
Edward V was only 12 when he became king, but within months he was declared illegitimate by Parliament and deposed in favour of his uncle, Richard, Duke of Gloucester, who became king as

Richard III. Within a few months, Edward and his brother, Richard, disappeared in the Tower of London; it is assumed that they were murdered by their uncle.

RICHARD III 1483–1485
A much maligned king, Richard III has gone down in history as the hunch-backed villain of Shakespeare's play. In reality he was physically fit, and an energetic, painstaking, and just ruler who enjoyed music and took great interest in education, endowing colleges at Cambridge University. His reign was short, however, for in 1485 he was defeated and killed at the Battle of Bosworth by Henry Tudor, the Lancastrian claimant to the throne.

THE TUDORS 1485~1603

The Tudor family were a Welsh family who could trace their descent back to the princes of independent Wales. Through his mother, Henry Tudor was the Lancastrian claimant to the throne and, after he became king, he married Elizabeth of York, daughter of Edward IV, thus uniting the two rival houses. The nobility had so weakened itself during the Wars of the Roses that the Tudors were able to wield considerable power, which they used to largely good effect. Parliament was kept under control, the economy was stimulated, and by the end of the 16th century, the English Renaissance was blossoming, reaching its peak in the works of dramatist and poet William Shakespeare.

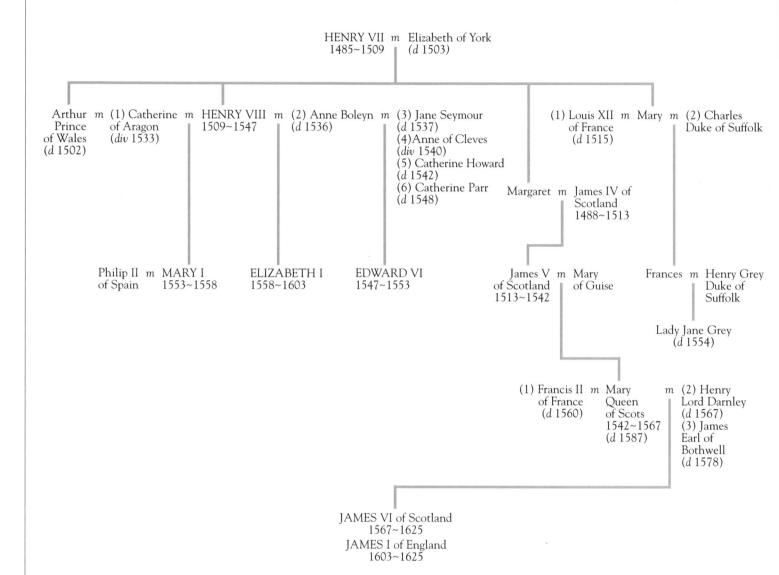

HENRY VII 1485–1509
Henry was a shrewd ruler who did much to reduce the power of the barons by banning their private armies and bringing them under legal control. His policies brought peace and prosperity to a nation tired of war.

HENRY VIII 1509–1547
At first Henry allowed his advisers to rule for him, but when he failed to get a divorce from his wife, Catherine of Aragon, he took power into his own hands, declaring himself head of the English Church and breaking the link with the Roman Catholic Church. Famously married six times, Henry was a capable, clever, but cruel ruler. The monasteries were dissolved and Henry seized their wealth for himself.

EDWARD VI 1547–1553
During the short reign of this boy king, the English Church moved closer to the Protestant churches of Europe.

MARY I 1553–1558
An ardent Roman Catholic, Mary restored the Catholic Church and burned many Protestants at the stake. In her brief reign, "Bloody Mary" became increasingly unpopular.

ELIZABETH I 1558–1603
Throughout her long reign, Elizabeth showed considerable skill in picking her advisers and ruled carefully and wisely. She restored the Protestant faith and defied the Catholic powers of Europe, notably Spain, which sent an armada to invade England in 1588.

THE HOUSE OF STUART 1603~1714

When Elizabeth I died childless in 1603, the throne passed to her distant relative, James VI of Scotland, thus uniting the crowns of Scotland and England. Although Protestant, the Stuarts were pro-Catholic; they were also firm believers in the divine right of kings to rule as they saw fit. Together these two characteristics led to continual conflict between King and Parliament that caused the execution of one king and the declaration of a republic in 1649 and the overthrow of another king in 1688. By the early 1700s, Parliament was supreme, and the rights of the monarchy severely reduced.

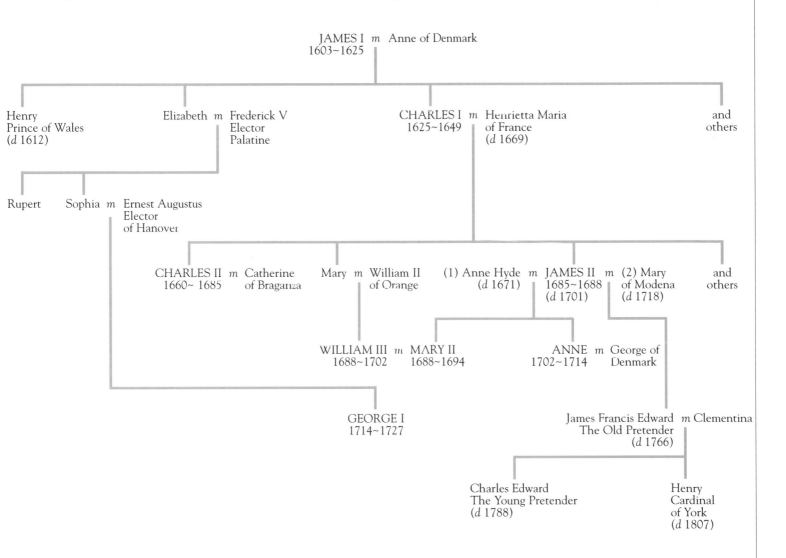

JAMES I 1603–1625
"The Wisest Fool in Christendom" ruled for long periods without Parliament, relying instead on his favourites for advice. He thus squandered the legacy of strong government left him by Elizabeth.

CHARLES I 1625–1649
A firm believer in his divine right to rule, Charles quarrelled with Parliament and governed without one for 11 years. In 1642 he tried to arrest five MPs, and civil war broke out, leading to the defeat of the king and his execution in 1649. The country then became a republic, but in 1653 Oliver Cromwell seized power and established a Protectorate, or monarchy in all but name.

CHARLES II 1660–1685
Restored to the throne in 1660, Charles's pursuit of pleasure after the Puritan zeal of the Commonwealth of 1649–60 attracted much controversy but also much popularity.

JAMES II 1685–1688
In the late 1660s James converted to Catholicism, and made it clear on his accession that he intended to restore Catholicism in Britain. His policies led to conflict with both Parliament and the Anglican Church, and he fled into exile in 1688.

WILLIAM III & MARY II 1688–1702
When William of Orange – a member of the Dutch royal family – was invited by Parliament to replace James II, it was agreed that he rule jointly with his wife, Mary. His main concern was to prevent French expansion in Europe, and so he involved British forces in lengthy wars against Louis XIV of France.

ANNE 1702–1714
Throughout her reign, England was involved in lengthy wars against France, conducted by the Duke of Marlborough. At home, union was achieved between Scotland and England.

THE HOUSE OF HANOVER 1714~1910

On the death of the childless Queen Anne, the throne passed to the Protestant rulers of Hanover. As German speakers from a landlocked state with no representative government, the Hanoverians found Britain a difficult and sometimes hostile country, but they worked hard to win acceptance in their new kingdom. By the time of Victoria, Britain was an industrialized country with a vast empire, and real power had passed from the monarchy to Parliament. Yet the royal family managed the transition well, and became a relatively uncontroversial and much-loved part of the British constitution.

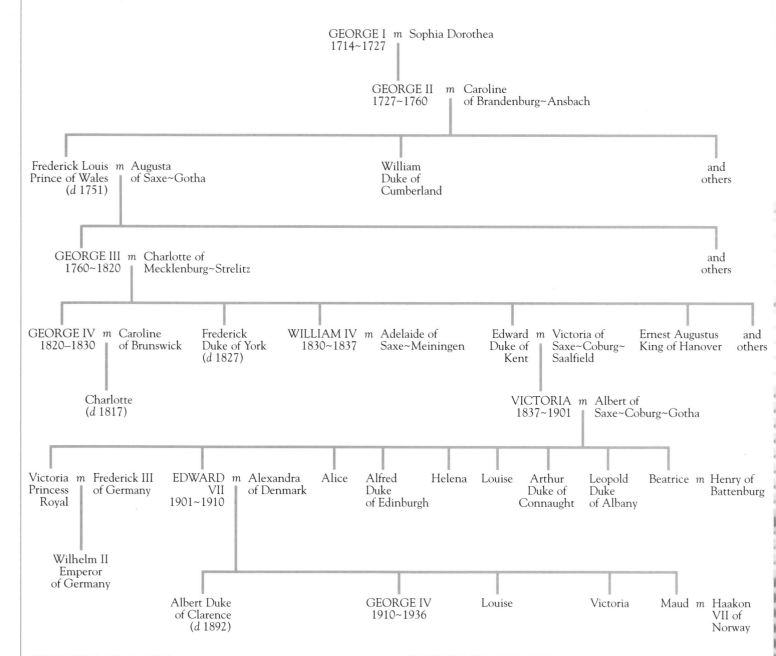

GEORGE I 1714–1727

Neither George I nor his son, George II (1727–60) spoke any English, and both faced revolts from Stuart claimants to the throne. They relied on political advisers to govern for them, one of whom, Robert Walpole, became the first Prime Minister in 1721.

GEORGE III 1760–1820

The first Hanoverian monarch born in Britain, George was a conscientious ruler who sometimes interfered too much in politics. From 1788 he suffered from a disease which made him appear deranged, and from 1811 his son ruled as his Regent.

GEORGE IV 1820–1830

An immoral Prince of Wales who lavishly supported the arts, George IV was an unpopular king. His brother, William IV (1830–1837) ruled during a period of great political reform.

VICTORIA 1837–1901

Britain's longest serving monarch, Victoria eventually presided over the world's largest empire. Ably served by her prime ministers, she relied on her husband, Albert, for support and was distraught at his early death in 1861. For the next 13 years she lived as a recluse, but returned to public life in 1874. Her Golden Jubilee in 1887 revealed the extent of her popularity.

THE HOUSE OF WINDSOR 1910~

Both Edward VII and his son, George V, were technically members of the House of Saxe-Coburg-Gotha but in 1917, at the height of World War I against Germany, the royal family removed all their German names and became the House of Windsor. Twice the monarchy has been involved in constitutional crisis: the first time in 1911 when George V was pulled into the struggle to reform the House of Lords, and again in 1936 when his son, Edward VIII, chose to abdicate. Yet despite these and more recent scandals, the monarchy has survived in good shape to face the new millennium.

GEORGE V 1910–1936
George came to power in the middle of a constitutional crisis caused by his government's determination to limit the power of the House of Lords and within four years he was leading a country fighting for its survival in World War I. Political and economic turmoil after the war added to the problems, yet George managed to keep the monarchy above politics and retained great popularity throughout his reign.

EDWARD VIII 1936
A popular Prince of Wales, Edward caused great controversy when he decided to marry an American divorcee, Mrs Wallis Simpson. The government objected and within months of his succession, he abdicated the throne.

GEORGE VI 1936–1952
Unexpectedly created king on the abdication of his brother, George proved a popular king who led his country through the horrors of World War II and restored the reputation of the monarchy shaken by his brother.

ELIZABETH II 1952–
Aged only 25 when she became queen, Elizabeth has presided over a massive transformation in Britain as empire has given way to Commonwealth and the country has joined the European Union. During the 1990s the monarchy's popularity suffered as three of her four children were divorced, notably the Prince of Wales and his former wife, Diana. Yet Elizabeth has retained her popularity.

KINGS & QUEENS OF SCOTLAND

The first king to govern the whole of Scotland was Malcolm II, king of northern Scotland, who conquered Lothian and Strathclyde in 1018–19. Scotland remained an independent country, despite constant invasions from England, until 1603, when James VI inherited the English throne as James I. The two countries were united in 1707.

REIGN	MONARCH	REIGN	MONARCH	REIGN	MONARCH
997–1005	Kenneth III	1124–1153	David I	1332–1341	Edward Balliol
1005–1034	Malcolm II	1153–1165	Malcolm IV, the Maiden	1341–1371	David II (restored)
1034–1040	Duncan I	1165–1214	William the Lion	1371–1390	Robert II, Stewart
1040–1057	Macbeth	1214–1249	Alexander II	1390–1406	Robert III
1057–1058	Lulach	1249–1286	Alexander III	1406–1437	James I
1058–1093	Malcolm III	1286–1290	Margaret, Maid of Norway	1437–1460	James II
1093–1094	Donalbane	1290–1292	Interregnum	1460–1488	James III
1094	Duncan II	1292–1296	John Balliol	1488–1513	James IV
1094–1097	Donalbane (restored)	1296–1306	Interregnum	1513–1542	James V
1097–1107	Edgar	1306–1329	Robert I, the Bruce	1542–1567	Mary, Queen of Scots
1107–1124	Alexander I	1329–1332	David II	1567–1625	James VI

RULERS OF WALES

When Wales was an independent country, it was ruled by princes, some of whom controlled only parts of the country. In 1277, Edward I of England invaded Wales, ending its independence in 1284; the two countries were united in 1536. Ever since 1301, it has been customary for the eldest son and heir of the British monarch to be invested as Prince of Wales; recent investitures have been in Caernarfon Castle.

WELSH PRINCES	
REIGN	**MONARCH**
999–1005	Cynan ap Hywel
1005–1023	Llewelyn ap Seisyll
1023–1039	Iago ap Idwal
1039–1063	Gruffydd ap Llewelyn
1063–1075	Bleddyn ap Cynfyn
1075–1081	Trahaern ap Caradog
1081–1137	Gruffydd ap Cynan
1137–1170	Owain Gwynedd
1170–1175	Cynan ap Owain
1175	David ab Owain
1175–1194	Rhodri ab Owain
1194–1240	Llewelyn ap Iorwerth
1240–1246	David ap Llewelyn
1246–1282	Llewelyn ap Gruffydd
1282–1283	David ap Gruffydd

RULERS IN SOUTH WALES	
1078–1116	Rhys ap Tudor
1116–1155	Gruffydd ap Rhys
1155–1194	Rhys ap Gruffydd

PRINCES OF WALES		
INVESTITURE	**PRINCE OF WALES**	**RELATION**
1301	Edward, *later Edward II*	Son of Edward I
1343	Edward the Black Prince	Son of Edward III
1376	Richard, *later Richard II*	Grandson of Edward III
1399	Henry, *later Henry V*	Son of Henry IV
1454	Edward of Lancaster	Son of Henry VI
1471	Edward, *later Edward V*	Son of Edward IV
1483	Edward of Middleham	Son of Richard III
1490	Arthur	First son of Henry VII
1504	Henry, *later Henry VIII*	Second son of Henry VII
1610	Henry	First son of James I
1616	Charles, *later Charles I*	Second son of James I
1640	Charles, *later Charles II*	Son of Charles I
1688	James, the Old Pretender	Son of James II
1714	George, *later George II*	Son of George I
1729	Frederick Louis	Son of George II
1751	George, *later George III*	Grandson of George II
1762	George, *later George IV*	Son of George III
1841	Edward, *later Edward VII*	Son of Victoria
1901	George, *later George V*	Son of Edward VII
1911	Edward, *later Edward VIII*	Son of George V
1969	Charles	Son of Elizabeth II

WARS & BATTLES

The history of the millennium has been disfigured by wars and battles, some fought over territory, others over religion or ideology. At first, the warfare was conducted by small, part-time conscript armies fighting with bows and swords, but the use of gunpowder after the 14th century revolutionized warfare. Today, wars are fought by professional armies using tanks and planes armed with hi-tech weapons delivered by missile and guided by computer.

MAJOR WARS & REVOLUTIONS

CRUSADES 1096–1291
European knights and adventurers fought in the Holy Land to keep the holy sites free from Muslim control; the Muslims expelled them by 1291.

100 YEARS' WAR 1337–1453
A long series of battles fought intermittently between England and France caused by the English claim to the French throne; by the end England held only the port of Calais.

DUTCH WAR OF INDEPENDENCE 1568–1648
Lengthy campaign by the Protestant Dutch to win their independence from Catholic Spanish rule. Dutch independence was finally agreed in 1648.

THIRTY YEARS' WAR 1618–1648
Began as a Catholic-Protestant struggle in Germany but turned into a conflict between the Hapsburg Empire and France.

ENGLISH CIVIL WAR 1642–1651
A social, religious, and military conflict between Charles I and Parliament which ended in his execution in 1649 and the declaration of a republic.

GREAT NORTHERN WAR 1700–1721
A lengthy conflict between Sweden and Russia for control of the Baltic which ended in Russian victory.

WAR OF THE SPANISH SUCCESSION 1701–1713
An inconclusive struggle between France and the rest of Europe over control of the Spanish throne.

SEVEN YEARS' WAR 1757–1763
Major European conflict between France and Austria against Britain and Prussia. Prussia expanded its territory while Britain expelled France from Canada.

AMERICAN REVOLUTION 1775–1783
War of independence fought by American colonists against British rule, leading to the independence of the USA.

FRENCH REVOLUTION 1789–1795
An uprising against the aristocratic rule of Louis XVI. The revolution led to the formation of a republic, the execution of the king, and the complete transformation of French society.

NAPOLEONIC WARS 1792–1815
A lengthy series of wars fought by Napoleon against other European power that saw Napoleon and France dominate Europe until his ultimate defeat at Waterloo in 1815.

MEXICAN-AMERICAN WAR 1846–1848
Disputes over land between Mexico and the USA led to war, which ended with the annexation of California and other southwestern states by the USA.

AMERICAN CIVIL WAR 1861–1865
Fought between 11 slave-owning southern states of the Confederacy and anti-slavery northern Union states, the war was won by the Union, and slavery was abolished.

FRANCO-PRUSSIAN WAR 1870–1871
After defeating Denmark and Austria, Prussia goaded France into war and defeated her in 1871, gaining land in eastern France and establishing a unified German empire.

RUSSO-JAPANESE WAR 1904–1905
The first modern conflict won by an Asian power against a European nation, showing Japan to be a major force in world affairs.

WORLD WAR I 1914–1918
International conflict between the German, Austro-Hungarian, and Ottoman empires against the Allies powers of Russia, France, and Britain led to an Allied victory and the collapse of four major European empires.

IRISH RISING 1916
The republican rising against British rule in Dublin on Easter Sunday led to six years of conflict before Ireland became an independent state in 1922.

RUSSIAN REVOLUTION 1917
Two revolutions took place in Russia in 1917: the first overthrew the tsar and established a liberal democracy, the second established the world's first communist state.

CHINESE-JAPANESE WAR 1931–1945
Taking advantage of Chinese weakness, Japan invaded the northern province of Manchuria in 1931. In 1937 it invaded the rest of the country, and was only defeated at the end of World War II.

SPANISH CIVIL WAR 1936–1939
Civil war between the left-wing Republican government and right-wing Nationalist rebels led to Nationalist victory and a Fascist government under General Franco.

WORLD WAR II 1939–1941
Caused by German aggression in Europe, the war spread around the world as Japan and Italy joined in with Germany, and the USA and USSR with Britain. The war ended in the defeat of Germany and Japan.

CHINESE REVOLUTION 1949
In 1911 the Chinese empire had been overthrown and a republic set up. Communists rebelled against the new government and in 1949, led by Mao Zedong, took over the whole country.

KOREAN WAR 1950–1953
Communist North Korea invaded capitalist South Korea, leading to an international force intervening to protect the South. A truce was called in 1953, which is still in force today.

VIETNAM WAR 1965–1975
Communist North Vietnam's attempt to unite the country brought the USA into the war in support of South Vietnam. After the US withdrew, Vietnam was united under Communist rule.

SIX-DAY WAR 1967
The third of four major wars between Israel and its Arab neighbours led to Israeli control over Sinai, the West Bank, and the Golan Heights.

IRAN-IRAQ WAR 1980–1988
After the Iranian revolution of 1979, Iran invaded Iraq to gain dominance over the Persian Gulf. The war ended with much loss of life but no advantage to either side.

GULF WAR 1990–1991
In 1990 Iraq invaded Kuwait to gain control of its oil supplies but was expelled the following year by an international force led by the USA.

FAMOUS BRITISH BATTLES

HASTINGS 1066
The Norman army of William the Conqueror crossed the English Channel and defeated the English army of Harold, beginning the Norman conquest.

BANNOCKBURN 1314
Continual warfare between Scotland and England after 1040 led to English rule over Scotland in 1296. The Scots revolted, and under Robert Bruce defeated the English at Bannockburn and won independence.

CRECY 1346
Longbows proved superior against crossbows when the English defeated a large French army at Creçy; the French lost around 10,000 men, the English less than 200.

AGINCOURT 1415
Henry V of England renewed his claim to the French throne and defeated a far-larger French army, thus proving the superiority of bowmen over mounted knights.

SPANISH ARMADA 1588
Philip II of Spain – the leading Catholic power in Europe – sent an invasion fleet, or armada, to conquer England, the leading Protestant power. The armada was defeated in the English Channel and sunk by storms.

NASEBY 1645
The decisive battle of the Civil War between Charles I and Parliament; the untried Parliamentary New Model Army, under Cromwell, overwhelmed the Royalist army.

THE BOYNE 1690
Deposed in favour of the Protestant William III, James II joined Catholic Irish forces fighting English rule. The two armies met north of Dublin: James was defeated, ensuring Protestant domination in Ireland.

BLENHEIM 1704
Britain declared war against France to stop it taking over the Spanish throne. Under the Duke of Marlborough, an Anglo-Austrian army defeated the French army and ended its domination of Europe.

TRAFALGAR 1805
Admiral Nelson's defeat of the French navy at Trafalgar gave Britain control of the seas and prevented Napoleon invading Britain.

WATERLOO 1815
A combined four-nation army, led by the Duke of Wellington, finally defeated Napoleon, ending his empire in Europe and restoring the monarchy in France.

EL ALAMEIN 1942
Allied forces led by General Montgomery defeated the Germany army under Rommel as it advanced towards Egypt, ending German control in North Africa.

D-DAY LANDINGS 1944
Allied forces led by US General Eisenhower landed in German-occupied France, in the largest seaborne attack ever. The invasion of France led to the defeat of Germany the following year.

PRIME MINISTERS

During the reign of Charles II (1660–85), the practice arose for the king to consult a few important ministers about affairs of state in his private apartment or "cabinet". By 1700 this Cabinet of ministers was in charge of the government, but it was not until 1721 that one of them, Robert Walpole, became the prime or first minister of the king. Most prime ministers were members of the House of Lords, and not all led political parties, but today the prime minister is always the leader of the largest political party in the House of Commons.

TERM OF OFFICE	PRIME MINISTER	PARTY
1721–1742	Sir Robert Walpole	Whig
1742–1743	Earl of Wilmington	Whig
1743–1754	Henry Pelham	Whig
1754–1756	Duke of Newcastle	Whig
1756–1757	Duke of Devonshire	Whig
1757–1762	Duke of Newcastle	Whig
1762–1763	Earl of Bute	Tory
1763–1765	George Grenville	Whig
1765–1766	Marquis of Rockingham	Whig
1766–1768	William Pitt the Elder	Whig
1768–1770	Duke of Grafton	Whig
1770–1782	Lord North	Tory
1782	Marquis of Rockingham	Whig
1782–1783	Earl of Shelburne	Whig
1783	Duke of Portland	Coalition
1783–1801	William Pitt the Younger	Tory
1801–1804	Henry Addington	Tory
1804–1806	William Pitt	Tory
1806–1807	Lord Grenville	Whig
1807–1809	Duke of Portland	Tory
1809–1812	Spencer Percival	Tory
1812–1827	Lord Liverpool	Tory
1827	George Canning	Tory
1827–1828	Viscount Goderich	Tory
1828–1830	Duke of Wellington	Tory
1830–1834	Earl Grey	Whig
1834	Viscount Melbourne	Whig
1834–1835	Sir Robert Peel	Conservative
1835–1841	Viscount Melbourne	Whig
1841–1846	Sir Robert Peel	Conservative
1846–1852	Lord John Russell	Whig/Liberal
1852	Earl of Derby	Conservative
1852–1855	Earl of Aberdeen	Peelite
1855–1858	Viscount Palmerston	Liberal
1858–1859	Earl of Derby	Conservative
1859–1865	Viscount Palmerston	Liberal
1865–1866	Lord John Russell	Liberal
1866–1868	Earl of Derby	Conservative
1868	Benjamin Disraeli	Conservative
1868–1874	William Gladstone	Liberal
1874–1880	Benjamin Disraeli	Conservative
1880–1885	William Gladstone	Liberal
1885–1886	Marquis of Salisbury	Conservative
1886	William Gladstone	Liberal
1886–1892	Marquis of Salisbury	Conservative
1892–1894	William Gladstone	Liberal
1894–1895	Earl of Rosebery	Liberal

TERM OF OFFICE	PRIME MINISTER	PARTY
1895–1902	Marquis of Salisbury	Conservative
1902–1905	Arthur Balfour	Conservative
1905–1908	Sir Henry Campbell Bannerman	Liberal
1908–1915	Herbert Asquith	Liberal
1915–1916	Herbert Asquith	Coalition
1916–1922	David Lloyd George	Coalition
1922–1923	Andrew Bonar Law	Conservative
1923–1924	Stanley Baldwin	Conservative
1924	Ramsay MacDonald	Labour
1924–1929	Stanley Baldwin	Conservative
1929–1931	Ramsay MacDonald	Labour
1931–1935	Ramsay MacDonald	National
1935–1937	Stanley Baldwin	National
1937–1940	Neville Chamberlain	National
1940–1945	Winston Churchill	Coalition
1945	Winston Churchill	Conservative
1945–1951	Clement Attlee	Labour
1951–1955	Winston Churchill	Conservative
1955–1957	Anthony Eden	Conservative
1957–1963	Harold Macmillan	Conservative
1963–1964	Sir Alec Douglas-Home	Conservative
1964–1970	Harold Wilson	Labour
1970–1974	Edward Heath	Conservative
1974–1976	Harold Wilson	Labour
1976–1979	James Callaghan	Labour
1979–1990	Margaret Thatcher	Conservative
1990–1997	John Major	Conservative
1997–	Tony Blair	Labour

POLITICAL PARTIES

Whig	An aristocratic group of leaders, rather than a political party, the Whigs supported constitutional liberty and limited social reform.
Tory	Originally a term of abuse to describe Irish Catholic rebels, the Tories were an aristocratic party which supported the monarchy, the Church of England, and strong government.
Conservative	Formed by Sir Robert Peel in 1834 as successor to the Tory Party, the Conservatives believe in moderate social reform and a commitment to traditional institutions. Many are now anti-Europe.
Peelite	Conservative supporters of Sir Robert Peel who left the party in 1846 in support of free trade. Many later joined the Liberal Party.
Liberal	Formed in the 1850s out of the Whigs, Peelites, and various radicals, the Liberals originally believed in free trade and free-market economics. Today the Liberal Democrats are pro-Europe and for electoral reform.
Labour	Formed in 1900 out of the trade unions and various left-wing parties, the Labour Party aimed to secure representation for the working class. Today "New" Labour is pro-Europe with moderately progressive views.
Coalition	Two or more parties joining together in government. The coalition of 1931–40 was known as the National Government.

US PRESIDENTS

Since the USA became independent from Britain in 1783, the country has had 42 presidents. Each president is elected for four years – the election is held in the November before he, or she, takes office the following year – and can now stand for only two successive terms. At first, party labels were weak, but the emergence of a Democratic Party in the 1820s and a Republican Party in the 1850s established a two-party system that has survived to this day.

TERM OF OFFICE	PRESIDENT	PARTY
1789–1797	George Washington	Federalist
1797–1801	John Adams	Federalist
1801–1809	Thomas Jefferson	Democratic-Republican
1809–1817	James Madison	Democratic-Republican
1817–1825	James Monroe	Democratic-Republican
1825–1829	John Quincy Adams	Democratic-Republican
1829–1837	Andrew Jackson	Democrat
1837–1841	Martin Van Buren	Democrat
1841	William Harrison	Whig
1841–1845	John Tyler	Whig
1845–1849	James Polk	Democrat
1849–1850	Zachary Taylor	Whig
1850–1853	Millard Fillmore	Whig
1853–1857	Franklin Pierce	Democrat
1857–1861	James Buchanan	Democrat
1861–1865	Abraham Lincoln	Republican
1865–1869	Andrew Johnson	Democrat, Unionist
1869–1877	Ulysses Grant	Republican
1877–1881	Rutherford Hayes	Republican
1881	James Garfield	Republican
1881–1885	Chester Arthur	Republican
1885–1889	Grover Cleveland	Democrat
1889–1893	Benjamin Harrison	Republican
1893–1897	Grover Cleveland	Democrat
1897–1901	William McKinley	Republican
1901–1909	Theodore Roosevelt	Republican
1909–1913	William Taft	Republican
1913–1921	Woodrow Wilson	Democrat
1921–1923	Warren Harding	Republican
1923–1929	Calvin Coolidge	Republican
1929–1933	Herbert Hoover	Republican
1933–1945	Franklin Roosevelt	Democrat
1945–1953	Harry Truman	Democrat
1953–1961	Dwight Eisenhower	Republican
1961–1963	John F Kennedy	Democrat
1963–1969	Lyndon Johnson	Democrat
1969–1974	Richard Nixon	Republican
1974–1977	Gerald Ford	Republican
1977–1981	Jimmy Carter	Democrat
1981–1989	Ronald Reagan	Republican
1989–1993	George Bush	Republican
1993–	Bill Clinton	Democrat

POET LAUREATES

Although he was never appointed Poet Laureate, Ben Johnson enjoyed special status as unofficial laureate when he received a pension from James I in 1616. Today the title – named after the laurel wreath that crowned ancient poets – is largely honorific, although the laureate is expected to produce poetry to mark important royal and national events.

DATE	POET	DATE	POET
1668	John Dryden	1843	William Wordsworth
1688	Thomas Shadwell	1850	Alfred Tennyson
1692	Nahum Tate	1896	Alfred Austin
1715	Nicholas Rowe	1913	Robert Bridges
1718	Laurence Eusden	1930	John Masefield
1730	Colley Cibber	1967	Cecil Day Lewis
1757	William Whitehead	1972	Sir John Betjeman
1785	Thomas Warton	1984	Ted Hughes
1790	Henry James Pye	1999	Andrew Motion
1813	Robert Southey		

ASTRONOMERS ROYAL

First appointed by Charles II in 1675, the title of Astronomer Royal was given to the director of the Royal Observatory in Greenwich until its closure in 1948. War damage, interference from the lights and smog of London, and the small scale of the building led to its relocation to Herstmonceux in Sussex. Today, the Astronomer Royal is based in Cambridge and the title is largely honorary, given to an outstanding astronomer, who receives approximately £100 per year.

DATE	ASTRONOMER	DATE	ASTRONOMER
1675	John Flamsteed	1910	Sir Frank Dyson
1720	Edmund Halley	1933	Sir Harold Spencer Jones
1742	James Bradley	1955	Sir Richard Woolley
1762	Nathaniel Bliss	1972	Sir Martin Ryle
1765	Nevil Maskeleyne	1982	Sir Francis Graham-Smith
1811	John Pond	1991	Sir Arnold Wolfendale
1835	Sir George Airy	1995	Sir Martin Rees
1881	Sir William Christie		

THE ACADEMY AWARDS

Every year, the Academy of Motion Picture Arts and Sciences in Hollywood, California makes its awards for the year. Prize-winners originally received the Statuette, but in 1931 it was renamed the Oscar when, legend has it, the Academy's librarian thought the figure looked just like her uncle Oscar. "Oscars" are now awarded in 24 different categories, although four are particularly prized: best film, best director, best actor, and best actress.

YEAR	BEST FILM	BEST DIRECTOR	BEST ACTOR	BEST ACTRESS
1927–28	Wings	Frank Borzage, Seventh Heaven	Emil Jannings, The Last Command, The Way Of All Flesh	Janet Gaynor, Seventh Heaven, Street Angel, Sunrise
1928–29	Broadway Melody	Frank Lloyd, The Divine Lady	Warner Baxter, In Old Arizona	Mary Pickford, Coquette
1929–30	All Quiet On The Western Front	Lewis Milestone, All Quiet On The Western Front	George Arliss, Disraeli	Norma Shearer, The Divorcee
1930–31	Cimarron	Norman Taurog, Skippy	Lionel Barrymore, A Free Soul	Marie Dressler, Min And Bill
1931–32	Grand Hotel	Frank Borzage, Bad Girl	Wallace Beery, The Champ and Fredric March, Dr Jekyll And Mr Hyde	Helen Hayes, The Sin Of Madelon Claudet
1932–33	Cavalcade	Frank Lloyd, Cavalcade	Charles Laughton, The Private Life Of Henry VIII	Katherine Hepburn, Morning Glory
1934	It Happened One Night	Frank Capra, It Happened One Night	Clark Gable, It Happened One Night	Claudette Colbert, It Happened One Night
1935	Mutiny On The Bounty	John Ford, The Informer	Victor McLaglen, The Informer	Bette Davis, Dangerous
1936	The Great Ziegfeld	Frank Capra, Mr Deeds Goes To Town	Paul Muni, The Story Of Louis Pasteur	Luise Rainer, The Great Ziegfeld
1937	The Life Of Emile Zola	Leo McCarey, The Awful Truth	Spencer Tracy, Captains Courageous	Luise Rainer, The Good Earth
1938	You Can't Take It With You	Frank Capra, You Can't Take It With You	Spencer Tracy, Boys Town	Bette Davis, Jezebel
1939	Gone With The Wind	Victor Fleming, Gone With The Wind	Robert Donat, Goodbye, Mr Chips	Vivien Leigh, Gone With The Wind
1940	Rebecca	John Ford, The Grapes Of Wrath	James Stewart, The Philadelphia Story	Ginger Rogers, Kitty Foyle
1941	How Green Was My Valley	John Ford, How Green Was My Valley	Gary Cooper, Sergeant York	Joan Fontaine, Suspicion
1942	Mrs Miniver	William Wyler, Mrs Miniver	James Cagney, Yankee Doodle Dandy	Greer Garson, Mrs Miniver
1943	Casablanca	Michael Curtiz, Casablanca	Paul Lukas, Watch On The Rhine	Jennifer Jones, The Song Of Bernadette
1944	Going My Way	Leo McCarey, Going My Way	Bing Crosby, Going My Way	Ingrid Bergman, Gaslight
1945	The Lost Weekend	Billy Wilder, The Lost Weekend	Ray Milland, The Lost Weekend	Joan Crawford, Mildred Pierce
1946	The Best Years Of Our Lives	William Wyler, The Best Years Of Our Lives	Fredric March, The Best Years Of Our Lives	Olivia De Havilland, To Each His Own
1947	Gentleman's Agreement	Elia Kazan, Gentleman's Agreement	Ronald Colman, A Double Life	Loretta Young, The Farmer's Daughter
1948	Hamlet	John Huston, The Treasure Of The Sierra Madre	Laurence Olivier, Hamlet	Jane Wyman, Johnny Belinda
1949	All The King's Men	Joseph L. Mankiewicz, A Letter To Three Wives	Broderick Crawford, All The King's Men	Olivia De Havilland, The Heiress
1950	All About Eve	Joseph L. Mankiewicz, All About Eve	Jose Ferrer, Cyrano De Bergerac	Judy Holliday, Born Yesterday
1951	An American In Paris	George Stevens, A Place In The Sun	Humphrey Bogart, The African Queen	Vivien Leigh, A Streetcar Named Desire
1952	The Greatest Show On Earth	John Ford, The Quiet Man	Gary Cooper, High Noon	Shirley Booth, Come Back, Little Sheba
1953	From Here To Eternity	Fred Zinnemann, From Here To Eternity	William Holden, Stalag 17	Audrey Hepburn, Roman Holiday
1954	On The Waterfront	Eliz Kazan, On The Waterfront	Marlon Brando, On The Waterfront	Grace Kelly, The Country Girl
1955	Marty	Delbert Mann, Marty	Ernest Borgnine, Marty	Anna Magnani, The Rose Tattoo
1956	Around The World In 80 Days	George Stevens, Giant	Yul Brynner, The King And I	Ingrid Bergman, Anastasia
1957	The Bridge On The River Kwai	David Lean, The Bridge On The River Kwai	Alec Guinness, The Bridge On The River Kwai	Joanne Woodward, The Three Faces Of Eve
1958	Gigi	Vincente Minnelli, Gigi	David Niven, Separate Tables	Susan Hayward, I Want To Live!
1959	Ben-Hur	William Wyler, Ben-Hur	Charlton Heston, Ben-Hur	Simone Signoret, Room At The Top

YEAR	BEST FILM	BEST DIRECTOR	BEST ACTOR	BEST ACTRESS
1960	*The Apartment*	Billy Wilder, *The Apartment*	Burt Lancaster, *Elmer Gantry*	Elizabeth Taylor, *Butterfield 8*
1961	*West Side Story*	Robert Wise and Jerome Robbins, *West Side Story*	Maximilian Schell, *Judgment At Nuremberg*	Sophia Loren, *Two Women*
1962	*Lawrence Of Arabia*	David Lean, *Lawrence Of Arabia*	Gregory Peck, *To Kill A Mockingbird*	Anne Bancroft, *The Miracle Worker*
1963	*Tom Jones*	Tony Richardson, *Tom Jones*	Sidney Poitier, *Lilies Of The Field*	Patricia Neal, *Hud*
1964	*My Fair Lady*	George Cukor, *My Fair Lady*	Rex Harrison, *My Fair Lady*	Julie Andrews, *Mary Poppins*
1965	*The Sound Of Music*	Robert Wise, *The Sound Of Music*	Lee Marvin, *Cat Ballou*	Julie Christie, *Darling*
1966	*A Man For All Seasons*	Fred Zinnemann, *A Man For All Seasons*	Paul Scofield, *A Man For All Seasons*	Elizabeth Taylor, *Who's Afraid Of Virginia Woolf?*
1967	*In The Heat Of The Night*	Mike Nichols, *The Graduate*	Rod Steiger, *In The Heat Of The Night*	Katherine Hepburn, *Guess Who's Coming To Dinner*
1968	*Oliver!*	Carol Reed, *Oliver!*	Cliff Robertson, *Charly*	Katherine Hepburn, *The Lion In Winter*
1969	*Midnight Cowboy*	John Schlesinger, *Midnight Cowboy*	John Wayne, *True Grit*	Maggie Smith, *The Prime Of Miss Jean Brodie*
1970	*Patton*	Franklin J Schaffner, *Patton*	George C Scott, *Patton*	Glenda Jackson, *Women In Love*
1971	*The French Connection*	William Friedkin, *The French Connection*	Gene Hackman, *The French Connection*	Jane Fonda, *Klute*
1972	*The Godfather*	Bob Fosse, *Cabaret*	Marlon Brando, *The Godfather*	Liza Minnelli, *Cabaret*
1973	*The Sting*	George Roy Hill, *The Sting*	Jack Lemmon, *Save The Tiger*	Glenda Jackson, *A Touch Of Class*
1974	*The Godfather Part II*	Francis Ford Coppola, *The Godfather Part II*	Art Carney, *Harry And Tonto*	Ellen Burstyn, *Alice Doesn't Live Here Anymore*
1975	*One Flew Over The Cuckoo's Nest*	Milos Forman, *One Flew Over The Cuckoo's Nest*	Jack Nicholson, *One Flew Over The Cuckoo's Nest*	Louise Fletcher, *One Flew Over The Cuckoo's Nest*
1976	*Rocky*	John G Avildsen, *Rocky*	Peter Finch, *Network*	Faye Dunaway, *Network*
1977	*Annie Hall*	Woody Allen, *Annie Hall*	Richard Dreyfuss, *The Goodbye Girl*	Diane Keaton, *Annie Hall*
1978	*The Deer Hunter*	Michael Cimino, *The Deer Hunter*	Jon Voight, *Coming Home*	Jane Fonda, *Coming Home*
1979	*Kramer vs Kramer*	Robert Benton, *Kramer vs Kramer*	Dustin Hoffman, *Kramer vs Kramer*	Sally Field, *Norma Rae*
1980	*Ordinary People*	Robert Redford, *Ordinary People*	Robert De Niro, *Raging Bull*	Sissy Spacek, *Coal Miner's Daughter*
1981	*Chariots Of Fire*	Warren Beatty, *Reds*	Henry Fonda, *On Golden Pond*	Katherine Hepburn, *On Golden Pond*
1982	*Gandhi*	Richard Attenborough, *Gandhi*	Ben Kingsley, *Gandhi*	Meryl Streep, *Sophie's Choice*
1983	*Terms Of Endearment*	James L Brooks, *Terms Of Endearment*	Robert Duvall, *Tender Mercies*	Shirley MacLaine, *Terms Of Endearment*
1984	*Amadeus*	Milos Forman, *Amadeus*	F Murray Abraham, *Amadeus*	Sally Field, *Places In The Heart*
1985	*Out Of Africa*	Sydney Pollack, *Out Of Africa*	William Hurt, *Kiss Of The Spider Women*	Geraldine Page, *The Trip To Bountiful*
1986	*Platoon*	Oliver Stone, *Platoon*	Paul Newman, *The Color Of Money*	Marlee Matlin, *Children Of A Lesser God*
1987	*The Last Emperor*	Bernardo Bertolucci, *The Last Emperor*	Michael Douglas, *Wall Street*	Cher, *Moonstruck*
1988	*Rain Man*	Barry Levinson, *Rain Man*	Dustin Hoffman, *Rain Man*	Jodie Foster, *The Accused*
1989	*Driving Miss Daisy*	Oliver Stone, *Born On The Fourth Of July*	Daniel Day Lewis, *My Left Foot*	Jessica Tandy, *Driving Miss Daisy*
1990	*Dances With Wolves*	Kevin Costner, *Dances With Wolves*	Jeremy Irons, *Reversal Of Fortune*	Kathy Bates, *Misery*
1991	*The Silence Of The Lambs*	Jonathan Demme, *The Silence Of The Lambs*	Anthony Hopkins, *The Silence Of The Lambs*	Jodie Foster, *The Silence Of The Lambs*
1992	*Unforgiven*	Clint Eastwood, *Unforgiven*	Al Pacino, *Scent Of A Woman*	Emma Thompson, *Howard's End*
1993	*Schindler's List*	Steven Spielberg, *Schindler's List*	Tom Hanks, *Philadelphia*	Holly Hunter, *The Piano*
1994	*Forrest Gump*	Robert Zemeckis, *Forrest Gump*	Tom Hanks, *Forrest Gump*	Jessica Lange, *Blue Sky*
1995	*Braveheart*	Mel Gibson, *Braveheart*	Nicolas Cage, *Leaving Las Vegas*	Susan Sarandon, *Dead Man Walking*
1996	*The English Patient*	Anthony Minghella, *The English Patient*	Geoffrey Rush, *Shine*	Frances McDormand, *Fargo*
1997	*Titanic*	James Cameron, *Titanic*	Jack Nicholson, *As Good As It Gets*	Helen Hunt, *As Good As It Gets*
1998	*Shakespeare In Love*	Steven Spielberg, *Saving Private Ryan*	Roberto Benigni, *Life Is Beautiful*	Gwyneth Paltrow, *Shakespeare In Love*

NOBEL PRIZE WINNERS

The Nobel Prizes are awarded annually for outstanding achievement in physics, chemistry, peace, and literature. The awards were established by the will of the Swedish explosives manufacturer Alfred Nobel and first awarded in 1901. An economics prize was added in 1969. The awards are made on 10 December, the anniversary of Nobel's death.

PEACE		LITERATURE
J H Dunant	1901	R F A Sully–Prudhomme
Frédéric Passy		
Elie Ducommun	1902	Theodor Mommsen
C A Gobat		
Sir William R Cremer	1903	Bjørnstjerne Bjørnson
Institute of International Law	1904	Frédéric Mistral
		José Echegaray
Baroness Bertha von Suttner	1905	Henryk Sienkiewicz
Theodore Roosevelt	1906	Giosuè Carducci
E T Moneta	1907	Rudyard Kipling
Louis Renault		
K P Arnoldson	1908	R C Eucken
Fredrik Bajer		
Auguste Beernaert	1909	Selma Lagerlöf
P H B Estournelles de Constant		
International Peace Bureau	1910	Paul Heyse
T M C Asser	1911	Maurice Maeterlinck
A H Fried		
Elihu Root	1912	Gerhart Hauptman
Henri La Fontaine	1913	Sir Rabindranath Tagore
–	1914	–
–	1915	Romain Rolland
–	1916	Verner von Heidenstam
International Red Cross	1917	K A Gjellerup
		Henrik Pontoppidan
–	1918	–
Woodrow Wilson	1919	C F G Spitteler
Léon Bourgeois	1920	Knut Hamsum
Hjalmar Branting	1921	Anatole France
C L Lange		
Fridtjof Nansen	1922	Jacinto Benavente y Martinez
–	1923	W B Yeats
–	1924	W S Reymont
Sir Austen Chamberlain	1925	George Bernard Shaw
Charles G Dawes		
Aristide Briand	1926	Grazia Deledda
Gustav Stresemann		
F E Buisson	1927	Henri Bergson
Ludwig Quidde		
–	1928	Sigrid Undset
Frank B Kellog	1929	Thomas Mann
Nathan Soderblom	1930	Sinclair Lewis
Jane Addams	1931	I A Karldeldt
Nicholas Murray Butler		
–	1932	John Galsworthy
Sir Norman Angell	1933	I A Bunin
Arthur Henderson	1934	Luigi Pirandello
Carl von Ossietzky	1935	–
Carlos Saavedra Lamas	1936	Eugene O'Neill
Viscount Cecil	1937	Roger Martin du Gard
Nansen International Office	1938	Pearl Buck
for Refugees		
–	1939	F E Sillanpää
–	1940	–
–	1941	–
–	1942	–
–	1943	–
International Red Cross	1944	J V Jensen
Cordell Hull	1945	Gabriela Mistral
J R Mott	1946	Hermann Hesse
Emily G Balch		
American Friends Service Committee	1947	André Gide
and Friends Service Council		
–	1948	T S Eliot
John Boyd Orr	1949	William Faulkner
Ralph J Bunche	1950	Bertrand Russell

PEACE		LITERATURE
Léon Jouhaux	1951	Pär F Lagerkvist
Albert Schweitzer	1952	François Mauriac
George C Marshall	1953	Winston Churchill
Office of the UN High	1954	Ernest Hemingway
Commissioner for Refugees		
–	1955	Halldór K Laxness
–	1956	Juan Ramón Jiménez
Lester Pearson	1957	Albert Camus
Georges Henri Pire	1958	Boris Pasternak
Philip Noel-Baker	1959	Salvatore Quasimodo
Albert Luthuli	1960	St-John Perse
Dag Hammarskjöld	1961	Ivo Andric
Linus C Pauling	1962	John Steinbeck
International Committee of the Red	1963	George Seferis
Cross, League of Red Cross Societies		
Martin Luther King Jr	1964	Jean Paul Satre
UN International Children's	1965	M A Sholokhov
Emergency Fund		
–	1966	S Y Agnon
		Nelly Sachs
–	1967	Miguel Angel Asturias
René Cassin	1968	Yasunari Kawabata
International Labour Organisation	1969	Samuel Beckett
Norman E Borlaug	1970	Alexander Solzhenitsyn
Willy Brandt	1971	Pablo Neruda
–	1972	Heinrich Böll
Henry Kissinger	1973	Patrick White
Le Duc Tho		
Sean MacBride	1974	Eyvind Johnson
Eisaku Sato		Harry Martinson
Andrei Sakharov	1975	Eugenio Montale
Mairead Corrigan	1976	Saul Bellow
Betty Williams		
Amnesty International	1977	Vicente Aleixandre
Menachem Begin	1978	Isaac Bashevis Singer
Anwar Sadat		
Mother Teresa	1979	Odysseus Elytis
Adolfo Pérez Esquivel	1980	Czeslaw Milosz
Office of the UN High	1981	Elias Canetti
Commissioner For Refugees		
Alfonso Garciá Robles	1982	Gabriel Garciá Márquez
Alva Myrdal		
Lech Walesa	1983	William Golding
Desmond Tutu	1984	Jarosalv Seifert
International Physicians for the	1985	Claude Simon
Prevention of Nuclear War		
Elie Wiesel	1986	Wole Soyinka
Oscar Arias Sanchez	1987	Joseph Brodsky
UN Peacekeeping Forces	1988	Naguib Mahfouz
Dalai Lama	1989	Camilo José Cela
Mikhail Gorbachev	1990	Octavio Paz
Daw Aung San Suu Kyi	1991	Nadine Gordimer
Rigoberta Menchú	1992	Derek Walcott
Nelson Mandela	1993	Toni Morrison
F W de Klerk		
Yitzhak Rabin	1994	Kenzaburo Oe
Yassir Arafat		
Shimon Peres		
Joseph Rotblat	1995	Seamus Heaney
The Pugwash Conference on		
Science and World Affairs		
Bishop Carlos Belo	1996	Wislawa Szymborska
José Ramos-Horta		
International Committee to Ban	1997	Dario Fo
Landmines, Jody Williams		
John Hume	1998	Jose Saramago
David Trimble		

Index

British Empire, 60, 171, 188
Britten, Benjamin (1913–76), **195**
Broglie, Louis-Victor Duc de (1892–1987), **163**
Bronstein, Lev, *see* Trotsky, Leon
Brontë, Anne (1820–49), **96**
Brontë, Charlotte (1816–55), **96**
Brontë, Emily (1818–48), **96**
Brothers Grimm, 80
Brown, James (1933–), **218**
Brown, John (1800–59), **88**, 128
Brown, Lancelot "Capability" (1716–83), **59**
Brown, Louise (1978–), **246**
Broz, Josip, *see* Tito
Bruce, James, 71
Bruce, Robert (1274–1329), **15**
Bruckner, Anton (1824–96), **102**
Bruegel the Elder, Pieter (c.1525–69), **33**
Brunel, Isambard Kingdom (1806–59), **90**, 117, 127
Brunelleschi, Filippo (1377–1446), **18**, 27
Buñuel, Luis, 184
Buonarroti, Michelangelo, *see* Michelangelo
Bunyan, John (1628–88), **47**
Burke, Robert O'Hara (1821–61), **99**
Burnell, Jocelyn Bell (1943–), **231**
Burns, Robert (1759–96), **69**
Burton, Richard (1821–90), **100**
Butler, Josephine (1828–1906), **103**
Byrd, William (1540–1623), **35**
Byron, Lord (1788–1824), **81**
Byzantine Empire, 7, 24

C

Cabot, John (1450–99), **22**, 23
Cabot, Sebastian (1474–1557), **22**
Cadbury, George (1839–1922), **112**
Cage, John (1912–92), **194**
Cagney, James (1889–1986), 153
Caillié, René-Auguste (1799–1838), **86**
Cairo, 7
Calhoun, John C. (1782–1850), **79**
Callas, Maria (1923–77), **206**
Calvin, John (1509–64), **32**
Camoëns, Luis Vaz de (c.1524–80), **33**
Canadian Pacific Railway, 154
Canute (c.995–1035), **8**
Cao Chan (c.1715–63), **59**
Capone, Al (1899–1947), **171**, 214
Carabobo, Battle of, 99
Caravaggio, Michelangelo Merisi da (1573–1610), **40**
Carlist War, 108
Carlyle, Thomas (1795–1881), 89
Carnegie, Andrew (1835–1919), **111**
Carnot, Sadi (1796–1832), **85**

Carroll, Lewis (1832–98), **107**
Carson, Rachel (1907–64), **187**
Carter, Howard, 206
Cartier, Jacques (1491–1557), 23, **29**
Cartier-Bresson, Henri (1908–), **190**
Cassat, Mary (1845–1926), **118**
Cassidy, Butch, 171
Castro, Fidel (1927–), **210**, 242
Catherine the Great, Tsarina of Russia (1729–96), **61**, 70, 73, 85
Cauchy, Augustin Louis (1789–1857), **82**
Cavendish, Henry (1731–1810), **62**
Caxton, William (c.1422–91), **21**
Celsius, Anders (1701–44), **57**
Cervantes, Miguel de (1547–1616), **37**
Cézanne, Paul (1839–1906), 109, **112**
Chadwick, James (1891–1973), **162**
Chain, Ernst, 147, 169
Chamberlain, Neville, 227
Chanel, Coco (1883–1971), **151**
Chaplin, Charlie (1889–1977), 153, **160**
Charles I of England (1600–49), **45**, 51
Charles V, Holy Roman Emperor (1500–58), **32**, 35
Chartist Movement, 112
Chaucer, Geoffrey (c.1340–1400), **18**
Chekhov, Anton (1860–1904), **128**
Chen Kaige (1952–), **236**
Cheng Ho (1371–1435), **18**
Chiang Kai-shek (1887–1975), **155**, 212
Chief Joseph (c.1840–1904), **113**
Chimu culture, 26
Chippendale, Thomas (1718–79), **59**
Ch'iu Chin, *see* Jin Qiu
Chomsky, Noam (1928–), **212**
Chopin, Frédéric (1810–49), **93**
Christian, Fletcher, 81
Christian Science Movement, 100
Christie, Linford (1960–), **242**
Christo (1935–), **221**
Church of Jesus Christ of the Latter-Day Saints, 88
Churchill, John, *see* Marlborough, Duke of
Churchill, Winston (1874–1965), **142**
Ciccione, Madonna Louise, *see* Madonna
Cid, El, *see* El Cid
cinema, **153**, 213, 225, 230
Cistercians, 9
civil rights, 212, 239, 245
Clapton, Eric (1945–), 220
Clark, William, 74, 89
Clay, Cassius, *see* Muhammad Ali
Clay, Henry, 108
Clemens, Samuel Langhorne, *see* Twain, Mark
Clive, Robert ("Clive of India") (1725–74), **60**, 69
Cobb, Ty (1886–1961), **154**
COBOL computer language, 187
Cockcroft, John (1897–1967), **168**
Cockerell, Christopher (1910–99), **191**

Cocteau, Jean, 172
Cody, William "Buffalo Bill" (1846–1917), **118**
Cole, Henry (1808–82), **91**
Coleridge, Samuel Taylor (1772–1834), **74**
Colette (1873–1954), **140**
Collins, Michael (1890–1922), **160**
Coltrane, John (1926–67), **209**
Columbus, Christopher (1451–1506), **22**, 23, 24
Comaneci, Nadia (1961–), **244**
Compton, Arthur (1892–1962), **162**
Compton, Denis (1918–97), **200**
computers, 187, **238**
Conan Doyle, Arthur (1859–1930), **128**, 156
Condorcet, Antoine Nicolas (1743–94), 125
Connors, Jimmy (1952–), **236**
Constable, John (1776–1837), **75**
convicts to Australia, 82
Cook, James (1728–79), **61**, 72, 78
Cook, Paul (1950–), **236**
Copernicus, Nicolaus (1473–1543), **26**
Copland, Aaron (1900–90), **176**
Corelli, Archangel (1653–1713), **52**, 55
Cortés, Hernando (1486–1547), 17, 23, 27, **29**
Coubertin, Baron Pierre de, 167
Coulomb, Charles (1736–1806), **63**
Cousteau, Jacques (1910–97), **191**
Crick, Francis (1916–), **198**
Crimean War, 82, 121, 124
Crockett, Davy (1786–1836), **80**
Crompton, Samuel (1753–1827), 73
Cromwell, Oliver (1599–1658), **43**
Crusades, The, 8, 9
Cruyff, Johann (1947–), **234**
Cugnot, Nicolas, 73
Culloden Moor, Battle of, 66
Cultural Revolution, 164
Curie, Marie (1867–1934), **135**
Curie, Pierre (1859–1906), **127**
Custer, George (1839–76), **112**
Cuvier, Georges (1769–1832), **72**

D

Daguerre, Louis (1789–1851), **82**
Daily Telegraph, The, 123
Daimler, Gottlieb (1834–1900), **108**, 148
Dalai Lama (1935–), 183, **221**, 252
Dali, Salvador (1904–89), **184**
Dalton, John (1766–1844), **71**
Dante (1265–1321), **14**, 27
Danton, Georges (1759–94), 69
d'Arezzo, Guido (c.990–c.1050), 8
Darwin, Charles (1809–82), **93**, 208
Davis, Bette (1908–89), **189**

Davis, Joe (1901–78), **177**
Davis, Miles (1926–61), **209**
Davy, Humphry (1778–1829), **76**
Dawkins, Richard (1941–), **228**
de Beauvoir, Simone (1908–86), **189**
de Champlain, Samuel (1567–1635), **39**, 45
de Gaulle, Charles (1890–1970), **161**, 241
de Klerk, F. W. (1936–), **223**
De Mille, Cecil B. (1881–1959), **148**
De Niro, Robert (1943–), **231**
De Valera, Eamon (1882–1975), **150**
Dean, James (1931–55), **216**, 238
Debussy, Claude (1862–1918), **131**
Declaration of Independence, 66, 76
Defoe, Daniel (1660–1731), **52**
Degas, Edgar (1834–1917), **109**
Delacroix, Eugène (1798–1863), **86**
Dempsey, Jack (1895–1983), **167**
Deng Xiaoping (1904–97), **185**
Descartes, René (1596–1650), **42**
Desprez, Josquin (c.1440–1521), **21**
Diaghilev, Sergei (1872–1929), **138**
diamonds, 61
Diana, Princess of Wales (1961–97), **243**
Dias, Bartolomeu (c.1450–1500), **22**
Dickens, Charles (1812–70), **94**
Dickinson, Emily (1830–86), **105**
Didrikson, Babe, *see* Zaharias, Babe Didrikson
Diesel, Rudolf (1858–1913), **126**, 164
DiMaggio, Joe (1914–99), **196**
Ding Ling (Ting Ling) (1904–86), **183**
Dior, Christian (1905–57), **185**, 224
Dirac, Paul, 155
Disney, Walt (1901–66), **176**, 225, 238
Disneyland, 238
Disraeli, Benjamin (1804–81), **89**
Dodgson, Charles Lutwidge, *see* Carroll, Lewis
Domesday Book, 8
Don Miguel of Portugal, 102
Donatello (1386–1466), **19**, 27
Donato, Donatello, *see* Donatello
Doppler, Christian Johann (1803–53), **88**
Dostoevsky, Fyodor (1821–81), **99**
Dowland, John (1563–1626), **38**
Drake, Francis (1540–96), **35**
Drew, Charles Richard (1904–50), **182**
Dreyfus, Alfred, 113, 187
du Pré, Jacqueline (1945–87), **233**
Dubcek, Alexander (1921–92), **204**
Duchamp, Marcel (1887–1968), **155**
Dunant, Jean-Henri, 132
Duncan, Isadora (1878–1927), **144**
Dunlop, John (1840–1921), **114**, 157
Dupin, Amandine Aurore Lucie, *see* Sand, George
Dürer, Albrecht (1471–1528), **26**, 27
Dutch empire, 49
Dutch East India Company, 45
Dvořák, Antonin (1841–1904), **114**
Dylan, Bob (1941–), 220, **228**

Z

Picture Credits

The publisher would like to thank the following for their kind permission to reproduce their photographs:

a=above; c=centre; b=below; r=right; t=top

Action Plus: 239tr; Chris Barry 23clb; Mark Pain 242; Neil Tingle 239cl, 244tl, 245cr.
AKG London: 2ca, 2tc, 20, 31, 47.
Allsport: Hulton Getty 157tr, 167bc. 206.
Arcaid: Viv Porter 121.
Arena Images: 202.
British Library: 130cr, 131cl.
Bridgeman Art Library, London/New York: 33tr, 34, 35, 55, 56, 68, 69, 106, 115br, 117, 167tl, 184ca; Bibliotheque Nationale, Paris, France 7tl, 12cl; Kenwood House, London 45tc; National Library of Australia, Canberra 2bc; Palazzo Medici-Riccardi, Florence, Italy 26tc; Private Collection 2br.
Christie's Images Ltd 1999: 50cr, 59br, 64cr, 102, 137, 149.
Colorsport: 231, 236.
Donald Cooper Photostage: 232cl.
Corbis UK Ltd: 2cra, 91, 96cr, 142, 147br, 152, 153cr, 168, 174, 194, 207, 215cr; Bettmann 153bl, 170, 179, 189, 195, 211bl; Bettmann/UPI 192cla, 198tc.
Charles Darwin Museum: 93.
E.T. Archive: 2ca, 67tc, 87.
Mary Evans Picture Library: 2ca, 2c, 2cl, 7tr, 8tl, 12cr, 14cl, 16tr, 17b, 24b,

28tl, 40, 42, 44, 51, 58, 90tr, 92tl, 94tl, 94tr, 95tl, 96bl, 100, 101tr, 108, 110cr, 111, 112, 118, 120, 122br, 123, 125cr, 125bl, 127, 129, 130, 13tl, 134tl, 141, 144, 147ca, 155.
Werner Forman Archive: 36bc.
Sigmund Freud's House, Vienna: 124.
Glasgow Museums: 157ca.
Robert Harding Picture Library: 204; John Zimmerman/FPG International 201.
© Michael Holford: 2tl, 6.
Hulton Getty: 75, 99, 101cl, 128, 143, 145tr, 145bc, 150, 151, 162, 175, 178, 184bl, 193bl, 208, 212, 213tr, 225bc.
Imperial War Museum: 158cl.
Kobal Collection: 85, 148tl, 165, 176bl, 181, 188cr, 228bl.
Lebrecht Collection: 126.
Lucasfilm Ltd: 232br.
Magnum: H. Cartier-Bresson 190; Philippe Halsman 182cl; Thomas Hoepker 229bc.
Marx Memorial Library: 97.
Moviestore Collection: 154, 156, 166, 171tr, 173, 177tl, 187cr, 200, 209, 216, 218tr, 230.
Musée d'Orsay, Paris: 109, 115tl.
National Gallery, London: 26.
National Maritime Museum, London: 7, 23tr, 60.
National Railway Museum, York: 73, 79.
N.H.P.A.: Trevor McDonald 191br.
Ann & Bury Peerless: 25.
Scott Polar Institute: 138tl.
Popperfoto: 119tl, 160, 163, 172, 174, 183, 186cl, 188cl, 191cl, 199br, 205,

214br, 219, 222, 225cra.
PowerStock Photolibrary/Zefa: 29.
Pushkin Museum of Fine Arts, Moscow: 148bc.
NMEC licensed illustrations: QA Photos Ltd 3br, 218bl, 247.
Redferns: 196, 197, 198bl, 220cl, 220cr, 223, 228tr, 177tr, 193cla, 244br, 246.
Rex Features: 164, 217, 221, 224, 237br; Chris Harris 210; Tim Rooke 243.
Royal Geographic Society: 140bc, 203bl.
Science Museum: 62, 66, 78tl, 119br.
Science Photo Library:, 215cl.
SuperStock Ltd.: 86tl.
Topham Picturepoint: 74, 84, 104, 211tr.
Universal Pictorial Press: 234, 241.
Courtesy of the Board of Trustees of the **Victoria & Albert Museum:** 185.
The Wallace Collection: 30tr, 41tr.
Peter Newark's Western Americana: 71, 81.
Wilberforce House, Hull City Museums: 70.

Jacket:
AKG London: Bibliotheca Reale Front cover 14.
Camera Press: Front cover 7.
Capital Pictures: Front cover 13.
Corbis UK Ltd: Front cover 3; Front cover 4, Front cover 11, Front cover 12, Front cover 22.
Mary Evans Picture Library: Front cover 1, Front cover 5, Front cover 8,

Front cover 19, Front cover 23.
Robert Harding Picture Library: Front cover 6.
Peter Newark's Pictures: Front cover 17.
Rex Features: Front cover 9, Front cover 20; Tim Rooke Front cover 2; Front cover 18; Tony Smith Front cover 21.
Science Photo Library: Front cover 10; NASA Front cover 15; US Library of Congress Front cover 16.

Additional photography by:
Dave King, John Parker, John Heseltine, Neil Lukas, Kim Sayer, Philippe Serbet, Roger Moss, Clive Streeter, Mike Dunning, Max Alexander, Stephen Oliver, James Stephenson, Tina Chambers, Norman McGraph, Susannah Price, Peter Wilson, Laurence Pordes, Paul Harris, Geoff Brighting, Demetrio Garrasco, Matthew Ward, Philip Dowell.

Illustrators:
Peter Dennis: 11; Sally Alane Reason: 14; Brian Delf: 19, 22-23, 36; Janos Marffy: 52.

Acknowledgments

Dorling Kindersley would like to thank the following people for their assistance with producing this book:

With special thanks to Leapfrog Press Limited

Index: Lynn Bresler

Additional editorial assistance: Melanie Halton, Martin Redfern, Carey Scott

Additional design assistance: Janet Allis, Polly Appleton, Ann Canning, Amanda Carroll, Ted Kinsey, Peter Radcliffe, Vicky Wharton, and especially Sheila Collins

Additional research: Jess Gloder, Jazz Wilson

Additional picture research: Franziska Marking

Film outputting: Graphical Innovations, London

BRIAN BORU BASIL II ALHAZEN LEIF ERIKSSON MURASAKI SHIKIBU AVICENNA GUIDO D'AREZZO CANUTE WILLIAM THE CONQ
HENRY II SALADIN MINAMOTO NO YORITOMO GENGHIS KHAN LEONARDO FIBONACCI LLYWELYN THE GREAT ST FRANCIS OF ASI
WALLACE ROBERT BRUCE MANSA MUSA GUILLAUME DE MACHAUT IBN BATTUTA PETRARCH EDWARD III KAN'AMI KIYOTSUGO
NAVIGATOR FRA ANGELICO JOAN OF ARC PACHACUTI WILLIAM CAXTON SONNI ALI JOSQUIN DESPREZ JAN VAN EYCK SAND
LEONARDO DA VINCI AMERIGO VESPUCCI LUDOVICO DE VARTHEMA VASCO DA GAMA DESIDERIUS ERASMUS NICCOLÒ MACH
MICHELANGELO BUONARROTI LUCREZIA BORGIA MONTEZUMA II XOCOYOTZIN FERDINAND MAGELLAN RAPHAEL BABUR I M
ATAHUALPA CHARLES V ANDREA PALLADIO JOHN CALVIN JOHN KNOX ANDREAS VESALIUS LI SHIH-CHEN LUIS VAZ DE CAMOËNS
DRAKE WILLIAM BYRD EL GRECO MARY, QUEEN OF SCOTS AKBAR TOKUGAWA IEYASU TYCHO BRAHE MIGUEL DE CERVANTES
HUDSON WILLIAM SHAKESPEARE JAMES VI AND I SAMUEL DE CHAMPLAIN CLAUDIO MONTEVERDI GUY FAWKES JOHANNES KEPLER
HOBBES SHAH JAHAN ARTEMISIA GENTILESCHI GUSTAVUS II ADOLPHUS RENÉ DESCARTES GIANLORENZO BERNINI OLIVER CRO
PASCAL SAMUEL PEPYS GEORGE FOX ROBERT BOYLE JOHN BUNYAN MARCELLO MALPIGHI CHRISTIAAN HUYGENS JAN VERMEER
JEAN RACINE APHRA BEHN SEKI KOWA ISAAC NEWTON RENÉ ROBERT CAVALIER DE LA SALLE BASHO WILLIAM PENN GOTTFRIE
DEFOE THOMAS NEWCOMEN GOBIND SINGH JONATHAN SWIFT PETER THE GREAT JETHRO TULL ROBERT WALPOLE ANTONIO VIVAL
FAHRENHEIT JOHN HARRISON FRANÇOIS VOLTAIRE WILLIAM HOGARTH DANIEL BERNOULLI ANDERS CELSIUS JOHN WESLEY BE
CHAN LANCELOT "CAPABILITY" BROWN DAVID GARRICK MARIA THERESA JEAN D'ALEMBERT THOMAS CHIPPENDALE ADAM SM
BOUGAINVILLE JOSIAH WEDGWOOD HENRY CAVENDISH RICHARD ARKWRIGHT GEORGE WASHINGTON (FRANZ) JOSEPH HAYDN JC
PAINE GEORGE III WILLIAM AND CAROLINE HERSCHEL MONTGOLFIER BROTHERS KARL WILHELM SCHEELE ANTOINE-LAURENT L
JOHANN WOLFGANG VON GOETHE JAMES MADISON JOHN NASH LOUIS XVI WOLFGANG AMADEUS MOZART JOHN LOUDON MCA
WOLLSTONECRAFT WILLIAM PITT THE YOUNGER WILLIAM WILBERFORCE ALEXANDER MACKENZIE ELI WHITNEY THOMAS MALTHU
VAN BEETHOVEN GEORG HEGEL WILLIAM WORDSWORTH MUNGO PARK RICHARD TREVITHICK ROBERT OWEN SAMUEL TAYLOR CC
AMEDEO AVOGADRO HANS CHRISTIAN OERSTED KARL GAUSS JOHN ROSS HUMPHRY DAVY JOSEPH GRIMALDI BERNARDO O'HIGG
GEORGE STEPHENSON NICOLÒ PAGANINI JOHN C. CALHOUN FRIEDRICH FROEBEL SIMON BOLIVAR CARL MARIA VON WEBER DAV
ROBERT PEEL LOUIS DAGUERRE AUGUSTIN LOUIS CAUCHY WILLIAM PARRY MICHAEL FARADAY CHARLES BABBAGE SAMUEL MOR
SADI CARNOT FRANZ SCHUBERT MARY WOLLSTONECRAFT SHELLEY HIROSHIGE ANDO CHARLES LYELL SOJOURNER TRUTH EUGEN
VICTOR HUGO JOHANN DOPPLER HECTOR BERLIOZ RALPH WALDO EMERSON NATHANIEL HAWTHORNE GEORGE SAND BENJAMIN D
NAPOLEON III HENRY COLE FELIX MENDELSSOHN EDGAR ALLAN POE LOUIS BRAILLE ABRAHAM LINCOLN CHARLES DARWIN WIL
BEECHER STOWE CHARLES DICKENS EDWARD LEAR DAVID LIVINGSTONE RICHARD WAGNER HENRY BESSEMER GIUSEPPE VERDI GE
TURGENEV JAMES JOULE JEAN FOUCAULT GEORGE ELIOT HERMAN MELVILLE WALT WHITMAN QUEEN VICTORIA JENNY LIND SUS
HELMHOLTZ MARY BAKER EDDY CLARA BARTON GREGOR JOHANN MENDEL ULYSSES S. GRANT LOUIS PASTEUR ETIENNE LENOIR
JOSEPH LISTER JOSEPHINE BUTLER HENRIK IBSEN LEO TOLSTOY JOSEPH SWAN FRIEDRICH KEKULÉ GERONIMO WILLIAM & CATH
NORDENSKJOLD GUSTAVE EIFFEL ALFRED NOBEL JOHANNES BRAHMS SITTING BULL WILLIAM MORRIS GOTTLIEB DAIMLER JAMES
CARNEGIE MRS BEETON ELIZABETH GARRETT ANDERSON GEORGES BIZET ERNST MACH GEORGE CUSTER PAUL CEZANNE GEOF
ANTONIN DVORÁK HENRY MORTON STANLEY PIERRE AUGUSTE RENOIR ARTHUR SULLIVAN JOHN WILLIAM STRUTT RAYLEIGH E
WILHELM RÖNTGEN MARY CASSAT "BUFFALO BILL" CODY PETER CARL FABERGE JESSE JAMES ALEXANDER GRAHAM BELL THOMA
LOUIS STEVENSON ANTOINE HENRI BECQUEREL MEIJI ANTONI GAUDI VINCENT VAN GOGH CECIL RHODES OSCAR WILDE PAUL EH
ROBERT EDWIN PEARY WOODROW WILSON SIGMUND FREUD J. J. THOMSON NIKOLA TESLA GEORGE BERNARD SHAW HEINRICH
GIACOMO PUCCINI ETHEL SMYTH MAX PLANCK BILLY THE KID GEORGES SEURAT PIERRE CURIE SVANTE ARRHENIUS ARTHUR CO
MELBA RABINDRANATH TAGORE MARY KINGSLEY CLAUDE DEBUSSY AUGUSTE & LOUIS LUMIÈRE KONSTANTIN STANISLAVSKI DAV
H. G. WELLS WILBUR & ORVILLE WRIGHT SUN YAT-SEN MARIE CURIE LUIGI PIRANDELLO FRANK LLOYD WRIGHT ROBERT FALCON S
VLADIMIR ILYICH LENIN JAN CHRISTIAN SMUTS MARIA MONTESSORI ROSA LUXEMBURG MARCEL PROUST ERNEST RUTHERFORD
ERNEST SHACKLETON HARRY HOUDINI LILIAN BAYLIS GUGLIELMO MARCONI W. MACKENZIE KING ARNOLD SCHOENBERG CHARL
ALI JINNAH FREDERICK SODDY ISADORA DUNCAN JACK JOHNSON LISE MEITNER CH'IU CHIN EMILIANO ZAPATA LEON TROTSKY JO
MUSTAFA KEMAL ATATÜRK BÉLA BARTÓK ALEXANDER FLEMING CECIL B. DE MILLE PABLO PICASSO JAMES JOYCE VIRGINIA WOOL
KEYNES CLEMENT ATTLEE WALTER GROPIUS COCO CHANEL ELEANOR ROOSEVELT F. D. ROOSEVELT HARRY TRUMAN D. H. LAWR
GARVEY ERWIN SCHRODINGER LE CORBUSIER MARCEL DUCHAMP BORIS KARLOFF CHIANG KAI-SHEK BERNARD MONTGOMERY AF
T. S. ELIOT CHANDRASEKHARA VENKATA RAMAN ADOLF HITLER LUDWIG WITTGENSTEIN EDWIN HUBBLE JAWAHARLAL NEHRU
EISENHOWER CHARLES DE GAULLE SERGEY PROKOFIEV ARTHUR COMPTON LOUIS DE BROGLIE J. B. S. HALDANE J. R. R. TOLKIEN ROB
NIKITA KHRUSHCHEV SHOJI HAMADA ROBERT MENZIES KONSUKE MATSUSHITE MARTHA GRAHAM RUDOLPH VALENTINO LASZLO
ENID BLYTON GEORGE GERSHWIN SERGEI EISENSTEIN BERTOLT BRECHT C. S. LEWIS HOWARD FLOREY ZHOU ENLAI PAUL ROBESON
ERNEST HEMINGWAY FRANCIS POULENC DUKE ELLINGTON JORGE LUIS BORGES ALFRED HITCHCOCK FRIEDRICH VON HAYEK KURT
WALT DISNEY ALBERTO GIACOMETTI LOUIS ARMSTRONG JOE DAVIS MARGARET MEAD LEE STRASBERG HIROHITO LINUS PAULIN
LOU GEHRIG AMY JOHNSON GEORGE ORWELL JOHN VON NEUMANN MARK ROTHKO BARBARA HEPWORTH JOHNNY WEISSMULLE
DING LING FREDERICK ASHTON ISAMU NOGUCHI SALVADOR DALI B. F. SKINNER GRAHAM GREENE DENG XIAOPING SIR JOHN GIE
GRACE HOPPER RACHEL CARSON W. H. AUDEN JOHN WAYNE GEORGES HERGÉ NIKOLAAS TINBERGEN LAURENCE OLIVIER FRANK W
HENRI CARTIER-BRESSON STEPHANE GRAPPELLI KWAME NKRUMAH ELIA KAZAN WILLIAM SHOCKLEY DOROTHY HODGKIN JACQU
JUAN MANUEL FANGIO JACKSON POLLOCK WOODY GUTHRIE WERNHER VON BRAUN PATRICK WHITE JOHN CAGE GENE KELLY LEA
THOR HEYERDAHL BILLIE HOLIDAY INGRID BERGMAN ORSON WELLES FRANK SINATRA STANLEY MATTHEWS ARTHUR MILLER R
RICHARD FEYNMANN LEONARD BERNSTEIN DENIS COMPTON INGMAR BERGMAN FANNY BLANKERS-KOEN BILLY GRAHAM NELSON
FRANKLIN ISAAC ASIMOV KATH WALKER JOHN PAUL II ANDREI SAKHAROV ALEXANDER DUBCEK JOHN GLENN JUDY GARLAND JA
MARIA CALLAS NADINE GORDIMER JACK KILBY MARCEL MARCEAU MARLON BRANDO ROBERT MUGABE MALCOLM X YUKIO MISH
II JOAN SUTHERLAND BOB FOSSE FIDEL CASTRO THEODORE MAIMAN SHIRLEY TEMPLE CHE GUEVARA ANDY WARHOL MAYA
YASSER ARAFAT ROGER BANNISTER (SIR) ARNOLD PALMER EDWARD O WILSON TED HUGHES NEIL ARMSTRONG JEAN-LUC GODA
TUTU LOUIS MALLE CORY AQUINO JAMES BROWN RICHARD ROGERS YURI GAGARIN HANK AARON BRIGITTE BARDOT HARRISON
ALLEN DALAI LAMA GIORGIO ARMANI CHRISTO SYLVIA EARLE ISSEY MIYAKE LUCIANO PAVAROTTI LESTER PIGGOTT GARY PLAY
GLASS DAWN FRASER DAVID HOCKNEY MARCIAN "TED" HOFF RENZO PIANO VALENTINA TERESHKOVA RUDOLF NUREYEV ROD LAV
BOB DYLAN JESSE JACKSON EDWARD ROBERTS PAUL SIMON JIMI HENDRIX MUHAMMED ALI DANIEL BARENBOIM ARETHA FRANK
WALESA KIRI TE KANAWA REINHOLD MESSNER PETER WEIR BOB MARLEY JACQUELINE DU PRÉ FRANZ BECKENBAUER AUNG SAN
ANDREW LLOYD WEBBER MARK SPITZ STEVIE WONDER STEVEN WOZNIAK SALLY RIDE NICKOLAY ANDRIANOV JIMMY CONNORS
NORMAN ALAIN PROST BJORN BORG OLGA KORBUT SPIKE LEE SUGAR RAY LEONARD JOE MONTANA MARTINA NAVRATILOVA SE
DIEGO MARADONA DIANA, PRINCESS OF WALES NADIA COMANECI WAYNE GRETZKY CARL LEWIS WYNTON MARSALIS MICHAEL J